INVARIANCES

ROBERT NOZICK

————

INVARIANCES

The Structure of the
Objective World

————

THE BELKNAP PRESS OF
Harvard University Press
Cambridge, Massachusetts
London, England
2001

Library of Congress Cataloging-in-Publication Data

Nozick, Robert
Invariances : the structure of the objective world / Robert Nozick
p.   cm.
Includes bibliographical references and index.
ISBN 0-674-00631-3 (alk. paper)
1. Relativity.   2. Truth.   3. Objectivity.   4. Ethics.   I. Title.

BD221 .N69 2001
110—dc21   2001035102

To Trude

The structure of my subjective world

Acknowledgments

Acknowledgments usually begin with intellectual debts, but I have reason to begin more personally here. In their order of appearance in this narrative: Marvin Kolodny, high school, college, and continuing friend, distinguished practitioner and professor of gastroenterology in Los Angeles, urged me to get to the bottom of some physical symptoms, and has provided excellent advice and continuing friendship; Andrew Warshaw, Chief of Surgery at Massachusetts General Hospital and Austen Professor of Surgery at Harvard Medical School, operated brilliantly six years ago, and again one and one half years ago, to remarkable effect; Robert Mayer, Professor of Medicine at Harvard Medical School, laser-minded brilliant clinician and chief of gastrointestinal oncology at the Dana Farber Cancer Institute, provided chemotherapy and radiation, keen medical judgment, good-humored cheer, and continuing excellent medical care (and even as this book goes to press, his knowledge and experienced intuition come to the rescue once again). Without the skill of these three men, this book, and its author, would not now exist. "Grateful" is not the word.

My wife Gjertrud Schnackenberg's love, dedication, and iron-willed determination that illness would not conquer have sustained me in these past few years and have continued to make my life wonderful in innumerable ways. I found that I had absolutely no desire or need to dwell upon the dangers to myself, and the writing of this book over the past seven years took up my spare attention. Consequently, the main emotional task fell upon my wife, who provided constant enormous love, care, and concern. Her own work of writing was seriously interrupted for several years, as mine was not, and I am overjoyed that the world now has her completed book, *The Throne of Labdacus*, which appeared last year. Readers of that magnificent work will understand how substantial are the mind and spirit that I live with daily, and how very privileged I am to do so.

To my parents' (Max Nozick and Sophie Cohen Nozick's) great love for each other and for me, I owe, ultimately, my optimistic view of life and of its possibilities. Or perhaps it is to their genes. In any case, I have been the great beneficiary.

During the writing of this book, many people offered helpful advice and comments. Timothy Williamson, Dagfinn Follesdal, and Elijah Millgram gave me detailed written comments on the whole manuscript, to its great benefit. I also received helpful comments and criticism on portions of the manuscript from (in alphabetical order) Carla Bagnoli, Ned Block, Scott Brewer, Marshall Cohen, Leda Cosmides, Tamar Gendler, Gilbert Harman, Stephen Kosslyn, Eric Maskin, Thomas Nagel, Derek Parfit, James Pryor, Hilary Putnam, Thomas Scanlon, Martin Seligman, Susanna Siegel, Alison Simmons, William Talbott, John Tooby, and Bernard Williams. My discussions of physics in particular have also benefited from the comments of David Albert, John Earman, David Malament, Timothy Maudlin, Simon Saunders, Abner Shimony, Mark Steiner, and Ady Stern. Neither my philosophical colleagues nor these distinguished and technically proficient philosophers of physics (and physicists) are responsible for any errors the book contains.

Earlier versions of parts of this book were delivered in the spring of 1997 as the six John Locke Lectures at Oxford University. I was first invited to deliver the Locke Lectures in 1978, and I declined. It took almost twenty years before I had material that I was happy to deliver, and I am grateful to Oxford for being willing to reinstitute the invitation. Portions of this book also were presented in three lectures at Notre Dame University, two lectures at the University of California at Berkeley, University College Dublin, Edinburgh University, two at New York University, and in lectures at Dartmouth, the Harvard Kennedy School Ethics Program, the University of California at Los Angeles, the University of Florence, the University of Rome, and the Ecole Polytechnique. An earlier version of Chapter 2 was delivered as the Presidential Address to the Eastern Division of the American Philosophical Association in 1997. I am grateful to these audiences for their attention and for their questions.

While writing this book, I was the recipient of a fellowship from the John Simon Guggenheim Foundation, which I gratefully acknowledge. The manuscript of this book was completed during an intensive and productive two-month stay at the superb and extremely beautiful facilities of the Getty Research Institute for the Humanities.

Contents

Introduction: On Philosophical Method   *1*

I. THE STRUCTURE OF THE OBJECTIVE WORLD

1. Truth and Relativism   *15*

Is Truth Relative?   *15*
Who Wants Relativism?   *21*
Truth in Space and Time   *26*
The Truth Property   *44*
Is a Theory of Truth Possible?   *48*
Is Truth Socially Relative?   *55*
Does Relativism Undercut Itself?   *64*
The Correspondence Theory   *67*

2. Invariance and Objectivity   *75*

Objective Facts   *75*
Admissible Transformations   *79*
Two Types of Philosophical Account   *83*
The Ordering of Objectiveness   *87*
Intersubjectivity   *90*
Objective Beliefs and Biasing Factors   *94*
Dimensions of Truth   *99*
The Objectivity of Science   *102*
The Functional View   *106*
Underdetermination of Theory   *111*
Rationality, Progress, Objectivity, and Veridicality   *114*

3. Necessity and Contingency   *120*

Epistemology of Necessity   *120*
Cross-Classifications   *126*
On the Supposed Necessity of Water's Being H_2O *128*
The Withering of Metaphysical Necessity   *133*
Explaining Away Necessities   *136*
Logical and Mathematical Necessity   *141*
Degrees of Contingency   *148*
The Nature of Actuality   *155*
The Ultimate Theory of the World   *161*

II. THE HUMAN WORLD AS PART OF THE OBJECTIVE WORLD

4. The Realm of Consciousness　*171*

The Function of Consciousness　*171*
Gradations of Awareness　*174*
The Context of Consciousness　*176*
The Zoom-Lens Theory　*180*
Synthesizing and Filtering Data　*190*
Common Knowledge　*197*
The Functions of Phenomenology　*205*
Mind-Body Relations　*218*

5. The Genealogy of Ethics　*236*

The Theory of Ethics　*236*
The Ubiquity of Ethics　*238*
Coordination to Mutual Benefit　*240*
Coordination via Ethical Norms　*243*
The Evaluation of Systems of Coordination　*253*
The Core Principle of Ethics　*259*
Normative Force and the Normativity Module　*267*
Evaluative Capacities　*274*
Higher Layers of Ethics　*278*
Ethical Truth and Ethical Objectivity　*284*
The Unpredictability of Human Behavior　*294*
Ethics and Conscious Self-Awareness　*298*

Notes　*303*
Index　*403*

INVARIANCES

Introduction: On Philosophical Method

Philosophy begins in wonder. How much of our view of the world is objective, how much is subjective? How much of what (we think) is true holds absolutely, how much is relative to our situation? Are truths only local or do some hold everywhere and always? Does ethics have an objective basis? Why are we conscious? What is the function of felt experiences in an objective world?

Previous philosophers, almost all of them, have sought to establish permanent truths in an enduring framework of thought; these truths were supposed to be absolute, objective, and universal. Details might remain to be filled in, but the essentials were meant to be in place and to stand firm for all time.

In mathematics, a fixed-point theorem states that all transformations of a certain type (for instance, continuous ones) leave at least one point in a certain space unchanged. The unchanged point is a fixed point of the transformation. It is not the point's intrinsic nature that leaves it fixed, however. Although every transformation may leave some point or other fixed, different points are left fixed by different transformations. No one point is left fixed by every transformation.

Philosophers, however, have sought points that remained fixed under all transformations, at least all the ones that were worth considering. Such points would constitute absolutely secure foundations for knowledge and values. The most prominent candidates for fixity were the *cogito* of Descartes, the sense data of the empiricists, and the necessary metaphysical truths of the rationalists. These points were supposed to be not only fixed but also fertile enough to support the rest of our knowledge and values. One by one, these purportedly certain, indubitable, and unassailable points have been shaken. And their fertility also was undermined. Little could be built upon them using only perfectly secure means of building.

The pragmatist Charles Peirce held, against Descartes, that nothing was indubitable. Each thing was open to doubt, although not all things at once.

Each thing could be doubted on the basis of other propositions that were, at that particular moment, not actually in doubt. Their turn could come later. Otto Neurath, followed by W. V. Quine, likened our situation to that of sailors who have to rebuild a ship at sea: while standing on somewhat rotten planks, they must repair and replace the others. Every plank sooner or later gets repaired. Everything is open to transformation. Nothing stays fixed. Even something as fundamental as the principle of noncontradiction can be open to questioning and to revision.[1]

Critics have nibbled at the edges of the position that nothing is immune to being modified or given up. Aren't the criteria for revising views themselves unchangeable? Could we ever give up the weakest principle of noncontradiction, which says that not for *every* statement p, is it the case that both p and not-p?[2] But even these objections are not decisive. True, it would, take a serious intellectual crisis to motivate a change as far-reaching as holding it is the case both that p and that not-p, for *every* statement p, so it is difficult now to imagine specifically how such a change would be justified or plausible.[3] Yet even if we cannot conceive of the details of a (justified) rejection of the weakest principle of noncontradiction right now, nevertheless a gradual process of change might lead to the giving up of any statement or criterion, including that very weakest principle, on the basis of other statements and criteria that have come to be accepted then. The fact that a particular theory has a fixed point does not show that this very same point must or will be held fixed by every plausible theory. And it does not show that the theory under consideration is unable successively to transform itself by using its own then accepted standards, so that this point and even these very standards get modified.

"But won't there be meta-meta- . . . -metacriteria that do not get transformed no matter what?" Even if such objections were accepted, their import would not be very great. You cannot get very far solely on the basis of saying that not every contradiction holds true,[4] and not much can be built upon (only) such rarified metacriteria. We might as well say that there are no fixed points, and no fixed metapoints either. (And that includes the statement just made.)

Any particular purported principle of reason might be given up, but must not reason itself stand always and eternally as the final arbiter of all intellectual claims? Must not reason remain always (as Thomas Nagel called it) "the last word"?[5] But what precisely is it that must endure? Not any particular statement or principle, for any one of those might be transformed or replaced or delimited or rejected. If it is said that Reason itself, rather than any particular statement of its content, must remain as the final arbiter, then we must wonder what precisely *that* is. If not as particular content, then the only sense in which reason must endure is as an evolving chain of descent. Reason will endure as whatever evolves or grows out of the current content of reason by a process of piecemeal change that is justified at each moment by principles which are accepted at that moment (although not necessarily later on), provided that each evolving stage seems close enough to the one immediately preceding it to warrant the continued use of the label "reason" then. (The new stage may not seem very similar, however, to a much earlier, stepwise stage.) That degree of continuity hardly seems to mark something which is a fixed and eternal intellectual point. It is little help to add that what will endure is some process of thought that, in human beings, will continue to have its significant locus in the prefrontal cortex of the brain unless and until genetic alterations and artificial prosthetic supplementary devices come to shift the physical location of reason's major activity.

My own philosophical bent is to open possibilities for consideration. Not to close them. This book suggests new philosophical views and theses, and the reasons it produces to support these are meant to launch them for exploration, not to demonstrate conclusively that they are correct. Similarly, my criticisms of some major competing theories or positions are not intended to refute them conclusively, merely to weaken them enough to clear a philosophical space in which the newly proposed views can breathe and grow. I state this aim here at the very beginning so that disclaimers do not have to be repeated constantly throughout. This is not a cautious attempt to avoid criticism by a diminution of ambition. The claim to be saying things that are new and philosophically interesting sticks one's neck out considerably.

The opening and exploring of new views, without aiming at their *proof*, is especially suited for expanding philosophical knowledge. The method of proof starts at a place or with a set of premises, and it goes on only to what can be proven on their basis. If there are some truths that cannot be reached from that starting place,[6] this method will limit the truth content of the philosophy that results. Furthermore, it does not make rational sense to restrict one's philosophical method to proof only, once it has been acknowledged that the view is not built upon certain and unalterable foundations anyway. Since the nonfoundationalist begins at a place that has not been proven or absolutely established, then since it is permissible to accept *some* things that have not been absolutely proven, why cannot one accept other such things as well?

Why might someone require that philosophical views be accepted only if they are provable from the starting place *P*? That requirement does not guarantee the truth of the resulting views, for *P* itself may not be true. It is true that the method of proof does guarantee that one will not add new independent falsehoods to one's views (although it does allow the addition of new false beliefs that are based, in part, upon falsehoods that *P* currently accepts). However, we also must notice that the restrictive nature of the method of proof may prevent one from *eliminating* some falsehoods currently residing within *P*, which the use of certain nondeductive methods might enable one to discard. For a nondeductive method might allow one, starting from *P*, to reach some new propositions that would be incompatible with those particular falsehoods within *P*, thereby prompting one to eliminate those falsehoods from one's current view. Through the nondeductive methods, *P* gets transformed by adding propositions to it and then by subtracting those (false) propositions that are incompatible with the new ones; thus a new view arises. Requiring that philosophers proceed only by the method of proof makes it impossible to eliminate falsehoods in this way. The method of proof is not as unalloyed a friend of truth as might have appeared.

An alternative method, the one I follow here, consists in a series of philosophical forays. Start at your current position *P*, and consider what is plausible, illuminating, intellectually interesting, and supported by reasons, given *P*. (These reasons should have weight but they need not be conclusive.) Finding something that is such, suppose that *it* is true and then consider what is plausible, illuminating, intellectually interesting, and supported by reasons, in its light in turn. Finding another thing that is such, consider what is plausible . . . And so on. This method does not mark out one unique path. Different things will be plausible, illuminating, intellectually interesting, and supported by reasons, given *P*, and these different things are not identical or perhaps even compatible with each other. Assuming one of these things, still further different things will be plausible, illuminating, intellectually interesting, and supported by reasons, given it, and these further things too are not identical or perhaps even compatible. So the proposed method will explore, or allow the exploration of, different pathways.

By following this method as outlined, we may eventually arrive at considering a view that is *not* plausible on the basis of the starting position *P*. (For the relation "*X* is plausible given *Y*" is not a transitive relation.) Should we limit the extent of our philosophical method only to what is plausible given our initial starting point? Some will indeed want to stop there. But I suggest that plausibility (from the standpoint of the initial position) should not be a constraint on exploration, so long as we follow a chain of reasoning of the sort described, and continue to reach something that is illuminating and intellectually interesting given *P.* No doubt, in seeking philosophical interest and illumination, we will want especially to explore the most plausible of the intellectually interesting and illuminating views.[7]

We should, however, limit the range of our forays to what is philosophically interesting and illuminating given our current position *P.* (This constitutes a limit because the relation "*X* is philosophically interesting and illuminating given *Y*" is not transitive, and so a chain of such connections can reach something that is *not* philosophically interesting and illuminating in relation to the starting point.) Of course, if we come to *accept* some of these new things (and aren't simply exploring them), then what is our current position will change from *P* to some new *P'*. Thereupon, what we foray into also will change. The domain of forays will both get extended and get restricted—extended, in that new things will be interesting and illuminating given *P'* that previously were not; restricted, in that some once interesting and illuminating views no longer will be so, given *P'*.

A comparison to physics is apropos. Physicists use nonrigorous messy mathematics for extended periods in order to make fast, fruitful, and promising progress on the problems that concern them. (Recall the state of the calculus before Weierstrass, and the path to renormalization methods in quantum field theory.) They are content to leave the task of cleaning up their methods to the mathematicians who follow in their wake. At present, string theorists explore many varieties of string theory, and just now they are beginning to peek at ways of unifying these in M-theory. They find interesting consequences (the theory yields gravity in a very natural way), they explore constraints such as supersymmetry for their fruitful consequences (without any very strong evidence that these constraints hold), they investigate the properties of a theory they have only sketched but not yet explicitly stated (in that *some* of its properties are known but the equations of the theory are not), and they use methods of approximation (perturbation theory) to get some grip on the consequences of the theory (and put little weight on the areas where they know these methods are greatly off the mark). All this theoretical effort, without coming close (at present) to touching down on particular empirical data or experiments. (Since string theory is currently the most exciting area of metaphysics, I return to it in Chapter 3.)

Although arriving at a range of new and philosophically interesting and illuminating theories is intellectually quite exciting, the mark of significant philosophical progress occurs when some of the different positions that the forays have managed to reach begin, not just to reside alongside each other, but to combine, integrate, and *knit together* to yield a new, illuminating, and interesting structure.

Even this outcome, of course, does not prove that one is on the right track, but it does make it more probable. For one cannot automatically always get some such group of separately illuminating and interesting pieces to knit together into a resulting structure that also illuminates these pieces and perhaps some new things as well. Such a series of disciplined philosophical forays would constitute what Imre Lakatos has termed a "progressive research program,"[8] if it continues to reach new illuminating positions that knit together into an interesting structure, especially if this structure fruitfully suggests, or provides a platform for, further forays that reach still further positions that satisfy these criteria.[9]

"But should we *believe* the results of this kind of philosophy?" This mode of philosophy is not designed to induce belief in something or the acceptance of it as true (beyond the belief that the theory is illuminating and interesting). Belief may eventually result if the view is plausible and best explains or unifies various things. Yet the philosophy, or that particular pathway to it, is not shown to be unsuccessful when it does not lead to belief (and this, not just because this method's other pathways might themselves lead to belief). Belief is not the only coin of the philosophical realm. There are new classifications and analyses and understandings, and there is the process of intellectual openness itself. Ones that do not eventuate in belief may get fulfilled in other ways. Aquinas led to Dante.

A philosophy's process may continue to hold intellectual interest because of its new methods of foray, its new ways of applying old methods, and its imagination and its daring. Future thinkers might be spurred to find analogues of these characters to fit their new intellectual situation. Twenty-five hundred years later, we still find reading Plato exciting—not for his *results*.

When I held earlier that there are no fixed philosophical points, I meant that there are no fixed philosophical concepts either. Yet certain concepts seem central, and locked into apparently immovable place by other concepts that they organize; they seem *guaranteed* to apply fruitfully. Evolutionary psychologists speak of an innate predisposition within us to understand and explain the world through certain categories and "theories," for instance, that the world consists of continuously moving physical objects, and that beliefs and desires propel other people's behavior and our own actions as well.

An evolutionary account of some of our fundamental concepts is both reassuring and upsetting. It is reassuring in that it holds that these concepts had enough of a grip upon the world that they aided reproductive success and were selected for. They must have got something right. Yet this selection does not guarantee their complete accuracy. The spatial concepts of Euclidean geometry were good enough to guide us practically, yet we now know that they are not, strictly speaking, accurately applicable to the world. So, when we see the world through an evolutionarily instilled conceptual structure, do we thereby know the way the world really is? Do we know the world—to use Kantian terminology—as it is *in itself*?

Since the time of Aristotle, philosophers have delineated and utilized fundamental categories of understanding: form, content, substance, property, causality, object, belief, desire, space, time, objectivity, truth. Some philosophers hold these categories to be inescapable, and necessarily accurate of the world. Kant retreated to saying that they necessarily apply to the world as we structure and represent it—they apply to appearances rather than to things in themselves.[10] More recently, some philosophers have reinstated the authority and validity of some of these traditional concepts on the basis of the *intuitions* that structure their philosophy; they treat these intuitions as data to which a philosophical theory must conform. However, an evolutionary explanation of these concepts undercuts their unquestionable authority, along with that of any intuitions they bring in their wake. No secure basis for a philosophical theory there!

One piece of the objective world, a piece that is instilled in our heads by evolution, is our theory of that world, and this theory is not necessarily strictly accurate. If someone questions a part of that theory, even calling into question the applicability of its basic categories, it is not sufficient, or appropriate, for philosophers to quickly argue the contrary position in a way that presupposes the valid application of these very concepts or of closely associated ones. Or to react in outrage, even when what is questioned are such central notions as objective truth, objective inquiry, and rationality.

Not even the applicability of the notions of belief and desire can be taken for granted. Two philosophers, Paul and Patricia Churchland, have recently claimed that these categories of "folk psychology" are seriously inadequate and will be replaced by the explanatory concepts of a developed neuroscience. Many philosophers have reacted to this view as earlier generations did to atheists, recoiling from their denial of the existence of sacred things. The denial of the folk-psychological categories might be incorrect, but it is not beyond the pale of possibility.

A philosopher should be open to radically different intriguing conceptual possibilities. At the least, their investigation will lead to deeper insight into the conceptual structure we find ourselves inhabiting or being inhabited by. Too often, philosophers insist that things *must* be a certain way, and they make it their business to close off possibilities. "Damn braces. Bless relaxes."[11]

It is a commonplace that advances in physics have radically overturned our evolutionarily instilled theories and concepts, and our common-sense theories. Space is not Euclidean, simultaneity is not absolute, the world is not deterministic, quantum events stand in (an ill-understood) relation to their being observed, and they also can have nonlocal correlates that are not mediated by intervening processes. Such an overturning of our traditional concepts can be disquieting and disconcerting. People go to great lengths to avoid this.

An instance is David Bohm's formulation of quantum mechanics, which has won some adherents among philosophers but few among physicists.[12] Bohm's theory is deterministic, particles have definite positions and trajectories, the wave function of the system refers to an existent entity that determines how the particles behave, there is no collapse of the wave function, and (as John Bell has emphasized) the theory does not require reference to an observer and it offers a homogeneous account of the physical world that is not bifurcated into a quantum part and a classical part. However, according to Bohm's view "the fundamental laws of the world are cooked up in such a way as to systematically *mislead* us about themselves . . . [the theory] recounts the unfolding of a perverse and gigantic conspiracy to make the world *appear* to be *quantum-mechanical*."[13]

Bohmian mechanics is a far more complicated theory than orthodox quantum mechanics. It is interesting that this deterministic theory of objective existents can be formulated. But what do we learn from that fact? At the beginning of the twentieth century, Henri Poincaré said that since the simplest geometry for space was Euclidean, and since all other facts could be assimilated into the Euclidean framework by complicating the (theories of) physics, Euclidean geometry was unassailable. It could not rationally be given up. Simplicity was important, others agreed, but the important simplicity was that of the overall theory, not just of one theoretical component, even if that one component is as large and extensive as geometry. If the greatest overall simplicity of geometry + physics can best be achieved by including a *non*-Euclidean geometry, then that more complex geometrical component will be included in the interests of the simplicity of our overall theory. Given that accommodations can be made elsewhere in order to maintain Euclidean geometry come what may, how could one discover that this inherited and apparently obvious Euclidean geometry was false, if not by subjecting it to such a test of overall simplicity?

Pierre Duhem has taught us that a particular theory can be maintained in the face of recalcitrant data by modifying auxiliary hypotheses. (It is less clear that a particular theory can always be combined with such auxiliary modifications to *explain* the empirical data.) What we learn from Bohm's efforts is that the traditional framework of a deterministic, objective theory *can* continue to be maintained and will explain the data if enough complications accompany it. But how shall we learn that such a familiar and apparently metaphysically compelling framework is mistaken unless we subject it to a test of overall simplicity of theory? We do not want to be stuck with our cave-man categories or our Newtonian categories forever; we want to be able to learn more, if indeed there is more to be learned. The physicists' rejection of Bohm's theory, a rejection that many philosophers of physics now look askance at, stems, I think, not just from the difficulties in giving it a relativistically invariant form but from the physicists' sense that Bohm's theory stands in the way of this further learning. And it should not surprise us that it takes time to achieve clear and precise formulations of new and difficult concepts, such as those of quantum mechanics. The concepts of the calculus, after all, had to wait from the time of Newton and Leibniz to that of Weierstrass for their clarification, and the formulation in terms of infinitesimals achieved clarity only with the recent work of Abraham Robinson.[14]

Philosophical thinking, too, can raise surprising conceptual possibilities, sometimes prompted by such scientific findings even though not entailed by them. Just as geometry does not stand alone but is part of an overall view, so too we do not seek the simplest or the most elegant philosophy but rather the best overall theory, and in the interests of this goal, philosophy, too, can be asked to renounce some of its previous apparent treasures. Philosophy's loss of its (presumed) foundational authority over all other disciplines is more than made up for by the external stimulation it now receives to arrive at more satisfactory, no longer *a priori*, positions.

We should expect that many of our evolved concepts will have defects, and we should be prepared to give up reliance upon them, at least in the specialized contexts in which their shortcomings are most evident. The need for such conceptual revisions or revolutions (and the direction they will need to take) cannot be predicted, nor can this need be avoided or warded off by any general device of conceptual purification such as Locke's empiricist criterion, Kant's critical one, or P. W. Bridgeman's operational definitions.

"But don't our evolved concepts constitute our fundamental mode of understanding? Doesn't understanding a phenomenon ultimately just come to being able to place it within our network of evolved concepts? So won't giving up these concepts leave us adrift, with no further hope of understanding?"

There is the alternative, though, of creating new concepts for the understanding of new phenomena, and then applying these new concepts to older phenomena as well. Einstein referred to scientific theories as "free creations of the human mind," and these creations include the concepts these theories employ. One physicist, Roland Omnes, has asserted that the task of interpreting quantum mechanics is not to find a classical description of quantum phenomena but to find a quantum description of all classical phenomena and facts, that is, to understand the older phenomena in terms of the new concepts.[15] Quantum mechanics paints a surprising picture of the world, and the task is not to capture or understand its surprises within our previous picture of the world, but rather to understand the world through the concepts appropriate to its surprises. (Since the task of developing fruitful new concepts can be extremely difficult, we do have reason not to toss our previous concepts aside lightly, without due cause.)

In investigating the functions of truth (true belief), objectivity, ethics, and consciousness, we will have occasion to keep our eyes peeled for relevant scientific theories and scientific data. Philosophy is not (wholly) an *a priori* discipline, so it must mesh with current knowledge and also pursue promising and puzzling leads stemming from that knowledge. We shall also seek to identify and separate the empirical substrate or aspect of philosophical questions and, to the extent that this is possible, to transform philosophical questions into factual, empirical ones. Thus, we will see that questions of whether truth is relative turn on the explanation of different groups' success in action, and also upon whether each and every truth registers throughout space and time. Questions about objectiveness depend upon the range of transformations under which something is invariant. Some questions about ethics depend, in part, upon why ethics is ubiquitous, and some questions about consciousness depend upon its biological function. Understanding why there is an objective world may depend upon cosmology.

Freud described the goal of psychoanalysis as "Where id was, there ego shall be." It would be far too strong, and also undesirable, to echo this and say, "Where philosophy was, there science shall be." Yet although the transformation of philosophical questions into testable factual hypotheses is not the sole method of philosophy, that sharpening of the questions *is* one way to open new avenues of progress. Another way is to pose new questions.

So let us begin.

I

THE STRUCTURE OF THE
OBJECTIVE WORLD

1

Truth and Relativism

Is Truth Relative?

Is truth absolute, or is it possible for truth itself to be relative? Is the view that all truth is relative undercut by the familiar question: is *that* view relative or not?

For some time now, I have felt uncomfortable with this quick refutation of relativism, a favorite of philosophers and one that I had often used in conversation. The argument is supposed to proceed like this. If the relativist position (that all truth is relative) itself is nonrelative, then it is false. And if it is not put so generally as to apply to itself, if it says that all *other* truths are relative, then what makes itself so special? If it manages to be a nonrelative truth, then why cannot there be other such truths also? So the view that the relativist position is itself nonrelative is unstable.

"Unstable" does not mean impossible, however. Suppose the relativist says that indeed there is one nonrelative truth, namely, the truth (R′) that states the relativist position, viz.

(R′)   All statements other than (R′), and other than deductive consequences of (R′), are relative.

Relativism is as true, he says, as it consistently can be.[1] (And this might be his reply to the question of why, even though the statement of relativism is a nonrelative truth, it does not follow that there are many other nonrelative truths.) Would the absolutist really be happy if there were only one absolute truth (along with its deductive consequences), and (R′) was that one? Is the absolutist satisfied simply if relativism is not *universally* true?

Or suppose that the relativist says that all (or almost all) of the *important* statements that we currently formulate and care about are merely relative truths. Perhaps there are some absolute truths that we haven't yet formulated and don't really care about, perhaps these are abstract structural statements about the framework of truths, but almost all the ones we know of, care about, and act upon are relative. Does the relativist need more than this? Would the absolutist be content if there exists at least *one* absolute truth, something firm that he can hang onto even if not do much with? (And will he be content if he merely can maintain that such a statement exists, but cannot specify which statement it is? Or will he be content if the one nonrelative truth is something like this: There exists one nonrelative truth and this very statement is it.) Won't this make the absolutist's victory hollow? Isn't the more important issue, or an equally important issue, the question of what proportion of the truths we believe, put forth, and act upon are merely relative?

Thus far I have imagined the relativist granting that some statement is nonrelative, namely, the statement of the relativist position itself (along with its consequences). Call this the relaxed relativist position. But what about unrelaxed relativism? Is the claim that relativism is universally and without exception true undercut by that familiar question: is this relativist view relative or not? It seems that surely it is, for if we suppose that the (unrelaxed) relativist position R (which holds that *all* truth is relative) itself is relative, then . . . Then what? Then it is only relative, and so what authority does it have over me; why should I believe it? The relativist might reply that although R is only relative, I fall within its domain. R is relative to a group I am in, or to a property that I have, etc. And so the relativist answer to the question of why I should believe R, even though it is merely a relative truth, is that it *is* true relative to something about me. So I am stuck with it as true. (And about that statement that R is true relative to something about me, I ask: is *that* statement only a relative truth? Yes, replies the relativist, and it too is true relative to something about me. And as to that something about me, I wonder: is its holding only a relative truth? Yes, the relativist replies, but . . .) If R is true relative to property P, and if I have property P and do not lose it through knowing that truth is relative (and knowing it is relative to P and knowing that I have P), then R *is* true relative to this property that I have, so shouldn't I believe it?

This makes it look as though relativism about truth is a coherent position, and that the quick and standard refutation is much too quick. And I think that relativism about truth *is* a coherent position; the relativist claim can be structured and stated so that it need not undercut itself. Moreover, the nonrelativist should think it is *desirable* that relativism be coherently formulable. For then *non*relativism (absolutism) about truth becomes a position with (Popperian) empirical content; it excludes something that is *possible*. That gives the nonrelativist position more bite and thus makes it more interesting.

To say that relativism about truth is a coherent position is not to say that it is the *correct* position. The relativisms about truth that have been formulated previously and that have great interest (for instance, that truth is relative to one's society, or one's sex, or one's economic class) are, I think, extremely implausible. However, philosophically very interesting, though socially less striking, versions of relativism can be formulated that *are* plausible. That I have reached this position surprises me. My original intent was to argue that relativism about truth was coherent *but false*. To give the nonrelativist position falsifiable content, I needed to produce formulations of how relativism *could* coherently be true, and doing this led me to notice interesting ways that relativism could well turn out to be true!

To proceed further, we need to understand more exactly what relativism involves. A property is relative only when there is an unobvious nonexplicit factor such that the presence or absence of the property (or the degree of its presence) varies with that factor. But this is not enough. The length of an object is different under different temperature conditions, yet this fact alone does not show that length is relative to temperature. Causal variation under different conditions is not the same as being relative. The different temperature conditions are exclusive; an object cannot have different temperatures at the same time. Whereas, when a property is relative to a factor, the different states of the factor can obtain simultaneously, in different respects. To ask simply whether or not the property is present, the relevant state of that factor must be specified.

The probability of a statement or of an event provides an example of something that is relative. The probability of a statement is relative to evidence. That probability will vary with different evidence, and that probability is not detachable from the evidence as something that holds as a freestanding fact.[2] And the probability of an event's having a certain property is relative to a reference class. Different classes into which that event falls will show differing percentages of events having the property in question.[3] To speak of the probability (period) of a statement or of an event, we have to take as given or to hold constant the evidence or the reference class. Indeed, this is not enough. Rather, we must speak explicitly of the probability of a statement relative to given evidence or the probability of an event relative to its being of a certain type.

There is a further feature to be mentioned when a property P is relative to the state of a factor. (This feature is implicit in the previous characterization, but it should be stated explicitly.) Suppose that the factor F to which the property is relative can take on different values or degrees, $F_1, \ldots, F_n$, and that these different values are not exclusive; they can hold in different respects. We have to add that no one of these different values is privileged, or superior to the others. They all are on a par, equally valid, or equally good, or whatever. If one of these values, say F_a, of the factor was privileged or superior, then the state of P relative to F_a could be picked out as defining the freestanding and nonrelative property P. Relativism must be egalitarian about the variations in the factor F.

In the Special Theory of Relativity, the length of an object will be measured differently by different observers traveling with different constant velocities with respect to the object. Put differently, the measured length of the object will vary according to its velocity with respect to an (inertial) observer. A privileged velocity of the object (or of the observer) could be used to pick out one (measured) length as its true, absolute length. Absolute space, if it existed, would provide a framework for defining an object's absolute length, namely the length that would be measured by an observer at rest with it in absolute space. However, within the Special Theory of Relativity there is no framework (such as absolute space) to pick out one inertial observer's position as better or more privileged than another's. The length of an object is relative to the motion of an observer.

A similar situation holds with respect to our example of probability. The probability of a hypothesis is relative to evidence, but if one batch of evidence could be picked out as privileged, for example, the total evidence that is available to us, then the probability of a hypothesis *simpliciter* might be defined as its probability relative to the total evidence. (This probability would shift, of course, as we acquired new evidence.) Or if one of the reference classes within which an event falls could be picked out as the most informative one with regard to the event, for example, the narrowest homogeneous reference class that includes the event, then the probability of the event *simpliciter* could be specified as its probability relative to this particular reference class.[4] Thereby would the relativity of probability be eliminated. However, no such specification of a privileged body of evidence or of a privileged reference class has been successful for this purpose. The notions of inductive and of statistical probability remain relative.

A property is relative, then, when its occurrence or value varies with some other factor, when the different values of this other factor can coexist, and when no one of this factor's values is especially privileged or superior to every other one.

Once the relativization is made explicit within the statement itself, however, it seems that the resulting statement (for instance, "The probability of hypothesis h relative to evidence e is greater than .5") is not itself relative. It states a relativity, but its statement of that relativity is not itself relative—or does not appear to be.[5]

We now are in a position to state what must obtain if truth itself is to be relative. Everyone agrees that the statement made by an utterance, e.g., "The book is on the table," will vary with or depend upon the meaning of the utterance and with what items in the world the terms in the utterance refer to. The correspondence theorist of truth holds that the truth value of the statement (made by the utterance in its context) also will vary with or depend upon the way the world is—e.g., upon whether the book *is* on the table. So much is common ground and does not establish any relativity of truth. Truth is relative only if it varies with some additional, less obvious factor.

A set T of truths contains relative truths if the members of T are true and there is a factor F other than the obvious ones (the meaning of the utterance, the references of some terms within it, and the way the world is), such that that factor F can vary, and when F is varied, the truth value (viz. truth or falsity) of the members of T varies. The different values of the factor can coexist, and they are on a par. So the truth value of the members of T is a *function* of factor F as well as of meaning, reference, and the way the world is.[6]

The claim that truth is relative to gender or race or class or culture or sexual preference says that variation in at least one of these factors would produce variation in the truth value of some statements whose content is not explicitly *about* matters of gender or race, etc.[7] Moreover, variations in these factors can hold simultaneously, and all variants in these factors are on a par; they are equal. If truth is relative to, for instance, anthropological culture, then different cultures can consistently coexist, and they (and their standards of truth) are held to be equally good. Relativism is egalitarian.[8]

Some recent formal theories of propositional content and the semantics of context-dependent statements may appear to leave no room even to state the position that truth is relative. I provide some technical discussion of these theories in a note,[9] but the conclusion I reach is of general philosophical interest and needs to be stated here. Relativism does not differ from absolutism merely by claiming that statements have the traditional truth values True and False but possess these traditional truth values only relatively. Rather, relativism about truth holds that truth values are of a new and different kind. A statement or utterance can have the truth value [true relative to factor F_1] or the truth value [false relative to factor F_2]. And when these factors are different, it can have both of these truth values at once. These truth values are structurally different and more complex than the traditional truth values, and they are intrinsically relative. No statement, the (total) relativist says, has the traditional truth value of true *simpliciter* or false *simpliciter.*

The position that truth is relative cannot be ruled out because of the arbitrary structural constraints of a theory of propositional meaning that was formulated and designed for purposes quite unconnected with issues of relativism in mind, especially since the relativist position can be formulated within a closely related but more expansive framework. A similar point applies to other restrictive theories in the philosophy of language, including those of sense and reference in the tradition of Gottlieb Frege. Before dismissing relativism as incompatible with these theories, a person would have to investigate whether cognate theories that allow relativism are possible.[10]

To say that *all* truths are relative is to say that each and every truth is a relative truth. The *absolutist* about truth says that not all truths are relative. He need not hold that all truths are nonrelative. He can grant that some truths are relative, in that their truth value can vary with variation in some unobvious factors, etc. He holds, though, that this is not true of all true statements. There are, he claims, *some* absolute truths, some true statements where there is no factor F (other than . . .) such that F can vary and the truth value of those statements varies with F.[11] Moreover, as we have seen, the absolutist wants to claim that the absolute truths are in some sense the important and fundamental ones (perhaps because all the relative truths are derivable from and explainable in terms of absolute truths, perhaps for some other reason).

The absolutist has a problem, it seems, of stating a position the relativist must deny. Suppose the absolutist says (A): there is an absolute truth. The relativist, conciliatory as always, then says: That (namely, (A)) is true for you but not for me. The absolutist then says (A2): There is an absolute truth and it is true for everyone.[12] The relativist then says: (A2) is true for you and your group but not for my group. The absolutist then says (A3): There is an *absolute* truth, and it is true for *everyone!* The relativist says: (A3) is true for you but not for me. The absolutist then says (A4): It is an absolute truth, which is true for everyone, that there is an absolute truth that is true for everyone. The relativist says: (A4) is true for you and not for me. The absolute says: I'm not going to let you always go up a level to refer to what I say. I am going to make a statement at an infinite number of levels, or make an infinite number of statements. Here it is, and here they are: (S1), that is, there is absolute truth; and (S2), that is, (S1) is absolutely true; and (S3), that is, (S2) is absolutely true; and . . . (And, relativist, please don't fail to notice these dots of infinite continuation.) But cannot the relativist quote all these, up to and including the dots, and say that all that is true for the absolutist but not for himself? Is there any way that the absolutist can state his position so that the relativist cannot go ahead and bracket it as only relatively true?

Whereas the absolutist cannot easily turn the tables on the relativist who says (R): all truths are relative. If the absolutist replies (F): (R) is false, absolutely false, then the relativist again can say (R2): (F) is true for you but not for me, and the absolutist's reply of (F2) (that (R2) also is absolutely false) only pushes further along a familiar path.

The absolutist's statement that there is absolute truth can be encircled and enfolded by the relativist, leaving the absolutist dissatisfied with what he has said previously. However, while the relativist's statement that truth is relative can be denied by the absolutist, it does not get enfolded by him, and so the relativist can rest content in having at least already fully conveyed his position. This symmetry does not show that relativism is true, of course, only that it is infuriating. To the absolutist, that is.

Who Wants Relativism?

The issues concerning relativism have generated much discussion, often quite heated. People very much *want* the issue of whether all truths are relative to turn out a certain way. It is worth pausing to consider why this is so. Why is so much passion aroused by this issue, and what determines which way people want the issue to turn out?

In classroom discussions and lectures, I have asked listeners whether *they* think that all truth is relative. (As *you* interpret the terms "relative" and "truth," is all truth relative?) I also ask them whether they *want* all truth to be relative.[13] Almost all have found themselves in the happy position of believing that things are the way they want them to be. Now, it *could* be that we adjust our desires to the realities of the situation, coming to want what (we believe) is the case. However, it seems more likely—doesn't it?—that in this case our (philosophical) belief about relativism follows in the footsteps of our desire. This gives one pause.

What determines which desire a person has about relativism? I shall offer some social-psychological conjectures about the factors that shape the desire, but I do not mean to say that the *truth* about relativism is relative to these factors. (Note that the philosophy to come is completely independent of my amateur psychological conjectures.)

Relativism about truth, along with cognate views such as that there are no objective facts and that all facts are "social constructions," is seen by its proponents as enhancing freedom. Objective facts are a constraint; they limit what one can do.

When we have various goals, the way to get to these goals is by performing actions that launch along paths to realizing these goals. Facts can therefore constrain the achievement of your goals. It may be a *fact* that the actions available to you do not begin any existing or possible paths that lead to achieving your goals. Or it may be a *fact* that every path that might lead to your goals unavoidably involves side effects that are significant (and unacceptable). Therefore, it can enhance your freedom and power if you are free of these constraints, if the facts that constitute them or underlie them are not objective facts.

On the other hand, the existence of objective facts, of particular ones that are believed to hold, can be desired because these facts are seen as a platform upon which to stand in pursuing your goals, as a means to get to your goals. If it is a fact that this path will lead from an available action to your goal, then that fact *enables* you to achieve your goal. If it is a fact that an action will have particular side effects and you do better to avoid these, then certain other available actions may facilitate this avoidance.

So which is the true character of facts, constraining or enabling? Clearly, facts have both aspects. (Rationality, too, can be seen as a constraint or as an enabling means.) If generally you are achieving your important goals, achieving them well enough even if not perfectly or optimally, if there are paths leading out from your actions that enable you to reach your level of aspiration, then you will view facts, in general, as enabling. If there are no such paths, however, then facts will appear to you mainly as constraining. Whether people welcome or oppose relativist doctrines depends, I conjecture, upon which of the two situations they are in.[14]

According to this explanation, the desire that truth be absolute arises from satisfaction with the particular truths that are believed to hold, and the desire that truth be relative stems from dissatisfaction with particular truths. The philosophical preference for absolutism or relativism, then, is a derivative one.

We therefore can understand why young people are more prone to favor and welcome relativism than the old. Younger people often are under the external constraining force of parental authority, and they may have fewer means or paths available to their goals. Older people, on the other hand, either are more likely to have discovered or acquired means to the realization of their goals or, if they were continually frustrated in their pursuit, to have lowered their level of aspiration and substituted other goals more easily achieved. Thereby they are likely to find the facts of the world less of a constraint to achieving the goals they actually have. (As for the unavoidable increasing constraints that they encounter as they age, they do not think that these being relative would make them any more escapable.)

However, the relativity of a truth is not the same as its alterability. Even if it is a nonrelative truth that my pen is on my desk, that is a fact easily changed.[15] Whereas if it is merely a relative truth that New York City is adjacent to the Atlantic Ocean or that capitalism outproduces socialism, these are not facts that are changed easily. Whatever these facts might hold true relative to, is not easily altered.

Why, then, would some people welcome relativism and assume that relative facts are less constraining? To account for such motivation, we need not assume that every relative truth is more alterable than any absolute truth. Still, for any given statement *p, p* almost always will be less constraining, or more alterable, or more escapable, if *p* is a relative truth than if it is an absolute one. For *p*'s being relative at least holds out the hope of escaping from its clutches, by losing the property relative to which it is true, or by moving into a group or culture relative to which it is not true. Even if you cannot change your own traits or situation, it might be liberating merely to know that someone somewhere isn't (or may not be) subject to that truth.

The desire to escape the reach of obdurate facts and compelling arguments can extend to the theoretical realm as well. It is this desire (and not the book's illuminating description of the texture of scientific practice) that accounts, I think, for the enormous public impact that Thomas Kuhn's *The Structure of Scientific Revolutions* has had since the 1970s. That was a time when many cherished theoretical positions on the political left faced very serious intellectual challenges and difficulties. Frederick Hayek and Milton Friedman produced powerful arguments about how markets operated and about how socialist systems failed to operate. These arguments were buttressed by "neoclassical economic theory" and also by evident and hard-to-deny facts about economic growth under capitalism, economic stagnation under socialism. What to do? Along comes Thomas Kuhn with his talk about different "paradigms," even in the apparently hard science of physics. To others (I do not say that this was Kuhn's motivation), Kuhn seemed to supply a ready way to avoid facing very strongly backed theories, criticisms, and data. A person (it was supposed) could rest secure within his own political paradigm, which was as good as any other competing theory, and he could feel licensed to ignore his own view's very evident difficulties. One simply said, "You have your paradigm and I have mine." End of discussion. Supposedly.

Increasing economic prosperity also has made it possible for people to be more relativistic, I think. In earlier times, people either had to adjust their beliefs and desires to a hard and difficult world or they failed to survive. They would have preferred, however, that the adjustment went in the opposite direction, that the world conformed to their beliefs and desires. Because prosperity fortunately enables life to be lived less close to the margin, it enables people to maintain whatever their current beliefs and desires are, at the cost of some loss of mesh with the actual world, to be sure, but without very dire consequences. By thinking that all truths or facts are relative, (it appears that) a person can hold that all his beliefs are true without change—relative to himself and his situation, at least. (On the other hand, increasing prosperity also might make some people more satisfied with their situation and hence less prone to relativism.)

The relativist sees the divisions among people as so great that truth cannot be the same for them; the nonrelativist (as we shall see) thinks the similarity in humans and in their environments is sufficiently great to make (the nature of) truth the same for all. Might people's different attitudes toward relativism also depend upon whether they *want* the divisions among people to be large and insurmountable? This puts the absolutist in a favorable light, allowing him to favor the unity of humankind. However, his opponents might see the absolutist as favoring unity on his own terms, in the belief that the one absolute truth is the truth as he sees it. And he might have the power to impose that view on others, or at least to compel their public assent to it. Thus, less powerful groups (women, racial minorities, homosexuals, minorities on the political left) appear to offer higher percentages (of vocal proponents) favorable to relativism, perhaps in resistance to the hegemony of the powerful. Current calls for "multiculturalism" come primarily from groups that view themselves as being subordinate.[16]

An alternative possible explanation for why some people especially welcome relativist views might be that these people are more tolerant in general. True, an absolutist about truth also might be tolerant, for an absolutist might well be a fallibilist, uncertain that he definitely has hold of the absolute truth that exists. And an absolutist who even is certain he knows some particular truth might be tolerant of those who are mistaken, while a relativist might turn out to be intolerant of various positions, especially of nonrelativist ones. Nevertheless, relativism might fit more easily psychologically, and hence more often, into an attitude that is tolerant of differences, and it could be their prior tolerance that predisposes some people toward relativism.

Many people who hold that all truths are relative also hold that many things, previously thought to be facts holding independently of human desires, beliefs, and choices, instead are "social constructions." This correlation, I think, reinforces our first tentative explanation for the desire that truth be relative, viz. it depends upon finding many central and (socially) important facts thwarting, frustrating, unpleasant, and undesirable. A "social construction" is not simply a fact unexplained by biology and other levels lower than the social. Consider such facts as the existence of educational systems or some other mode of transmission of adult knowledge to younger people, or the existence of armies or defensive forces to protect a society from outside attack. (I mean the existence of these general institutions, not the particular forms that they take.) These might well be universal facts constant across all societies that last for at least two generations.[17] Such institutions or practices would be social facts but not "social constructions," for we would understand the point and rationality of such institutions and see their practical necessity. A social construction, on the other hand, is *arbitrary*—or at any rate there is no good reason, no justifying reason, for its existing or for its being anything like the way it is. Whether or not it can easily be changed (and some social constructions might have come to be deeply embedded), a social construction is something without *authority*.

Hence, the thesis of social constructionism often is selective rather than universal. Only those things are held to be social constructions that the speaker wishes were different and holds to lack any authority; therefore, they do not have to be adapted to or obeyed or adhered to.[18] Because social constructions are arbitrary, it is perfectly permissible to alter them, to go against them, to violate them.

When all facts are viewed as social constructions, then facts (in general) lose authority. They need not be accepted as limitations upon what one might do. Some objective facts are *obdurate;* while we may wish they were different, we discover that they cannot (easily) be changed. Hence they have to be taken account of, be worked around, and be granted a certain, perhaps grudging, respect. (It is such facts that Freud's reality principle bids us to recognize.) If all facts are social constructions, however, then since they lack all authority, we would do better to devote energy toward changing undesired social facts rather than adapting to them or contouring our institutions around them.

The theory that some particular thing is a social construction may be an illuminating theory and even a correct one. However, it cannot be that *everything* is a social construction; it cannot be that all truths and facts and things are social constructions.[19] For to say that something, for instance gender differences, is a social construction is to say that there are social processes that cause this phenomenon to exist or to take a certain form. If gender differences are a social construction, then it is a fact that certain existing social processes produce those gender differences. And *that* fact—that those social processes exist and produce gender divisions—is not itself a social construction. (Or, if it too is a social construction, the fact that it is, is not itself a social construction.) William James tells the story of a person approaching him after a lecture and saying, "The world rests on a large turtle." "And what does the turtle rest upon?" James asked. "Another turtle," said the person. "And what . . . ," began James, who then was interrupted: "Professor James, it's turtles all the way down." There cannot be social constructions all the way down.

It is worth noting that even if all truth turns out to be socially relative, it does not follow that anything and everything holds true. If all truth is relative, then every truth holds relative only to some factors or other, and not beyond. (For every truth, there then will be some factor relative to which it does *not* hold.) It is a different matter to claim that each and every statement has the status of being a relative *truth*. That would entail that for each and every statement, there is some factor relative to which it holds true. So if someone makes a statement, and defends himself against criticism by saying that every truth is relative, one can reply that, nevertheless, his previous statement is false. There may be no factor relative to which *it* holds true (in which case, its denial will be absolutely true), or even if there is, that factor need not apply to the speaker. What could have been true in someone else's mouth in some other situation is false when he speaks. Relativist doctrine does not save him.

Truth in Space and Time

When he presented the principle of noncontradiction—that a statement and its denial are not both true, that no statement is both true and false—Aristotle had to state it sharply to avoid various apparently obvious counterexamples. Cannot it be both raining and not raining? In different places—raining in Boston, not in New York. And can't it be both raining in a certain place and not raining in that place? Raining there on Monday, not there on Tuesday. And can't it be both raining in a place at a time and not raining in a place at a time—raining softly there then and not raining hard there then? So Aristotle stated his principle of noncontradiction carefully. Nothing is both true and false at the same time in the same place in the same respect. It is that fully and exactly specified thing which cannot be both true and false.

It is not surprising, then, that almost all philosophers have held truth to be timeless. If it is true today that it is raining, while yesterday it didn't rain, since "It rains today" is an incompletely specified proposition, no statement or proposition changes its truth value from one day to the next, despite appearances. Specify the date, the time, and the place, and that completely specified tenseless statement will be timelessly true. It is true at every time and place that it rains in Boston, Massachusetts, on June 13, 1998. Fully specified truths, since they have their times and places built into them, are timeless and placeless.

Almost all philosophers, therefore, agree that a fully specified proposition or statement would have a fixed and unvarying truth value. W. V. Quine held that the vehicle of truth is (or could be viewed as) "eternal sentences," that is, sentences with timeless verbs and all temporal indicators explicitly included.[20] This trivial formal device seems to guarantee the timelessness of truth.

I think, however, that the timelessness of truth is a contentful empirical claim, one that might turn out to be false. In order to make it possible even to state this possibility, let our ascriptions of truth to statements speak explicitly with two temporal indices, one referring to the time of the events the statement describes, and the second referring to the time when the statement is true. Thus, consider the statement stating that event E occurs at time t_j. In ascribing truth to this statement, we must state explicitly the time at which it is true. We shall have to say things of this form: It is true at time t_k that event E occurs at time t_j. And this might be compatible with its being true at another time t_m that event E does not occur at time t_j. (And false at time t_m that event E occurs at time t_j.) The truth of even fully specified statements, then, would be relative to time.[21]

It is interesting that Aristotle is a notable exception to the general philosophical consensus that truth is timeless. For Aristotle (according to the usual interpretation) held that it is neither true nor false to say beforehand of a future contingent (undetermined) event that it will happen. If a sea battle is to be fought on Tuesday between two opposing fleets, and on Monday it is undetermined which fleet will win the battle, perhaps because victory depends upon commanders' decisions that themselves are free and undetermined, then on Monday it would not be true to say, "The first fleet will win the battle tomorrow" and on Monday it would not be true to say, "The second fleet will win the battle tomorrow."

Aristotle's root intuition here, I think, is this one. A statement is true at a time only if something holding at that time makes it true, fixes it as true, constitutes it as true, determines that it is true, makes it determinate that it is true. We might say that for something to be true at a time, there has to be information at that time that fixes it as true. Here, though, information does not mean something that is known but facts that hold. For something to be true at a time there must be facts that hold *at that time* in virtue of which that thing is true; there must be facts holding at that time that make it true.

Because Aristotle believed that which fleet is victorious in tomorrow's sea battle depends upon future decisions of the captains that are not now determined or determinate, he believed that there are no facts holding now that will make one fleet, or the other, victorious later, and so he believed that it is not now true that the first fleet will win the battle, and it is not now true that the second fleet will win the battle. It is not simply that the battle has not yet taken place. It is not yet true which fleet will win.

But cannot we always say, when a statement holds at a certain time, that in virtue of that fact it also was true earlier that it will hold at that later time? The correspondence theorist will assert that a statement is true when it corresponds to a fact, and not merely to a future fact. The root intuition behind the correspondence notion of truth extends to saying that a statement is true at a time if and only if it corresponds to a fact holding at that time. Yet it might seem that we always can trivially postulate additional facts (with appropriate tenses) that will mirror, at all other times, any fact that holds at any time. However, if we take an ontology of facts (or of what underlies them) seriously—as a correspondence theorist of truth must— then we should not multiply facts capriciously, beyond necessity. (Consider how one would react to someone who said that whenever a new object comes to exist, there must always have been previously existing ghostly anticipators of that object.) The question is whether there really *are* such mirroring facts that actually do hold at each of the other times. I doubt that purely philosophical arguments can settle such an ontological question. Indeed, it is difficult even to formulate a criterion that will distinguish real facts or changes from their linguistic simulacra.[22] Those who attempt to mandate the timelessness of truth by stipulation or fiat or verbal legerdemain may prevent us from discovering the interesting empirical nature that truth actually has.

The notion of its being determinate at a time that an event occurs at another time, of its being determinate at a time that a statement holds true at that other time, is an important one that is worth investigating. What are this notion's properties, and to what extent, and in what way, is it actually realized and instantiated in the world?

Some may say that this is all well and good but it is quite a different matter from the topic of *truth*. Determinately holding is one thing, being true is another. I do not want to quarrel over what may be a verbal issue. I do think that "determinately holds" is the interesting and important notion. If determinateness turns out to be more rooted in time and space, its span drastically smaller, than once was thought, then whatever apparent distinct content the further notion of "true" may have is drained of interest because of the way the world is, the way we have learned it to be. It is determinateness that stitches the universe together, or fails to do so. A timeless truth that floats free of determinateness is a nonscience fiction.

The standard theories of tense logic hold that the following statements are true; indeed, they hold these to be necessary truths.[23]

(A)   If it is true at a time that event *E* occurred at an earlier time, then it is true at that earlier time that *E* occurs at that time.

(B)   If it is true at a time that event *E* occurs at that time, then it is true at all later times that *E* did occur at that earlier time.

(C)   If it is true at a time that event *E* occurs at that time, then it is true at all earlier times that *E* will occur at that later time.

I believe that quantum mechanics makes it plausible that each of these statements (A)–(C) is false. (One might say that quantum mechanics makes it plausible that these statements are sometimes false, but since they are asserted with full generality, if they are false in some cases then they simply are false.) If these statements are false, they certainly are not necessary truths of tense or of any other logic. I do not say that quantum mechanics *demonstrates* that these statements are false, merely that their falsity fits with a plausible reading of quantum mechanics that equates determinateness and truth.

What quantum mechanics does show is that the following corresponding statements about determinateness do not (always) hold true.

(1)   If it is determinate at a time that event *E* occurred at an earlier time, then it is determinate at that earlier time that *E* occurs at that time.

(2)   If it is determinate at a time that event *E* occurs at that time, then it is determinate at all later times that *e* did occur at that earlier time.

(3)   If it is determinate at a time that event *e* occurs at that time, then it is
        determinate at all earlier times that *e* will occur at that later time.

I begin by listing some phenomena of quantum mechanics. (The remainder of this section is somewhat technical.) The first phenomenon is
well known.

The two-slit experiment. Photons are fired from a source toward a thin
barrier containing two slits, which may be opened or closed. Behind the
barrier is a sensitive screen that registers what impinges on it. When both
slits are opened, with no detector active at either slit, the far screen shows
interference phenomena characteristic of waves, even when the photons are
released very slowly. (When either slit alone is open, the far screen shows a
pattern of hits characteristic of particles, but this is not incompatible with a
wave phenomenon.) When both slits are open, with an active measuring
device at one slit, the far screen shows a (noninterference) pattern of hits
characteristic of particles.[24] Moreover, an active detector at one slit, even
when it does not register a passing particle, is sufficient to nullify the interference pattern.

The delayed-choice experiment. The decision whether and where to activate a measuring instrument to detect along which of two widely separated
tracks photons have come can be made long after the photons have been
emitted and have entered along one or another (or both) tracks. If the measuring device is not activated, the interference pattern is exhibited; if it is
activated, the noninterference pattern characteristic of particles that have
traveled definitely along one or another of the tracks is exhibited. If a detector is present at one of the slits in the two-slit experiment, the light will
behave like particles and not exhibit interference patterns on the screen. If
no detector is present, the light will behave like a wave and exhibit interference patterns on the screen. Delayed-choice involves delaying the choice of
whether or not there is a detector operating until *after* the light has passed
the plane containing the two slits. John Wheeler imagined this situation
could be realized astronomically with light from quasars, with a heavy gravitational object such as a galaxy bending the light around it into two curved
paths that meet at a far distance (and cross if they are not intercepted.) An
observer at that distant place, e.g., earth, can decide, long after the light has
passed the galaxy, to set up a detector where the two paths come together
again (so that interference will be shown) or to set up a detector later along
a path, after they cross, recording the action of particles.[25]

Merging streams. If light of +45-degree polarization is fed into a horizontal/vertical detector (a forward polarizer) and then both streams are fed into a reversed polarizer, reuniting the streams, the light emerging from this second polarizer will have +45-degree polarization (as measured by a later ±45-degree detector). Is it that the initial +45-degree light that was fed into the horizontal/vertical detector did *not* have a measurement made upon it, since it was immediately fed into a reversed polarizer that merged the two streams, or that it did have a measurement made but this measurement was erased? In either case, the light coming out of the second horizontal/vertical (reversed) polarizer now has the original +45-degree polarization. The two horizontal/vertical polarizers together did not do what either alone would do, namely, produce a stream of half +45-degree polarization and half −45-degree polarization.

The erased measurement. Within the Schrodinger wave formalism, a measurement of a system by a device establishes a correlation between the states of the system and the device. It is possible, however, for this correlation to be erased. (Since the Schrodinger equation is time-reversal invariant, it is physically possible for the process to be run backward, with the measured particle and the measuring particle or system interacting again to reach the noncorrelated state, even though people may not themselves be able to manipulate this precise a reversal.) If that happens, the information in that measurement is lost irretrievably.

Things are less clear if a measurement (to yield a particular result) involves a collapse of the wave packet. Is it possible for this to proceed backward through the collapse to the previous superposition? (It is another question whether one can make that happen.) If so, a definite measurement involving a collapse can be erased.[26] In the view of Martin Scully, "it should be possible to gain information about the state of a quantum phenomenon, thereby destroying its wavelike properties, and then restore those properties by 'erasing' the information." A group led by Raymond Chiao performed experiments to reinstitute interference patterns in a way that seems to indicate that "a collapsed wave function can be put back together again."[27]

After collapse of the wave function, there is no fact holding afterwards that makes it determinate what the wave function was before the collapse. With the two-slit experiment, a mark on (that part of the wave function of) an electron that passes through the righthand slit will eliminate the interference pattern. But if that mark and all traces of it are erased (perhaps the electron has emitted a photon that is reflected back by a mirror so that it gets reabsorbed into the electron), an interference pattern reemerges. If there was a collapse whose traces have not been erased, and that collapse eliminated half of the wave function, it then is impossible to tell what the whole wave function had been beforehand. (One can know, however, that the previous wave function was such that it gave a nonvanishing probability to the situation that was got to after the collapse.)[28]

All actualities can have effects. (Put more pointedly, what cannot have an effect is not an actuality.) Something X has property P only when that can affect the properties of something (else), only when it is possible that there is something (else) Y and a property Q such that X's having P affects Y's having Q. X's having P does not require actually affecting something else; it just has to be *possible* that there exists a thing that X's having P affects.

In some cases, quantum theory excludes this latter possibility. For some properties P in some situations, when no measurement is made of X's having P at time t_1, when no measurement is made of whether or not X has P, it is not possible (according to quantum theory) that there is something that X's having P at time t_1 affects.[29] Such an affecting would itself be a later measurement by a device at time t_2; it would not be an effect of X's being P at the earlier time t_1. Quantum mechanics, on the usual interpretation, tells us that a definite property exists only insofar as it can possibly affect something. And let us add that a measured entity continues to have a property only as long as it is possible that there is something (some other "measuring" device) whose properties it (does or) can affect.

Recall now the case of the erased measurement. A measurement of system S by device D entangled the states of S and D, but now the process has been reversed, the states of S and D no longer are entangled, and the measurement information is irretrievably lost. (If we say there was a collapse of the wave packet, we should have to say that the collapse has been reversed.) The usual appeal to macroscopic systems or to irreversible effects in discussions of measurement is designed to fix the stability of the measuring device's (or of what it affects) being in a certain state so that the information that this is so never becomes (in principle) nonrecoverable. When the only measurement of X's having P (a certain position, say) is *completely* erased, then X's having had P can no longer affect any other thing's having any property. Thus, it no longer is determinate that X had P. It no longer is true that X has P or that it *had P!* The effects of X's having P were, in turn, erased so as not to be able to affect anything further; so X's having had P does not, at that later time, hold.

This may seem reminiscent of verificationist views about past events. "Do you mean to say," asked incredulous objectors to the verifiability criterion of meaning, "that a statement about the past now is meaningful only if we presently are able, in principle, to verify it?" However, the position put forward here is *not* a verificationist one. I *do* mean to say, though, that it is true now that a system was in a past state only if it now is true that some differential effect of that past state continues.[30] However, it need not be the case now that the particular differential effect can be *discovered* or *verified*. When Aristotle held that there were no facts holding on Monday that determined or fixed the victor of the sea battle on Tuesday, his point was not that on Monday it could not be *verified* who would win the coming battle. If there were facts holding on Monday that determined the victor on Tuesday, even if these facts could not be detected or verified on Monday, and even if no one was aware of the kind of connection there was between such facts and a victory the next day, nevertheless it would be true on Monday that one particular fleet, say the Athenian fleet, was going to win on Tuesday. The issue isn't what can be verified or what can be found out on Monday. The issue concerns what actually holds on Monday.[31]

Let us separate two issues. The first concerns the concept of its being fixed and determined at a time that some event occurs at another time. We can investigate the properties of this concept, its interrelations with other concepts, and what general and what particular statements using the concept actually hold true in our universe. If our universe were a deterministic one then the following would hold: if it is fixed and determined at time t_j that event E occurs at time t_j then it is fixed and determined at all earlier times that event E occurs at time t_j. If, instead, our universe is not a deterministic one, then there is (or at least can be) at least one event E and a time t_j such that it is fixed and determined at time t_j that event E occurs at time t_j yet not fixed and determined at some particular earlier time that event E occurs at time t_j. And we need not restrict attention to earlier events. It might be fixed and determined at time t_j that event E occurs at time t_j yet not be fixed and determined at some *later* time that event E occurs at time t_j. What the actual properties are of the "fixed and determined" notion is an empirical question.

These two general statements, corresponding to (2) and (3) above, are shown to be false by the stochastic character of quantum mechanics. On our assumption that truth is identical with determinateness, the stochastic character of quantum mechanics is sufficient to show the falsity of the (purportedly necessary) principles of tense logic, (B) and (C) above. The argument against (1) and (A) above was more complicated, and required something in addition to the general stochastic nature of quantum mechanics. It needed to invoke the delayed-choice experiment in a realist way. No current realist interpretation of quantum mechanics interprets the delayed-choice experiment; Wheeler himself used the delayed-choice situation as a *reductio* of realism. Our argument against (A) and against (1) therefore depends upon some realist interpretation of delayed-choice that remains to be developed. There is no guarantee that this can be done. However, we can say, at least, that the price of a realist interpretation of delayed-choice is the denial of (1) above, and also (on the assumption that truth is identical to determinateness) the denial of (A) above.

The notion of whether some event's occurring at a time is fixed and determinate at another time clearly is an important one. A separate issue is how this important notion is connected with the notion of truth. Shall it be identified with that notion? This would capture Aristotle's intuition that on Monday the truth about the victor of the battle on Tuesday is indeterminate. It is not merely that the victor cannot be known or verified on Monday but that, since no facts holding on Monday determine who will be the victor, there is no truth holding on Monday that specifies Tuesday's victor.

The contrasting view that truth must be timeless denies the following proposition. For a truth to hold at a time, there must be a basis for it to hold then, that is, there must be facts holding then that fix that truth as also holding. But what is the usefulness of the timeless notion of truth if it floats free of such a factual basis? How would we discover that truth is not timeless—surely an interesting discovery, if true—if we insist on defining or contouring truth so that its timelessness is guaranteed?

It is worth exploring a view of truth at a time that identifies it with being fixed and determined or determinate at that time. (Readers who insist on the timelessness of truth can read on, interpreting the discussion not as concerning truth's holding at a time but as concerning truth's being fixed and determinate at a time. Later, perhaps they will relent and see the point and the plausibility of the identification.)

This view of truth as mired in time may seem incompatible with a correspondence theory of truth, according to which a statement is true if it corresponds to the facts. But are the facts, the fully complete facts (which correspond to fully specified statements), themselves timeless? If not, then a correspondence theory will hold that a statement is true at a time when and only when it corresponds to facts which hold at that time.

Quantum mechanics has led some theorists to maintain that facts themselves can be said to be relative. Although the relativity they speak of is not a relativity to time, it is instructive to look briefly at these claims. (If the facts themselves are relative, then a relativist might concede that truth is always and everywhere correspondence to the facts, but hold that since facts are relative, so also is truth.) The "measurement problem" in quantum mechanics is that of understanding how measurements can yield definite results when the system being measured is in a superposition of states, since it follows from the laws of quantum mechanics that a measuring device interacting with such a system also will move into a superposition and show interference properties. The time-dependent Schrodinger equation, when applied to the interaction of a measuring device with a system in superposition, does not yield the measuring device going into one particular state (rather than into a superposition). John von Neumann held that there were two kinds of changes in a quantum mechanical system, the continuous change (in accordance with the Schrodinger equation) that occurs when the system evolves in the absence of a measurement, and a discontinuous change that occurs when a measurement is made (the "collapse of the wave packet"), which yields a particular definite measured value.

As one route out of the apparently intractable measurement problem, the literature of quantum mechanics offers some interpretations that explicitly make the quantum-mechanical facts relative. (I follow the secondary literature here.) Simon Kochen interprets the measurement situation as follows. When two systems in superpositions interact, one being a measuring device, each one *relative to the other* has one or another definite value; each relative to the other is in a definite state.[32] However, the total combination, relative to the entire outside environment, still remains in a superposition and exhibits interference features. So a system has a definite property *relative to* a measuring apparatus that it interacts with, but not relative to the outside world that "witnesses" the two systems. On this interpretation, there is no collapse of the wave packet, no discontinuous event that constitutes an exception to the Schrodinger equation. Furthermore, the smear of the indefiniteness of a superposition is not ever present, at least not so relative to the measuring apparatus. While both are in a superposition in relation to the outside world, one is not in a superposition relative to the other.[33]

Quantum mechanics is our most fundamental theory of the microlevel, so if, according to it, all definite facts (involving conjugate variables) are definite only relative to states of measuring systems, then we are well on our way to holding that all facts (or at any rate, all the physical facts that are reducible to quantum mechanics) are relative. (The Schrodinger equation itself would not thereby be held to be relative.) The Kochen interpretation certainly has not been established as the definitive interpretation of quantum mechanics; still, it is a possible interpretation, one that avoids the difficulties of the von Neumann interpretation with its collapse of the wave packet, and it illustrates how almost all (definite) facts could turn out to be relative.[34]

Perhaps facts can be relative, but can it be a relative matter whether some entity is real or not? Some say yes. According to the laws of quantum fields in curved space-time,

> Accelerated observers just above a black hole's horizon must see the vacuum fluctuations there not as virtual pairs of particles but rather as an atmosphere of real particles. This startling discovery revealed that *the concept of a real particle is relative*, not absolute; that is, it depends on one's reference frame. Observers in freely falling frames who plunge through the hole's horizon see no real particles outside the horizon, only virtual ones. Observers in accelerated frames who, by their acceleration, remain always above the horizon see a plethora of real particles.[35]

Our brief reference here to quantum mechanics and to cosmology indicates how these very basic theories might lend themselves to the conclusion that facts are relative. Facts needing a temporal index may not be such a wild idea, after all.

According to the view we are exploring, the truth about the past is not fixed. This lesson of the erased measurement is reinforced by the delayed-choice experiments. Some people have concluded that delayed-choice implies that the observation we now choose to make causes long-past events to have occurred (and others have objected to delayed-choice because they think it implies this). Delayed-choice does have the implication that truths about the past are not fixed in the way that people thought, but we must be careful in stating precisely what this involves.

The erased-measurement situation shows that the (previous) second purported truth of tense logic is false. Something can be true at a time, yet it not be true at a later time that it was true at that earlier time. The erasure of the effects of the measurement erases the truth that the measurement revealed. The delayed-choice experiment can be interpreted to show that the first purported truth of tense logic is false. It can be true now that a certain event occurred at an earlier time, although it was not true at that earlier time that the event occurred then. It was true at that earlier time that the particle was in a superposition then, but it now is true that the particle followed a particular path then and was not in a superposition then.[36] (The delayed-choice experiment admits this interpretation but does not require it, since the usual formulation of quantum mechanics offers a consistent description according to which it now is true that it was in a superposition back then. We can say, though, that any realist view that could be developed that keeps Wheeler's lessons from delayed-choice would also amount to a refutation of (A).) And the falsity of (C) is shown, one might plausibly argue, by the randomness of what the wave packet collapses into.

These results should not be very surprising to proponents of the standard view of quantum mechanics. This, the Copenhagen interpretation (named after the Danish physicist Niels Bohr's city of residence), holds that a system is not in a definite state in the absence of an actual measurement showing it to be in that state. (And also, let us add, using the Einstein-Podolsky-Rosen criterion, when it is not true that a measurement definitely, with probability 1, would show it to be in that state.) If actually registering at a time (or definitely being such as would register at that time) is necessary for the system's being in a definite state at that time, then it is not a large step to saying the following. A necessary condition for its being true at another time t_2 that a system is in a definite state at this time t_1 is that the system's being in the state at time t_1 can possibly register at time t_2.

With erased measurement, it no longer is true that the particle was in that measured state then. Speaking more carefully, there is a time t_1 and there is a later time t_2 such that it is true at t_1 that the particle is in that state at t_1, but it is not true at t_2 that the particle is in that state at t_1. What about the statement that a measurement is (was) made, which does not state the result of that measurement? It is true then that a measurement is made then, and it can be true now that a measurement was made then. (The fact that a measurement was made, that there was a correlation then between a state of a particle and a state of the measuring device, has left a trace now. What has not left any trace is the particular result of that measurement.)

In this sense, what holds true at a time can be incomplete; it can have holes. It holds true now that some measurement was made then, but nothing holds true now about what measurement resulted then, and so nothing holds true now about what the state of the particle was then.[37] It could, for example, be true at time t_2 that p-or-q held at time t_1, although it is not true at time t_2 that p held at time t_1, and it is not true at time t_2 that q held at time t_1.[38] Since the set of truths that hold at a time is incomplete, there is a need to study what logic appropriately applies to them.

With delayed-choice, it is true at time t_1 that the particle is in a superposition at t_1, yet it is not true at t_2 that the particle is in a superposition at t_1.[39] With erased measurement, things can be opposite. It is true then (at the time of the earlier measurement) that the particle is in a particular state then, but it is true now that the particle is (was) in a superposition then. Delayed-choice can collapse a previous superposition; erased measurement can reinstate it.

Truth is tentative. Before the discoveries of quantum mechanics, the question whether what once was true always will be what once was true, automatically received an affirmative answer. Now the answer turns out to be negative, or at least "not necessarily." "Once a truth, always a truth" does not necessarily hold. Truth does not necessarily stay fixed.

For it to be true at time t_2 that some entity or event E has a property P at time t_1, it must be possible (at t_2) for E's having P at t_1 to affect some Y's having some property Q at t_2. If all effects, and all possibilities of effects, are erased, it no longer is true at those later times that E had P at t_1. But what if exactly those same effects of E's having P at t_1 also could have been produced by some other thing Z's being R at t_0 (without E's being P at t_1)? The strongest form of the view under development—the form that I tentatively put forward here—holds that (the possibility of) the later effects of E's having P must not only exist but also allow the *unique recoverability* of the fact that E had P at t_1.[40]

We have discovered as a (possible) consequence of quantum mechanics a relativity of truth, and of facts, to time, to the existence of effects at a time.[41] I do not claim that quantum mechanics entails this, merely that it is a plausible interpretation of quantum mechanics, a plausible hypothesis about what else holds if quantum mechanics does.[42]

The Copenhagen or Aristotelian motivations about determinacy lead to a theory that makes truth relative to a time. A statement is true at a time only if its truth is fixed and determinate (by facts that hold) *then*. The possible relativization of truth to time, depending upon the results of physics, is a surprising result but a digestible one. However, the view (that a statement is true at a time if and only if it holds true in virtue of a fact that holds at that time) can be extended even further. Since conceptual change is easier to accept one small step at a time, prudence dictates my not immediately pushing this line of thought to its furthest limit. A consequence that seems like a *reductio ad absurdum* of a view when it comes in one big leap will be treated seriously if the way to it has been paved by already assimilated steps. Nevertheless, I press on.

It seems natural, even if somewhat less intuitive, to extend the theory to include spatial location. A statement is true at a place only if its truth is fixed and determined (by facts that hold) *there*. It was quantum mechanics (or temporal indeterminacy) that motivated viewing truth as relative to a time; it is Einstein's Special Theory of Relativity that motivates making truth relative to a place. (Indeed, because relativity theory treats space and time in a unified way, as space-time, it would be unnatural *not* to extend our theory to include spatial location.) Because the velocity of light is finite, an event E can occur at place p at time t, yet no effects of E occur at other places at that same time t or at distant places at some particular (sufficiently close) later times. It takes time for the effects of E's occurrence at p, for the news of its occurrence there, to arrive elsewhere. We therefore cannot ask simply whether it is true at t that E has occurred at place p. We also have to ask *where* that is true. It is true at place p that it is true at t that E occurs at p (at time t), but it need not be true at other places r (at time t) that E occurs at p at t. The news has not reached these other places yet; it has not registered at those other places yet; it is not yet fixed and determinate there. (Here we must suppose that E at p is not causally determined by some earlier event E' that also registers at the other place r in question, where r at t *is* in the future light cone of E', or else r at t could carry the information that makes it determinate that E occurs at p.)

It is an empirical question whether truth is timeless, and also whether it is spaceless.[43] There is no necessity about it. The universe could be such that truth is neither. And according to current physical theory, it seems that truth holds at a place-time.

The forward light cone of an event E is a spreading (at the speed of light) spatial volume whose events can be causally affected by E (which is at the point of the cone). The backward light cone of an event E is the spatially converging spatial volume (coming to a point at E) of events that can causally affect E.

As a first approximation, we might say that the only truths that hold at a place at the current time are of two sorts. First, those truths concerning events in the backward light cone of (an event at) that place at the current time. In that case, the statement that event E happened at place p at time t can be true at some later place X at a later time t' yet not be true at another later spatially even more distant place Y at that same later time t', because p at t is in the backward light cone of X at t' but not of Y at t'. The second sort of truth that holds of a place at the current time concerns those future events that are determined by what holds at that place at the current time. It is true here-now that some later event will occur there-later only if factors that hold here-now are sufficient to determine that event there-later.

It is true here-now that event E occurs there-then only if there-then (or some uniquely recoverable sufficient cause of E at there-then) is in the backward light cone of here-now (and so could affect here-now) or if there-then is in the forward light cone of here-now and is causally determined by factors holding (now) at here-now, or if E at there-then has some uniquely recoverable sufficient cause C, where C is in the backward light cone of here-now *and* is uniquely recoverable from this spot. That is *one* restriction.

We are not yet quite done with the complications. It is not exactly "causally affect" that is in question. For quantum mechanics is a nonlocal theory. Events at one place-time can fix, that is determine according to scientific law (but not a *causal* law, so they do not causally determine), an event outside the first event's forward (or backward) light cone.[44] An event of measuring the spin of a particle here-now as $+\frac{1}{2}$ fixes the spin of a correlated particle there-now as $-\frac{1}{2}$. It is true here-now that the correlated particle has a spin of $-\frac{1}{2}$ there-now. So truth is *not* restricted within the light cone after all. What is true here-now are not only statements about events light-cone-linked (with chains of unique recoverability) to here-now. Nonlocality can extend the tentacles of truth more widely.[45] What is true here-now are statements about events there-then that are fixed by events and facts holding here-now. Generally this will be within here-now's (or its recoverable cause's) past and future light cone, sometimes more narrowly because of erased measurements, sometimes more widely because of nonlocal fixing of facts.

To take the step to indexing truth to a time (because of the delayed-choice and erased-measurement experiments) is one thing. To also index truth to a place, because of considerations from Special Relativity, is another matter that raises its own special problems. Are there truths at a point instant? Truths in a room?[46] Does which truths hold there depend upon which person is there and what he knows, upon which books are there and what sentences it contains? Perhaps there is some way to define the information in an object, and so in a space-time volume, and thereby to define what holds truth there-then, as fixed by the information that holds there-then and by what holds elsewhere-elsewhen that scientific laws are able to (uniquely) connect with the information that obtains there-then.

The theory that relativizes truth to place-times is *not* verificationist. It does not depend upon what we know or upon what anyone knows. It does depend upon *determination,* upon what facts holding at some place-times *fix* about other place-times.

And such determinate fixing might turn out to be sparser than we had assumed, with the consequence that truth is much more localized than we previously thought. Do physical laws permeate the universe so that they hold at each and every place-time? Or does contemporary physics tell us that our universe contains very few place-times (Leibnitzian monads) that mirror whatever holds elsewhere? There can be interfering factors between place-times, when the causal laws linking them hold only all things being equal; in that case, whether the truths that hold here fix what holds elsewhere depends upon whether interfering factors (and which ones) actually did operate. But apart from this, it seems that what is true locally does not determine the structure of the global space-time.[47] If the physics we discover greatly fragments and localizes the facts that hold, some philosophers may recoil from seeing truth itself as similarly localized. Instead, they might define truth *period* as what is fixed by the (logical) union of the facts that hold at each of the place-times at those place-times. But that would make the timelessness (and spacelessness) of truth a derivative and definitional thing that corresponds to nothing real beyond a disjunction of the scattered facts, which nowhere are actually gathered and registered. The apparently weighty reasons for holding that truth must be timeless (as well as the intuitive counterexamples to opposing views) may come to be seen as dependent upon, and derived from, a conceptual framework that itself is undercut by a physics that roots its facts in local space and time.[48]

Where st is a place-time or spatiotemporal region, "It is true at st that p" behaves like "It is determined at st that p." Because Aristotle believed the outcome of a future sea battle might be undetermined by current facts, he believed that it is not now true that such-and-such a fleet will win the sea battle.[49]

An appealing and standardly imposed condition of adequacy on a theory of truth is:

(C)   It is true that p if and only if p.[50]

A theory that relativizes truth to place-times cannot easily endorse this condition, in its full strength, but it can put forth some consequences of it. One consequence, stated in terms of something being determinate at a place-time, would be:

(D)   It is determinate at place-time st that [it is determinate at place-time st that p] if and only if it is determinate at place-time st that p.

As a statement about truth, this corresponds to:

(T)   It is true at place-time st that [it is true at place-time st that p] if and only if it is true at place-time st that p.

However, even though we have restricted this statement to one and the same space-time, it will be too strong to assert the implication from right to left if there can be enough information at *st* to make it determinate there that *p* yet not enough to make it determinate there that it *is determinate* there that *p*.[51] If such a situation can obtain, then only the following weaker condition can be put forth:

(D')   If it is determinate at place-time *st* that [it is determinate at *st* that *p*], then it is determinate at *st* that *p*.

Putting this conditional (but not biconditional) proposition in terms of truth, we have:

(T')   If it is true at place-time *st* that [it is true at *st* that *p*], then it is true at *st* that *p*.

Condition (T'), unlike condition (C) above, does not allow the term "true" to be eliminated from the sentential context "It is true that *p*."[52]

But what of statements (D') and (T') themselves; are these also relativized to space-time? And is the theory of truth as relativized to space-time itself also relativized to space-time? Are quantum mechanics, which suggested the relativization of truth to time, and relativity theory, which suggested its relativization to space, themselves also relativized to space-time? More generally, mustn't there be some topmost level stating a truth *without* a temporal index, so that at this topmost level there are unrelativized truths? Mustn't the very theory we are stating here be stated as a truth that is *not* relativized to time?

To say that truth is relativized to time is not to say that there is no truth that holds at every time, that is, no truth for which it is true at every time that it is true at every time. Perhaps statements (D') and (T') and quantum mechanics and relativity theory all are such. However, such omnitemporal truth would not be a feature of the notion of truth but instead a feature (if it turned out to be so) of the universe as it concerned these particular truths. And there is no necessity that somewhere up the line there *must* be some such omnitemporal truth.

Suppose there isn't any omnitemporal truth, at any level up the line of generality or at any metalevel either. We can state this position as the following statement (which only *might* be true; whether it is true depends upon what the universe actually is like):

(S)   For every statement *p*, there is a time t_i such that at time t_i *p* is not true.

Now what about statement (S) itself? If it is true and it applies to itself, then there is some time when it is not true. Provided that time is not now, the time when I am asserting it, there will be no paradox. There will be a moment, call it t_j, when it is true that there is a statement, call it M, that is true at all times. But that moment is not now, that moment need not last for long, and at all other times M will be false. The proponent of an omnitemporal truth does not want there to be just one time when a statement is omnitemporally true but for that to hold (of that particular statement) at *all* times. This, however, does not follow merely from an argument that applies (S) to itself.[53]

The theory of truth presented here is not a theory about space-time that itself is outside space-time. Truths *outside* space-time are a remnant of Platonism, and, whether or not that structure holds for necessary truths, it is inappropriate for empirical truths. Our theory places truth *within* space-time.

We might say that truth is *weakly spatiotemporal* when there is some (fully specified) statement that holds true in some place-time but does not hold true in every place-time.[54] Truth is weakly spatiotemporal when there is at least one truth that doesn't register everywhere and everywhen. This is compatible with there being a particular and quite small spatiotemporal region where every truth registers. (I add "quite small" because if we let the region be large enough—all of space and time—then each truth will register somewhere within that region.) Let us call such a region in which every truth registers an omniscient region. All truths that hold anywhere are fixed and determinate there. We might say that truth is *strongly spatiotemporal* when there is no omniscient region, no point or small place where all truths register and hold.

Quantum mechanics has led us to maintain that truth is relative to a time. And the considerations that led to this conclusion, when consistently pursued, lead to the further view that truth is relative to a time and place. Truth is relative to spatiotemporal position. Spatiotemporal position is a surprising and unexpected factor in the context of truth, and all spatiotemporal positions are equally good. So the present view counts as *relativism about truth*. It might aptly be described as the *Copenhagen Interpretation of Truth*.

This Aristotelian-Copenhagen interpretation of truth is not put forward as a necessary truth about truth. I do not claim that truth *must* be rooted in space-time. What character truth actually has is an empirical question. But notice how strong are the conditions that must be satisfied for truth to be space-timeless. For any truth that holds at a place-time *st*, it must also be determinate at all other place-times that this truth holds at *st*. Let us say that, in this case, this truth *registers* at every other place-time. Moreover, for truth to be space-timeless, the fact that this truth registers at each and every other place-time must also register at each and every place-time, and so on up the line. And all this must hold, all the way up the line, for every truth that registers at any place-time. This exhibits the structure that in the case of shared knowledge among different persons has been termed "common knowledge," so let us term such infinitely extended registering, common registering. Truth transcends being rooted in space and time only when there is common registering, throughout all of space and time, of each and every local fact. Only then does Truth subsist in its own Platonic realm.

The Truth Property

This position that truth is relative to place and time is a far cry from social relativisms wherein truth is relative to a culture or to a sex or gender or to a social position. The correspondence theory of truth says that a statement is true if it corresponds to the facts. Adding references to the places and times where these facts are fixed and determined does not appear to make any reference to anything social. So (according to the correspondence theory) must not what is true for one person be true for all? How can truth vary from person to person, group to group, or society to society? Won't a statement that is fully specified (and contains no indexical expressions that refer to a society or group) be true for every society or group, if it is true for any one? From its being true *period*, doesn't it follow that it is true for everyone? How, then, can we even make sense of relativism about truth?

In *The Nature of Rationality*, I wrote:

> It seems reasonable to think that our original interest in truth was instrumentally based. Truths served us better than falsehoods and better than no beliefs at all in coping with the world's dangers and opportunities. Perfectly accurate truth was not necessary, only a belief that was *true enough* to give (more) desirable results when acted upon. What was wanted were "serviceable truths," and to be serviceable, a belief need not have been precisely true. Truth, then, would be rather like what Rawls has called a primary good, something that is useful for a *very* wide range of purposes, almost all, and hence that will be desired and bring benefit (almost) no matter what our particular purposes might be. So we might desire true beliefs and come to be concerned with truth because true beliefs are useful for a very wide range of

purposes. However, that would leave our concern with truth instrumental—at least originally.

Was William James right, then, in saying the truth is what works? We might see James as depicting the *value* of truth, not its nature. Rather than hold that truth simply is 'serviceability,' we can construe truth as that property, whatever it is, that underlies and explains serviceability. If one property underlies the serviceability of various statements about different subject matters, that property will have to be very general and abstractly stated. The various theories of truth—correspondence, coherence, etc.—then would be explanatory hypotheses, conjectures about the nature of the property that underlies and explains serviceability. (And if it turns out that the serviceability of different kinds of statement is explained by distinct properties?)[55]

In general, it is better to act upon truths than upon falsehoods. We more often achieve the goals of our action when the beliefs they are predicated upon are true. Not every time, however. We can imagine cases in which a belief is false, yet acting upon it happens to dovetail with what is true in the world so as to produce that action's success, that is, the achievement of the goal that was aimed at. And sometimes an action that is based upon the truth will fail. The best way that a goal might be reached, or even the only possible way, need not be guaranteed to reach it. Nevertheless, as a statistical matter, we more often achieve our goals when we act upon the truth.

Now, consider those statements or propositions that we frequently are successful in acting upon, and also those statements that we usually are unsuccessful (or are less frequently successful) in acting upon. What do the statements in the first group have in common (that statements in the second group lack)? We can view theories of truth as presenting the property these statements in the first group share, the property that explains why (more frequently than otherwise) we are successful in acting upon these statements. Some would hold it is the property of corresponding to the facts that explains the greater statistical likelihood of success in action, others that it is coherence, and so on through the range of theories of truth.[56] Facts, however, are not merely components of hypotheses about the beliefs upon which you act to *successfully* achieve your goals. Facts also are encountered more directly when they thwart your achieving your goals (as you act upon false beliefs). You sometimes discover facts by bumping up against them.

We need to refine this view of truth. Truth is not the one property that the statements in the first group have in common, for there is not just one such property. All the statements will have the property of being expressible in under 327 words, for instance.[57] The truth property not only is common to the statements in the first group, it *explains* why the statements in the first group are (as a statistical matter) more often successfully acted upon.[58] Although its instrumentality is what identifies the truth property, we can (come to) care about truth (and what has that truth property) intrinsically.

Not every possible explanation of why some statements can be successfully acted upon would count as a theory of truth, though. If God (existed and) were constantly intervening to sometimes produce success in action, sometimes not, then what the statements in that first group would share is "being temporarily favored by God as a basis of action," but this property would not count as a truth property. In such a case success in action would not depend upon truth at all.[59]

There will be some appropriate general condition that a property must satisfy for it to qualify as a truth property. (Perhaps that condition is Tarski's condition that S is true if and only if p, where "p" is replaced by a sentence of the language and "S" is a name of that sentence; or, in the case of our theory that truth is rooted in space and time, some weakening of that condition, such as (T') above, but this time treated as a condition that must hold true of truth, not as one that must in each case be provable via a truth definition.) We may understand the statement that truth is socially relative as claiming that there are alternative and different truth properties (each of them satisfying that appropriate general condition) which explain different people's, or groups', or cultures' success in action. The people not only are acting upon different beliefs; their success in action is explained by different truth *properties*, according to which different particular propositions are true.[60]

The success in action I speak of is a success in achieving the particular goals of the action. A biologist who espoused Mendelian genetics in Stalinist Russia might be less successful than his Lysenkoist colleagues in avoiding labor camps in the Gulag. Does this mean that a biologist in the Soviet Union is more likely to succeed acting upon a falsehood? No, a biologist who wishes to achieve the goal of avoiding imprisonment in a labor camp will be more likely to succeed if he acts upon the truth about what will elicit such persecution, and a biologist who wishes to raise plants with certain characteristics will be more likely to succeed in this goal if he acts upon the (Mendelian) truths about genetics.[61] The times when acting upon a false belief actually will help achieve a goal involve that belief's dovetailing with a very particular situation, and also the action's being aimed at a very particular dovetailing goal. The success will be a pinpoint success; the false belief is not a good basis for achieving other goals in different situations in which it also could be acted upon. Its success is not robust.[62]

It may be wondered whether success in action is even an indication of the belief's truth. It is not just that the belief acted upon may be only approximately true, or approximately true in a certain domain for certain purposes, but enough so to yield success. Navigation in accordance with a geocentric theory leads to successful goal achievement, yet that theory is not true, even approximately. Rather, its *consequences* are close to the truth, concerning the particular goals of navigation. So the geocentric theory is in the set of beliefs that we act upon successfully, yet it is quite false. What is needed, therefore, is a two-stage theory. The success of acting upon some beliefs is explained in terms of their having the truth property. The success of acting upon other beliefs, which do not have the truth property, is explained in terms of some of their consequences' closely matching the consequences of beliefs that themselves *do* have the truth property. (A full and knowledgeable explanation would show why the consequences do closely match.) In both cases, what explains success in action is, ultimately, the truth property.[63]

There are, however, cases in which seeing the probability of danger or failure as lower than it is—a false belief—helps to sustain someone's action or courage, and so raises the probability of success above what it would be if the person's belief were completely accurate. (Alternatively, overestimating a danger can lead a person to be more cautious and hence to avoid that danger.) Belief affects motivation, which in turn affects the likelihood of success. And sometimes a belief about the probability of success, or about recovery from some disease, initially false, can be made true by wholehearted adherence to it. Normally, we think truth is independent of what we think about it. But thinking a placebo is effective helps to make it so. However, such phenomena are relatively rare. We would have a very different notion of truth if, for a vast segment of our beliefs, the act of believing affected the probability of the belief's holding true.[64]

We have presumed thus far that each and every truth is *wholly* true. Yet, rather than just flat-out success or total failure in acting upon various beliefs, there can reliably be different degrees of success in action upon different beliefs. And these differences can be counted upon; beliefs have differing degrees of accuracy. (A general belief may differ in its degree of accuracy across different situations; its degrees of accuracy may fall along a gradient.) If the truth property that underlies the differing degrees of success in action itself can come in degrees (if, for instance, there can be different degrees of correspondence to the facts), then we might aptly speak of *degrees* of truth. Different purposes in action then might require (or make do with) differing degrees of truth.

Is a Theory of Truth Possible?

Various objections have been raised in the literature to the very possibility of an illuminating theory of truth. It is held that we can use different vocabularies to divide up the world, different terms to describe the world. Just as a jigsaw puzzle carves up a picture into different shapes, so too a language is able to carve up the world into various configurations. We use terms like "chair," "house," "nation-state," and "river," but some other culture and language, it is said, might divide things quite differently, for instance having a term "zanzar" that refers to anything which is either a chair or a river or half of a house.

However, even if terms embody arbitrary divisions of the world, it does not follow that the statements or propositions made with these arbitrary terms are not true. Define an "ourth" as anything that is either a chair or a river or half of a house or is identical with Grover Cleveland. That is, according to us, an arbitrary term. Be that as it may, it is *true* that all zanzars are ourths. And it also is true that the object in the corner of my office is a zanzar, and that Grover Cleveland is an ourth but not a zanzar. The arbitrariness of the constituent terms does not make the truth of these statements an arbitrary matter. We may not be much interested in statements composed of these arbitrary terms, but that lack of interest and that arbitrariness do not affect whether these statements are true. Statements with gerrymandered terms can be true, and statements with quite natural terms can be false, as is the statement that there are no giraffes in the United States right now.

It also is maintained that the world itself does not have any natural divisions intrinsic to it. Hence, our terms do not "cut nature at its joints."[65] It is not clear what or whose theory of truth requires that nature be so cut. Perhaps the idea is that, with no intrinsic character to things and no natural boundaries awaiting description, truths do not correspond to anything existing independently of our descriptions. Thus, some say that we cannot describe the world in its character as undescribed. If the world did come divided into objects having intrinsic natures, then apparently these natures would hold apart from our descriptions, and so if our terms did match or fit these intrinsic natures, we would be succeeding in describing the world as it is when undescribed. However, the world does not come already carved up and awaiting these, or any, particular descriptions.

Should we think of the world as it is undescribed as a homogeneous blob, infinite in all spatial and temporal directions? Any description is an arbitrary division, an arbitrary imposition upon the world's homogeneity. (But homogeneous according to which descriptive terms?) Such a world, however, would not lend itself to the differentiating descriptions that we do offer. Our terms would gain no grip on, or in, that undifferentiated unity.

Even if the world (as it is undescribed) does not uniquely determine its correct description, it can be described in a range of ways but not in all possible ways. And only a range of worlds, not all possible ones, can be described by the terms and concepts that we do use. The world has the potentiality to be described by some terms and not by others.[66] Hence, when we do successfully describe it, even though our description is not the unique possible one, this does show us something about the world "as it is undescribed," namely, that particular undescribed world lends itself to this particular description. The description thus describes the (undescribed) world in its potentiality.

It also is said that truths are statements or sentences, and so are dependent upon the existence of a language; therefore, truths did not exist before any languages did (somewhere or other in the universe). The question "What kind of thing is 'true' a property of?" is a vexed one. Each existing answer faces its own formidable problems. (Some hold that the vehicle of truth is an abstract entity that is not language-based. This entity is termed a proposition; there are problems about its identity conditions.) But even if the vehicle of truth is a sentence or a statement, this does not show that what *makes* the sentence or statement true, what it corresponds to, also depends upon language, and so did not exist before language did.[67] Some would add that there weren't any facts either before the existence of language, because facts just are languagelike entities that were hypostatized to match language's true sentences. (P. F. Strawson has written that facts and true sentences were made for each other, but, as we shall see, we needn't suppose that each true sentence has its own separate fact.)

It has been held that it is empty and unilluminating and circular to say that people are successful in achieving their goals (when they act upon a belief) because their belief is true or because it corresponds to the facts, since the only reason we have for thinking that the belief is true is that the goals of the action are achieved. Similarly, it has been held that it is empty and unilluminating and circular to say that scientific hypotheses and theories yield correct predictions because they are true or because they correspond to the facts, since the only reason we have for thinking the hypotheses and theories are true is that they yield correct predictions.[68]

Let us linger for a moment over the issue of circularity. Suppose a person has a heart attack of a certain sort, and this is explained as being caused by a particular kind of structural defect in the heart. Yet the only reason for thinking that person did have that structural defect is that he died of that kind of heart attack. That appears to be an objectionable circle. (Why did the bridge collapse? It had a structural defect. Why do you think it had that structural defect? It collapsed.)

It *would* be a circle if we said that event A caused event B, and event B caused event A. Here, the causes go in a circle. It also would be a circle if we said that event A is our reason for believing event B occurred, and that event B is our reason for believing that event A occurred. Here, the reasons go in a circle. However, it is *not* a uniform circle to say that event A caused event B, and that our reason for thinking event A occurred is that event B occurred. Here "causes" goes in one direction, and "is a reason for thinking" goes in the other direction. It is not evident why this kind of nonuniform circle is objectionable.

There might be existing well-confirmed hypotheses that all heart attacks of this type are caused by that specific kind of structural defect, and that all bridge collapses of this type are caused by that type of structural defect. Every one of the large number of cases that we have examined in the past fits this generalization. Every such heart attack was found, upon independent physical examination, to occur along with that structural defect. We have good reason to believe that all are, and so we have good reason to believe that this particular one is, even though we have not (yet) performed an independent examination to discover the existence of the defect in this case. It is not circular to explain the heart attack by the existence of the defect, even though our only reason for believing that the defect did exist in this case is that the person did have the heart attack.

In the case of the link between belief and truth, however, we do not have this kind of direct statistical evidence. We do not establish background generalizations through an independent ascertainment of the truth of the belief (or hypothesis) and then discover that its truth is highly correlated with successful action (or successful scientific prediction).

Instead, we have an explanatory hypothesis: what explains success in action (or prediction) is that the belief (or hypothesis) is true. This hypothesis is not trivial, for there are alternative explanations. It might be that the success occurred by accident this one time. This explanation will be increasingly implausible, though, the greater the number of successful actions or correct predictions based upon that particular belief or theory. Recall the earlier objections to the claim that success in action is an indication of truth. There are ways, the objection held, that false beliefs can lead to successful action or prediction. (For instance, a false belief might inspire a person's confidence, which leads to successful action.) The existence of alternative hypotheses to explain successful action or correct prediction gives content to the claim that in a given case (or in most cases) it is the truth of the belief that is the explanation. If we can check whether these alternative hypotheses do hold, and if we can eliminate them, that will leave the truth of the belief or theory as the most reasonable explanation extant.

One of the alternative explanations in the case of scientific prediction, though, is not easy to eliminate. One can successfully navigate according to the geocentric theory, which is false, because its predictions in this particular domain match or approximate the predictions of the true heliocentric theory. One can successfully make predictions according to Newtonian theory, which is false, because its predictions in certain domains match or approximate the predictions of the true theory of relativity. It always seems to be a possibility that our correct predictions occur, not because the theory we are using is true, but because in this domain it matches some other true theory that has not yet been formulated or dreamt of. This does not mean that we now should abandon our current theory. And it certainly does not mean that we should abandon the notion of truth. For this alternative explanation *invokes* the notion of truth, not for our current theory but for some alternative unspecified one.

We have considered whether there is any bar, in principle, to stating a correct *theory* of truth. It also may be wondered whether we ever do state any (completely accurate) truths. Our language could have some false metaphysical assumptions built into it (assumptions about substances and attributes, or whatever). Such assumptions may be only roughly accurate but accurate enough to have been built into our cognitive apparatus by the processes of evolutionary selection. There may be assumptions that are so deep that we do not yet notice them, yet everything we say might be infected with their metaphysical inaccuracy. (Even our current mathematical formalisms, and hence also the mathematical formulae of our physics, might embody some such assumptions.) Perhaps, then, we have yet to state one completely accurate truth.[69]

Euclidean geometry might be a useful way of viewing physical space, evolutionarily instilled but not strictly accurate. Could even the notion of truth itself be one that is evolutionarily instilled but not strictly applicable? Paul and Patricia Churchland have argued that our ordinary psychological notions of belief and desire are components of a theory (folk psychology) that might be defective and nonreparable; these notions might be destined to become defunct when a fully accurate psychological theory comes along.[70] Is the notion of truth part of (what we might call) *folk epistemology,* which conceivably is a defective theory that might also be replaced, along with its component notion of truth? If truth is that property of some beliefs that explains why acting upon those beliefs, in contrast to others, leads to the achievement of the goals of the action, then the theory of truth finds its place as *part* of the theory of mind. Within the structure of belief-desire psychology, it marks truth as the property of acted-upon beliefs that is conducive to the realization of desires. So if future neuroscience were to undermine the notions of belief and desire, could the associated notion of truth lag far behind? It seems plausible, however, that whatever such a neuroscience will substitute for beliefs, for instance, neural networks of a certain sort or in a certain state, a concept that plays a somewhat similar role to that of truth then will apply to this substitute to somehow connect the neural networks or events to the way the world is.

Does the denial of fixed philosophical points, of fixed and guaranteed intellectual categories and truths, open the way to chaos? Some postmodernist writers seem to think that if there are no self-evidently compelling axioms or methods that are knowable *a priori,* from which all truths (or at least the vast majority of the ones that we care about) can be established, then all truths are relative or somehow nonobjective. If "foundationalism" fails, then objective truth totters—or so we are told. "No judgment is or could be objective in the classic sense of justifiable on totally context-transcendent and subject-independent grounds," Barbara Herrnstein Smith writes. In this allegedly classical sense, "the only reasons that count as 'good' ones are those that are certifiably deduced by pure reason from universally valid, transcendentally necessary principles."[71] Charles Sanders Peirce, who formulated the first explicitly nonfoundationalist view—he called it "pragmaticism"—certainly did not believe that foundationalism's failure entails relativism about truth.

Richard Rorty has claimed that the notions of truth, correspondence to the facts, rationality, and objectivity all stand in the way of (what he holds to be) desirable social consequences; so these should be replaced by other concepts (such as solidarity) whose adoption and use will better lead to those consequences.[72] This position seems to embody empirical claims: that adopting certain concepts will lead to certain social results, that continuing to use other concepts will impede the reaching of certain social results. Presumably, Rorty believes it is true (or a fact) that his proposed conceptual reforms will lead to those results. Sooner or later, it seems, a proponent of Rorty's position must claim and affirm that certain things will in fact lead to other things, that this indeed will occur in the world, given the way the world is. And if these statements can correspond to the way the world is, why not other statements as well? (Or would Rorty say that these statements do not correspond to the way the world is, but that our accepting them has certain beneficial consequences? But then, is it a fact that . . . , etc.?)

Recent postmodernist theorists have excoriated the notions of objective truth, objectivity, and rationality, holding these to be empty and valueless notions, mere masks for privilege and power. The arguments that have been provided for such strong and startling claims can be countered or shown to be confused or inconclusive, yet this rebuttal does not dispose of the postmodernist position. Let me explain.

In *The Examined Life,* I offered the following interpretation of Zen enlightenment within Buddhist philosophical theory.[73] The self is a theoretical posit, and once its existence is accepted, everything falls into place around it; everything is seen through the filter of that one theoretical piece. Through meditative practice (and theoretical reasoning), one comes to realize that the self does not exist (the "no-self doctrine"). Eliminate (the belief in the existence of) the self, and everything else then falls into a quite different pattern and gestalt. (In the familiar drawing of gestalt psychology, if you follow the direction to see that part of the drawing not as a women's chin but as a nose, the whole picture looks very different. It is a picture of something else entirely.) Since the posit of the self organizes every other piece, it is difficult to argue against it. The other pieces, already in their organized place, create a space that requires the self, which only it can fill. It therefore is difficult to make a *local* argument against the self. An alternative global picture is needed.

Consider a jigsaw puzzle containing ten pieces that do fit together in a pattern, yet if you put those pieces together *that* way, then you cannot fit together the rest of the pieces to complete the puzzle. Those ten pieces *do* interlock, but their total interlocking shape fits nowhere; you have to disperse those pieces and start again in order to successfully complete the puzzle. (It would be fiendish to manufacture a puzzle of this type unannounced.)

Might some central philosophical notions, such as *objective truth,* be impervious to a *local* counterargument? Other conceptual pieces, once in their place—a place they acquired because of this central piece—can be used to protect the central piece, or to reinstate it if it gets temporarily displaced. These other organized pieces leave a hole that only that one particular central philosophical piece can fill. Yet they have been organized *that* way by the central piece with its particular shape. No wonder the other pieces leave *that* shaped a hole. Quine presents an image of some statement not easily being given up because it is central to many other things.[74] But this central purported truth might be held in place by other things that *it* placed into their positions. If these other things were positioned differently, they might hold something else in place. Or nothing.

Postmodernism questions central pieces of long-standing philosophical views. The apparently compelling local arguments against postmodernism are not decisive, I suggest, because the local pieces they rest upon have their place and connections to the central pieces *because of* those very central pieces that postmodernism puts under question.

A *global* argument against postmodernism will pit (a cleaned-up version of) the current position against an alternative global postmodernist view and argue that the former is superior. But is this comparison to be made and judged by the standards and criteria of the current view or by those of the postmodernist view that purports to replace the current view? This issue is not insurmountable, for the standards of comparison themselves may turn out not to be controversial, in that the two views may share them. Also, there is no guarantee that a view will count itself superior to another, even according to its own standards. However, we currently are at an earlier stage of the discussion. The alternative global postmodernist view, the one that rejects currently central philosophical pieces and places many other pieces in a new pattern, has not yet been built. So we don't know yet what it is that is to be compared.

Arguments that say that such an alternative global postmodernist view *cannot* be constructed also might rest upon local, even if very central, pieces of the current view, and hence be inconclusive. Still, such arguments can show how very great would be the new view's intellectual cost, by showing how much (of what currently is central) that new view would have to give up. (Proponents of the new view might welcome these costs, holding that the greater the havoc wreaked upon the old view, the better.) However, pointing out the unavoidable costs of the new view will not tell us what might be its great and compensating benefits. We cannot know these until the new view has been constructed and operates for a while to show its own unexpected consequences. (After all, the once-reigning religious worldview could have made a structurally similar argument about costs against the nascent secularism that challenged it, yet this would not have sufficed to demonstrate its superiority.)

Even someone who rejects postmodernist theories can welcome their existence, for they force us to look anew at some fundamental notions—a quintessential philosophical task. The challenges and errors of the postmodernists have the beneficial effects that John Stuart Mill describes in discussing liberty of discussion. Although I have spoken of someone's constructing and assessing a global postmodernist theory, this seems to be the last thing existing postmodernist theorists want to do. They would claim, in justification, that there can be no such global theory or "totalizing narrative," yet an induction from particular past failures (such as Christian eschatology or Marxism) does not establish this claim. In any case, it is so much easier—and apparently so much more fun—to sabotage the existing theory. However, the irresponsibility and the intellectual confusion of much postmodernist writing do not entail that the theories and concepts it attempts to undermine are secure.

Is Truth Socially Relative?

We now can return to our initial question of whether truth is socially relative. It is obvious that the very same statements are not serviceable for everyone. The statements that serve an engineer may not serve an artist; the statements that serve a person in the frozen tundra may not serve someone in the tropics. However, the same property underlies the serviceability of these different statements, and that one property is what gets demarcated by a theory of truth—so says the nonrelativist.

Yet the general characterization of truth does not require that it be one and the same property that underlies serviceability for every society, group, economic class, and sex. The general characterization leaves it open whether two groups can differ in their truth property. It might be distinct properties that make statements serviceable to members of different groups. For each group, truth is what underlies and explains serviceability, but what *does* this for the different groups is different. What truth is, is fixed by its (particular kind of) explanatory role in explaining serviceability,[75] but the situation of groups can be so different that the explanation of serviceability in their two cases must differ. What truth is, truth's nature, is different for the different groups. This constitutes a social relativism about truth.

The notion of serviceability is explicitly *relational*. Something is serviceable *for* some person or *for* some group. The underlying property that explains this relational serviceability need not itself be relational, however. For instance, being digestible by human beings is a relational notion (and what is digestible by animals that digest cellulose is not digestible by us), yet having certain chemical structures (the property of substances that underlies their being digestible by the human digestive apparatus) is a monadic, not a relational, notion. But even if what always underlies serviceability is a monadic, nonrelational property, the truth property would be relative if different groups had different nonrelational truth properties.

We should distinguish three ways in which truth can be relative. First, the notion of truth can be relative by containing a (perhaps inexplicit) factor that can vary. Second, the truth property can be relative in that it varies from group to group (or it is explicitly relational and refers to groups that differ). Particular truths can turn out to be relative too, even if the notion of truth itself is not relative and neither is the truth property. Einstein identified some truths about spatial and temporal intervals as relative (to the velocity of an observer) although the notion of truth itself (and the truth property) was not (held to be) a relative notion. So the third way in which truth can be relative is that every particular truth turns out to be relative.[76]

The truth property is socially relative, I said, when what explains serviceability for two social groups are two distinct properties. Even if we doubt that this is a fully coherent notion, it is one to explore, for it offers social relativism its best chance of being true. If that chance turns out to be small, even on the most favorable conceptual suppositions, that will be instructive.

Surely, though, there will be considerable overlap in the explanatory properties. The members of each group need to avoid bumping into objects, place food in their mouths, tell day from night, and find their way back home. Won't it be the very same property of statements, call it *P*, that enables them to do this? Won't their supposedly distinct truth properties each have to include *P* as a subpart or conjunct, and hence won't they overlap? However, while the distinct truth properties must apply to some of the same statements that *P* applies to, thereby overlapping in what they apply to, these truth properties needn't apply in the same way. Their extensions (what the properties apply to) will overlap but their intensions (their defining characteristics) need not. The overlap of the extensions of the two truth properties may be enough to explain why the two group's beliefs are serviceable yet, nevertheless, the two truth properties are different. (There are some things that one applies to that the other one does not; their extensions overlap but are not identical.) The two group's different needs will be differentially encompassed by the two differing truth properties, and even for the statements marking the groups' common needs, the two different truth properties provide different (but overlapping) explanations of serviceability.

Some philosophers (leaving issues about groups aside) have held that different properties underlie and explain the serviceability of beliefs in such different areas as mathematics, ethics, interpersonal relations, and beliefs about objects as different as elementary particles and ordinary middle-sized perceptible physical objects. Could there be a different explanatory property for each of these areas, without any one overarching property that includes each as a subproperty?[77] (Yet the respective truth properties of statements from different areas must mesh to some extent, since we sometimes successfully reason by combining such truths; for instance, mathematics is applied to formulate theories of the social domain.) Similarly, two groups' truth properties may each be conjunctions that overlap (intensionally as well as extensionally) in one conjunct yet differ in their other conjuncts. One property might aid members in the first group in their interpersonal relations (and hence be a conjunct of their truth property), while another property might aid members of the second, differently situated social group in *their* interpersonal relations.

The correspondence theorist might object that we do not know of two plausible proposals about truth properties; there is only one, his, viz. that correspondence to the facts is the truth property. However, the point that the truth property may not be unique does not require proposing a completely different theory of truth. For correspondence theorists themselves disagree about how to formulate the correspondence theory of truth and what exactly the correspondence truth property is. Consider then two plausible proposals about the details of the correspondence theory of truth that yield two interestingly different specifications of the truth property, both of which fall under the general rubric of "correspondence." Must one of these proposals be the right one and the other wrong? The difference between the two (correspondence) truth properties might match the differences in the situations of the two groups. Could not each theory *correctly* state the truth property of a *different* group? Even a confirmed correspondence theorist, therefore, might countenance relativism about truth.

Let us summarize. The general *characterization* of truth that we offered is *relational.* Truth is what explains a person's or group's success in action; it is what is serviceable *for* the person or group. The *truth property,* which explains the relation of serviceability for a person or group, may be a non-relational property that statements can have apart from their relation to a person or group.[78] *Social relativism* about truth is the claim that *different* nonrelational properties P_1 and P_2 are the truth properties for different groups; P_1 explains the relation "serviceable for group G1" while P_2 explains "serviceable for G2." Nonrelativism holds that the same nonrelational truth property underlies these two relations (serviceable for group G1 and serviceable for group G2).

What specific arguments might be offered for the claim that truth is socially relative? Suppose that the different domains (of ethics, of impersonal facts, and of people's motivations) *do* have different truth properties underlying them. So far, no social relativism. But different groups of people (as delineated by economic class or race or gender or sexual preference or whatever) are differently situated in a society; they have different power, status, and influence. Because of the groups' different situations, statements in the different domains are differentially important to their members. Perhaps the powerful people do not have to be very concerned about understanding other people's motivations because they do not need, very often, to gain the spontaneous willing cooperation of others. They can shape people's behavior by issuing commands or payments, without paying close attention to the nuances of those people's motivations and concerns. Since (beliefs from) different domains are important to different groups, the underlying property that explains their successful goal-achievement will vary. Since the different groups will have different truth properties, truth is relative to the group. So runs one argument for the relativity of truth.

To this it might be objected that everyone should use a differentiated truth property, and the very same one, of this form: truth property P_1 in domain D_1, property P_2 in domain D_2, . . . , property P_n in domain D_n. Rather than each person's using the one truth property across the board that serves him best in the domain that is most important to him (given his social position), every person should use the same more differentiated property. It will serve everyone well across all the different domains. However, there are cognitive and computational costs (and costs in effort) in using a differentiated truth property. It may not be worthwhile for members of particular groups to incur those costs. Cost-benefit analysis might show that it is more rational for each person to use a rule of thumb utilizing *one* truth property—which one that is depends upon which group the person is in. In doing this, the person will not often go far astray. To be sure, an unlimited being for whom there are no such costs might use a perfectly differentiated truth property. But does this show that relativism is false or that it is true?

Here I have spoken of what property it is rational for each group *to use*. Earlier, however, the truth property was identified by its explanatory role. It is that property of beliefs that explains the (statistical) success in acting upon them. It need not be the property that the people are acting *on,* in the sense of adverting to or consciously taking into account or computing in accordance with. Won't that underlying explanatory property be the differentiated property? Here is where the analogy to different domains is imperfect. The specification of the one common differentiated truth property (that explains *everyone's* success in action) would have to refer explicitly to people's differentiated social roles and situations. The one common truth property, therefore, would have to be a conjunction, something like the following: P_1 if you are an entrepreneur, and P_2 if you are a hired employee, and P_3 if you are a slave, and P_4 if you are a priest in an animistic sect, and P_5 if you are speaking to someone more powerful than yourself and unable to deceive him about your ultimate aims, etc. This does make truth appear nonrelative in its form, because the same truth property applies to everyone, but at a cost. All the relativization that a social relativist could desire has been explicitly incorporated into the (conjunctive, socially differentiated) truth property itself.

Success in realizing the goals of an action depends upon the goals aimed at, the action done, and the nature or state of the world. The action a person performs depends, in turn, upon his goals, upon his beliefs (about the nature of the world), upon the range of alternative actions that might be done, and upon the decision rule he uses to select a particular action (given those goals, beliefs, and possible actions). Hence a person's success in realizing his actions' goals depends upon *all* of these factors.

If truth is that property of beliefs that explains the successful achievement of goals, then (in principle) truth might vary with, and be relative to, the nature of the world (as the correspondence theory holds) and also to the particular kind of goals the person pursues. (For it has not been excluded that different properties of belief would explain success in achieving different kinds of goals.) Moreover, and more surprising, truth might vary with, and be relative to, the *decision rule* the person uses to choose among actions. For it also has not been excluded that it would be different properties of belief that explain success in achieving goals under different decision rules. One property of belief might fit the decision rule of maximizing expected utility, a second property might fit the decision rule of satisficing, while a third property of belief might fit the decision rule of minimaxing.[79] Might the truth property also be relative to how rational people are, or to the way in which they are rational? Would some completely irrational decision rule give rise to a different truth property? Should we demarcate the range of rational decision rules by saying these are the ones that give rise to some particular truth property, such as correspondence?[80] I do worry that I may have followed out the implications of a roughly accurate view of truth—truth is what explains success in acting upon beliefs—to the point where its lack of perfect fit begins to show. Is the possible relativity of truth to a decision rule a new and interesting discovery, or is it a *reductio* of taking the starting point too literally?

A relativity of truth also might bring in its wake a relativity of logic. Valid rules of logical inference are identified as those that preserve truth. Different truth properties might be preserved by different rules. If truth is relative and can vary from group to group, then there is the possibility that the rules of logical inference also will vary and so be socially relative. (A relativity of logical rules is not entailed by the relativity of truth, however. Even if truth differed from group to group, these different truths could be preserved by the very same rules.)

The absolutist is claiming, on our construal, that people are similar enough in their nature, their environments, their human situation, and their mode of decision that the very same truth property underlies the successful actions of them all. The absolutist believes in the unity of humankind. The relativist, on the other hand, on our construal, claims that the commonalities among people and their situations are too weak for all people to share a common truth-predicate. The differences in the nature of people, or their social positions, or their environments, or their decision rules, are so great, he says, that different properties of belief are needed to explain why these different people tend to be successful in acting.[81]

The relativist, therefore, is making a very strong claim, and faces the difficult explanatory task of coming up with several different specific properties that do explain the successful actions of different (or differently situated) persons. The absolutist, on the other hand, needs to formulate only one theory, albeit one of wider scope. I myself find the social-relativist claim about truth—that truth is relative to culture, or social class, or gender, or sexual preference—highly implausible. The commonalities among people and the unities of human nature and the human situation are sufficiently great, I think, to make people's truth property identical. The social-relativist claim that we are denying is a coherent claim, however. When we deny *this* relativist claim, we exclude a coherent possibility and thereby say something with empirical content. The truth property is not socially relative. Not all particular truths are relative to culture or social class or gender or sexual preference. I want to say something even stronger. *None* of them are.[82]

Yet I do have to note the possibility that similar situations might not converge to the very same truth property. Similar situations might lead merely to *similar* truth properties. In that case, truth properties would have a linear relation to situations, and this *would* constitute a social relativism about truth, albeit a mild one. But if some social relativism does result with a well-behaved linear relation of truth property to situation, the situation is more striking if the relation of truth property to situation is nonlinear. Very similar situations then would have very different truth properties. Relativism then indeed would be, in the technical sense, chaotic. Across the actual range of human situations, it is an empirical question whether the relation of truth property to situation is converging, linear, or nonlinearly chaotic. My own bet, or guess, is for convergence.[83]

I seem to be left with putting forth nothing more than a belief or a guess that truth is not socially relative. Nonetheless, since I *am* now saying that the commonalities among people and their situation are sufficiently great that truth is not relative to culture or social class or gender, etc., how can I also have said, near the beginning of this chapter, that it is highly plausible that truth *is* relative? Phrasing the issue in terms of the unity of human nature, and of humankind, leads to a further widening of purview in considering the relativist position. The relativist about truth claims that the truth property can vary among different groups. Different specifications of the groups yield different relativist claims.

There are four versions of the claim of *Actual Relativism on Earth*. Among past, present, or future beings on Earth, some two have different truth properties. There is the wider claim of *Actual Relativism in the Universe*. Among (past, present, and future) actually existing beings anywhere in the universe who have beliefs, some two have different truth properties.

There is the claim of *Possible Relativism on Earth*. This comes in two versions. First, some actual beings elsewhere in the universe, if they were on Earth, would differ from the Earth's human inhabitants in the truth properties that explained their successful actions here. Second, some possible beings could exist on Earth with a different truth property here from that of actually existing people. The Earth's environment is not powerful enough to constrain every organism here that is capable of belief to the same truth property. There is the still wider claim of *Possible Relativism in the Universe*. There are possible beings, capable of existing in the actual universe (and capable of having beliefs), who would have different truth prop-

erties. The actual universe is not so uniformly ecologically constraining everywhere (including in interstellar space and in black holes) as to restrict all
possible beings to the very same truth property, wherever these beings
might be.[84] Finally, there is the claim of *Relativism in Possible Universes.*
Among the different possible universes (one of which is the actual one) and
the different possible beings capable of existing in them (who are capable
of having beliefs), some two beings (either in the same universe or in different universes) differ from each other in their truth properties. So at least
one also differs from us. (And might we or beings very similar to us have a
different truth property in the very different environment of some other
possible universe?)

Now, I am as absolutist about truth as the next person—or so I had
thought until I considered these different relativist positions. Which ones
does the absolutist mean to contest? The first two relativisms about actual
beings on earth, surely, the absolutist will deny, but after that things begin
to be cloudy. By the time we reach science-fiction cases about other beings
in this universe, not to mention other possible universes, who would confidently deny or care about denying *those* relativist positions? There is absolutism enough (for now) if the truth property does not vary among (actual)
human beings existing thus far and in the foreseeable future; future en-
counters with extraterrestrials might press other questions upon us. Nevertheless, if one of the latter positions on the list did hold, that would show
that truth *is,* in an interesting theoretical sense, relative. Relativism would
be a philosophical truth, though not a practical concern. So perhaps our
(philosophical) question should be, not whether truth is relative, but in
what way truth is relative. How relative is it?

To say that truth is relative is an incomplete specification. To answer the
question of whether all truth is relative, we must ask *relative between whom?*
It is not relative (I believe) between myself and any other contemporary human being. (It is not relative to any factor in which we differ.) It may well
be relative between human beings and other existing or possible beings in
the universe. Even when there is such relativity, still, for any particular
question at issue between two groups, we can ask whether *that* question can
be resolved on the basis of statements that the (different) truth properties
of the two groups lead them both to accept. Just as scientific observation need not be theory-unladen, but merely neutral enough or acceptable
enough for the proponents of whatever theories actually are under consideration to be able to resolve the issues among *those* theories, so too statements need not be (absolutely) nonrelative, merely acceptable enough to

groups with differing truth properties to enable them to resolve the particular questions they are concerned with.

If (as I believe) actual human beings have enough in common to give them the same truth property, we can ask what the specific basis of our common truth property is. What specifically is it that people share that suffices to make truth nonrelative among them? What is it about the combination of human nature and the human physical and social environment that makes the same property (of beliefs) explain people's successful actions? And how contingent is this basis, and therefore our truth property; how sensitive to variation in this basis is our particular truth property?[85]

If the answer to the question "Is truth relative?" turns out to be "yes" when we take the very widest view across possible beings and possible environments, then the interesting question becomes "How relative is truth?" How wide is the group that shares the same truth property with us, and in how wide a range of environments does that sharing continue?[86]

Scientific knowledge changes people's possibilities of action; it provides more efficient means for achieving goals, and it opens new alternatives. In every human culture, acting upon the accepted results of scientific inquiry will lead to more successful achievement of the goals of particular actions undertaken. (This does not mean that there cannot be serious and significant unintended consequences of these actions.) We might see the spread of science then, its results and its consequent practice, as a force driving us, if we do not already share it, to the same truth property. Far from being relative truths, scientific results tend to make everyone's truth property the same across cultures.[87] In this sense, science unifies humanity.

Our investigation of the concepts of absolute and relative truth has encountered, not a dichotomy but a gradation. The factor that a truth is relative to may be wider or narrower. Is the truth relative to larger or smaller regions of space-time? Is it relative to characteristics shared by all groups of rational creatures, or only to characteristics had by some groups, and how wide a range of groups is this? The narrower the extent of the factor that a truth is relative to, the more relative the truth. The wider the extent, the less relative. If the truth is relative to characteristics shared by almost every possible region and almost every possible group of individuals, then, although it is not wholly absolute, it comes close; it is minimally relative. At the limit, one tiny step more, it is absolute. It is an empirical question how extensive the characteristic is that a particular fact or truth varies with, and so it is an empirical question how relative a particular fact or truth is. On the dimension that runs from the (wholly) absolute to the (completely) relative, many truths fall in between.

Does Relativism Undercut Itself?

We have been led not only to hold that relativism about truth is coherent but to think that truth (probably) *is* relative to spatiotemporal region and, when the purview goes beyond actual human beings, that it also is relative to a group in an environment.

Relativism about all truth faces a question of its own coherence that more particular relativisms do not, for the statement of a particular relativism (e.g., ethical relativism) need not itself be a statement *within* that particular domain (e.g., ethics) that is claimed to be relative. It may be a statement *about* the domain but not be within it, and so not even appear to apply to itself.

How can relativism about truth, of the sort we have been considering, be consistently stated? When I am in group G1 and I say

(1) P_2 explains serviceability for the members of another group G2,

if this statement is true, what truth property am I using, the one incorporating P_1, which underlies the serviceability of *my* group's statements, or the one incorporating P_2, which underlies the serviceability of theirs?

If I, a member of group G1, am putting forth statement (1), then if it is true (relative to me), it must have property P_1. But that doesn't mean that G2's statements that are spoken of also must have property P_1, or that I need to accept P_2 as the property adequately underlying the serviceability of my beliefs.

When I put forward statement (1), or put forward the more general statement

(2)   For different groups, different properties underlie and explain the serviceability of their beliefs,

I am claiming that both statements (1) and (2) are true, and hence that both do have my truth property, which, whether or not I know this, is P_1. I need not be claiming that the members of every other group, with the differing truth properties underlying serviceability for them, must recognize (1) and (2) as true. Consider now the statement

(3)   Statement (1) has property P_1.

I accept that as true, for (3) has property P_1, the property that underlies the serviceability of *my* group's statements. However, someone else from another group need not accept (3) as true, for statement (3) itself may not have the property that underlies serviceability for the members of his group, and hence may not have the property that for them constitutes truth.

To the standard question of whether the relativist *consistently* can state his relativist doctrine, the answer seems to be yes. However—the relativist will be quick to note—it does not follow that his doctrine, consistently stated, will be accepted by every group, or even be true for every group. That depends upon what their truth property is, and whether *it* applies to statement (2). Thus we have the possibility that one group affirms relativism as true and another denies it, where each group is not merely uttering the truth as they see it but asserting what *is* true according to their truth property.

Does the absolutist contradict the relativist? He does deny that truth varies with some factor (of type) F, and this the relativist affirms. Someone may wonder, however, whether these two are talking about the same thing when they both speak of "truth," since they have different truth properties. Notice, first, that it is not given that their truth properties are different. The relativist is claiming that there *are* different truth properties, but the one he himself is using need be no different from the one a particular absolutist uses.[88] In that case they are talking about the same notion of truth, and the claim of one of them, in terms of that notion, will be false. But even if they are using different truth properties, still, as they speak, they both can be using the same general notion of truth, namely, "that property, whatever it is, that underlies people's successfully acting on certain of their beliefs." (And both of their general notions also can include the requirement that the truth property satisfy (some appropriate weakening of) the Tarski condition that S is true if and only if p.)

The (weak) absolutist denies that all truths are relative, but he may grant that some truths are. What reason is there to grant that there is such a category of relative truths? Once it is known what factor F a particular truth p is relative to, cannot we formulate the nonrelative truth "p holds relative to F," and doesn't this (as C. I. Lewis suggested) obviate the need for any relative truths at all? Cannot, and should not, the relativity always go explicitly within the truth, which then itself is nonrelative; why need it lurk outside the truth to cloud it?

There is this reason to continue to speak of relative truths. We may not know how to state a truth as absolute because we do not yet know a ground-floor absolute framework relative to which it holds, one that explicitly mentions all the factors with which truth could vary. Nevertheless, someone might maintain that the notion of relative truth is secondary because it is eliminable by reference to the *existence* of an absolute framework, whether or not we know what that framework is, as follows:

> Statement S is relatively true if and only if there exists a framework F, such that F is a ground-floor framework, and "S is true relative to F" is *absolutely* true.

The notion of relative truth would be eliminable because all statements using it would be replaceable in context by statements using only the notion of absolute truth. However, not only are we not yet in a position to specify what that absolute framework is; we are not yet in a position to say that there *is* such an absolute framework. Must there, after all, be a ground floor? Could not there be an infinite number of deeper and deeper frameworks? (Compare the question of whether there must be a deepest physical theory, or whether there could not be an infinite number of levels of depth.)

Is it necessary to go all the way to a ground-floor framework, though? Once the factor F relative to which p is true is known, cannot we state, not just that p is relatively true, but that "p is true relative to F" is itself true? Yes, that last statement will itself be true, but the question is: will it be a relative truth, holding only relative to still further factors, or will it be an absolute truth, for whose own truth no further factors need be stated or invoked or depended upon? The person who means to replace all (purportedly) relative truths by nonrelative ones that make explicit the relative factor F needs the statement that mentions the factor F to be true without itself depending upon some further different factor. That is a very large task. In the meantime, I want to be able to say that it is true that I am now typing at the computer. There should be some notion of truth that enables me to do this without being committed to any particular ground-floor absolute framework of factors, beyond which truth cannot vary, and even without being committed to the existence of some such ground floor or other. The notion of relative truth fits the bill.

Relativism about truth seems to make it parochial and limited. ("That is just *your* truth." Even when the "you" is quite widespread, the truth's limits still are discernible.) Someone might argue for correspondence as the universal truth property as follows: the truth property is what explains success in acting upon beliefs; if a belief is a representation of the world that guides our actions, then surely any being acting upon a belief will do better acting upon an accurate representation—and that constitutes correspondence.

But an accurate representation is not the same as a true one,[89] and "more accurate" does not necessarily mean better. The greater accuracy might make the representation too confusing or too difficult to work with, as does a map with too many details. What is wanted is something accurate enough for the purposes. (Is "true" just being accurate enough for most *normal* purposes, and as purposes shift over time, or vary from group to group, can truth also then shift or vary?) Belief is an intermediate mechanism statistically connected to inclusive fitness.[90] Yet when combined with certain goals, such as a desire to commit suicide immediately, accurate beliefs might ill-serve inclusive fitness. Other organisms might have different intermediate mechanisms that do not involve separate beliefs at all, but rather some entities that (we would say) join beliefs and desires in certain combinations only, and so leave these organisms less vulnerable to accurate beliefs in the service of harmful desires.

If truth is tied to beliefs and representations, and to their function in guiding action, then we can consider alternative functional substitutes that also guide behavior but do not involve beliefs or representations or some analog of the notion of truth. Our own mode of cognition and of action might be treated in a wider comparative theory of different modes of cognition, behavioral guidance, and reproductive survival. Such a theory also might make truth appear somewhat parochial, not (as relativism does) by saying that truth varies from person to person, or group to group, or place to place, but rather by saying that truth appears only in certain contexts, those that are belief- or representation-guided; in other contexts, truth does not even get a grip. Such a view, too, would make truth more limited than the absolutist believes, not by making it relative but by making it *local*. This view of truth's locality would gain force if combined with the claim that the other modes of guidance are equally conducive to survival and reproduction, and also equally "good," however that is to be spelled out. (It would beg the question, though, to say that since these latter modes do not involve truth and so do not involve the special kind of knowledge *that something is the case*, they cannot be equally good.) Truth may be local, not just if it is relative but if it gets a grip only within certain action-guiding structures, the ones that involve beliefs or representations.

The Correspondence Theory

There is a form for defining truth common to many specific definitions.[91] *S* is true if and only if there is a *p* such that *S* says (only) that *p*, and *p*. Apart from technical difficulties, this form leaves much to be desired. The first part, that there is something that *S* says, that what *S* says is (that) *p*, seems to be something to be illuminated by a theory of language. How it is that language can state something about the world is an intricate question, but it is not the question of truth.[92] So, the piece of the definition of truth (of the above form) that seems especially to concern *truth* is the part that *follows* "there is a *p* such that *S* says (only) that *p*." Here one might expect something like "and *p* is a fact," but instead we simply get "and *p*," the mere repetition of *p*. So much the better, hold proponents of the redundancy and disquotational theories of truth. Yet we want something more. If the above form indeed could serve as a definition of truth, then what we want is not (simply) a definition of truth. We do not want a completion of

S is true if and only if _____,

where the right side includes "and *p*," when *S* is a term of the metalanguage that refers to the declarative sentence substituted for *p*. Rather, we want to understand what it means to say that *p* holds, for any declarative *p*. We seem to want a completion of

p if and only if _____,

a completion that provides something more illuminating than the trivial "*p* if and only if *p*." And here we might expect that *p* will be analyzed into components (such as objects, properties, relations), and that we will be told what relations or combinations these components must stand in for *p*, in general, to hold.

We seem to want a *general characterization* of truth.[93] Not every general characterization will do, however. Consider the coherence theory of truth. There seems to be no reason why our universe should be the most coherent one, no reason why all actual truths should be members of the most coherent set of statements. It seems possible that another universe might be more coherent than the actual one, and also that sufficiently imaginative and skilled science-fiction writers might describe such a more coherent universe. Suppose it were the case, though, that the actual universe *is* in fact the most coherent possible universe, according to some criterion of coherence. All the actual facts are explainable by *one* ultimate law, etc. Suppose, further, that it is an accident, a brute fact, that the actual universe is the most coherent possible one; it could have been otherwise. Then the coherence theory of truth would give us a characterization—and not just a list—of the set of all (actual) truths. But it would not delineate what truth would be if the universe were different, if some other universe were the actual one. It would not characterize what truth is in every possible world. Perhaps a longer list could give us, in extension, a delineation of truth in each possible world. But what the philosopher wants, it seems, is a general characterization of truth in any possible world, an illuminating statement of what all truths have in common in virtue of being truths.

Suppose the physicists' hopes of a final unified theory (of everything) were realized. All facts are explained by, and follow from, one fundamental law L_1. Then we can say that S is true if and only if S follows from L_1. (L_1 also is one of the things that follow from L_1.) This is a general characterization of truth, not simply a list, and it would give us a deep characterization of truth in the actual world. However, since there could be other universes built around other fundamental laws or sets of them, this characterization would not delimit truth for those other universes. We might say: it would be a theory of *what is true* but not a *theory of truth.*

A theory of truth is a general characterization of truths in any possible world. If we had a deep theory of what is (actually) true, we might be less interested in a characterization of truth for any possible world. That latter task might strike us as like wondering how many angels can dance on the head of a pin. Those things—angels, other universes—don't exist, and the subjunctive questions (if angels did exist, how many could . . . ; if another universe were actual, what would truth be there?) might seem less than pressing, and their answers less than illuminating.

Consider, as an analogy, the question of what constitutes a good wine. Someone might be content with a list, drawn from an encyclopedia of wine. X is a good wine if and only if X is from this vineyard in the year 1983 or X is from that vineyard in the year . . . etc. Suppose the disjunction covers all vineyards through the last year (after which year all the vines are destroyed and there are no further wines made from grapes). We would have a list of good wines, and so have defined "good wine" in extension. But we would not have a characterization of good wines, a specification of what they all have in common. Suppose, instead, that someone does produce such a general specification, listing the properties of good wines. Now we know what makes something a good wine. Yet it might be objected that those things would not be good wines if the atmosphere of the planet were different, or if the laws of chemistry were different, or if differently constituted organisms were drinking them. What is wanted, says this objector, is a general characterization of "good wine" for each and every possible world. It is not so clear that we *would* desire this, and such a thing might have to be so general and abstract (applying as it must to every possible world) as to be unilluminating.

We can distinguish the *breadth* of a general characterization, the range of possible worlds in which it applies, from the *depth* of a characterization, how much it tells us, and explains, about the actual things of that kind. And there might be a tradeoff between depth and breadth. Still, we might want more than an account for the actual world; we might also want an account for worlds very similar to the actual one. Each trait, depth and breadth, is a virtue, and different purposes might lead us to seek different types of accounts.

I have said that we want to know what, in general, must hold if (any) p. One answer would be provided by a final theory of the one ultimate law L_1: p if and only if p follows from L_1. This does tell us when p (actually) holds. However, we might want, not simply a characterization of when p holds, even one that applies to other possible worlds, but a *microtheory* of when p holds, of what makes p hold. This would be a theory that looks within the structure of p itself, and delineates how p's holding depends upon the components of p.

One sort of theory (though perhaps one that is not "micro" enough) speaks of facts. What must hold if p, is that p corresponds to a fact. The correspondence theorist holds that the truth property, or more modestly *our* truth property, is correspondence to the facts. But then we want a theory of what components make up a fact, and how they do this, and also a clear statement of what the relation of correspondence is. Such an approach raises familiar and troublesome questions: are there negative facts, what are facts composed of, do they exist alongside ordinary entities in the world, and so on.[94]

In a criticism of J. L. Austin's presentation of a correspondence theory of truth, P. F. Strawson tells us that facts are entities cooked up to be precisely what true statements state. For every true statement, a corresponding fact is reified. However, facts and true statements are not, as Strawson complained, made for each other. Not every true statement requires a distinctive fact as the one it states; different true statements can state and correspond to the same fact.[95]

The relation of a true statement to a fact or set of facts is a complicated one. Not every separate true statement states a separate fact. Nonatomic truth-functional statements in the propositional calculus are made true by the truth values of their component statements. If no facts make p true, then not-p is true.[96] Whatever facts make p true or make q true make p-or-q

true. Whatever facts make p true and make q true make p-and-q true. There needn't be an additional conjunctive fact, p-and-q, which makes the statement that p and q true.

The truths of molecular propositional calculus statements are built up from the truth values of their component propositional parts. The truths of the predicate calculus, Tarski taught us, are built from the satisfactions of their component nonmolecular open statements. The truth of a definite description statement, for instance, "The man in the corner has property P," Bertrand Russell held, is built from the satisfaction of its components. If some person has the property P, and that person is the man in the corner (which Russell analyzes, within the scope of the existential quantifier, as: x is a man in the corner, and for all y, if y is a man in the corner then y is identical with x), there need be no additional *fact* that the man in the corner has the property P. That statement is made true by the previous facts, without the existence of any additional fact. A true statement is made true by facts (or by their absence), yet there need not be any separate fact that it (alone) states.

Other relations, in addition to the ones listed above, are components of the "makes-true" relation. Philosophers of science have described scientific reduction: one theory T_2 is reduced to another theory T_1 when (in the simplest case) all the laws of T_2 can be derived from the laws of T_1 along with linkages (equivalences) of terms in T_2 to terms in T_1. Thus thermodynamics is reducible to statistical mechanics, when temperature is identified with the mean kinetic energy of molecules. A statement that the temperature in a room is such-and-such is made true by a fact about the mean kinetic energy of the molecules in the room. There is no additional or separate fact about temperature that makes this statement true.[97]

Similarly, truths of constitution might enter as components of the makes-true relation. When one object O is composed of entities $o_1, \ldots, o_n$ in certain relations, then it is truths about $o_1, \ldots, o_n$ in these relations that constitute and make true the statements about O. Correct philosophical analyses also will constitute components of the makes-true relation. If S knows that p is analyzed as p's being true, S's believing that p, and (for instance) S's belief that p tracking the truth that p, then this will enter into the truth definition, specifying what makes true someone's knowing something. If X at time t_2 is the same object as Y at earlier time t_1, if and only if X is a continuer of Y, X continues Y closely enough to be it at the later time, and X is Y's closest continuer at time t_2, then this will enter into the truth definition, specifying what makes true something's being the same object as an earlier one.[98] The truth of someone's knowing something, or of one object's being the same as an earlier one, is asymmetrically dependent upon the analyzing clauses. The analyses of the analytic philosopher then might be seen as increasing understanding not only of the notion that is analyzed but also of the notion of truth, in that it specifies particular components of the makes-true relation.

Another component of the makes-true relation might be specific forms of supervenience, wherein one property or fact holds in virtue of others that it is completely derivative from.[99] Some philosophers have held that ethical facts supervene upon nonethical facts, and that mental facts supervene upon neurophysiological and more broadly physical facts. When one fact is supervenient upon another, rather than two facts' being present, it seems that there are two true statements, but only one (underlying) fact. The one fact makes both statements true.[100]

The makes-true relation itself can be construed as a supervenience relation. By utilizing it, or its clauses, a definition of truth shows how some truths are supervenient upon others. The truths in a world w_i that are not made true by any other truths in that world, and so are not supervenient upon any other truths in that world, we might term absolutely *subvenient* in that world w_i.

Not only can the truths vary from one possible world to another; the makes-true relation can also vary from one world to another. Strictly, we should subscript a makes-true relation, indicating the world w_i in which it holds. It seems that two worlds could have the same set of first-level truths yet differ in their makes-true relation, and hence in the way they are constituted.

A definition of truth for a world w_i will divide into two general parts. First, it will list (or do the equivalent of listing) the subvenient truths of world w_i. This is the base clause of the definition of truth for that world. Second, it will (recursively) specify all other truths of w_i as made true by w_i's subvenient truths, in accordance with w_i's makes-true relation.

This will give us a definition of: S is true in world w_i. We can advance to a definition of S's being true (period) by adding that one of the worlds in which S is true is the actual world. (S is true if and only if there is a world w_i such that S is true in w_i and w_i is the actual world.) A theory of truth, then, needs to specify what it is for a world to be the actual world. I turn to this in Chapter 3.

It has been complained against Alfred Tarski that in the base clause of his definition of truth he simply lists the "atomic" predicates and gives their satisfaction conditions.[101] By introducing the makes-true relation, which adds clauses to Tarski's recursive machinery, we have reduced the number of predicates (and so derivatively of truths) that must simply be listed. Some of Tarski's atomic truths will not be absolutely subvenient. Still, the definition of truth in world w_i continues to contain a list, the list of the absolutely subvenient predicates (and so derivatively of truths) of w_i. This surd quality is eased somewhat by the fact that to obtain a definition of true (period), we add that w_i is the actual world. We shall have to see later whether this reference to actuality suffices to provide the further common quality of truths that critics of the simple list desire.

How is it that Tarski himself has managed to avoid speaking of actuality? He does not offer a definition of S's being true in world w_i, and then add that w_i is the actual world. He simply proceeds to offer a definition of S's being true *(simpliciter)*. He is not concerned with modality and sees no need to speak explicitly of possible worlds or any functionally similar notion. He simply states the truth conditions for atomic sentences within the actual world, and he is able to do this, without *mentioning* actuality, simply by speaking *within* the actual world. The Tarski procedure can be repeated in any possible world to define truth there (and we also have added clauses to his recursive procedure). He offers a particular instance of it, specific to the actual world. But since he has not explicitly specified the application of his general procedure to the actual world, since he has not explicitly demarcated the notion of actuality but merely has relied upon the fact that (as he assumes) he is speaking within the actual world, he has not explained the notion of actuality and hence has not explained the notion of truth *(simpliciter)*, even if he has succeeded extensionally in marking out all the actual truths.[102]

There is no reason to believe that we already know all the components of the makes-true relation, all the different ways (in the actual world) in which a statement can be made true. (This relation of being made true is an asymmetrical one; a statement is true *because* of what it is made true by.) We are not yet able to state all the relations that facts stand in to the true statements that they make true. Hence, we cannot now put forward a substantive and complete correspondence theory of truth.[103]

There is another reason why we cannot yet state a substantive and complete correspondence theory of truth. We do not yet know what the components of facts are. Are there ultimate components (absolute atoms)? There is a temptation to say that the components are things or objects, their properties and their relations. But this accords too well with grammatical categories, and so it raises the suspicion that linguistic units are being projected as ontological categories. Of course, another possibility is that these are accurate ontological units, and humanity very early got hold of them in its formation of corresponding linguistic categories. But how did we get so smart so early? One might grant that humanity got hold of a division that served it well enough, but that is no reason to think such categories will occur in our eventual best explanatory theory. What will our theories end up with as the components of those facts which stand in the makes-true relation to all true statements? Will these be particles, strings, fields, space-time manifolds, mental states, all of the above, or none of them but something as yet undreamt of? We are not yet in a position to say. Relativism does not follow, however, from this lack of final ontological knowledge.

Although we cannot yet specify the makes-true relation, and although we cannot yet specify the components of the facts marked by this relation, nevertheless we can hold that something about the world makes true statements true. This is, I grant, a weaker statement than I would wish to put forth. It is merely the doubly existentially quantified statement that there exists something about the world, and there exists some specification of the makes-true relation, so that a statement is true when that thing about the world stands in that specified relation to the statement. Weak as it is, however, some people seem to want to deny it.

We do not have to say, though, that this something which makes statements true is *facts*. Perhaps our explanations need not halt at the level of *facts*. It is not clear whether facts are an additional ontological category that we must countenance, or whether they too are reducible to some combination of the ultimate ontological components.[104]

To know the correct and deep theory of truth's nature requires far more than the mere ability to state particular truths. It requires a knowledge of the ultimate dependence relations, and of the ultimate explanatory and ontological factors. A theory of truth, therefore, arises closer to the end of inquiry than to its beginning. Do not be surprised that we have not reached it yet.

2

Invariance and Objectivity

Are there objective truths and facts? If so, are there also subjective facts and truths, or is the adjective "objective" redundant when applied to facts? Can beliefs be objective? Is objectivity in beliefs always a virtue? (In the present climate of opinion, one has to ask whether it ever is a virtue.) Is objectivity just a male trait? Worse, is it (in the current phrase) merely a "white, heterosexual, male" trait? (The complete contemporary locution is "dead, white, heterosexual males." What I really object to is the "dead" part. Leaving aside the vapidity of assuming that the only statements worth attending to are very recent ones, it is not nice to pick on people when they cannot fight back.)

The notions of "objective" and "subjective" are contrasting notions, at least insofar as objects and subjects themselves contrast. Something is objective when (or to the extent that) it is determined in its character by the features of an object; it is subjective when it is determined in its character by states such as consciousness, emotions, and desires that are intrinsic to being a subject.

The objectivity of a fact or truth depends upon its own content and character; the objectivity of a belief depends upon the character of the process that gives rise to the belief. It depends upon what kind of factors the belief is based upon, and how. The objectivity or subjectivity of a belief can crosscut the objectivity or subjectivity of the fact believed; all four combinations are possible.[1] I begin with a discussion of objective facts, turning later to the objectivity of beliefs.

Objective Facts

There are three strands to our ordinary notion of an objective fact or objective truth. First, an objective fact is accessible from different angles. Access to it can be repeated by the same sense (sight, touch, etc.) at different times; it can be repeated by different senses of the same observer, and also by different observers. Different laboratories can replicate the phenomenon. What can be experienced only at one instant by one sense modality of one observer is indistinguishable from random noise and does not (securely) count as an objective fact.[2]

The second mark of an objective truth, related to the first, is that there is or can be intersubjective agreement about it. And the third feature concerns independence. If *p* is an objective truth, then it holds independently of people's beliefs, desires, hopes, and observations or measurements that *p*.

The three features of objective truths (accessibility from different angles, intersubjectivity, and independence) certainly are in need of elaboration and refinement, if only to meet the counterexamples to thinking of them as individually necessary and jointly sufficient. We also may wonder how the notion of independence fares in the light of quantum mechanics.[3] However, it is a fourth and more fundamental characteristic of objective truth that I want to investigate here. An objective fact is invariant under various transformations. It is this invariance that constitutes something as an objective truth, and it underlies and explains the first three features (to the extent that they hold).

That invariance is importantly connected to something's being an objective fact is suggested by the practice of physicists, who treat what is invariant under Lorentz transformations as more objective than what varies under these transformations. P. A. M. Dirac writes, "The important things in the world appear as the invariants . . . of . . . transformations."[4] Einstein taught us that spatial distance and temporal distance are relative to an observer; their magnitudes will be measured differently by different inertial observers, and spatial and temporal intervals are not invariant under Lorentz transformations. However, inertial observers will agree about another, more complicated interval between events, involving not just spatial separations alone or temporal separations alone but a particular mixture of the two, namely, the square root of the square of the time separation minus the square of the spatial separation. This more complicated interval *is* invariant under Lorentz transformations. The principle of relativity of Einstein's Special Theory holds that all laws of physics are the same for all inertial observers; they are the same in every inertial reference frame, and so are invariant under Lorentz transformations.

That an interval involving *both* temporal and spatial separation is invariant, while no simpler interval involving only temporal or only spatial separation is invariant under Lorentz transformations, is the reason why talk of a unified *space-time* is significant. It had been possible since Descartes simply to add a fourth dimension, time, to the three spatial dimensions of Euclidean geometry and thus to locate each event in space and time by four coordinates, three spatial and one temporal. However, according to pre-Einsteinian notions of physical processes, time intervals and spatial intervals and the simultaneity of events all could be assessed and accurately measured by all inertial observers as identical, whatever their state of relative motion. The temporal dimension (it was thought) showed invariant temporal intervals, all on its own, and the spatial dimensions showed invariant spatial intervals. The joining of spatial and temporal dimensions (as these were conceived before Einstein) is a mixture and not a compound. Their joining is not a new ontological entity. Whereas, after Einstein, unified *space-time* is a true ontological entity, *for only it, and not its lesser dimensional parts, shows something that is invariant under Lorentz transformations.* And what it shows to be invariant, though defined by a formula in terms of other quantities, is not defined solely, or in this case at all, in terms of quantities that are themselves Lorentz invariant. Hermann Minkowski put forward the strong ontological claim in 1908: "Henceforth space by itself, and time by itself, are doomed to fade away into mere shadows, and only a kind of union of the two will preserve an independent reality."[5]

We already are familiar with the notion of invariance under transformations with less technical material. It is forty degrees outside as I write this sentence. Does it follow that it will be twice as hot on a day when it is eighty degrees outside? No. The temperatures I referred to were measured on the Fahrenheit scale, and although 80 is twice 40, when we measure the corresponding temperatures on the centigrade scale, we do not find that one is twice the other.

The procedure for measuring temperature on the Fahrenheit and centigrade scales allows different units and different zero points. In the familiar formula $F = (9/5)C + 32$, the "9/5" arises from the fact that the units of temperature differ on the two scales, and the "$+32$" reflects their different placement of the zero points. On such scales of measurement, the ratio of two numbers has no fixed significance but is an artifact of a particular scale. One quantity's being twice another is not invariant under the transformation $F = (9/5)C + 32$. Also, the difference or interval between two temperatures $(T_1 - T_2)$ has no fixed significance on these scales. What does have significance is the *ratio of two intervals, $(T_1 - T_2)/(T_3 - T_4)$*. This ratio will be the same on each scale of measurement, and it is invariant under positive linear transformations. The two scales are equally good scales for measuring temperature; anything that varies with the scale of measurement is not an objective fact about temperature.[6]

It is important to discover that a magnitude, previously considered absolute, is relative. It also is important to discover what magnitudes are invariant under the relevant transformations, and so still qualify (in that respect, at least) as absolute. Einstein later regretted that he called his theory "relativity theory" instead of naming it "Invariantentheorie."

To understand something, we want to know the transformations it is invariant under and also the transformations it is *variant* under. (To adapt the subtitle of Bertrand Russell's book on human knowledge, we want to know the "scope and limits" of its invariance.) In addition to the usual requirements on knowledge that p be true and that the person believe it, the tracking account of knowledge I presented in *Philosophical Explanations* contains an invariance condition and a variance condition. The fourth condition (of that book) states that if p were true the person would believe it. This is an invariance condition: the belief is invariant under subjunctive changes that maintain its truth value. The third condition states that if p were not true, the person wouldn't believe it. This is a variance condition: the belief varies under a subjunctive change of its truth value.

The physicist discovers basic invariances in the world, and the ordinary macro-objects and macrofacts we encounter also show invariances, at a different level from the invariances of the physicist. A bottle's shape or color does not change as we rotate it or move it from one place to another.[7] It is important for people (and other animals) to know some of these invariances, for they often mark continuing facts that we can use to predict the behavior of entities, and upon which we can base our behavior toward them. Evolution has shaped our sensory apparatus to give us the capacity to detect these invariances. The psychologist of perception James Gibson has argued that there are invariances in the stimulus energy flux that reaches our sensory receptors, and that these invariances correspond to permanent properties of the environment; hence, the (higher-order) invariances in the stimulus energy can give us information about the invariances in external objects.[8] The detection and extraction of invariants is also a central feature of Edwin Land's retinex theory of color vision.[9]

One program for ontology is to delineate the kinds of things there are, the different ontological statuses things have, by the set of transformations these things are invariant under. (Here we parallel Felix Klein's thought in classifying geometric objects, and geometries, by the kinds of transformations they are invariant under.) These transformations can be used to define or identify a thing's "mode of being." Macbeth's "dagger" is invariant under some transformations involving Macbeth (such as ones involving where he is standing) but not under ones involving other observers. The appearance of wetness on the road is invariant under transformations of observers, but the point of observation must be held fixed. Physical objects or higher-order relations concerning them are invariant under a wide range of transformations. A pain, a mirage, a fictional character, a table, an elementary particle are invariant under different sets of transformations. The transformations define, and demarcate, something's ontological category.[10]

Admissible Transformations

A property or relationship is objective when it is invariant under the appropriate transformations.[11] There are at least two types of transformation to consider. A transformation can be a *mapping*, a function from one set to another set (possibly the same one). (This is the notion used in mathematics.) To say that something is invariant under a transformation, in this sense, is just to say that when certain things have a property, other things also have this property. Second, a transformation can be an actual dynamical *change* or alteration of things through time, so that the very same things, though present, are changed in some way (which is compatible with the continued existence of those things). Properties invariant under such dynamical transformations, however, are not changed; they still apply to the entity. It is this notion that is used in the literature on identity through time. These different types of transformation might be appropriately used for different subject matters.[12]

If we say then that an objective fact is one that is invariant under all admissible transformations, how is it to be determined which transformations are the admissible ones? Simply to identify these transformations as the ones that leave all the objective facts invariant would not give us an independent understanding of the nature of objective facts. The notion of invariance under transformations cannot (without further supplementation) be a *complete* criterion of the objectivity of facts, for its application depends upon a selection of *which* transformations something is to be invariant under. Unless there is an independent criterion to specify which transformations something must be invariant under in order to be objective, it seems that the invariance criterion can only *transmit* objectivity—if this is objective, then that is—but it cannot provide the basis of *all* objectivity. Where, then, does the prior objectiveness come from?

We do not begin with an *a priori* criterion of objectivity, one that is unchanging and that holds necessarily. Instead, we start historically with a certain notion of objective facts, and with a certain (provisional) list L_1 of them. These facts support a view that certain other facts L_2 are objective. (Einstein's two postulates, for instance: that the laws of physics take the same form in all inertial frames—the principle of relativity—and that in any given inertial frame, the velocity of light is the same, whether the light is emitted by a body at rest or by a body in uniform motion.) These other facts L_2 entail that certain transformations T_1 are admissible, and that invariance under these transformations is a legitimate test of the objectiveness of a fact. Some of the "facts" on the original list L_1 fail this test (of invariance under T_1) and so are dropped from the list, leaving a revised list L_1', and now it is $L_1' + L_2$ that constitute our list of objective facts, along with those further facts L_3 that we noticed only when we went looking for additional things that were invariant under T_1. New scientific investigations yield new facts L_4, entailing that certain other transformations T_2 are admissible, and . . .

Not only are new transformations added, some get dropped. If well-confirmed theories that are our only explanation of certain phenomena fail to be invariant under certain transformations, these transformations will be dropped from the list of admissible ones. The Special Theory of Relativity provides a particularly clear and illuminating illustration of this process of alteration in the set of admissible transformations.[13]

The development of our understanding of objective facts is a stepwise process, involving mutually modifying knowledge of new facts and of new admissible transformations. (We might say that the two notions of objective facts and admissible transformations are brought into "reflective equilibrium," but we must notice that there also is continual new input into this process, viz. the new explanations of new phenomena that we come upon.) To understand the notion of an objective fact, then, we would need to understand this stepwise process and the standards it embodies; to understand the starting place, and why it was appropriate; to understand what transformations are admissible according to our current view, and why they are; and to present a general description that would encompass past, present, and future views.

The stepwise process and its standards are part of the subject matter of philosophy of science. These standards may themselves presuppose certain views of what specific facts hold (and what ones could not hold), along with general views on what counts as an objective fact. However, in the stepwise process these views and standards themselves can undergo successive modification.

The starting place is fixed by the phenomena and by the invariances that evolution has shaped us to notice and take account of. It would have served our ancestors well (according to our current view) to notice some facts or approximations of facts. Organisms that had the capacity and tendency to do so would tend more successfully to leave offspring with similar capacities and dispositions.

Our current view in physics gives great prominence to very general and abstract symmetries and invariances. These range from invariances across spatial position and in time, to covariant formulations of laws in general relativity, to group theory in quantum mechanics, to symmetries and supersymmetries in particle physics.[14]

Amalie Emmy Noether showed that for each symmetry/invariance that satisfies a Lie group, there is some quantity that is conserved. Corresponding to invariance under translation in space, momentum is conserved; to invariance under translation in time, energy is conserved; and to invariance of the law under the addition of an arbitrary constant to the phase of the wave function, apparently electrical charge is conserved. So it is not surprising that laws that are invariant under various transformations are held to be more objective. Such laws correspond to a quantity that is conserved, and something whose amount in this universe cannot be altered, diminished, or augmented should count as (at least tied for being) the most objective thing there actually is.

The story of changing standards in the stepwise process above is not just a matter of shifts in which invariances and symmetries are important. It can involve coming to take symmetries and invariances seriously in themselves, and not simply as a heuristic clue to further facts. Steven Weinberg writes:

I once went back to the original literature of the 1930's on the earliest internal symmetry principle in nuclear physics, the symmetry . . . between neutrons and protons, to try to find the one research article that first presented this symmetry principle the way it would be presented today, as a fundamental fact about nuclear physics that stands on its own, independent of any detailed theory of nuclear forces. I could find no such article. It seems that in the 1930's it was simply not good form to write papers based on symmetry principles. What was good form was to write papers about nuclear forces. If the forces turned out to have a certain symmetry, so much the better, for, if you knew the proton-neutron force, you did not have to guess the proton-proton force. But the symmetry principle itself was not regarded, as far as I can tell, as a feature that would legitimize a theory—that would make the theory beautiful. Symmetry principles were regarded as mathematical tricks; the real business of physicists was to work out the dynamical details of the forces we observe. We feel differently today. If experimenters were to discover some new particles that formed families of some sort or other like the proton-neutron doublet, then the mail would instantly be filled with hundreds of preprints of theoretical articles speculating about the sort of symmetry that underlies this family structure, and, if a new kind of force were discovered, we would all start speculating about the symmetry that dictates the existence of that force.[15]

Because there is no *a priori* demarcation of all the admissible transformations[16] and because our knowledge of these grows over time, perhaps the only general statement we can make is *very* general: An objective fact is one that is invariant under all admissible transformations. Not only has our history of investigations taught us that objectiveness is invariance under all admissible transformations; we also have learned (*a posteriori*) that the admissible transformations marking an objective fact (as described by our fundamental theory) form a mathematical *group*.[17]

Eugene Wigner showed that if one starts with the Hilbert space approach to quantum mechanics, and adds relativistic invariance, then there must be two invariants for a particle, its *mass* and its spin. Are the objective properties of particles, then, the ones that are invariant under relativistic transformations? What is the importance of starting with the Hilbert space representation? If one started with another representation and looked for relativistic invariants, would one be able to reach mass and spin, or anything else that was interesting? Or must one start with the right/deepest mathematical representation of a theory? We might hypothesize as follows: For our fundamental theory F, there is *some* mathematical representation M, and there is some set of transformations T such that the basic properties or entities (or whatever) B are what is invariant under T, in the representation M of F.

This suggests a three-way project of mutual adjustment. Find *new* transformations T_i, so that (only) B are invariant under these and old transformations. Formulate a new theory F, or a new mathematical representation M of it, so that B are the invariants of F under T_i. Modify your view of the basic objective entities and properties B so that B are the invariants of F under T_i. Our fundamental theory and list of admissible transformations and list of basic objective properties and entities are brought into mutual equilibrium. And such equilibria can be disrupted by the discovery of new facts, which then propels the construction of a new theory and a new search for equilibrium. (And from the new transformations that have been formulated to fit the newly discovered facts, new testable predictions may result.)

Perhaps every theory of a certain sort can be given a covariant representation, so the requirement of covariance is no constraint upon the content of a theory;[18] but once we possess the covariant representation under which the equations stay the same for all coordinate systems, the quantities in the (covariant) equations are the real and objective quantities.

In physics, the invariances that have been discovered hold only up to a certain level. General Relativity does not exhibit invariances under global Lorentz transformations.[19] We do not know of transformations that there is invariance under at every level (except perhaps the transformations that go with the conservation of charge). If objectivity is invariance under all admissible transformations, then is *anything* objective?[20]

Should we speak of *objectivity-at-a-level,* and claim that something is absolutely objective if and only if it is objective at all levels? Perhaps nothing is objective at *all* levels, but when the objectivity of X fails when it reaches a certain level, there always will be a Y at that other level which is objective at that level. If there were an infinite series of levels, then at every level there could be objectivity, without there being the same objectivity at each level.[21]

Two Types of Philosophical Account

A philosophical account of an important philosophical notion (such as objectivity) can aim at two different goals. It can aim to present the necessary truths that hold specially about that notion (which some think of as all the truths specially about it that hold universally in every possible world). Alternatively, a philosophical account can aim at presenting the deepest truths that actually hold about the notion, the truths that underlie all other truths actually holding of the notion whether or not these truths hold in every possible world. (Some think of such an account as presenting the actual essence of the notion, as it is exhibited in this world.)

Each type of account has its virtues. The necessary truths tell us what must hold true of the notion, in any universe in which it is exhibited. Those truths will be broad, although they also may be a little thin, giving up depth of content for breadth of application.

The presentation of the deepest truths about, e.g., objectiveness, as it is exhibited, will give us a deeper understanding of its nature. Although it tells us specifically about its character in the actual world, such an account also will be general. It will tell us about every actual instance of the notion. However, it will not tell us what *must* hold true wherever objectiveness might possibly rear its head, the features it must exhibit wherever it might appear.

We can distinguish (as we noted in Chapter 1) the *breadth* of a general characterization, the range of possible worlds in which it applies, from the *depth* of a characterization, how much it tells us, and explains, about the actual things of that kind. We do not have to choose between the two pure kinds of philosophical account. For complete understanding, we might offer both. Should a philosophical theory of the nature of a notion, then, be an ordered pair, consisting of the deepest actual truths about those things exemplifying the notion, and of the totality of necessary truths about any possible exemplification of that notion? (Let us not argue about which of these should come first.)

We are not limited in our analyses to the extremes of maximum breadth and maximum depth. There are tradeoffs possible between the two, yielding an account of intermediate depth and breadth, not so wide as to apply to all possible worlds, not so deep as to apply only to this world and to very similar ones. Each trait, depth and breadth, is a virtue, and different purposes might lead us to seek different types of account, different combinations of breadth and depth.

Our account of objectiveness illustrates another way in which depth and breadth can be combined, not by an ordered pair or by tradeoffs but by a unified account containing a parameter that varies. The special necessary truth about objectiveness, the one that it exhibits in all possible worlds, is the *broad* notion of being *invariant under all admissible transformations.* What varies from world to world is the list of admissible transformations, and this is connected with variation in the laws that hold from world to world. The *deep* notion of objectiveness (for a specified world) is that of being *invariant under specified transformations.* Which transformations these are cannot be known *a priori* but only through the bootstrap process of scientific investigation.

I do not mean to say that there cannot be objectiveness in domains other than science or that there can be objectiveness in these other domains only if the scientists' transformations apply there also. Science discovers the admissible transformations for the domains it investigates and explains. Advances in each domain of knowledge will discover the admissible transformations (if such there be) central to *that* domain. The questions of how, if at all, the objectiveness in each domain relates to the objectiveness in all other domains can be faced only after the respective sets of transformations have been uncovered.

The extension of the framework of invariance, transformations, etc. to other areas is a promising program of research that is worth pursuing, I think. The hope is that it actually will lead us to notice illuminating new phenomena in other areas, for instance, that it will help to explain aspects of our experience of the arts.[22] However, there is no guarantee that this attempt will succeed; mechanically dragging labels such as "transformation" into new areas and applying them to no particular illumination would constitute failure.

Invariance under specified transformations explains the three marks of objectiveness mentioned earlier (namely, accessibility from different angles, intersubjective agreement, and independence from the observer and the theorizing mind), at least in the actual world. Perhaps there could be a world of strange construction where this underlying notion, invariance under the specified transformations of *that* world, does not give rise to the three marks there. Still, the objectiveness of the facts or truths there will be delineated by this underlying notion of invariance under that world's specified transformations.

The notion of invariance under transformations leads us also to a particular account of a scientific law (which also illustrates our discussion of the two kinds of philosophical account). Eugene Wigner has pointed out that the division of the welter of scientific facts into laws and initial conditions enables us to abstract the generalizations that are invariant across space and time, leaving the variant to the realm of initial conditions.[23] (The cosmological initial conditions of the universe as a whole, which underlie some other things we treat as laws, might be classified, for certain purposes, as akin to laws.) A scientific law gives us a stronger form of invariance than a generalization that happens to hold.[24] Writers in the Humean tradition, such as Carl Hempel and Ernest Nagel, have formulated criteria for a law that involves certain invariances (e.g., across individuals, places, and times).

R. B. Braithwaite added that a law is subsumable under more general true laws or theories. Of every law other than the ultimate ones, we can add to this that it is a true generalization that exhibits certain invariances $I_1, \ldots, I_n$, and that it is subsumed under some other more general statement that also is a true generalization satisfying certain (further?) invariances. Indeed, of every law that is not either ultimate or one step next to it, we can say that it is subsumed under some other more general true statement with these features (of exhibiting certain invariances and also of being thus subsumable).

What of the ultimate true generalizations, which subsume all the others? We can mark an ultimate law as one that is a true generalization that exhibits certain invariances, *and* that subsumes many levels under it that are true generalizations exhibiting invariances, and that is not subsumed itself by any other true invariant generalization. The ultimate generalizations are not subsumed themselves, but they do a lot of subsuming; they subsume *many* levels of true generalization.

We can add the further invariances that have been discovered to hold, e.g., Lorentz invariance, to the list of what writers in the Humean tradition require for a generalization to be a law (viz. that it states invariances or constancies that hold across individuals, places, and times). A law, then, will be a Humean generalization, satisfying the conditions discussed above, that in addition itself satisfies various specified invariances. Not only does what the law describes satisfy invariance conditions, but so does the statement of the law itself. For instance, an equation may be invariant under a group of transformations of its parameters, so that the equation is identical (unchanged) after these transformations. (The symmetry of an equation needs to be distinguished from the symmetry of its set of solutions.) Einstein's Principle of Relativity requires that laws take the same mathematical and logical form in all inertial reference frames. Einstein's Principle of Equivalence requires that in any small freely falling reference frame the laws of physics are the same as they are in an inertial reference frame in a gravity-free universe. The principle of general covariance requires that laws take the same form in every reference frame, not merely in all inertial frames.

Recently, we may have learned another somewhat wider characteristic of fundamental scientific laws. If they themselves do not satisfy specified symmetry and invariance conditions, then they stand in a specific relation to other statements that do satisfy these conditions; namely, they arise by spontaneous breaking of the symmetries in these latter statements.

These additional conditions on a law, stated by the particular invariances, serve to rule out many purported counterexamples to the Humean account of law. The standard examples of accidental generalizations do not exhibit these invariances (in their subject matter or in the statement of the laws themselves) or follow from statements that do in the way that more specialized laws follow from more general ones plus boundary conditions.

One feature that distinguishes laws from accidental generalizations is that laws support subjunctive inferences (e.g., "If the object were dropped, it would travel at velocity v after n seconds"). On the possible-worlds account, or representation, of subjunctive statements, these speak about what would hold true in (a band of) the closest possible worlds.[25] It seems that the more transformations an actually true general statement is invariant under, the wider is the band of close-by worlds it holds true in. Hence, the wider the range of transformations a generalization is invariant under, the stronger will be the subjunctives that it supports. Invariance under transformations thereby bestows a certain modal status to generalizations.

Notice that under this account, a law will be a Humean generalization (usually subsumable under others) whose content and whose statement satisfy various invariance conditions (or which arises via broken symmetries from statements that do satisfy these conditions). That is the broad account of a law. The deep account, delineating the nature of laws in this universe, will specify the particular invariance conditions they satisfy. The nature of scientific laws is discussed further at the end of Chapter 3.

The Ordering of Objectiveness

The three components of the ordinary notion of an objective fact admit of degrees. There can be more or fewer routes by which a fact is accessible, it can admit of greater or lesser intersubjective agreement, it can be more or less independent of our beliefs and desires. Can we use the notion of invariance under admissible transformations to specify a notion of degrees of objectiveness?[26]

It seems promising to hold that one property is more objective than another when the first is invariant under a wider range of (admissible) transformations than the second is. More precisely, the set of transformations the second is invariant under is a proper subset of the set of transformations the first is invariant under.[27] Invariance thus gives rise to a partial ordering of things in terms of how objective they are. The ordering is only partial because it gives no answer to the question of which property is more objective when the two sets of transformations are disjoint, or when they overlap without one being included in the other.

Topological properties are invariant under homeomorphisms while metric properties are not. Are metric properties therefore less objective than topological ones? Is the distance between two points less real or less objective than the connectedness of a space? Can the distance between two points be less objective than a torus structure? There might be equal agreement about the two facts, metrical and topological, and even more agreement about the first metrical fact if the tear in the topological structure is tiny. A more guarded position would hold not that the topological properties are more objective than the metric ones but that the topological properties are deeper, more fundamental, more *basic*. Alterations that change

other properties leave them untouched, while no alteration of the topological properties leaves all the metric ones unchanged. The metrical properties, however, are *sharper*.

I prefer to see the matter less cautiously, as follows. Something's invariance features are an important part of the explanation of its score according to the three usual criteria of objectiveness (avenues of access, amount of
intersubjective agreement, amount of independence of the knower). The
object's or property's score on the three usual dimensions will not depend
only upon its invariance features, however; it also will depend upon the environment the thing is in. Given two things, a certain environment might
not bring out or make evident the second thing's lesser objectiveness, and
so this second thing might achieve as high an actual score in these common
symptoms of objectiveness as the first does. The additional transformations that the first thing is invariant under might not, in that environment,
give rise to any superiority in actual objectiveness scores according to the
three usual notions. Other possible environments, however, would bring
out the difference. The additional transformations could and would explain
a higher objectiveness score according to the three usual criteria in some
possible situations and environments other than the actual ones. If things
had been different in a certain possible way, the first thing *would have* been
more accessible than the other, or been the subject of more intersubjective
agreement, or been more independent of the knower's characteristics. So
even if the first thing's score is not actually higher, it can be more objective
than the second in virtue of an actual fact, namely, that it is invariant under
a superset of transformations. This seems to be a good reason to say that
the superset criterion is sufficient for greater objectiveness,[28] and that it
should not be artificially limited. (Do these considerations show that the
object associated with the superset is more objective, or only that it could
be more objective, only that it is potentially more objective?)

We *could* see something's objectiveness as its actual score along these
three dimensions. That would make of objectiveness an occurrent property; call that the thing's *surface objectiveness*. Or we might see something's
objectiveness as its disposition to have a certain objectiveness score, and so
as the features that form the basis of this disposition; these underlying features explain the objectiveness score it has in this environment and also the
objectiveness scores that it would have in all other possible environments.
(Here, variation in environments also would include variations in the features of the beings having access to the thing and reaching agreement about
it.) Call this the thing's *underlying objectiveness*. It is this latter notion that is

theoretically more fundamental and more interesting. The temptation to say that two things can be equally objective even when the transformations the first is invariant under is a superset of the transformations the second is invariant under stems, I think, from focusing upon the two things' actual objectiveness scores, upon their surface objectiveness rather than upon their underlying objectiveness.[29]

When one set of transformations is not included in another, however, we will not get an ordering through the inclusion relation alone. Some weighting of transformations will be needed to generate an order. In music, for example, a transformation from one key to another keeps intervalic structure invariant but it loses the particular emotional flavor of a particular key. On the other hand, a transformation within a key might keep the emotional flavor—it is in the same key—but change the intervalic structure. Taking both transformations together generates no order. Is intervalic structure or emotional tone more objective? That would require weighting the transformations; merely listing them does not answer the question. (Other transformations also can be considered, e.g., what is preserved and what is not when the instrument that the melody is played on is changed.)

If one set of transformations T_1 is a proper subset of another set of transformations T_2, then fewer properties will be invariant under T_2 than are invariant under T_1. We might get to such a large set of transformations T_n such that only *one* property is invariant under all these, and so that one property counts as the most objective actual property, the only fully objective property. Could we not add another transformation, arriving at a set T_{n+1} such that *no* property was invariant under all those transformations, and so have to conclude that nothing was completely objective? Some would hold that this is paradoxical. However, if the additional transformation is well motivated (perhaps some things do satisfy it, but these things don't satisfy all the members of T_n), then we are *imagining* a way in which something can be more objective. There just is nothing actual which *is* that objective. There is no reason to think that something in our universe, or our universe itself, is the most objective thing that there *could be,* the most objective conceivable thing. It is not a necessary truth that the most objective conceivable or possible thing exists, and it is desirable that our notion of degree of objectivity have the consequence that there could be a thing more objective than anything that actually exists.

When p is an objective fact, will it also always be the case that it is an objective fact that p is an objective fact? Abbreviate "p is an objective fact" as Op. For all p, is it true that if Op then OOp? If the OO-thesis does not hold, then we can define the *level of objectivity* of a fact p as the largest number of O's that truly precede p.

To say that p is objective, to say that Op, is to say (1): p is invariant under a set T_i of admissible transformations. To say that it is an objective fact that p is objective, OOp, is to say (2): that (1) is invariant under a set T_j of admissible transformations. Either this set of transformations T_j that makes Op objective is a different set from the set T_i of transformations that makes p itself objective, or this set of transformations that makes Op objective is the very same set of transformations that makes p objective. At some point up the hierarchy of levels one would expect that the set of transformations repeats (but not, I would guess, at the very first level up).

We have followed the lead of the physicists in seeing invariance under (admissible) transformations at the heart of the notion of objectiveness. How well does this notion apply outside of physics to what we ordinarily term objective facts? Some perceptual psychologists have tried to apply the notion; I mentioned Gibson's work earlier. I have been reluctant myself to formulate any transformations under which ordinary statements or facts are invariant. The obvious ones that spring to mind tend to be trivial and unilluminating translations of the original three criteria of objectiveness into the jargon-talk of transformations, e.g., that the truth of a statement is invariant under transformations that map one perspective into another, or one observer into another, or one context for interpreting indexical expressions into another. What is needed is a sustained investigation of the particular transformations that mark the subject matter of areas other than physics. Only then will we be able to assess the fruitfulness of the suggestion that objectiveness can, in general, be understood as invariance under transformations. There certainly is no guarantee that it *will* turn out to be fruitful elsewhere, but the possibility is worth pursuing.

Intersubjectivity

I began by listing three components of our ordinary notion of an objective fact: an objective fact is accessible from different angles, there is or can be intersubjective agreement about it, and it holds independently of our beliefs, desires, and observations. It is because an objective fact is invariant under specified transformations that it has these three traits. Let us concentrate here upon intersubjective agreement. Intersubjective agreement can be taken as evidence for objectiveness. Different people agree because there is an objective fact that they have access to, and they agree in the results of that access. But there can be intersubjective agreement without an objective fact—everyone else in Salem thinks she is a witch—and there can be objective facts without intersubjective agreement.

Is something an objective fact because it is intersubjectively agreed to, or is it intersubjectively agreed to because it is an objective fact? Which of the two is basic and which derivative? Do we converge upon calling "objective" what we intersubjectively agree to (when this intersubjective agreement is common knowledge), and would this make objectiveness a social creation or construction? Yet why is there such a social consensus behind some statements and not behind others? If the *only* distinguishing mark of objective facts was intersubjective agreement, so that objective facts simply were the subset we intersubjectively agreed to, in that case intersubjective agreement would *make* something an objective fact or *create* it as an objective fact.

However, if there is something about the fact that p that explains why we intersubjectively agree that p, something of the right sort (and not, e.g., merely that p has been socially inculcated into each of us), then it is *that* which constitutes the objectiveness of p. Or at any rate, if there is one kind of characteristic (of the right sort) that for many statements p_1, p_2, p_3, . . . explains why we intersubjectively agree to them, then it is in this that the objectiveness of the p-facts resides. It is the feature of the p's that enables there to be intersubjective agreement to them that makes these p's objective facts.

And that feature, we have held, is p's being invariant under all admissible transformations. It is this that explains why p is (or would be) intersubjectively agreed to. It is not enough simply and dogmatically to say, "We agree to something because it is an objective fact." We need to find an objectiveness property such that we can see (at least sketchily) *how* that property produces (or tends to produce) intersubjective agreement. And with invariance as the objectiveness property, we are able to do this.

We then can say that intersubjective agreement may be our route to discovering objectiveness, and so in that sense be *epistemically prior* to objectiveness, but that nevertheless objectiveness (that is, invariance under all admissible transformations) explains the intersubjective agreement and so is *ontologically prior* to it.[30]

Our speaking of objective facts has not been pleonastic. There also are facts that are not objective ones. That I am now thinking of a particular number, and what number that is, is not, according to our criterion, an objective fact. There are not different routes of access to what number I am thinking of. Yet, that I am thinking of that particular number is *some kind* of fact. Call this a subjective fact. Is an objective fact one that there *is* different access to (one that has been differently accessed) or one that there *can be* different access to? On either view, a fact that once was subjective (a fact of that kind) can *become* objective, either because different access actually occurs, or because different access becomes possible.[31]

Wittgenstein described a situation in which regions of the surfaces of plants would cause pain to people who touched them, and the people then would speak of pain patches on the plants.[32] We can add to Wittgenstein's example by imagining that everyone is, and must be, in contact with the plant at the very same time. Would they then be having a subjective experience of the plant? The term "subjective" may get its grip only against a background of actual or possible variation. These people cannot differ in their experiences of the plant, but since their other pain experiences do differ in their time of occurrence, the notion of "subjective," once established for those other pains, might also apply to the experiences induced by the plant. To reduce the variation even further, we need to imagine a *sui generis* experience that is imposed upon everyone simultaneously: everyone is always lying down with his or her eyes fixed open, and each day everyone simultaneously sees the (nonblinding) Sun. With such multiple access without the possibility of variation among people, we will not speak of individual, subjective experiences. Variation with multiple access (each of us will feel pain at the different times that we feel the plant) allows subjectiveness to get a grip. Subjectiveness comes to full flower when there is variation without multiple access.

Why are some facts subjective? They are in our heads/minds/brains. We have de facto privileged access to them, while others have no sensory receptors registering them. Do *we* have physical receptors that register them, or do they (somehow) just register in our minds, as part of its activity? To be sure, other people can examine our brains, and the bloodflow to certain sectors can be registered in PET scans. As knowledge grows, kinds of facts may *become* objective that once were accessible only to one person. (And can a previously objective fact *become* subjective because multiple access to it is lost?)

The ultimate upshot of the brain's neuronal activity, the only cells to which neurons lead that are not themselves other neurons, are glands and motor cells. The brain produces changes in the internal state of the body, and it produces muscular movement. In each case, originally, it was the internal state of the body—the states within the body's physical boundaries—that the brain worked to improve, altering the body's chemical activity, moving it to a region of different temperature, etc. To do this, the brain monitored the internal state of the body to detect when changes needed to be made. The detector was inside the body, and, being itself another bit of fragile matter, it also needed to monitor and care for itself. The monitor is another organ that needs to be cared for, and this can occur only if it monitors itself, or monitors some other organ that also monitors it. There is privileged access to these internal states by other organs and systems internal to the body; only they register these internal states and respond to them. Some facts are subjective, that is, accessible only to one organism, because other organisms had no pressing enough need to detect them to lead evolution to give them the equipment to do so.[33]

Intersubjective access is one of the marks of objectiveness. When there is no intersubjective access to a fact, yet when that fact is invariant under transformations that play a central role in our theories, should that fact be termed subjective or objective? According to quantum mechanics, there may be certain situations of measurement in which an observer simultaneously holds a determinate belief about the results of two measurements, and these measurements are repeatable by that observer with the same result, yet the physical dynamics of the situation make it in principle impossible (according to the principles of quantum mechanics) for anyone else to have access to these facts simultaneously.[34] If these facts have sufficient stability to be invariant under various important transformations, they may be held to be objective even though they are not intersubjectively available. Intersubjective availability is a mark of objectiveness, not a necessary condition for it.

If, according to Nietzschean perspectivism, there were some constraints upon perspectives, and there were some things that are invariant across all the admissible perspectives, it is these things that would possess the greatest objectiveness. What is invariant under transformations of observers from humans to crickets is more objective psychologically than the features applying only to human observations, and than the features applying only to cricket observations. Even if the two organisms divide up the world differently, some relations between the human categories might map onto corresponding relations among the different cricket categories, and this isomorphic psychological structure would be more objective than what varies between the organisms.

Objective Beliefs and Biasing Factors

We turn now to the topic of the objectivity of belief. A judgment or belief is objective when it is reached by a certain sort of process, one that does not involve biasing or distorting factors that lead belief away from the truth. A judge in a courtroom is supposed to be objective and unbiased. If she has particular ties to a party in the case, or a particular interest in the outcome of the case, she must remove herself from participation. For it is difficult to shield off the effects of such factors, and they tend to lead one away from the truth.

A judgment or belief is *rational*, relative to certain epistemic goals, if it is reached or maintained by a process that is effective and efficient at achieving those epistemic goals. It would be too stringent to require that the process be *optimal* in achieving those goals. Perhaps another process is superior, but if this process is not far inferior, then a belief arrived at through it may well be rational.[35]

On these construals, objectivity and rationality are connected. Nonobjectivity lessens rationality. If a belief is arrived at by a process in which biasing factors that lead one away from the truth play a significant role, then that process will be less effective and efficient in arriving at the truth, and so, to that extent, less rational—at least as judged by a stringent optimizing criterion of rationality.

The objectivity of a belief is determined by, and derived from, the nature of the process by which it arises (and is maintained). An objective belief can turn out to be false. (So too can a justified belief.) What led the person to this false but objective belief will not, however, have been the operation of biasing factors. Also, a nonobjective belief may turn out to be true. Though shaped by biasing factors that tend, *in general*, to lead away from the truth, in some cases a person's belief happens upon the truth despite the biasing factors.

Being "biasing" is not an intrinsic feature of a factor; it depends upon the role that factor plays in the overall process of arriving at belief. Within one process, a factor may retard finding the truth; within another process that same factor may be neutral or even may aid in discovering the truth.[36] The crucial question is whether the overall process is biased against discovering certain truths, not whether a component is. Under the American system of criminal justice, to convict someone of a crime all twelve jurors must agree upon a guilty verdict. Any potential juror whose mind is (unalterably) made up or who is especially likely to favor one verdict is open to challenge and to exclusion from the jury. Jurors are supposed to be unbiased. Perhaps juries would better arrive at the truth, however, under a system that intentionally admitted two biased jurors, one for each side (who are able to argue their convictions during the jury's deliberations), with the votes of only eleven of the twelve jurors being required for conviction. It is an *empirical* question whether under this alternative system juries would more frequently arrive at the truth than in a system wherein all jurors individually are unbiased.

Since individual biases can be constrained and contained within systems such as the interpersonal system of scientific investigation and (perhaps) the jury system just described, and since such biases might even perform some positive role there, when bias is unavoidable we can attempt to devise various structures to counteract it and perhaps even to utilize it, against its own biased wishes, to arrive at the truth.[37]

Biasing factors tend to reduce reliability, but in certain structures they do not, and so they do not make those structures nonobjective. Emotions themselves need not be biasing either, and do not necessarily make judgment subjective. Israel Scheffler has emphasized the useful role certain emotions, such as a passionate concern for the truth, may play in cognition.[38]

These considerations raise a doubt about the frequent claim that science should be value-free. Consider this argument:

(1)   Science should be objective.
(2)   Values are not objective.

Therefore,

(3)   Values should not be introduced into science or play a role there.

That is to say, science should be value-free. The truth of this conclusion might be contested by denying the second premiss. Science could contain values, and even make value assertions, and still be objective *if* values themselves are objective. The objectivity of values is a large question; here we are concerned with a smaller point.

This argument for a value-free science (based upon the premiss that values are not objective) implicitly assumes the following additional premiss, which we might call the Contamination Premiss:

When something that is not objective is introduced into a subject or plays a role there, it makes the subject nonobjective.

Yet we have seen that something nonobjective might play a role within a subject or area without making that thing itself nonobjective. It depends on what that role is, and what other structures limit or direct the consequences of such individual instances of nonobjectivity. Hence, the implicit premiss is false as it stands, and needs to be formulated more carefully if the common argument is to be at all plausible.

An objective fact is one that is invariant under (all) admissible transformations; an objective belief is one that is arrived at by a process in which biasing factors that tend to lead one away from the truth play no role. What links these two themes? It is not sufficient to note that an objective process is a good way to arrive at beliefs about objective facts, for it is a good way to arrive at beliefs about subjective facts too. An objective belief does tend to exhibit a certain invariance, though. Because the process that generates the belief shields it from being determined by biasing factors, the belief tends to be invariant under a change in biasing factors, under a transformation in what desires, emotions, etc. the person possesses. This explains why we take "subjective" to be the opposite of "objective." The judgments that result from the operation of subjective factors, many of which tend to be biasing, are not invariant under transformations in these factors, and hence lack objectiveness.

How should we describe a belief that arises by a process in which biasing factors happen to play no role, although the process itself does not shield belief from being affected by some kind of biasing factor or other? There might be different levels or degrees of objectivity. The lowest level of objectivity is reached when no biasing factors actually *did* operate; the next level when no biasing factors did operate and none of certain specified kinds *could* operate; and the highest level when the process of belief formation (about that topic) is insulated from the operation of *any* kind of biasing factor. The two highest levels of objectivity in belief would exhibit invariance under various transformations, although the very lowest level would not.

When there are biasing factors that do play a role in the formation of belief, they may operate to differing extents. Some biasing factors may tend to lead one *further* away from the truth than do other biasing factors; some biasing factors may *more frequently* lead one away from the truth than other factors do. We may combine these two aspects of bias, the probability of divergence from the truth and the extent of divergence from the truth, into one measure of the weight of a biasing factor, viz. the expected divergence from the truth that it produces.[39] And when several biasing factors are operating simultaneously, then, taking careful note of whether the factors bias in the same direction or not, we can estimate the total bias they are expected to produce. So it is not simply a matter of a belief's being objective or subjective. For some purposes, we do better to speak of *degrees* of objectivity (or of subjectivity).

In saying that an objective belief is one that arises by a process in which biasing factors that tend to lead one away from the truth play no role, I have taken an externalist and an instrumentalist view of the objectivity of belief. Someone might hold that objectivity is an intrinsically valuable characteristic of belief. John Dewey emphasized how something which starts as instrumentally valuable in reaching some end *E* can come to be held to be intrinsically valuable. We can add that its being held to be intrinsically valuable can itself be instrumentally valuable, either because holding it thus also is conducive to the particular end *E* or to some different end. Whether or not one can maintain an instrumentalist theory of all intrinsic value—and it is worth considering the extent to which one can—it is plausible to maintain that this is the case for whatever intrinsic value is attributed to objectivity.

Even if the value of an objective belief is instrumental, some will hold that the objectivity of a belief is better defined by its resting upon (objective) *reasons,* rather than by its instrumental connection to the truth. Instrumentality will not thereby be avoided, however, if the reason relation itself is defined by an instrumental connection to the truth. It seems plausible to think that the fact that p is a reason for believing q if there is a general type-type *factual* connection (which may be a statistical one) between p and q (that is, between the truth of facts of some type that p falls under and the truth of statements of some type that q falls under), so that believing q (partly) on the basis of p is conducive to believing the truth. The apparent self-evidence and *a priori* character of the reason relation might be explained by there having been evolutionary selection for a factual relation's coming to seem self-evidently valid.[40]

There has been much discussion of whether historians' and social scientists' explanations of phenomena, or even their descriptions of these phenomena, are or can be objective. Values and policy preferences affect the topics, questions, and problems investigators select for study; they affect the descriptions they offer of these phenomena and the explanations that they formulate and consider. Ernest Nagel holds that despite all this, the social-scientific results can be objective if the ultimate explanation or hypothesis that is accepted is based upon the evidence and the data that are gathered.[41] If one controls the bias in the selection of evidence (which evidence is

sought, considered, and weighted as trustworthy), then the objectivity of
(social) science, Nagel holds, resides in the (objective) assessment of the
extent to which that evidence supports a hypothesis or explanation and
makes it acceptable or better supported than another. There has not yet
been formulated, however, an adequate inductive logic or theory of comparative confirmation; there is no mechanical procedure or algorithm to
answer how well supported a hypothesis is, and that very program of inductive logic may be misconceived. Fixed and explicit adequate general
rules for assessing evidence, if they were seen to be followed, would be sufficient, though, to show that the assessments were objective. However, the
lack of such rules does not entail the nonobjectivity of the assessments. Social scientists might still agree about the extent to which given evidence
supports a hypothesis, that is, agree about which hypothesis is most worthy
of acceptance in the light of the evidence. (They might disagree, however,
about how much evidential support was necessary to make a hypothesis *acceptable,* if this depended upon their evaluation of what social phenomena
might follow from acceptance of the hypothesis.) In the absence of explicit
rules of evidential assessment, though, actual disagreement will make it difficult to tell who, if anyone, is objective and unbiased. One indication of
lack of bias would be a person's acceptance of a hypothesis that goes *against*
the grain of his or her own desires and values.

Ernest Nagel concentrated upon showing that scientific objectivity is
possible in principle, even in the social sciences. One might also wonder,
though, how often it is actual. If it rarely is so, and if it is very difficult for it
to be so, then the question arises whether the best strategy is to attempt to
make it *more* objective. If objectivity will not in fact actually be reached,
then there is the structural possibility (discussed by writers in economics
under the label "second best") that getting closer to it is not an improvement.

Some writers have questioned not just the possibility or the frequency of
objectivity but its desirability. Is objectivity a male notion? Are claims to
objectivity merely claims by the powerful to cover over relations of dominance? Or should we instead construe apparent attacks on objectivity as attempts to improve it? Including the views and perspectives of those who
previously were ignored is to include data which an adequate social theory
should take account of, and hence is a way to protect against basing theory
upon a biased selection of data. Nor must these others, themselves, present
an objective view of the matter, for their own subjective view is important
as data, and its very subjectivity may be needed to counteract the very dif-

ferent subjective data that previously had been used as the basis of theory. If subjectivity is introduced to redress an imbalance and counter a previous bias so that the whole system then is unbiased, this introduction is not a rejection of objectivity but an affirmation of it. Moreover, we have seen, emotions and intuitions themselves may be appropriate components of an objective process for arriving at beliefs if their presence makes the process more reliable or effective in arriving at the truth or at its cognitive goals.

Dimensions of Truth

An objective view of things is valuable, but it is not always what is needed or what will serve us best. Sometimes we take a subjective view, thinking how a situation will affect us, seeing what opportunities it offers us for action, rather than looking impartially at its effects upon everyone. Indeed, it might take too long to start with such an objective view and then compute or figure out what we need to know in that situation in order to act immediately, namely, the effects of the alternative actions upon ourselves.

A fact that we act upon need not have the highest degree of objectiveness. It need not be invariant under *all* admissible transformations. What we need to base our actions upon are facts that are invariant enough, facts whose variation under some transformations will not affect the action's achieving its intended goals. The action's being done and the goal's being achieved also might not be invariant under all admissible transformations—similarly for the conditional that if the fact holds, then if the action is done, the goal is achieved. What is necessary is that these less than completely objective facts mesh. Their range of nonvariation overlaps to provide a sufficient basis for the achievement of the goal.

Facts should be represented in an objective way for the purposes of scientific theorizing. For other purposes, an organism might represent a fact in a way that suits it especially for immediate action. When will an action be based upon an objective representation of the fact? Andy Clark writes,

This is again to exploit a kind of action-centered . . . internal representation in which the system does not first create a full, objective world model and then define a costly procedure that (e.g.) takes the model as input and generates food-seeking action as output. Instead, the system's early encodings are already geared toward the production of appropriate action . . . Action-oriented representations thus exhibit both benefits and costs. The benefits, as we have noted, involve the capacity to support the computationally cheap guidance of appropriate actions in ecologically normal circumstances. The costs are equally obvious. If a creature needs to use the same body of information to drive multiple or open-ended types of activity, it will often be economical to deploy a more action-neutral encoding which can then act as input to a whole variety of more specific computational routines. For example, if knowledge about an object's location is to be used for a multitude of different purposes, it may be most efficient to generate a single, action-independent inner map that can be accessed by multiple, more special-purpose routines. It is, however, reasonable to suppose that the more action-oriented species of internal representation are at the very least the most evolutionary and developmentally basic kinds. And it may even be the case that the vast majority of fast, fluent daily problem solving and action depends on them.[42]

To write on the nature and value of objectivity is not to deny to subjectivity its own proper place and value.[43]

Our investigation of the concepts of objective and subjective (like that of absolute and relative truth) has encountered a gradation, not a dichotomy. The three strands of objectiveness (accessibility from different angles, intersubjective agreement, and holding independently of people's beliefs, desires, and hopes about it) all admit of degrees. And being invariant under admissible transformations, which accounts for these strands, also admits of degrees. A fact or truth can be invariant under a wider or a narrower group of transformations. When the transformations that one truth is invariant under is a (proper) subset of the transformations that another truth is invariant under, then the second truth, invariant under a wider set of transformations, is more objective than the first.[44]

We also have investigated an additional notion of objectivity, that of the objectivity of a belief. A belief is objective when it arose (and is maintained) by a process in which biasing factors that tend to lead one away from the truth do not play any role. However, when there are such biasing factors that do play a role, these may operate to differing extents. Some biasing factors may tend to lead one further away from the truth than do other biasing factors; some biasing factors may more frequently lead one away from the truth than other factors do. These two aspects of bias, the probability of divergence from the truth and the extent of divergence from the truth, can be combined into one measure of the weight of a biasing factor, viz. the expected divergence from the truth that it produces. And when several biasing factors are operating simultaneously then, we can estimate the total bias they are expected to produce. So it is not simply a matter of a belief's being objective or subjective. (Three beliefs, produced in different ways, can all differ in their degrees of objectivity or of subjectivity.) There are degrees of the objectiveness of a fact, and there are degrees of the objectivity of a belief. Objectivity, too, is a dimensional matter, and much falls between the poles of the (wholly) objective and the (completely) subjective.

So we have two orderings of truths: from totally objective to extremely subjective, and (the subject of Chapter 1) from wholly absolute to extremely relative. Any given truth can be located at a position along each of these two orderings. We can idealize and imagine that each ordering is a complete ordering, and, idealizing further, we can suppose that numerical values can be given to a truth's position along each ordering. Each ordering, then, is a *dimension,* and we can suppose that these form the axes of a two-dimensional space. Each truth, then, possesses a position within this space.

The philosophical tradition seems to assume that some of these positions are better than others: absolute truths are better than (more) relative ones, objective truths are better than (more) subjective ones. But how valuable types of truth are on specific occasions depends upon what you want or need to do with them then. If I want to pick up a pen, I need to know where it is in relation to my hand. If I want to catch a baseball that has been hit over my head, I need to know its speed relative to the speed at which I am moving. More absolute descriptions might well underlie these relative truths. But such more absolute descriptions might not serve me well, for I might not be able to compute from them the information that I need in the time available to me to act. What I need to know, and hence to compute from the absolute information (if that is what I am given initially), is where the object is and where it will soon be *in relation to me.* Relative information may be just what I need, and so be better information for me to start out with, when my goal also is a relative goal, a goal of putting something in a certain relationship to myself. Going through absolute truths may not merely be unnecessarily roundabout given my goals; it may be an impediment (or a total barrier) given my limited time and limited computational ability. It may be that the goal of formulating a scientific theory is to reach statements as absolute as possible, but in testing such a theory we also will need to lean on many relative truths in order to build our experimental apparatus, get it into the right place at the right time, and find the switch that turns it on and sets it going.

Similarly, a subjective truth may be more to the purpose than a more objective one. If I need to be motivated to act, then a description of a situation that rings true to me, and that fits the particular feelings I have, may galvanize me more effectively than a more objective description that takes account of all aspects of the situation and is neutral among all perspectives. A description that is invariant under transformations from one emotion to another may grip and move me less than a description that is colored by the first emotion, the emotion with which I actually do respond to the situation. Objectivity is not always what we seek, or need.

What is objective about something, I have claimed, is what is invariant from different angles, across different perspectives, under different transformations. Yet often what is variant is what is especially interesting. We can take different perspectives on a thing (the more angles, the better), and notice which of its features are objective and invariant, and *also* notice which of its features are subjective and variant. Each kind of feature, and its status, is interesting. The bent of some people may be especially to notice the invariant features, the bent of others may be especially to notice the variant ones, yet each kind of knowledge can be important in different contexts.[45]

Different degrees of objectiveness and different degrees of relativeness will suit different purposes and needs. An accurate philosophy, an objective philosophy, will note this obvious fact, and will dispassionately depict the virtues of differently located truths for different situations. To be sure, in a time (such as the present) when many announce the view that objectivity is impossible and is, in any case and in all respects, undesirable, or announce that all truths are relative to social position, then it will be important to defend the possibility and the value of objectivity and absoluteness. However, this states only part of the truth. One also must acknowledge the legitimate function and importance of relativeness and subjectivity.

We can distinguish three issues: whether there are any nonrelative truths, whether anything we know is a nonrelative truth, and whether we know *of* something that it is a nonrelative truth. The first is an interesting theoretical issue. For practical action, we rarely will need our beliefs to be completely nonrelative, much less to know that they are so. It usually will be enough that they hold relative to the space-time volume of Earth or (if we are sending out exploratory spacecraft) of the solar system, and hold relative to human intelligence. For each truth that we act upon, we might consider the breadth of the whole domain we need it to be true relative to. Rarely, if ever, will this be a universal domain.[46]

The Objectivity of Science

Let us turn now to the general question of whether science is objective. First, a very brief sketch of the past seventy years or so of the philosophy of science. Karl Popper presents an appealing picture of science as formulating sharp theories that are open to empirical testing and to empirical refutation. Scientific theories are not induced from the data, but are imaginative creations designed to explain the data. Writers in the logical positivist tradition (Hans Reichenbach, Carl Hempel, and Ernest Nagel) elaborated the hypotheticodeductive view of scientific theorizing and testing. Call this (or a combination of these) the standard model of science.[47]

In treating Popper together with the logical positivists, I leave aside his distinctive anti-inductivist position wherein the degree of corroboration of a hypothesis is a purely *historical* description of the severity of the tests that the hypothesis already has undergone and survived; and no justified inference can be made that a better-corroborated hypothesis is more likely to survive its next test than a worse-corroborated one is, or than it was before it first was tested.[48] It is worth pointing out that Popper cannot consistently combine this doctrine with his acceptance of the doctrine that the wider the variety of circumstances under which a hypothesis is tested, the more severely it has been tested; repeating the same test over and over again does not (any longer) constitute severely testing the hypothesis.[49] (Therefore, Popper's philosophy of science is, in a certain way, *incoherent*.) We severely test a hypothesis *H* by checking the hypothesis in those circumstances in which, if *H* is false, its falsity is most likely to show itself (and we assess this likelihood according to our background beliefs). After *H* has passed a test in an area, it would not be as severe a test, not the severest test, to check *H* again and again and again in that same area. Checking *H* in another area now becomes its severest test. This can only be because after the initial test has been carried out and passed, the probability that *H*, if false, will show its falsity in that first area goes down. (It is not that the probability of *H*'s showing falsity in some other area goes up.) This means that: probability (*H* passes its next test in area *A/H* already has passed tests in area *A*) is greater than probability (*H* passes its next test in area *A/H* has *not* already passed tests in area *A*). Otherwise, repeatedly rechecking *H* in area *A* would continue to be the severest test of *H*. But this means that *H*'s passing severe tests eventually does provide some inductive support that *H* will pass the very next test of that sort. The assessment of *H*'s *past* degree of corroboration, that is, the historical assessment of the severity of the tests that *H* already has passed—a central feature in Popper's philosophy of science—therefore involves some inductive assumption.[50] Notice, in passing, that testing theories by pushing them to their limits under unusual circumstances leads scientists to identify the transformations the theories are invariant under, and thus to formulate theories in their most objective form.

Complications of the standard model abounded. (Some of these complications Popper foresaw, and attempted to incorporate in his view.) Here are some of the complications:

1. Isolated statements or even theories, Pierre Duhem claimed, are not subject to refutation by themselves, because, by themselves, they do not imply any particular observational data. Auxiliary hypotheses are needed also to derive observational predictions (for instance, hypotheses about the propagation of light, about the functioning of our measuring instruments, and about how our own perceptual apparatus functions).

2. Theories are not given up unless a better theory is available. Testing is best seen as differential testing that occurs *between* formulated theories, rather than just of one theory alone.

3. Theories might be rendered immune from refutation by *ad hoc* modifications. Popper formulated a methodological rule barring these, but there is no clear demarcation between a wise modification that reformulates a theory and an *ad hoc* one that merely preserves it in the face of recalcitrant evidence. Imre Lakatos proposed looking at a series of theories formulated within a research program, and he attempted to formulate criteria to determine if this series was progressive or degenerative.[51]

4. The data itself are not completely solid and are not completely independent of theory. Sometimes it is the data that are dropped or discredited, rather than the theory. And data and observations are shaped by the theories held by the scientist, and are reported in terms of these theories. Such "theory-laden" observations and experimental procedures are used to establish the facts that then are used to test theories, including the very theories they are laden with.[52]

5. There are no rules or algorithms to determine the acceptance of a scientific theory. There are different desirable features of a theory that may conflict (fitting data, explanatory power, accuracy, scope, precision, simplicity, theoretical fruitfulness, and so on). There also are different conceptions of each of these desirable features; moreover, different weightings can be given to these features. No explicitly formulated and accepted rules precisely resolve questions about the acceptance of theories, and there is much leeway for scientists to disagree. Thomas Kuhn sometimes put this more colorfully: accepting a new theory is like a psychological gestalt switch or (more colorfully still) like a religious conversion.

6.   Much scientific work takes place within a tradition of what kind of work is fruitful, what questions are worth asking and working on, what kinds of answers are acceptable, and so on; scientists normally work within a "paradigm."

7.   Theories are underdetermined by the data.

There have been two kinds of reactions to these complications for the standard model, a radical reaction and a defensive one.

The radical reaction holds that these features undermine the objectivity of science.[53] The theory-ladenness of observations means that theories cannot (easily?) be refuted, for the theories themselves shape the observational reports, and thereby make it likely that these reports will fit together with the theories. Work within a paradigm makes science "path dependent," in that the past history of science and of what theories have been accepted by scientists partly determines our current formulation and acceptance of theories, which therefore is not simply a function of the data available to us. If different theories had been formulated earlier, science would have taken a different path, with different procedures being invoked and different observations "reported," and hence different theories later being accepted. The current theories of science are path-dependent historical products. The lack of agreed-upon rules to determine theory acceptance makes such acceptance a matter of subjective judgment, or the product of non-rational social forces, or of other factors such as gestalt switch and conversion which are not governed by reason. Notice that the radical response frequently accepts the notion of objectivity that went with the standard model, and concludes that since *this* notion is not satisfied, there is no objectivity to science. Another response might attempt to formulate a more nuanced notion of objectivity, one according to which science is objective despite the complications.

The defensive reaction follows this path.[54] The theory-ladenness of observation does not guarantee that it will comport with the theory that loads it. People concluded that the Earth revolved around the Sun, despite having previously thought differently and so "observing" the Sun to rise. Proponents of different theories might agree about an observation, or observational report, that differentially tests the theories, and so agree about whether a given theory is compatible with the data.

The meaning of scientific terms might vary from theory to theory, but still scientists might be *referring* to the same things in the world, and their different predictions about these things might be comparable and intersubjectively agreed upon, across the competing theories. Although there are not precisely agreed-upon rules of theory choice, rationality does not require such explicit rule-following. (I can add the following point. The literature on parallel distributed processing systems shows how complicated tasks might be accomplished, effectively directed toward a goal, without following any explicitly formulated rules that are adverted to. The activity simply is the result of the weighted connections in the network, which themselves were shaped by some feedback rule.)

Moreover, although there might not be a complete ordering of theory preferability, relative to given data, there might be a partial ordering that is enough to decide the question scientists are facing. One theory might best another according to all the criteria, or it might be that the vague weights that are given to the different criteria are within a range that is constrained enough to determine particular theory choices. Hence, science can be rational and objective *despite* the factors that complicate the standard model.[55] Thus ends my sketch of recent philosophy of science.

The Functional View

If I had to choose one of these responses to the complications to the standard model, I would choose the defensive one. However, there is another response that is possible: that science is rational and objective, not despite the complicating factors but (in part) *because* of them. The complicating factors play a role in the advance of science. They contribute to the progress of science, to science's rationality and objectivity. (Note that these are different notions that the literature tends to jumble together. A factor that aids the progress of science might make its objectivity more difficult; there might be tradeoffs among these notions, etc.) Let me explain.

It would not be rational to start science from scratch at every moment. Things that have been learned can be built upon, not just to save time and effort but to enable us to get farther, to learn more. This point is not restricted to science but concerns human activities and endeavors in general. In building a brick wall we do not support each layer independently; we let each be supported by what comes below it. In teaching a subject, we do not teach it in a new language unknown to the students, which they must learn; we teach it in a language they already know. We do not start from scratch unless we have to. It would be irrational always to begin at the very beginning.

We can make more, and deeper, empirical predictions by utilizing several theories and assumptions rather than just one. Not only do we thereby learn more things, but also we subject our theories to a more severe test, for their inaccurate consequences might be apparent to us only when they are wielded jointly.

Using our already supported theories to make and to report observations enables us to look farther, at further and deeper consequences. Perhaps only an experimental physicist will see a certain particle in the trail in a Wilson cloud chamber, but given the existence of an evidentially supported theory that tells us what this trail indicates, it would be foolish to report only bare phenomenal seeings, even if such were possible. Only by standing upon our existing theories can we reach to predictions yielded by theories still further from "bare" observations. Similarly, it is rational to work within an existing paradigm that has some successes to its credit. Thereby we build upon its resources as we elaborate it further, and we learn from its further applications in new domains.

We should notice that the notion of observation uncontaminated by theory is, in any case, an evolutionarily naive notion. Consider how we see egg-shaped figures as convex or concave, depending upon the pattern of bright light and shadow.[56] No inference or conscious interpretation takes place. Rather, we see these three-dimensional facts in accordance with the (default) assumption that light comes from above. This is a long-standing and general enough fact (light comes from the Sun or from the moon; regular ground-level illumination such as fires are a late and relatively infrequent phenomenon) for the evolutionary process to have built it into our very mode of observation, structuring it. If light does come from above, then for a convex figure, the light will be at the top, the shadow at the bottom, while for a concave figure, the darker portion will be at the top, the lighter one at the bottom. When those shading patterns obtain, we automatically see the three-dimensional structure of the object accordingly.

Another way of putting the matter is that evolution has built the equivalent of certain inferences or theories *into* our observations, selecting for structures in our visual system (the pattern of excitations and inhibitions in our neuronal wiring) so that, given certain stimulation of sensory receptors, we see things a certain way. Those wiring patterns which led our ancestors to see the world (roughly) the way it was, were selected for. We don't need to *infer* from the sensory stimulation that things in the world are a certain way; evolution has made the inference for us. Try as we might, we cannot bring the theoretical content of our observations down to zero, for evolution itself, even if it has not maximized the accurate theoretical content of the observations, has placed it at a level much above zero.

Evolution has not produced completely accurate observations though, for interesting reasons. Consider Mach bands, which are lighter and brighter bands seen at the border of a dark and a light surface, or around a dark object against a light background. The gradient of perceived brightness is not proportional to the actual brightness (as measured by the intensity of the light reaching the retina), and this difference can be explained in terms of the pattern of neuronal wiring, including adjacent inhibitory connections. Our perceptual experience is *not* linear with the physical phenomenon, but this "distortion" serves the function of accentuating and making more salient the boundaries of an object, which it is useful to notice quickly.[57] The particular pattern of neuronal wiring that produces Mach bands leads to an increase of accuracy in one respect, and to an inaccuracy in another; there presumably was evolutionary selection for this wiring because the benefits of perceiving boundaries outweighed the costs of the inaccuracy. Evolution seeks to give us a *useful* picture of the world, in preference to a fully accurate one. A similar point applies to the adaptation of sensory receptors, wherein receptor potential declines with a sustained stimulus.

What could observations with zero theoretical content be like? Would there be no internal wiring that recorded things one way rather than another; in the stream of processing of stimulation patterns, would none automatically be taken, through the wiring, as indicating the presence of certain physical phenomena? Would this be at all desirable (supposing that we could imagine what it would be like)? Would it be better to start from (evolutionary) scratch, having learned nothing from our ancestors' long experiences of what facts typically produce which stimuli? If so, there is no reason to stop at our human ancestors. How far down the evolutionary scale of our origins do we have to proceed to find observations that are uncontaminated by any instilled (framework of) facts? Must uncontaminated science be done only by amoebae? When, or if, we find such primitive organisms, we will not have discovered organisms that know more, and more accurately, than we do about the world. The more evolution has laden our observations with accurate theory, the better.

It is not only evolution and accepted theories that shape scientists' observations. Often, the data gathered in laboratories are smudged, presenting an unclear picture. Scientists clean up these data to find some clear picture that they reveal; the data then are taken to support and confirm this picture. Scientists themselves might worry about the validity of this process. The clear picture was not accepted or expected beforehand; that particular theory did not shape the presentation of the data. What shaped it was the desire to find support for some particular theory or other. If only one laboratory existed, with just one scientist interpreting its data, this would create problems for holding that scientific theories are objectively supported by the data. But often there will be other scientists in that same laboratory who also will have to find the same pattern as the most convincing one emerging from the smudged data. And other laboratories will attempt to replicate the experiment. Will they, in performing as similar an experiment as possible, extract precisely the same pattern as the best cleaning up of their own smudged data? If so, there is sufficient objectivity in the reported observations to constitute confirmation of the theory. To be sure, when the other laboratories already know which pattern the first laboratory claimed to observe, this knowledge may bias and thus contaminate their own process of extracting (what they take to be) the best cleaned-up pattern from the smudged data. The other laboratories' confirmation of the theory by finding the same pattern in the data would be firmer if it were wholly independent. Yet such dependence, when it exists, is counteracted to some extent by the competitive desire of scientists to originate *new* theories that the data support.

What of the path-dependence involved in building our current science upon past advances in knowledge? Had we not built upon particular earlier theories and research traditions, and followed the path they pointed to, we might be accepting very different theories now. (We could not be accepting any very powerful theories, though, unless we had built upon some theories or other—a different path but path-dependence nonetheless.)

Scientists who work within a paradigm are making this *local induction:* a paradigm that has solved some recalcitrant problems (without failing significantly yet) probably will succeed in solving its next problems. Temporarily at least, working within the paradigm constitutes a good research strategy.

However, the existence of Kuhnian revolutions shows that scientists are not *stuck* in the paths they find themselves upon. They can shift to another, very different theory, one so different that some philosophers are led to hold that the theories (or theorists) cannot speak to or understand each other. Scientists *can* leave a previous path for a new one. There may not be precise rules for doing this. (Or there may be rules that are agreed to by proponents of both competing theories—a point from the defensive response.) But even if Max Planck is correct that the older generation dies out before it unanimously accepts a theory, the younger generation of new scientists does move almost uniformly in one direction. Presumably they do this because, unburdened by an investment in the old theory, they can more neutrally compare the virtues of the new and the old. (Another explanation: their incentive is to concentrate upon the new, for it is here that the largest contribution remains to be made.) And individual differences in the time it takes for scientists to become convinced of a new theory can have positive functions for the institution of science, as Kuhn points out. We can add that gestalt switches may be needed to *understand* a new theory, but that does not show that they play any further role in the decision to *accept* that theory. And if such switches, or even conversions, play a role in individual decisions to accept and work further upon theories, deriving new predictions from them and subjecting them to new tests, still, being impressed and convinced by such results need not depend upon any switches or conversions. Perhaps such agreement and conviction comes years later, after all the interesting choices have been individually made by those willing to run theoretical risks. But who said that the objectively correct choice must be immediately evident? If the owl of objectivity flies only at night, so be it.[58]

If, contrary to fact, all choices about acceptance were made according to given fixed rules, wouldn't this raise the worry that science is strongly path-dependent, dependent upon the particular path *these* particular rules are a part of? That there are not always such rules, and that there is a way of hurtling oneself over to a very different place, one that can rationally be evaluated later, remove some of the sting from the charge of path-dependence. The lack of such fixed and fully determinate rules of acceptance, then, is a virtue, not a defect.

The replacement of an old paradigm by a new one might occur as follows. The old paradigm accepts certain criteria C (e.g., successful precise predictions) for judging a theory, and the theory component of the new paradigm surpasses the theory part of the old paradigm by these very criteria, or by the most important one of them (as judged by the old paradigm). So the old paradigm judges that the new theory is a better theory than the theory component of the old paradigm itself. Notice that the new paradigm need not give the criteria C as much weight as the old paradigm gave them. It might compliment itself according to different criteria D. Still, the move will be made to the new theory. Reaching the new theory, one tends to accept the new paradigm associated with it, and also to accept D, the new criteria for a good theory which are part of the new paradigm, and which that paradigm's new theory satisfies very well (and better than the old theory did).[59] These new criteria D are accepted because the new theory satisfies them. Accepting D is part of the move to a new paradigm. (The new criteria D come to seem important when the new theory satisfies them, and the paradigm associated with that new theory gives these criteria importance.) An example is the move to the Special Theory of Relativity. This theory satisfies various invariance and symmetry principles, and so criteria giving these great weight in assessing a theory come to seem like good criteria. They emphasize the kinds of features the new theory has, that other theories to be developed also might have. Scientists direct their activities toward searching for new theories that also satisfy these new criteria. A sequence of such changes, each one seen locally as progress, might, bit by bit, alter or even reject all the initial criteria. By the (perhaps temporary) criteria of the very latest stage, its current theory is superior to each preceding one.

Underdetermination of Theory

The underdetermination of theory seems a different matter, however, serving no apparent function while raising uncertainty about the truth of any theory we accept. Let us look first at *whether* theories are underdetermined by the data, and second, at the implications this underdetermination might have. Theories are underdetermined by the data when more than one theory can explain the data. However, we do not yet have an adequate account of explanation that enables us confidently to assert such underdetermination. What further conditions, in addition to being Hempelian in form, must our explanations satisfy? Might not these further conditions drastically narrow the range of acceptable explanations, perhaps to just one? Hempel requires that explanations be given in terms of laws. In the light of our earlier discussion, we can add that these laws must satisfy various invariance conditions (or be derivable, via broken symmetries from statements that satisfy these conditions). Following Wigner's lead, we can add a further requirement, namely, that we formulate a mathematical representation of our fundamental physical theory, and find a set of transformations such that the fundamental properties of entities are the invariants under those transformations of the fundamental theory as so represented. A theory that meets this further desideratum is to be preferred, as is a fundamental theory that is invariant under the widest range of admissible transformations and so itself exhibits a high degree of objectiveness.

If these additional constraints (or desiderata) alone do not reduce the number of explanation candidates to one, perhaps they will do so in combination with further conditions yet to be discovered. We cannot say that theories *must* be underdetermined by the actual (much less, by all possible) data, for the conditions that an acceptable explanatory theory must meet are not given *a priori;* they are things that we learn as we go along. There is no reason to believe we know all such conditions already.[60]

However, our existing theories *are* underdetermined by the data (insofar as the currently known conditions for explanation can say). What are the implications? Would we be better off if our theory was *not* underdetermined? This would mean either that our theory did not go beyond our data at all (but then at best it would give us only a compendious repetition of the data) or that it did not step far enough beyond our data to also allow in, as an alternative, another theory.

In that case, for our theory to be a powerful description of the world,

a.   our data itself would have to be quite robust, matching the robustness of the actual world, or
b.   the world itself would have to be quite thin, matching the thinness of our actual data, or
c.   theories would have to be quite sparse in the space of possible theories, so that there was only *one* between our thin data and the robust world.

Our actual data, however, are not robust enough to reach almost all the way to a powerful theory of a thick world. Our observational data are one small consequence of the laws that hold, and sometimes are quite distant from the most basic processes. For things to be different, our observations and data would have to be "in the round" and deep. In that case, although we could not get very far beyond our observations, we would not need to, for those observations would reach all the way to the basic structure of the world; they would be observations *of* the basic structure of the world, a direct experience of underlying laws, of elementary particles, and of the structure of space and time. In that case, science would not exist—it would be unnecessary. We would know its results already, *by observation.* (And we are fortunate that our ancestors did not face such strong selective pressures against observing merely particular aspects of surface manifestations, for then *those* ancestors would not have successfully survived to give rise to us.)

On the other hand, if the world were (less robust than it is, but) as thin as the observations we actually make (a far more meager group than all actual and possible observations), we would not need to risk reaching far beyond our observations, for there would exist nothing robust to reach toward. I shall not pause to discuss what such a thin world might be like—would it be an *objective* world?—or what of value would be absent in it.

The first two alternatives (a and b) collapse the distance between our data and the world. The third alternative maintains that distance but leaves the interval between data and the world underpopulated. Just one possible theory can live there. Strong constraints on what a theory or adequate explanation is could keep that population down to one, as I have noted. If those constraints stem from the nature of our limited powers of understanding, however, they are an uncertain guide to the truth. But suppose that the constraints do reflect a fact F about the actual world, about what, in the world, is capable of giving rise to (and explaining) what. In that case, there would be ontological determination of theory; the world would make just one theory true. Still, we might ask whether *that* fact F is entailed by our data or underdetermined by it. There will be *epistemic* underdetermination of theories, even if there is ontological determination, if, so far as we can know, facts incompatible with F also will be compatible with our data and will not necessitate those particular F-based constraints upon explanation. Suppose that, in fact, only F is compatible with our data, because F *does* hold and so gives rise to the very constraints that make F the unique choice from our data, and hence, because of F, in general only one theoretical explanation is compatible with any given data (and so ontological underdetermination of theory by data is false). Still, perhaps we cannot know all this on the basis of our data (without *already* knowing F), and so epistemic underdetermination holds sway. Over time perhaps we can learn that fact F, but at the present time, data epistemically underdetermine theory.

For creatures with thin data in a robust world, epistemic or ontological underdetermination may indeed be an unavoidable fact of life, but does either have a role or function in propelling scientific progress? They do propel the *existence* of science; we would not need an organized activity of science if our observations reached all the way to the most basic processes. They do propel the gathering of more data, in an attempt to decide between particular theories, or to test one theory in the area where we believe it is most likely to go wrong.

Perhaps the gathering of data might go on even without underdetermination of theory. Even if only one theory T could explain the existing data D, there still would be the possibility that the data D are brute facts having *no* explanation, so that further data would have to be gathered to determine if T held true. (And the falsity of T might continue to be possible, even though its replacement by another *theory* was not.) So continued data gathering might be spurred, even without underdetermination of theory in the sense of two alternative theories' being compatible with the data. There still would remain a certain underdetermination: compatible with any data *D* would be the *one* explanatory theory compatible with it, and *also* the statement (incompatible with the truth of that explanation) that the data *D* have no correct theoretical explanation. (The truth of "everything has some correct theoretical explanation" might itself be underdetermined by our data.) A gap between data and theory spurs the gathering of further data to gain new knowledge about the world.

The fact that our theories reach farther than our data shows how far extended the reach of our theories is—a cause for celebration, not for lament. To be sure, the further we reach, the more our theories become susceptible to being wrong or being overthrown in new ways. (Recall, though, that the observational data presuppose the regularities and incorporate the theories that evolution has instilled.) However, also, the further we reach, the deeper our understanding goes. This deeper understanding also points toward new obtainable data that, when gathered, make less shaky some previous moves beyond the then existing data.

Rationality, Progress, Objectivity, and Veridicality

It may be granted that the complicating factors on the list do perform some positive function in the progress and rationality of science, but cannot they, at the same time, also be biasing factors that interfere with science's objectivity? Whether a factor is biasing—we already have seen—is not an intrinsic quality of that factor. It depends upon the nature of the overall system within which that factor operates. Do other factors within the system of science control or counteract (what otherwise would be) the bias of the factor in question? Can some factors on this very list of complications control or counteract other factors on the list?

The theory-ladenness of observation might be counterbalanced by using the conjunction of several accepted, jointly consistent, distinct theories to derive predictions so that no one theory dominates or determines our observation; by the personal bias of scientists who favor their own new theory, and so do not see the world through the lens of the old theory; and by requiring increasingly greater precision of prediction beyond what uninstrumented observation can bring. The underdetermination of theory might be counterbalanced by having to construct a theory that can be integrated with (modifications of) past successful theories; also, working within a paradigm will provide additional criteria (beyond compatibility with the data) that constrain new theories. However, the tendency to work within a paradigm also is counterbalanced by the incentive structure that rewards scientists for new breakthroughs, by an insistence on explaining all relevant replicable data so that anomalies cannot persistently be ignored, and by pressing for new integrations of existing theories (e.g., of the four fundamental physical forces), which cannot be done within the existing paradigm. To be sure, that these factors oppose each other does not show that they exactly counterbalance, but such exactness is not necessary to ensure that over time no one factor dominates all others to push science in the direction of its own particular bias.

We therefore can see the possibility of a third response to the complications of the standard model, a response that is neither radical nor defensive but one that delineates the role of these factors in contributing to the rationality and the objectivity of the scientific endeavor, and so gives us a better understanding of precisely how science *is* rational. Call this third response the *functional response.*

It is not necessary, of course, to uniformly offer this third functional response for each of the complicating features (theory-ladenness, underdetermination of theory, working within a paradigm, etc.). It is possible to hold a mixed view that combines the second and the third responses. On this mixed view, some features on the list *do* play a positive role, contributing to scientific progress, and other features, though not playing such a role, still do not prevent scientific objectivity. Such a mixed view, nevertheless, might hold that on balance the complicating features do play a positive role in effecting scientific progress.

Why are the methods of science successful in finding out about the world? How sensitive are these methods to the particular nature of our world? We want a robust method that works for a range of worlds—after all, we do not start out knowing the particular character of our world (beyond what evolutionary selection has built into us as it operated within our world's past). Yet the effectiveness of a method probably will depend upon how specifically tuned it is to the character of the actual world. As we learn about the world by using the methods of science, we refine these methods to make them perform more optimally in the kind of world we have discovered there to be.[61] As our knowledge grows, our scientific methods should become more world-specific, that is, better suited to a narrower variety of worlds, and so more effective in the actual world.[62] Effectiveness and specificity vary together. Nevertheless, we want the methods to be open to the possibility that we have gone wrong, and to enable us to detect that we have done so.[63]

We can list some general features of the actual world that are especially conducive to the success of our current methods of investigation. Our science proceeds via stratified levels: stratified vertical levels of reduction, and stratified horizontal levels of analysis. There are separable problems with approximately true solutions, separable events that can be explained (with reasonable adequacy) without concomitantly being able to explain all other events. There are manageable scientific problems within striking distance of current knowledge. (That is what science graduate students seek when they ask their advisers for a dissertation topic.) The world is linked by manageable problems, and it is partitionable into separate topics; there are questions that can be answered separately. And the (adjacent) levels of explanation, and of reduction, also are within striking distance of each other.

We now can sort out and keep distinct, at least roughly, the notions of the rationality of science, of the progress of science, and of the objectivity of science. Science is *rational* when its processes effectively and efficiently achieve its goals: discovering truths, rejecting falsehoods, uncovering explanations, making precise and accurate predictions, and so forth[64] (perhaps we also should add: and its goals themselves also are rational or reasonable). Science *progresses* when it continues to further achieve its goals, by discovering more truths, accepting fewer falsehoods, uncovering deeper explanations, extending the domain of things that can be explained scientifically, unifying the explanations it offers, making more precise and more accurate predictions, and so forth. Science is *objective* when (differential) human factors do not systematically and irremediably point it away from certain kinds of truths or toward certain kinds of falsehoods.[65] And, we can add, science is *veridical* to the extent that it presents an unadorned description of the world and its processes—nothing but the truth—or (more leniently) to the extent that the adornments of its theories eventually will drop away.

Each of the factors on the complicating list (Duhemian considerations, theory-ladenness of observation, underdetermination of theory, working within a paradigm, etc.) might differently affect the distinct goals of scientific rationality, scientific progress, scientific objectivity, and scientific veridicality. It is worth investigating this in detail. For now, I can simply say that theorists who think the list of complicating factors impugns the objectivity of science owe us an account of objectivity according to which objectivity does stumble before the complicating factors, yet which does not demand that science be infallible or omniscient and does not impugn the objectivity of a system because of the apparent nonobjectivity of one of its components.

Since my argument for the functional view thus far has tended to focus upon the progress of science and also, assuming it is rational to organize science so that it does progress effectively, upon the rationality of science, let us say something more about scientific *objectivity*.

Science will be objective when no extraneous factor diverts it from accurately finding out the truth. It might seem that the complicating features on the list do divert it, but we have seen that we cannot determine that a factor is biasing without knowing the role it plays in an overall process. How it initially strikes us is not enough. (An individual scientist's bias in favor of his pet theory might lead him to search for evidence why a competing theory is wrong, and thus perform a function within a system in which not everyone has that very same bias, provided that he is not powerful enough to block others in their inquiries or to compel their support of his own theory.) Still, doesn't the list of complicating features show that (the choice of) which scientific theories are accepted (at any given time) must depend upon some factors in addition to what the world is like? And doesn't that, all by itself, indicate nonobjectivity?

What root idea of objectivity would this conclusion involve?[66] There are two ways in which science can deviate from stating all and only the truths, corresponding to the type I and type II errors discussed by statisticians. Science can accept some false statements, or it can fail to accept some true ones. Since science is at any time incomplete and nonomniscient, it cannot be that simply failing to accept any particular truth counts as making science nonobjective. Science would be nonobjective if there are some particular types of truths that must forever be beyond its ken, or if some truths are much harder to discover than others, and not merely because of their greater depth but because of the character of scientific practice or method. In such a case, let us say that science is *blinkered*.

Similarly, since science is fallible it will accept some statements that are false; but, again, this alone does not suffice to make it nonobjective. Science will be nonobjective if there are certain false statements that it must accept, or if its falsehoods fit a pattern, if there are certain topics it is more likely to accept falsehoods about, or certain kinds of falsehoods it is more likely to accept, *and* these fall into a pattern of being due to human biases or cognitive limitations.

Since science is not infallible or complete, an objective science cannot be required to make its theories a function only of the world. However, its theories should not be a function also of systematically biasing factors. Science might be (in the terminology of C. S. Peirce) "self-correcting" in overcoming particular biases for particular theories. But if some particular biasing factor continues to operate, now favoring one inadequate theory and next favoring another, or if science continues to maintain some theory because one biasing factor after another favors it, then biasing factors would have more than a temporary influence, and so would interfere significantly with the objectivity of science. Perhaps science is objective when its theories are a function only of the world, of random factors, and (perhaps) also of temporarily biasing factors that do not systematically blind it to certain types of truths or predispose it to certain types of falsehoods. It is far from evident that the list of admitted complicating factors shows that science is biased and so is nonobjective in this sense.

In its broadest form, the question of veridicality asks to what extent our view of the world contains features that are due to our method of knowing or representing the world. Can we disentangle these artifacts from the way the world itself is?

Color phenomena present an illuminating example. There is an objective physical phenomenon, surface reflectance, whose detection is biologically important because of its correlation with other phenomena. Our biological apparatus detects information about surface reflectance in a particular way that imposes some structural organization upon it. Wavelengths are continuous, yet color is psychologically experienced as organized into bands. There is a psychological discontinuity, an experienced psychological categorization, where there is a physical continuum.

We have been able, however, to discover this nonisomorphism between the physical continuity of wavelengths and the psychological phenomenon of color bands. By using our senses and our accompanying reasoning power, we have discovered that our sensory organization imposes additional structure. Thus, in this case we have been able to disentangle the objective nature of what is perceived from the additional structure due to our perceptual apparatus, by independently investigating the physical reality and investigating our perceptual capacities (including their neurophysiological basis) to discover a lack of isomorphic structure. We could have used different senses (vision, hearing, touch), each with their own special structuring, to discover the special and distinctive structuring of any one sense. To the objection that this would not identify any structuring that was commonly imposed by all the senses (but only identify a sense's *distinctive* structuring), we can point out that even using one sense to investigate itself can yield the conclusion that it imposes its own structuring, along with information about what that imposition is.

Our investigations have used scientific reasoning in addition to perceptual information. So one might wonder whether such reasoning introduces structuring of its own. However, there seems to be no bar in principle to using one component of scientific reasoning to discover artifactual structure introduced by another component, or even to using one component to discover its very own artifactual structure. For there is no guarantee that a component's artifactual contribution (or that of scientific reasoning as a whole) must remain invisible to itself, especially when that one component (or kind of reasoning) investigates itself from as many angles as it can. To be sure, the possibility remains that there is some structural artifactual contribution that it makes that it is never able to detect itself.

"Whoever it is that discovered water, it wasn't a fish," someone once remarked. How can we discover that something is an artifact if it is omnipresent in all our ways of investigating and representing the world, and present to an equal degree in each so that there are no variations in its character to make it noticeable? What is present everywhere, the thought runs, cannot be discovered, because it contrasts with nothing. Even if it could be detected somehow, could it be discovered to be an artifact that was due to the combined operation of scientific method plus our (or every rational being's) cognitive apparatus, rather than being part of the basic fabric of reality?

A clue might exist in its very inescapability. The feature would seem not just universal but *necessary*. Such necessity should raise the strong suspicion that it originates as an artifact of methods of discovery or representation. (I do not say that such a broadly Kantian explanation of necessity is the only possible one, but I do not know of another equally plausible one.)

At one time, philosophers held that necessary statements constituted a structured domain of central and fundamental truths to which all other truths conformed. The next chapter will delineate the waning of the notion of metaphysical necessity in this past century and, despite some encouragement that notion has received recently, will further that implosion. Philosophers might decry this shrinking of (what some think to be) their domain of investigation. And they might mourn, in the loss of necessary statements, what might have seemed the most objective statements there are: statements whose truth is invariant across all possible worlds. However, this cloud of philosophical decline contains a silver lining, for the fewer necessities there are, the more veridical our beliefs can be. We shrink necessity in order to make room for veridicality.

3

Necessity and Contingency

Epistemology of Necessity

Necessary truths are statements or propositions that *must* be true; their truth could not have been otherwise. Necessity, as standardly conceived, marks the strongest form of invariance: invariance across all possible worlds. A necessary truth is true in all possible worlds, something is possible when it is true in at least one possible world, and something is impossible when there is no possible world in which it is true. A contingent statement is true in at least one but not all possible worlds, and that contingent statement is a contingent truth when it is true in the actual world. Necessary truths are invariant across all possible worlds, contingent ones across only some.[1] No wonder necessity lures philosophers. It is the flame, the philosopher the moth.[2]

We can ask whether the philosophical notion of necessity is coherent, and whether it has important application.[3] *Are* there any necessary truths? If so, what makes them necessary, what gives rise to them? And what is the epistemology of necessity? How can we know (or have sufficient reasons for believing) that a particular truth is necessary?

That the notion of necessity itself is not perfectly clear is indicated by controversies concerning different systems of modal logic, which were formulated by philosophers and logicians to capture the notion of necessity. Philosophers' intuitions have differed over which of the various systems of propositional modal logic is the correct one, and there seems to be no evident way to decide. It is not simply that the different systems have been proposed for different kinds of necessity (logical, metaphysical, physical), with each system being appropriate for its own kind. The disagreement extends to which system correctly applies to each particular kind of necessity. Quantified modal logic presents further problems and questions that, once again, philosophers and logicians have differed over.[4]

I am skeptical about the extent of necessary truths, and about their status. And I shall maintain that there are no interesting and important metaphysical necessities. Moreover, I attempt to formulate a position according to which even logical and mathematical truths are not, at the most basic level, ontological necessities. I do not claim to demonstrate this last proposition; my aim is merely to place it within the philosophical pale, and to sketch a way in which it might turn out to be true.

I begin with the epistemological question, for if you are confident or convinced that you know that certain truths are necessary, you also will be confident that the notion of necessity is a coherent one with significant application. Therefore, you will think that any arguments purporting to show that there are no metaphysical necessities must be mistaken. That confidence needs to be undermined.

How can we know that certain statements are necessarily true? The following, which fits one current philosophical methodology, might seem to be a way. A general statement *S* will be a candidate for being a necessary truth when it is, so far as we know, true, and we do not see how it could be false. We test its candidacy for necessity by trying to think up counterexamples to *S*, possible cases in which *S* would be false. If strenuous efforts by ourselves and others fail to find such a possible counterexample, we tentatively conclude that *S* is a necessary truth.

We might construe this inference as an inductive one. (All the possibilities we have examined fit *S*; therefore, all possibilities do.) Or we might construe it as an inference to the best explanation. (The best explanation of why we have failed to find a possibility where *S* is false is that there is no such possibility.) This explanation will have to compete with and show its superiority to other explanations, for instance, that there is a possible case in which *S* is false but we have been too unimaginative (thus far) to think of it.

It is easier to think of possibilities than of necessities, easier to know that something is possible than that it is necessary. Whatever is necessary is possible, but not vice versa. So to say that something is possible is to make a weaker statement than the claim that it is necessary. (On Leibniz's possible-worlds account, to say that something is possible is to say that it holds in at least *one* possible world, while to say that it is necessary is to make the stronger statement that it holds in *all* possible worlds.) Moreover, to say that something is possible is weaker than to say that it is impossible, for to say it is impossible is to say that it fails to hold in *all* circumstances (all possible worlds), while to say it is possible is to say merely that there is at least *one* circumstance (one possible world) in which it holds.

People are good at thinking up possibilities but not perfect at it. We often think of a possibility by *imagining* a situation, yet imagination does not perfectly overlap with possibility. Some things we imagine may not really be possible—we just think they are—and there may be possibilities we cannot imagine, at any rate not without the development of a whole alternative theory that embeds such possibilities. (It could not be imagined as isolated possibilities that there existed more than one parallel to a line through a given external point, or triangles whose angles did not sum to 180 degrees. This required the development of an elaborate theory of non-Euclidean geometry.) People may disagree about whether an imagined or described case really is possible.

That people have a talent for thinking up possibilities, but only a negligible talent for directly assessing necessities, fits the methodology of the mode of philosophical work described above.[5] Candidates for necessity are tested by examples and purported counterexamples, with disagreements arising sometimes about whether a particular case really is possible.[6]

Such debates would be avoided if we possessed a faculty of reason that could directly assess the possibility of general statements and of their denials. This faculty would deliver a judgment about whether *S* was possible or not, whether not-*S* was possible, and hence whether or not *S* was necessary. However, we do not appear to have such a faculty, and it is implausible that evolutionary processes would instill that within us. Since our ancestors evolved in the actual world, there were no selective pressures to reward accuracy about all possible worlds, and there was no handicap to being right only about the actual world. To be sure, the most efficient mechanism to lead our ancestors to truth about the actual world might also correctly encompass other possibilities, but it is highly implausible to think it would encompass *all* possibilities, no matter how different from actuality. A roughly accurate faculty for generating or imagining possibilities might have served our ancestors well in deciding upon actions, but there would not have been selection for a faculty powerful enough to generate *all* logical possibilities.[7] More-limited faculties bear no disadvantage in the actual world. We therefore should be wary of concluding that a statement *S* is necessarily true, simply because we and others have been unable to generate a counterexample to it. If our imaginative capacities do not generate all the possibilities there are, or even a random or representative sample of these—if we are able to imagine only possibilities of a certain sort—then *S*'s truth may not extend to possibilities we cannot imagine.

Evolutionary considerations can illuminate the scope and limitations of the *a priori* knowledge human reason purportedly delivers. In *The Nature of*

Rationality, I discussed two philosophical views concerning reasons for belief.[8] The *a priori* view, holds that a reason *r* for a hypothesis *h* stands in some relation *R* to *h*, such that the faculty of reason can apprehend that this (structural?) relation constitutes one of support. Reasons are things the mind has the power to recognize. The problem is this: why expect that *h* actually will be true when *r* is true and *r* stands in the relation *R* to *h*? The second view, the factual view, holds that *r* is evidence for *h* when it stands in a certain contingent factual relation to *h*. In *Philosophical Explanations,* I claimed that the evidential connection is a factual relation, and presented an account of it in terms of the tracking relation between evidence and hypothesis (and in terms of probabilistic approximations of that relation). The factual view seems to leave out what most strikes the *a priori* view, namely, that in particular cases the reason connection appears (almost) self-evident.

Therefore, in *The Nature of Rationality* I suggested that a combination of these two views is more adequate. A reason *r* for *h* is something that stands in a certain factual connection to *h*, while the contents of *r* and *h* stand in a certain structural connection that appears to us strikingly to make *h* (more) believable given *r*. The reason relation is a factual connection that appears, apart from experience, to be one of support.

This concordance between the two views is not just a fortunate preestablished harmony. What gets the two views to combine is evolution. It is desirable to act in accordance with a factual connection, and one way to do this is to act upon *reasons* (which involves *recognizing* a connection of structural relation among contents) that match the factual connection. Hence, this recognition itself might have been useful and have been selected for. The attribute of a certain factual connection's *seeming* self-evidently evidential to us might have been selected for and favored because acting upon this factual connection, which does hold, in general enhances fitness. *It is not the capacity to recognize independently existing valid rational connections that is selected for. Rather, there is a factual connection and there was selection among organisms for that kind of connection's seeming valid,* for noticing that kind of connection and for such noticing's leading to certain additional beliefs, inferences, and so on. There is selection for recognizing as valid certain kinds of connection that *are* factual, that is, selection for them coming to seem to us as *more* than just factual.

This evolutionary selection might be an instance of the Baldwin effect. Those whose "wiring" makes the connection seem closer to evident learn the connection faster, thereby gaining a selective advantage, and they leave offspring distributed around their own degree of finding it evident. Over generations, then, there can be movement toward finding it more and more self-evident.

Something's seeming self-evidently true to us does not guarantee that it ever was, strictly, true. Consider, by analogy, what we now say of Euclidean geometry: that it is true enough for almost all practical purposes, that it is undetectably different, in the small, from spaces of small constant curvature, but that, strictly, it is not true (of, as we say, "physical space"). If there had been selection for Euclidean geometry's seeming self-evidently true, that would have served our ancestors well. Nothing would have been gained by selection for some other geometry. Believing that alternative and making inferences automatically in accordance with *it* would not have bestowed any selective advantage (in *that* environment); also, the costs in terms of the neurological resources devoted to having this alternative geometry seem self-evident might have been great. Moreover, "intuiting" this alternative geometry might not have been within reach of what random mutation (in the absence of stepwise selective pressures) could produce from the genetic endowment that existed then. This alternative geometry, literally true, would not have been selected for as what seemed self-evidently true to us. Given Euclidean geometry's close approximation to the truth, and given the attendant advantages of its seeming self-evidently true to us—advantages including quickness of inference, believing serviceable (approximate) truths and avoiding other, more divergent falsehoods—we can imagine that there was selection for Euclidean geometry's seeming self-evident; we can imagine that Euclidean geometry was selected for as our form of sensibility. Nevertheless, Euclidean geometry is, we now believe, strictly speaking, false as a theory of physical space. I do not claim that this evolutionary story *is* the true account of Euclidean geometry's seeming self-evident, but it is a plausible one. The apparent self-evidence of a connection's holding (by virtue of some other manifest structural feature or relation) is no guarantee that it does hold in fact.

We might make a similar claim about the "self-evidence" of deductive rules of inference and of the principles of logic themselves. Are they necessary, or is all of traditional *a priori* knowledge to be swept into the evolutionary bin? Some writers have claimed that the principles of logic are neither necessary nor knowable *a priori;* even if we now do not have a formulated alternative, certain intractable phenomena—of quantum mechanics or whatever—might drive us to revise even our principles of logic. Our point here is more modest. To explain why such principles seem self-evident to us, one need not invoke their necessity. It might be enough that they are true, even if only contingently, even just "true enough"—recall the example of Euclidean geometry—and that they have held true for long enough to leave an imprint upon our evolutionary endowment. This position is not open to Quine's cogent objection that all logical truths cannot owe their truth to convention, because the principles of logic themselves need to be invoked to derive the infinite number of consequences of the conventions.[9] We are not explaining the truth of logic but its apparent necessity. If the principles of logic do hold contingently true—true-enough anyway—then processes of evolution could instill (not their truth but) their seeming self-evidence. (There is no bar to assuming their truth in deriving the consequences of their being instilled as self-evident.)

What is the moral for the methodology that philosophers follow when they assess candidates for necessary truth by attempting to imagine counterexamples, calling upon "intuitive" judgments, etc.? The strength and depth of our intuitions about statements cannot be used as powerful evidence for their necessity when those statements are of a kind such that selection would lead to strong intuitions of their self-evidence even if they were (only) contingently true. The philosophers' explanation of why something seems evident to us on its face is that it is an inescapable necessary truth, one whose falsity cannot be coherently conceived. The evolutionary account provides an alternative possible explanation for why a truth might appear self-evident. And evolution also might instill as evident something that is only an approximation to the truth, and hence not strictly true at all—Euclidean geometry need only have been "true enough." Intuition is an extremely frail reed upon which to build a philosophy.[10] If our intuitions of necessity, and our inability to imagine otherwise, can be accounted for without assuming the existence of necessities, should we believe there are any such necessities at all?

Philosophers who give great weight to intuitions need to offer some account of why such intuitions are reliable and are to be trusted; at least, they need to sketch how we would have acquired a reliable capacity of this sort. Descartes based his confidence in thought processes that involve "clear and distinct ideas" upon the existence of a good God who would not deceive him. Upon what do contemporary philosophers of intuition base their claims? Of course, if the purpose of such philosophy is merely to codify and systematize the intuitions that (for whatever reason) are held, then a philosophy built upon intuitions will need no further basis. And it will have no further validity.

Cross-Classifications

There is an additional reason for skepticism about any purported necessity concerning a particular object.[11] We can imagine two alternative complete systems of classification that divide the world quite differently. Suppose one classification is ours and the other is the Alpha Centaurians'. These different classifications are driven by different interests and purposes, by the organisms' places in different ecological niches, where they face different dangers and opportunities. These two cross-classifications are equally good, as judged by the purposes of those who use each. An entity x is classified differently within each system of classification, grouped with different entities.[12] The two classifications utilize different categories and connect them with different further categories.

It is fruitful to think of an object's essential properties as those that underlie and explain many of the object's other properties.[13] The two classifications will attribute different essential properties to the same entity x, for they will be concerned with explaining different groups of other properties. Whether a trait is held to be an essential or an accidental trait of an entity will depend upon how deeply it is embedded in the (explanatory) network of that entity's other salient traits. Since the two classifications pick out different traits as salient, they also will differ in which traits they hold essential.

Our claim here about the bearing of alternative classifications upon purported necessities about an object differs from the claim that the possibility of different classificatory schemes shows that the truths formulated within one classification are unsteady or are merely relative. The arbitrariness of a classificational scheme does not entail the arbitrariness of the truth claims made utilizing it. Two concepts may each be gerrymandered concepts, but nevertheless it can be an objective fact whether everything that falls under one of the concepts also falls under the other. Whether it is necessary to use those concepts is a different question from whether, given that those concepts are being used, a statement formulated in terms of them is true or not.

Truth is independent of a classificatory scheme, but necessities about an object are not.[14] Although we and the Alpha Centaurians differ in our classifications, we can agree about the truth of statements that use the terms of one of the classifications. We can agree that x is E_1 (where E_1 is a salient class within the Earth classification) and also that x is an A_1 (where A_1 is a salient class within the Alpha Centaurian classification). We will disagree, however, about whether x is necessarily A_1. The Alpha Centaurians will hold that be-ing A_1 explains and underlies all other of x's salient traits, while we will deny this because we disagree about what x's salient traits are.[15] We even can agree that being A_1 *does* explain x's having many other specific traits $A_2, \ldots,$ A_n, where these are traits salient to the Alpha Centaurians but not to us. La-boriously, we have learned to identify these traits (or classes), but we cannot see why anyone would take note of them, much less focus upon them. (Similarly, the Alpha Centaurians may agree that E_1 explains and underlies x's other traits $E_2, \ldots, E_n$, yet show similar puzzlement about why we pay any attention to these other traits.) After understanding our different eco-logical niches, though, we each will understand why the other has come to find different traits worth attending to.

That we and the Alpha Centaurians assign the same nonmodal predi-cates to an object is enough to show we are talking of the same object, even though we and they do not pick out the same subset of these predicates as salient. (Hence, we do not attribute the same necessities to these objects.)[16] It might be objected that we and the Alpha Centaurians are talking of dif-ferent objects because we are talking of things with different essential prop-erties, and hence different identity conditions. But this fact comes too late. Identity is *based upon* and is a function of essential properties, which are based upon (and are a function of) the important and salient properties, which are based upon . . . which is based upon (and is a function of) the in-terests and needs we have (or of the interests that the Alpha Centaurians have). This fact of what is based upon what shakes the status of necessities about an object by showing how *unfundamental* and derivative a notion it is. Even if our agreement about all the (nonmodal) properties of x were *not* sufficient for us to be speaking of the same thing, and even if different *(de re)* necessities defined different objects, nevertheless such necessities come too high in the chain of what depends upon what, of what is a function of what. They are, at best, superficial facts.[17]

Once we come to see how the two classifications differ, won't we come to see the claim that x is necessarily or essentially E_1 as relative to a scheme of classification? It holds relative to our own scheme of classification, but not relative to the Alpha Centaurians' scheme. In their scheme, x *is* E_1 but is not essentially so. How then can claims about what properties x necessarily has, claims that are merely relative to a scheme of classification, be seen as ex-pressing an ontological necessity?

People are similar enough to all other people that *truth* is not relative (among people)—so I said in the first chapter. We could be different enough from Alpha Centaurians, however, that *necessity* would be relative. Since the claim of necessity extends everywhere, the fact that we could be sufficiently different from some other possible being is enough to show that necessity *is* relative. Even if one holds that truth too is not absolute, necessity partakes of still further relativeness.

On the Supposed Necessity of Water's Being H_2O

Saul Kripke and Hilary Putnam have argued that the chemical composition of a substance is essential to it, so that water is necessarily H_2O. Empirical scientific investigation is needed to discover this (so it is an *a posteriori* truth), yet it is necessary, nonetheless.[18] The reference of the term "water" is fixed by what is around here, where the term is used. Since water is H_2O on Earth, then, as that term is used by us, "water" will refer only to H_2O, even if we use it to refer to substances on other possible worlds. If it is not composed thus of hydrogen and oxygen, a colorless, odorless, drinkable substance in another such world will not be *water*. Since in any possible world in which it exists water is H_2O, the statement that water $= H_2O$ is true in all possible worlds, and hence is a necessary truth.

We may lay out the Kripke-Putnam argument explicitly as follows:

(1)   Water is H_2O in the actual world.
(2)   If water is H_2O in the actual world then water is H_2O in every possible world.
(3)   Therefore, water is H_2O in every possible world.
(4)   If something holds in every possible world then it is necessarily true. (For necessity just is truth in all possible worlds. That may even be the *definition* of necessity.)
(5)   Therefore, it is necessarily true that water is H_2O.

Because empirical investigation is necessary to establish premiss (1), it is not known *a priori* that water is H_2O, and so we have an example of a necessary truth that is not known *a priori*. So runs the argument.[19]

I want to say that the statement that water $= H_2O$ is a contingent statement. Even if it is true in all possible worlds, it is only contingently true here on Earth. That would mean that being true in all possible worlds is not sufficient for necessity, so the *definition* of necessity as truth in all possible worlds is mistaken. Premiss (4) of the argument is to be rejected.[20]

In the actual world *A,* water is H_2O, and also (despite the previous note, let us grant that) in *A* it is true that if water is H_2O (in *A*) then on every (accessible) possible world, water is H_2O. That water is H_2O is a truth *exportable* from *A* to every other (accessible) possible world. By that I mean that its truth (when evaluated) on these other possible worlds is determined by, and dependent upon, its being true (when evaluated) in the actual world *A*. If in *A* it were false that water is H_2O, then it would be false on those other worlds also. For what "water" (as used by us) refers to, on every world, depends upon what chemically composed substance the term refers to in the actual world *A*. However, this dependence is an asymmetrical dependence. Water's being H_2O in the actual world does not similarly depend upon its being H_2O in any other particular possible world. Water is H_2O elsewhere *because* it is H_2O in the actual world.[21]

In the other (accessible) possible worlds, the truth that water is H_2O is an *imported* truth, imported from the actual world *A*.[22] Let us say that a truth is an *indigenous* truth on world w_i if it is true on world w_i, and its truth there is not imported from another possible world. (No other possible world to which w_i is accessible exports this truth to w_i.) Leibniz held that a necessary truth is true in all possible worlds. Saul Kripke holds that a necessary truth is true in all accessible possible worlds. (A truth *p* of a world w_i is a necessary truth of w_i if and only if *p* is true on all worlds accessible from w_i.) Neither Leibniz nor Kripke provides us with a sufficient condition for necessity. We need a more stringent condition.

A necessary truth is something that is indigenously true on all (accessible) possible worlds. A truth is a necessary truth *(simpliciter)* on w_i if and only if *p* is an indigenous truth on all worlds accessible from w_i. And a truth is a contingent truth *(simpliciter)* on w_i if and only if *p* is true on w_i and *p* is not a necessary truth *(simpliciter)* on w_i.[23] This does not bar something as a necessary truth when it is not completely home-grown. There may be general necessary truths, rooted in no particular possible world. What it does bar as a necessary truth is something that, though true everywhere, is true on some possible worlds only because it is imported there from some other particular possible world(s).[24]

On the account I have proposed, the statement that water is H_2O is a contingent truth here on Earth. It is true here, and although it is true on all possible worlds accessible from here, its truth is not indigenous there, so it is not necessarily true here.[25] Something can just *happen* to be true in the actual world (without any *must* about it), even though the actual world exports that truth to all other (accessible) possible worlds and so is completely surrounded by worlds where that statement is true.[26]

Suppose that a well-motivated further development of the many-worlds interpretation of quantum mechanics, one of the currently existing interpretations that is well regarded by physicists, leads to their proposing a theory in which water has another chemical structure, XYZ, in another possible world. Should the philosopher tell the physicist not even to consider such a theory because it violates some (purported) necessary truth that is established by philosophical argument? Surely not. Some philosophers defending the Kripke-Putnam line might say that, in this case, the physicist is discovering the actual chemical structure of water, which is more complicated than we thought. That structure of water turns out to be: H_2O in the actual world A, XYZ in possible world w_1, QRS in possible world w_2, etc. However, this seems to abandon the theory that the structure and composition of water in the actual world fixes its structure and composition in every possible world.[27]

Philosophers always believed that it was a contingent truth that water was H_2O until the Kripke-Putnam argument came along, an intriguing argument that meshed with an attractive formal machinery. (Yet the argument, from the beginning, did seem to have something fishy about it, in the way it pulled its remarkable conclusion out of the hat. In this respect, it resembled that most famous of all fishy philosophical arguments, the ontological argument for the existence of God.) At least some things retained their hard-won contingent status, though, things such as the structure of physical space. It once was thought to be a necessary truth that space was Euclidean, but with the development of non-Euclidean geometries and the advances of twentieth-century physics, it became clear that this statement has a contingent status—indeed, that it is false. Even if, after the development of alternative geometries, the experimental results of physics and their theoretical explanation had shown that space *was* Euclidean, this would have been a contingent truth that was shown to hold. But on the Kripke-Putnam line of argument, *is* the geometry of space contingent? The term "physical space" refers to what is around here, to the receptacle that we find ourselves in, to this universe's receptacle, and doesn't it refer rigidly? If the receptacle holding objects in another possible world had a different structure, would it be *physical space*? ("It would be *their* physical space," you might say, but that is like saying that the colorless odorless potable substance in that possible world would be *their* water, even though it did not have the structure H_2O.)[28] Mustn't those following the Kripke-Putnam line of argument say the following? Twentieth-century physics has shown that previous philosophers were wrong in saying that physical space is necessar-

ily Euclidean, but philosophers have drawn the wrong conclusion in holding that the structure of physical space is contingent. Instead, it is a necessary truth that physical space, or rather space-time, is a four-dimensional
Riemannian manifold of nonconstant positive curvature.[29] (And would
something in another possible world be physical space if its curvature was
not determined somehow or other by the matter distribution in its space-
time, even if not precisely in accordance with Einstein's particular field
equation? So isn't the fact that the structure of space-time is thus determined another necessary truth?) I take this application of the Kripke-
Putnam line of argument to constitute an objection to it, indeed a *reductio*
of it.[30] If, instead, I have discovered what will be hailed as a new metaphysical necessity, that only shows how uninteresting the claim can be that
something contentful is metaphysically necessary.

Kripke also has claimed other truths as being necessary, for instance,
truths of origin: a person necessarily comes from the particular fertilized
egg cell that he came from. A different fertilized egg cell (though of exactly
the same genetic and chemical composition), a different person. This, of
course, makes very important the criteria of identity of the originating entity. And the tale must be taken further, to the origins of the particular fertilized egg cell, to the gonads that produced the sperm cell and to the ova-
ries that produced the egg cell, and further still to the entities from which
these originated, etc. For each of these origins will in turn be necessary, and
won't these relations of necessity be transitive, so that it will be a necessary
truth that a person originated from anything that he stands to in the ancestral of the (relevant) "originated-from" relation? Carried back far enough,
these consequences are highly implausible, and nothing of theoretical interest has thus far been built upon such purported necessities.

The notion of the identity of something plays a crucial role in these arguments purporting to uncover metaphysical necessities. "If *this*" (pointing to
water) "had a different chemical structure then it would be different stuff; it
wouldn't be the same thing." Some changes in a property make the same
thing different in some respect; others make it a different thing. Suppose we
grant that our *concept* of the identity of a thing is connected to what
changes (or additions to or lacks in its properties) would make it a different
thing. Still, couldn't we have had a different *conception* of a thing, according
to which the aforementioned differences in property would not make for a
different thing, but differences in other properties would make for a different thing?[31] Not a change in the underlying chemical structure but a change
in the salient surface qualities, for instance, might make for a different stuff.

Even if our own conception of the identity of something is connected to its underlying explanatory structure or to its origin ("different structure, different thing," "different origin, different thing"), aren't there other conceptions that would differently specify the general concept that has to do with identity and sameness? Is it a necessary truth that the identity of something be specified by one of these conceptions rather than another? If different conceptions are equally valid, or even if a second conception, though inferior to the first, nevertheless is within the pale of acceptability, then any truth tied to one of these conceptions will not cut very deeply.[32] If you wish, you can call the ascription of a property to something whose identity would be different if it lacked that property, a "metaphysical truth." But since that change in identity occurs only upon a particular conception of the thing's identity, these "metaphysical necessities" will hold, as necessities, only relative to the particular conception. They will not cut deeply enough to be *ontological* truths.

Elegant structurings and formalizations (such as are provided in Kripke's presentation of modal logic) may give the illusion that some significant subject matter is thereby revealed. However, some formalizations may reveal nothing existing. (A consistent formalization of the notion of the Trinity, hard to achieve, might show that it is, despite appearances, coherent and consistent, but it would not show that anything existing answers to that notion.) And one consistent structuring and formalization might be countered by another, different one that is close by. Should simplicity then suffice to select one formalization over another? Not if its price is a distortion of the subject matter. Although it may be more complicated to speak of "true in all accessible possible worlds" rather than simply of "true in all possible worlds," the former structure may better fit the philosophical facts. Accessibility was an interesting wrinkle in the previous account that yielded interesting and unexpected structure. Even in mathematics, what is wanted is the most interesting and powerful structure, not the simplest one. Although "indigenously true in all (accessible) possible worlds" may be more complex than "true in all accessible possible worlds," it too may have its compensating virtues.

We should not let the glitter of a formalization, even when it yields some acceptable consequences, persuade us to accept its application *in toto*. A theory with even some successes is still open to falsification, and although we are reluctant to abandon a theory in the absence of a better theory, nevertheless we may know that the first theory, despite its elegance, stumbles and fails before recalcitrant material.

The Withering of Metaphysical Necessity

Once upon a time Metaphysical Necessity was a proud category, encompassing a vast range of important interconnected truths. Now it has been reduced, at best, to a scattering of odd statements. Let us recall its glorious days of yesteryear. *Every event has a cause*—gone with the formulation of quantum mechanics. *Space is Euclidean*—gone with the formulation of consistent non-Euclidean geometries and their adoption in contemporary physics. *Space has constant curvature*—gone with General Relativity. *Space has three dimensions*—questioned with the Klein-Kaluza theory of the early 1920s, and abandoned in superstring theory's formulation of twenty-six and ten dimensional spaces, with many dimensions folded in. *For any two events, one temporally proceeds the other, or the other proceeds it, or the two are simultaneous*—modified in Special Relativity. *Nothing travels backward in time*—but in quantum electrodynamics, antimatter going forward in time is equivalent to (ordinary) matter going backward in time. (John Wheeler went so far as to wonder whether all objects could be made of the same one electron repeatedly going forward and backward in time.) And Kurt Godel discovered that some solutions to the equations of general relativity admit time travel.[33] *The world exists in a definite state independently of our observations*—shaken by quantum mechanics. *One solid object cannot move through another one*—yet quantum tunneling allows this as possible. *Space is simply connected*—but not in certain solutions of the equations of general relativity.

You might think that an insight into metaphysical impossibility could save the physicists much useless work by thereby excluding something as physically possible.[34] Things seem to have worked in the other direction, though. Driven by a need to explain strange data, physicists formulate theories that countenance what previously was held to be metaphysically impossible. When those theories succeed in accounting for the data, they become candidates for a true description of physical reality, and *ipso facto* are viewed as metaphysically possible. Even if the theory later turns out to be (physically) false, our changed conceptions count it as metaphysically *possible*. I have claimed in Chapter 1 that quantum mechanics gives us reason to believe that even the fixity of facts and truths about the past is not a necessity. The physical tail wags the metaphysical dog.

If all these apparent necessities fail, then which metaphysical necessities hold secure? What does this shrinkage of the domain of metaphysical necessity leave us with? There remains an uninteresting collection of isolated truths, purportedly metaphysically necessary. *Nothing is red and green all over at the same time.* If objects, and not merely particles, can travel backward and forward in time, the same object can be in two places at the same time and have two colors (all over) at the same time. (I shall say something more about the color incompatibility below.) The apparent metaphysical necessities that remain, if any, will be a paltry lot, shrinking continually over time. They are nothing to build a science around and nothing to build (any important part of) a philosophy around.[35]

One additional purported necessity has received much attention recently. It has been claimed that true identity statements (composed of rigid designators flanking the identity sign) are necessary.[36] A rigid designator R that denotes a in the actual world will denote the same thing in any possible world (in which a exists).[37] The standard example involves the proposition: Hesperus = Phosphorus. In the actual world, there is one planet at the location of Venus that can be seen from the earth in the morning and in the evening. Once thought to be two stars, the evening star was named "Hesperus" and the morning star was named "Phosphorus." In the actual world, Hesperus = Phosphorus. Suppose that in some other possible world w_1, there are two bright planets approximately in the position of Venus (they are the second and the third planets from the sun). One of these is visible from the earth in the morning, the other in the evening. Each of these has an equally good claim to being the closest counterpart in that possible world to Venus in the actual world. Now what are the counterparts in world w_1 of Hesperus and of Phosphorus in the actual world? *Must* the actual Hesperus and the actual Phosphorus have the very same counterpart in world w_1, simply because in the actual world Hesperus is the same as Phosphorus? Isn't it plausible to say that the counterpart of Hesperus in world w_1 is the planet seen from Earth in the evening, and the counterpart of Phosphorus in world w_1 is the planet seen from Earth in the morning? Since, in world w_1, these are two distinct planets, in that world Hesperus is not identical with Phosphorus. Hence, that identity does not hold in all possible worlds, and it is not a necessary truth that Hesperus = Phosphorus.

Consider the relational sentence "X is the best counterpart in world w_i of Y in world w_j." According to what we have said, this is not an extensional context in the place for Y (or for X). To be sure, if we assume that this context is extensional and not intensional, then there will be an argument for the necessity of identity. But to assume that these contexts are extensional is to presuppose that identity is necessary. And why should we do that?

Another way to put the question is to ask whether (and why) identity must be a transitive relation when it holds between entities in different possible worlds. It would be rash, I think, to assume that because identity is transitive when it holds among entities, all of which are in the same possible world, that it must be transitive as a relation between entities in different possible worlds. (Compare: people have the intuition that if one set contains everything a second set contains, plus some additional things not contained in the second set, then the first set contains a larger number of members than the second set does. But it would be rash to extend this intuition from finite sets to infinite ones; there is a gulf between those two kinds of things. Similarly, there is a great gulf between the character and nature of identity statements about entities in the same possible world and identity statements across possible worlds.)[38]

Even quasi-analytic truths succumb to new feasible possibilities. Consider the apparent synonymy of "mother" and "female biological parent," yielding the statements that *all mothers are female biological parents,* and *all female biological parents are mothers.* Suppose that current or future sex-change operations can transform an adult male into an adult female, and vice versa. (Perhaps current surgical procedures affect only surface qualities, but imagine advances that install reproductive organs that do function, with gamete-producing cells to match the new host's genetics.) If a male has been a biological parent of a child, and he undergoes a sex-change operation that transforms him into a female, even though he now is the parent of the child and is a female he does not become the child's *mother.* (The child does not come to have two mothers.) "All female parents are mothers" is not a necessary truth (or an analytic one); neither is "All mothers are female parents," for the mother of a child may have been transformed so that she no longer is female. Nor should we think that "mother" is synonymous with "biological parent who is female at the time the child is born," for the male can have the sex-change operation during his mate's pregnancy; and "mother" is not synonymous with "biological parent who is female at the time the child is conceived," for artificial insemination and storage of sperm enable a male to donate sperm and undergo a sex-change operation before the conception of the egg cell. Should we hold "mother" synonymous with "biological parent who is female at the time the gamete is produced," and can we be confident that further technological developments, for instance, time travel, will not provide counterexamples to this? Is the mother necessarily the female producer of the gamete? Perhaps not; perhaps we had better say the producer of the female gamete, that is, the egg cell. But will all future reproduction that involves naturally produced genes require them to be transmitted in gametes? And so on.

In the face of new feasible possibilities, either existing (purported) synonymies do not guarantee the necessary truth of the corresponding (biconditional) statements, or the meanings are reshaped so as to maintain the purported necessary truths (but why will the meanings always be reshaped in that congenial way?) or new, more complex statements (for instance, that all mothers are biological parents who are female at the time the gamete is produced) get formulated that are supposed to hold necessarily even in the face of the currently newest possibilities—but still newer feasibilities are ever flowing in upon us.

While necessity may be a notion of little importance or application, the notion of possibility may be of very great importance. How can it be that one modal notion, possibility, is of great importance while another, necessity, is of vanishing concern? There can be possibilities, possible worlds if you wish, without there being necessities, statements that hold of *all* possible worlds.[39] The possibilities (the worlds of possibility) can be so diverse as to defy characterization in terms of a general truth.[40]

Although the possibilities are infinitely diverse, we may be so limited in our imaginations as not to be able to conceive of counterexamples to particular purported necessities. Our imaginations might be limited because there were evolutionary advantages to having such a narrowed imagination, or because there was no special evolutionary advantage to having an imagination of completely unfettered inventiveness (so this was not selected for or instilled). Lack of invention is the mother of necessity.

Explaining Away Necessities

It is worth looking in more detail at one of the isolated purportedly necessary truths, the proposition that nothing can be red and green all over at the same time.[41] Seeing what underlies this truth will suggest a general way to understand the status of many purported necessary truths.

Let us list some general features of color, as we perceive it. Color (as we perceive it) comes in bands or categories, showing qualitative differences. Although the precise boundaries that mark off one color (concept) from another may vary from culture to culture, different cultures will agree in which shades they take to be best or paradigm instances of a color (e.g., which shade is the best shade of red).[42] Wavelengths of light vary continuously, but colors as perceived vary discontinuously, or at least not uniformly with the wavelength. A small difference in wavelength may correspond to a large difference in the color perceived. (The difference between wavelengths x and y may be equal to the difference between wavelengths y and z, yet the perceived monochromatic colors (that came closest to) corresponding to x, y, and z may be such that y is seen as more different from x than it is from z.)[43]

Second, some combinations of colors are not perceived or (apparently) even imaginable. We can see a bluish green or a reddish yellow but not a reddish green or a yellowish blue. Red and green are opponent colors, as are yellow and blue. Third, there is the phenomenon of color constancy. The color of an object looks to be (almost) the same color despite great changes in (the spectral composition of) the ambient light, which can range from sunlight to shade outdoors to a tungsten or a fluorescent bulb indoors. An adequate theory of color, and of our perception of it, should explain how colors come in bands, why there are opponent colors, and why there is color constancy.

Why cannot something be (seen as) red and green all over at the same time? Suppose that color is surface spectral reflectance (along with other objective wavelength phenomena),[44] and that these physical properties have certain additional characteristics only in relation to human perceptual apparatuses.[45] That is what an adequate reduction of the notion of color would hold. The color at a point (or small area) is the proportion of incident energy of each wavelength that is reflected at that point (or in that small area). No point (or small area) can have two different colors simultaneously because no point can simultaneously reflect different proportions of incident energy of a given wavelength. And there is no possibility here of saying that a point does have both colors (in the way it could be bluish-green) because the two colors that have been chosen here, red and green, are opponent colors. This is so because the Red and Green cone mechanisms pair in feeding into concentric single-opponent cells; one feeds into the center, the other into the surround, and their actions are opponent. And pairs of Red and Green single-opponent cells oppose each other throughout the receptive fields of double-opponent cells.[46]

The exact wiring of double-opponent cells is not currently known, but the general structure of double-opponent cells can explain the (psychological) phenomenon of opponent colors, e.g., why there is no reddish green or yellowish blue. When a pair of cone mechanisms, such as Red and Green (or such as Yellow and Blue) oppose each other throughout the receptive fields of double-opponent cells, there will be no possibility of experiencing a reddish green (or a bluish yellow).[47]

The identification of color with surface spectral reflectance shows why no point can have two distinct colors, leaving aside the possibility of both blending in some third color. And the wiring of Red and Green cone mechanisms into single and double-opponent cells shows why no such blending is possible with red and green to produce a reddish green; it explains why these two are opponent colors. The phenomenon of color constancy through changes in ambient light also is illuminated by double-opponent cells.[48]

The particular wiring pattern of cells, which cones feed how into opponent center-surround cells, is contingent. There is no necessity there, no metaphysical necessity at any rate. So there is no necessity (or at best only a "relative necessity") in the color phenomena and in the limits on color phenomena that this wiring explains.[49] Between the physics (the relation of color to surface spectral reflectance) and the physiology (the existence of double-opponent cells), the reductive explanation of the color phenomena shows them to be wholly contingent (or, at best, physically but not metaphysically necessary).

A true necessity is invariant under reduction. A "necessity" that is not invariant under reduction is only apparent. When we see what a phenomenon reduces to, and thereby see what explains it, if what does the explaining itself is not necessary then there will be no necessity left. A necessity reduced to the nonnecessary is no necessity at all.[50]

Not all purported necessities will be open to the same kind of explanation. However, this one kind does suggest a general strategy for investigating and understanding such purported necessities. Given an apparent necessity that *p*, search for an explanation of it and see whether the apparent necessity of *p* is preserved under that explanation. That explanation need not be a reduction; some nonreductive explanations also will not leave apparent necessities intact.

Consider the suggestion in Wittgenstein's *Tractatus* that some necessities are due to "the method of projection." I think he means something like the following. Each method of drawing a two-dimensional map of a three-dimensional sphere (for instance, the standard Mercator projection) distorts some characteristics and relationships. A person might think that a certain feature shown in the map is a feature of the surface of the Earth; looking at many such maps exhibiting that same feature, he might conclude that the feature is a necessary one. It can be due, however, to that particular method of mapping a spherical surface onto a plane. Although a map drawn according to that method of projection *has to* have that feature, other methods of projection would not imprint that same feature, and so other maps would not exhibit it.

Perhaps language too resembles a method of projection, in that some features that appear to be necessary features of the world are artifacts of the way a particular language, or even any language, operates to represent the world. One task of the philosophy of language is to discover the most general modes of linguistic representation in order to isolate their imprint, the features they impress upon the world.

Cognitive science and neuroscience are beginning to investigate other, nonlinguistic modes of representation. Some are languagelike, as with the so-called language of thought; others, such as modes of visual imagery or the modes of representation that are used by neural networks as parts of perception-action systems that operate in the physical world, apparently are not.[51] These modes of representation, too, may leave their imprint: artifactual features that pertain not to the world but to the method by which it is represented.

One day it will be a fruitful program, I think, even if it is too early now, to explain the apparent necessity and inescapability of various statements as products of various modes of representation.[52]

Even if each mode of representation imprints certain features upon the world, these modes may differ in which features they imprint. We may discover, then, that an apparently necessary feature of the world as verbally described is absent in other, nonlinguistic representations of the world that are equally adequate, and so is not a necessary feature after all.

Might there be features that would be imprinted upon the world by any and every possible mode of representing it? If so, we then would face the question of whether these features are truly necessities in the world, or are simply the imprints of the representing of the world (in some way or other). We might have enough of a grasp of the shared character of linguistic and all other possible modes of representation to see that, whatever the state of the world, any mode of representation itself would be sufficient to imprint a certain feature. That would be a reason to doubt that the world itself does have that feature.

I do not envision one unitary theory of all (apparent) necessity. Some apparently necessary truths will have reductive physical explanations, others will have neurological explanations, others explanations in terms of mechanisms of representation, while others might be due to convention.[53] These diverse explanations may show the truths to have a relative necessity—one relative to the holding of the explanatory factors. The question is whether these explanatory factors themselves are (even apparently) necessary. If not, then what they give rise to is no real necessity at all, no intrinsic and objective ontological necessity. In such a manner, we might mop up the separate stray apparent necessities. Perhaps even *all* of them.

Various necessities can be handled in this manner, but there lingers a question about veridicality. A mode of representation, we have said, can give rise to isolated apparent necessities that it imposes as an artifact in the course of its describing the world. But it also might *shade* or color everything that it describes. How then can we hold that our theories or descriptions or other representations of the world are veridical, in the sense of containing nothing but the truth?

We can use the imprinted (apparently) necessary statements to figure out the mechanism by which the mode of representation works (much as visual illusions have been used to detect how the visual mechanism works). Once that operating mechanism is known, perhaps we can figure out how it shades everything, and then also correct for that shading or subtract it. Thereby, we would get to more veridical statements, even if not *completely* veridical ones.

This raises three further points. First, couldn't there be a mode of representation that shades everything but doesn't give rise to imprinted (apparent) necessities? How could we detect that mode's mechanisms of operation and correct for its shading? However, there might be *other* routes, other than imposed necessities, to discovering the mechanism of the mode of representation, for instance, other kinds of illusion it produces. Thereby, knowing the mechanism, we could infer what shading it would produce and then correct for that. Second, might there be modes of representation that do shade and also do impose necessities, but since we haven't yet noticed these necessities we haven't yet uncovered the mechanisms? We therefore would not yet have corrected for the shading, and so would not yet have complete veridicality. Of course, there *could* be such currently unnoticed shadings. We do not know everything yet. However, there is no bar in principle to discovering and correcting for each such shading, even for all such shadings. Third, there are (apparent) necessities that, as it happens, we cannot yet explain by the operation of a mode of representation (or in any other way). Therefore, supposing that the correct explanation of one of these is a mode of representation and that it is shading very many things, there might be shading we don't yet know about. True, but this establishes no bar to improving the veridicality of our statements in the future.

Logical and Mathematical Necessity

Stray isolated necessities are one thing, logic and mathematics are another. There we have a body of systematically related truths, tightly linked in structures that are extremely useful and fruitful. And it seems that these *must* hold true. Even if there are no metaphysical necessities, still there do appear to be mathematical and logical necessities, and *their* basis is unclear. What gives rise to them? Is their necessity (though not their truth) to be explained away as only apparent? Or, if these are true (and nonrelative) necessities, what is their basis?

Although there presently exists a vast and intricate literature on logical and mathematical *truth,* there is only some writing on logical necessity, and hardly any writing on mathematical necessity. It is fair to say that these topics are not yet well understood. Also, the area is filled with intellectual minefields. Only fools rush in. Yet I do want to say something to indicate how logic and mathematics might be construed as *not* consisting of a body of necessary truths.

You may well resist this position, or even think it is absurd. Of some particular mathematical (or logical) proposition, you may be convinced, you may be certain, that it could not be false. You are convinced that it holds necessarily. I myself, however, have been greatly impressed by the fact that mathematicians have produced startling results to show that things that seemed self-evidently to be impossible really are possible. Can one solid ball be cut into a finite number of pieces, and these pieces then be rearranged (by rigid motions) to form two solid balls, each the same size as the original one? "Impossible!" you say. "It is a necessary truth that this cannot be done." Yet the Banach-Tarski theorem shows that this *can* be done.[54]

My situation is this one. For any mathematical statement p, including very simple ones such as $3 + 2 = 5$, if the mathematicians at my university announced that they had defined or discovered some new and remarkable mathematical objects for which that statement did not hold (it breaks down, they say, for "2-dimensional 1-adic representations associated to classical cuspidal modular forms," or for "irreducible complex representations of the reductive group over a local field," or for "semimodular irreducible cyclotemic fields of Shimura varieties"), and if mathematicians elsewhere agreed, then I too would believe them. In the intellectual division

of labor about such matters, and given mathematicians' track record, I accept their authority. (And no matter how extraordinary their claim, I do
not feel that I have to withhold belief until I have labored through the
proofs myself.) It is epistemically possible for me that the mathematicians
will announce this, and it also is epistemically possible for me that they will
be correct in what they say. Should your situation be so very different?

Let me emphasize that the remarks that follow are meant to be suggestive
only. Perhaps a very different line of thought might better explain away the
apparent necessity of logic and mathematics than anything presented here.
Some possibilities have been surveyed already. According to the evolutionary explanation, some general truths (or propositions close enough to the
truth), although themselves contingent, would be instilled to have the pa-
tina of necessity. Arriving quickly at beliefs or making prompt decisions
would have great advantages, and this speed would be aided by limitations
in our capacities to imagine other possibilities. As the example of Euclidean
geometry shows, these limitations can be part of an interconnected structure of nonisolated (almost) truths. The inability to imagine the falsity of
the mathematical and logical truths would be part and parcel of other limitations (or side effects of the neurological structures selected to produce
these other limitations). The logical and mathematical truths would be
contingent truths dressed in the clothing of necessity.

Does this explanation of necessity explain or comport with "the unreasonable effectiveness of mathematics in the physical sciences"?[55] Let us distinguish four questions. In what does the truth of logic and mathematics
consist? Why do logic and mathematics hold true? In what does the necessity of logic and mathematics consist? Why are logic and mathematics necessary? The evolutionary explanation is not meant to answer the first two
questions about truth. It leaves open the issue of why the propositions of
logic and mathematics continue to bear truthful fruit in correct predictions
in far-flung further applications. The explanation of necessity is different,
however, and it only needs to reside alongside whatever ultimately explains—we offer no explanation here—the truth and effectiveness of mathematics.[56]

The same point applies to necessities that are imprinted by modes of linguistic or other representation. It is only necessity that these imprint, not
truth.[57] Why do these methods of representation happen to imprint necessity upon what is true (enough)? That does not "just happen." Only those
methods of representation whose projected features comport well enough

with truths manage to survive the biological and social processes of selection. Whatever methods make egregious falsehoods seem like necessary truths quickly fall by the wayside.

There is more. The imprinted necessities of the methods of representation are not simply these method's side effects. The limitations in conception or imaginability, and the quickness of inference or thought, that these limitations bring in their wake can be part of the reason why those particular modes of representation, rather than closely similar ones, were selected. These would therefore be *functions* of the mode of representation, not side effects. So the evolutionary explanation of (apparent) necessity and the representational mechanism explanation of it are not two separate and disconnected explanations. Evolutionary selection works on the representational mechanisms.

As a set of propositions about the world, logic may be (approximately) true. As an instilled part of our cognitive mechanism, it also provides the framework through which we filter data in order to arrive at an objective truth about the world.

An objective fact is one that is invariant under all admissible transformations. Such a fact has a certain stability, fixity, and multiple accessibility. Our theory of the world does not attempt to account for all random sensory events, some of which are merely noise, internal to the operation of our bodily sense organs and neural machinery. These are filtered out by neurophysiological and psychological processes *before* we begin to construct a theory of objective phenomena. Similarly, empirical science does not try to account for all observations or for all the events of observings. It accounts only for the replicable observations, those constant and stable enough that there is a regularity to be accounted for: under such-and-such conditions, so-and-so is observed.[58]

People who are schizophrenic lack adequate filters for the disparate material that all people encounter. They fail to ignore flashes at the periphery of their field of vision or stray motions or cells drifting across their visual field or odd bodily sensations or coincidences of events (such as when two different people happen to look at them, or when a noise occurs simultaneously with a sighting). These people attempt to construct one coherent story or theory that accounts for all of this, giving a place to each and every bit. That way madness lies, or paranoid conspiracy theories. The schizophrenic's alogical thinking is a product not of bad translation but of bad filtering.[59] First, a person needs to identify what is a candidate for a place in the objective world by filtering the noncandidates; only afterward does he build a theory of how the objective world works and of what pattern it exhibits.

I conjecture that logic functions as a filter to weed out data that can safely be ignored. Only what is stable enough and structured enough to pass the tests of logic need be examined further to detect what particular invariances it exhibits. In dreams, if things or events violate (are represented as violating) the principle of noncontradiction by simultaneously showing contradictory properties, this just shows the subjectivity of dream material. Having a dream is a part of the objective world, but the content of the dream is not. It would be desirable to investigate in detail how the particular pieces of currently standard logic might function as filters.

The filtering mechanisms are not restricted to logical principles. At every stage along the neural pathways that begin with sensory receptors, data are integrated and synthesized, and nonintegrable data are not passed along further.

The pieces of standard logic function to filter the data of the world, but the filtering could be done differently. Some logical system or other contributes to the filtering, but no one particular system is required. Standard logic is the system we possess, perhaps one that was evolutionarily instilled, but this does not mean it is unchangeable. Indeed, modifications in standard logic have been proposed. Intuitionist logicians have proposed abandoning the law of the excluded middle and certain forms of *reductio ad absurdum* proofs; alternative logics have been proposed to cope with the vagueness (and higher-order vagueness) of the terms of ordinary language, a vagueness that opens the way to sorites arguments; quantum logicians have proposed revising standard logic, and if their proposals have not found favor this is not because they flout necessary truths but because they do not sufficiently illuminate the puzzles of quantum theory; multivalued logics have been proposed to assign to statements *degrees* of truth; because of lack of progress in finding convincing solutions to the logical antinomies and paradoxes, paraconsistent logics have been proposed in which contradictions hold true but rules of inference are modified so that these contradictions do not entail every statement.[60]

The principles of standard logic, and of the alternative systems of logic, rule out of consideration various (kinds of) *putative* facts. From a standpoint within these principles, what are ruled out are *merely* putative facts, statements that just appear to be supported by data and experiences. From an external point of view, in examining someone else's system of principles that are more restrictive than our own, we might say that their principles are not necessary—for some things they rule out are countenanced as possible by our own principles—or even that their principles are false—for they rule out things that our principles not only fail to rule out but (in conjunction with other principles) conclude are true. The filtering account that we offer is meant to account for the apparent necessity of statements. It does not have the consequence that some statements that our principles of logic rule out actually do hold; it does not imply that some statements we deem to be necessary actually are false.[61]

It might be said that if standard principles of logic were given up, that would amount to a change in the meanings of the terms involved, for instance, a change in the meaning of "not." These new logical principles then would not be denying what the earlier ones affirmed, and so their acceptance would not impugn the status of the earlier principles as necessary truths—so runs the defense of the necessity of the standard principles. However, if a series of well-motivated steps might lead to the reasonable abandonment of any particular principle of logic (even though all cannot be abandoned at once), the claim that under the old meanings the old logic held necessarily is greatly weakened. If it held necessarily, what could motivate a change in the meanings? Perhaps it could be supplemented, but how could it be given up when it holds necessarily of everything there is? Of what worth are truths that, though necessary, are so useless as to be set aside while the serious theoretical work takes place (for good reason) within other systems of thought? The old truths might be necessary, but they no longer would be *needed*.

There is an interaction between the stringency of the filter and the coherence of the resulting theory or story. If it is impossible to reach a coherent theory with a given filter, one should try a more stringent filter of that same sort. Since that more stringent filter eliminates more data, the subset of data that remains may now fit a coherent pattern that the wider class of purported data violated. (If no strengthening of a filter of that sort fits the pattern, try another type of filter.) On the other hand, if it is very easy to find a coherent theory of the data that have passed through a given filter, if many theories fit those data equally well, then relax the filter so that even more data are admitted. This will limit the number of theories (or the ease in finding a theory) that fit those now-expanded data. One also can increase the stringency of the standards of coherence. Levels of aspiration move up if it is easy to achieve given goals, and they move down if it proves to be extremely difficult or impossible to achieve those goals.[62] So too the degree of stringency of the filter, or of the standards of coherence, adapts to the ease or difficulty of formulating coherent theories of the data.

We are built to detect an objective world in a way that adapts to the recalcitrance of the world. We filter data to a shape that yields things that are invariant under various transformations. However, there is no guarantee that the particular filters and procedures we use *will* discover a coherent pattern of objectiveness, given the specific unfiltered data the world presents. Success with *those* procedures tells us something about what the world is like. And we gain confidence in what that tells us when further successful predictions are made on its basis. We are able to modify or even discard some of our built-in filtering criteria, and also even the criteria that specify the goal of coherence. (In addition, as we have seen, the set of admissible transformations that marks what is objective changes over time.)

This does not mean that the objective world is our construction. Our picture of the objective world is sensitive to our malleable criteria of objectiveness and to our procedures for filtering data to arrive at a coherent account, but it also is sensitive to what the world is like. If the world were different, those *particular* procedures and criteria would not yield any stable account of an objective world; so when they do, this tells us (something of) what the world is like. Still, while those particular procedures might not yield an account of an objective world unless the world presented it with data of a particular character, won't it be true that whatever kind of data the world presents us with, there will be some filters or other, some procedures and criteria that, from those data, will then yield an account of that world as objective? That is not clear. But even if there were a guarantee that, for any data, some procedures or other must yield an extensive account of an objective world, that *these* specific procedures do so reveals the world's particular character.

I have focused thus far upon the apparent necessity of the truths of logic. Something should be said, however briefly, about mathematics, with its truths of great and far-flung effectiveness. We focus upon set theory, within which all of mathematics can be modeled. (Category theory too is of fundamental philosophical importance.) Set theory itself contains an axiom, the axiom of infinity, that guarantees that there is (at least) a denumerable infinity of objects. This axiom, from the very beginning, struck people as lacking the necessity that a truth of logic should have. (It seemed logically possible for it to turn out that the world contained only a finite number of particles, for space and time to be finite and quantized, etc. Was an infinity of abstract objects any more necessary?) The axiom of choice holds that for any infinite set of (disjoint) sets, there exists a selection set containing exactly one element from each one of this infinity of sets. This axiom also was controversial as a basis of mathematical reasoning, and therefore held to be noninevitable and optional (and so as nonnecessary, if not false), as were the many statements proved equivalent to it or proved on its basis. Moreover, given the undecidability of the continuum hypothesis within standard set theory, some theorists (including Paul Cohen, who proved that undecidability) proposed formulating a non-Cantorian set theory that would stand as an alternative to standard set theory, just as non-Euclidean geometry stands as an alternative to Euclidean geometry. Neither set theory would hold necessarily.[63]

Similarly for arithmetics. With independent axioms for number theory, of course, one can vary each axiom to form a new variant theory. (And just as the terms of Peano arithmetic were definable and its axioms derivable within set theory, so would the terms of these variant arithmetics be definable and their axioms derivable, for these theories too could be modeled within set theory.) Would every such variant define a different mathematical structure with different objects as its subject matter, or would some variants be speaking of the same natural numbers yet be making different claims about their properties? Not every such variant theory would be theoretically fruitful in allowing the proof of interesting and powerful theorems. Had there been these equally powerful alternatives, it would be an empirical question which one was most applicable to (which aspects of) the world. Clearly, under those circumstances, arithmetic would not constitute a body of necessary truths. Does the necessity of arithmetic, then, rest upon the fact that there are no powerful close alternatives? (And is this fact necessary, or itself contingent?) Even if Peano arithmetic stands unrivaled in its fertility, couldn't there be some phenomenon that one of the weaker alternatives suits better?[64]

The topic of logical or mathematical truth seems to be *prior* to the topic of logical or mathematical necessity. Yet part of the difficulty of explaining why a statement of logic or mathematics holds true—not wherein its truth consists but *why* it holds true—may be connected to the apparent necessity of logic and mathematics. It is difficult to find a reason why a thing is this way rather than that way if there is no *that* way that it could be. To the extent that explanation is contrastive, it will be difficult to provide (nonreductive) explanations of necessary truths. I have suggested that representational or filtering mechanisms limit our conceptions and imagination, and that these limitations might prevent our conceiving of the explanatory contrasts. The existence of these mechanisms, however, does provide a relevant possible explanation, not of why necessities hold but of why some things appear to be necessary.

Degrees of Contingency

Philosophers of modality count with three numbers: 0, 1, all. Something is impossible when it is true in no possible world, something is possible when it is true in at least one possible world, and a necessary truth is true in all possible worlds. A contingent statement is true in at least one but not all possible worlds; that contingent statement is a contingent *truth* when it is true in the actual world. Necessary truths are invariant across all possible worlds, contingent truths across only some.

When a contingent truth varies across possible worlds, how contingent is it? It is instructive to attempt to formulate a measure of a statement's *degree* of contingency. Only if a statement is a conjunction that completely describes a world (the actual world or some other one) will it hold only in that world. Otherwise, it will hold true of more than one possible world.

It seems reasonable to say that the fewer the number of possible worlds in which a statement holds true, the more contingent it is. So as a measure of a statement's contingency we might think to take the ratio of the number of worlds in which the statement does *not* hold to the total number of possible worlds. A statement that holds in 1/4 of the possible worlds will be 3/4 contingent; a statement that holds in 1/8 of the possible worlds will be 7/8 contingent.[65] However, if there are an infinite number of possible worlds, and these include an infinite number in which the statement holds and an infinite number in which it does not, that ratio will be ill-defined or will not serve our purposes exactly.[66]

Measure theory in mathematics is a theory of the size of a set, where this is not interpreted as the number of points within the set. If we suppose we are given, or have at hand, a general measure of the worlds in which a statement holds, the simplest measure of its contingency would be the ratio of the measure of the worlds in which it *doesn't* hold to the measure of all possible worlds.[67] The higher the ratio, the more contingent the statement is. This ratio, however, seems to be exactly what Rudolf Carnap thought of as 1 minus the *a priori* probability of a statement, which was the ratio of the measure of the worlds in which the statement held to the measure of all possible worlds.[68] Is a statement's degree of contingency then simply the complement of its *a priori* probability? The more probable, the less contingent?

Such information about a statement's absolute degree of contingency might not be precisely what we seek. Consider a random event on Earth, prima facie highly contingent, which might, however, occur in very many possible worlds quite different from the actual one. How contingent a truth is *here* will depend upon how frequently it holds true in possible worlds that are similar to the actual world. David Lewis has developed a representation of possible worlds in a similarity space, with a comparative metric of distances from the actual world.[69] Consider a sphere of radius r centered about the actual world. Since the choice of r will be somewhat arbitrary, and may vary in different inquiries about contingency, I shall relativize the notion to the choice of radius r. We then can say that the *degree of r-contingency* of a statement S is the ratio of the measure of possible worlds within the sphere of radius r centered about the actual world where S does *not* hold true to the measure of all possible worlds within that sphere.

In these terms, we might raise the question of how contingent our evolutionarily selected categories of understanding are. How distant are the closest worlds where these particular categories would *not* have been selected for (not because of variations and accidents in the particular course of the evolutionary history but) because in those worlds these categories would have significantly decreased fitness?

We still have not arrived at a notion of degree of contingency that is significantly different from (the complement of) probability. True, we no longer are speaking of the ratio of the measure of the worlds in which S doesn't hold to the measure of all possible worlds, which is the complement of the *a priori* probability of S. However, by turning instead to a sphere centered about the actual world, we simply speak of the complement of the *conditional* probability of S, given that some world similar to the actual world holds. A shift from unconditional to conditional probability is a shift from one notion of the probability family to another; it does not get us to degree of contingency as a new notion.

Let us begin again. We often are concerned with how narrow the path is that led (or would lead) to S, given a certain starting point. Even in a deterministic system, the range of initial conditions that lead to a particular state might be quite small. Starting with a range of initial states, the laws of process of the system might be (somewhat) *convergent,* leading them all to the same end result or at least to end results less distant than their starting points. Or the laws of process of the system might be *parallel,* neither reducing nor enlarging the original differences. Or the laws of process of the system might be *divergent,* enlarging the initial differences. Very small initial differences in state might, through the operation of nonlinear laws of process, be magnified into very significant differences. Chaos theorists write of sensitive dependence upon initial conditions to describe this situation. Proponents of the Weak Anthropic Principle also emphasize how very narrow is the range of initial conditions that would lead to a universe supporting stable material objects and life.[70]

Stephen Jay Gould has argued that the existence of organisms like us is highly contingent, depending upon a sequence of historical events that easily could have been very different. At very many historical moments, the branches of life that eventually did lead to us could have become extinct.[71] How particular were the conditions that would lead to us? How wide a range of initial conditions would have led to the very same, or to a similar enough, result?[72] (Evolutionary theorists speak of convergent evolution.)

This raises an interesting issue concerning time. Suppose, only for the purposes of our argument here, that something very much like Gould's claim is correct and that the evolutionary line that led to us depended very tenuously upon particular conditions holding very long ago, and that if different conditions had held then, the forces of evolutionary selection would not have led to similarly conscious and intelligent beings. (I myself tend to doubt that this is so.) How contingent does that make our existence?

Consider another example. Suppose that very recently a nuclear war easily could have occurred (or that it would have occurred under only slightly different conditions, for instance, if the Cuban missile crisis had taken a slightly different course), and also suppose that if this war had happened then all human life on earth would have been extinguished.[73] This would make the current existence of human life a highly contingent matter. Next, suppose that a very long time ago, perhaps the time that Gould speaks of, the particular evolutionary path that led to us was very tenuous, and easily could have not continued on to us or to anything like us, and also that it would not have taken a path to us under some particular circumstances very similar to the ones that then obtained. Yet suppose also that since that crucial long-ago time, human existence has been secure; no circumstance similar to anything that did obtain since then would have threatened it. This second scenario does not, I think, make current human existence highly contingent. According to this scenario, human existence once was highly contingent but now it no longer is. Time makes a difference.

Not everything that depends upon an earlier highly contingent event (as a necessary condition) is itself highly contingent. Contingency fades over time; it has a half-life. The features of our physical universe that are due to a very early spontaneous breaking of a symmetry are not now—are no longer—highly contingent. We could formulate another, more absolute no-tion, under which the degree of contingency is preserved under necessary conditionhood: nothing is less contingent now than any one of its neces-sary conditions ever was. However, that is not our actual notion—at any rate, it is not the one I am exploring here.

Suppose that S is true in the actual world. Consider some possible world W that differs from the actual world at some point back in time, and gives rise to not-S. I want to say that the further back we need to go to find this difference that would lead to not-S, the less contingent S now is. And the greater the difference that is needed to lead to not-S, the less contingent S is (at least insofar as shown by world W). It is difficult to combine the two factors, the time difference and the dissimilarity of W from the actual world, into one single measure.

Things would be simple if the further back in time a difference between worlds is, the greater the current dissimilarity will be between them. This amounts to saying that the laws of process of the system are divergent, en-larging whatever initial differences there are at a constant rate. If we mea-sured the degree of contingency of S (when S is true in the actual world) by the closeness of the closest possible world in which S is false, then since a difference a long time back would correspond to a large current difference, that possible non-S world would not be very close currently. Hence *it* would not show that S is highly contingent.[74]

This approach makes clear why in a deterministic world whose laws of process are *parallel*, the fact that the differences that give rise to a non-S world go back as far as the big bang does not have the effect of reducing the degree of contingency of S. For in a universe whose laws of process are par-allel, if only a small difference all the way back then was needed to produce non-S now, then it was only a small difference yesterday that also marks non-S, and that will be a world very close to today's actual world.

The closer a non-S world is to the actual world, the more contingent S is. We can equate the degree of contingency of S in today's actual world to the degree of closeness of that closest non-S world.

Degree of contingency of S (in today's actual world) = MAX (degree of closeness of a non-S world to today's actual world).

The greater that degree of closeness, the greater S's degree of contingency.[75] Because degrees of closeness (or similarity) to today's actual world enter into the formula, the degree of contingency of S differs from any delineated (complement of the) probability of S.[76]

Even when a crucial factor is recent and produced great divergence, this need not make the current facts highly contingent. Was the terror a contingent fact in the Soviet Union?[77] Some argued that it was due to peculiar features of Stalin's personality (although we know now that Lenin's personality was not so very different in its ruthlessness).[78] Others have argued that the terror was intrinsic to the Soviet system and to the Bolshevik program[79] or, at any rate, that because of Lenin's centralization of the Bolshevik party, the persecution and banning of opposition parties, and the banning of Bolshevik party or of Central Committee factions in 1921, there was no institutional barrier remaining to the concentration of power in one person's hands and to the consequent forced collectivization and terror.[80] Suppose that the latter view is correct, but that it was a highly contingent matter that the Bolsheviks succeeded in taking power, either because a more intelligent tsarist regime could have avoided a revolution, or because more-effective Mensheviks could have avoided a successful Bolshevik putsch.[81] The recentness of the highly contingent Bolshevik success in seizing power in 1917 does not make it highly contingent that there was a terror in the 1930s, for the Russia of that latter date included an established Bolshevik system. The process in Russia from 1917 to the 1930s was a strongly divergent one. Small differences in 1917 made for large and catastrophic differences later on. Therefore, the relevant question is whether worlds very similar to *that* one as it was then, in the 1930s, not in 1917—perhaps with different leaders (but ones who could have come to power under that system) or slightly different institutions—also would have included a terror. Because the successful Bolshevik Revolution produced massive changes in Russia very quickly, when we ask about the terror twenty years later, the closest possible world (in 1936) in which there is *no* terror is very far away from the then actual world. The terror of 1936–1939, therefore, was *not* highly contingent.

When a radically new system or situation is established by a recent highly contingent event that is its necessary condition, the ensuing events within the system are not thereby inexorably infected with high contingency. For their contingency will need to be assessed in terms of what occurs later in worlds closely similar to that established world then.[82] (That holds as well within individual lives that are created through highly contingent events of fertilization.)

How might we make use of this temporal notion of contingency? First, it might be correlated with ease and difficulty of change. The more contingent something is, the easier it is to change; the less contingent, the harder to change. Ease and difficulty might be measured by the energy or effort it takes to make the change. The fit of degree of contingency with ease of change is not perfect, however. It might be a highly noncontingent fact that something is created having a property that will spontaneously change (or be very easily changed) after a certain time. Nevertheless, ease of change will tend to vary with degree of contingency.

A delineated notion of degree of contingency might illuminate the nature of explanation. Typically, an *explanation* shows something to be less contingent than it otherwise appears. An explanation of a fact or regularity seeks the least contingent truth that yields that fact or regularity.[83] Subsuming the fact or regularity under a *law* is a way of showing it to be less contingent. The law itself is less contingent than the fact it explains, holding in a wider range of worlds. And although the initial conditions themselves may be contingent, by virtue of the subsuming law the fact itself will hold (at least) in *all* the close-by worlds where those initial conditions also do hold.

Let us eliminate the reference to how contingent something otherwise might appear. An explanation of some thing (e.g., an event or law) shows that thing's (maximum) degree of noncontingency.[84] It does that by showing how far away is that (closest) world where the thing does not hold. Subsuming some thing under a scientific law, then, shows that thing's degree of contingency in the r-band of worlds around the actual world where that law holds true, by focusing attention upon those worlds containing the requisite initial conditions. In *all* such close-by worlds where the same initial conditions hold, the law guarantees that the event also will occur. We also then can see that establishing an event as random also constitutes an explanation of it by marking its exact (and hence its maximum) degree of contingency.

Does an explanation presenting something as an event in a chaotic system show it to be highly contingent? The butterfly's flapping its wings in China may be highly contingent, but by the time the storm system has reached the United States, it can be both difficult to change and also significantly noncontingent. The time since the originating event may be short, but as a result of the nonlinear dynamics, the divergence that this event has caused from what otherwise would have occurred now is very great. The distance between these possible worlds has increased so that the storm in the actual world is, by now, highly noncontingent.

An explanation of some thing shows exactly how contingent that thing actually is. It exhibits its degree of contingency. Recent writers have emphasized the role of unification in explanation.[85] Integrating some phenomena with others, unifying them via a law or by some other means, ties them together into a larger package. Henceforth we know that an alteration in one of the tied phenomena would involve alterations in the others as well. So the closest world in which one of the phenomena is different is a world in which *all* the unified phenomena are different; hence that closest world is further away than would appear (in the absence of the unification). The unifications effected by laws or theories thereby reduce the degree of contingency of the phenomena that fall under them, that is, the unification exhibits how noncontingent these phenomena are. Hanging together, they avoid the contingency of hanging separately.

Our discussion here suggests also another (looser) notion of necessity that might be explained as follows. It is necessary that q when there is a p such that p is true, and p makes q true, and q's degree of contingency is below a certain threshold. It is highly noncontingent that q. To the simpler statement without the final conjunct, viz. that q is necessary when there is a true p that makes q true, it might be objected that q cannot be necessary in this situation unless its cause p also is necessary. Alternatively, it might be objected that this makes everything in a deterministic system necessary. However, we can apply here our earlier point that q can be highly noncontingent even when the p that makes q happen is itself highly contingent. When p makes q true, q can be said to be necessary when its degree of contingency is below a certain threshold. And this may occur even when the degree of contingency of the cause p is considerably above that threshold itself, even if p is recent, provided that circumstances then diverged sufficiently greatly. It is this loose notion of necessity—something is necessary when it is highly noncontingent—that seems to capture much of the ordinary, as opposed to the philosophical, talk of "necessity."

We might even say that the earlier p, once highly contingent, no longer is so. Not only does it give rise to q's that are not contingent; its own degree of contingency *changes*. Back then, it was only a short distance to the closest non-p world, but now it is a very great distance to a world where p had not happened. So contingency turns out to have an unexpected temporal index. It is relative to a time. We cannot simply ask how contingent S is in a given world W (whether the actual world or some other possible world). Instead, we must ask how contingent S is in a given world W at a given time t. According to our formula, that will be assessed by (weighted) similarities of other worlds to that world W *at that time t*. In the first chapter, we saw that truth might be relative to time. We now see that a truth's degree of contingency might also be relative to time.

Philosophers generally have sought or even craved high degrees of non-contingency, and they have developed theories that both widen the zones of noncontingency and increase the degree of noncontingency within these zones. What motivates philosophers, not just to want to know how contingent things actually are, but to *want* things not to be very contingent, and consequently to develop theories which satisfy this desire?

If the world is less contingent, then less still remains to be explained or to be in dire need of explanation. However, it is not just a desire to reduce the remaining intellectual tasks that is at work here. The greater the contingency there is, the less our understanding of why things are one way rather than another.[86]

The Nature of Actuality

I proposed in Chapter 1 an amplification of Tarski's recursive schema to specify the makes-true relation in a possible world w_i and thereby to define the notion of truth in world w_i. S is true *simpliciter* when there is a possible world w such that S is true in world w, and w is the actual world. Therefore, in order to understand the notion of truth *(simpliciter)*, we must specify what it means to say that a particular possible world is the actual one. An analogous problem will face anyone whose theory falls under the general schema for an account of truth which says that S is true if and only if there is a p such that S means that p, and p. For, as we have seen, the first part ("S means that p") falls within the purview of a theory of language, or semantics, or the philosophy of language, and it does not especially illuminate the nature of truth, while the second part ("and p") offers incomplete illumination. We need something more like "S is true if and only if there is a p such that S means that p, and p is a fact" or "S is true if and only if there is a p such that S means that p, and p holds." (I do not mean to foreclose the *ontological* question of whether p refers to facts, or states of affairs, or situations, or events, or things and their properties and relations, or whatever. A full account of truth will specify what kind of entities it is that stands in the makes-true relation to statements.)

Once we reject simply ending the account with "and p," we must add some *verb* after p. Which verb is appropriate will depend upon the answer to the ontological question. If p refers to a fact, we will need to add that p is a fact that *holds;* if p refers to a state of affairs, we will need to add that p *obtains;* if it refers to a situation, we will need to add that the situation is *realized;* if it refers to events, we will need to add that these events *occur* or *hap-*

pen; if it refers to objects, we will need to add that these objects *exist;* if it refers to something else, we will need to add that this thing is *real* (or, in some traditions, that it *is* or has *being*). If the account of truth refers to a possible world ("*S* is true in world *w*"), then we will need to add that this world is *actual.*

We would like to understand what is involved in something's holding, or obtaining, or being realized, or occurring, or existing, or being real, or being actual. Call this the *ontological* question. Some of these notions might be explained in terms of others, but all raise similar issues. Is there some way to break out of this circle of notions, or are they so fundamental that they cannot be explained in terms of anything else? Any adequate theory of truth will have to face the ontological question in one or another of its forms.

Let us suppose, to focus our attention and in accordance with Chapter 1, that we have a general account of a statement's holding true in some possible world, utilizing the makes-true relation of that world and that world's set of absolutely subvenient truths. In terms of this account we can explain what it is for something to exist, occur, etc. in that possible world. This narrows our ontological question to this one: what is it for a possible world to be *actual?* Can we explain this, or are we stuck with (to paraphrase James Joyce) the ineluctable modality of the actual?

David Lewis has presented a theory according to which "actual" is an indexical term, referring when used in any possible world to that very world. Just as "here" in a statement refers to the place where the utterer of the statement is, so "actual" refers to the possible world where an utterer is located. All possible worlds are on a par (this is Lewis's "modal realism"), and each one is correctly termed "actual" by its own inhabitants.[87] (Some possible worlds will not have language-using or sentient inhabitants, and so will not be "actual" *to* anyone. A possible world is a world that could be actual—so it usually is thought, yet on Lewis's account it is impossible for some possible worlds to be actual.) Lewis's theory treats all possible worlds in an undesirably symmetrical fashion.

What stronger claim do we make, then, when we say of our world that it is the actual one? (An occupant of some other possible world, after all, would say the same thing of his world.) Is it that our world contains us? But his possible world contains him and his friends. The situation seems symmetric between his world and ours. Is it that my world is actual because it contains *me,* and because I exist?[88] (You may say the same.) But a denizen of any possible world would say that *he* exists. Is it that I cannot doubt that I exist, or that I can extinguish such a doubt by rehearsing a Cartesian argument? But could not a character in a work of fiction also recite such an argument, and does his stating it prove that he exists?[89] (And even if I do indubitably and certainly exist, even if my consciousness has some particular quality that can be realized only in actuality, identifying existence and actuality by this route does not tell me in what actuality consists. An epistemological route to actuality, even one that is certain, is not the same as an ontological understanding of actuality.) To insist that my religion is the correct one, or that the custom of my society is the appropriate one, merely because it is mine seems unduly parochial.

The nonsymmetrical theory that we need, it seems, would present a general description D that applies only to the actual world, a description that not only marks it as the actual world but that successfully bears the burden of *explaining* why that world is the actual one. Such a description would provide us with an answer to the ontological question. This requirement on the description is a stringent one and is not easily satisfied, even by very powerful descriptions. A complete description of the actual world would apply only to it but would not explain why that world is actual. A statement of the initial conditions of the actual world and of the laws governing it, supposing that the world is deterministic, would explain everything *in* the actual world, but it would not explain why *that* world is actual. Every other possible deterministic world also would have its own laws and initial conditions, and hence there also would be a description that would uniquely pick *it* out.

The following paragraphs are quite speculative first attempts at an answer. Perhaps they will spur others to do better.[90]

We now are looking for a general description of the actual world that would explain why it is the actual world. Derek Parfit formulates the notion of a property special enough to explain why something having it exists in "Why Is There a Universe?"[91] Some possible worlds would fit some description or other that would explain, if that world were actual, why it was. Other possible worlds will have no such explanatory property hold uniquely of them. We may not know why something with that property exists or must exist, but the property is so special that it would be too great a coincidence if a world existed and it also had that property yet there was *no* explanatory connection between its existing and having that property. Let us call such a property a sufficient explanatory property (an SEP).

A sufficient explanatory property will place a world at the end point (or some other special point, perhaps the exact center) of some (salient and special) dimension D. For example, when the dimension is degree of complexity, being the simplest possible world would be an SEP, and so would being the most complex possible world. Other dimensions will give rise to other SEPs, for instance, the familiar ones of being the most perfect world, the best of all possible worlds, and the most beautiful world. Parfit terms a situation of various possible worlds existing a *global* possibility. (One global possibility is that all possible worlds exist, another is that none do, another is that several of a certain sort do, etc.)

We can build the following line of thought on Parfit's notion. Let us suppose that all possible worlds exist that *do* fit some general description or other that would explain their actual existence, supposing they do actually exist. So what we have supposed is that one particular global possibility holds, namely that all possible worlds exist that have some SEP or other.

Not all logically possible worlds, not all logically consistent worlds, are at the end or some other special point of a specially salient dimension. Not every consistent world possesses an SEP. Only the worlds that do possess SEPs exist. (Shall we say that only the ones that possess SEPs really are *possible*, thereby delineating a notion of real possibility that is narrower than logical consistency?)

When we suppose that one particular global possibility holds, namely that all possible worlds exist that do fit some general description or other that would explain their actual existence, supposing they do actually exist, we have offered what itself is a special description, call it N, of that global possibility. And this description is one that would explain why it holds if indeed this is the global possibility that does hold. N is itself an SEP.

And why is N the property of the global possibility that holds, rather than some other description that would uniquely describe and explain some other global possibility if it held? Why is N the SEP that holds rather than some other SEP? N is the least restrictive description (one level up); it admits *all* descriptions that would explain the actuality of possible worlds. Being the least restrictive description is itself an SEP along a dimension that SEPs are arrayed along.

And why, two levels up, do we have "least restrictive description of the global possibility" as the description that explains why N holds, rather than some other description of some other global property? What description at the third level picks out "least restrictive description" at the second level? What SEP does being the least restrictive description itself have? Shall we say that at the third level also it is the least restrictive, or the least arbitrary? Or shall we say that there is only *one* least restrictive one, while there are many that tie for most restrictive (and so these are not special enough to explain why the actuality is as they describe), and that there also are many in-between ones that therefore are less special than the extremal one of being least restrictive? And so at some level do we reach the description of "most special descriptive property," an SEP that continues to apply to itself at still higher levels? By this route, we might hope to arrive at an explanatory description that applies (downward through various levels) uniquely to the actual world, or at least that applies only to those of the possible worlds that do exist. Call this the Least Arbitrary Theory.

We can find an example of an SEP that is not at the end of a special dimension but smack in the center, in an analogue of Richard Feynman's formulation of quantum mechanics. According to that path-integration formulation, all possible ways that something can happen, all ways that are given positive probability in the wave function, affect the result that does occur.[92] The analogue of Feynman's procedure would be to hold that the framework of all actual physical possibilities, set by the laws of the actual world, or (alternatively) the wave function of the actual world, is simply the average of all logical possibilities. Our world might not be a special world at the end of a salient dimension, but simply *an average world.* But being exactly average might itself be a special characteristic.

The sum over all possibilities offers a structural and general criterion of actuality, which is an advantage. The form of the theory is that the actual world is some function (in this case, the average) of all possible worlds. That is a desirably neutral form, less arbitrary than starting with *given* initial conditions. However, it still leaves the question of which particular function relates the actual world to all the possible ones. We might, at this point, seek the least arbitrary function, and hold it is that one that satisfies the most symmetry conditions, and that will be the *averaging* of all the possible worlds. (Are there some differential weights to the averages, and do those also satisfy some symmetry conditions? Won't maximum symmetry require giving each world equal weight?)

Recall again David Lewis's theory that "actual" is an indexical term, referring when used in any possible world to that very world, and recall also the view that identifies a world as uniquely actual simply because it is the world that we are in. If we seek a theory of actuality that is neither indexical nor parochial, then that theory will have to use some general description that explains why a (possible) world is actual. If we add that the general description should be the least arbitrary one (so as to avoid the question "Why does that arbitrary theory hold?"), then our theories are considerably restricted. Examples are the two theories we have presented, the Least Arbitrary Theory and the Feynman-like theory.

We have offered an account of actuality in terms of Parfit's notion of a sufficient explanatory property. All worlds are actual that possess some SEP. This does not get us to a unique actual world, for there are different SEPs. And given a dimension along which an SEP is located, this dimension might present two SEPs, one at each extreme end; even one such SEP might allow more than one actual world if different worlds can tie in having a maximal score along that dimension, that is, if different possible worlds can equally possess that particular SEP.

This theory does not yield the one unique actual world that we may have hoped for, and countenancing more than one such opens the notion of truth to a new relativism: whether or not a statement is true might be relative to which actual world (of the several such) is being considered. Moreover, I must express some worries about the notion of a sufficient explanatory property. What determines whether something is a sufficient explanatory property? Is it not what we find to be explanatorily pleasing? Won't this be relative to our own conceptual scheme, sense of simplicity and elegance, notion of surprisingness, and so on? For each logically possible world w_j, cannot some possibly quite artificial dimension be cooked up so that the world w_j falls at some extreme end of that dimension? To demarcate the sufficient explanatory properties, must we first find an objectively correct solution to Nelson Goodman's problem of "grue" and "bleen," and to all analogous problems?[93] Some might claim that this shows a further way in which truth is relative. Actuality is dependent upon SEPs, and which properties are SEPs, and which dimensions they are arrayed along, are relative matters, relative to the features of a conceptual scheme and to the past history of conceptual development that makes some properties explanatorily illuminating and sufficient explanatory properties. On this view, actuality would be relative, not because it is indexical but because it is explained in terms of the notion of a sufficient explanatory property that itself is a relative notion. This would make the notion of truth relative, not in the innocuous sense that "true in world w_i" refers to a possible world but because "true in the actual world" refers to a notion, actuality, which itself is relative to features of a conceptual scheme. However, if the notion of an SEP cannot be specified in a more objective manner than this, it would not be an appropriate basis for an ontology of actuality. What is needed is a sufficient explanatory property that cuts so deeply (that we are confident) that its specialness is not the product or effect of human psychology but rather an independently existing deep structural divide that we discover, one that distinguishes whatever possesses it from what does not.

The Ultimate Theory of the World

Physicists seek a theory that will unify all known forces of nature. Four forces currently are known: the strong force, the weak force, electromagnetism, and gravitation. String theory, and its generalization in the nascent M-theory, is the most promising (and the most recent) attempt to accomplish this unification. Within string theory, charges and masses arise from the vibration of strings, and this vibration is affected by the space within which it occurs. If there were additional spatial dimensions branching out orthogonally from each point within the standard three-dimensional space, if there were finite dimensions curled up in so tiny a form that we have not yet noticed them, and if these dimensions took a particular form or shape, then this might yield the four forces of nature as we know them.[94] Currently, space-times of ten and eleven dimensions are being investigated.

But these additional curled-up finite dimensions, if they are to yield the forces that we know, may have to be very strangely shaped indeed, not simply tiny circular loops emerging from each point of three-dimensional space, but grotesquely complicated and contorted figures, known as Calabi-Yau spaces or shapes. These have been investigated by mathematicians (starting with Calabi and Yau). There are many thousands of such shapes that could give rise to a universe of our type, and additionally there are untold numbers of such shapes that could give rise to universes of types other than ours. Discovering that one such contorted Calabi-Yau shape could give rise to our exact universe would seem to leave the physics of this particular universe very contingent indeed. The question would remain unanswered: why do the additional spatial dimensions take that one particular Calabi-Yau shape rather than any of the myriad others that could be taken?

Finding such a particular shape might well constitute a unification (and not just a conjunction) of the four known existing forces by showing how they all arise from or within one particular mechanism. Hence we see that a unification of all known forces can be different from a removal of all contingency. For unless the particular Calabi-Yau shape generating our universe had some very special property (such as being the *simplest* Calabi-Yau shape) that holds uniquely of it, that shape would provide a unification, yet it would hold very contingently. For it seems possible that any of the other Calabi-Yau shapes also could have held.

Might not these intuitions about possibility be all wrong, though? The intuitions are shaped, after all, on a subuniversal scale. An analogy would be intuitions about infinity. Intuitions grounded in finite numbers do not extend to the infinite; for instance, no finite set can be placed into a 1–1 correspondence with a proper subset of itself, with nothing left over, yet an infinite set can be. So, too, might not our intuitions about what is possible for the universe as a whole, intuitions that are grounded in experience of only small parts of the universe, be inaccurate and unreliable? We think that other universes are possible, that other Calabi-Yau-shaped dimensions, in addition to our own, are possible. Maybe they really are not.

But why not? They can be consistently described, after all. Mathematicians have done so. Yet perhaps the mathematical theories that describe these other shapes are not actually consistent. Since Godel, we have known that we cannot prove the consistency of a system (powerful enough to express elementary number theory) within the system itself, that is, without using even more powerful means than the system itself embodies. And we have known since the discovery of the paradoxes (that is, inconsistencies) of intuitive set theory that a theory can appear consistent and transparent and also generate many appealing consequences yet still harbor contradictions. Unknowingly, it can discuss or treat of what are actually impossibilities. Not everything that looks consistent really is possible.

Our language, including our mathematical language, is a representational device that has worked reasonably well in the domains, and on the scales, that we have used it in thus far. Still, this representational system may not be the best possible one, and in particular, like naive set theory, it may present impossibilities as possible. Our actual universe, and the Calabi-Yau figure that generates it, appear within our representational system as just one possibility among others. But perhaps in a better representational system it will appear as *unique*. There, the particular Calabi-Yau space that generates our physics will be the *only* one that can be represented. If that were the case, the actual universe would not (appear to) be contingent, after all.

String theorists currently study space-times of 10 or 11 dimensions. These numbers themselves seem quite arbitrary. Even if they are convenient to yield the actual physics of our universe, why was there exactly that number of dimensions; why not 27, or 5,395,647? Even a space of zero dimensions is not so very special. Zero is just one finite number among the others.

The string theorists concentrate upon space-times of 10 or 11 dimensions because various constraints that they find it plausible to impose upon a theory, constraints such as supersymmetry and the constraint that there be no more than one time dimension, have the consequence that there are no more than eleven dimensions.[95] Yet there might be occasion to relax these constraints in the future.

It would be interesting to investigate the structure and the consequences of a string (or of the related brane) theory with a denumerable infinity of dimensions. This would contain as many dimensions as there are natural numbers 1, 2, 3, . . . Things would be very nice, of course, if there were only one such theory that was constructable, and if it yielded the physics of our universe. Infinity would be a very special starting point indeed. One couldn't easily ask why there is a denumerable infinity of dimensions rather than some (particular, arbitrary) finite number.

One also might investigate the structure and consequences of a string (or brane) theory with a continuum of dimensions, that is, the number of dimensions that is the same as the number of points on a line. (All lines, no matter what their length, have the same number of points, and this is more points than there are natural numbers, more than a denumerable infinity of points, as was proved by Georg Cantor. If the continuum hypothesis is correct, the number of points on a line is the very next order of infinity that is greater than a denumerable infinity. There is no distinct kind of infinity that comes between these two. And you don't get more points by going up from a line to a plane.) Again, things would be very nice if there were only one such string theory that was constructable, and if it yielded the physics of our universe. That too would be a very special starting point, and one couldn't easily ask why there is a continuum of dimensions rather than a denumerable infinity, or some still higher order of infinity.[96]

So here is one form that an ultimate theory might take. It is the unique physics of a string or brane theory with a denumerable infinity or continuum of spatial (and hence space-time) dimensions. (The previous sentence states an SEP.) Might there be *two* actually existing worlds, one with a denumerable infinity and the other with a continuum of dimensions?

Another possibility is that the number of space-time dimensions might change or evolve. Physicists currently are investigating ten or eleven dimensional space-times. It would be very satisfying if one could show that starting with a denumerable infinity of dimensions, the system would evolve in time so as eventually to collapse to ten or eleven dimensions. That history would leave such a ten- or eleven-dimensional space-time as nonarbitrary, since it would arise from a nonarbitrary starting point. (We might then wonder whether it has yet reached its stable final number.)

But where does space-time itself come from? Brian Greene reports that, within string theory, space-time can be viewed as stitched together from many strings undergoing the same orderly graviton pattern of vibration. This would constitute what is called a *coherent* state of strings. A theory of the origin of space-time, then, would see it as arising from something else, from an *incoherent* state of strings, which occurs in no place (space doesn't yet exist) and at no time (for time also doesn't exist).[97]

What is being imagined, then, is a more primitive form of space, call it S_{10}, and a more primitive form of time, call it T_{10}, as the arenas within which there are strings or branes (or more primitive versions of these too, call them B_{10}) in incoherent states. Within these arenas, B_{10}, which is "located" in S_{10} and T_{10}, evolves through T_{10} to become strings in (ten- or eleven-dimensional) space-time. (In following our previous line of thought, it might be seen whether these more primitive forms could give rise to strings in a denumerably infinite space-time or in a space-time with a continuum of dimensions.) And perhaps B_{10}, S_{10}, and T_{10} all arise from even more primitive branes B_9, located in an even more primitive space S_9 and time T_9, which evolved through T_9 to become $[B_{10}, S_{10}, T_{10}]$. We can continue tracing this process backward until we reach an underived and nonevolved initial most-primitive state, call it $[B_0, S_0, T_0]$. It would be interesting to know what character this might have.

Eventually we might reach the following situation. We start with the premiss that some universe exists. And we add the premiss that it is not arbitrary what universe exists.[98] From the premiss that a nonarbitrary universe exists, we might then reach the conclusion that a universe exists that is generated by a string or brane theory of infinite dimensions, one that has (or began with) either a denumerable infinity of dimensions or a continuum of dimensions. (Or perhaps we might reach the conclusion that both of these nonarbitrary universes exist.) Thereby would the degree of contingency of the actual world be maximally reduced. I don't claim, though, that it is reduced to zero, or that the actual world would be shown to be necessary. Have we formulated here, though, a *surrogate* for the ontological argument, the best substitute that secular money can buy? It would be difficult for someone to ask *why* an arbitrary universe doesn't exist, or to complain that it is arbitrary that one doesn't. (Does this person think that arbitrariness is the natural state, or not?)

Another form of deep explanatory theory also has been investigated. A number of theorists have suggested reproductive models in cosmology, wherein some universes give rise to others, bubbling out as component parts.[99] John Wheeler added the idea that an "offspring" universe might not be identical with the universe that gave rise to it; it might vary somewhat. Lee Smolin then took the step of applying evolutionary considerations directly to cosmology.[100] Those particular characteristics that enable a universe to give rise to progeny, and are themselves inherited by the progeny universes, will be selected for. Within such an evolutionary cosmological scheme, one might try to explain traits of the present universe as traits that would be selected for and hence possessed by almost all universes.

Smolin argues as follows. Within the framework of known physical laws, new universes can develop out of black holes. There will be selection for universes good at producing further universes, that is, good at producing black holes. Black holes come from collapsing stars. Only some values of physical constants are conducive to producing such stars, and so there will be selection for universes with those precise values of the physical constants. If we assume that our universe is a typical member of the collection of actual universes, this yields the prediction that the values of fundamental physical constants in our universe will be close to optimal for producing black holes, that is, that slight variations in these constants will cause a falling off in the production of black holes (and hence of progeny universes). Smolin lists further assumptions of his model: that the parameters of the initial universe (or of one of several initial universes) and of all those created from it are such that each one gives rise to at least one universe; also, that the form of the physical laws does not change from parent to child universe, but the values of the parameters change at random in small ways. The first universe is short-lived and gives rise to another slight variant, and so on until one is reached at random that gives rise to several progeny via black holes, and these give rise to further ones, some variants of which are even more fecund in universes, so that such traits spread in the population of universes. (It also will be illuminating to relax Smolin's assumptions of fixed laws in order to see what laws might be generated from random beginnings within a more general evolutionary model.) These ideas are suggestive and original, and they raise further questions.[101]

It is not clear that Smolin's framework does allow us to say what the vast majority of universes will be like. Let us grant that universes that do not reproduce themselves will be sparse among universes, and that being a producer of black holes is conducive to reproduction. There might be another method M_2 of reproduction that is vastly different from that method M_1 operating within our universe and its immediate ancestors. This other method M_2 would not merely vary the values of parameters of the laws of the actual universe; it would involve different laws. Such universes would exist as a result of a process that happened to generate an initial one of them, from which the remainder are descended. Suppose that universes of our sort, reproducing by method M_1, are quite fecund. Every such universe gives rise to 10^{10} descendants, and so does each of these descendants, so we end up with quite a lot of them. However, the other method M_2 is even more fecund: every such universe embodying it gives rise to 15^{25} descendants. Universes of our type, though quite fecund, constitute a minority of the total number of universes, so it is surprising that ours has the character that it has. Nevertheless, even if universes of our sort are outnumbered, it still might be explainable that ours has the character it does, provided that well-structured probabilistic explanations do explain even low-probability outcomes, when these occur.[102]

Smolin's framework is a very suggestive one and opens possibilities for explaining the holding of fundamental laws. Consider the question of why the world is quantum mechanical. The question is not what evidence there is that the world *is* quantum mechanical—that evidence is overwhelming—but why the world takes that quantum-mechanical form. What makes quantum mechanics hold?

The framework of evolutionary cosmology might provide an answer. Suppose that quantum-mechanical laws, and their accompanying non-locality, enable universes to be longer-lived, and hence these laws raise the probability of their universe's lasting to reproductive age and long afterward. Hence, most of the existing universes should exhibit a quantum-mechanical character. For instance, if quantum mechanics, through its superluminal influence, contributes to the homogeneity and hence to the long-term stability of wide-scale universes, and if nothing else that is feasible would contribute to this as well, and if large and stable universes will yield more progeny universes, then large, stable universes would tend to be quantum mechanical.[103] We then would have a (possible) explanation of why quantum mechanics holds in this universe that we inhabit.

Might quantum mechanics also contribute to the generative potential of a universe, making it more likely that it will give rise to progeny universes? Consider the hypothesis that new universes might be produced within black holes. The *existence* of black holes does not depend upon quantum mechanics. Their existence follows from gravitational collapse creating an entity so dense that the escape velocity from it is greater than the maximum possible velocity (the speed of light). However, how black holes behave as their volume is squeezed, and so whether they give rise to another universe "on a bounce," will depend upon quantum-mechanical effects and upon the nature of quantum gravity. Hence quantum mechanics might play a role in whether, and how, progeny universes are given rise to. That would add another place for quantum mechanics within an evolutionary cosmology, viz. in the generating process (as well as in the character of the result).

If quantum-mechanical universes reproduce more (by reproducing more frequently or by producing a larger litter), and if that is a heritable trait, and also if they survive better, then we would expect the characteristic of being quantum mechanical to move to fixation in the population of universes. That is, we would expect all universes to be quantum mechanical.[104] In such a case, we might even be in a position to speak of the *function* of quantum mechanics in precisely the sense that the evolutionary biologist speaks of function.[105]

Earlier we considered a vast generalization of Feynman's path-integral approach by treating the actual world as an average world, the average of all the possibilities. We then faced the question, in arriving at such an average, of what weights each of these possibilities possessed. We might now suggest that it is only stable worlds, or worlds of a sufficient stability, that enter into the average. Better, let the weight of each world as it enters into the computation of the average be that world's degree of stability (i.e., expected long-livedness). We live in an average world, but not in a world of average stability, because the more stable worlds carry greater weight in determining what is the (weighted) average.[106]

These thoughts about the cosmological evolution of quantum mechanics are *extremely* speculative, I admit, and they are likely to fall by the wayside. But perhaps explanations can be offered for other physical traits of the universe. Charles Peirce (in a discussion of induction) said that universes are not as plentiful as blackberries. But what if they are? Might we thereby gain insight into why general laws exist, why there is great simplicity in the theory of the universe, in what form induction holds, and so on? Beginning with some number of universes of random character, most of which are infertile, by chance some might have the capacity to reproduce themselves, and to give rise to heritable traits. Notice that here we do not retain Smolin's assumption that the laws of our universe hold, with evolutionary processes only setting their parameters. Instead, start with a (large?) number of random universes with different laws, and some with no laws at all. By chance, among these randomly existing universes, several short-lived ones temporarily are able to replicate themselves. Once that process begins, it is off and running. By formulating a Generalized Framework of Evolutionary Cosmology which drops Smolin's particular assumptions (e.g., that the laws of quantum mechanics hold in every existing universe), one might explain how some laws, and how particular ones, move to fixation in a population of universes. Thereby one might explain, rather than just assume, the emergence and existence of these laws in a typical universe.[107]

Might such an evolutionary cosmology even have implications for issues concerning mathematical and logical truth and necessity? It would be remarkable if some (purported) necessities could return by this backdoor route, with their character as *necessary* being explained as (somehow) conducive to any universe's survival and reproduction. Would we conclude from this type of explanation that the purported necessities were necessary after all, or that they were not? (Or would the question of their necessity be transcended?)

Within evolutionary cosmology, scientific laws might be viewed as the heritable structure of a universe, akin to what in biology would be an organism's genetic endowment. An evolutionary process requires heritable traits, variation, and selection. A universe with scientific laws has sufficiently stable structure to endure to reproductive age, and a structure that (with variation) can be passed on to its offspring. Laws constitute a universe's heritable traits, and the vast majority of the population of universes will be law-governed. That's why there are scientific laws.

Why is there an objective world? According to our account in Chapter 2, this is the question of why our universe contains things and laws that are invariant under various transformations. Within an evolutionary cosmology, the invariance of scientific laws under transformations might contribute to their heritability. If the reproductive process of universes changed every trait, so that no trait of an offspring universe was identical with that of its parent, then there would be no heritable traits. (On the other hand, if no trait ever changed in any respect, there would not be the variation upon which selection acts.) Suppose that the reproductive process of a universe U involves a transformation T. The offspring universes of U will differ from their parent in accordance with the transformation. If a particular law L is invariant under that particular transformation T, then if L is a trait of the parent universe, it also will be a trait of the offspring (assuming that none of the other reproductive transformations alters L).

Invariance under transformations thus increases the heritability of a law. The greater the transformation that a law is invariant under, and the wider the number of such transformations, the greater its heritability. The vast majority of the universes that exist through the processes of cosmological evolution, therefore, will exhibit laws that are invariant under a wide range of significant transformations. *Evolutionary cosmology gives us objective worlds.* Such invariance, we have seen, is exactly what constitutes objectiveness.

II

THE HUMAN WORLD AS PART
OF THE OBJECTIVE WORLD

4

The Realm of Consciousness

The Function of Consciousness

Consciousness, the conscious awareness of things, plays a widespread role in our lives and our thoughts, and in our conception of ourselves. So it is not surprising that philosophers have devoted considerable attention to it. A large number of fundamental philosophical issues concern consciousness. There are value issues: Is consciousness the *only* valuable thing? Why not live in an experience machine? How central is consciousness to the value of our lives? (Writers on immortality would not be pleased to learn that we *do* continue after death, but in a state akin to a permanent coma.) There are ethical issues: Why does consciousness have ethical weight, so that it is one of the properties in virtue of which a being is owed ethical behavior?

There are epistemological issues: Do we know anything other than our own experiences? Do we know, how can we know, that we are not living in an experience machine, floating in a tank in a laboratory near Alpha Centauri, being given exactly the experiences that we already have had? And might a prelude to our being removed from the tank be that the scientists, to cushion the shock, have fed us the experience of reading about this question in a philosophy book?[1] And how can we know that another being is consciously aware of anything, instead of always simply acting as a nonconscious automaton—the problem of other minds?

There are metaphysical issues: Is something's status as real just constituted by experiences cohering in a certain way? There is the mind-body problem: What is the relation of conscious experience to neurophysiological and to physical happenings?

Yet, despite the ubiquity of consciousness in our lives, it is surprisingly difficult to say what consciousness does, what consciousness is *for*. What is its function, and why is consciousness necessary for that function? How does consciousness, that apparently most subjective of things, fit into an objective world?

Whatever conscious awareness does, there may be some other (logically or biologically) possible way to accomplish that task. The function of conscious awareness need not be something that only it can do. Even if there could be some other way to get blood around the body, still, the function of the heart is to circulate the blood. An alternative mode of circulating the blood would involve different organs, different machinery. That machinery does not exist, and, without it, the heart is needed to accomplish the task. The rest of the bodily machinery that actually exists, by itself, cannot circulate the blood. The heart adds something, and it makes a difference. That is why it was selected for. To ask about the function of consciousness, therefore, is *not* to ask what could not be done, in principle, without consciousness' being present. It is to ask what consciousness actually does, what (in its actual context) it serves to do. It does not matter if that same thing could be done in a vastly different situation by other means not involving consciousness.[2]

That consciousness serves to do a certain thing is not enough to mark that as its biological function. Consciousness might be a side effect of organized brain structure that was developed for other purposes.[3] Selection shaped the brain to perform those other functions, and the neural structures, once they existed, gave rise to (or even constituted) consciousness, and so also get used for that further activity. Consciousness can do something, even something important, without that constituting the biological function of consciousness. Only if the actual history of selection for instituting the brain's structure or—it is important to add—for maintaining that structure over time involves the brain's doing what consciousness specially enables it to do, will doing that be what consciousness is *for*. By and large, I will be concerned with what consciousness specially enables us to do. The answer, and the neuroscientific information connected with this answer, may, however, provide some grounds for thinking that this activity of consciousness constitutes its function.

We want an answer about the function of consciousness to come at the right level of detail. If consciousness does have a function, it would no doubt be true, but not illuminating, to be told that the function of consciousness is to aid in maximizing inclusive fitness. That does not distinguish the function of consciousness from that of other biological organs; the heart also aids in maximizing inclusive fitness. For consciousness, we want to know something comparable to saying that the function of the heart is to circulate the blood. And we want to know not just what particular difference consciousness makes, but *how* it makes this difference, how it is that consciousness accomplishes its task.

Any adequate theory of the function of consciousness should cohere with neuroscientific knowledge about processes and events in the brain. Whatever the function of consciousness is, it must be something that the brain is able to carry out. This means, at the very least, that current knowledge must not already show that some purported function is not feasible. For instance, the facts of sensory transduction of different sensory inputs into one kind of signal make it impossible (or highly doubtful) that the function of qualitative experience (although it might provide information about the world) is to provide a certain specified type of information that mirrors the world.

It also means something that is more interesting. The neurological correlates of consciousness should be something that does (underlie) the carrying out of *that* function. We should be able to see how the neurological correlate does implement this function.[4] Moreover, we should see how the detailed contours of that neurological correlate serve to implement this function, and this should lead to the prediction and discovery of new and surprising psychological facts (or at least to the explanation of previously known puzzling facts) about the limits, errors, illusions, and peculiar contours of that functional activity.[5] Compare the way in which neuroscientific knowledge about vision helps explain certain visual illusions; the way in which neuroscientific knowledge of memory processes helps explain certain limitations and failures of memory; and the way in which neuroscientific investigations of visual imagery explain limits of the spatial extent and resolution of images.[6] In a similar fashion, a theory of the function of consciousness should be able to predict new and surprising details and consequences of, e.g., the damage to the striate cortex producing blindsight (and also make predictions for parallel phenomena, if these exist, involving other sensory modalities, e.g., for "deaf-hearing").

If some activity or result is the function of conscious awareness, if the brain was shaped to carry out that important function, then some broad, previously puzzling features of brain activity, such as the extraordinarily large amount of back projection and crosstalk, should find an intelligible place as serving and implementing that function. We then should be able to understand why that (previously) puzzling feature exists.

In investigating the function of consciousness here, we do not seek a philosophers' *definition* of consciousness or its necessary and sufficient conditions. An accurate delineation of whatever a term applies to need not tell us that thing's function, and an understanding of its function need not precisely delineate exactly what satisfies the term. Yet even non-Aristotelians can recognize that knowing something's function is a great step toward understanding it.

Gradations of Awareness

We distinguish *conscious entities* from nonconscious ones, people from stones, according to their capacities. Among entities possessing the capacity, we distinguish those that are in a *conscious state* (awake, activated) from those that are not. And we speak of those who are conscious (conscious entities in a conscious state) as being *conscious of* something, being aware of it, and (sometimes) of having a conscious experience with its own felt quality. It might not be simply a matter of yes or no, but of more or less. Each of these might come in degrees: the greater the capacity, the more conscious an organism is; the more activated the state, the more conscious it is; and the greater one's awareness of something, the more conscious of it one is.

The basic notion is the third one, *being aware of something.* To be a conscious being is to have the capacity to be aware of things; to be conscious (awake, activated) at a time is to have the power at that time to be aware of things. Being consciously aware *of* things is the point of consciousness.[7]

There seem to be two kinds of conscious awareness, one involving a qualitative feel or phenomenology, one not. Sensory experience (visual, auditory, tactile, gustatory, etc.) gives us awareness of objects, events, processes, facts in the world. We are consciously aware of these objects, events, etc., and our sensory experiences of them have a certain qualitative feel. Conscious awareness, however, need not distinctively involve sensory experience. I can think about an intellectual problem, and be aware of doing so, without any distinctive sensory experience. I can remember that $2 + 2 = 4$, and be aware of doing so, without any sensory experience or any experience with a qualitative feel; I can remember an event, and be aware of doing that, without any current (external) sensory experience. For each of these kinds of conscious awareness (the kind with a qualitative feel that sensory experience involves, and the kind of nonsensory mental states of awareness without any qualitative feel), we can ask what such conscious awareness is for: what does it do, what was there selection for its doing?

Being consciously aware of things is the point of consciousness, but what is the point of awareness? Awareness enables organisms to contour and fit their behavior to objects, facts, and aspects of situations (that they are aware of). Taking account of facts, present or distant, in one's behavior tends to make one fare better than simply stumbling around blindly.

Since there are different grades of awareness, there are different levels or kinds of fitting behavior to circumstances. Differing degrees of fit can be achieved through different grades of awareness. We should not be too quick to denigrate a low grade of awareness from the standpoint of a higher one. Even quite minimal levels of awareness can be better than none at all. Some people have wondered how a complex organ such as the eye *could* have evolved, when it is composed of interconnected parts, all of which contribute to, and seem essential to, its functioning. Isn't it too great a coincidence that they all arose simultaneously? However, Richard Dawkins has pointed out that no such lucky coincidence is needed. The slightest sensitivity to light confers an advantage (e.g., in detecting the presence of a predator blocking light), as compared to no light sensitivity at all. Each primitive stage and component of increasing sensitivity would be selected for, as would their further developing and their dovetailing together.[8] Similarly with other limited kinds of awareness that are not visual.

We can identify what seem to be seven increasing gradations of awareness. (However, perhaps there are fewer if some of these different descriptions actually pick out the very same level.) At the first level of awareness, an external object or situation or an internal state *registers* upon an organism. At the second level, it *registers that it registers* (where this is not merely the same thing registering again). At the third level, the organism is *aware* of something. (Might this be identical with the second level?) At the fourth level, the organism is aware that it is aware of the thing. We can term this *conscious awareness*. At the fifth level, the organism *notices* the external object or situation or internal state, or some of its aspects. (Is this identical with the fourth level?) At the sixth level, the organism pays *attention* to that. At the seventh level, the organism *concentrates* upon that thing. (There also are two further gradations that might usefully be considered: *absorption* and *flow*.)[9] The first grade, registering without conscious awareness, might seem to be no kind of awareness at all. However, the surprising phenomenon of blindsight shows that this impression is misleading.[10]

In a case of blindsight, a person (with damage to a portion of the primary visual cortex) reports that he is having no visual experience, that he is not seeing anything, yet when he is asked to guess whether he is being presented with a large drawing of an X or an O, he succeeds in answering correctly significantly above a chance level.[11] Here we seem to have a case in which the X or O figure does register on the person, yet he is not aware of its registering. Stretching language somewhat, we might say that he is aware of the figure but is not *consciously aware* of it, in that he is not aware that he is aware of it.

A driver can drive absentmindedly for miles along a road, engrossed in thought, and then suddenly realize to his surprise that he has driven some distance, and perhaps even has arrived at home. He did not drive off the road, so the earlier fact that he was approaching a curve certainly registered upon him; he responded to it by some turning of the steering wheel. What gradation of awareness does this driver occupy? Are the curves simply registering upon him, or was he aware of the curves? Was it that he was not consciously aware of them, in that he was not aware of being aware of them? Or should we say that he was consciously aware of them but was not noticing them? He certainly was not paying any attention to them.[12]

It is clear what the lowest grade of awareness does for us, as compared to no grade of awareness at all. (Here, I use the term "awareness" not for the third level but as a general term for all gradations, with registering at the lowest end.) Without things', facts', and situations' somehow registering upon us, we could not guide ourselves through the world; we could not act to use or to avoid objects. But what is the function of *conscious* awareness? Why is simple registering not always sufficient; what does that extra thing (the awareness of the awareness, the conscious awareness) enable us to do that could not be done, or done as well, in its absence?

Gradations in awareness enable, and hence are correlated with, gradations in capacity to fit behavior to aspects of situations. The greater the level of awareness of situations, the more finely and subtly the behavior can be matched to aspects of these situations. Since increased capabilities of matching behavior to situations brought accompanying benefits (as measured by increases in fitness), there was selection for these capacities.[13]

The Context of Consciousness

Let us begin a more detailed investigation of the function of conscious awareness. Many biological tasks get handled at a subconscious level, for instance, circulating blood, maintaining heartbeat, maintaining bodily temperature within a certain range, dilating the pupils of the eye, blinking when an object moves rapidly toward the eye. Consciousness is not needed to do these things, and it might get in the way.

In certain situations, there is one best thing to do. When an object is moving rapidly toward the eye, blinking protects the eye against injury. We could imagine circumstances under which blinking yields a worse result; for example, someone will kill you if you blink right then. But, in general and frequently enough, blinking when an object is moving rapidly toward your face is the best behavior available to you. And it was the best behavior available to your ancestors. There was evolutionary selection for performing that behavior in that situation. It now is hardwired, and done automatically.

In many situations in which there was one best thing to do in response to concurrent or very recent stimuli, in which one and only one thing maximized inclusive fitness, there was evolutionary selection for machinery that produced this behavior automatically. There was no need to choose among other available alternatives, and no gain from doing so. (Indeed, a conscious choice might slow an organism's reaction time, to its detriment.) When there was one right answer repeatedly in our evolutionary past, consciousness is not necessary to find it now.

However, because some organisms frequently enough face choices with no uniformly best alternative, prefixed rules were not wired in to make the selection automatically (or at any rate, evolution did not actually wire in such rules). The *context* for the operation of consciousness is a choice point, where evolution has left unsettled what is to be done. Being a choice point (from the point of view of evolution) is necessary for being a context of consciousness. Whether something is an (open) choice point, and so a context for consciousness, normally will not itself be a choice point. Evolution will have decided *that* automatically for the organism.

That something is an *evolutionary choice point* does not entail that it is a point at which the *organism makes choices*. At evolutionary choice points, it will not be prefixed what the organism does, but the organism's behavior may be determined at random or by some process that we would not term *choice*, e.g., Pavlovian conditioning or even perhaps operant conditioning. Nevertheless, the fact that evolutionary choice points are the context for consciousness suggests that the function of consciousness is somehow to aid in (or set the stage for) the making of choices.[14] We are conscious of what is or might be useful for choice. (Other "choices" have been made for us by evolution.) However, this does not yet tell us the particular function of consciousness. To know that, we need to know precisely how consciousness helps in choice; which particular aspect of choice-behavior does consciousness serve?

Let us first consider in more detail why organisms make choices at all. It is useful for organisms to behave, to move in different ways under different environmental or internal circumstances, to turn toward light, to get out of the heat, to move away from a nearby predator, to somehow change their own internal states. The local world is not completely uniform through space and time, and organisms do better under some conditions than under others; they do better in some environments than in others, and in a given environment they do better in one internal state than in another. Organisms have ways of registering their internal state and their environmental situation, and also ways in which this information differentially affects their motion. They have means of movement (in higher organisms, muscles and effector neurons), and they have sensory receptors that register environmental or internal facts or changes, and they have some connection, direct or indirect, between the receptors and the effectors. In human beings, all neurons that do not connect only with other neurons connect with muscles or with glands. The ultimate (biological) purpose of all the neuronal machinery is to change the body's position (by moving limbs or the whole body) or to change (or to maintain) its internal state, that is, to change it from what it otherwise would or might be.[15] (Should whatever more particular functions we find for consciousness and for intelligence therefore fall within the category of enabling brains to carry out these tasks and functions to better result?)

The body has the capacity to move and change itself, and it does so non-randomly. Random motion sometimes might help but it could just as easily harm. The body changes in response to changing internal or external information. Some aspects of the world are so fixed, insofar as the situation of the body is concerned, that the body does not have to register information about these aspects. If it simply behaves a certain way, that behavior will fit its situation. But other aspects of the external or internal environment vary, and different behavior is appropriate to those differing states. The body is not hard-wired to produce that behavior always and under all conditions, but only under certain detectable, that is, registrable (at better-than-chance level) conditions.

When these conditions are such that they are detectable by one or a combination of sensory organs, and when one behavioral response is reliably the best under these conditions, and when these conditions and their linkage with that particular behavior's being best held for long enough to be taken account of by evolutionary processes, then the behavior can be wired in as a simple reflex, which is activated under these conditions.[16]

The current world, however, is also different in its various specifics from the world in which our ancestors' (and our) simple reflexes evolved. But these ancestors also evolved modes of linking behavior to (evolutionarily) more transient conditions, through Pavlovian (classical) conditioning and through operant conditioning. By these means, behavior can usefully be linked to phenomena that are transient on an evolutionary scale but somewhat constant recently. Recently certain behavior in certain circumstances has led to certain beneficial consequences that were reinforcing or pursued as goals (because these consequences have been correlated over evolutionary time with enhancements of fitness). It is useful for current behavior to be attuned to such recent information. Although these recent specifics are new, the fact that some recent specifics or other matter is a long-standing one that was constant enough for evolution to take account of. Evolution provided our ancestors with a fixed (hardwired) capacity to take account of certain kinds of recent varying specifics. (Simple reflex behavior may be activated by information about wholly current phenomena, but the link between such phenomena and the desirability of the behavior is not itself a recent one.)

However, in certain circumstances, the most desirable behavior (as measured by its influence on inclusive fitness) cannot be prewired because it is not a function of combinations or correlations of current sensory information. There is not just one simple observational correlation to be found out or acted upon. The desirability of the action may depend on inferred properties, for instance, and the properties toward which optimal inference should be directed might depend also upon what alternatives for action are currently available, which itself is not a simple observational fact. The desirability of the action also may depend upon a variety of factors whose proper weight is context sensitive, where the contexts in their fully relevant particularity are so rarely repeated that no prewired rule will serve.[17] This suggests that consciousness plays some crucial role in the flexible adaptation of behavior to circumstance, but how exactly does consciousness do this?

The context of consciousness, we have said, is a choice point that evolution has left unsettled. It is plausible that consciousness gives decision processes a flexibility beyond that of prewired decision rules and the (unconscious) analyses that these utilize. The exact nature of this flexibility and the exact role that consciousness plays in it need to be elucidated.

It is useful to classify the kinds of possible views on the function of consciousness. (I leave aside the view that consciousness has no function.) The function of consciousness can be individual, to bring some benefit to the being who is conscious, or it can be social, to benefit other conspecifics. Under individual views, the function of events of consciousness can be to aid the individual in concurrent (or shortly successive) action or it can be to aid in later action, for instance, by placing something in memory so that it is available to automatically and nonconsciously guide action in the future. (An extreme version of such a view would hold that current action never is guided by current consciousness but only guided automatically by the effects of previous conscious awareness.)

Consciousness might aid the individual in his current choices in any of the following ways. It could add to the registering of some fact in the environment (such as takes place in blindsight) an additional *registering of that registering*, which aids in the more subtle control of action. It could aid in the *classification* of environmental facts, and hence in drawing upon knowledge and behavioral routines that are linked with particular classifications. Consciousness could aid in *feedback upon ongoing action* to enable it to more precisely fit the environment and achieve its goal. It could aid in selecting information relevant to choice from the vast welter of available information. It could facilitate more-extensive processing of information and more-complex weighing of facts that play a role in choice. Consciousness could aid in the ranking or reweighting of wants, desires, and goals in situations in which these conflict. And it could be the arena in which (nonpresent) answers to problems are figured out and developed through the gathering and weighing of diverse and previously unconnected considerations, and the drawing of implications from them.

The Zoom-Lens Theory

The *function* of conscious awareness is to enable action to be more accurately, precisely, subtly and flexibly oriented to the world. (I shall speak of other *roles* of consciousness at this chapter's end.) The truth property is that property of beliefs that explains why (statistically) we are more often successful in achieving the goals of our actions when we act upon such beliefs. Truth is what we do better acting upon. Awareness and conscious awareness enable us better to act upon the truth or facts. To act *upon* something involves having some representation of it, whether in beliefs or in states of (phenomenological) awareness. The capacity to have beliefs about matters that are not presently before us widens the range of facts to which we can fit our actions.

How exactly does awareness operate to fit behavior to situations? Let us consider (what we might call) the zoom-lens theory of attention, according to which the function of attention is to allow details to be zoomed in upon and enlarged. Stephen Kosslyn has discovered that when people follow the instruction to visualize something, the same part of the brain's visual cortex is activated as is activated when they see. The operations of visualization use the brain's machinery of vision. Also, when people are asked to visualize an elephant and then to zoom in on portions of their visual images, they are able to do so, and they report that when they get too close, the whole elephant overflows their image "screen" so that they no longer are visualizing all of it.[18] These data are very suggestive.

I hypothesize that paying attention to something enlarges the amount of the brain's resources that are devoted to that item, and that coordination of behavior to details can take place only when those details have received a certain amount of magnification through a certain quantity of the brain's (relevant) resources' being devoted to them. The registering that occurs with blindsight does not involve conscious awareness, and so it does not make possible zooming in upon details for a closer look; hence it does not enable the coordination of behavior to those details.[19] (Are films such a popular entertainment form because their visual devices, such as closeups and zoom shots, match the modes of awareness' working?)

The lower threshold of things within an organism's current conscious awareness consists of those things it can zoom in upon for closer attention. Conscious awareness by itself, leaving attention aside, brings greater ability to match behavior to situations than does the mere registering involved in blindsight; consider how one can react to things in one's peripheral vision that are unattended to. Yet each of these things within consciousness can be selected for closer attention when some lower level of processing marks it as relevant to the organism's goals or well-being. Conscious awareness was selected for because of the benefits it brings in contouring behavior to situations, as compared to the benefits of mere registration. Attention is a later evolutionary addition that rides piggyback upon the capacity of conscious awareness. The capacities and mechanisms of attention were selected for because of their attendant increases in the coordination of behavior to situations. And concentration, I think, is an intensification and a fixation of attention. It is a more intense form of attention, and is more resistant to being diverted by other items; when it is diverted, there is a tendency for it to return to the item of previous attention. Concentration is attention on a strong and short leash.

These hypotheses about registering, about conscious awareness, and about attention can be put to empirical test. Each gradation will involve its own specific tests. The tests will look in two directions, downward toward the more extensive (or intensive) utilization of neural machinery involved in greater gradations of awareness, and outward toward the more subtle fitting of behavior to situation that higher gradations of awareness enable. The overarching hypothesis is that the more extensive (or intensive) the utilization of neural machinery is, the more subtle can be the fitting of behavior to aspects of situations.

How extensive a portion of the brain can mere registering involve, and what sort of gross activities does it enable? Might some drugs prevent or slow down attentional zooming and magnification, and what are their effects upon the matching of behavior to situations? I shall focus upon just one level of particular philosophical interest, the line between mere registering and minimal awareness (and leave the formulation of other empirical tests to perceptual and cognitive neuroscientists).

Awareness is useful in, and necessary for, making behavior contingent upon a fact, and for executing behavior contingently upon a fact. There are four ways, of increasing sophistication, in which my behavior can depend upon a fact p. First, the holding of this fact can cause me (to choose) to do the behavior. Second, I can choose to do the behavior because the familiar fact that p obtains. Putting this more minimally, the holding of the familiar fact that p can be a *discriminative* stimulus for my doing the behavior.[20] Third, p can become a *new* discriminative stimulus for the behavior, and this can happen in two ways: either because p is a previously unfamiliar fact, or because the previous contingencies had not linked the already familiar p with any reinforcement. Or fourth, I can decide to perform the behavior contingent upon p's obtaining. I can decide: if p obtains, perform the behavior; if p does not obtain, don't perform the behavior. It is the third of these ways, I suggest, that marks the threshold of (the function of) awareness, or perhaps it is of conscious awareness. Awareness (or conscious awareness) is needed to act upon a *new* discriminative stimulus.[21]

This leads to a prediction. If some animal with the capacity to be subject to operant conditioning and to act upon discriminative stimuli has damage done to the area of its brain corresponding to the striate cortex, presumably producing blindsight, then that animal will *not* be able to be operantly conditioned to perform behavior contingent upon a new (visual) discriminative stimulus, e.g., to press a bar when (and only when) an "impossible" figure such as a Penrose triangle is present. The Penrose triangle may register upon the animal, but since it will not be consciously aware of the

Penrose triangle, it will not be able to be conditioned to behave contingently upon its being present. My hypothesis is that (conscious) awareness of p is necessary for behavior to become contingent upon p, whether through p's becoming a new discriminative stimulus for the behavior or through a decision to make the behavior contingent upon p.[22] (Recall that something can be the function of conscious awareness without its being physically impossible that *in another context* that thing could happen in the absence of conscious awareness.)

The blindsighted person is able to answer correctly when prompted with a question. Learning facts about blindsight, and the fact that he is blindsighted, the person might prompt himself to exhibit behavior B in the presence of a circle, by constantly asking himself to guess if there is a circle before him and to do B when he guesses yes. (He will need to be consciously aware of guessing yes.) But it will not be possible, through selective reinforcement, to newly condition the blindsighted person to do B when he is presented with a circle at that place in his visual field. Such is the prediction, based on the hypothesis that conscious awareness is necessary for installation of new discriminative behavior. However, many, many repetitions of a stimulus can give it the status of an old stimulus so that operant conditioning to it as a discriminative stimulus then can take place, or can take place more quickly.[23] (And some stimuli may never have been new, in that the preparedness for them is prewired.)

Simple reflexes, according to our discussion of the context of consciousness, are instilled by the evolutionary process that has closed the choice point about what behavior to emit in those circumstances. If the function of awareness (above mere registration) is to guide behavior at choice points (that evolution has left open), then such awareness should not be necessary for simple reflex behavior to occur. It is a prediction of this account, then, that when an object moves quickly toward the eye of a person with damage to the primary visual cortex, in the blindsight portion of his visual field, that person will blink. The simple reflex is not dependent upon any grade of awareness higher than registration.

Are there organisms that can be operantly conditioned but not conditioned to a discriminative stimulus? It would be illuminating if different gradations of awareness (starting with mere registering) were necessary for different levels of conditioning: for classical Pavlovian conditioning, operant conditioning, operant conditioning to a discriminative stimulus, and operant conditioning to a new discriminative stimulus. Is some representation necessary for operant conditioning to take place, but not for Pavlovian conditioning? Might Pavlovian conditioning without awareness take place when there is biological preparedness of the connection between stimuli, with awareness required for Pavlovian conditioning with biologically unprepared connections?[24] Might the gradation of awareness necessary for a certain task be dependent upon the cognitive architecture of the system, for instance, whether it is a distributed system or a von Neumann architecture?

Conscious awareness is necessary for *learning* discriminative behavior, for acquiring new discriminative behavior. Perhaps already learned discriminative behavior can be unrolled automatically, without the organism's becoming consciously aware of the discriminative stimulus. But new discriminative behavior, behavior B's becoming contingent upon p, cannot be learned in the absence of conscious awareness of (the discriminative stimulus) p. So runs our hypothesis, and it leads to the following prediction: it will not be possible to condition a rat to emit behavior on a discriminative stimulus that is new to that behavior, if that rat's striate cortex has been suitably impaired.[25] However, stimuli presented to the blind field might cue or affect other subsequent behavior.[26]

Various quirky psychological facts might complicate our picture of the function of conscious awareness as enabling new discriminative behavior. Should the hypothesis be refined so as not to run afoul of such facts? Or are these facts leftovers from more primitive brain structures that have hung on? Conscious awareness adds a far more effective and efficient way whereby behavior is (made) contingent upon facts, but the earlier capacity of unconscious (scraps of) registering, useful in comparison to no registering or differential behavior at all, has remained in place and still is detectable in directed experiments.

The current hypothesis sees an important part of the function of consciousness as residing in producing *future* discriminative behavior. The blindsight person may be able to unreel the results of past operant conditioning, but he will not be able to appropriately register, for (near) future use, conditioning to new discriminative stimuli. However, the blindsight person also is not able to subtly guide his current behavior, even when faced with familiar discriminative stimuli. His motor behavior is not precisely attuned to the contours of the objects he is presented with. Reaching for something, his hand does not form a contour precisely anticipating the contour of the object to be grasped. Preparation for future action cannot be the sole function of consciousness.

Let us turn, therefore, to the function of consciousness in current behavior. A stimulus presented to a blindsight person registers upon that person (he guesses what is presented at better than chance), but it does not register upon him that it registers. How does the registering that something registers help in the subtle guidance of behavior, and how shall we understand such registering one level up? Is there a difference between a first-level registering's being passed further along a system, and its registering that it has registered?

First, consider what psychologists and neuroscientists call *coarse coding*, which involves two registerings at the same level. How can the precise wavelength of light that reaches the eye be recorded? Wavelengths are continuously arrayed, and if retinal cells were specialized to record a precise wavelength, there would have to be infinitely many (indeed, a nondenumerable infinity of) such cells. That is too many! A retinal cone cell responds to a range of wavelengths, but it does not respond equally to each wavelength in that range. The cone varies in its frequency of firing, and it fires more rapidly in response to some wavelengths than to others. With wavelengths arrayed along the x-axis and frequency of firings measured along the y-axis, a cone cell shows a normal distribution, firing most rapidly with the wavelength to which it is maximally sensitive. For every other wavelength, the brain cannot read that wavelength from the rate of firing, for the same rate will intercept the normal distribution curve at two places. However, if two or three types of cones are present, and if these overlap in the wavelengths to which they are sensitive but differ in the wavelengths to which they are maximally sensitive, then from the different firing rates of the three cells the brain can reconstruct which particular wavelength they are receiving. Each cell gives coarse information about the incoming wavelength, but in combination the information they jointly give is fine.[27] You can make a silk purse from many sows' ears.

The blindsight person, too, has information that has registered coarsely. Another registering at the same level, as in coarse coding, might refine it further. But so also might a registering of this first registering. Must that second registering itself be a fine one, or can it be coarse too, while the result of the two together turns out fine? Suppose the registering of consciousness is not a spike but another curve of distribution added onto the first, amplifying it in a way that distinguishes some part of that first coarse curve. (Compare temporal coding.) The initial registering coarsely registers an external fact, and the registering of this registering, while coarsely registering the initial registering, enables finer information about the external fact to be extracted. If even a crude response to our own registering of some thing Y (made possible by this registering's also registering) gives us the ability to respond more subtly to Y, that would mark the function of conscious awareness. The metaregistering would enable a more subtle response to the Y that is originally registered. (The function of registering is to adapt behavior to facts, and the function of conscious awareness is a more subtle adaptation.) These remarks are meant to be suggestive only, and to raise the question of the ways in which the further registering, one level up, might facilitate more-precise guidance of behavior.

Why does a registering at that next level constitute conscious awareness of what has registered at the first level? Couldn't it *all* stay unconscious, both first level and metalevel? Compare the similar question for the theory that consciousness is constituted by registering at a particular place (or in a particular system) in the brain. Why does registering *there* constitute consciousness? Could two such theories take in each other's washing by saying that metaregistering constitutes consciousness because it registers at that place (or in that system), and registering at that place (or in that system) constitutes consciousness because that is metaregistering?

It is another approach I wish to pursue here. Suppose, as with blindsight, that some thing Y in the environment registers on a person, and there is some crude response or adaptation that he makes or is able to make to Y. So far, no conscious awareness of Y. Next, suppose that this registering of Y (and the tendency to at least crudely respond to it) itself registers and is crudely responded or adapted to. We are supposing that this second-level registering and crude response (to the first-level registering and crude response to Y) makes possible a more subtle response and adaptation to Y.

Thus far, we have discussed one isolated instance of a two-level structure. Next, let us suppose that an organism has more general capacities, perceptual capacities to register and crudely respond to various forms of energy (heat and light and pressure and . . .), and that it also has a general capacity to register and crudely respond to these first-level registrations and crude responses to the various forms of energy. This general capacity, which has registered these different first-level registrations and crude responses, is also able, let us suppose, to integrate and to produce some representation of them and then to crudely respond or adapt to this resulting representation.

The nature of representation is a topic that currently is under active discussion by philosophers and cognitive scientists.[28] Perhaps a criterion for a representation must be stated in terms of what happens one level above *it*. An integration of registrations constitutes a representation when it itself registers and is integrated along with other things of its type, and then is (at least) crudely responded to at that next level (where, standardly, in the case of evolutionarily produced representations, it functions as an information-bearing state to produce adaptive behavior). A belief is one kind of representation; physiological states and states of neural networks may well constitute other kinds.

In *Philosophical Explanations,* I presented the view that knowledge involves a belief that subjunctively tracks the truth of what is believed: if *p* weren't true, the person would not believe that *p*; and if *p* were true, the person would believe that *p*. This structure can also be applied to representations or representational states other than belief, with the result that we, or our bodies, may know things when states of our neurons or other parts of our body represent and track the truth or existence of various things in the world (including other states of our body). The absence of quotation marks around the word *know* is intentional.

I conjecture that there is conscious awareness of *X* when a number of conditions are satisfied: (1) There is registering of *X* along with a consequent ability to crudely respond or adapt to *X*, as part of a capacity to register and crudely respond to a broad range of phenomena. (2) There exists a more general capacity to register and crudely respond to such first-level registerings and crude responses. (3) There is a capacity, moreover, to integrate these first-level registerings and consequent abilities to crudely respond into a *representation R*. (4) This representation *R* then is registered and crudely responded to. (5) All of this produces (in accordance with our earlier hypothesis) very subtle and finely tuned responses to *X*. (6) Finally, this representation *R* (or further representations of it or of representations of . . . it) satisfies a further important condition that we shall discuss after further machinery is developed later.[29] (The body can know things without conscious awareness when there are representations that, although they track phenomena, do not satisfy this further important condition.) I leave until later the question of whether (1)–(6) constitutes the *basis* of conscious awareness, or whether this just *is* what conscious awareness is.

If the function of conscious awareness is to adapt our behavior finely to phenomena and to circumstances, then the function of conscious awareness of what we are doing, planning, thinking, desiring, and feeling will be to adapt our behavior finely to these phenomena so that they can be taken precisely into account, redirected, altered, or controlled. We might term these kinds of conscious awareness *self-consciousness,* reserving the term consciousness-of-self for another phenomenon.

We can briefly list some other possible functions of conscious awareness. Conscious awareness might aid in current action by playing a role in feedback processes that modify ongoing current action. Visual feedback about the new distance between a hand and an external object and about the orientation of the body in space can aid in appropriately modifying the hand's motion or the body's posture to enable a launched movement to more exactly reach its destination. The conscious awareness that is lacking in blindsight might be necessary for the operation of subtle feedback controls. The registration without conscious awareness that does take place in blindsight might be insufficient for such feedback mechanisms.

Conscious awareness might play a role in the classification of stimuli. To classify something as a member of a kind is to invoke or make accessible already stored information about (typical) individuals of that kind, and so to bring to bear that information upon current action. If conscious awareness is necessary for the identification and classification of the kind of object one is encountering, it would be needed to utilize stored information about such entities to produce a more precise contouring of behavior.

Consciousness might be needed to isolate and highlight that part of the information available to an organism that is (possibly) relevant to its choice. Much past information that has registered in memory will be irrelevant to the current choice point, and even much current information that is registering is not relevant to the current choice. (The degree to which my foot was pressed against the floor five minutes ago was not relevant to my choice then of what sentence to type next.) Even with relevant perceptual information, the process by which it arises is normally not relevant to choice; we normally do not need to be aware of the neuronal connections or firings that produce our seeing something, or even of the fact that we have neurons at all.

It would be inefficient, if not impossible, to utilize all the information that is available to us in each and every choice. In some way, then, a subset of the available information must be marked out, that part of the total information available to us that is possibly relevant and will be used in making the choice. This subset is the information that will feed into the organism's choice mechanism.[30]

We cannot simply say, though, that conscious awareness is the drawn boundary around the relevant subset of information or what saliently marks it as what is to be attended to and intensively processed. For why cannot the boundary drawing or marking be done outside of conscious awareness, with the information feeding into and functioning within the mechanism of choice? How does conscious awareness *help*?

Conscious awareness might make relevant information more perspicuous and more intelligible, so that it can be more readily taken in and remembered. Sensory consciousness might be an illuminating display mechanism, a way of making sense of information by placing it in an intelligible gestalt.[31] Recall the children's pastime of connecting the dots to form a recognizable picture. The dots of data (or particular bits of information) can be connected into an overall picture that makes it easier to recall and to use this information, and easier to see its relevance to particular projects and choices.[32]

The great welter of information stemming from past impingements on sensory apparatus stands in complicated confirmation relations to a vast range of statements. It would be cumbersome, costly, and unnecessary for an organism receiving new information to continually recompute and bring the probabilities of *all* statements up to date via some Bayesian procedure.[33] Given the organism's particular goals and the actions now available to it, only *some* statements will specially need to be reevaluated. Placing these statements into a new gestalt might be a quick and rough method that approximates reevaluating their probabilities. Conscious *beliefs* might be an illuminating display of the cognitive relevance of all this information, placed in an intelligible gestalt. Current consciousness can be used to bring up to date and modify what is stored in memory, while memory also can be used to modify or fill out the reports of current consciousness.

Some choice mechanisms might function *automatically*, below the level of consciousness, but if you are consciously aware that a choice is to be made, you can decide to seek further information when the information currently available yields no desirable option. To some extent, this too might happen automatically, with the current options' desirabilities registering automatically and, when these are beneath a certain threshold, a signal then being sent to seek further information or options. Still, this process might be guided better by conscious awareness. As with perceptual registering, the awareness of awareness of Y may yield more subtle control over responses to Y, and more-differentiated responses to more subtle Y's.[34]

If the function of conscious awareness is to play some role in adapting behavior to changing facts, then we should expect such conscious awareness to come into play only after it is determined (or in the later stages of determining) that something (probably) is indeed a fact. Most of the work of testing whether something *is* a fact should take place through neural processing that remains beneath the level of conscious awareness. Only after it passes a certain number of tests for being worth considering will a particular stimulus rise to the level of conscious awareness.

Some philosophers have asked whether we can ever know anything other than our own conscious experiences. If the function of conscious experience is to enable us to conform our behavior to external facts and to act differentially upon such facts, if the function of consciousness is to give us usable awareness (and knowledge) of external facts (or of our own bodily facts), then if it carries out its function, something will be registering upon us other than the experiences themselves. (And if we *also* are aware of the experiences themselves, then these other things will have even more decidedly registered upon us.) The prison the solipsist lives in is one of functionless experiences.

Synthesizing and Filtering Data

The function of conscious awareness, I have suggested, is to enable behavior to be contingent upon (new) facts that register upon an organism, and to enable that behavior to be precisely contoured or adapted to that fact. Even more grandly, it functions to enable behavior to be weighed and contoured in relation to different facts or considerations whose vectors individually point in conflicting directions. Hence we should expect that a stimulus will not rise to consciousness unless it is a good candidate for representing a further fact about the environment (or the organism). That it *is* such a candidate will be determined automatically, nonconsciously.

At all levels in the nervous system and brain, some data are passed along, while other data that are checked for consistency and concordance with still further data but fail these automatic tests are stopped or dropped. The nervous system constantly must deal with the following question: Does some datum stem from random firings of neurons, is it just noise in the nervous system, or does it indicate something more substantial? The data that are passed along are merged with other streams of data, passed further along, partially filtered out as they are checked for consistency with yet more data streams with which they then are merged yet again, and so on. Of unsynthesized data we are not conscious at all. The more levels of synthesis that have taken place, and the more different the data that have been synthesized, the more conscious we become of the resulting representation.[35]

Something is objective, we said earlier, when it is approachable from different angles. Differently angled approaches do not have to involve any synthesis; the different avenues of approach, by different senses, persons, or methods, at different times may simply exist side by side and be concordant. To be sure, we provide some unification of these by hypothesizing that there is one objective fact that they all are diverse routes to. In this case, however, it is not the routes themselves that are unified; the unification is provided by the routes' destination.

Different routes to the same fact may increase the reliability of our judgments. This increase is exhibited by the analysis of vision at the neural level.[36] Binocular vision *fuses* data into new synthesis.[37] One recent article on the role of multiple cues in seeing three-dimensional shapes distinguishes three possible ways in which cues can interact.[38] One cue can veto another, completely overriding it; or the information from two cues can be pooled in a simple linear estimation, for instance, cues for two different depths are combined, with weightings, to yield the expected value of the depth; or before there is an estimate of the depth from either cue, one cue can provide information that affects the interpretation of the other one.[39] Integration is not limited to the action of each separate sensory mode. The response of some neurons to multisensory stimuli is greater than the sum of their responses to each of the separate stimulations, and the rules that govern neural multisensory integration have been investigated.[40]

Binocular vision takes two different streams of data, or two representations, and merges or synthesizes them into one unified representation. Synthesizing the data streams is not simply a matter of holding them side by side, as in a box, but of merging them into a third further representation that incorporates each of these two streams.

I conjecture that it is such merging of data that underlies consciousness. Consciousness involves the meshing of different streams of data into a unified synthesis or representation. Objectivity involves the approachability of the same fact or object from different angles. Whether different streams of data *can* be given a unified representation is a *test* of whether there is some objective fact present that is approachable from different angles. (And the actual unification of the data streams indicates an actual multiangled approaching.) Subjective consciousness, therefore, is a mark or test of objectiveness. To test for objectiveness may be (part of) the function of subjective consciousness.[41]

In human beings, the cerebral hemispheres overlap greatly in the information they process. Might it be that each hemisphere provides a different angle on the world, and the enormous communication between hemispheres checks to see if the angles (can be made to) mesh?[42]

The tests that filter out certain data use standards of consiliance that themselves were selected for from among many possible standards. Particular standards that served well and led to reproductive success were inherited; the same holds for particular procedures of synthesis.

Synthesizing data is not, however, an infallible test of objectiveness.

Something might be approachable by different routes, and hence objective, although these different routes cannot be synthesized into one psychological or neural representation. In the other direction, synthesis could occur although nothing objective corresponds to what is synthesized.[43] Moreover, we can have subjective experiences of things that are not objective facts, e.g., in hallucinations or dreams. (Are these partial mimics of objective syntheses which are not caused by external stimuli but start higher up the pathways of synthesis, even within the cortex itself?) Fallible though it be, subjective consciousness is our major access to objectiveness.[44]

Evolution has given us the capacities to detect objective facts. Since our capacities are not infallible and can malfunction, our ability to detect objective facts incorporates some redundancy. Checks are made to see if a single-track detection mode has malfunctioned or encountered noise, etc., by comparing one detection mode's results with that of another.[45] Only if these jibe do we conclude that we are facing an objective fact. Thus, evolution instills multiple routes onto objective reality. (Is reasoning itself one of these routes, or is it best construed as a metamode of meshing other routes?)

When data are integrated, they are passed further along processing streams for further synthesis. The higher the degree to which data can be integrated, the more they indicate an objective fact, and hence the more likely it is that they should be taken account of in choice. Data rise to consciousness when they are synthesized, and this integrated information is then passed on to (or toward) some place, or transformed into some state, that gives it a greater role in decisional processes.

The objective facts are what choice needs to take account of. The objective facts are what a chooser needs to make his behavior contingent upon. The function of conscious awareness is to be aware of objective facts, so that behavior can be performed contingently upon them, and only when data pass the tests of successive syntheses are they marked as registering an objective fact. Just as idiosyncratic data do not rise to the level of being the topic of scientific explanation—science explains only the regularities of repeatable phenomena—not all stimulations rise to the level of consciousness.

However, as we noted in Chapter 2, a fact that we act upon need not have the highest degree of objectiveness; it just needs to be invariant enough. A fact can be tested for objectiveness, and pass such a test, without the organism's then representing it in an objective way. It can be represented in a way that suits it especially for immediate action.[46]

Data that do not pass the test of integration with other data are treated as insignificant noise, not worthy of notice as an objective fact. The damage to the striate cortex (cortical area VI) that produces blindsight still allows projection from the lateral geniculate nucleus to cortical areas beyond VI, but whatever projects to these further areas is insufficiently strong or insufficiently integrable to signal an objective fact, to signal it strongly enough that one becomes consciously aware of it.

Earlier we said that conscious awareness of some thing X, the registering of the fact that X has registered, is necessary for the keying of behavior to X as a new discriminative stimulus. In general, it is desirable to key behavior to a discriminative stimulus only when that stimulus constitutes an objective fact. Things rise to consciousness, we now have said, only when the data that represent them exhibit sufficient unity and integration to possibly represent an objective fact. Conscious awareness tests for the objectiveness of the facts to which behavior is to be keyed. And conscious awareness gives the power of subtle adjustment to objective facts, and adjustment to more subtle objective facts. Thus do the strands of our theory of consciousness mesh.

It now is known that different aspects of the external world are analyzed along separate channels. Surprisingly, it turns out that color, shape, and motion are generally analyzed by different cells within different processing streams,[47] although recent studies show there is some overlap in the sensitivities of cells in different areas. It has been found through empirical studies that many such aspects are represented in the brain through (what are termed) topographic maps. When the stimulation to various sensory cells is processed and affects cells further inward, the order of the spatial relations among the stimulated sensory cells is preserved in the neuronal cells to which they project, to which they send their signals. When retinal cell Y is between retinal cell X and retinal cell Z, Y will project further inward to a cell Y′ that is between the X′ and Z′ that X and Z respectively project to. And so on for different stages of projection inward, with the firing cells in each stage forming a (topologically stretched but structure preserving) picture or map of the pattern of firing cells at an earlier stage. (At least fifteen of the visual areas in the macaque monkey are known to be retinotopically mapped.) Such an arrangement is convenient in avoiding the necessity for densely crossed wires. But does this "analog," picturelike character of the representation have any further significance? If the particular wiring connections were maintained but the particular positions of the cells were discontinuously shifted so that the later topography altered, would not all brain functions remain the same?

I believe that topographic mapping has a significance beyond the engineering consideration (about the dense crossing of wires) that recommend it, but it is difficult to put one's finger on its precise significance. We can begin with this. Although every topographic mapping can be altered into a nontopographic one by the discontinuous movement of cells, not every nontopographic mapping can be transformed into one that is transitively topographic over many stages.[48] A topographic mapping is not necessary, but that it is *possible* tells us something about the sensed array.

Topographic maps seem to have an intimate connection to felt qualities of experience, to phenomenology. My believing something, and my conscious awareness of the belief, seem to have no detectable phenomenology,[49] and also do not, so far as we currently know, involve significant multilevel topographic mapping. Sensory arrays, however, do involve topographic maps, and these are of two sorts: those which are centered about the body and the relation of things to parts of the body, and those which map the positions or mutual relations of things in objective physical space. The transforming of one of these kinds of representation to another is crucial for understanding physical movement and the successful grasping of seen objects.[50]

We have *experience*, an awareness through or accompanied by a phenomenology, of things that can be given a kind of spatial representation. This involves space itself, objects in physical space, happenings in parts of our body, and also sounds and smells emanating from spatial locations. It also involves spacelike realms that can be represented by transitive relations among "locations" (e.g., some tones are higher than others). More precision would be desirable here, to state exactly what mathematical relations constitute the relevant notion of "spacelike."[51] Whatever it turns out to be, it will be (mathematically) possible to give such spacelike representation to things that we do not experience as having a phenomenology. What we do experience is what we *do* give such a spacelike, topographic representation to. Evolution has shaped us to give such a representation to only *some* of the kinds of things to which it can be given, perhaps because there would be no special purpose to such a representation in some cases, or perhaps because in some cases such a representation, though having a point, was too complicated or abstract mathematically to be evolutionarily feasible.

The information about color, form, orientation in space, and motion that is analyzed separately somehow is brought together. We are aware of moving, round, red objects. And the information is brought together correctly, for when we see two objects, the moving, round, red one and the stationary square blue one, we do not become aware of a moving square red one. How does the brain integrate the separately analyzed information and bind it together? This question has been termed "the binding problem."[52]

How can we get from "Something is red" and "Something is round" to "Something is red and round"? One way is to have a system of names, wherein each entity receives one name, and no two entities receive the same name. "Joe is red" and "Joe is round" will together imply "Joe is red and round." Another way is to use spatial locations. Two things cannot be in the same place at the same time, or at least this holds well enough for identification purposes. (A sound that comes from directly behind an object may lead us to attribute it to the object.) If red and round are located at the same place, then there is something that is both red and round. If red and noisy are located at the same place, then some red thing is making noise. Since different attributes are analyzed and represented in the brain by different topographic maps, this suggests that coordination among topographic maps (color and form, and auditory space), through signals sent between them, may be the basis of binding information together. The various topographic maps can be brought into consistent coordination and representation by signals across them and by signals sent back from later stages that affect the earlier maps. What are bound together are things having *corresponding positions* on different topographic maps. The known but puzzling large amount of neuronal crosstalk and back-projection would be for the purpose of coordinating topographic maps, and also for (the before-mentioned) tests of concordance between different data streams, and for the filtering out by backtalk of some data earlier in the stream (because of their lack of concord with existing syntheses later in the stream of processing).

Motion may be an especially potent source of integration; if color and form, red and square, not only occupy the same stationary place, but move together through the same places (through the same parts of the visual field when the head is stationary, or through the same motion-adjusted paths) on their respective maps, then there exists a red square. Not only could binding occur through the coordination of positions in different topographic maps,[53] but the extent to which multiple topographic maps from different sense modalities can be coordinated (through crosstalk and feedback) can help to test whether there is an objective fact, or an object, out there.[54]

This procedure need not be guaranteed to be accurate, but it may be accurate enough to be what evolution actually has installed. A check on a hypothesis about binding would be whether it provides a basis for the construction of "binding illusions." These would be suitably constructed stimuli that trick the binding process into producing an experience of properties inhering together in one object, although that does not occur in the presented world or the presented stimulus.[55]

Let us now combine our various themes. I conjecture that X has an experiential quality, a felt phenomenological quality only if X is synthesized information that is represented in some topographic map, which is coordinated, spatially and temporally, with other topographic maps (enabling binding to take place), thereby producing a representation of the objective fact, and this further registering is suitably passed on. (The specification of "suitably"—I shall offer one in the next section—constitutes the content of the important condition that was mentioned in the text preceding note 28.) Roughly put, X has an experiential quality when it is topographically represented information that rises to conscious awareness.[56] (I shall say much more about phenomenology in the later section that is devoted to that topic.)

But passed on to where? We might be tempted to say: toward the decision apparatus, to register there.[57] But is there any such "decision apparatus" to speak of? The context of consciousness may indeed be evolutionary choice points, but this does not imply there exists in the brain any specialized or localized decision apparatus. And the best current evidence seems to indicate that there is no such one central locus, whether of decision or of anything else. The human brain, it seems, is a massively parallel distributed system of innumerable interconnections, not only forward along hierarchical pathways but also cross-connections and back connections. This has often been noted in the recent literature. We can ask, though, *why* there isn't any such central decision locus. Is there a special disadvantage to such an architecture that explains why evolution didn't produce it, or is there a special advantage to the distributed system? We shall return to this question below.

Martha Farah usefully distinguishes the following three types of theories of conscious awareness: that it involves a particular part or system of the brain, that it arises from a high degree of integration of different systems in the brain, and that it arises from a particular threshold of activity or activation in the brain.[58] Bernard Baars sees consciousness not in the sending of particular kinds of processed information to any one (decisional) place, but in the widest broadcast of messages to all the specialized unconscious processors in order for them to take account of this information in their (unconscious) work.[59] But why does this constitute consciousness rather than a very widespread and extensive (blind) registering? Rather than a localized blindsight, why isn't this just (the equivalent of) blindsight *everywhere?* Let us reconsider the kind of registering that conscious awareness involves.

Common Knowledge

If the registering of something can occur without conscious awareness of it—this is shown by blindsight—why cannot a registering of that registering also occur without conscious awareness of the external thing that was registered, or of its prior registering? If there were one central hierarchical place in the cortex of the brain to which all signals get sent, we might say that a signal reaches consciousness when it registers *there*. The puzzle would remain, however, of what it is about registering there that constitutes something as conscious. Why does something's registering there, in contrast to registering in any other place, make us conscious of it? This question would arise even if that place played some central role in our decision-making processes, at the crucial link between receptor and effector neurons. And, as we have said, the best current evidence indicates that there is no such central locus of decision.

Rather than speaking of a signal's registering in one crucial (hypothesized) place—something that does not illuminate *why* that phenomenon gives rise to consciousness—we might follow Baars and speak of signals or messages being sent ("broadcast," in his terminology) everywhere, and even of their registering everywhere. This gives very widespread registering, but it does not provide a registering that something registers.

There is an important notion in the literature of game theory, the notion of "common knowledge," wherein each person in a group knows that *p*, each knows that each of the others knows that *p*, each knows that each of the others knows that each of the others knows that *p*, and so on up the line.[60]

What we need for our present purposes in understanding consciousness is not just widespread (or even universal) registering, and not just widespread registering of widespread registering but something like common knowledge of universal (or widespread) registering.[61] Conscious awareness, I hypothesize, involves registering all the way up the line. This involves *p*'s registering everywhere (in the relevant parts of the brain), its registering everywhere that it registers everywhere, its registering everywhere that it registers everywhere that it registers everywhere, etc. It involves *common registering*. We might say that consciousness is the brain's common knowledge.

Recall, now, our earlier discussion of conscious awareness, in which a number of conditions were listed: registering of X and the ability to crudely respond to it; registering of this registering by a general capacity that provides a representation of these registerings and (at least) crudely responds to this representation, thereby more finely responding to X, where this representation satisfies some further important condition that was not then specified. Here, I suggest that this further condition states that the representation is commonly registered, as part of a system of such common registration.[62]

The difference that knowledge's being common can make is illustrated in this well-known puzzle. Two perfect reasoners are in a room and each has acquired, unbeknownst to herself, a mark on her forehead. Each can see the mark on the other person's forehead but not on her own. A friend enters the room and, in the hearing of each, says, "At least one of you has a mark on her forehead. At the end of one minute raise your hand if you know whether or not you have a mark on your own forehead." A minute passes, and neither one raises her hand. Each one knows that the other has a mark, but neither one knows that about herself. The friend then says, "At the end of the next minute, raise your hand if you know whether or not you have a mark on your own forehead." Each person then raises her hand and says she knows she has a mark on her own forehead. Each one has reasoned as follows: "If I did not have a mark on my own forehead, the other person would have seen that and, having been told that one of us in the room did have such a mark, she would have realized that person must be herself, and so she would have raised her hand at the end of the first minute. Since she did not raise her hand then, she must have seen that I had a mark on my forehead, so now I know that she did see this, and so at the end of this second minute I raise my hand to say that I *do* have a mark on my own forehead." Each one reasons similarly, and so both raise their hands.

Next, suppose a situation in which there are three people in the room, all with marks on their forehead, and the friend enters the room and says that at least one of them has a mark on her forehead, and that they are to raise their hands at the end of a minute, etc. At the end of the first minute, and also at the end of the second minute, no one raises her hand, but at the end of the third minute each of the three persons raises her hand to say that she herself has a mark on her forehead. Each one has reasoned to that conclusion as follows: "Suppose that I do not have a mark on my forehead. Each of the others would see that. Then at the end of the second minute, each of the others would know that they themselves had marks on their forehead, for if they too did not, the other one would have raised her hand at the end of the first minute, knowing that she alone was the person with a mark. Since neither of them raised her hand at the end of the second minute, that must mean that I *do* have a mark on my forehead, and so I now raise my hand to say so at the end of the third minute." More generally, and I will not carry the reasoning further here, if there are n persons in the room, and a friend makes the announcement, then in the first $n - 1$ minutes no one raises her hand, but after n minutes each of them realizes that she herself has a mark on her forehead.

Now imagine that the situation is slightly different. There are two people in the room with marks on their foreheads, a friend comes in and, *without* announcing that at least one person in the room has a mark on her forehead, simply asks the two people to raise their hands after one minute, then after two, etc., when they know whether or not they themselves have a mark on their forehead. In this situation, each one knows that at least one person in the room has a mark on her forehead, for each sees that the other one does. However, neither knows that the other person knows that at least one person in the room has a mark on her forehead, since neither knows what the other person sees. So neither one can reason, after one minute or after two minutes or after three minutes, etc., to the conclusion that she herself has a mark on her forehead. What the situation lacks is what the public announcement in the first version of the story provides, namely common knowledge that at least one person in the room has a mark on her forehead. Similarly with a larger number of people in the room having marks on their foreheads; suppose there are three of them. In this case, each one *will* know that at least one person in the room has a mark, and each will know that each one knows this, for each can see someone with a mark that the other person also can see. However, the lack of common knowledge means that no one of them can reason to a solution based upon a premiss that there are as many depths of iterated knowings (that at least one person has a mark) as there are persons marked. (Rather, the most they can use as a premiss in their reasoning is one less number of iterated knowings than the number of persons who are marked.) Common knowledge makes a difference to what these (perfect) reasoners can figure out.[63]

Consider another type of example from the literature on common knowledge.[64] Two separated divisions of one army can attack an opposing army from different sides, and if both attack simultaneously, they will defeat the opposing army, while if only one attacks (or attacks first) it will be destroyed. Neither general commanding a division will attack if he is not certain that the other one will attack simultaneously. The generals can communicate only by messenger. Can they successfully coordinate their attacks? If the first general announces in a message to the second general that he will attack first thing the next morning, he will not know that this messenger has got through, and since the second may not have received the message, the first general will *not* attack (despite having sent his message) the next morning. Moreover, the second general realizes this, and will not attack, even though he has received the message (and the first general realizes this fact that the second general will not attack, also). Things are not changed if the second general sends a messenger back to the first general, saying that he has received the first general's announcement of his attack, for even if this messenger from the second general does get through to the first general, the second general will not know this fact, and so will not know that the first general will attack and so he himself will not attack. (Moreover, the first general knows this, and so he will not attack either.) A third messenger does not help the situation. What is lacking in this situation is what is necessary for their coordinated attacks, namely, common knowledge that the first general's message was received by the second. No (finite) number of messengers sent back and forth is sufficient to establish this common knowledge.

Common knowledge, therefore, is extremely useful in situations in which simultaneous and coordinated action can produce good results, while action by only one or a few parts will produce extremely bad results. Common knowledge (or common registering upon separated parts in a disaggregated system) enables the joint coordinated action to take place safely. If a massively parallel distributed system is able to perform computations that a more hierarchical architecture (adhering to the same energetic requirements) cannot do, this will be worth little if the disaggregated system does not act in unison, thereby opening itself to the dangers of only some parts' taking (or cooperating in) an action.

The virtues of parallel distributed processing systems have been expounded in the literature. Such systems have flexible access to stored information; they generalize smoothly and fill in missing details; they can find the right result despite a probe that contains errors or is incomplete (this has been termed "graceful degradation"); they are powerful general learning devices and are very speedy because of their parallel operation.[65]

We now can add a further reason why there isn't a centralized hierarchical system of decision and action, whereby one central decision locus makes a decision and sends commands to all the relevant executory parts. It can send commands, but will all the separated executory parts have received them, and will each part register that all the others have received them, *and* that all the others have registered this further fact, etc.? (It is not sufficient if each part sends a return signal to the center saying that the first message has been received. And if the central locus sends a second signal to the parts saying that it has received all the return signals, will each part register that all the other parts have received this second signal?) Common knowledge in a disaggregated system overcomes this problem.[66]

Earlier we remarked that something can perform a function in a context without that thing's being necessary to that function in every context; something else might accomplish that function in another, very different context. If a parallel distributed architecture exists and was selected for because of the virtues listed above, then common knowledge can perform an important function within such a distributed system, which is its context.

In a disaggregated system in which unified simultaneous action produces good results while staggered action or action of only some parts might lead to disaster, common knowledge is needed to coordinate the simultaneous joint action. Consciousness is what coordinates a distributed system in simultaneous joint action—that is the *function* of consciousness. That is accomplished by common knowledge, common registering within the system, and it is this common knowledge which (when added on top of the other conditions) constitutes consciousness.

Common knowledge can also operate to *prevent* separate action in certain situations. How can a purely speculative trade of a stock take place between two rational individuals? Each knows the other is willing to trade; that indicates that the other's estimate of the future price of the stock differs from his own. (So each one then wonders whether he should rely on his own estimate.) Each then takes this information about the other into account, and if they still differ, that constitutes further information each must take into account. Can two such rational individuals with common knowledge of their differing estimates continue to differ if they follow the same decision rule (for which actions to perform under which circumstances)? A theorem by the game theorist Robert Aumann proved that they cannot "agree to disagree" and perform different actions.[67] Just as these separated individuals acting according to the same decision rule must act identically under conditions of common knowledge, perhaps an analogous result obtains for separated parts acting under a certain regime in a system of common registering; they cannot simply "go off on their own." It may be the phenomenon of common knowledge that maintains the unity of the self—and also that enables the coordination of somewhat unreliable parts.[68]

We have listed two fundamental functions of consciousness, to coordinate a distributed system in simultaneous joint action, and to enable behavior to depend upon a new discriminative stimulus. There are some obvious general connections between these two functions—such accurately tuned joint actions are necessary precisely when urgent new situations are recognized—but it would be desirable to link the two functions more closely. Common knowledge, common registering, is a very strong condition, of course. Perhaps a more nuanced view would distinguish different levels of consciousness that correspond to different depths of the registering (i.e., registering everywhere, registering everywhere that it registers everywhere, etc.).

How is such common (or at least very high-level) registering brought about? The human brain contains billions of neurons, billions of synaptic connections, and it is ever shifting among its *trillions* of possible total states of connection. Here is vast scope for the forward propagations, back-propagations, and cross-projections exhibited among various parts of the brain. This vast array of connections keeps each portion fully informed of what the other portions are informed of, and also fully informed that the other portions also are fully informed, up many levels in the registering hierarchy. The brain is a very busybody place, where each part minds every other part's business, including that portion of every other part's business wherein it minds every other part's business.

The transmission of any finite number of discrete signals back and forth is insufficient for common knowledge, as we saw in the example of coordinated attacks. How, then, might common registering that literally extends an infinite number of levels up be brought about? A string A's frequency of vibration can be affected by the frequency of vibration of a close-by string B, and vice versa.[69] Under some conditions, strings might be brought into vibrating at the same frequency. Each string registers the vibration of the others, and if the others are unchanged then, by not changing further itself it also registers that the other registers its own as identical and as registering that of the other as identical, etc. Many such strings might be brought into a harmonious chord of common registering, indicating that each is vibrating at the very same rate as *all* the others.

There has been recent investigation of the hypothesis that consciousness involves synchronized firing at 40 megahertz.[70] If the rate of firing of each affects the rate of firing of the others, then synchronized firing, aided by the reentrant networks emphasized by Gerald Edelman,[71] might constitute the brain's being in a state of common knowledge. This common firing is a *global* property of the brain, dependent upon the action of the individual parts and upon their synchrony. The busybody brain registers common registering when it registers firing everywhere else yet registers no deviation elsewhere from its own rate of firing. (Such a deviation would cause its own rate of firing to change.) It "hears" only the note that it itself is playing.

The synchrony these theorists speak of, however, is a synchrony in time, not an induced identity in frequency of firing. Neuronal oscillations might provide an instance of what we seek, if these oscillations can be coupled so as to establish cortical resonance.[72] Or perhaps the neurological phenomenon of the requisite type remains to be discovered. I conjecture that there is some neurological phenomenon wherein separated neurons or parts of the brain are coupled in a way that can bring them into a uniformity of action that would not occur if any significant number continued to perform differently; the continuation of one part's action thus constitutes a sign to it that all parts are "on the same wavelength," that each one registers that all the others are on that same wavelength, etc. Philosophers are not accustomed to proposing empirically testable and falsifiable conjectures, but since that is precisely what a fruitful theory about consciousness should yield, I resign myself to sticking my neck so vulnerably out.

I said earlier that registering in a particular *place,* any particular place, would leave the pressing question of why *that* constitutes consciousness. Similarly, we can ask: Why does the common registering delineated here constitute consciousness? Why is it any more satisfactory than registering in a place? However, we would expect consciousness to turn out to be a global property of the brain, and to involve the most extensive registering of registering. Common registering (in the technical meaning of that term) fits the bill exactly.[73]

We would hypothesize, then, that the registering involved in blindsight does not extend to a common registering throughout the cortex—we know already that blindsight is produced by lesions in certain portions of the visual cortex. If we combine our claims that conscious awareness enables fine motor guidance, and also the conditioning of behavior to new discriminative stimuli, with the claim that conscious awareness crucially involves common registering, we reach the conclusion that common registering enables fine motor guidance and the conditioning of behavior to new discriminative stimuli. We already know that common registering facilitates far-flung instantaneous coordinated firing. It would be instructive and desirable to push the theory of what common registering enables and facilitates to the point where it connects up more closely with what conscious awareness is known to accomplish.

The notion of common registering might help to clarify the relationship of sleep to consciousness. We are not quite unconscious when we are asleep, yet we are not fully conscious either. And when we dream, aren't we conscious of the dream content—or are we? It is interesting, therefore, to discover that some *parts* of the brain can be asleep while others are not. More precisely,

> There is recent evidence from studies in monkeys that the process of falling asleep may not occur synchronously in the entire brain. The animals were trained to perform a visual search task while the activity of their cortical neurons was being recorded. At times the monkeys became drowsy, and the neurons in the extrastriate cortical area V4 exhibited the typical sleeplike burst-pulse pattern and no longer responded to the visual stimuli. In spite of this "neuronal sleep," the animals continued to perform the visual task, which indicates that their primary visual cortex was still responsive. Thus, a portion of the cerebral cortex may "fall asleep" while another is still performing a behavioral discrimination that has become automatic.[74]

In these cases, there is not the intense cross-communication of parts of the brain that gives rise to common registering.

However, not only is there not common registering in this case, there is not even universal registering. Our hypothesis is that consciousness involves common registering of universal registering, or at least the registering of this many levels up. An experiment to test this sharper hypothesis would need to produce universal registering without common registering, and even without registering many levels up of the registering of universal registering. Will the subject under those circumstances then report or indicate conscious awareness? Perhaps sleep and dreaming, and other intermediate phenomena of consciousness too—not quite unconscious, yet not quite conscious either—involve registration beyond the very first level but only to very low levels, certainly not to the level of common registration.[75]

This does not mean, however, that consciousness is simply a matter of flow-chart linkages. If coordinated synchrony indeed is necessary for consciousness, and *if* this can be produced only by the direct causal interaction of physical parts—as with strings vibrating or cells firing so as to bring themselves to do this in unison—then consciousness requires more than a finite number of message and information linkages. It requires certain kinds of physical realization or instantiation in order to generate even more interconnective harmony than the flow diagrams indicate or can produce.

This would give consciousness a very physical basis indeed. Consciousness does not just happen to be physically instantiated. The medium is part of this message. However, this does not entail that consciousness can be embodied in, or emanate from, animal protoplasm only. It does mean, though, that an attempt to build a conscious machine will involve more than very clever and intricate programming. It also will involve very delicate physical engineering.

Since common registering is a very stringent condition, we might consider surrogates that often might serve in its stead. Evolution, after all, might settle for a statistical approximation of common registering. Since when something is universally broadcast, very often every relevant component will in fact receive it, Baars's universal broadcasting, or, better, some significant strengthening of it that does not require the equivalent of an infinite number of levels of registering, might serve as a statistically satisfactory surrogate for common registering.[76]

With regard to registration, we can distinguish its depth from its scope. The depth indicates the number of levels that registration reaches: it registers that it registers that . . . that it registers that p. The scope of the registration indicates how widely it registers that p, through which of the brain's various areas and subsystems. If surrogates that fall short of full common registering *can* give rise to some conscious awareness, the degree of conscious awareness that p will depend on both the depth and the scope of p's registration.[77]

We have focused upon the role that common registering (among the relevant parts of subsystems of the brain) plays with regard to conscious awareness. Common registering, or one of its surrogates, might also play an important role in establishing the *unity* of a conscious subject.[78]

We have seen what common (or multilevel) registering especially enables an organism to do, namely to jointly coordinate the action of separated parts in situations in which action by only some will be disastrous. The supposition that common registration *is* the basis of consciousness tells us much about the function of consciousness in general.

The Functions of Phenomenology

Phenomenology is connected with topographic maps, with information in spatial arrays. Examples are visual experience and auditory experience. Digitally formulated verbal thoughts, even ones that we are consciously aware of, do not have any corresponding phenomenology. Why isn't visual and auditory information presented only verbally, propositionally, in conscious thoughts? The density of the information is too great for propositional presentation (where the propositions do not include continuous variables). Vector coding of information gives rise to a very large combination of discriminable situations. Four kinds of sensory receptors, each with 10 levels of activation, give rise to 10,000 different four-element patterns.[79] Ten thousand different names or terms would be too great a cognitive burden, but (almost continuous) discriminable experiential "feels" can make these distinctions.[80]

Not all of conscious awareness has an accompanying phenomenology. However, if there is a function to conscious awareness, then there is a function also to phenomenology in the case of information so dense that it cannot be presented in distinct verbal thoughts. Phenomenology is a way to bring that dense information into conscious awareness. So our earlier discussion of the functions of conscious awareness provides the function of phenomenology too. And perhaps phenomenology enables some of these previous functions to be performed especially well, e.g., increasing the saliency of certain information and bringing out patterns in information. Once these things are consciously noticed, they can be investigated more closely, and further related information can be called upon. (Why, on the other hand, is not all information represented phenomenologically? Why is there verbal representation at all? We shall return to this question later.)

In an earlier section I said that conscious awareness of X involves a registering and crude ability to respond to X, which itself registers and is synthesized along with other things into a representation that itself is registered and (at least) crudely responded to. According to this, there can be conscious awareness of X without any phenomenology. There is phenomenology when what is represented is continuous or dense information, and this involves some mode of analog representation or topographic mapping. And there is awareness of phenomenology when, in addition, there is conscious awareness of these representations as presenting material that (ostensibly) is continuous or dense in a mode of presentation that itself is (apparently) analog.

There could be different strengths of connection between phenomenology and density. The strongest would be that phenomenological feeling occurs only when dense information actually is represented. A weaker connection would hold that phenomenological feeling can occur (even when dense information is not actually represented) but only when the sparser information that is represented is of a type that can take a position in a dense array, and when the capacity now actually representing this (sparser) information has in the past presented this type of information in a position in a dense array. (Typically, this capacity will have been selected for or expressly designed for the representation of densely arrayed information.) A still weaker connection would hold that phenomenological feeling can occur (even when neither of the foregoing holds) but only when capacities are involved that have represented other types of information in dense arrays. In this last case, discrete information might acquire a phenomenological feel by capturing or utilizing the machinery whose function it is to represent dense information. (So it might be with the phenomenological representation of tastes, if gradations of taste are not effectively continuous and conducive to mathematically "spatial" representation, or if someone is born with fewer than the normal number of taste receptors and distinguishable categories.)

One possibility is that qualitative experiences, qualia, occur because theory, even rather low-level theory about objects in the world, is underdetermined by data. Just to register the data doesn't get prelinguistic animals very far. An *experience* of the world might be a way of fixing upon one hypothesis among the many that fit the data. The hypothesis (or interpretation of the data) that the animal acts upon is the one presented phenomenologically (since the animal is not capable of linguistic formulations of the hypothesis or interpretation).[81] If the function of qualia is to specify one interpretation of the data for prelinguistic organisms, such experiences might continue also for linguistic organisms. Even for them, experiences would be an automatic and effortless way to interpret the (underdetermining) data. And the experiences then might be put to other uses, also. The "seeing as" phenomena with the two-dimensional drawing of a three-dimensional cube, the duck-rabbit, etc., show the perceptual system easily switching between two experiential presentations of different interpretations that are underdetermined by the data.

There is a difference, though, between saying that there is a function to phenomenology, to *some* phenomenology or other, and that there is a function to *that* particular phenomenology. Up to what level of the particularity of the phenomenology can we ascribe a function?

There is a function to there being *a phenomenology,* some phenomenology or other. There also is a function to *the structure of the phenomenology.* Two things in the world stand in a certain relationship R to each other. Two brain states register these two things and give rise to two experiential states that stand in a relationship R' to each other; where R' matches R in certain structural features, for instance, both are asymmetrical transitive relations. An asymmetric transitive relation between the experienced pitch of tones parallels the asymmetric transitive relation between the frequencies of sound waves.[82] Some dimensional aspects of the experience are isomorphic in structure to dimensional aspects of the world which they represent.[83] Evolution selects for such isomorphism in the structure of representational experiences because this enables aspects of the world to be read off aspects of experience.

There is a function to there being *specificity to the phenomenology*. The specificity enables us to distinguish things in the world. Absolute specificity would be this: when two aspects of the world differ, then respective experiences of these aspects also differ. However, there are limits to the specificity of our experiences. Color chips A, . . . , Z can be arrayed alongside each other so that A matches B (it is impossible to distinguish A from B just by looking at the two of them), B matches C, . . . , and Y matches Z, yet A can be visually distinguished from Z. A and Z are not exactly the same color, and since "exactly the same color as" is a transitive relation, some two adjacent colors in the sequence must differ in the exact colors they have even though they match visually.[84] The existing difference between some two adjacent colors falls below what psychologists term the "just noticeable difference." Our experiences of the world, though acute, are not perfectly acute. Our experiences are not as specific as the world is. (Still, two adjacent colors A and B might be told apart if there is some color, H say, that matches B but does not match A. We can then infer that A differs from B although we cannot see the difference between them just by looking at the two.)

I have said that there is a function to there being a phenomenology, to its structure, and to its degree of specificity. There also will be a function to *where* a sensation is felt, for instance, to induce the organism to lick or to tend to that bodily part. And there will be a function to the *valence* of the feeling or sensation or phenomenological state. Is it positive or negative; how positive or negative is it? Let us consider each of these aspects, too, as part of the *structure* of the phenomenology. But given that these structured aspects already are fixed, is there a further function to the *particularity* of the phenomenology, to the particular feel or qualia that it has? There is no function to *that* particularity, I claim, as opposed to another particularity of the same structure and specificity.

It may seem that every time an aspect of phenomenology has a function, I incorporate it into the structure or specificity of the experience. Is there any content, then, to my claim that there is no function to the particularity of phenomenological aspects that are beyond structure and specificity? Yes, there remains this contentful claim. After all aspects with a function are incorporated into the experience's structure, there will remain still other particular phenomenological aspects of the experience. These, by hypothesis, will have no function, and they can freely vary (within the structure) without affecting the function.

The specific particularity of the experienced qualities could hardly have an informative function, given the phenomenon of sensory transduction. All incoming energy that is sensed (light, i.e., electromagnetic energy, mechanical energy, thermal energy, sound waves, etc.) is transduced by specialized receptors into electrical impulses.[85] Transduction is the changing of information from one form to another. Receptors change stimuli into nerve signals, and effectors change these nerve signals into mechanical or chemical responses.[86] Information about the stimuli is transmitted to the central nervous system by conducted action potentials.

The *intensity* of the stimulus affects the rate or number of evoked action potentials. The intensity of the stimulus is coded as larger receptor potentials, which propagate electronically, and which cause a greater number and a higher frequency of action potentials. Not only do stronger stimuli increase the frequency of firing; they also activate a greater number of receptors. So the intensity of a stimulus is also encoded in the size of the responding receptor population.[87] The *duration* of the stimulus affects, and is encoded in, the discharge patterns of rapidly and slowly adapting receptors. (During a period of constant stimulation, the receptor adapts, and its action is damped down.)

Now if every kind of stimulus is transduced into electrical energy, into conducted action potentials—it is not electrons that are transmitted along the axon, but changing action potentials—then what distinguishes light from sound from pressure? All are translated into electrical impulses.[88]

Ultimately, these impulses are received somewhere, and apparently are transformed into different kinds of experience: visual, auditory, pressure, pain, heat, and so on. Let us not yet wonder *how* this occurs—let us think about what is occurring.

The brain might identify what kind of stimulus energy incoming action potentials represent by *labeling* each pathway the electrical impulse can come in along. These labels might be X, Y, Z, W, P, or they might be the words "light," "heat," "smell," "temperature," "sound." Notice that these labels *refer to* the pathways, and thereby to the kind of stimulus that begins propagation along these pathways. The labels do not *resemble,* and they do not need to resemble, the initiating energy. Similarly, the different qualitative feel to different sense modalities might just be labels indicating the kind of receptor the information originates with, having no particular (nonstructural) resemblance to the (source of the) incoming energy.

The brain keeps track of which electrical impulses, which action potentials, come from which kinds of stimuli by sending the impulses along different pathways (or conceivably by different signal codes) and by keeping track of which pathway (or code) is which. Its method of keeping track, however, need not end up with labels *or with experiences* that are anything like the original stimuli.

We could imagine another possible way the brain could work. After the nervous system transforms the different kinds of energy into one kind of energy and sends it along different pathways, it then could, somewhere in the brain, transform that common energy back into the different original kinds of energy. It could transform the electrical impulses transmitted along pathways that begin with thermal energy back into thermal energy, thereby producing a hot spot in the brain. It could transform the electrical impulses transmitted along pathways that begin with mechanical energy back into pressure in the brain. And so on. But what purpose would these retransformations serve? Hot spots or pressure in the brain would not be at all desirable. The brain does not retransform the action potentials back into the original kind of energy.[89]

The question is: does the brain transform the action potentials back into anything that *resembles* the original stimulus energy, into anything that is *like* that energy? We tend to think that the kind of experiences we have is just that. We think that our experiences resemble or picture or match what is out there. (A notable denier of this was John Locke.) But do they, and what would it mean to say that they do, given that the stimuli are not literally reproduced within the brain, heat with heat, pressure with pressure, etc.? And it is not clear even what reproduction would be in other cases. Chemical receptors capture the tastes of the food, but what would it mean to reproduce those tastes in the brain? Would someone else have to eat the brain to discover if this had been done? Or do we mean, reproducing within the brain, the very chemical content of the food? (And what would be the *point* of that?) Some relations do get reproduced within the brain, as we saw in our discussion of topographic maps.

Supposing we could get the meaning of this straight, would it serve any purpose if our experiences did resemble what was out there? Would it serve any biological function; would it have increased fitness so that there would have been selection for an apparatus that produced such resemblance? Once we have a phenomenological awareness of the world with sufficient specificity, with structural aspects isomorphic to the structure of the world, there is no further function to be served by a particularity of experience that (in some way) matches or pictures the particular quality of the world—let us suppose for the sake of the discussion that this is a clear notion. If such a particularity in matching did somehow arise, there would be no selective pressure to maintain it. For it would confer no benefit. Any mutation that altered the particularity while maintaining the structure and specificity of the phenomenology would fare as well, and could spread in the population by genetic drift. I do not mean only a mutation that shifted the quality of the experience along the same dimension (as color changes with the aging human eye), but also mutations that would produce a "reversed spectrum" or even mutations that would produce a crossing of the modalities of sensory experience—always, of course, supposing that the structure and the specificity of the phenomenology would be maintained.

We could experience *sounds,* that is, have experiences indistinguishable in their qualitative characteristics from our current kind of auditory ones, when we ate foods. Chewing some foods would produce sounds we liked; chewing other foods would produce experiences of discordant sounds. We would seek out the nicely sounding food. And sound waves would produce structured taste experiences, from which we could locate objects in space. There is no more reason (leaving structural features aside) to think that tastes are like the chemical composition of food than that heard sounds are.[90] Indeed, both taste and smell, each modality having its distinctive phenomenological feel, are experiences of chemical composition. Is chemical composition more accurately rendered by, more like, one kind of experience than the other?[91]

Frank Jackson has described a situation of a woman with normal vision who spends her life in a room containing only objects that are black or white or various shades of gray. Nothing there is colored. She is taught all scientific facts about color, and all facts that are known about the colors of various things. Yet, when she later is taken out of the room and sees colored objects, it seems that she learns something that she did not previously know, for instance, what the color red is.[92] Colors, of course, have various aspects or dimensions that themselves are continuous or dense. When the woman saw only black and white and shades of gray, she had a qualitative experience of these, in a mode of representation that itself was (apparently) analog, but not one as *dimensionally* rich as what color experience presents. So, since while she was in the room she was told all the known facts about color, including the number of dense or continuous dimensions had by colors, she knew that she was not herself experiencing colors or anything like it, since her existing visual phenomenology did not then exhibit the requisite dimensionality. So while in the room she knows that she is not having dense or analog representations of (the fullness of) colors. And so she expects to learn something when she leaves the room, and indeed she does.

Another person will not have my phenomenology if that person is not consciously aware, or is consciously aware yet does not possess any phenomenology, because she is without representations of continuous or dense phenomena, or does possesses such representations but these are of a lesser dimensionality than mine. These are sufficient conditions for a difference in phenomenology, yet they are not necessary. These and all other structural conditions can be met, yet her phenomenology nevertheless can differ from mine.

With phenomenology being such a powerful and useful mode of awareness, why isn't all our awareness phenomenological? Why does some of our conscious awareness involve digital linguistic/semantic entities with (little or) no phenomenological feel? Why do our thoughts have the character that they do?[93]

Phenomenological states are especially well suited for representing dense arrays of information. Many facts and aspects of the world (such as the surface reflectances at many spatial points) affect our neural states, which somehow produce experiences that represent the world. Being consciously aware of the world or of our states (as the blindsight person is not) enables various effects to take place beyond what the neural states can automatically unreel.

There are many other states of our brain that do not correspond to external perceptual stimuli and are not constituted by topographic maps. These states are beginning to be investigated in parallel distributed processing (PDP) networks wherein neurons are connected in multilayered vast networks with varying and ever-shifting weights on the synaptic connections. Such states also are present in nonhuman animals. These PDP states also can unreel automatically to produce behavior, and they spontaneously form new groupings and classifications of stimuli. Yet, just as with perceptual states, there are advantages to conscious awareness of these PDP states. If *these* PDP states are represented so that we are consciously aware of them, then we can better alter them, control them, combine them with other states, sequence them, utilize them in decisions, and so on.

I suggest that *thoughts,* that is, linguistic or at any rate semantic items, are the *representation* of such parallel distributed processing neural states. Thoughts in words or wordlike entities are the way in which these PDP neural states present themselves to us. The reason that linguistic thoughts do not have a phenomenology is that linguistic thoughts themselves *are* a phenomenology, the phenomenology of neural parallel distributed processing states. Semantic content is *the way in which (certain) neural states feel to us*. (I feel that at best I am groping toward an insight here; I would be far more comfortable if I understood my own proposal more clearly.) A book on thought might be titled *The Phenomenology of Neural Networks*.

But don't thoughts represent the external world? Neural PDP states represent the external world, and thoughts are the phenomenological representation of these states. In this case at least, the representation relation is transitive; thoughts represent the world. (Encoding of a text represents the text and through doing so represents what the text represents. Written texts, at least at first, represented verbal speech and thereby represented what the speech did. Use/mention distinctions came later.)

If linguistic thoughts are the phenomenology of PDP states, and (given the vast number of neurons we possess and their vast number of actual, not to mention possible, interconnections) if these states are effectively dense, then why isn't their linguistic representation also dense? Instead, the linguistic representation groups these states into rough equivalence classes, perhaps grouping them differently depending upon different purposes we hold. In effect, it quantizes a (multidimensional) continuum. It would be illuminating to investigate the special advantages, in this case, of a digital representation of such richly complex, constantly changing neurophysiological material.

The qualitative characters of sensory states do not themselves *have* qualia (or, if they do, these further qualia do not have qualia); they just *are* qualia. Similarly, thoughts that, for instance, $2 + 2 = 4$ don't have qualia; they just are the qualia of states of the brain.[94]

We now can repeat the series of questions we considered earlier concerning the phenomenology of sensory and perceptual states. Is there a function to there being *a* phenomenology of neural parallel distributed processing states? Yes, as we mentioned three paragraphs ago. Is there a function to the structure of the phenomenological states? Some of the linguistic/semantic structure is useful for the formalities of inference, and if these inferential relations parallel relations among the PDP states (or among facts the PDP states are appropriately connected to), then this aspect of linguistic structure will have a functional role. Is there a function to specificity in linguistic representation? No doubt it does give more precision and accuracy. There will not, however, be a distinct thought for each distinct connectionist state. Close connectionist states (with slightly different weightings or geometric configurations in state-space)[95] will present as the same thought, just as close shades of color will phenomenologically be within just noticeable differences. (And can some very close connectionist PDP states, even the very same state, be presented in different thought contents, for instance, "He is a brother" and "He is a male sibling"?)[96]

But given that there is some phenomenology (that is, some linguistic or semantic representation or other) of a certain structure and degree of specificity, is there an additional function to the particularity of the linguistic representation? We might put the question as follows: is there a function to the *particular* meanings that are used?

Quine's thesis of the indeterminacy of translation holds that the "meaning" of any sentence could be different (or translated differently), yet if this were accompanied by sufficient compensating structural changes throughout, there would be no behavioral difference occurring and all objective facts of sensory stimulation would be accommodated.[97] For example, instead of referring to continuing physical objects, terms would refer to temporal stages of such objects, with the identity relation correspondingly modified (so that "x is the same object as y" becomes "x and y are co-stages of the same object"). Since, according to Quine, there are no irreducible semantic facts that go beyond the fit of behavior to objective facts of stimulation, there is no fact of the matter about which of these two translations of identity-talk is the correct translation of someone else's sentences (and indeed no fact of the matter about what your own thoughts mean; indeterminacy of translation begins at home), although you will (quite naturally) offer them a homophonic translation. Meanings can be permuted so that no difference is made. The *particular* meanings, the particular character of the semantic or linguistic items, make no difference provided that certain structural and specificity conditions hold.

Quine's thesis of the indeterminacy of translation can be seen as a *consequence* of the view that semantic items are the phenomenology of (certain) neural states. We already have seen that the particularity of a phenomenology can vary freely within the structural and specificity constraints. Not only do the permutations of meaning envisioned in Quine's indeterminacy of translation call to mind the "reversed spectrum," they are an instance of the same general phenomenon![98]

A system of representation by qualia or by semantic items will contain features that "are not inherent in the phenomena" represented.[99] Some structural or other features will not correspond to features represented. Yet certain of these structural features may be inescapable so long as that specific system of representation is being used, and those features may get *imputed* to the world. Artifacts of the particular system of representation used, they may come to seem necessary and inherent features of the world. This is unlikely to happen with certain features of systems of representation. With writing, we do not impute features of the typeface used, or of upper or lower case, to the world. We are aware that these stem from our particular mode of representation, perhaps because we can switch freely between different systems of representation. With maps, it takes somewhat longer to learn what is a feature of the world, and what is due to the particular method used to project a (portion of a) sphere onto a plane surface. (Recall the distortions of the Mercator projection.) Other such structural features might be effectively invisible to us, at least for a time, and give rise to the illusion of necessary truths. We have seen that there is a function to the existence and the structure and the specificity of phenomenological representation. We have held, however, that the particularity of the representations within these functional limits itself is *non*functional. It is an error when this nonfunctional particularity is imputed to the world or projected onto it.

Although there is no function to the particularity of experienced qualities, the particularity that holds can be very important to us. We have been wired to pay attention to particular qualities, to find some reinforcing and to find others punishing. Those contemporaneous with our ancestors who did not find sexual activity reinforcing did not, voluntarily, engage in child-producing activities. We are descended from those who possessed the heritable trait of finding that activity pleasurable. Still, it seems that there could have been a different particular phenomenological quality to sexual activity that also was found reinforcing and also led to that same behavior with the same frequency. The activity's feeling precisely like *that* does not seem necessary for motivational purposes. Something different that was equally pleasurable and exciting and intense would have done equally well. A fondness for certain tastes motivated our ancestors to take in substances needed for nutrition, growth, and survival, but other qualitative tastes that were found similarly enticing would have served as well.

The particular quality of the phenomenology has no biological function, given that the structure, specificity, intensity, and rewardingness of the phenomenology are held constant. Nevertheless, we do pay close attention to those particular qualities, distinguishing them from other, similar qualities.

Thereby we derive information about precise states of the world or of our bodies. Someone who ignores the particular qualities of the phenomenology will lack some discriminative knowledge. This seems somewhat paradoxical. Those particular qualities have no function, yet we need to pay close attention to those very qualities. How can that be?

Few Americans can pick out the correct drawing of a Lincoln penny from among other drawings that show the head in different orientation or the printing in different places, despite the fact that we encounter pennies every day. However, we do not need to know how to distinguish real pennies from very similar purported pennies, which the world does not contain. It would be inefficient to store in memory full information about an object or kind of object. All we need is just enough information to distinguish an object or event from all (or most) other known actual cases. Even though people in the United States frequently handle pennies, there is no need for them to notice or remember the precise information about the orientation of Lincoln's head and where the writing is located, for people's daily tasks do not involve making these distinctions. We *do need* to tell pennies from nickels from dimes from quarters, and we store in memory enough distinguishing features (color, approximate size, etc.) to perform this task. The particular orientation of the face on the coin is *not* one of the features useful in making these discriminations. There is a maxim of need to know. Don't know more than you need to; don't store more information than you need to. What a given person needs will depend upon his situation, tasks, occupation, etc., and upon what other things he actually has encountered that he needs to distinguish this case from. A coin dealer will remember more about common coins than you or I will.[100]

This storage of partial information also accounts for the unreliability of eyewitnesses to events. They are unable to distinguish the person they saw at the crime from all other actual persons. They have stored only enough information to distinguish the perpetrator from the people they actually have seen, but they have not stored (and so cannot remember) enough detail to distinguish him from a similarly described person that the police have found. It is the predicted or expected needs that shape what information we save, and how we save it, and our memories will be as reliable as we later need them to be only when our actual later needs are in accord with the needs that were anticipated. When the later needs are unexpectedly stringent, as in criminal identification, we get noticeable memory errors.[101]

We now can understand why we often do pay close attention to the particular qualities of an experience. The way in which these particular qualities differ from the qualities of other (actual) experiences tells us that (and how) the cause of this experience differs from what caused the other experiences.[102] To know this fact about the situation we are in is to possess valuable information.

The actual particular qualitative ways in which this experience differs from other experiences gives us valuable information, but that information could, in principle, be conveyed by other qualitative differences. What is important is that experiences differ. We look to the particular characteristics of the experiences to determine whether they do differ, and by how much. It is the fact of differences that is important, not the fact of *those* particular differences. It is important, therefore, that experiences corresponding to different external circumstances differ in qualitative ways, but it is not important that they differ in precisely *those* particular qualitative ways. It is some particularity or other that matters—not that special particularity. Nevertheless, what we have to pay attention to is the particularity that there actually is, which is—as it happens—*that* one.

The central focus of our discussion thus far has been the informational impact of qualitative experience. Do we find some additional role for *a* phenomenology, even if not for that particular one, in the phenomena of reward and punishment, of reinforcement, operant conditioning, and motivation? Does phenomenology extend down to some organisms that lack the capacity for being operantly conditioned? A machine could be constructed with some distinguished state (with no pretense to a phenomenology) so that whenever any behavior causes it to go into that state, the probability increases of its repeating that behavior. Totaling the pluses and minuses seems sufficient for a pattern of reinforcement to occur; why must anything be experienced? People do learn from a match or mismatch between the anticipated reinforcement and the received reinforcement, and we modify our behavior accordingly, but couldn't this occur with registration but no experience?

What role does phenomenological awareness play in the functioning of reinforcement and of emotions? Are there analogs of blindsight with reinforcement? If a person is given a reinforcement of which he is not consciously aware, how will the results of this differ from the usual case of conscious awareness? Will there be only crude behavior control and adaptation in the motivation case, as in the informational case, so that in each case qualia give us more subtle and refined adjustments?[103]

To all hypotheses about the function of felt qualia, it might be objected that this can be (and is) carried out by the neurology that (on the identity or supervenience theory) underlies the phenomenology. Why then are the qualia needed? However, that particular neurological capacity and configuration might exist and have been selected for *because* it gives rise to those qualia that then accomplish their function.[104] While the neurology alone, without qualia, could do the job, there would not *be* that neurology, there would not have been a process of selecting for it, had it not given rise to qualia. And certain neurological configurations would not have made the organism more fit had they not given rise to more salient or better-grouped qualia (within the qualitative psychological space that affects generalization gradients and thus affects behavior). More on this later.

Mind-Body Relations

What is relevant to the function of phenomenology (we have held) is that it is *a* phenomenology with a particular structure and degree of specificity; the particular character of the experiences is not relevant. The function of a phenomenology determines that phenomenology only up to isomorphism. But what of the aspects that can vary within that isomorphism (e.g., the precise way in which something feels)?[105] If phenomenology does have a precise character, even if the particularity of that precise character performs no special function, there will be a question about the ontological status of this phenomenological character and of its relation to physical processes.

The literature on the mind-body problem often is extremely heated. Writers often are angry at, or contemptuous of, those who hold an opposing view. It might be interesting to diagnose why this is so. There is the value-laden nature of the subject matter, yet the literature on free will is far less agitated. (Have passionate polemicists disproportionally entered the mind-body topic? If so, why?) Whatever the correct explanation, I myself do not feel at all heated about the topic. It is not a matter of religious conviction for me. (Indeed, religious conviction is not a matter of religious conviction for me.) The nature of the mind-body connection is, I think, an empirical question. Or it can be turned into one.

Various theories of the mind-body relation have been proposed in the philosophical literature, including the identity theory, functionalism, anomalous monism, supervenience, epiphenomenalism, dualism. Despite disagreement about what is the correct theory, the literature agrees that *just one* theory is the uniformly correct one. However, it is possible that one of these theories applies to certain mental items or aspects, while another one of the theories applies to other mental items or aspects. There may be no *one* mind-body relation.

The thesis that mental states are identical with physical ones usually is stated by drawing upon the model of identity embodied in the reduction of one scientific theory to another. One scientific theory is reducible to another one if the first theory is deducible from the second theory in combination with statements connecting the concepts of the two theories. The process of reduction itself may show limitations in the theory intended for reduction, and so some approximation of that theory, more limited in its scope, may be what gets deduced. (One does not require a reduction of every feature mentioned by the candidate theory for reduction; some of those features may be discarded as inaccurate or misguided.) Thus thermodynamics is reduced to statistical mechanics: the laws of thermodynamics follow from those of statistical mechanics along with the correspondence of the temperature of a gas with the mean kinetic energy of its molecules. So runs the account offered by Ernest Nagel; a modification has been offered by Paul Churchland and C. A. Hooker.[106] On this latter account, within the reducing theory one deduces an image or isomorph of (some of) the laws of the reduced theory, and the pairings of concepts (such as temperature and mean kinetic energy) are there to exhibit the isomorphism. The paired concepts will refer to the very same thing, and so the correspondence between them will be an *identity,* when the reduction goes smoothly. (Since smoothness is a matter of degree, this seems to make the line between correlation and identity somewhat arbitrary, as it also makes the question of how many different kinds of entities there are.)

The claim that conscious experiences or states of conscious awareness are identical with physical states of the human organism seems incredible to many people. The two things just seem so very different! It appears absurd to view them as (even possibly) identical. To assess this dismissal, we must look more carefully at the question of identity. Suppose there is a deduction or isomorphic mirroring of one (modified) theory by another. What is required of the correspondences between notions A and B of the two theories for them to refer to the *very same* entity, property, event or state? If there is to be identity, there will be at least a universal correlation between the two. An entity has or instantiates A if and only if it has or instantiates B. (That correlation is already stated in the reduction.) We want more than A and B always going together, though, more than each always being present when the other is. By Leibniz's law, two things are identical only if they have the same properties. We want A and B, therefore, to have the very same features. A and B will have the same features if laws about B have isomorphic parallels in laws about A, and if nonlawlike truths about all B's have isomorphic parallels in true statements about all A's. (And vice versa.)[107]

However, for identity to hold between A and B (and so between instances of A and instances of B), we want them not only to have corresponding features up the line, but to have the *very same* features. We want, that is, that there not only be some correlate G that an A has whenever a B has *F;* we want that A to have that feature *F* itself. We started with a correlation (between A and B), and we wondered when it would constitute identity. We then looked to their having exactly the same features, yet by phrasing this in terms of the correlated second-level features *F* and *G,* we seem to have encountered the same problem again, this time one level up, of finding a condition beyond correlation that is sufficient for identity.

Two entities are the same only if they have the same properties—they cannot differ in their properties—but are the entities guaranteed to be the same when they do have the same properties? Leaving aside the examples discussed in the literature on the identity of indiscernibles (e.g., two spheres of the same size and material in an otherwise empty infinite space), in general, a difference between entities will be marked by a difference in their properties. And if they have correlated but different properties A and B, a difference in those properties will, in general, be shown by a difference in the properties of these properties. And if *these* properties themselves have different but correlated properties F and G, then a difference in these latter properties will be shown, in general, by a difference in *their* properties. Barring extremely unlikely coincidences and very artificial situations, somewhere up the line a difference will show itself in a lack of parallelism, a lack of universal correlation.

It is reasonable to believe that two things are identical if they are (universally) correlated, if their properties are universally correlated, if the properties of their properties are universally correlated, and so on all the way up the line, *unless* it is evident that the situation is one of the extremely unlikely or artificial ones in which the principle of the identity of indiscernibles breaks down.[108] When every aspect of one phenomenon is mirrored, all the way up the line, by an aspect of the other phenomenon, then (barring one of the evidently exceptional cases) it is reasonable to conclude that the two phenomena are not two but one. It is reasonable to conclude that they are identical. (Notice that this criterion of mirroring all the way up the line no longer is tied to the notion of the scientific reduction of one theory to another.) What we have proposed here is not an ontological criterion of identity but an epistemic criterion of when it is reasonable to believe that identity holds.

Why have people held that the mental or experiential could not be identical with the physical? The mental or experiential seems different from any physical phenomenon (even if it is correlated with one) because it has aspects or properties that are different from any physical property. For example, there is a *perspective* involved in experiences that does not apply to the physical, there is *a way that it is to be* that does not apply to the physical, there is a *raw feel* that doesn't apply to the physical, *a felt phenomenological quality* that nothing physical has. (And there also are the obvious properties of *seeming different from a physical event* and *not feeling like a physical event.*)

But how do we know that *these* properties cannot be had by physical events, that they are not themselves properties of physical events? Could not some type of physical event occur in the brain whenever there is a conscious experience, or a perspectival phenomenon? Only *RN* has access to *m*. Does that show *m* cannot be physical? *RN*'s perspective gives him a unique relation *R* to *m*. However, why cannot this be paralleled by a unique physical relation *R'* that *RN* stands in to a physical thing *e* that *m* is correlated with? To stand in *R'* to some entity *e is* to have the unique perspective. Why not? Could there not be a property of brain events that they instance only when something occurs with a felt phenomenological quality, or even a physical property that correlates with something's seeming different from a physical event?[109] Aspect *N* is the aspect of "not feeling like a physical happening," but *N* gets correlated with some aspect *N'* of neuronal states and firing, which occurs whenever some psychological item doesn't feel like a physical happening. *N'* is the physical aspect or occurrence that the identity theorist claims *is N*.[110]

"Well, there might be physical properties correlated with these psychological properties, but they would not be (identical with) these very same psychological properties." But why would they not be identical? Is there some trait had by each, or even by one, of these psychological properties that no physical property has? What is that trait, and how is it known that no physical property has it? Isn't that because (it is thought that) no physical property *can* have it? And is that because that trait has some further trait which (it is thought) no physical property has (because none can have it)?

My claim is that the philosopher who is convinced that the mental is distinct from the physical, who believes that the two cannot be identical, has in mind some trait *T* that distinguishes the two, whether this is a trait of the experience or a trait of a trait of the experience, or whatever. Yet he does not know, I think, that this trait *T* is not paralleled by a physical trait that universally corresponds to it.[111] If there *were* a parallelism of traits, *all the way up the line,* would this philosopher still assert or be convinced that the mental and the physical were not identical?[112]

I have held that a sufficient condition for the nonidentity of two properties A and B would be that A has an aspect *F,* and there is *no* aspect *G* of B that is (universally) correlated with *F.* My proposed criterion for concluding that identity holds amounts to this: conclude that identity holds when this sufficient condition (of nonidentity) is not satisfied. This is plausible as an epistemic criterion: when the parallelism holds all the way up the line, then (except in certain very special situations) conclude that the two are identical. However, the proponent of the nonidentity of the mental and the physical may hold that this is not enough, on the ground that the proposed criterion of identity does not logically entail that there is identity. (I agree that there isn't that entailment.) Even if it is epistemically sufficient, it is ontologically insufficient. Yet what other criterion is there *to use?* Does the non–identity theorist have a criterion of his own to propose? (It is not enough for him just to sit back and say, "That is not enough.")

One objection to the identity of the mental and the physical has carried great weight in the literature.[113] The mental can be realized in many different materials, in organisms composed of different substances from our standard protoplasm. What is important to the identity of the mental, therefore, seems to be a certain structural and functional organization rather than the particular stuff out of which it happens to be made in our case. So runs the argument from "multiple realizability."[114]

Consider another notion of something with a function, *food.* Food is something that can be broken down by a body's enzymes and chemicals; it can be digested, with the resulting chemicals and physical elements circulating through the body and absorbed to give the body energy and material for growth. A substance that is food for one kind of organism may not be food for another that is unable to digest it. So the notion is implicitly relative: *food for organism O.* (And is *O* a *type* of organism, or a particular one? Is food for the lactose- or gluten-intolerant person the same as it is for the rest?) So the (relative) notion of food is specified functionally, by causal interconnections marking what can be done to it for what biological purposes. Is there one common chemical specification of what constitutes food for people? Given the number of different digestive enzymes and their specific chemical targets, I think it more likely that there is a disjunction of chemical structures that constitutes the underlying basis of the dispositional concept "digestible by a normal human being." What gets absorbed is a disjunction too: of essential amino acids, essential fatty acids, essential elements, and carbohydrates. The original specification of human food is functional, but what human food *is* is specifiable by a disjunction, the disjunction picked out by that more unitary functional specification. (But how unitary is the functional specification itself, mentioning as it does substances that provide a source of energy *or* a source of material for growth and for structural components?) Does all this make one an identity theorist about human food or a functionalist? That question does not seem to be very interesting.

When we extend our purview to other animals here on Earth, different foods are digestible by them, and (for all I know) the chemicals that form the disjunction of what they absorb also differ from the chemicals for human beings. So we have a disjunction of substances and chemicals that constitute food for human beings, a disjunction of such disjunctions that constitutes food for organisms on Earth, and perhaps a wider disjunction for food in the universe. (I leave aside the social aspect of food, which concerns not just what is digestible and absorbable but how cultural factors shape what humans choose to ingest.) Such disjunctions do not stand in the way of interesting identities.

Jaegwon Kim has emphasized the possibility of limited reductions in the philosophy of mind. These specify the physical nature of some mental item for a particular type of organism (rather than specifying the unitary physical nature of that mental item for all actual or possible organisms).[115] And if other organisms find slightly different uses for ingested chemicals, won't we still be able to recognize these as food, just as we might recognize other beings' items as mental even when they do not exactly match the functional connections of any of *our* items. Perhaps there is a general functional characterization of food for an organism, as perhaps there is for a mental item of any organism; but using these functional characterizations to identify the more particular items and their underlying disjunctions does not commit us to a functionalism that denies anything of significance to identity theories.

When each species ingests different food yet, for each species, we can offer a chemical description of what constitutes food for it, then it is correct to say that that *is* what food is for that species. And, as in the case of the lactose- or gluten-intolerant person, the subject of the description can be drawn more narrowly than the species. (If other animals chew and swallow some substance that we also chew and swallow, but the chemicals they absorb from this substance are disjoint from the chemicals we absorb from it, are we eating the same food?) In answer to the question of why the same

term "food" gets applied in these various cases, a functional characterization of food can be offered in reply. Similarly, when different species carry
pain in different material substrata, in cells of different sorts or even in sili-
con instead of protoplasm, it still can be correct to say of one species that
that *is* what pain is for that species. (And the subject of the description can
be drawn more narrowly than the species.) In answer to the question of
why the same term "pain" gets applied in these various cases, a (partly)
functional characterization of pain might be offered in reply, for instance, a
state involving experiences that are undesired (in part) for their own intrinsic or felt qualities, which state typically is produced by physical injury or
damage to physical organs.[116] However, notice that this characterization decidedly does not endorse "functionalism" about pain. If something involving experiences is undesired for its own intrinsic (or felt) qualities, then if
another thing performs many of those same functions yet involves no experiences, or if the experiences it does involve have no intrinsic (or felt) qualities because of which they are undesired, that never-felt or differently felt
kind of thing will not be pain.

Our discussion here has been confined to considering whether the functionalist's claim of multiple realizability, if true, is fatal to the identity theory. If our earlier discussion of consciousness is on the mark, however, then
the multiple realizability of consciousness, and of whatever depends upon
consciousness, turns out to be a tricky matter. For the common registering
intrinsic to consciousness requires a particular kind of material for its realization, one in which the requisite physical reverberations occur. Consciousness is not simply a matter of the functionalist's flow diagrams linking stimuli to internal states and to response. Or, if common knowledge is
built into a specification of these flow diagrams, then these flow diagrams
themselves can be realized only in very particular kinds of materials. I do
not say that only one material can do the job. There may be room, still, for
more than one realization. But one cannot just assume that the multiplicity
will turn out to be very great.

I have said that the mind-body relation is an empirical question. The
identity theory could be true; mental events and experiences and consciousness might be physical happenings and capacities. The identity theory could be false. It is a question of whether, *in fact*, there are sufficient
parallelisms that all aspects of the mental, all the way up the line, have a
correlate with something physical. We do not yet know whether this is so.[117]

However, as I said at the beginning of this section, perhaps there is not
just *one* mind-body relation that holds. Different aspects or components of
the mind might stand in different relations to the body.

Here is one such possibility. Those aspects of conscious awareness that mark its biological function might be type-type identical with neurophysiological states, while such an identity might not hold of the nonfunctional aspects. For example, there being a phenomenology of a particular structure and degree of specificity—something that has a function—would be identical with some neurophysiological events, states, and processes, whereas the particularity of the phenomenology of the qualitative states, a particularity that does not have a function, would not be type-type identical with the physical.

Thus, the neurological correlate of consciousness might be something that carries out the function of consciousness, yet consciousness might have features, accidental to its function, that are not paralleled (all the way up the line) by features of consciousness' neurological correlate. Consciousness might acquire some added features *inessential* to its function. The only things that get reduced are the functional features of consciousness. The identity theory then would apply to the functional essence of consciousness. Whatever features consciousness has in order to carry out its task and function *are identical* with neurological events, processes, and structures. The by-the-way features consciousness has acquired, an accretion on consciousness or an arbitrary filling in of it, are not identical with neural phenomena (but stand in some relation other than identity to these phenomena). This kind of nonidentity, however, would be cold comfort for the non–identity theorist. It would not give him what he wants, namely, something *important*'s being nonidentical with the physical. (He might say that it is important that something or other, even something nonimportant, be nonidentical with the physical—but why should this be so?)

The particularity of phenomenological quality might fit this general description of a by-the-way feature. We have held that there is a function performed by there being some phenomenological qualities or other that stand in certain structural relations to still other phenomenological qualities, but that there is no function to the *particular* content and feel these qualities have. (Given what the function of consciousness is, we do not need more accurate contentful knowledge than the structural experiences provide.) The property of having a phenomenology with a certain structure, therefore, might be identical with a physical property, while the particularity of the phenomenology might be an additional psychological trait supervenient upon the physical or even (although I doubt this) an additional trait (which is nonsupervenient) that varies freely within the bounds of the physical.

People vary in their neurological wiring just as they vary in other physical characteristics such as the size, shape, and location of their hearts. We might predict that there will be more resemblance in their traits that have been selected to perform a certain function than there will be in traits not so selected (even when these traits are side effects of the selected traits). If the specific particularity of the phenomenology performs no function and was not selected for, we might expect it to vary from individual to individual. That does not mean that in the case of one given individual, the particular character of the phenomenology floats free of his physical states. The relevant physical states that give rise to the particularities of the phenomenologies might vary from individual to individual, while each physical state fully determines its own accompanying phenomenology. (In this case, there might be token-token identity, or supervenience without identity.)

Jaegwon Kim has distinguished weak from strong supervenience of the mental upon the physical. The first involves a dependency of the mental upon the physical in the actual world; the second involves the same dependency of the mental upon the physical in all possible worlds. It is worth pointing out that these are not the only two possibilities. There are degrees of supervenience between weak and strong. These degrees are a function of two factors: the extent across possible worlds of some sort of weak supervenience or other of the mental upon the physical, even if not the same exact supervenience that obtains in the actual world; and the extent across possible worlds, even when the extent is not universal, of exactly the same supervenience that obtains in the actual world. Suppose that indeed there is (weak) supervenience in the actual world of the mental upon the physical. If that very same dependency does hold in some possible world, there will be transworld supervenience between the actual world and that particular possible world.

Let us now ask how close the closest possible world is in which that particular dependency of the mental upon the physical does not hold. And how close is the closest possible world in which there is no weak supervenience at all, even of another sort, of the mental upon the physical? The answer to these two questions will give us the *degree of contingency of the supervenience* of the mental upon the physical that holds in the actual world. It would be very illuminating if the supervenience of a particular phenomenology upon the physical is not very contingent (even though it is not necessary, since it is not strong supervenience); in that case, the very same phenomenology depends upon the very same physical states in all close-by worlds. And it would be very illuminating if the supervenience of *some* phenomenology or other upon those same physical states (which phenomenology is supervenient upon in the actual world) was even less contingent. And still less contingent might be the dependence of some phenomenology upon some physical states or other.

Nevertheless, there will remain an issue of understanding why certain physical states give rise to conscious awareness or qualitative experience. Why don't those physical states simply have their consequences without any conscious accompaniments? Or why aren't the physical states accompanied by different conscious states, states other than the ones that actually accompany them? When the connection between the physical states and the conscious states they underlie is a contingent one, there seems to be room for this question yet no evident way to answer it. Can one avoid or shortly answer the question by maintaining that the conscious state is *identical* with the physical state, and that this identity is a necessary one, holding in all possible worlds? Claims that such identities are necessary if they hold at all, are currently widespread. (But they are not without difficulties.)[118] Yet one continues to want to ask: why is the physical property identical with this consciousness property rather than with that one, or with none at all? To be told that the properties just are identical, and they have to be, is unsatisfactory. And to be instructed that it is not that they "just" are identical, rather they necessarily are identical, does not eliminate the question of why precisely that identity holds.

However, according to the account we have sketched, even if we do not know *why* precisely that identity holds, we do know quite a lot. Suppose there are many physical states $P_1, \ldots, P_n$, and only some of these give rise to or are identical with states of conscious awareness. We do not know why some do, or why the ones that do are connected to those particular conscious states. Yet, if there indeed is a function to conscious awareness, then there would be selection for organisms whose constitution gives rise to some physical states that are connected to states of conscious awareness. Moreover, there would be selection for organisms whose constitution gives rise in certain circumstances to those physical states that are connected to precisely *those* states of conscious awareness that are useful in those circumstances. These are states whose informational content or focus aids in the performance of finely adaptive activities, that is, states whose causal consequences are, in that kind of external and internal context, finely adaptive.[119]

So once a function of conscious awareness and of qualitative experience is identified, we can see why there would be evolutionary selection for states of conscious awareness, and hence for the physical states that underlie them. (To forestall an objection, we need to recall that the circulation of blood can be the function of the heart even though there are other logically possible or even physically possible ways to get blood circulated. In those particular bodily surroundings, however, the heart serves and is needed to do so.) We can see why there would be evolutionary selection for states of conscious awareness, states whose causal consequences *depend* upon their being states of conscious awareness, even if there were possible other ways, not involving conscious awareness, to accomplish the same functions in different circumstances and bodily environments.[120]

Will this necessarily leave an "explanatory gap" so that we cannot explain why that physical state gives rise to precisely *that* phenomenology?[121] Assuming that we understand why it will give rise to any phenomenology at all, that is, to some phenomenology or other, we can understand why it will give rise to a phenomenology with the structure of that particular one. Suppose that physical state S_1 gives rise to a phenomenology P_1 of a certain structure (and its having that structure is explainable), and physical state S_2 gives rise to a different phenomenology P_2 of the very same structure (and its having that structure is explainable). The qualitative differences in the phenomenologies have a physical basis, in that they depend upon different physical happenings and states. But must it remain an enigma why physical state S_1 gives rise to the particular phenomenology P_1 rather than to the phenomenology P_2 of exactly the same structure? Must this remain a brute fact? The differences in the phenomenologies might be comprehensible, however, even though they have no function. Suppose that one phenomenology P_1 involves somewhat brighter hues throughout than P_2 does, and its physical basis S_1 involves, e.g., more rapid firing of neurons than S_2 does. The explanation of the increase in brightness is the increase in the rapidity of the neuron firing. This is very crude, of course, but it makes the point that the differences in the qualitative feels of the phenomenologies might be traceable to physical differences that make those qualitative differences comprehensible. (Even though someone certainly will object that the brighter hues could equally well go with the slower firing of neurons.)

If the mental and the physical are *non*identical, could the systematic relationship between the mental and the physical reveal their nonidentity in some additional way, other than by their lack of parallelism at some level up the line? The non-identity supervenience theorist claims that there is a systematic connection between mind and body that exhibits features incompatible with (or in tension with) identity, while the identity theorist claims that all systematic connections between mind and body are compatible with identity. We need to hear what these features are that are incompatible with identity.[122] To sharpen the issue between these theorists is not to make a claim about which one is right.

I have emphasized that the truth about the mind-body relation may not be uniform. There is the possibility that some mental items are identical with physical ones, others are supervenient but nonidentical, while still others are (dualistically) nonsupervenient. I myself tend to think that the identity theory has been given unduly short shrift recently, and that it should be the default position, to be maintained as the one uniform truth in the absence of compelling evidence against that. I also am extremely skeptical about the third dualistic possibility, but the issue is to be settled by empirical investigation, not by *a priori* arguments. Will investigation discover parallelism everywhere all the way up the line, or will it sometimes discover correlations between properties whose distinctness is revealed by some structural fact, or will it find a decided lack of correlation somewhere that shows some mental feature is not even supervenient upon the physical? These are empirical questions. It is best to keep an open mind.

The identity theory connects in a surprising way with the question of the function of consciousness. We can ask what consciousness actually does, and also we can ask why consciousness is needed to do that. Couldn't the underlying causal connections involving physical states and bodily motions accomplish all that consciousness does, *without* the presence of conscious awareness? To ask what consciousness does is, on the identity theory, to ask what the physical states that are identical with states of consciousness do. What these physical states do (that other physical states do not) is lead to close coordination in parallel distributed process systems, subtle kinds of fitting of behavior to environment, certain kinds of monitoring of behavior, etc. But why can't all that be accomplished by the physical causal connections concerning those physical states, without these states' giving rise to or being identical with states of conscious awareness?

The answer is that if the states were not states of conscious awareness, they would not have *those* causal connections.[123] This is an example of what Donald Campbell and Karl Popper have called "downward causation." No nonphysical influences act to produce particular physical events. However, not all physical laws and causal relations are deducible from some set of fundamental physical laws that apply to all physical states, whether or not these are identical with states of conscious awareness.[124] All the consequences of conscious states are in accordance with physical law, but the laws stating some of these consequences are not deducible from or reducible to underlying general physical laws of unrestricted application (plus bound-

ary conditions). The only physical laws that delineate these causal consequences of conscious states (that is, of the physical states that are identical
with conscious states) are *restricted* laws that apply only to the physical
states that are identical with conscious states. The logical-positivist thesis of
the unity of science, therefore, is denied.

However, on this view, the physical world is causally closed, in that there
are no (caused) physical events whose causal antecedents are not in the
physical realm. (Causal closure does not require that the physical universe
be deterministic, only that the physical events that *do* have causes have
physical ones.) Conscious states do have causal consequences in the physical realm. They are not causally inert. But since the producers of these
causal consequences are conscious states that (by hypothesis) are identical
with physical states, the chain of causal antecedents does not lead out of the
physical realm.[125]

To the question of why conscious awareness is needed, of why the same
underlying physical states cannot produce the same causal results without
any conscious awareness being present, the answer is that without conscious awareness, those physical states would not have those particular results. The laws according to which they do have those particular results are
special laws that apply only to states that are identical with conscious states.
Consciousness is different.

But *are* there any such specialized laws that apply only to certain specialized states and that are not derivable from more general laws of unrestricted application? Yes, there are, according to our currently best and
most fundamental and precisely accurate theory, quantum mechanics. For
according to the standard interpretation of quantum mechanics, as expounded by John von Neumann, when a physical system in a superposition
comes into contact with a measuring device or with a human observer
(who is treated as another physical system), there is a collapse of the wave
packet, and the measurement device or human observer observes one particular result.[126] Yet this collapse of the wave packet is not a consequence of,
or an instance of, Schrodinger's equation, which is the fundamental equation of quantum mechanics. According to Schrodinger's equation, in that
particular measurement or observation situation, the device or human observer also goes into a superposition, and so does not make any one unique
observation. Thus, on the standard interpretation, the collapse of the wave
packet and the making of particular observations is not a consequence of
the most general law of quantum mechanics. It is a unique phenomenon
that occurs only when a system in superposition interacts ultimately with a

physical system that is a conscious human organism. The measurement problem in quantum mechanics is the puzzle of understanding why unique observations occur.

My aim is not to join others in deriving murky conclusions about consciousness from the murky mysteries of quantum mechanics. I invoke quantum mechanics only to support the view, by example, that the thoroughgoing reducibility of all laws to a select general few (the unity of science) does not hold, or at least need not do so. That the wave packet collapses is not derivable from Schrodinger's equation. Moreover, that failure of derivability comes precisely at the point where physical systems that are identical with conscious beings interact with physical systems in a superposition.

If we did want to connect consciousness directly with quantum mechanics, we would need to gain some understanding of why measurement by conscious observers collapses the wave packet.[127] And that might constitute a test of a particular theory of consciousness. What is it about consciousness, as that theory construes it, that would collapse the wave packet and produce an exception to the operation of Schrodinger's equation, an otherwise universal law? On the theory presented in this chapter, that question becomes: why does the common registering (in a distributed mechanism of a certain sort) of a quantum measurement on a state in a superposition, rather than sending that mechanism itself into a superposition of observing this and observing that, instead collapse the wave packet and put the mechanism into a particular state of observation? Is there something about such a common registering that makes it especially difficult to reverse or to erase?

On the view we are presenting here, the quantum mechanics of the collapse of the wave packet, rather than requiring that conscious states float free of physical states, dovetails with the view that conscious states are *identical* with physical states. States of consciousness are not ontologically special, but they are *nomologically special*. Special laws do apply to these states, laws that are not derivable from the most general laws that apply to all physical states, including those that are not identical with consciousness. (What other states, in addition to the states identical with consciousness, are nomologically special?)

I do not claim to understand fully the possibility of nomological specialness that I have adumbrated here. Were the laws governing physical states that are identical with states of consciousness (laws that, by hypothesis are not derivable from the other most general fundamental laws) always lurking there, ready to spring into action when the newly complex physical material evolved or otherwise came into being? Was it determinate earlier, that is, was it true earlier, that those laws would be the ones to govern the more complexly structured matter, only this was true as an independent underivable fact, without any domain of application existing yet? That seems implausible. Are the previously universal laws like a set of axioms for number theory, with the new laws that emerge being like Godel sentences that are unprovable, underivable, from the axiomatic laws? Yet did the underivable laws nevertheless hold true all along? If not, why was it these particular underivable statements, and not some others, that became the laws governing the newly emergent physical structures? Moreover, if some newly emergent physical structures elude the operation of the previously universally applicable general laws, why must their behavior be subject to any new laws at all? Couldn't these new structures (although they came to exist as a result of the operation of laws of previously universal applicability) emerge as outlaws?

In view of these formidably difficult questions, it may seem philosophically extravagant, and excessively humanocentric (or animocentric) to consider postulating nomological specialness merely in order to accommodate consciousness.

Recall again the explanatory structure of evolutionary cosmology that was discussed in Chapter 3. We compared physical laws to the genetic constitution of an organism that is passed on (with some mutations or transformations) from generation to generation. But any set of laws powerful enough to contain number theory will contain (by Godel's theorem) an infinite number of undecidable statements. Some things will hold true in each such universe that do not follow from its fundamental laws. Will any of these things be physical truths, as opposed to statements of pure number theory? If some phenomenon is so complex in its structure that the propositions describing it and its behavior are not derivable from the "axioms" constituting the laws of its universe, and if it is intertwined with mathematical statements of number theory that are complex enough to constitute undecidable statements within that universe's lawlike structure, then either that phenomenon will be subject to some emergent law, or its behavior will not be governed by any law at all.

Will this phenomenon's behavior constitute a trait that will be passed on to descendent universes? Not if it is unlawful. But suppose that the law governing its behavior, once arising as an underivable special law, somehow is added on to the existing corpus of (fundamental) laws as a component of the "genetic" structure that is transmissible to descendent generations. In that case, the trait would be transmitted. But why would it get added in this way, as an additional "genetic axiom" of that universe's genome? Within evolutionary cosmology, the following two (heritable) traits might themselves have spontaneously arisen and then have spread in a population of progeny universes because of their tendency to preserve advantageous random mutations. First is the trait of giving rise to some law or other to govern a new physical structure that arises that is not subject to any law derivable from the existing set of the universe's laws. Second is the trait of transmitting any law given rise to (by the first trait, in the way just described) to the next generation of that universe's progeny. These two traits, in combination, would produce heritable traits and preserve the advantageous ones, that is, the ones that increased a universe's individual fitness.[128]

We thus would expect that universes produced by the processes of evolutionary cosmology would contain some emergent laws. Wouldn't this lead to a great proliferation of laws, though? Wouldn't it make even the current degree of unification in our physical theory unlikely? A good question. There might be a process that combines the newly emergent laws with the previous fundamental one(s) into a new unification, so as to better transmit them all. (We know that the newly emergent law is *compatible* with that universe's previously existing laws, for it is independent of them.) Such a unifying mechanism might itself be a third heritable trait that spontaneously arose and then spread because of its advantageous consequences.[129] Thus, we might expect universes to exist which are by and large susceptible to explanation by a unified theory, but which have (only) a few emergent laws that (temporarily) stick out. These particular recalcitrant laws will get incorporated into unifications in the next generation of universes. But a universe's line cannot step into the same theory twice, for freshly emergent laws are ever flowing in upon it.

This chapter has examined gradations of awareness; these range from registration, to registration of registration, to awareness, to conscious awareness, to noticing, to attention, to concentration. Different gradations of awareness subserve different kinds of guidance of current behavior, different kinds of accessibility to memory later, and different roles in the process of planning future behavior. Each level or gradation of awareness involves the activity of a certain fraction of the relevant portions of the brain, as is shown in various measurements of brain activity. (At the time I write, the current methods of measurement include positron emission tomography and functional magnetic resonance imaging.)

But why couldn't these more advanced and subtle guidance functions be performed automatically, without rising to the level of awareness? Each of these functions, performed in human brains as they actually are constituted, requires the activation of a certain fraction of the relevant parts of the brain subserving those functions. Having at least that fraction involved just *is* reaching that level of awareness. Still, why must that fraction involve any awareness?

For the involvement of that fraction of the relevant part of the brain to be able to serve the subtle and advanced guidance functions, the relevant subparts of that part must be in the closest intercommunication. This involves the registering of its activities throughout that part of the brain, the registering of that registering, and so on up to (an approximation of) common registering. And that common registering is a grade of awareness. Each increase in the gradation of awareness corresponds to a larger relevant portion of the brain's being in a state of common registering.

Can we describe achievable capacities that would yield a computer that was aware or conscious of something? If the capacities are achievable, we need not be stingy with them. Sufficient conditions for awareness are the goal. (A later investigation might attempt to pare these down to the minimum that could achieve awareness.)

The computer will utilize representations. Some of its states will be information-bearing states, in that they stand in certain connections to the world, and they function in a wider system, in an adaptive way, as information states.[130] We can add the capacity for dense representations of dense external or internal information. This, we have said, is the basis of phenomenology. (In giving the computer a capacity for phenomenology, we are not claiming that such a capacity is a necessary condition for being consciously aware of something.)[131] We also provide the computer with a zoom-lens capacity. The computer can magnify an item ("zooming in"), it can shift from one item to another, it can diminish the resources it devotes to an item. The computer can regulate the amount of "attention" it pays to something, that is, it can regulate the extent of resources and time and processing power that it devotes to some item, according to the goals that were built into it or that it modified in accordance with its routines. Above certain levels of magnification, it is able to respond more subtly to details of items.

The machine also can be given nonphenomenological representational states, its "beliefs," which represent situations or aspects of the world that guide its behavior (given its goals) and that are modifiable (in accordance with Bayesian or other procedures for modifying its representational states) on the basis of information that has been registered and magnified.

It not only has goals toward which it is teleologically directed in the sense of modifying its behavior to pursue these goals, it also represents these goals. It possesses multiple goals that are thus represented, and it uses procedures to modify these goals, to establish priorities among them, etc., procedures that themselves are modifiable in accordance with its higher-level procedures (which perhaps also can be used to modify themselves).

We have a computer, then, upon which aspects of the environment register as informational states which are reacted to; which can regulate its focusing upon portions of this registered information, zooming in on some, connecting it with others; which in accordance with its goal states and representations of them can resist being diverted to "paying attention" to other topics, that is, devoting cognitive resources to them; which utilizes dense representations of dense informational arrays in the world to guide and modify its behavior in intricate fit to absent as well as to present (belief-) represented aspects of the world, the degree of intricacy of the fit depending upon the amount of attention, that is, the portion of computational resources, devoted to these aspects of the world.

How different is this computer from you and me? It represents dense areas of the world in dense representations, it zooms in upon and focuses attention upon some aspects of what is registered and represented, it acts upon the basis of representational (belief) states, its behavior can be precisely contoured to aspects of the world to the extent that it pays attention to these aspects, and so forth. What we have described here, I think, is a computer that is conscious. You don't think so? See if you can convince it that it isn't.

This chapter has devoted its primary attention to what the *function* of our capacity for conscious awareness is. I should at least mention the *roles* that conscious awareness plays in our lives. There are the important things we use it for, there are kinds of conscious awareness we most seek and value, and there are ways (beyond its biological functions) in which conscious awareness shapes our lives. Conscious awareness underlies and shapes interpersonal courtesy, artistic creation and artistic appreciation, ethical behavior, and scientific understanding. And also philosophy. To focus only upon the function of conscious awareness is to present an impoverished view of consciousness. We need to understand, to assess, and to appreciate its roles as well. A task for a lifetime, happily.

5

The Genealogy of Ethics

The Theory of Ethics

How can ethical statements be true, if truth consists in correspondence to the facts? Are there special kinds of facts, ethical ones, and if so, by what route do we discover them? Not, apparently, by everyday observation or by scientific experimentation and theorizing. How else can we discover them? The history of philosophy is abundant with unsuccessful attempts to establish a firm basis for ethical truths. Inductively, we infer that this task is unpromising.

Some recent writers have retreated to a more modest aim than truth: ethical *objectivity*. If there is an objective process that will lead all people to accept certain ethical statements, then (it is thought) that alone is sufficient grounding for these statements. Their objective character is sufficient surrogate for their ethical truth; perhaps that objective character even establishes them as ethically true. On this view, if objective procedures of ethical reasoning (or ethical justification) lead to agreement upon particular statements or principles, that suffices to establish these statements, if not as true then, at any rate, as a (practical) basis for our common life—and that is all that we need. Ethical objectivity is the central notion; ethical truth is (at best) a derivative one. So runs the view.

Whether a judgment is objective, we have seen, depends upon the process by which it is arrived at, and upon how that process is related to reaching the truth. A judgment is objective if it is arrived at by a process in which (certain sorts of) distorting factors that bias against finding the truth do not play a role. A judgment might be termed *strongly* objective when it is arrived at by an effective and efficient process for reaching the truth. If there do exist ethical truths, then it is clear why we would want our ethical judgments to be objective, in each of these senses. When they are objective, they are more likely to be true.

But why is ethical objectivity a virtue, if there are no ethical truths that independently hold? And how is ethical objectivity to be specified, if not as what reliably or best leads to ethical truths, or as what is not diverted from the truth by biasing factors? We could, of course, haul over the specification of objectivity from some other arena, from science or mathematics or everyday factual investigations, and say that ethical objectivity is just the same as one of those objectivities. But why think that objectivity in ethics should be identical to one of those? If ethics differs from those realms, perhaps the attitude or mode of investigation for reaching those other truths is not suitable for discovering the truths of ethics. What is a biasing factor may differ from realm to realm. (Maybe dispassion is needed in science, but empathic emotion serves best in ethics.) However, if we are supposing that there are no independent ethical truths, we cannot wonder whether some other kind of process is best for discovering them. But then why should we use a process that is based elsewhere and justified there by its success in arriving at truths, to arrive at our ethical judgments? Why should what elsewhere is a biasing factor play no role in ethical judgments, when there is no independent truth that factor can bias us away from? Allowing what normally are distorting factors to play a role in one's judgments will not lead one away from the truth, if there is no such truth to be led away from. (Indeed, under those circumstances what would it mean to call a factor distorting?) Isn't importing the notion of objectivity from elsewhere simply *fetishism?*[1]

One common process in arriving at ethical agreement is to appeal to shared ethical intuitions. This process has been criticized often. Might not our intuitions be due largely (or wholly) to shaping by societal forces and to cultural conditioning? If so, would not the resulting ethical principles purportedly justified on the basis of the intuitions be as contingent and variable as the particular social factors that produce such intuitions? Or might not such intuitions (or rather their basis that underlies the later cultural elaboration) have been instilled in the evolutionary process because the holding of such intuitions was conducive to the maximization of inclusive fitness?[2]

If the origin of our ethical intuitions does not connect these intuitions directly with the truth of their content, it is difficult to see why (once we understand this) we should continue to give those intuitions normative weight. Why does fitting *those* intuitions, even in a sophisticated process that brings them into reflective equilibrium, count as a justification?

And why should justification be given such a primary place within ethical thinking?[3] It seems highly implausible that ethics exists in order to facilitate justifying our behavior to others. Justification is a complex and sophisticated activity, whereas the ethical regulation of behavior predates that.

Certainly, norms that regulate behavior, some of which are continuous with patterns of sanctioning behavior among primates, predate practices of justification. Ethics does not exist in order for behavior to be justified, and the extent to which an already existing ethics is shaped by the ease or possibility of its justification should be left as an open question for investigation, not taken as an *a priori* constraint upon (the content of) ethics.

If ethics does not exist in order to facilitate justifying our behavior to others, why *does* it exist? What is ethics *for?* What is the function of ethics?

The Ubiquity of Ethics

It seems that any answer to the question of what the function of ethics is will have to be an *ethical* answer (or at least a normative one); it will have to say what ethics *should* do or say what its function *should* be.

We can try to avoid or at least to postpone this issue by asking a descriptive question. Every known society has some ethical norms or other, some ethical rules or prohibitions or goals. Ethics is an anthropological universal. No society says that everyone may do whatever he or she wants to under all circumstances. What is the explanation of this ethical ubiquity—that *every* society has some ethics or other? Let us ask this as an anthropological question, a non-normative question. Why is ethics there? Why is ethics *everywhere?*[4] (And we may well find ourselves in a better position to discuss what detailed content ethics should have, or to justify ethics, after we understand why ethics exists.)

First, a bit of clarification. Sociologists and anthropologists agree about the universal presence of norms, of some norms or other, yet they disagree about the precise definition of norms. I said that all societies have some norms about behavior—no society says that everything goes all the time— but this does not by itself show that every society has *ethical* norms. It is not obvious how to demarcate ethical norms from other norms, including enforced laws, rules of etiquette, etc. Later, I will make a pass at circumscribing ethics, but the claim that ethics is universally present does not require any such definition. We all can know *that* it is there without being able to agree upon a definition of *what* is there. *You* provide the definition or demarcation of ethics that you find most plausible, and see if ethics, so construed, isn't a feature of all societies.

However, it is an anthropologically plausible definition (or list of defining characteristics) that is needed, one that is not committed to a particular ethical view or even to the view that there are any objective ethical truths at all. A Kantian who says ethics is present only when people are doing what is right for its own sake, out of reverence for the (moral) law, would be providing too narrow a definition. Compare the task of defining religion in order to investigate its presence and characteristics in different societies. We would not want to follow Kierkegaard in demanding that inner purity of heart be present for religion truly to exist. Moreover, an atheist anthropologist should be able to recognize a religion when he sees one; the identification of a religion does not depend upon agreeing that there indeed is religious truth, or that there does exist an external object of religious worship. Similarly, the definition of ethics should be broad enough to tell when *an ethics* is present, without being committed to any particular ethics or even to view that there exist any ethical truths. My claim is that any suitably general and suitably neutral identification of *an ethics* will find that some ethics or other is present in every society.

It seems plausible that ethics is ubiquitous across societies because it performs a function that humans in association everywhere have found extremely important, even necessary.[5] Perhaps ethical capacity of some sort was biologically instilled in order to aid in this function; perhaps ethics is so important a cultural tool that every society (or at least every society that has survived for some time) has found its way to culturally instill it. In either case, the presence of ethics is associated with this function. What, then, is this important function of ethics?

It might be said that the function is obvious: to do what is morally right, or to be a good person. Enough people in every society have some ethical discernment and want to act rightly; therefore, ethics exists as a universal institution. This provides an ethical description of the function of ethics. Why is there ethics? Because there are ethical truths that people discern, and want to follow, and want to pass on to their children, etc. The basis of the ethical truths is left open (perhaps it is divine edict), as is the origin of people's (partial) knowledge of them (perhaps it is a divine gift).

Because the basis and status of ethical truth are so unclear, we cannot present an account of ethics and of its function that *starts* with the notion of ethical truth and the desire to do what is right. We need a function that is not described in explicitly ethical terms. It might be objected that this will necessitate a demeaning reductionistic view of ethics. The only suitable function for ethics is an ethical one—so it might be held. There is a difference, however, between a function's being ethical in the sense of ethically desirable, and the function's being specified in explicitly ethical terms. For example, saving the lives of children might be something that is ethically desirable; it might be an ethical goal even though "saving the lives of children" is not a description of that goal in explicitly ethical terms. We seek a naturalistic description of the function of ethics, a specification of its function in nonethical terms, and a naturalistic explanation of why some thing or practice or institution performing this function is to be universally found. And we will feel more comfortable if the function of ethics, once stated, is something that itself can be seen to be ethically desirable. To be sure, something will be seen as ethically desirable in the light of the ethics that gets established by the performance of that function. But there is no guarantee that every function will bask in whatever light is given off by what serves it. For instance, even if all ethical standards turn out eventually to serve inclusive fitness, inclusive fitness does not, by our ethical standards, seem to be especially ethically desirable. Let us turn, then, to the task of naturalistic explanation.

Coordination to Mutual Benefit

My actions are connected with yours when the outcome of some action of yours varies, depending upon what I do. My actions can affect the outcome of one of your actions. Our actions are mutually connected when my actions are connected with yours, and yours with mine. Frequently, the actions of different people are mutually connected and the outcomes are nontrivially affected. This is the background that gives rise to ethics.

The function of ethics, of ethical norms and ethical beliefs, is to coordinate our actions with those of others to mutual benefit in a way that goes beyond the coordination achieved through evolutionarily instilled desires and patterns of behavior (including self-sacrificing behavior toward biological relatives). The coordination that ethics achieves is more extensive and better adapted to new and changing circumstances and opportunities.

Animal biologists have studied the benefits and bases of interlocking or coordinated or cooperative behaviors among organisms of the same or of different species.[6] Mere proximity (and hence acting to maintain this proximity) can enable each to benefit from the presence of the others, from the bodily warmth the others emit or the alternative targets they provide to predators. More particular interlocking behavior is widespread. Biologists have been especially interested in explaining how evolution gives rise to behavior wherein a cooperating individual bears some significant costs, for understandably this has constituted a puzzle. Yet we should not forget that evolution instills much behavior that is completely and clearly in the individual organism's interests yet interlocks with the behavior of others to produce magnified benefits to all concerned. Still, these interlocking behavior patterns are instilled by the evolutionary process, which thereby saves the individual organisms the burden of having to be genius enough to figure out the benefits to themselves of this pattern of behavior. More specifically, biologists have discussed the behavior patterns in fish of intraspecific cleaning, cooperative foraging, egg trading among hermaphrodites, nonbreeding helpers at the nest, alarm pheromones, and mobbing behavior; the behavior patterns in birds of cooperative hunting, food calls, food sharing, alarm calls, and mobbing behavior; the behavior patterns in mammals of grooming behavior, alarm signals, coalitions for mutual defense, alloparenting, i.e., dispensing of "parental" behavior to young who are not one's own, cooperative hunting, and (in the case of dolphins) caregiving; the behavior patterns in primates of grooming, cooperative hunting, cooperation in intergroup conflicts, alarm calls, and alloparenting; and a host of behavior patterns in the complex organization of eusocial insects.[7]

The evolutionary mechanisms giving rise to these patterns of behavior also are of great interest. It is known that a parent will sacrifice itself for the survival of direct offspring. The line of the gene coding for such behavior would continue in these direct descendants, and so such behavior would serve the parent's individual fitness and be selected for. By what mechanisms, though, would genes coding for behavior that reduces an organism's own individual fitness (as measured by the number of its direct descendants) be selected for? Would not such genes, in fact, be selected against?

There has been much discussion of kin selection and its widened notion of fitness, *inclusive* fitness. Selection takes account of the effect of genetically determined behavior on the propagation of these causative genes in other organisms that share them by common descent. According to the often quoted statement, an organism will sacrifice itself for the survival of (at least) two full siblings or (at least) eight full first cousins, etc., and in so doing the gene determining such sacrificial behavior will not be diminished in the population. Since it has a one-half chance of being carried by each full sibling, a one-eighth chance of being carried by each full first cousin, etc., these surviving organisms (on average) will continue to carry at least as many copies of the gene as was carried by their sacrificing relative. A precise mathematical formula was presented by W. D. Hamilton.[8]

There also has been study of reciprocal altruism, whereby individual selection would take place for cooperative behavior toward nonrelated reciprocatingly cooperative organisms.[9] An action *A* which itself diminishes the reproductive fitness of organism O_1 (by amount D) will be undertaken if it raises the probability (by amount p) that another organism will act to sufficiently raise the reproductive fitness of organism O_1 by amount R (where $p \times R$ is greater than D) so that there is a net gain in O_1's reproductive fitness. Organism O_2 might be the beneficiary of O_1's action A, and it, or its relatives, might in turn reciprocate to benefit O_1. Reciprocal altruism involves each organism's performing actions which *directly* diminish its own reproductive fitness, yet which bring a compensating *increase* in its own reproductive fitness through a reciprocating action by the other organism. Each trades an action that costs it something in reproductive fitness (in exchange) for a reciprocating action from the other that returns a greater reproductive benefit. A genetically based tendency to be a reciprocating altruist will be selected for, and this will occur even if the other reciprocating altruists in the interactions act that way not because of genes that code for that behavior but for other reasons or causes.

And there also has been investigation of whether behavior that is individually disadvantageous, even by the widened criterion of inclusive fitness, might in specific circumstances be selected for by a process of group selection: though lessening in percentage within its group, the absolute number of individuals behaving that way nevertheless increases because of the behavior's beneficial effects upon the total number in that group as compared to some other competing groups.[10]

It is worth noticing that the Hamilton Rule for selection for a gene G coding for actions that benefit another yet reduce *individual* fitness, that is, the rule that marks the actions that increase *inclusive* fitness, depends upon the actual probability that the benefited organism also shares the gene G, for *whatever* reason it shares that gene. The rule does not actually depend upon the acting organism and that other organism's sharing the gene G by virtue of common descent. The two organisms do not have to be related at all.[11] The coefficient of biological relatedness is one of the ways in which that particular probability can arise, but it is merely one of these ways.[12]

This point is worth mentioning because it provides a double perspective on reciprocal altruism. Suppose that both I and a nonrelated individual with whom I interact have a hereditary tendency to behave altruistically to those who reciprocate altruistically, and that this tendency is coded for by the same gene, the same DNA sequence. My altruistic action benefits me in the long run, by the exchange process that Robert Trivers described; it raises my own individual (and also inclusive) fitness, and, if it is a heritable trait, it will be passed on to my descendants. *Moreover*, it also propagates the tendency to reciprocal altruism by increasing the individual (and inclusive) fitness of the other organisms who also possesses that same gene, in accordance with Hamilton's Rule. Thus, there is even stronger selection for genes for reciprocal altruism than might appear. To be sure, there will be such stronger selection for the behavioral trait, even if it is coded for by different genes in different individuals. Among biological relatives, however, the very same genes will be the focus of this double process of kin selection and reciprocal altruism.

Intricate as the animal behavior patterns are, they are limited in their ability to coordinate behavior to mutual benefit with nonpresent nonrelatives, and to generate new kinds of coordinated cooperative behavior for new situations that differ from long-standing ancestral ones. This is a familiar type of point with regard to the evolution of new mechanisms of behavior. Animals that locomote in reaction to changing local conditions have advantages over stationary entities; organisms that are subject to Pavlovian conditioning can exhibit a wider range of self-beneficial behavior than organisms capable only of behavior through simple reflexes; organisms that are subject to operant conditioning can exhibit a wider range of self-beneficial behavior than organisms capable only of Pavlovian behavior; and presumably intelligent organisms capable of conscious thought, planning, control of impulses, etc. are similarly advantaged over Skinnerian ones in their ability to respond to, and adapt to, new and changing circumstances, dangers, and opportunities. Our higher capacities have been selected for because of the benefits they bring.

Coordination via Ethical Norms

Guiding our behavior by ethical norms is another piece of our higher capacities, and it too brings benefits in extending the realm of cooperative activity beyond what is reached by fixed instilled patterns of behavior.

Factual beliefs coordinate our actions to the world, facilitating the achievement of our goals. Ethical beliefs coordinate our actions, each to each other's, so as to achieve mutually beneficial action. One person cannot directly will another's actions. It is because individuals control some of their own actions,[13] or because the costs of another's doing so are very great, that coordination is needed. And it is because people know that their actions are interconnected that coordination is undertaken.

The coordination of ethics should be distinguished from other modes of coordinating behavior. You can coordinate your action with that of another person who is unaware that you are doing so, following him because you know he is going to a place you want to reach (although you do not yourself know the precise route). And someone can coordinate his behavior with that of another person who knows he is doing this, or trying to do so. A killer follows his intended victim, who attempts to evade him, and each might think about what the other will expect him to do, and about what the other will expect him to expect, so as better to reach his own goals (of capture, or of escape). Game theory, with its accompanying equilibria notions, describes how actions can be *strategically* coordinated.

Ethics exists because at least sometimes it is possible to coordinate actions *to mutual benefit*. (This is a significant part of the distinctiveness, referred to above, of ethical coordination. I do not say, however, that every coordination to mutual benefit is distinctively ethical.) In a situation in which our actions are interconnected, my *security level* is the amount that I can guarantee myself (by an appropriate choice) no matter what you choose to do. Consider, for each of the actions that it is possible for me to choose, what the worst outcome or payoff is that I might end up with. (What I end up with if I do an action might also depend upon what you choose to do.) Now consider the action that has as its worst possible outcome a better (or no worse) outcome than any of the other worst outcomes that might result from the other actions. If I perform that action, I am guaranteed to end up at least with that action's worst payoff, and that payoff is my potential security level in my choice situation. I can guarantee myself at least that much. (And I cannot guarantee myself more.)

In many situations in which two people interact, there will be some combination of their actions whereby both do (strictly) better than their potential security levels in that situation. There is room for them to cooperate, to coordinate their actions to mutual benefit. Notice that both people maximizing their security level can end up above those security levels, even without further coordination. (For each secure action might be defending against some action of the other besides the one that maximizes that other person's security level.) Is the baseline for ethics what each receives when each chooses the action that maximizes his security level, rather than the security-level payments themselves? Ethical norms and rules are not so precisely attuned to the details of individual situations; the actual payoffs accompanying joint security-level maximization are too variable, I think, to be taken account of by ethical norms, which deal with the repeatable features of situations.

It may be risky, however, for me to perform some other action in order to get above my potential security level, for (unless these two actions tie in their worst outcomes) that performed action will have some possible outcome which is worse than my potential security level, a level I can guarantee for myself by acting differently. I am well advised to perform an action that risks going beneath my security level only if the other party will not act so as to land me with my (non-security-maximizing) action's worst possible outcome.

It is a fortunate fact that the world presents us with many opportunities for coordinated action to mutual benefit. Indeed, one must invoke quite elaborate science-fiction scenarios to imagine a world with no opportunities at all for cooperation to mutual benefit. Even the situation of two species' competing for the very same ecological niche, or of one species' being useful to the other only as food, will present opportunities for cooperation *within* each species.

Coordinated action to mutual benefit is of four sorts. The first sort involves action toward a joint goal that the parties share and desire. An animal is preying upon our village, and no one of us is able to drive it away alone. What is needed is our acting in concert. The second sort involves complementary actions toward our separate goals. I want some food that you have grown; you want some tools that I have made. We engage in voluntary exchange to improve our situations, I to improve mine and you to improve yours. This need not, although it can, involve our each having the joint goal of acting to the mutual improvement of both of our situations. The third sort involves our each wanting wholeheartedly to pursue our separate goals without diverting energy and attention to protecting this activity, and our person, from the predation of the other. We each adhere to noninterference, refraining from murdering, enslaving or stealing from the other. More likely, this involves an exchange: I exchange my refraining for your refraining, and I will refrain only provided that, and only so long as, you continue to refrain, only so long as you do not take steps (or make an attempt) to interfere. There also is a fourth sort of coordination: coordinating your interactive behavior with those who also are acting on the same norms and principles of interactive behavior—that is, with those who you know are, and those who know you know this, etc., so that you coordinate your behavior with those acting in common knowledge of acting on those same norms and principles.

Voluntary exchange and cooperative coordination of behavior involves many opportunities for separate benefits that improve each participant's situation. There is a danger in people's coming together for this purpose.

One may seize the other's possession, or person, forcing an involuntary transfer or even enslavement. It is fortunate that very frequently the net benefits of (continued) voluntary exchange and cooperation are greater than the net benefits of the immediate involuntary exchanges. Someone whose possessions are seized will not soon return for another "exchange" with you, and a willing participant in exchange may give you greater benefits than even the labor of a slave, taking into account the greater productivity of personally beneficial labor and the costs of forcing the slave to continue in that involuntary status. (It has been said that even slavery at one time constituted an advance over what preceded *it*, namely, being killed as a means to the plundering of one's possessions.)

Adherence to patterns of voluntary cooperation is personally beneficial, and a reputation for such adherence brings further rewards in the further cooperation with others that it induces and facilitates.[14] Moreover, being someone who finds coordinating behavior to mutual benefit enjoyable or gratifying in itself, apart from the specific benefits involved in that particular act of coordination, will make one a more promising and steady cooperative partner in the eyes of others, if that trait is perceived by them. The trait of enjoying cooperative activity might be evolutionarily selected for, given the individual benefits it brings of increased (opportunities for) cooperation with others. We therefore might be beings who have been shaped to enjoy (and to prefer) achieving our goals through interpersonal coordinative and cooperative activity.

No doubt, one of the impetuses to extending the sphere of voluntary cooperation beyond the immediate family, or village, or group is the perception of the benefits that this brings, benefits whose net amount is greater than that of involuntary control over others. With much backsliding, that has been one important component of the history of what ethical progress there has been. Sociologists have delineated the later extension of the domain of impersonal behavior governed by impersonal and neutral rules, and the benefits these bring.

Ethics arises when frequently or importantly there are situations offering opportunities for mutual benefit from coordinated activity. (By "importantly," I means that there are some situations in which the utility difference for both parties between their security levels and the amounts they can gain by coordinated activity is *very* great.) There are various structures that such situations can exhibit. More particular theories might hypothesize that one of these structured situations plays a more important causal role than others in the arising of ethics across different societies, but I present no such more particular hypothesis here.

That ethics has the effect of facilitating coordinated activity to mutual benefit does not show that this is the *function* of ethics. For that to be so, having that effect would have to play a role in the creation or maintenance of ethical institutions, practices, and systems E. There would have to be some homeostatic mechanism, evolutionary or social, that shapes and selects norms to have this effect, an operating homeostatic system whose goal state is "norms having the effect of facilitating coordinated activity to mutual benefit," which homeostatic system produces and maintains the ethical system E.[15]

I do not say that *all* coordination of activity for mutual benefit is distinctively ethical. Perhaps other modes of such coordination are ethically desirable, but they may not count as distinctively ethical activities themselves.[16] Coordination to mutual benefit can be the function of ethics without ethics' being the only thing to have that function. The function of a car may be speedy transportation, but other things also may perform this function. What distinguishes an automobile need not be a special function that it, and only it, has, but rather a special way in which it carries out this function, or a special means by which it does so. Similarly, the function of ethics can be coordination of activities to mutual benefit even though other things do this also and even have it as their function too. What distinguishes ethics might not be a narrower function but the particular way in which it carries out this general function. In this case, a full explanation of the ubiquity of ethics would say also why every society not only has some way of carrying out the general function but also carries it out in the specifically ethical way.

Perhaps what is distinctive about the ethical means is that it involves norms that get internalized and followed even on occasions when others are not directly observing or in a position to sanction deviation from the norms. A *normative statement* is a statement that a person or group of persons ought (or is required, or is permitted) to do act A in circumstances C. A *norm* is an organized or institutionalized pattern of social rewards and punishments for doing or not doing A in circumstances C. A norm, then, corresponds to a normative statement that is generally enforced. And a person *internalizes a norm* when the person has a disposition to behave in accordance with a normative statement in the absence of social sanctions for deviations from the normative statement.[17] The usefulness of the internalization of norms is clear, both in reinforcing and protecting other modes of cooperation to mutual benefit, and in filling the gaps that these other modes leave.[18]

It might be of interest to present some (rough) criterion or definition of an ethics, even though the accuracy of this particular criterion is in no way essential to the further course of our theorizing in this chapter. An ethics is the most weighty principles or values concerning interpersonal relations (or relations of self and other, including self and animals, or self and environment) that mandate behavior that may be opposed to one's desires of the moment, where these principles or values are not backed solely (or predominantly) by the consideration that other people will punish you if you deviate.

This definition has various desirable features. It does not follow from it that every society necessarily contains an ethics, for a society might not limit behavior at all, or the sole mechanism of such limitation might be the punishment others inflict when they detect transgressions of the limitations. Also, it does not follow from the definition that ethical considerations must be more weighty than any other kind of consideration. Some principles or values that are not about interpersonal behavior might turn out to be more weighty than ethical ones in certain situations, e.g., religious principles or aesthetic considerations. However, the definition does not say that ethics is limited to interpersonal behavior; principles or values that did not apply to interpersonal behavior would not count as ethical, but they can extend more widely than that. Something other than (or in addition to) punishment by other people must support the principles or values for them to be ethical principles or values. This other thing may be internalization of the principles, the conviction that the principles or values are right or good in themselves, punishment of violations by God, or whatever. What matters is that ethics is enforced or maintained by something in addition to (human) social sanctions. (Motivation by socially bestowed rewards, however, might do the job, as in the case of Homeric behavior motivated by a desire for undying glory.) The statement of the definition also does not specify any particular function of the principles or values, so it is compatible with this definition that the function is to make people behave in accordance with the interests of local powerful persons, for instance.

We should note how minimal the mutuality of benefit might be that norms of mutual benefit govern. There might be norms of exploitation: if you serve him (to his benefit) then he will not kill you, which benefits you, at least in contrast to the situation in which he *does* kill you. Do the highwayman and his victim follow norms to mutual benefit; if the highwayman kills his victim after the money has been turned over, does he violate some norm? X could come up to Y and seize his goods, but that takes effort on X's part. He must grab, immobilize, and perhaps knock out Y. So instead, X says, "I will kill you unless you hand over your money." We may suppose that killing Y is even more effortful for X. (If X refrains from killing Y in order to return and steal from him again, does his not killing Y constitute some cooperation to their mutual benefit?)

In choosing a course of action, the highwayman X faces a decision between the effortful falling upon Y and forcibly immobilizing him or knocking him out, then taking his money on the one hand, and threatening Y with death if the money is not turned over on the other. To announce the threat gives warning to Y, thereby giving him more opportunity to resist, and this might eventuate in X's losing the fight. But it also can save X the costs of actually fighting with Y. So X must make a calculation of what best serves his interest.

A norm might emerge for such situations: give the other person a chance to comply, and don't kill or injure him after he complies. Such norms would be in the general interest of highwaymen. If the second part is frequently violated, and compliant victims are frequently killed or injured afterward, then (when this becomes known) few will comply, and highwaymen then must follow the more arduous path of actually fighting with their victims. In theory, highwaymen might even discipline other highwaymen who violate this norm, in order to maintain the general reputation of highwaymen with their potential victims.[19]

Are there norms of victimhood also? It is not a norm that one should not tell anyone of the robbery. Indeed, telling the story may spread a highwayman's reputation for letting the victim go after compliance. The highwaymen may enforce the rule that the victim is not to chase after them and attempt to kill them, but this will not thereby get instilled as a norm in the victims. Not every rule that is imposed by others becomes a norm of behavior. Norms must be maintained (by sanctions or social pressure) by those *within* the group to whom those norms apply. Even rules for children's behavior, imposed by adults, do not become norms for the children until the children become old enough, and willing enough, to enforce these rules themselves.

We therefore should distinguish two levels to which rules can be internalized, thereby becoming norms. First, the group to which the rule applies itself enforces the rule upon its recalcitrant or disobedient members. It no longer is simply a rule imposed from outside the group. A necessary condition for this step from a rule to a norm would be that there are enough interactions within the group that violations of the rule can be noticed, and violators sanctioned. Second, the person enforces the rule upon himself; he follows it even when no others are around to notice or enforce its violation. A hypocrite is someone who enforces a rule upon others but not upon himself. Even such a person can contribute to the stability and enforcement of the rules by his sanctioning of others.

Does ethical coordination go beyond what game-theoretic reasoning (combined with factual information) can reach? We do not yet know the limits of game-theoretic reasoning—the subject still is developing—and perhaps it will come to yield the full content of ethical cooperation. It seems unlikely, however, that people in all societies would intuitively have reasoned their way to such complex game-theoretic conclusions, long in advance of the explicit development of game theory. Even if game theory (in some future stage or by some yet undiscovered application) could reach something coextensive with ethics, that would not be the route that was followed to make some ethics or other a universal fact of human society. Ethics might be the functional equivalent of such a game theory, but it would not be its result. Even a society that did possess such a sophisticated game theory might need ethics as a summary or rule of thumb for those who would not constantly reason their way to the ethical result via the game-theoretical route.

That cooperative activity is possible to mutual benefit does not yet say how these benefits are to be divided. Where on the contract curve will a bargain be struck? Where should it be struck? John Rawls has suggested that the problem of justice is that of dividing the benefits of cooperation.[20] Particular ethical questions arise within and about the framework of cooperation. However, the general purpose of ethics is to serve coordinated activity for mutual benefit. Ethical norms and ethical restrictions on behavior are to facilitate and ensure such coordinated activity. This does not explain the particularity of ethics; rather, it explains why there is ethics rather than nothing. (Compare: one can distinguish the task of explaining why the facts are a particular way from that of explaining why there is something rather than nothing.)

Ethical norms exist to facilitate or ensure cooperation to mutual benefit, and among these norms are norms of distribution that exist to govern who receives what amounts of these attainable benefits. The two effects of norms can be analytically distinguished but cannot easily be disentangled. For a norm that facilitates coordination to mutual benefit often will affect the shares of these benefits that each party receives. If the facilitation had been done differently, the parties' respective shares would be different. On the other hand, a norm that specifies how benefits are to be assigned or divided will contribute to facilitating cooperation to mutual benefit, for such cooperation will not take place (or will be far less likely to take place) in the absence of some norm or other that specifies an assignment or division of benefits.

A norm that says "Move from a Pareto-suboptimal situation to one or another of the Pareto-optimal situations" might be geared only to the first task, coordination to mutual benefit, without being geared to the second, the assignment or division of the benefits. But this abstract norm will not be put into effect in two-person situations without the existence and operation of some norms that include the second type of content.[21]

It might be asked which of these functions, the facilitation of cooperation to mutual benefit or the division of the benefits, is *the* function or is *the more important* function that explains the existence of societal norms. For a two-person situation, we can view norms as mandating or facilitating a move from the status-quo point O to a particular point P on the Pareto frontier, or at least as excluding certain (though perhaps not all) Pareto-suboptimal points (including the status-quo point O), and also perhaps excluding certain of the Pareto-optimal points from being the result. For instance, among the Pareto-optimal points, the extremes of almost all the benefits of cooperation going to one or the other of the parties might be excluded by a norm.

The question can be asked: which function is more important to the existence of norms in general, getting significantly away from the O point or moving toward one of the division points rather than another (for instance, favoring more the benefiting of person II than of person I)? But at this very general level the question is an obscure one.[22]

The questions need to be cut more finely. Why is there any norm at all about the matter? Because a norm facilitates cooperation to mutual benefit. Why is there this particular norm rather than that particular norm? Here various answers are possible. Perhaps because the norm can be followed more easily, or because its violations can be detected more easily, or because it is less costly in time, energy, or resources to follow it—these factors fit within the rubric of facilitating mutual benefit. Or perhaps because this norm benefits these people more than those, while that norm benefits those people more than these, and these people had the greater resources or greater power or greater authority to affect which norm got instituted—these factors fit within the rubric of assigning or dividing the benefits.[23]

Within one individual's mind, the amount of concern about an incremental benefit seems to depend upon the proportion of the total amount that it constitutes an increment of. In buying an expensive product such as an automobile, people do not care about, or urgently bargain over, or comparison shop to avoid a small percentage of the total price, for instance, to get to pay $25,500 rather than $25,700. Yet a $200 difference in price can make a big difference in the purchase of a $600 set of stereo speakers, and in that case one might travel across a city to save that amount. (And there will be "framing" issues here that will affect behavior. Are stereo speakers for the automobile a separate item, or part of the car?) One would therefore predict that if the amount to be gained or lost by fighting or serious conflict is a small percentage of the benefits to be gained by cooperation, then the parties will not concentrate very hard on distributional issues. (Indeed, the reason for our tendencies to focus upon percentages rather than absolute amounts and to give little weight to small percentages of the total at stake may be that such tendencies were selected for precisely in order to facilitate cooperation to mutual benefit.) Of course, these percentages may be different for different parties, and framing issues also can arise here as well, so that even with apparently equal amounts at stake, the parties will behave differently because of the different totals that they see these amounts as percentages of. Clearly, the processes of cooperation to mutual benefit can be very complex.

Nietzsche, of course, takes a more cynical view of norms, especially those of Christianity. These constitute a "slave morality," imposed by the individually weak and powerless to prevent the strong from living fully and expansively in ways harmful to the weak. Such norms do not, in Nietzsche's view, work at all to mutual benefit. (It has often been remarked that if the weak have succeeded in doing this, then they are, at least as a group, stronger than the strong—or at least smarter.) Someone might hold that norms are instituted and maintained by the powerful to bring about acquiescence in hierarchical inequalities on the part of the less powerful.

These alternative hypotheses should not be dismissed (or accepted) automatically. It is an empirical question what the function of ethics is, and that question needs to be decided by evidence. It would be instructive to specify what evidence would need to be gathered to decide between our hypothesis about the function of ethics, and specific alternative hypotheses. Of course, different theories about the function of ethics might be combined. Ethics, from the beginning, might have had various effects, and these effects might have contributed to different extents to its existence and maintenance. (And the extent to which a specific factor contributes to the maintenance of ethics might be different at different times.) The question would then become: what is the most important function of ethics? Or more quantitatively, where F might be coordination to mutual benefit, or the subordination of the less powerful, or whatever: to what extent or degree is F a function of ethics (at that particular specified time)? We may presently lack the information to answer this, and we also may lack an adequate framework for assessing how important the various causes of a phenomenon are.[24]

That norms exist in order to facilitate cooperation to mutual benefit tells us why norms exist but not how they come to exist. Did foresightful and influential people institute norms in their group because they foresaw its beneficial results? And did this group initiate norms of particular content (among all the different ones that might facilitate cooperation to mutual benefit) because they foresaw that these particular norms would especially benefit themselves?[25] Or did some groups stumble blindly upon norms, while other groups without norms, or without ones that effectively facilitated cooperation to mutual benefit, fell by the wayside as a result of ineffective coping with the hazards of nature or of other, better-coordinated societies? Did norms grow and evolve within societies from the concatenated interactions of individuals by an invisible-hand process?[26] Or did all three processes in tandem create the ubiquitous phenomenon of norms? These questions about the *how* of norms are interesting and important; formal models of these processes need to be developed and investigated further. For our purposes here, though, knowing the *why* of norms is sufficient.

Yet this "why" of norms seems to be an explanatory one, not a justificatory one. Does it give a person any reason to adhere to particular norms in the face of temptation or reason not to do so? Does it give norms with any normative force? (Does it leave them with any?) These are important questions, but before turning to them, we need to consider some further details about systems of coordination and cooperation to mutual benefit.

The Evaluation of Systems of Coordination

Ethical beliefs facilitate closer coordination and voluntary exchange among people. They also underlie the operation of more-impersonal markets and exchange. Ethical beliefs coordinate our actions with the actions of others also acting on those very same ethical beliefs, and also with the actions of others acting on different beliefs. These beliefs facilitate the achievement of our individual goals, and of joint goals, and also the achievement of widespread social goals.

It would be churlish not to mention that over historical time we have learned more about the coordination of activities, not just about face-to-face coordination but also about institutional arrangements that facilitate coordination and enhance it, most notably, the market. The market is an institutional process whereby individual actions and plans are coordinated.[27] The earliest forms were stumbled upon, but once set going, they generated their own elaboration, aided by the judicious improvements intentionally introduced to remove impediments or to sharpen their functioning.[28] History has taught that one extremely good way to coordinate actions is through the market and its associated private spheres, individual rights, property rights, financial and capital markets, and so on. Socialism may once have appeared to be more efficient and productive because it introduced more explicit and conscious attempts at coordination. But these, we have learned, are not more conducive to coordination than are the spontaneous adjustments of individuals responding to their local circumstances on the basis of their local knowledge, coordinated through a widespread market and price mechanism. And the theoretical understanding given by the literature on the impossibility of rational calculation in a socialist society undergirds and explains this historical experience.[29]

We can see ethics as one particular mode of cooperation and coordination, distinct from and touching upon markets, private property, government activity, and other institutional modes. It would be a very large task, not one to be undertaken here, to discuss all these modes of coordination and their respective appropriate spheres.

Since coordination can take many different forms, what limits the variety of coordination schemes? If societies differ in their situations (for instance, in climatic or geographical factors, in social history, in inherited social situation) so that what norms or rules best further coordinated activity to mutual benefit varies from society to society, then does ethical truth (or the correct ethics) also vary? Since the details of social cooperation and the division of its benefits remain open, does this not also bring room for some relativism about ethics? Will all human societies or all societies of rational creatures have certain things that are common to their coordination schemes? Are these ethical invariants, and hence objective? Even if they exist, these invariants may not be enough for a complete code of behavior or for complete coordination; the extra pieces needed for such completion will not themselves have invariant content across all societies. In the Venn diagram of societies' moral beliefs, there may be a common overlap, but each society also will have some beliefs special to it and to its circumstances. Even if one mode of coordination arguably is best in some ecological niche, the social and biological pressures may not be strong enough to drive the society to that result. Actual ethical codes may not optimize coordination.

In the first chapter, we described relativism about truth as holding that truth is a function of some unobvious factor, and varies with variation in that factor. (In addition, relativism is egalitarian, in that different values of that factor are held to be equally good.) The relativist, then, is committed to a theory of what something (such as truth) depends upon and varies with. The ethical relativism we are considering here does not specify any factor whose variation determines variation in ethics. Instead, it simply says that there is *room* for such variation; nothing excludes it. We might call this position *latitudinism*. It maintains the egalitarianism of full relativism—all the variation is equally good—but it is not committed to (the existence of) any factor that the variation is *relative to*.

From the fact that all societies will have some norms or other to encourage and regulate social coordination and to discourage some activities that interfere with social coordination, it does not follow that there are any specific norms by which people guide their behavior that all societies will share. In a recent discussion of moral relativism, Gilbert Harman writes:

> It may be that *murder* is always considered wrong, if murder is defined as "wrongful killing." But few societies accept *general* moral prohibitions on killing or harming other people. There are societies in which a "master" is thought to have an absolute right to treat his slaves in any way he chooses, including arbitrarily beating and killing them. Similarly, there may be no limitations on what a husband can do to his wife, or a father to his young children. Infanticide is considered acceptable in some societies. When moral prohibitions on harming and killing and lying exist, they are sometimes supposed to apply only with respect to the local group and not with respect to outsiders. A person who is able successfully to cheat outsiders may be treated as an admirable person. Similarly for someone who is able to harm and kill outsiders. Any universally accepted principle in this area must verge on triviality, saying, for example, that one must not kill or harm members of a certain group, namely the group of people one must not kill or harm.[30]

Harman goes on to write in a note to this passage: "There will be universal truths about moralities . . . Perhaps all moralities have some rules against killing, harm, and deception . . . The existence of universal features of morality is compatible with moral relativism." Since Harman construes relativism as denying that anything is absolute (and not merely as affirming that something is relative), he must be focusing not upon (what he terms) universal features (such as the existence of certain kinds of rules) but upon the rules and norms themselves.

Harman supposes that the universal and invariant features of morality are that each society has some norms or other against killing, harm, and deception. The specific content and details of these norms will vary from society to society. So there seem to be no statable norms that are invariant across all societies. This is misleading, however, for there are these: not every killing is (morally) permissible; not every harm is (morally) permissible; not every deception is (morally) permissible. However, these shared norms are not specific enough to significantly guide or control action, and they are not norms that anyone consciously follows. (For all I know, they are formulated here for the first time.) Perhaps we should not even call them "commonly shared norms"; rather, they are commonly shared *implications* of norms (though not implications that are commonly drawn). Within this general framework of (commonly shared implications of nonspecific) norms, there will be all the variation exhibited by the different schemes of coordinating activities to the mutual benefit of all, or of only some.

Are there criteria that we can propose for evaluating coordination schemes? (And are these conditions that each society would accept, even if they do not actually have coordination schemes that satisfy these conditions?) What makes for closer and more desirable coordination? The utilitarian might suggest that issues of division are secondary. Since cooperation to mutual benefit is the function of ethics, the only thing that matters is the total amount of benefits thereby gained, that is, the size of the social pie.[31] Others will seek further criteria concerning the division of these benefits, and how mutual it is. Some will say that maximizing the total over time leads to the largest absolute share for everyone, even eventually for those at the bottom, and so questions of division are secondary; others will not see the matter thus.

Different factors, therefore, provide room for ethical variation among societies. What best serves cooperation may differ from society to society because of the different situations (geographical, historical, social) of these societies. The same conception of ideal cooperation may lead to different schemes and norms of cooperation in different circumstances. And these societies also may differ in their conceptions of what best serves cooperation, that is, in their conceptions of "serves" and of "best"; will it be a maximizing or a side-constraint view, will it emphasize duties or rights, etc.? There is much room for legitimate variation within the general framework of serving cooperation.

Can we say at least that more-efficient schemes of cooperation are better? That one scheme is better than another if it consistently leads to (strongly) Pareto-better situations, that is, situations in which all people are better off? However, simply because the purpose of cooperative schemes is (consistently) to lead to some situation or other that is better for all (in the group of voluntary cooperators) than their respective security levels, it does not follow that every such situation is deemed better, or that the more it is Pareto-superior, the better. For various reasons the people may prefer less efficient payoff combinations that have (in their eyes) other desirable qualities. For instance, the move to a Pareto-better situation may increase the amount of inequality in a society. Those societies that greatly value equality will not deem every situation that is Pareto more-efficient to be better. Can we at least say that a society will deem one situation better than another if it is Pareto-better and also not less egalitarian? But inequality is not the only possible bar to welcoming Pareto efficiency. A Nietzschean society might see some degree of inequality, and opportunity for it, as providing an arena for people to show their Nietzschean virtues.

One writer has said of the Pareto-optimality (efficiency) criterion, "40 years ago the new welfare economists agreed that it was the only indisputable principle on which legitimate welfare analysis could ever develop."[32] Indisputable? Hardly. If there is not invariant agreement across societies (or within our own society) over the Pareto-better criterion, all the more will there be disagreement over the more specific criteria for cooperative processes and the division of benefits that theorists have discussed. These include explicitly normative criteria: for instance, *anonymity*, which requires that the welfare of different people be interchangeable, an unacceptable norm in monarchical and aristocratic societies, as well as in those societies favoring military conquest of other societies; the egalitarian *Pigou-Dalton principle*, which says that a transfer of (nonnegative) utility from one person to another does not decrease social welfare if the first's utility is greater than the second before and after the transfer—the Nietzschean objects; *issue monotonicity*, which requires that when the set of feasible cooperative outcomes expands, the received utility of no person should decrease, which is violated by a decline in blacksmiths' income when automobiles are introduced; *population monotonicity*, which requires that when the number of agents entitled to a share of the cooperative surplus increases, and no new cooperative opportunity arises, then the utility of the original persons should not increase; *separability*, which requires that a decision between two alternatives can ignore the persons who receive exactly the same utility in the two alternatives; the *Shapley value*, which gives each person the average of his marginal contribution to all coalitions containing him. And the disagreements will continue over proposals about how the benefits of Pareto optimality should be divided, that is, where on the contract curve the division should be made. This includes informal principles such as George Homans' principle of justice that people's rewards from an activity should be proportional to their investment and contribution;[33] the *Nash solution* to the two-person bargaining game, which requires the maximization of the product of the differences between each person's allocated utility and the utility he would receive if no agreement is reached; and David Gauthier's *relative concession* solution to the two-person bargaining game, which requires minimizing the greatest relative concession that any participant makes. The literature on the fair division of a resource also proposes and utilizes various normative conditions. A division is *envy free* when every person thinks he or she received the largest or most valuable portion of the resource, that is, a share not smaller or less valuable than anyone else's—there are contexts in which envy-freeness and Pareto efficiency are incompatible. A division among *n* persons is *proportional* when each person receives what he or she perceives to be at least $1/n$th of the resource. When a division is envy free, each person thinks his own allocation is as good as each other person's, and would not prefer to exchange his for another's. And a division is said to be *equitable* when each receiver thinks he values his own allocation as much as any other person values his or her own allocation. The literature also includes criteria of coherence among judgments (such as *independence of irrelevant alternatives,* which requires that if a preferred distribution among a wider set of alternatives also is in a narrower set, it continues to be a preferred distribution among that narrower set), and it includes structural conditions (such as various continuity conditions) that facilitate the derivation of particular normative results.[34] None of these conditions, useful as they be mathematically for deriving particular results, is likely to be acceptable across all cultures (or across all persons within our own culture).

Of course, since the work of Kenneth Arrow,[35] it has been known that not all appealing criteria can be simultaneously satisfied by a social-choice mechanism. The criteria themselves were not thought objectionable in isolation. The surprise, and disappointment, was that in combination, they proved impossible to satisfy jointly. Here, we have noticed that some normative views will object to many proposed criteria (such as Pareto optimality, anonymity, and issue monotonicity) on an individual basis, and so these criteria will not be acceptable across all societies.

Pareto efficiency holds that one situation is better than another if all are better off in the first than in the second (strongly Pareto-better) or if some are better off in the first and none are worse off (weakly Pareto-better). People's being better off, however, is not the only thing that a society can (come to) care about. We can extract from the notion of Pareto efficiency the notions of strong and weak dominance, however, and apply it not to the preferences or well-being of people but to the values of society. A society embracing values $V_1, \ldots, V_n$ (and no other values) will deem one situation better than another if, for every one of these values, the first situation does better than the second (strong dominance); or if for some of these values the first situation does better than the second while for none of these values does it do worse (weak dominance).[36] Perhaps each and every society will agree to this Value Dominance criterion of betterness, but since they may differ in their particular values, the criterion does not provide a common value or specific norm but a common metavalue.

The Core Principle of Ethics

I am willing to see some pieces of ethics as objective and other pieces as relative, but relativism is carried too far when it says that every system of norms of coordination is as acceptable as every other one, no matter how limited its domain of cooperation or how exploitative it is toward people outside that domain. We need something more positive and more delimited. So let me recommend one general norm of social coordination and cooperation. The view I am recommending is very closely intertwined with the notion of cooperation to mutual benefit. It makes mandatory the widest voluntary cooperation to mutual benefit; it makes only that mandatory; and it (in general) prohibits interactions that are not to mutual benefit, unless these are entered into voluntarily by all parties, or unless these interactions (such as the act of punishing another) are in response to previous violations of the principle or to preparations to violate it.[37] Yet, despite this close intertwining, the principle put forward is not entailed by the function of cooperation to mutual benefit. I do not claim that this particular norm is deducible from the descriptive (or explanatory) fact that the function of ethics is to specify and to facilitate some social coordination to mutual benefit. I am not trying to derive this normative *ought* from a descriptive *is*. Instead, the principle specifies one particular way in which cooperation to mutual benefit can proceed, and it holds that way to be normatively binding.

It is desirable to extend the realm of people who benefit from coordination and cooperation. A group G1 should extend social cooperation to G2, if this can be done in some way that benefits those in G2 and improves (or does not worsen) the situation of the people in G1. (What if it can be extended to G2 in this way, and also to G3, but not to both?) However, a group is not required to extend cooperative relations to another group with whom it has no interactions, at the cost of lessening the benefits to itself. (This, of course, constitutes a point of division between libertarian and other views, as does the great extent of the range of permissible voluntary coordination of activity that is countenanced. It would be hasty for non-libertarians to conclude, though, just because they are not willing to accept *all* cooperation to mutual benefit, that facilitating and governing such cooperation cannot be the originating function of ethics.)

Game theorists define the *core* of a game as all of those payoff vectors to the group wherein no subgroup can do better for itself acting on its own, without cooperating with others not in the subgroup. Some games have empty cores. In such games, there is no distribution to a group such that no subgroup can do better for itself on its own. A standard example is the game of three people dividing an amount of money, $1,000. If two out of the three people agree upon a division, that will determine how the money is divided. An equal division of [333⅓, 333⅓, 333⅓] is inferior, for the first two people, to a division of [500, 500, 0]. The subgroup consisting of the first two people can do better on its own (by instituting the second division) than with the first division, so this first division is not in the core. (In the terminology of game theory, the first two people *block* the equal division.) Yet the second division is inferior, for the last two people, to a division of [0, 501, 499], so these last two people block the second division, which therefore is not in the core. Yet the first and third persons do not do as well with this third division as they would with a division of [500, 0, 500], so the third division also is blocked, and so is not in the core. It becomes clear that for this game, no division of the $1,000 is in the core. The core of that game is empty.[38]

Notice that all the blocking coalitional subgroups in this game themselves have their favored distributions blocked by still other coalitional subgroups, which themselves get blocked in turn. As an empirical matter, in actual fact, the stability of some distributions may be maintained by social divisions among people that prevent certain subgroups from forming coalitions or even considering doing so. And the significance of some divisions (racial, ethnic, religious, class, sex) may be fostered or exacerbated by an existing coalition that benefits from the way in which such divisions prevent the formation of alternative coalitions that would block its own favored distribution.

I now want to describe a multistage process whereby cooperation between distinct groups gets established. Here is the first stage. Suppose that there are two distinct groups, G1 and G2, which do not cooperate or interact together, and that the two separate distributions D1 and D2 to each of these groups is within the cores C1 and C2 of their separate games. No subgroup of either group can split off by itself and do better than it does in its own group's actual distribution.

Group G1 will unanimously favor (or at least no member will oppose) extending cooperative relations with G2 when each member of G1 will fare at least as well (and some will fare better) under the new, enlarged cooperative arrangement's distribution D3 as he or she fares under D1. (Similarly for group G2 and D2.) This can be accomplished in two ways. Either each member of G1 fares better directly, or the total received by G1 in cooperation with G2 increases by an amount sufficient to compensate any member of G2 who might fare worse under the new arrangement, and this compensation actually is paid. Suppose that G1 consists of two people, A and B, who produce a total of 6 between them, and they split this evenly, each receiving 3. (Alone, let us suppose, each can produce nothing.) Group G2 contains only one person, who is producing 1 on his own. Together, suppose that the three people can produce a total of 9. Cooperation will be extended if the new distribution gives A and B more than 3 each, and gives C more than 1, thereby improving everyone's situation. One example of such a distribution is D4: [3 and $\frac{3}{4}$, 3 and $\frac{3}{4}$, 1 and $\frac{1}{2}$]. That distribution D4 does not divide the 9 evenly, and it also does not divide the increase of 2 over the previous total evenly. Moreover, supposing that A and C together could produce a total of 7, the distribution D4 is not in the core, since A and C each could do better with a distribution D5 of [4, 3] than they do under the distribution D4.

However, it is no requirement of the first stage that a wider sphere of cooperation involves movement to a new distribution that is in the larger core. (We may suppose that the previous lack of friendly contact between the groups makes it impossible for a cross-group blocking coalition actually to form.) The new distribution need only surpass what each got under the old distributions for cooperation to be mutually beneficial. The principle of the first stage says that cooperation should be extended between groups when it results in a joint distribution that is (weakly or strongly) Pareto-better than the existing one of no extended cooperation (and also better than what the continuation of that scheme of noncooperation would be), in that some people's distributional shares increase while no one's is worsened.

Over time, however, the cooperation between the two groups will lead to a weakening of the barriers between them. It will be possible for subcoalitions consisting of members of the previously separate two groups to form. Such a subcoalition must now receive a distributive share equal to what it could receive alone. Now the distribution to the total enlarged group must be in the core of that larger game. This is the mark of an integrated society, and it is the principle governing the second stage of extended cooperation between groups. These two stages are illustrated, in rough form, by the history of voluntary immigrant groups in the United States. Their initial situations constituted an improvement over that in their country of origin (*ex ante*, it certainly was expected that there would be an improvement), but group barriers prevented their receiving what they would have from some distribution in the core. However, their children faced increased actual coalitional opportunities, and their grandchildren, as adults, were full members of the group G1, and full participants in a distribution from its core. (Because African Americans were brought to the United States in slavery and subject to strong caste restrictions afterward, their subsequent history, unfortunately, has been different.)

The actual distribution in a society that widens its range of cooperation, either by incorporating new immigrants within itself or by extending the domain of trade, will be the result of some mixture of the two stages. The distribution will tend to move to one in the core, but with some stickiness. (The first theorem of welfare economics says that the allocation of a market economy will be in the core, but the conditions of this theorem abstract from the sticky factors that stem the equal formation of all possible subcoalitions.)

This two-stage process cushions persons or subgroups in G1 against the shock of extended cooperation with G2, that is, against the worsening of their position that would occur if some (subset of) members of G1 formed their own coalitions with (some) members of G2, without regard to how this affected the other members of G1 who remained outside this new coalition. Thereby, it allows the extension of cooperation between groups to take place without fierce opposition. Interethnic conflict, I conjecture, sometimes arises or gets inflamed when such intergroup subcoalitions are beginning to come into effect. Those members of G1 who see their own position worsened or threatened by the coalition of other members of G1 with (some) members of the previously separate or subordinate G2, are led to support drastic curtailment of the cooperation with G2, even to the point of driving them away or slaughtering them. ("The members of G2 are taking over," they say, or are told by leaders who see exacerbating this conflict as a route to their own power.)

I have spoken until now about extending cooperation with another group in a way that benefits the members of both groups. The other facet of this is not to extend relations with group G2 in a way that worsens the situation of G2 (without their consent). The resulting distribution should not be such that G2 could do better on its own, not interacting with G1. This excludes a group G1's murdering the members of G2 or enslaving them for the benefit of G1.[39] Such prohibitions apply also within the group G1 itself. There should be no subgroup S within G1 such that S does better on its own, without any interactions with the rest of G1, where S alone would actually constitute a stable coalition. This excludes G1's enslaving or greatly oppressing a subset of its members. The norm we are proposing is that of *voluntary cooperation,* the norm of unforced cooperation. We might appropriately term this *the core principle of ethics.*[40]

The actual process of widening cooperation with another group may not be a Pareto improvement; it may leave some members of G1 worse off. What then determines whether cooperation *will* get expanded, if not a unanimous vote or agreement among the initial n persons? I conjecture that a *descriptive* theory of the following sort holds. There is a subgroup of the n persons, call it the *power subgroup* of the n persons, that has the power to extend cooperation past the n if such extensions benefits all the members of this subgroup, and that also has the power to block extensions of cooperation past the n persons. (Note that there may be different overlapping power subgroups.) Cooperation will be extended if and only if some power subgroup favors its extension, thinking it will (in the short run or the long run) benefit (or at least not lessen the position of) each and every one of them. A power subgroup may be mistaken, of course, and the extension of cooperation may turn out to work to the detriment of some of them, but such cooperation, once extended, may create a new power subgroup and hence be irreversible. Historically, the extensions of cooperation to further groups—trading with the others rather than conquering or enslaving them, dropping tariffs and trade barriers, etc.—has been impelled, I think, by power subgroups' coming to think such extensions are in their own interests. It is fortunate that many such extensions have been, or seemed to be, in the interests of then existing power subgroups.

There are four types of norms that we can illustrate in the economists' diagram of an Edgeworth box containing that football-shaped figure formed by two facing indifference curves (representing no interaction), with a lace astride the middle. The first type of norm says not to worsen the situation of another, that is, don't forcibly move the person below his indifference curve of no interaction. The second type of norm mandates cooperation to mutual benefit, that is, moving to somewhere within the boundaries of the two curves. The third type of norm mandates efficiency, that is, moving to the contract curve within the figure, that shoelace line of points such that no other point is more preferred to one of these by both parties. The fourth type of norm would be distributive norms, giving further instructions for where on the contract curve the interaction should land.

It would be extremely instructive to see how much of ordinary ethics, for instance, as presented in W. D. Ross's lists of *prima facie* duties,[41] can be encompassed by the first three types of norms, and similar ones. (These include norms that facilitate or guide cooperation to mutual benefit; norms that protect, foster, or maintain cooperative activities for mutual benefit, or norms that guide such activity, as with principles of dividing benefits; norms that mandate behavior for response to deviations from the above norms; and norms that foster virtues and dispositions that maintain patterns of cooperative behavior.) I do not claim that *all* the ordinary ethical views that we wish to maintain can be so encompassed. We shall consider later how ethics gets extended beyond its basis in coordination to mutual benefit.

Notice that the norms I have presented governing coordination to mutual benefit have two sides. They encourage the extension of such coordination and cooperation. And they also *forbid* one kind of interaction that is not to mutual benefit, namely, interacting with another (or with others) in a way that forces that other (or them) to be worse off than if you or your group had not interacted with him (or them) at all. (It is not that all interactions are required to be of mutual benefit. A person may *voluntarily* choose to interact with others in a way that benefits them yet is to his *own* detriment.) So the ethics of coordination to mutual benefit has the two sides: that of encouraging the extension of mutually beneficial cooperation and that of restricting or forbidding (certain kinds of) detrimental interaction.[42] The first of these sides might seem to make of ethics a self-interested activity, but the second decidedly restricts the way in which self-interest can be pursued. The ethics of coordination to mutual benefit is not the same as ethical egoism.

One part of the history of moral progress consisted in the extension of the domain of ethics to those previous excluded from its full concern—to people in the next family, in the next village, to slaves, to neighboring cities, to women. (And discussions occur now about the extent to which ethics should be extended to animals, or to fetuses.) *Moral progress* frequently is thought of as the discovery or instantiation of long-standing (perhaps eternal) preexisting moral truths. Society always should have satisfied these truths, and now it has come to do so. However, there is another kind of moral progress. A group previously was compelled to accept less than its baseline vector or was not interacted with at all. Conditions change so that an extension of cooperative coordination to include this group becomes feasible and desirable, in that the previous group of cooperators, or a power subgroup of it, realizes (or believes) that this extension is in its own interests. The previously existing social, technological, etc. conditions may not have favored such an extension—not all in the group or in any power subgroup would have benefited from the extension under those previously existing conditions. We are fortunate to live under conditions that favor more-extensive cores, and less conquest, slavery, and pillaging, less imposition of noncore vectors upon subgroups. Perhaps we moderns should take less credit for the moral progress that changing conditions (which in part were caused by the earlier extensions of cooperation) have made feasible and desirable.[43]

A second kind of moral progress consists in the shrinkage of the domain of mandatory morality. Cooperation to mutual benefit is seen no longer to require such extensive regulation of an individual's activities, of religious beliefs, of sexual behavior. A domain of liberty and personal autonomy is established and extended. A third kind of moral progress involves the development of higher levels of ethics. We shall discuss this in a later section.

A more extensive web of civilization makes a more extensive range and domain of cooperation more feasible. Unfortunately, we also have learned how fragile are the extensions of the domain of cooperation, and how easy it is for that domain to shrink: from internationally to only within a nation; from within a nation to only within one of its ethnic groups. The ease with which political demagogues can provoke such shrinkage testifies to the power of the more narrowly based norms—these do stipulate *some* (perhaps very intense) cooperation—and to the relative weakness and instability of the wider domain. It is an urgent task to generate mechanisms and devices to impede the easy reversion to narrower, violent loyalties.

The subject of this chapter is ethics, not political philosophy or the proposal of institutional political structures. Yet I do have a proposal about a voting system for legislative positions (in single representative legislative districts) that has not (to my knowledge) been suggested before. Since it may help alleviate the problem of tyrannical majorities, it is worth considering and exploring.

I call this mechanism *Winner Take Proportional All.* A legislature is divided into legislative districts. The winner of the election in an electoral district is that candidate who receives a majority of the votes or, failing that, the candidate with a plurality in that election. (Or the candidate with a majority in a runoff election; perhaps the choice of whether to hold a runoff election can be decided previously by the district itself.)

Once serving in the legislature, a legislator casts a fractional vote, equal to the fraction of votes that he received, of all of the votes cast in the election that elected him. (In two-person elections, that fraction will be between $\frac{1}{2}$ and 1.) The number of votes a bill receives in the legislature is the sum of the fractional votes of the legislators who vote for the bill. A normal bill passes if it receives a higher sum than the votes opposing it (or perhaps a majority of the votes eligible to be cast).[44]

The advantages of this system are these. It gives candidates an incentive to build a large winning coalition of supporters, for this will give him a larger vote and hence greater power within the legislature. It gives eligible voters an incentive to vote in elections, for their cast votes have a continuing effect, whether they vote for the winning candidate or for a losing candidate. (Voters for the winning candidate contribute to the fraction of a vote he is able to cast, and voters for other candidates contribute to the diminution of that fraction.) And voters are encouraged to follow politics more closely, since, in one way or another, their votes do count. More to our current concern, the system places divisive candidates, who are able to win only a bare majority of the voters in their district, under a disadvantage within the legislature. They have a minimal vote there. Yet, because each district is a winner take (proportional) all district, the system does not lead to a legislature that is hobbled by many of the disadvantages of a system of proportional representation. Such a legislative structure, with its incentives for large majorities within districts, seems likely to dampen a legislative politician's reversion to narrow group interests.

We return now to our consideration of ethics. The function of ethics is to protect and promote voluntary cooperation and coordination between people, to guide this cooperation (through norms of division of benefits), and to demarcate the domain of such cooperation (which people are to be the participants); also, to specify what is to be done when the above rules, norms, etc. are *not* followed, that is, to specify norms of response to different kinds of noncooperation (should it be met by boycott, punishment, retribution?); and to guide or mandate character virtues relevant to cooperation, and to people's response to noncooperators. Ethics is universal because the possibility of beneficial coordination and cooperation is universal, and because all such possibilities are not exhausted or exploited by instinctual behavior unguided by concepts and norms.

If the central function and basis of ethics is cooperation to mutual benefit, then ethics, too, holds in space and time. What the content of ethics is there and then depends upon the existing opportunities for cooperation to mutual benefit. This does not mean that every society is immune to moral criticism. A society can be criticized for not recognizing the more extensive possibilities for cooperation to mutual benefit open to it, or for not pursuing those opportunities that they do recognize, or for not developing further opportunities when these are clear. So ethical truths can hold in a society even when the society does not recognize or follow those truths. Nevertheless, the particular ethical truths that hold for a society do depend upon the opportunities for cooperation to mutual benefit that exist in the social circumstances of that society.

If ethics is universal across societies because of the possibility of fruitful coordination of behavior to mutual benefit, then ethics may not *apply* to enduring situations in which coordination to mutual benefit is not possible. (In societies in which fruitful cooperation *is* possible, ethics will carry over to govern temporary situations in which such coordination is impossible.) So, we might say, ethics also is relative to the possibility of fruitful cooperation. The *existence* and applicability of ethics will be relative to the possibility of cooperation, while within those contexts in which fruitful cooperation is possible, the content of ethics may be relative to other factors.

Will there be *some* other norms that exist and apply to enduring situations in which no coordination to mutual benefit is possible? Certainly norms from situations in which cooperation to mutual benefit is possible can be generalized and extended to these other situations, but it is difficult to see how ethics could originate in such situations; and perhaps it is unlikely that it would long continue if permanently (it was known that) no cooperation to mutual benefit was possible, even to the limited extent of mutually benefiting from reciprocally leaving each other alone.

Normative Force and the Normativity Module

What can be said to someone who does not wish to aid in or participate in the carrying out of the coordinative and cooperative function of ethics? Or to someone who wishes partially to participate, but to deviate when he calculates that this is decidedly in his interests and that he is likely (enough) to get away with the unethical action? Why should he be moral? Why should someone be cooperative in any nonrepeated prisoners'-dilemma situation? The considerations we have put forward about the general function of ethics do not answer these long-standing, theoretically troubling questions.

Yet the fact that these problems *have* been so long-standing and still remain unresolved theoretically can be taken as confirmation of our thesis about the function of ethics. To say that it is having a certain effect that is the function of ethics is to say that ethics does have this effect and that ethics was selected for (and maintained) because it has this effect.[45] However, the process of selection does not require that the effect be present always. This is clear in the biological case in which a mechanism that gives an organism a statistically better chance of survival and reproduction will be selected for. The mechanism needn't give each organism a better chance in every situation or guarantee survival in any. Giving enough organisms in a population a better chance in enough situations will constitute enough of an edge for the mechanism to spread in the population. This is compatible with that mechanism's working to the (survival or reproductive) detriment of a particular organism in some particular situation. That organism would have been better off if the mechanisms had been turned off right then.

If adherence to certain norms generally works to coordinate people's behavior to mutual benefit, that may be enough to (biologically or culturally) select for those norms, or for the society to instill them, and such coordination will be the function of those installed norms. Yet there will be particular situations in which adherence to that norm does not work out to mutual benefit and, in particular, not to one party's benefit. Why should that person follow the norm then? There may even be specific individuals who, in general, are better off not following that norm. Why should those individuals usually comply with it?

These are familiar and difficult—some say intractable—issues in ethics. The utilitarian faces the question of whether to follow a rule that generally works to the greatest good when he is in a particular situation in which following that rule produces less good than some other action would. (This is the question of act versus rule utilitarianism.) There also is the question of whether always to pursue only one's own interest, even to the detriment of others. (This is the question of ethical egoism.) These are not just questions a theorist puzzles over; they are issues an actor has to face who recognizes a divergence between self-benefit and mutual benefit, or between mutual benefit in general and mutual benefit on a particular occasion.

We have seen that such divergences will occur when norms exist because they statistically have advantageous effects. We might hope that a theory of the function of ethics would resolve such theoretical quandaries and practical difficulties. Yet it is the very fact that ethics does have a function, and the nature of the statistical standard that produces it with that function, that also produce the quandaries and difficulties. An appeal to the function of ethics cannot be sharp enough to resolve these problems, unless that function has strayed considerably from the (statistically based) initial function. And that extended function, just because it is extended, will have less authoritative weight than the original function that made of ethics a ubiquitous phenomenon.[46]

But does the theory I have presented depict ethics as having normative force? True, it is the explanation of why there are any norms at all, and of why those norms, as part of their own content, command or demand obedience. Yet still it may be wondered whether the norms that the theory describes, if they exist for those described reasons, although they contain commands and demands as part of their content, themselves do have an independent normative force that makes demands upon our obedience.

Notice that even if our theory were not a theory of the existence and normative force of ethics—suppose ethics exists and has normative force for quite other reasons—it still could be the explanation of the universal spread and recognition of that independently existing ethics, and of the widespread conformity to it. That occurs because, whatever the other basis of its existence and normative force, ethical norms (as a whole, statistically and in general) *do* serve cooperation to mutual benefit.

That small-scale cooperation among people is mutually beneficial surely has been a long-standing fact about the human past, not to mention the situation of our primate ancestors. One would expect that evolution has shaped us to be creatures adapted to coordinating our behavior with close others of the same species. This shaping is imperfect, to be sure, given the occasionally large benefits of noncooperation or of betrayal of cooperative schemes. We are partially cooperative creatures, built also to monitor the actions and reputations of others and to enforce cooperative coordination through social (or even physical) sanctions. We have been biologically built to live in an ethical realm, that is, a realm of *some* limitation of behavior in order to serve some cooperative coordination. And cultural shaping has extended these tendencies significantly, though not far enough to make us (all) citizens of Kant's Kingdom of Ends.

An innate human predisposition, evolutionarily instilled, for cooperation to mutual benefit,[47] even if not of infinite weight in competition with motives of self-interest, might be sufficient to induce us largely to cooperate, and to *want* to cooperate to mutual benefit. Of course, those in the Kantian tradition would hold that this is insufficient to yield normative force; it simply is an existing (almost) universal motivation and desire. This is better than nothing, surely. But is it enough to yield ethics as we understand it?

In *The Concept of Law*, H. L. A. Hart describes the *internal attitude* toward the law as one that people take when the mere fact that the law requires them to do something counts for them as a *(prima facie)* reason to do it, and also as a *(prima facie)* reason to criticize others who fail to act in accordance with the law. Similarly, we accept a nonlegal norm when we take such an internal attitude toward it, and we think that our noncompliance with that norm requires some overriding reason.

We human beings have a capacity, not simply to instinctively perform particular behavior that is cooperative, and not simply to calculate what is in our own best interest and then to behave cooperatively to mutual benefit as a result of such a calculation, but to *guide* our behavior by a norm. Once a norm is accepted we do not upon each occasion recalculate the benefits of following it, nor do we choose to accept a norm initially as a result of such a calculation. We are creatures who are amenable to being inducted into a world of norms. We are poised to learn norms as we are poised to learn a first language. We simply need to be shown, or told, what the local rules are.

The capacity for following norms and the predisposition to follow some norms or other—norms of the local group, of our young peers, of our parents and elders—is innate. It will be helpful to consider this as a specialized capacity, a "normativity module." (I think it unlikely that it arose as a side effect of some other function of a large and complicated brain.) Certainly the benefits of being able to discern, and being predisposed to follow, the local rules of speech and of behavior have been very large.

Our earlier discussion distinguished various aspects of a norm of behavior. It is a regularity of behavior that is enforced upon others; these others are expected (wanted and required) to internalize the regularity and to regulate their behavior by it; and they are expected to contribute to the enforcing of the regularity upon the behavior of others, and expected to expect others to internalize it.

Internalizing a norm will, according to contemporary cognitive psychology, involve some psychological *representation* of the normative rule, but this need not involve any conscious awareness of the details of the norms that we follow, as is illustrated by the grammatical rules and norms of public behavior whose making explicit required sophisticated theoretical effort.[48]

The benefits of a capacity to follow norms and a tendency to do so are great. Attentiveness to the negative attitudes of others in reaction to one's behavior, even when these attitudes are not normative, is useful. A person's explicit calculations about the chances of successfully avoiding detection by others often are faulty and highly fallible. Internalizing a norm, and the attendant behavioral conformity this brings, help to prevent significant mispredicted punishment.[49] (Is it important for the internalization of norms that the socialization into particular ones occurs early, before the individual develops confidence in his capacity to calculate what is in his own interests? Might a rational, self-interested adult who is not cognizant of the degree of his own fallibility resist the full internalization of moral norms? When in Rome, an adult may do as the Romans do, but will he also internalize the norms they follow?) In addition to the individual benefits that a heritable capacity for normative behavior brings, some group selection also may operate, in that it may be beneficial for the survival of local groups to contain norm followers and internalizers.

So let us suppose that there has been evolutionary selection for our normative capacity and receptiveness. There has been selection for a normativity operator within our cognitive and emotional apparatus, an operator that attaches an internal "ought" to certain behavior or patterns of behavior. Some things ought to be done, other things ought not to be done. We learn these rule-governed patterns and we behave in accordance with them, not solely or mainly because of incentives, because of carrots and sticks, but because we are not by nature unruly creatures. We are, in fact, ruly ones. We are predesigned to follow the local rules (although we can grow to reject them) and to take the fact that something is required or forbidden by a local rule as a reason for or against doing it.

Hume was right that an *ought* cannot be derived from an *is*. Something's normative status does not follow from facts, and it is not part of any best hypothesis that explains facts. Yet when we are young and are presented with certain facts, facts about the pattern of behavior of others nearby, including their pattern of approving and reproving other behavior, these facts enter into and fill our preexisting (but heretofore largely empty) normative boxes.

An *ought* cannot be derived from an *is*; normativity cannot be derived from descriptiveness. Yet the descriptive fact that we do have biologically instilled normativity boxes and operators (as, I conjecture, is the case) can

be given a thoroughly naturalistic and non-normative evolutionary explanation. Normative receptiveness and normative capacities were selected for,
as were other behavioral predispositions and cognitive and psychological
capacities, because of the benefits they bring. The internalization of norms
expands the sphere of (possible) mutually beneficial cooperation, and the
formulation of new norms enables cooperative behavior to adjust to
changes in local circumstances. It is because of the advantage given by the
available benefits of norm-guided cooperation (to mutual benefit) that the
capacity for internalizing norms, and the disposition to do so, have been selected to spread in the population.[50]

Consider again the person who asks why he should be moral, either on
this particular occasion or (as in the case of the ethical egoist) ever. Does he
wish that no one had been born normatively susceptible? No; he benefits
from living in a society in which people largely adhere to some norms of
coordination to mutual benefit. Does he wish that he had not been born so
susceptible? No; for otherwise he could not have learned any language, and
so could not even have formulated any principle of ethical egoism. Does he
wish that he had been born with a more limited susceptibility, one that got
him to learn and follow all norms except for ethical ones that mandate coordinating behavior to mutual benefit? No; for such an antisocial being
would have been detected and then killed or abandoned or exiled early in
life. Does he wish that he had been only susceptible enough to internalize
ethical norms until he was old enough to pretend to others to do this and
so avoid retaliation and punishment? Evidently, he does. Has he taken account of the fact that there is a tendency to overestimate one's chances of
success in evading detection and punishment, and that the capacity to internalize norms may exist partly to counteract such calculative mistakes
about the personal consequences of norm violation? Perhaps he has, and
nevertheless he believes that he now faces a clear case in which the violation
of an ethical norm will be in his own interests. Does this leave him with any
reason to be ethical now? Has our account of normative force explained it,
or explained it away? (Has normative force gone the way of necessity? Even
a theory of necessity that grants that something is necessary but denies that
it is necessary that the something is necessary may make of necessity something insufficiently deep ontologically.)

Are norms *binding?* Thinking that norms are binding, authoritative, inescapable, etc. may itself help to avoid any tendency to fallible calculations
about improving one's situation through norm violations. The belief that
normative force goes all the way down may have instrumental value in con-

trolling one's own behavior. Stating this belief aloud may help others to control their own behavior, and also provide them with the confidence to undertake interactions with you without costly surveillance. (Evolutionists also have theorized that certain costly displays—the peacock's tail—are signals to potential mates of how very healthy and sturdy one is; only such organisms could carry such a handicap.[51] Might the adherence to ethical constraints upon behavior be an illustration of the handicap principle?)

Yet a theory that explains the normative force of ethics in part by mechanisms and purposes that do not carry such normative force all the way down, may seem to undercut or diminish ethics by making it (at some level) escapable or avoidable or contingent. Actions performed from a calculation of personal benefit or of what serves mutual benefit, whether in a particular situation or in general, seem to have prudential force but not moral force. Will it suffice for normative force that moral norms are internalized, and followed even when their violation will not be detected? When moral norms are evidently internalized, the other party can trust that you will carry out your part of the coordinated action, even if personal calculation recommends otherwise, and hence, being able to depend upon your action, that party will engage in a wider range of cooperative activity with you. So a tendency to internalize such norms has been selected for, because of how it increases the extent of cooperation to mutual benefit. There still is (amoral?) calculation here, only this time not done not by the individual person but (implicitly) by evolution. More is involved, though. People who internalize moral norms feel shame, guilt, remorse if they violate them. The tendency (uncontrollably) to feel, and to show that one feels, these emotions provides others with information about one's reliability as a participant in cooperative endeavors. But the tendency to feel these "moral" emotions may have been selected for, precisely for these reasons.[52] So does a psychological tendency to feel these emotions give morality the requisite normative force? The mere existence of (a tendency to) these emotions is not enough; it is important that these emotions be appropriate. So add that one not only feels these emotions but also believes that it is appropriate to feel these emotions when norms are violated. A tendency to this belief, too, can have been selected for. Suppose that we travel all the way to a Kantian disposition to act from respect for the moral law. Couldn't this itself (not the Kantian *theory* but its psychological basis or underpinnings) be a psychological disposition that was selected for because of the firm reliability it gives one in the eyes of others as a participant in cooperative activities?[53] What is needed, it may be said, is not any bit of psychology, any occurrence of emotion or belief or reverence or of a tendency to these—for these things all may receive a naturalistic explanation—but rather that the emotion or reverence actually *be* the correct and appropriate thing to feel and act from. Anything short of that, it may be said, leaves ethics shorn of sufficient normative force.

Explaining the existence of ethics or of its normative force at a level that does not itself assume or state or entail the correctness or force of morality (all the way down) seems to undercut the validity of ethics, or at any rate not to provide all the authoritative backing for it that is desired. Yet to explain ethics in a way that does assume its validity is to presuppose part of what needs to be explained, and hence to provide a theory that is incomplete.[54] Philosophical critics of the attempts at complete explanations are right to take them very seriously, for whatever apparently solid ground they stand upon in making their criticisms is itself in the process of being explained, and perhaps explained away. (We shall return to questions about normative force later in the chapter.)

Evaluative Capacities

In addition to capacities for imbibing and for following norms, human beings also possess capacities of *evaluation*. Human beings possess four general mechanisms for regulating behavior: pleasures and pains; desires, wants, and preferences; evaluations; and norms. Not only do we have desires and wants that we act upon; we also evaluate things in the world as good or bad, as better or worse, and we shape our desires accordingly. We also can evaluate our desires and wants themselves, and consider whether particular ones are good or bad things to possess and to act upon. What is the function of such an evaluative capacity?

Suppose we start with beings who have wants and desires. They also are able, when desires conflict or when the realization of one desire is seen to interfere with another, to determine which desire is stronger and to act upon that one. Let us also suppose that they possess second-order desires, desires about desires that lead them sometimes to eliminate or to damp down the strength of desires that they desire not to have.[55] What (additional) benefit does an evaluative capacity bring to such a being?

We want some things as means to other things that we already (want to) want. As a result of a particular calculation of effectiveness in a particular context, a desire for one thing generates a particular and localized desire for something else that is a means to it. Yet some things, such as sufficient food, physical speed, and health, serve as helpful means toward a wide variety of ends. After enough experience of this, it is unnecessary and inefficient continually to recalculate and assess their effectiveness for reaching our ultimate ends in each particular context. An evaluation of some thing as good therefore might have its origin as a summary of the generalized effectiveness of that thing as a useful means toward many ends, and hence mark the general desirability of possessing that means. (The capacity to keep track of exceptions to these generalizations also would be useful.)

Once several evaluations are made, *generality* makes its appearance in the evaluative realm. The different multipurpose means X, Y, and Z are evaluated as good. It is noticed that these have some common property P, and the generalization is tentatively made that other P's also are good, that is, that they too will be able to function as multipurpose goods. A generalization over existing evaluations thereby extends them to other evaluations, and also to other levels of evaluation.

A capacity (to evaluate and) to have one's actions be guided by one's evaluations gives a person greater control over her actions by making her less subject to the push and pull of existing desires, including the existing second-order desires she happens to find herself with. Desires and wants can be for particular objects or kinds of objects, and they need not involve or invoke any general characteristics. Evaluations, on the other hand, see something as good or bad in virtue of some sharable characteristic that it possesses. If I evaluate X's as bad in virtue of characteristic C, then my desire for all X's is damped down, including the particular X I find myself faced with, and my desire for any C also is damped down, including C's of a type (non-X) that I have not hitherto encountered. To the extent that I can control my evaluations, I also can control my desires.[56]

Evaluations enable us to manage, oversee, and guide our desires because of the widespread network of considerations that they are responsive to. Evaluations do not stand in isolation individually. They form a system, at least a loose one, and they must cohere to some extent. Therefore, some of them, or the vast majority of them together, exert pressure upon the others. They push and shape the others to fit.

We evaluate objects and situations and actions and character traits and people and institutions and societies and ourselves, and we feel uncomfortable if these evaluations are too disparate and discordant. Positively evaluated people should not have too many negatively evaluated character traits, positively evaluated actions should not produce too many negatively evaluated situations, negatively evaluated objects should not be the focus of too many of our own desires, positively evaluated societies should enable positively evaluated people to flourish, and so on. Evaluations bring one another into line.

The initial importance of evaluations, to repeat, is in guiding our own conduct through the greater control they give us over our existing desires. We suppress some desires, damp down others, and acquire yet others, if not directly as a result of the evaluation that it would be good to have those further desires, then indirectly through that evaluation's leading us into situations in which it is more likely that we will acquire those desires or will find them socially reinforced.

Just as norms are more adaptable to changing circumstances than are inherited desires and inherited patterns of behavior—it takes less time for a norm to change than for biological selection to institute new behavior—so too are an individual's evaluations more adaptable to changing circumstances, and to local ones, than are norms, which are more lethargic and slower to change. A capacity for evaluating objects and desires is an extremely useful capacity to possess. It is one that might well have been selected for, or, if it exists as a beneficial side effect of another combination of capacities, it might have helped to maintain the existence of these other selected-for capacities.

How do particular evaluations arise initially? Are the ones that we make arbitrary? We may suppose that certain tendencies to evaluation themselves were first selected for because they fitted a range of circumstances. These tendencies might mandate evaluations of type E_1 in circumstances C_1, evaluations of type E_2 in circumstances C_2, etc. And tendencies to evaluation, fixing as they do upon general characteristics, also interknit with our cognitive capacities; they followed paths these cognitive capacities laid out for other reasons, perhaps for reasons of understanding rather than immediate action. When various evaluations were made, a common underlying basis for these evaluations would be sought. Theories would be spun.

The normative and the evaluative capacities interacted. Once there were incipient general standards of evaluation, norms themselves could be subjects of evaluation to be judged as good or bad, better or worse. And evolutionarily selected desires and patterns of behavior might get incorporated into norms: "Care for your offspring"; "Help members of your family"; "Cooperate with those who evidence a willingness to cooperate with you for mutual benefit." When certain conditions were met, new evaluations could get solidified into an individual's new norms or be plugged into existing ones. If you evaluate certain ways of being as bad, then you are led to a norm mandating not being those ways; if certain desires are evaluated as bad, you are led to a norm mandating not having these.

When a person holds conflicting evaluations, these need to be weighted, or reconciled, or to have priorities established between them. Perhaps this could all happen automatically beneath the level of conscious awareness. If conflicting desires are like vectors with directions and lengths, there might be some automatic process of computing their vector sum. Conflicting evaluations, however, might come with directions but without lengths; their reconciliation might require a conscious arena. In any case, once the capacity for conscious awareness exists, the awareness of a conflict in evaluations and attention to the process of revising or reweighting these evaluations will bring greater flexibility in evaluation, a more precise fitting of evaluations to the choice situation, and a greater knitting together of these particular evaluations with the person's other standards of evaluation. The results of this conscious contouring of evaluations will set precedents to guide future choices as well.[57] (As with a legal system, such precedents will carry some weight, yet be overturnable in new circumstances.)

Once norms are in place, along with capacities for evaluation and a search for the evaluations' underlying consistent basis, we are launched upon familiar paths. I do want not to be treated a certain way; not only do I possess this desire, I evaluate that treatment negatively. What makes it bad is some feature of mine or of the treatment. Given my cognitive capacities, when this evaluation is combined with my other evaluations, (often but not necessarily) it generalizes into an evaluation of that type of treatment as bad, whether done to me or done to anyone (or at least when done to a favored wider class of persons: my family, my group, my tribe).[58] Later, there will be similar pressure to expand this evaluation beyond the favored group to include everyone.

We care not only about ourselves but about our offspring. No one says that a mother who races into a dangerous situation to save her child is acting stupidly or irrationally. We also care about other relatives, and such caring is held to be good. What marks the limits of when such caring for others is good? The actual explanation of the extent of our previous instinctive caring may be the mechanism of kin selection, but (in the absence of evolutionary knowledge) it will not be obvious why biological relationships bear such significance. What theoretical understanding, then, can people reach of the boundaries of appropriate caring? True, relatives may be more likely to cooperate with you or come to your aid in situations of need, but shouldn't that then be the basis of caring for others: care for those who are likely to cooperate with you or to come to your aid in need? By such a process of attempted understanding of the basis of caring behavior that already is acknowledged to be good, the appropriate domain of that behavior may get extended, eventually (by some) to include all of humanity. Also, religious explanations of the creation of peoples may have marched, hand in hand, with ethical expansions of the domain of caring, with each propelling the other eventually to include all of humanity. The mechanisms through which the domain of ethics gets extended need not involve only beliefs that are true.

The normative capabilities and evaluative capacities are open-ended ones. They are not destined to travel along one particular track. Once they exist, they take on a life and a direction of their own.

Higher Layers of Ethics

Ethics and our normative capacities arise because they extend the domain of coordination to mutual benefit beyond that which is accessible through evolutionarily instilled behavior patterns plus operant conditioning. Capacities of evaluation provide greater means of controlling our desires, and hence of controlling our behavior. However, once ethics of some sort exists, once our normative boxes and operators are in place and prepared to receive content, and once our evaluative capacities are functioning, ethics can get extended beyond its originating function.

The principles that apply in one domain might get extended to another; the metacriteria that the principles fit might get applied in reasoning to formulate other principles or to modify some existing ones. The range of principles thereby might get extended beyond the range or possibility of mutual interpersonal benefit. Principles might get formulated about behavior toward helpless beings with whom no mutually cooperative interaction is possible (fetuses, animals) or to currently nonexistent beings (future generations). Principles can come to be accepted which are favored by general criteria consonant with principles of mutual cooperation, but which mandate that in certain situations someone ends up below his security level or makes very serious sacrifices. The plant that first takes root in the soil of cooperation to mutual benefit can migrate to other ecological niches, extended by our conceptual and intellectual abilities.

Moreover, our inherited susceptibility to normative instruction means that we will (at least initially) adopt and conform to the existing normatively guided patterns of behavior that we are presented with and taught, whether or not *those* presented norms (are designed to) serve coordination to mutual benefit. Once these other norms originate, for whatever reason, they too are imbibed early. Their way is eased later, when following them is not to our current benefit, if they possibly are to our own future benefit or to the benefit of those, perhaps kin, whose well-being we already care about. The more generally norms are formulated, or the more general are the stated principles from which they follow, the more likely they are to encompass an actual or potential semipersonal benefit that is cared about.

Even principles whose focus is clustered about coordination to mutual benefit need not always operate, in every situation, to people's mutual benefit. Principles that generally operate to mutual benefit might not do so in some particular situations, yet these principles might continue to be applied and followed in those situations. Principles that once served both parties may no longer do so because of changed circumstances, yet these principles might linger on and continue to be adhered to. Particular principles of behavior might be instituted because it is thought that they will benefit all, but this belief might be mistaken. And sometimes principles might be proposed and propagated only because they serve the interests of some, yet they might be accompanied by arguments maintaining that all do benefit.

Serving cooperation in one way or another, among some group or another, even though this was the originating function of ethics does not remain its sole function. Since different functions can be added, by a process of extension that takes some portion or aspects of cooperative principles and applies them to new domains, or takes existing evaluations and pushes them in a new direction, and since the direction and extent of that extension are not uniquely determined, there is yet further room for variation in different societies' ethical norms. Once we advance beyond *the* function of ethics, once we advance beyond the one original function to the multiple functions it can come to possess and be given, the question of which functions ethics *should* have comes to the fore as an ethical question to be discussed within a society's own ethical theory. Moral reformers do not simply propose extending the scope of application of existing principles to new groups; they also propose novel moral purposes and goals. This does not mean that a society automatically will use its current ethical theory to endorse that theory's current functions. In the case of science, the criteria and standards for assessing a theory, though born with and established by one successful theory, then can favor another theory that does better by those very standards. That second theory can bring along its own standards, ones it holds important and satisfies well, and these new standards then can come to replace the previous ones. So too in the case of ethics, existing views of function, and the principles these endorse, can then lead to the criticism of some extant functions and to the discovery and acceptance of others. The enterprise that begins in cooperation to mutual benefit, in normative capability, and in evaluative capacity goes on, as we know, to further heights.

In *The Examined Life*, I distinguished the following levels or layers of ethics.[59] The first layer is the *ethics of respect*, which corresponds to an (extended) ethics mandating cooperation to mutual benefit. Here there are rules and principles mandating respecting another (adult) person's life and autonomy, forbidding murder and enslavement, restricting interference with a person's domain of choice, and issuing in a more general set of (what have been termed negative) rights. The second layer is the *ethics of responsiveness*, which is based upon an underlying notion of the inherent value of (all) individuals. It mandates acting in a way that is responsive to people's value, enhancing and supporting it, and enabling it to flourish. The third layer is the *ethics of caring*, which ranges from concern and tenderness to deeper compassion and love. In its full development, this layer mandates nonharm, *ahimsa* and love to all people, perhaps to all living creatures; it often is motivated by religious feeling or by an identification with all living beings. The final layer, what I termed the *ethics of Light*, calls for being a vessel and vehicle of Light (in the special meaning I there gave to that term, which encompassed the dimensions of truth, beauty, goodness, and holiness). Socrates, Buddha, and Jesus, along with various lesser-known *rishis, tzaddiks,* saints, and sages point the way.

These layers stand in intricate relations to one another. Each level is more basic than the next higher level (respect is more basic than responsiveness) and is the ground from which the higher layer grows. The higher layer is to be followed when it conflicts with the more basic one but only in accordance with a principle of minimal mutilation of the lower.

A complete and a satisfying genealogy of ethics would delineate the steps that carry one to these further layers. (Are higher levels of awareness needed for higher layers of ethics? What is the role of conscious awareness in the transition to a higher level?) A first step may be the hypothesizing of *value* as the object and basis of acts of evaluation, and then developing a consistent delineation of value. This leads one to the layer of responsiveness to value, or at least to its threshold. What further steps—the word "mechanisms" does not seem quite right here—can take one further?

Perhaps each layer effortlessly (though not inexorably) gives rise to the next. The domain of coordination to mutual benefit is expanded ever more widely, and the basis for this is found in traits common to all human beings. We hypothesize a basis in value for our evaluations that it would be good to extend cooperation more widely, and we delineate an inherent value to human capacities of choice, of self-consciousness, of norm following, and of evaluation (and later to the trait of actually seeking value). We then respond to these capacities in others as we respond to valuable things in general, appreciating them, preserving them, nurturing them, protecting them. Our *actual behavior* in this manner, at this level, interacts with our capacities of emotional responsiveness, including emotional responsiveness to (what we perceive as) value, and these capacities, at least in some individuals, get extended to compassion or love for all people and all living creatures, and to adherence to nonharm to them. This actual behavior and its attendant nobler emotions lead to a deeper and more encompassing evaluative vision of the good and its intertwining with other aspects of the universe, a vision that has taken different forms in humanity's great ethical and spiritual seers.

I do not say that each layer entails the immediately higher one, or that the progression of development through these layers is inevitable. Living and behaving at each layer, though, with its attendant changes, may make the next step a natural one to take. It may come to seem that the vector that has brought one to the current layer naturally extends to the next layer, and that the next step will continue the previous path and fulfill it.

This is merely a sketch that extends a genealogy of ethics to its higher layers, or rather a gesture at a sketch, a placeholder for the insights and the details needed to fill in and animate the general structure of (nonentailed and noninevitable, yet appropriate and fulfilling) growth to higher ethical levels. I do not say that the ethics of each higher layer is more obligatory. It just is lovelier, and more elevating.

The different levels of ethics have a different status. The ethics of respect, largely specified by what I have called the core principle, is the part, the *one* part (I think), that is (that should be) mandatory across all societies. In saying this, I am putting forward a particular normative position: that the further ethical levels are matters of personal choice or personal ideal.[60] Even if these further levels are not mandatory for all societies, some particular society may attempt to make one or another of these further levels mandatory *within it*, punishing those members of the society who deviate or fall short. I also believe—this is an additional component of my own position, presented in *Anarchy, State, and Utopia*—that no society should take this further step. All that any society should (coercively) demand is adherence to the ethics of respect. The further levels should be matters for a person's own individual choice and development.

Can we understand why people disagree so about which levels of ethics are to be mandatorily imposed? Evaluations can classify things as good, bad, or neutral. They also can rank things as better or worse, even to the extent of talking about how much better or worse one thing is than another. (To be sure, the classificatory notions also involve some ranking, in that good things are better than neutral things, which in turn are better than bad things.) The detailed rankings in goodness are more useful, and more necessary, in complicated choice situations, yet they require far more information than do the simple classifications, and hence they are difficult to generate. One means of generating a detailed goodness-ranking of things in one fell swoop is to match their degree of goodness with their known positions along some other dimension. The stronger someone is, the better. The more nonperishable food one possesses, the better. We might term this *the Principle of Proportional Ranking:* rank things according to their place along some other dimension. Such a generalized principle might well have been built into our cognitive architecture by the evolutionary process. Notice that ranking things in goodness is only one application of this principle. The more extensively this principle is followed, the greater will be the correlation of things' rankings across different dimensions. And some things might get arrayed along another dimension in proportion to their already specified goodness.

To what degree, then, should a level of ethics be enforced and imposed? It would be natural, in accordance with the Principle of Proportional Ranking, to answer that the more important the level is, the greater should be its enforcement.[61] The question then becomes: what determines the importance of a level of ethics? Is a level more important the higher it is, so that the most inspiring and saintly behavior is what is to be not only the most admired but the most demanded and the most enforced? Is a level more important, the more it enables and encourages people to live (some particular vision of) the most desirable human life? Or is a level more important the more it is necessary to the functioning of nonviolent relations, so that rights of noninterference are what are to be most strongly mandated and enforced, thereby preserving room for people to pursue their own ends and goals?[62] My own reply (as regards the question of coercion and enforcement) has been the last one, but I cannot help but notice that this has been a minority view thus far.[63]

Once we have hypothesized value as the basis of our evaluations, the question of normative force takes on a different character. The first book of Plato's *Republic* asks the question of why an individual with a magic ring (the Ring of Gyges) that would make him invisible and able to get away with any crime should be moral. Glaucon challenges Socrates to show that the just life is the best one; that it is better even to be just yet seem to others not to be, with the consequence of being treated harshly by them, than to be unjust yet seem to others to be just and so be honored and treated well by them. The *Republic* describes the soul or psyche of the ethical person as harmoniously ordered, with the rational part ruling the courageous and appetitive parts, in contrast to the soul of the unethical person, which is clashing and conflicted, with the lower parts often dominating the higher. I want to focus upon the structure of Plato's argument, not upon the question of whether he does show that the person whose soul is harmoniously ordered will indeed behave in the ways that the Greeks (and we too) have held to be ethical.[64] Plato does not demonstrate that the person with the harmoniously ordered soul will be *happier*. Rather he presents a picture of a more appealing way to be, a more ordered and beautiful way, a way that is more desirable and valuable than that of the disordered and conflicted soul. What Plato invokes here, and depends upon, is our view of value. Which kind of life is most valuable? A complete theory would explicitly present (and support) a general theory of value according to which being an ethical person is a more valuable way to be. The answer, then, to the question "Why should I be moral?" is not the trivial one that you morally should be moral. Rather, being moral instances and realizes a more general kind of value, and you should be moral because it is (according to this more general value) a better way to be. The unethical person may not care about being more valuable (when he realizes what value is), but his not caring about this just reinforces his lesser value. The unethical person, then, is not getting away with anything. But the sanction is a value sanction. Such, at any rate, is one attractive and promising theoretical route to giving normative force to ethics.[65]

It may seem that we have presented a theory with too many epicycles. Ethics is rooted in coordination of activities to mutual benefit, but some ethical principles do not operate to mutual benefit, and some modes of coordination (such as that in Thomas Schelling's "coordination games") may not strike us as ethical.[66] What begins in coordination to mutual benefit can get extended to quite different arenas, in part by reasoning and metacriteria rooted in principles that govern action to mutual benefit, in part because our capacities include normative boxes eager to be filled with content. Ethical obligations to oneself might get added as a further epicycle, perhaps construed as involving the coordination of one's present actions with one's future and past ones. The exercise of evaluative capacities leads to still further extensions. And that is just the beginning of the story, one which continues, according to our sketch of the higher ethical levels, with further optional but permissible steps.

Doesn't this theory involve too many qualifications, extensions, and caveats? I too would prefer a theory with a neater shape, one with no spokes extending out from the center, but I do not know of an alternative such theory that is adequate. The present theory sees ethics as something rooted in the governance of opportunities for cooperation to mutual benefit but which grows (slowly) outward from there, eventually reaching, in some cases, the loftiest heights of the ethical and spiritual imagination.

On the other hand, one might complain that the theory is too inclusive, in that there is no behavior that it could not be stretched to account for. One wants an explanatory theory to be wide enough to include whatever does occur (within its domain) in the world. A narrower theory could not be the whole explanation of that domain. Yet an explanatory theory should explain why things are one way rather than another, and thus should exclude things' being some other way. The theory should possess Popperian content. Is there any possible ethical content, then, that could not be got to by the various mechanisms envisioned in our theory? There is. One would not expect any society to have norms that say "Never cooperate with anyone else under any circumstances" or norms that mandate violating every previous agreement when this can be done undetectably or norms that mandate killing all of the society's young (when there is otherwise no threat to them). It also is unlikely that a society will *forbid* most people to act against their own interest when that action is greatly to the benefit of others in that society. Admittedly, these are easy cases. Others would require more elaboration.

Ethical Truth and Ethical Objectivity

How does the notion of *truth* apply to ethics? Our previous discussion of truth contained two stages: first, the characterization of true beliefs as (statistically) conducive to success in achieving the goals of action—this presented the general notion of truth and marked the value of holding true beliefs; second, the identification of the truth property, the property that underlies and explains such success in action. The proponent of the correspondence theory of truth says this: some of our beliefs tend to have the actions that are based upon them achieve their goals because these beliefs correspond to the facts. That discussion of truth presumed that the beliefs (whose statistical success in action was being investigated) were factual beliefs, nonevaluative and nonethical ones. After discovering the truth property for factual beliefs—let us suppose that it is (some form of) correspondence to the facts—we then can investigate whether some ethical statements can and do have that very same truth property. Are there ethical statements that correspond to the facts; are there ethical facts, and are there ways that statements can correspond to them?[67]

A straightforward way in which ethical statements would be true is if they possess for themselves the factual truth property F. Less straightforward would be to say that ethical statements have some property E that is analogous to F. It differs from F in a way that befits the difference between ethics and empirical facts, yet does *not* differ in a way that conflicts with what we think of as truth. The two properties, E and F, may each be instances of some more general property that reveals something important about the nature of truth.

Another strategy would be to apply the general notion of truth, in terms of success in action, directly to ethics, without going through the stage of specifying the truth property for factual statements. Ethical statements can be acted upon, and if some lead to more success in goal achievement than others, cannot we identify the truth property for ethical statements as the one that underlies *their* serviceability, the one that underlies and explains the success in acting upon *those* statements? And it might seem more reasonable to so determine the ethical truth property directly. For why should we care about ethical statements' having the property that makes factual statements serviceable, if that very property does not also make ethical statements serviceable? And if what we value is the serviceability of ethical statements, if that is why we care about finding ethical truths, then why not investigate that serviceability directly to discover what truth in ethics is, by seeing what characteristic ethically serviceable statements share? What kind of serviceability, though, is it that ethical statements (are to) have; what counts as success in acting upon ethical beliefs?

I propose to consider the extent to which ethics parallels the structure that we have uncovered in the clearly factual arenas. If there is a very significant parallel, we then can ask whether this shows that there *are* ethical truths, or (if not) whether the parallel shows that ethics is sufficiently *truthlike* to put our worries about its status to rest.

The biological function of sensing the world is to guide our physical movements and actions so as to improve our situation. Doing better than random motion or stasis counts as an improvement. It is not just current perceptions that guide our actions. Through memories of past perceptions, or through inferences from them, or through evolutionarily instilled approximately accurate cognitions, beliefs incorporate past information that is not presently perceptually available to us. The function of beliefs is to guide our movements and actions so as to better achieve our goals. Beliefs are effective when they succeed in so guiding our actions. We may generalize the notion of the truth property of beliefs to speak of the *effectiveness property* of beliefs. Their effectiveness property is the property that explains their effectiveness in carrying out their function. That function is what defines the general notion of truth and marks the value of holding true beliefs. The effectiveness property of beliefs, then, just is the truth property (for instance, according to one prominent theory, correspondence). This explains the effectiveness of some beliefs, that is, the (statistical) success of actions based upon those beliefs. This wordy excursus has a point. It prepares us to speak of the effectiveness property of ethical statements, the property that enables ethical statements to carry out *their* function, which function may be different from the function of factual beliefs. Ethics still can parallel factual beliefs even if ethics does not have the truth property of factual beliefs. The parallel is this: ethics and factual beliefs each can have their own effectiveness property that explains how they are able to carry out their respective functions. In the case of factual beliefs, their effectiveness property is the truth property. An interesting question is what the effectiveness property of ethical beliefs is.

These are ways of investigating the topic of ethical truth or its analogue. What about the investigation of ethical objectivity? An objective truth, we saw earlier, is marked by three characteristics. It is accessible from different angles; it is or can be interpersonally agreed to; and it holds independently of the beliefs and experiences of the observer or thinker. There is a fourth property of objective truths and objective facts (or at least of the fundamental ones in physics): objective truths are invariant under all admissible transformations. The list of admissible transformations, for instance, the Lorentz transformations, is not given *a priori* but is discovered in the course of scientific activity and scientific advance. Just as the truth property of belief underlies and explains its role in goal-achieving action, what we termed the objectiveness property underlies and explains the three marks of objectiveness. Our claim was that being invariant under all admissible transformations is the objectiveness property; it explains the other three marks of objectiveness.

We also can ask what objectiveness property it is that explains inter-subjective ethical agreement. If there is no such property, and if certain principles simply *are* agreed to, then the parallel to factual truth would seem to break down, and so would the normative weight of intersubjective agreement. (If the social-contract tradition aims at nothing more than agreement, without any independent basis for ascribing normative weight to this agreement, then its foundations and its results are frail.)

We have uncovered two notions of objectivity. An objective fact is one that is invariant under admissible transformations. The larger the number of admissible transformations a statement is invariant under, the more objective it is; a fully objective fact is invariant under all admissible transformations. And an objective belief or judgment is one that arises through a process that does not tend to be directed away from the truth by the operation of biasing factors or, more strongly, one that arises through a reliable and effective process for arriving at true beliefs. Call what an objective fact has, *objectiveness,* and call what an objective judgment has, *objectivity.*

The characteristics of the process that effectively and efficiently reaches true beliefs, the characteristics that play a role in its reaching these, we can call its *objectivity characteristics.* In the factual case, these characteristics standardly are held to include lack of operative bias toward different ways the truth might turn out, basing belief upon the evidence, dispassionate and unemotional evaluation of that evidence, and so on. A process for reaching belief that exhibits these characteristics is an objective process; it is objective because a process with these characteristics is effective in arriving at the truth.[68]

That is all quite a mouthful, I know, but it demarcates the notions of truth, objectiveness, and objectivity—and their interrelations—in the factual case. If ethics can conform to this structure, or can parallel it, then it too can embody and exhibit a desirable objectiveness and also (objective) truth.

The parallel structure for ethics, then, would present (1) a function for ethical statements (this corresponds to the function of beliefs in yielding successful actions); (2) an effectiveness property shared by statements effective in carrying out that ethical function (this corresponds to the effectiveness property, viz. truth, for factual beliefs); (3) transformations that ethical statements sharing that effectiveness property are invariant under, which constitutes their objectiveness (this corresponds to the admissible transformations factual statements are invariant under); (4) a reliable process for arriving at statements showing the effectiveness property (this corresponds to an objective process for arriving at factual beliefs); and (5) the objectivity characteristics holding of this reliable process (this corresponds to the characteristics of being unbiased, dispassionate, weighing all the evidence, etc., in the factual case).

I would feel happier if what follows were motivated by new and independent ethical insight, which it then attempts to codify. Instead, what we have discovered about truth, objectivity, etc. is used to structure preexisting ethical material. The ethics does not spontaneously give rise to the structure. Still, if ethics does to a significant extent fit the structure and get illuminatingly organized by it, then the resulting parallelism of factual and ethical structures, however it first originated in our thinking, may serve to illuminate and to solidify truth and objectivity in ethics.

We already have discussed the function of ethical statements at length. We now shall consider the effectiveness property that enables them to perform this function, the invariances these statements exhibit, the process that is most effective in arriving at such statements, and the characteristics this process has. It will be useful to begin with the objectivity process.

A legal judge is held to be more objective when he or she has no particular tie to the outcome of the case. Being a relative of one of the parties to a case, or an investor in a company being sued, shows a personal involvement not conducive to objective decision, that is, to arriving at a just verdict. A just verdict must stem from impartiality.[69] Similarly, ethical theorists have held that accurate moral judgment must arise (or, at least, best arises) from lack of personal involvement. The objectivity characteristics of the process must eliminate or mask or shield one from distorting involvements. This distancing should be seen as a feature of the process by which an accurate moral judgment best arises and is tested, not as a component of the psychological state ("distant") of a person who is in the midst of moral action.

There have been different specifications of the precise form this distancing from personal bias takes. Adam Smith held that correct moral judgments are those that would be reached by an "ideal observer" having full knowledge of the facts who is not personally involved in the outcome of the action but who has a lively, full, and sympathetic concern with how all parties are affected. Roderick Firth has elaborated this type of theory, describing an observer who knows all nonethical facts, who imagines this information vividly, who is without interests in particular persons, times, or places and without special passions toward persons or objects.[70] John Harsanyi, working within the economists' tradition of social choice theory, held that an objective judgment about which of two social states was ethically better could be made only (or made best) by someone who did not know which of the various different people he was, hence who did not know how each of the states would affect him personally. Harsanyi said this person should assume (or act as if) he had a equal chance of being each of the persons in the society, and then rationally choose one of the social situations. This leads to a derivation of the utilitarian principle that maximizes the total utility in the society.[71] John Rawls followed a similar path, holding that an objective moral choice is one made behind a "veil of ignorance" that prevents a person from knowing which of the people in the described society he is (or into which of the major social groups he falls).[72] It is interesting how a very delicate (and, in itself, unmotivated) distinction in the distancing situation—when you do not know which person you are, do you have a knowledge of an equal probability of being each person or do you have no knowledge of the probability at all?—leads to a significant difference in the principle (utilitarian or the difference principle) that is yielded. So no such argument from neutrality, all by itself, could justify a particular rule. This listing of theories in which ethical objectivity is held to involve a certain kind of distancing from one's own position in the situation could be extended.[73]

Objective ethical truths, in turn, are held to involve a certain symmetry or invariance. (There is an intimate connection between symmetry and invariance features.) The Golden Rule mandates doing unto others as you would have others do unto you. Similarity in treatment stems from impartiality. Related principles of justice and right hold that an action is right (permissible, wrong) for you only if it is right (permissible, wrong) for any similar person in similar circumstances. Kant's categorical imperative holds that it is right to act upon a maxim only if it can be willed to be a universal law. Henry Sidgwick formulated the (as he termed it, "self-evident") principle that "It cannot be right for A to treat B in a manner in which it would be wrong for B to treat A, merely on the ground that they are two different individuals, and without there being any difference between . . . the two which can be stated as a reasonable ground for difference in treatment."[74] A standard condition of social-choice theory is that the socially chosen alternative be invariant under a permutation of people. The ethical status of an action or policy is invariant under transformations that substitute one person for another.[75] An ethical statement is (held to be) objective when it exhibits this kind of generality, although ethical theories differ about the particular such invariance they require or impose. And theorists also differ about the status of this generality requirement: is it a normative requirement or, as R. M. Hare claimed (invoking the analytic/synthetic distinction), is it a consequence of linguistic facts? Note how Hare's theory shows the difficulty of clearly distinguishing the objective process from the invariance characteristics. Hare's objective process for deciding upon ethical principles involves reversing roles and asking yourself whether you would be willing to have that same principle apply to you if you were in the other role, and so it has invariance built into it.[76]

In science, there is no *a priori* criterion that selects the admissible transformations, invariance under which constitutes something as an objective fact. This is discovered in the course of scientific progress. Is there some *a priori* criterion that demarcates the ethically admissible transformations? Did the evolutionary process instill some transformations as a criterion that fitted kin-selective behavior? Did the social and historical experience of (extending) cooperation to mutual benefit then modify and extend this list?

An objective process for arriving at ethical judgments, one that exhibits the objectivity characteristics of distancing, yields statements that exhibit invariance under various transformations. Thus, the process yields statements showing objectiveness. This degree of parallelism to the factual case is encouraging. The circuit can be completed by specifying a function of ethics and describing an effectiveness property of ethical statements. It then should turn out that statements achieving the function of ethics (that is, having that effectiveness property) also exhibit the kind of invariance and objectiveness found in statements yielded by the objectivity distancing process for arriving at ethical judgments. Objectivity in ethics then would be grounded in the fact that it yields statements that are effective in carrying out the function of ethics. And this function, at least initially, is that of coordinating behavior to mutual benefit.

I have considered three themes about ethics: the objective and unbiased choice of ethical principles, the invariance features of ethical principles, and the coordinative function of ethics. It now is time to put these together in a thesis that claims (roughly) the following.

Unbiased and distanced choice of ethical principles leads to ones with invariance properties that, in virtue of those invariance features, are effective in achieving the goals of ethics: the protecting, fostering, or maintaining of cooperative activities for mutual benefit; the guiding of such activity (as with principles for dividing benefits); mandating behavior for response to deviations from the first two goals listed; and fostering virtues and dispositions that maintain patterns of cooperative behavior.

That principles with invariance features work effectively in this way no doubt depends upon various factors that it would be desirable to investigate. What assumptions about the cognitive capacities and motivational dispositions of people must hold? What general facts about the situation of the society, its level of economic development, technology, transportation, information storage, etc. must hold? And so on.

The principles of coordinated activity in early societies were not highly symmetrical; they often involved enslaving others, murdering for booty, etc. To be sure, the material situation of these early societies differed from ours, and more symmetrical and invariant principles have come to function importantly in the impersonal dealings of far wider, materially wealthier societies. The rule of law, bureaucratic rationality, the transition from status to contract, from gemeinschaft to gesellschaft—all these impersonal and general devices contributed to the possibility of a large coordinated society of nonrelatives that functioned to its members' greater benefit, and they contributed also to the society's ability to mobilize resources and physical force in its competitive relations with other societies.[77] Is it that only recently have we arrived at knowledge of timeless, objective moral truths, which were not evident in earlier societies that used asymmetric principles of coordination? Or did their situation make significantly more symmetric principles unfeasible?

We now might understand the philosophers' concern with justification, in terms of the coordinative function of ethics. Principles that are justifiable according to a society's existing and accepted criteria of justification—whatever those criteria are—will be more readily agreed to, and hence will tend to function more effectively (all other things being equal) in guiding social cooperation. (However, these considerations do not establish the strong claim that justifiability is a condition of adequacy that any ethical doctrine must meet.) Within justification processes of specified sorts, principles exhibiting invariance features might be more readily agreed to and accepted.

With regard to objectiveness in the factual arena, we found earlier that intersubjective agreement was epistemologically prior—it was our route to discovering that a truth is objective—while invariance was ontologically prior—it specified the nature of objectiveness and it underlay and explained the intersubjective agreement. We might see proposals about reaching interpersonal agreement in ethics, and about reflective equilibrium, in this light. Such agreement and equilibrium may be our route to coming to know that something is an objective truth, but only when, and because, this agreement is explained by other objectiveness properties (such as the relevant invariances in ethics) that contribute to carrying out functions of ethics.[78]

Ethics only begins because of opportunities for cooperation for mutual benefit and it then spreads into other arenas, partly by the application of the metacriteria that first apply to principles governing cooperation, partly through societal inculcation filling our normative boxes with that society's content. So won't there come to be *multiple* functions to ethics, functions that range beyond cooperation to mutual benefit? Since no compelling criterion picks out exactly which further functions are to be included for ethics, or the precise weights that they are to be given, this only reinforces the previous points about the leeway offered for some relativism. (However, writers also have argued that there are not precise weights to be given to the various desiderata for scientific theories in deciding which theory to accept, so ethics may be no less objective than science in this respect.)

Is the parallelism between ethics and ordinary or scientific facts sufficiently great to group ethics as true and as objective? I have not claimed that there are (irreducible and nonsupervenient) ethical facts, such as a *fact* that it is wrong to murder, so that some ethical statements are true when they correspond to this fact which they state. There are facts, however, that underlie an ethical norm or principle against murder, namely, that such a norm or principle provides a framework for and facilitates the coordination of activity to mutual benefit. Ethics does not float free of facts such as these, which determine the effectiveness of ethical beliefs in achieving the goals of ethics.[79]

What is the effectiveness property of ethics, though, and is it exactly the same as the effectiveness property, that is, the truth property, of factual statements? Or, at least, is it sufficiently like the factual truth property that ethics is *truthlike?* We are not yet in a position to state the truth property for factual statements, or so I argued in the first chapter. There I said that a substantive account of correspondence lies in the future, *after* we have discovered all the various modes of "making true" (including Tarskian logical structure, scientific reduction, and supervenience) and the various ultimate components and structures of facts. Similarly, we should expect that a substantive account of the ethical truth property will at least await advances in a theory of what makes for successful coordination. It seems unlikely, however, that the two effectiveness properties, the one for factual beliefs and the other for ethical ones, will turn out to be the same.

However, the goals and functions of factual and ethical beliefs differ. The function of our capacity for factual beliefs is to have actions based upon them that successfully achieve the goals of the action; the function of ethical beliefs is to have actions based upon them that successfully yield a more intensive or extensive coordination of activity to some mutual benefit. If, however, we see this function of ethical beliefs as marking the general goal of ethical actions (viz. yielding or facilitating a more intensive or extensive coordination of activity to some mutual benefit), then cannot we see successful ethical action as just a subspecies of successful action? Do the differences between the factual and the ethical effectiveness properties correspond to the differences between the respective functions of these two kinds of belief? If so, is the parallelism close enough to constitute a "kind of truth" for ethics?[80]

Or will this question matter so very much? Once we see ethics as having a function, and ethical statements as effectively carrying out this function, will whether ethical statements are *true* continue to seem important? Isn't truth important, after all, mainly because *it* has a function? If the function of factual beliefs (viz. success in achieving goals) is important, then so also is the function of ethical beliefs (viz. success in achieving the particular goal of mutual benefit by a particular kind of route, coordinated activity). Won't the effectiveness property of ethical beliefs, whatever that turns out to be, be as important as the effectiveness property of factual beliefs (whatever that turns out to be)? If ethical beliefs had the truth property of *factual* statements, but this did not enable the ethical beliefs to carry out the function of *ethics,* then such ethical "truth" would not be worth very much. It is the effectiveness property of ethics that we want ethical beliefs to have, not the effectiveness property of factual beliefs, unless the latter happens to coincide with the former. And so won't the respective kinds of effectiveness and the respective accompanying kinds of objectiveness (that is, invariances under different transformations) both turn out to be important?

There appears to remain one significant structural difference, though, between factual truth and "truth" in ethics. Since the ubiquity of ethical norms is a result of a selection and since the selection process is statistical in nature, the initial (general) function of ethics—I have claimed that it is coordination of behavior to mutual benefit—will allow situations and cases in which acting in accordance with the norm does *not* serve the function. Should an individual in such a situation follow the norm or violate it in order to pursue the functional goal directly? The existing function of ethics does not say. And why must a person pay any kind of attention to the function of ethics, when doing so is not in his individual interest? Since the function is not sharp enough to resolve these long-standing ethical quandaries, the effectiveness property of ethics also will be fuzzy. Surely factual truth is in better shape than that!

Yet factual truth too shows comparable lacunae. Because of the interplay of diverse factors in producing the outcomes of action, acting on true beliefs will bear only a statistical connection to success in achieving the goals of the action. And in particular cases, acting on false beliefs may lead to greater success in the achievement of particular goals (as when someone who optimistically overestimates his chances of success does better in his action) and even in the general achievement of goals (as when someone who overestimates how well his peers regard him does better in career success and in general happiness than someone with a strictly accurate view of how he is regarded).[81] So should a person always follow the general norm of believing and acting upon the truth, or should the person set or encourage himself to deviate from this path in particular cases? This is the act/rule question. There also might be an egoism question. Should you follow the truth property that underlies the success in action of people in general or, if these diverge, should you follow the property that underlies your *own* success in action? It is a fact that the function of belief and action, and of the cognitive and emotional and motor capacities that underlie behavior, is to yield differential behavior that serves inclusive fitness, and it is a fact that the function of belief in particular is to guide action so that it is based upon the truth (or upon what is true enough). But these facts do not answer or settle the questions that were posed. The function of (factual as opposed to evaluative) belief, the function of true belief, is not sharp enough to say.

If the structural situation is the *same* with factual as with ethical belief, why then have there been salient and prominent long-standing quandaries about ethics (follow the best norm or do the best act? pursue my own interest or pursue the general good?), yet no corresponding salient and prominent quandaries about factual truth? We care about the ethical issues because their resolution directly affects others. The corresponding issues about factual truth are more private, affecting others only indirectly if at all. So nobody else much cares. But in neither case, factual truth or ethics, can these corresponding issues be conclusively resolved.

Yet some have insisted that the conclusive resolution within ethics of the issue concerning why one should be moral constitutes the crucial test of a theory of ethics.[82] It seems overly ambitious to expect or demand that an ethical theory accomplish what a theory of factual truth cannot.

The Unpredictability of Human Behavior

Why has it been so difficult for psychologists to formulate an accurate predictive theory of chosen human behavior? Why have psychologists been unable to account for more than 50 percent of the variance in human behavior? To the answer that human behavior is extremely complex, it has been replied that everything appears complex until a good theory of it has been developed. Before the laws of motion were discovered, for all anybody knew, the color of objects or their past history or any number of other factors together might have been relevant to their motion. Motion appears simple only *after* the laws of motion are discovered. For much human behavior, however, empirical data do show that many factors are relevant to subsequent behavior, in that they are correlated with it in a way that seems to indicate causal connection. So let us grant that human behavior is complex; it is complexly caused, and that explains why we don't yet have a good theory of it.

But *why* is human behavior so complexly caused? We are creatures who are built so that our chosen behavior depends upon very many factors, including subtle and not easily discerned present factors and also innumerable factors in our history, as well as our varying inherent temperaments. But why are we built like that, and not in a simpler fashion? After all, what has causal impact upon us is a function of the way we are constituted. Why has evolution constructed us so that these many different factors have an effect upon us, factors that often are resistant to even the psychologists' attempts at discernment? Even siblings, raised by the same parents in the same home, are subject to differences in their microenvironments that produce large differences in their personal development.[83] The studies by psychologists of character traits (such as honesty) show that (the expressions of) these traits are highly variable across different contexts.[84]

One possible answer is that which decision is best often depends upon subtle differences and distinctions, so complex causation of behavior is needed to match behavior to a complex array of reasons relevant to optimality. However, many of the factors that psychologists have discovered are relevant to the causation of behavior do not seem attuned to, or correlated with, aspects of optimality, and all the more so does this hold for the effects upon behavior of evanescent factors, both external and internal. We need to search elsewhere for an explanation of the unpredictability of much behavior.

It is plausible to think that a major factor behind the explosive enlargement in the size of the human brain was the need of our ancestors to anticipate and counter the actions of reasonably intelligent conspecifics in situations of conflict of interest, when these others also were trying to anticipate and counter actions. As with evolutionary arms races between predators and prey, each developing further skills and abilities to match the improvements in the skills and abilities of the other, bit by bit human brains developed to match (or slightly surpass) the developments in the brains of conspecifics. Survival of the fittest led to survival of the brainiest.

This chapter has emphasized the benefits to be gained from people's voluntary cooperation to mutual benefit. That opportunities for such mutual benefit are so widespread has been a major factor, I have held, in the development of norms of behavior and in their extension to wider groups of people.

Yet not every interaction is a cooperative one, not only between groups but also between individuals who are members of the same group that does engage in widespread internal cooperation. Many are the conflicts between the interests of people, including those conflicts over mates or opportunities or resources central to the reproductive success that (biologists hold) drives the evolutionary process.

In such situations, people sometimes act antagonistically toward others, or even violently toward them. They aim at their own benefit. They often succeed by doing something unexpected, surprising the other person by their actions or stratagems. They want to act in a way that the other has not predicted, so that the other cannot effectively counter their own action in a timely fashion.[85] Yet a person would not be served by being completely unpredictable in all his actions. Such total unpredictability, if evident to others, would preclude these others from having enough confidence in the person's behavior to cooperate with him to mutual, and hence to his own, benefit.

What a person might most want or benefit from is to be reliably predictable in situations in which his best action is to cooperate to mutual benefit, and to be largely unpredictable in situations of conflict of interest. Not completely unpredictable even there, for he might want and need his probable future retaliatory responses to be well enough known to deter others from certain actions. A person even might want not to be predictably *rational* in conflict situations, for such predictability might enable opponents to box the person in, confident that his own best interests in avoiding injury or suffering will constrain him from reacting violently or aggressively in that constrained situation. A perceived chance of his behaving irrationally might deter others from pushing him into too much of a corner.[86]

My suggestion, then, is that our behavior is complex because the evolutionary process shaped us to be creatures whose behavior was significantly unpredictable by our conspecifics; unpredictable to them, despite their possession of a (possibly innate) belief-desire framework of psychological explanation and prediction.

Varied mechanisms might contribute to this unpredictability. A tendency to have one's behavior be shaped by many past factors whose individual strengths or vector result would not be known to others. A tendency to act on the basis of current subjective psychological states. (Are some subjective psychological states not intersubjectively available to others, not because they have no need to know them and so have not evolved means of doing so, but because these kinds of states, which affect your behavior, are *shielded* from the knowledge and predictive ability of others?) A tendency to impulsive behavior, spurred by evanescent whims or momentary facts. A tendency to be moved by factors one is not oneself aware of, so one cannot reveal or signal them to others as a basis of prediction.[87] A tendency to have one's actions governed by nonlinear dynamics so that they are sensitively dependent upon initial conditions, and so decidedly beyond the resources of other people's predictions, or even of one's own in advance. Our hypothesis would predict that these kinds of factors would operate far more strongly in situations of conflict than in situations in which significant gains are possible from cooperation to mutual benefit.

These speculations are meant merely to open a line of inquiry, one that needs to be continued by game-theoretic models that specify what kinds of degrees of predictability would be optimal for an individual, and also by models that specify which kinds and degrees of predictability would be evolutionary stable strategies.[88] The cost of such unpredictability might be some unavoidable spillover, or seepage, into cooperative situations. If the greater the unpredictability in conflict situations, the greater the spillover to cooperative ones, then selection may have limited how unpredictable most people can be even in conflict situations. (Of course, there may be individual variation in these characteristics.)

An amount of unpredictability of behavior may not simply be a side effect of other things that were selected for because of the benefits they directly yield, for instance, complex decision processes. Such unpredictability may have been directly selected for. Our mode of behavior may be a compromise between our ancestors' need for their behavior to be predictable to some others in order to coordinate and dovetail their actions (or to deter them from harmful actions), and their need to be unpredictable to others in some conflict situations, when these others have developed capacities of prediction that use publicly available knowledge and their own past observations of behavior. If the unpredictability of human behavior has a biological function, that is, an evolutionary function, then it is no surprise that psychologists have found their task a difficult one. In principle, the more detailed and intensive scientific investigations by psychologists could yield results that more casual investigators or observers have been unable to achieve. But that hasn't happened yet.

I have said that a person would benefit by his behavior's being unpredictable in situations of conflict yet predictable in situations in which coordinated behavior can lead to mutual benefit. Norms may facilitate predictability in cooperative contexts by pointing to or mandating cooperative behavior (within the group, in those contexts) *and* its being common knowledge in the group that those are the norms. If, for whatever reason (including but not limited to a match between the norm and the person's self-interest), it is known to be more likely that a person will adhere to the norm than to perform the same behavior in the absence of the norm, then the existence of the norm will increase predictability (in cooperative contexts). One function of norms is to increase the predictability of cooperative coordinated behavior in contexts in which mutual gains are possible. This serves to increase and to intensify the amount of cooperation.

It has been said that norms fill a gap left open by rationality, for instance, mandating cooperative behavior in prisoners'-dilemma situations.[89] But norms may also reinforce rationality and thereby lead to predictability. A norm to perform behavior that already is rational may make it more likely that the person will perform that behavior. It is far easier to get to common knowledge that such-and-such is the norm, and to get to common knowledge that people tend to obey the norms in their community, than to get to common knowledge that something is the rational thing to do in a certain situation, and that those people will behave rationally in such situations. If people predicted solely on the basis of rationality considerations, common knowledge of rationality would be necessary for them securely to perform certain actions (whose good results depend upon the other's acting coordinately). When such common knowledge of rationality is absent or difficult, norms can function to fill that gap in predictability.

It was in our ancestors individual interests to interact cooperatively with others, and hence to behave predictably to others, to a very considerable extent. There was a selection at the level of the individual for the normativity module.

Ethics and Conscious Self-Awareness

A conscious awareness of self often is said to be the attribute that marks us as human. It enables us to reflect upon our own behavior and goals, and to develop complex forms of human culture.

It also is crucial to the guidance of action by norms. A person who guides his own behavior in accordance with norms must have some self-consciousness. He has to know what action he is performing, what his intentions are, whether an intended action violates the norm, how to manage his own behavior to avoid violating the norm, and so on. These are sophisticated capacities that are not exhibited (so far as we know) below the level of primates; the extent, if any, to which other primates have a conception of themselves is a matter of current experimental investigation.[90] We would expect, then, that someone with significant defects in the capacity for conscious self-awareness also would have an impaired capacity to guide his own behavior by norms.

Animals are able to engage in cooperative behavior, but normative guidance makes possible closer and more adaptable cooperation in novel situations, to the parties' mutual benefit. The capacity for conscious self-awareness, and its underlying neural basis, might well have been selected for precisely because it does enable and facilitate such mutually beneficial and mutual fitness-enhancing behavior.[91]

If conscious self-awareness *was* selected for because it makes us capable of norm-guided behavior to mutual benefit, then the position of ethical egoism is placed under great tension. As a normative position, ethical egoism holds that each person ought to maximize his or her own self-interest. If self-awareness is part of the self's interest, then ethical egoism has to give great weight to conscious self-awareness. In any case, carrying out the ethical egoist position requires the presence of conscious self-awareness. A being without awareness of self could not consciously pursue his own self-interest.

Yet if the function of conscious self-awareness is cooperation to mutual benefit, that is, ethical cooperation beyond the mandates of egoism, then the ethical egoist has a serious problem. Not that the position is contradictory—a capacity *can* be used against its biological function. But the position is in substantial tension.

Let us examine more closely the relationship between function and value. Not everything with a function is valuable (consider instruments of torture), and some things without any further function are of intrinsic value. Could a functional object be valuable, though, without its function's being of some value? Recall the question of whether anything is valuable other than conscious experiences. ("Why not plug into an experience machine?") In earlier discussions, I spoke of how we want to connect with what actually is the case, and think it is valuable to do so.[92] It would be nice to be able to say something stronger: if the function of conscious awareness is to enable our actions to conform more closely to aspects of the world, then conscious awareness cannot be valuable without its also being valuable to have actions conform more closely to aspects of the world. So not *only* conscious experiences have intrinsic value. (Similarly, given the *function* of the phenomenological qualities of pleasure and pain, one should be reluctant to conclude, with Benthamite utilitarians, that the only valuable things are pleasures, the only disvaluable things are pains.)

But what if something once did have a function but that function now is vestigial, or is no longer adaptive, or is no longer needed? If the extraterrestrial beings who offer us the experience machine will take care of all our other (physical) needs, so that we no longer need to contour our behavior precisely to features of the world in order to survive, then must something else (continue to) be valuable in addition to conscious experiences? If the Romans made certain coins in order to glorify emperors, mightn't we now find that the coins are (aesthetically) valuable, without holding that the glorification of emperors also is valuable?[93]

It does not follow from something's being valuable and having a function that the function that is performed (or the state that is reached) also is valuable. Things would be different if that thing with a function were valuable *because* it performs the function. But since something that performs (or performed) a function might be valuable for some reason other than performing this function, in that case the function itself (and the state it reaches) need not be valuable too. Therefore, someone could agree that ethics originates in the function of coordinating activity to mutual benefit, yet hold that ethics now is valuable because of additional functions that it has acquired, and even that coordination to mutual benefit is not (and never was) itself valuable. And someone (who rejects all norm-following when it conflicts with his own self-interest) could grant that the function of self-consciousness was to enable norms to be internalized and adhered to, yet maintain that self-consciousness now is valuable for other reasons, and always was.[94]

Still, if conscious self-awareness *was* selected for because it makes us capable of ethical behavior, then ethics, even the very first layer of the ethics of respect, truly is what makes us human. A satisfying conclusion. And one with some normative force.

There are no fixed points in philosophy, or in human development either. What is human may change. Forthcoming genetic and neuroscientific knowledge will make possible great alterations in our inherited human nature and in our intellectual powers; and our descendants also may encounter vastly different intelligent beings from elsewhere. (What ethics will they need, or be moved to create?) We do not know what the philosophy of the future will be like; we do not even know what the *philosophers* of the future will be like.

It is not possible (for us) to look at a child and know what the adult he will grow up to be will look like, yet we are able to look at an adult and see how he came to be from the child he was whose photograph we now see. So too we can hope, even though we cannot picture the philosophers of the future, that, whatever substances they are made of and whatever beings they are descended from and whatever new things they discover and whatever new questions they pose and whatever complex interconnections they stand in to alter their boundaries and levels of consciousness and cognition, they will be able to look back upon us and recognize us as kin.

Philosophy begins in wonder. It never ends.

Notes

Introduction

1. Aristotle noted that this principle has to be stated sharply to withstand various putative counterexamples. That a liquid is hot at one time and cold at another or at one time is hotter than one substance and colder than another, is not a case of contradiction. The principle of noncontradiction, he said, should read: "The same attribute cannot at the same time belong and not belong to the same subject and in the same respect." It also might be necessary, Aristotle noted, to add other qualifications to the principle.

Yet even with all qualifications in place, the principle still might be questioned, I think. Here is one way. Suppose that an object changes from being red to being black or that it just ceases to exist. If time is continuous (or even if it is dense), then between any two instants there are an infinite number of other instants. There is no very next instant after any given one. So with a changing object in continuous time, either there will not be a last instant when it is in one state or there will not be a first instant when it is in the other. An object that changes in color from red to black either will have a last instant when it is red but no first instant when it is nonred, or it will have a first instant of being nonred but no last instant of being red. (In the language of mathematics, either the interval of its being red is closed to the right and the interval of its being black is open to the left, or the interval of its being red is open to the right and the interval of its being black is closed to the left.) Yet there seems to be no special reason to describe the change in one of these ways rather than the other. (We might think that every new state must begin with an interval that is closed to the left, leaving old states to dribble off in open intervals. If there were strong arguments for this—I know of none—they would give force to the notion of a direction of time.)

Therefore, it might be suggested that when an object changes its state, there is *both* a last instant of one state *and* a first instant of the other. If time is continuous, and if there are no instants when the entity is in neither state, no instant when it is neither red nor nonred, then the last instant of the first state and the first instant of the second state would be the very same instant. There would be an instant when the object is both red and black, that is, both red and not red. And, in the case of the object that ceases to exist, there would be an instant when the object both exists and does not exist. These contradictions hold only for an instant, though; it is no wonder that we do not notice them.

I do not claim, when time is continuous, that the correct way to conceive of change definitely involves two closed (and overlapping) intervals. Yet it seems arbitrary to choose one of the two alternative ways to knit together intervals that are exhaustive yet not overlapping. We can avoid such arbitrariness by countenancing instants (but no more than instants) of literal contradiction. If we accepted such delimited and motivated exceptions to the principle of noncontradiction, if the principle of noncontradiction were thus given up as an *exceptionless* principle, Logic would not crumble, Reason would not totter. (Therefore, it would be overreacting to argue, solely in order to avoid such delimited contradictions, that time must be quantized. Stronger considerations within physics would be required to show this.)

2. See Hilary Putnam, "There Is at Least One *A Priori* Truth," in *Realism and Reason,* vol. 3 of *Philosophical Papers* (Cambridge: Cambridge University Press, 1983).

3. Might a theory of potentiality hold that each contingent statement has a manifest truth value and a latent one, although only one of these truth values shows itself at any given time?

4. On the occasion of Putnam's retirement dinner in 2000, I commented upon "Putnam's doctrine that there is at least one *a priori* truth, namely, that you can fool all of the people some of the time and you can fool some of the people all of the time, but that you cannot, all of the time, both fool all of the people and not fool all of the people. This is extremely reassuring."

5. Thomas Nagel, *The Last Word* (Oxford: Oxford University Press, 1996).

6. I refer here to truths in addition to those stated by the system's Godel-sentences, for Godel showed that any system *P* powerful enough to express elementary number theory will have some truths or other, indeed an infinite number, that are not provable within that system.

7. It would be premature to try to list tasks in order of priority: whether to explore the most plausible among those views that tie for highest in philosophical interest and illumination, or to explore these maximally interesting views in proportion to their plausibility, or to explore somewhat less interesting views if they are considerably more plausible.

8. See Imre Lakatos, "Falsification and the Methodology of Scientific Research Programmes," in *Criticism and the Growth of Knowledge,* ed. Imre Lakatos and Alan Musgrave (Cambridge: Cambridge University Press, 1970), pp. 91–196.

9. In *Philosophical Explanations* (Cambridge, Mass.: The Belknap Press of Harvard University Press, 1981), I pointed out other defects of the philosophical method of attempting to prove conclusions conclusively, and I proposed instead that philosophy could be aimed at the goal of explanation, in particular the explanation of how various things are possible (in the face of some reason or argument to think that they are not). New, interesting, and illuminating explanations certainly would fit within the picture I am currently presenting, but other things would as well. There might be philosophically interesting and illuminating views or theories that aren't *explanations* of current material (or resolutions of quandaries, etc.) or explanations of how certain things are possible. These theories could just open new and interesting intellectual territory, raise new philosophical questions that we don't know the answer to, and so on.

10. Within his theory, Kant cannot assert strictly that they do *not* apply to things in themselves, although it would be a great coincidence if they did.

11. William Blake, "The Marriage of Heaven and Hell," 1793.

12. See David Bohm, "A Suggested Interpretation of the Quantum Theory in terms of 'Hidden' Variables," I and II, reprinted in *Quantum Theory and Measurement*, ed. John Wheeler and Wojciech Zurek (Princeton: Princeton University Press, 1983), pp. 369–396; idem, *Causality and Chance in Modern Physics* (London: Routledge and Kegan Paul, 1957); B. J. Hiley and F. David Peat, eds., *Quantum Interpretations* (London: Routledge and Kegan Paul, 1987); James Cushing, *Quantum Mechanics* (Chicago: University of Chicago Press, 1994).

13. This is David Albert's description in *Quantum Mechanics and Experience* (Cambridge, Mass.: Harvard University Press, 1992), p. 169. Albert finds this "conspiracy" an appealing feature (a similar conspiracy is evident in Albert's "many-minds" theory); others may disagree.

14. See Abraham Robinson, *Nonstandard Analysis*, rev. ed. (Amsterdam: North-Holland, 1974); and James Henle and Eugene Kleinberg, *Infinitesimal Calculus* (Cambridge, Mass.: MIT Press, 1979). John Bell has written: "Surely, after 62 years, we should have an exact formulation of some serious part of quantum mechanics . . . fully formulated in mathematical terms, with nothing left to the discretion of the theoretical physicist . . . 'apparatus' should not be separated off from the rest of the world into black boxes, as if it were not made of atoms and not ruled by quantum mechanics"; J. S. Bell, "Against 'Measurement,'" in *Sixty-two Years of Uncertainty*, ed. Arthur Miller (New York: Plenum Press, 1990), p. 17. In his acerbic attitude toward current formulations of quantum mechanics, is Bell now playing the role that Bishop Berkeley played toward the calculus?

15. When it is impossible, Omnes says, "to express the basic concepts of the theory while staying within the bounds of common sense . . . it is then imperative to follow the opposite way, namely, to reformulate the categories of thought belonging to common sense that are used for action and experiment within the conceptual language of the theory. An interpretation should then consist in recovering the language and framework of common sense . . . from the principles of the theory. The interpretation of quantum mechanics consists in re-expressing the phenomena and the data within the conceptual framework of the theory"; Roland Omnes, *The Interpretation of Quantum Mechanics* (Princeton: Princeton University Press, 1994), p. 98.

1. Truth and Relativism

1. (R′) explicitly refers to itself, and to its consequences, as the sole exceptions to its widespread claim.

2. If the probability of a hypothesis *H* relative to evidence *E* is .9, we cannot simply add that *E* obtains, and so conclude that the probability is .9 *period*. For the probability of that same hypothesis *H* relative to different evidence *D* might be .7, and that different evidence *D* also might obtain. The two inferences from the foregoing statements, all of which can hold consistently together, would lead to the in-

consistent conclusions (when taken as detachable, freestanding facts) that the probability of *H* is .9 and the probability of *H* is .7.

3. What is the probability of the event of your reading through all of this book? It is a philosophy book, and you read completely *n* percent of those that you begin; it is a book published by Harvard University Press, and you read completely *m* percent of those that you begin; it is a book that you began reading in a particular period (such as summer vacation), and you read completely *p* percent of such books; and it is a book that was acquired in a certain way (purchased by yourself, a gift from a friend, borrowed from a library), and you read completely *q* percent of those books. Now the event of your now reading this book is a member of all of these different reference classes, and if we suppose that the different percentages of completion in each of these classes represent different probabilistic tendencies to complete books of that sort, then (on the basis of this information alone) there is no freestanding statement of the probability *simpliciter* of reading this book completely. You ask, "And what is the percentage of reading completely the books that belong simultaneously to all the above classes?," asking for *more* information. Think of this as a case in which this very book happens to be the only book meeting that condition, and so there is no such additional statistic yet.

4. On the principle of total evidence, see Rudolf Carnap, *The Logical Foundations of Probability* (Chicago: University of Chicago Press, 1950), pp. 211–213; and Carl Hempel, "Inductive Inconsistencies," in his *Aspects of Scientific Explanation* (New York: Free Press, 1965), pp. 63–67. On the specification of a reference class, see Hempel, *Aspects of Scientific Explanation*, pp. 394–403; and Ellery Eells, *Probabilistic Causality* (Cambridge: Cambridge University Press, 1991), chap. 3.

5. What then would it mean to say that everything is relative? Everything would be relative only if there were an infinite number of factors (properties), each one relative to something else that itself is relative to something still further, and so on. No ground-floor factor would exist that is nonrelative, and for every statement *S* stating that *p* is relative to factor *F*, there would be a further factor that *S* is relative to. Our concern, however, is not whether everything is relative but whether truth is.

6. Since this other factor *F* also will be a part of the world, does it get included in the way *W* that the world is? It might be helpful to delimit the relevant part of the way the world is, so that it does not itself include *F*. Should we say that the relevant part of the way the world is, *W*, refers not to the whole world but to the spatio-temporal portion of the world picked out by the statement *p*, or (since some statements can be about the whole world, e.g., "the universe is finite") rather to those aspects of the world that *p* states explicitly to hold? In that case, *W* (referring to parts and aspects of the world) also depends upon the particular statement *p*, and so is some function *f* of *p* (and perhaps also of *M*, the meaning of the utterance, and of *R*, the referents of its terms). And the relativist is claiming that there is another factor *F*, in addition to *M*, *R*, and the delimited *W*, with which the truth value of *p* varies.

But if the relevant part of the world *W* is the aspect that *p* describes, then why not specify it simply as *p*? The relativist claim then would become: the truth value of *p* is a function of *M*, *R*, *p*, and *F*. However, once *p* is placed in there, how can *F* also be needed, unless the fact *p* itself is some function of the factor *F*? On this view, truth is relative only if the facts also are relative. To avoid that claim at this point, we presume there is some way of specifying the aspect of the world that *p* talks about, other than by *p* itself.

7. Our account sees the claim that truth is relative as holding that there is some factor, other than the meaning of the utterance, the reference of some of its terms, and the way the world is, such that the truth value of a statement varies with variation of the factor. What determines which factors make for relativism and which ones go on the list of permissible factors that do not produce "relativism"? The nonrelativist always knew that the truth value of a descriptive statement would vary with the way the world is; the statement, after all, is trying to describe the world. He also knew that the truth value would vary with the meaning of the terms of the utterance making the statement; the same utterance that in English, given its English meaning, states a truth might in another actual or possible language, given its different meaning there, state a falsehood. No disturbing relativism there. Yet if truth value varies with culture, race, sex, nationality, or social class, that variation will constitute "relativism." It would be desirable to characterize what demarcates the harmless factors, relativity to which does not constitute relativism, from the factors that make for relativism.

Also, could it turn out that the apparently harmless factors (meaning, reference, and the way the world is) themselves are relative to further factors, and that these further factors themselves are not completely harmless? For instance, much recent literature holds that meaning is holistic, not possessed by statements in isolation but only by larger theories, or that reference is indeterminate. Might not these complications make meaning or reference itself introduce a disturbing relativism? On issues concerning holism, see W. V. Quine, "Two Dogmas of Empiricism," in his *From a Logical Point of View* (Cambridge, Mass.: Harvard University Press, 1953), pp. 20–46; idem, "Five Milestones of Empiricism," in his *Theories and Things* (Cambridge, Mass.: Harvard University Press, 1981), pp. 67–72; Robert Nozick, "Experience, Theory, and Language," in *The Philosophy of W. V. Quine*, ed. Lewis Hahn (La Salle, Ill.: Open Court, 1986), pp. 340–345; Jerry Fodor and Ernest Lepore, *Holism* (Oxford: Blackwell, 1992); Christopher Peacocke, "Holism," in *A Companion to the Philosophy of Language*, ed. Bob Hale and Crispin Wright (Oxford: Blackwell, 1997), pp. 227–247.

8. How shall we classify the position that holds that a property varies with variations in factors that can coexist but are not equal?

9. According to these theories, the meaning of a statement is specified by the conditions under which the statement holds true. (It might be thought of as the set of all possible worlds in which the statement holds true.) The proposition expressed by an utterance or sentence functions like, or is associated with (or, on some views, is identical with) a mapping of all possible worlds onto the truth values True and False. Different such mappings specify different propositions. (To avoid the consequence that any propositions whose truth values match in all possible worlds

have the same content, additional conditions have been proposed to yield finer-grained specifications of content, starting with Carnap's proposal of intensional isomorphism.)

The truth value of some utterances, such as "I am happy now," depends upon who produces it and when. More generally, some utterance's truth value depends upon the context in which it is produced. All relevant features of the context of a discourse situation (such as time, place, person who utters the sentence, who else is present) can be represented by an index, an *n*-tuple of these factors. David Kaplan proposed that the character (meaning) of such a contextually dependent sentence type can be represented as a mapping of these indices onto propositional content. In accordance with the previous account of propositional content, Kaplan proposed that the character of a contextually dependent (indexical) sentence would be a mapping of contextual indices onto [mappings of possible worlds onto truth values]. (See David Kaplan, "Demonstratives," in *Themes from Kaplan,* ed. Joseph Almog et al. [Oxford: Oxford University Press, 1989], pp. 481–563.) In order to take account of contextual factors that not merely are drawn upon by a sentence's meaning but that *affect* the meaning of a token utterance of the sentence, Robert Stalnaker has defined the notion of a propositional concept, which is a mapping of possible worlds (representing the context in which the utterance is produced) onto propositions. (See Robert Stalnaker, *Context and Content* [Oxford: Oxford University Press, 1999], pp. 12–16, 78–95, 117–129.) However, we need not draw upon that further apparatus here.

Let us term the factors that some have held that truth is relative to, factors such as culture, sex, etc., potential *relative factors.* If we attempt to state the content of a relative truth within the framework just presented, we might represent it as a mapping of the values of these relative factors (American, Polynesian, male, female, and so on) combined with possible worlds onto truth values (or of relative factors onto propositions). But this mapping would just present a purported relative truth as stating an indexical proposition. Since the existence of indexical statements is uncontroversial, while the existence of relative truths is not, this formal representation cannot capture the notion of a relative truth.

Consider the sentence within the Special Theory of Relativity, "The length of a particular object *O* is 2 meters." If this holds true, it is relative to the velocity of an inertial observer. Yet the propositional content of the statement is not captured by a mapping of different observers' relative velocities mapped onto [possible worlds mapped onto truth values]. The statement is not an indexical statement which is true in that particular context. That context can coexist with other contexts in which the inertial observer measuring the object is traveling at a different relative velocity. Instead, that sentence is associated with a mapping of possible worlds onto pairings of truth values and inertial observer velocities. The sentence is *true for* an inertial observer at a certain velocity relative to the object. The sentence is true relative to an observer at that velocity. We need to parse this as follows. One truth value the sentence has is [true relative to an observer at that velocity].

The relativist holds that a similar situation obtains with regard to statements in general. If the meaning of a statement is to be specified in terms of its truth conditions, by a mapping of possible worlds onto truth values—I myself would not insist upon this apparatus—then these truth values must be of the appropriate sort. According to the relativist, there will or may be truth values such as [true relative to American culture], [false relative to you], [true relative to being male]. Propositional content then is specified by, or associated with, mappings of possible worlds onto these more complexly structured truth values. And the character of indexical statements too will be specified by Kaplan-like mappings of context n-tuples onto [mappings of possible worlds onto ordered pairs of truth values and relative factors].

10. See also my remarks later in this chapter on the inconclusiveness of local arguments against postmodernism.

11. I have described relativism as the doctrine that all truths are relative, while absolutism is the doctrine that some truths are absolute. This has the advantage of making absolutism the denial of relativism, but we might prefer a more symmetrical description. Strong relativism is the doctrine that all truths are relative; strong absolutism is the doctrine that all truths are absolute (= nonrelative); weak relativism is the doctrine that some truths are relative; weak absolutism is the doctrine that some truths are absolute. Weak relativism and weak absolutism are compatible. In the text I shall continue to refer to strong relativism as relativism, and to weak absolutism as absolutism.

12. Alternatively, the absolutist might reply that she does not understand the notion of "true for a person" or "true for a group" and ask the relativist, please, to explain what *he* means by this. I treat this issue in later sections.

13. We can more sharply distinguish those people who want truth to be absolute from those who want particular truths to be absolute, by asking them to preferentially rank the following four situations: what you want to be true *is* what is true, and what is true is absolute; what you want to be true *is* what is true, and what is true is relative; what is true is not what you want to hold true, and what is true is absolute; what is true is not what you want to hold true, and what is true is relative.

14. It is not simply a matter of facts' being enabling or constraining; if constraining facts importantly bar things a person wants *not* to occur, he may welcome them and so be prone to see them as nonrelative.

15. Or (to take account of the philosophical view that facts are timeless), it is easy to make it the case that the opposite fact holds about a closely following time.

16. Perhaps people also want their beliefs or views to be backed by something that is strong. A dominant view, the view of the majority or a powerful elite, is backed by the power of its proponents. A view that is not held by the majority or by a powerful minority nevertheless can be backed by stronger reasons or arguments that indicate it is in accord with the way things really are. A view that is not strong in either of these two ways loses, unless the standard of superiority via greater strength itself is denied. Hence socially weaker groups whose views cannot lay claim to stronger reasons may claim that all truth (or all in a certain contested domain) is relative. Those with power on their side, either social power or the power of reasons, feel secure enough in the strength of their views to maintain absolutism.

17. On the structural prerequisites of society, see Marion J. Levy, *The Structure of*

Society (Princeton: Princeton University Press, 1952); and idem, *Modernization and the Structure of Societies* (Princeton: Princeton University Press, 1966).

18. The social constructionist might claim that all I am saying is that the notion of a "social construction" is itself a social construction, and that what we apply that label to is socially determined. And he might be happy to concede that this is so. However, he then cannot use the fact that something is a social construction as a *reason* for denying it authority, since the lack of authority must come first. Applying the label to something, though, helps to denigrate it further.

19. Whether or not any writer of substance has maintained this view, it is so much in the air that it is worth discussing explicitly.

20. W. V. Quine, *Word and Object* (Cambridge, Mass.: MIT Press, 1960), pp. 191–195. Indexical sentences such as "I am here now," however, are not easily translated (without loss of content) into eternal sentences.

21. See Arthur Prior, *Past, Present and Future* (Oxford: Oxford University Press, 1967), p. 15.

22. See Sydney Shoemaker, "Time without Change," in his *Identity, Cause, and Mind* (Cambridge: Cambridge University Press, 1984), pp. 49–51; and Robin Le Poidevin, "Change," in *The Routledge Encyclopedia of Philosophy,* vol. 2 (London, 1998), pp. 274–276.

23. What follow are statements tailored to the discussion of quantum mechanics that is to follow. In the usual symbolism of tense logic, we have as axioms or theorems: if p then GPp (if p is the case then it always will be the case that p [once] was the case); if p then HFp (if p is the case then it always was the case that p will be the case). These are formulas (AO) c and d in John Burgess, "Basic Tense Logic," in *Handbook of Philosophical Logic,* ed. D. Gabbay and F. Guenthner, vol. 2 (Dordrecht: D. Reidel, 1984), p. 95.

24. The wave description is as follows. The wave function is defined over configuration space, not physical space. When the detector is present, the wave function splits in the configuration space and does not come back together, so there is no interference.

25. See John A. Wheeler, "The 'Past' and the 'Delayed-Choice' Double-Slit Experiment," in *Mathematical Foundations of Quantum Theory,* ed. A. R. Marlow (New York: Academic Press, 1978), pp. 9–48; idem, "Law Without Law" in *Quantum Theory and Measurement,* ed. J. A. Wheeler and W. H. Zurek (Princeton: Princeton University Press, 1983), pp. 182–213.

26. If not, collapse establishes a direction to time, but not one that seems to have a relationship to the more familiar directions. See the discussion in Bernard d'Espagnat, *Veiled Reality* (Reading, Mass.: Addison-Wesley, 1994), pp. 455–460.

27. See John Horgan, "Quantum Philosophy," *Scientific American,* July 1992, p. 98.

28. See Ady Stern, Yakir Aharonov, and Yoseph Imry, "Phase Uncertainty and Loss of Interference," *Physical Review A* 41, no. 7 (1990): 3436–46.

29. I refer to situations in which there was not an earlier measurement of whether or not X had P that was not obviated by a later measurement of a complementary property.

30. That is why the discussions in the literature of quantum mechanics focus upon irreversible macroscopic events and effects, things that never completely go away.

31. For a discussion of issues concerning the denial of bivalence for past statements, though motivated by verificationist concerns, see Michael Dummett, "The Reality of the Past," in his *Truth and Other Enigmas* (Cambridge, Mass.: Harvard University Press, 1978), pp. 358–374.

32. The states will be defined in terms of special properties appropriate to the dynamics of the interaction.

33. I take my description of Kochen's interpretation from Lawrence Sklar, *Philosophy of Physics* (Oxford: Oxford University Press, 1992), pp. 191–193, who refers to Simon Kochen, "A New Interpretation of Quantum Mechanics," in *Symposium on the Foundations of Modern Physics*, ed. P. Lahti and P. Mittelstaedt (Teaneck, N.J.: World Scientific Publishing, 1985). One does not want to rest too much upon Kochen's relativism, since the modal theories of quantum mechanics are very similar to Kochen's view, but without its accompanying relativism. It also is not clear to me what Kochen's interpretation says about the state of the whole universe or about the situation in which the measured system and the measuring device are complementary and add up to the whole universe.

34. Gordon Fleming has offered a Lorentz-invariant theory of wave collapse within quantum mechanics. On this theory, photons are polarized or unpolarized *relative to* a hyperplane, and all hyperplanes are given equal status. So the photon can be polarized relative to one hyperplane and also unpolarized relative to another. Similarly, measurement events can be both deterministic and stochastic *relative to* (different) hyperplanes. (I follow the description of Fleming's theory in Tim Maudlin, *Quantum Non-locality and Relativity* [Oxford: Blackwell, 1994], pp. 208–212, who terms this "a radically new ontological conception of the world.")

35. Kip S. Thorne, *Black Holes and Time Warps* (New York: W. W. Norton, 1994), p. 444. Thorne's explanation continues as follows: "How is this possible? How can one observer claim that the horizon is surrounded by an atmosphere of real particles and the other that it is not? The answer lies in the fact that the virtual particles' vacuum fluctuational waves are not confined solely to the region above the horizon; part of each fluctuational wave is inside the horizon and part is outside. The freely falling observers, who plunge through the horizon, can see both parts of the vacuum fluctuational wave, the part inside the horizon and the part outside; so such observers are well aware (by their measurements) that the wave is a mere vacuum fluctuation and correspondingly that its particles are virtual, not real. The accelerated observers, who remain always outside the horizon, can see only the outside part of the vacuum fluctuational wave, not the inside part; and correspondingly, by their measurements they are unable to discern that the wave is a mere vacuum fluctuation accompanied by virtual particles. Seeing only a part of the fluctuational wave, they mistake it for 'the real thing'—a real wave accompanied by real particles—and as a result their measurements reveal all around the horizon an atmosphere of real particles. That this atmosphere's real particles can gradually evaporate and fly off into the external Universe is an indication that the viewpoint of the accelerated ob-

servers is just as correct, that is, just as valid as that of the freely falling observers. What the freely falling observers see as virtual pairs converted into real particles by tidal gravity, followed by evaporation of one of the real particles, the accelerated observers see simply as the evaporation of one of the particles that was always real and always populated the black hole's atmosphere. Both viewpoints are correct; they are the same physical situation, seen from two different reference frames" (p. 444).

Describing the ideas of Stephen Hawking, Josh Boslough writes (*Masters of Time* [Reading, Mass.: Addison-Wesley, 1992], p. 186): "If such an event [the creation of pairs of particles] were to occur . . . at the event horizon of the black hole . . . one of the particles could be trapped by the black hole's enormous gravitational field. The other particle could escape if it were positioned just slightly farther away from the all-consuming event horizon. If somebody happened to see this, it would look like the surviving particle had actually been ejected by the black hole."

Since these phenomena occur in quantum field theory, where particles are states of underlying fields, it might be argued that particles no longer count as objects there, and so it is not shown that *objects* and their existence are relative.

36. We might try to use the delayed-choice experiment to deny the following: If event e_i occurs at a time, then it is true at that time that e_i occurs at that time. However, it is not clear (on our view) that this is a coherent statement. On other views it is, though, and hence we would deny, or object to, their asserting this.

37. On the many-minds interpretation also, there is nothing to prevent all memory of a particular outcome of a measurement from being wiped out, while there remains the memory that a measurement was made and that it was thought to have a determinate result. See David Albert, *Quantum Mechanics and Experience* (Cambridge, Mass.: Harvard University Press, 1992), chaps. 6, 8.

38. There will not be this same hole if the time is held constant. If it is true at time t_1 that p-or-q holds at time t_1, then it is true at time t_1 that p holds at time t_1 or it is true at time t_1 that q holds at time t_1. Intuitionist mathematicians, however, may have other reasons for maintaining that such holes exist.

39. According to realist views. Collapse views will say that at every time it is true that the system was in a superposition back then, and that at every later time after the measurement it is true at that later time that the system is not in a superposition at that later time.

40. Various weakenings of this very strong condition might be worth formulating also. Proponents of quantum logic have suggested that logic might be revised on the basis of quantum-mechanical considerations. We can add that if whether something is recoverable depends upon the strength and the character of the methods of inference that are used, then quantum mechanics might provide an empirical test or clue to what the correct methods of inference are. If it is differential effects that allow unique recoverability, must this be recoverability with certainty, or will very high probability be enough, at least in circumstances when rules allow the inference to the occurrence of that particular event? Could the truth later that the event occurred earlier depend upon issues about evidence and inductive logic, and might quantum-mechanical experiments be used to decide between alternative principles

of inductive logic if, for instance, some inductive logics predict interference phenomenon in some experiments while other inductive logics, for those very same experiments, do not?

41. It would be worthwhile to investigate the empirical consequences and predictions of this, for instance, about what would be discovered if time travel occurred. I have spoken, thus far, of the truth of statements about past events, but this relativity could be generalized to include statements about laws. These statements about laws also could be relative if laws do change and if all traces of earlier laws get wiped out. In that case, to say that a law holds at a time is itself a truth relative to a time.

42. The formalism of the wave function can give a consistent story about the wave passing through both slits even when a detector records a particle at one slit. In delayed choice, it can say there was a wave then around the galaxy, even with a particle collapse now. The wave function is complete; the wave goes both ways no matter where the detector is placed or whether it is there. Nothing about the particle is changed by where you put the detector. Even if the detector is put in one place, the collapse doesn't change the antecedent wave function, which can be described as always going one way. (I am indebted to Tim Maudlin and to Harvey Brown, who emphasized the possibility of nontensed wave-function descriptions to me in conversation.)

A consistent story of the unreduced wave is one way to describe things, but until the measurement problem is solved we will not know that (only) it will suffice. The path I have followed in the text is another possible way to describe things, though it is not forced upon us by quantum mechanics. I have wanted to discuss quantum phenomena without being tied to a particular theory or formalism (but also have not wanted to be incompatible with the standard theory by too much).

43. Should the Kochen relative-state interpretation of quantum mechanics be seen as saying that (certain) truths are relative to (the information at) a place-time?

44. Alternatively, one might hold that quantum nonlocality *is* a causal effect, and that quantum mechanics is incompatible with Special Relativity.

45. For a careful discussion of nonlocality and the connections it involves, see Tim Maudlin, *Quantum Non-Locality and Relativity* (Oxford: Blackwell, 1994).

46. Distinguish its being true *within* a spatiotemporal region that *p* from its being true *throughout* (that is, in every part of) a spatiotemporal region that *p*. If it is true throughout spatiotemporal region *st* that *p*, and it is true throughout spatiotemporal region *ST* that *q*, then (supposing that *r* logically follows from *p & q* in standard logic) it will logically follow that it is true throughout the intersection of *st* and *ST* that *r*.

47. See David Malament, "Observationally Indistinguishable Space-times," in *Foundations of Space-Time Theories,* ed. John Earman, Clark Glymour, and John Stachel, Minnesota Studies in the Philosophy of Science, no. 8 (Minneapolis: University of Minnesota Press, 1977), pp. 61–80.

48. However, one should not overestimate the restrictiveness of holding that truth is identical with determinateness. It is not a consequence of this view that "There exist events outside of *st*'s past and future light cone" is not true at a given spatio-

temporal point *st*. For at *st* it is determinate both that there are events *E* in its past light cone and also, because of laws that hold everywhere, that *E* has events in its own future light cone that are outside *st*'s light cone. (But is it determinate at *st* that all points in the forward light cone of whatever is in *st*'s backward light cone are subject to those same laws?)

49. Of course, the Aristotelian position needs to be stated carefully so as to not beg the question. For if, as opponents of Aristotle's position think, it now is true, though not determined, that a certain fleet will win the battle, then a current truth, namely that one, *does* fix which fleet it is that will win. However, the opponents too should not beg the question.

50. This condition goes back to Gottlob Frege and to Frank Ramsey, if not to Aristotle's *Metaphysics*. Alfred Tarski has put forward a metalinguistic version of this, which, using Quine's corner-quotes, can be stated as: ⌜*p*⌝ is true if and only if *p*.

51. Can a theory be developed of the conditions under which it is the case that for the smallest volume *st* where it is determinate that *p*, only in a larger volume *st'* will it be determinate that it is determinate at *st* that *p*?

52. Deflationist, redundancy, and disquotational accounts of truth depend upon such eliminability. According to them, to say that a proposition is true is, in the above context, merely to say that *p*. (See Frank Ramsey, "Facts and Propositions," reprinted in his *The Foundations of Mathematics and Other Logical Essays* [London: Routledge and Kegan Paul, 1931]; W. V. Quine, *The Pursuit of Truth* [Cambridge, Mass.: Harvard University Press, 1990], pp. 79–82; Paul Horwich, *Truth* [Oxford: Blackwell, 1990].) Since the theory that truth might be rooted in space and time does not automatically allow the eliminability of the term "true" in this context, if truth does indeed turn out empirically to be so rooted, then it is a consequence of this that deflationist and redundancy theories are incorrect. For now, we can at least say that such theories are premature. On their contention that no contentful theory of truth is needed or is possible, see note 56 below.

53. Does holding that truth is relative to a place-time mean that every statement explicitly has to index what is said to a place-time and so also to index that indexing, *ad infinitum*? No, not every statement has to be explicitly prefaced with a temporal operator, just as not every statement has to be prefaced by Frege's assertion sign. However, it is a condition on assertion that (to put it roughly) I should assert now only what I now believe is true-now. With regard to the delayed-choice experiment, suppose at time t_2 I say that

(1)   It is not true at time t_1 that *E* occurs at time t_1.

and

(2)   It is true at time t_2 (later than t_1) that *E* occurs at t_1.

At time t_2, do I also want to say:

(3)   It is true at t_2 that it is not true at t_1 that *E* occurs at t_1?

Is (3) compatible with (2)? (I thank Derek Parfit [personal conversation] for this question.)

These two statements, (3) and (2), *are* compatible. If (3) is asserted at time t_2, I can utter (3), and also at t_2 I can drop the initial "it is true at t_2" from any statement I utter at time t_2. Dropping this from (3) yields statement (1), which I also will assert at time t_2. And (1) also is something I will have been willing to assert at time t_1. Everything is (or so it appears) consistent.

54. When something holds true at one place-time, we should distinguish its not holding true in some other place-time (it may not have a truth value there) from its being false in that other place-time. Can the latter obtain, and if so, under what conditions?

55. Robert Nozick, *The Nature of Rationality* (Princeton: Princeton University Press, 1993), p. 68.

56. And some theories, deflationist and redundancy theories, would hold that there is no one property explanatory of successful action. These theories give up prematurely on the possibility of an illuminating generalization and explanation where one might hold. (See also note 52 above.) Paul Horwich formulates this statement: a person is more likely to be successful in achieving his goals acting on p than he is acting on non-p, if p. (See his *Truth*, pp. 23–24, 44–47.) It would be interesting to formulate the deflationist *explanation* of the following more general statement: If one person is more likely to be successful acting on (the fully specified) p than on not-p, then all people are more likely to be successful in acting on p than on not-p. It is not my purpose here to refute the deflationist position—that task is pursued by others in the technical literature—but rather to pursue the contours of an alternative full-bodied explanatorily illuminating view of truth, whose possibility the deflationist denies.

57. And, since the statements in the first group that are actually acted upon are finite in number, they also will share the property of holding in some particular nonactual possible world, call it W_{12}, a world where they are true but where other propositions hold that are false in the actual world. So "holding in world W_{12}" is a property that is shared by the true statements actually acted upon, but also is shared by many actually false statements. Being a common property of the beliefs that actually were successfully acted upon is not enough to make something the truth property.

Should we try to use features of the propositional calculus to further narrow the property, saying that truth is that property the statements in the first group have in common, which is such that every statement or its negation has that property, no statement and its negation has that property, etc.? Even if we could zero in on truth in this way, it would be better to have such statements (such as excluded-middle and noncontradiction) turn out to hold of the truth property, rather than to define the truth property by means of these statements so that they must hold.

58. To get such an explanation, it is not enough, about a common property, to add the subjunctive that if a statement were to have the property, it would be probably successfully acted upon. This subjunctive follows from "most of the atomic propositions holding in the previously described world W_{12} are true also in the actual world," yet "holding in world W_{12}" is not the truth property of (atomic propositions of) the actual world.

59. Unless God is intervening to guarantee success in exactly those cases in which, and because, the person is acting on a true belief.

60. One cannot argue that if the full Tarski condition is satisfied then there cannot be different and divergent truth properties (by arguing that *p* has the first truth property if and only if *p*, and *p* has the second truth property if and only if *p*, so therefore *p* has the first truth property if and only if *p* has the second truth property). For the full biconditional Tarski condition is not necessary to delimit a truth property. Also, proponents of each truth property who adhere to the Tarski condition will assert that their property does satisfy the condition, but, since they will disagree (as a consequence of having divergent truth properties) about which propositions are true, each consequently will see the other person's truth property as denying the application of "true" to some true propositions, and hence will deny that it does satisfy the Tarski condition.

One also might be tempted to argue that, according to theories that meaning is a function of truth conditions, variations in truth properties must bring along differences in the meaning of propositions, and so people in different cultures are not disagreeing about the truth of the same propositions, so the possibility of relativism about truth cannot even be stated. See pages 19–20 above for a comment upon why this type of restrictive argument is unsuccessful.

61. We have viewed truth and the truth property as part of the explanation of a being's successful achievement of aims in its actions. However, it might be objected, could there not be a purely contemplative being that had beliefs that were true, even though it did not act at all? In two ways, our theory still might enable us to call that being's beliefs true. The first way involves a subjunctive attribution: that being's beliefs have the property that would explain the success in action he would have if he were to act on the beliefs and were successful. (This would not apply straightforwardly to a being who necessarily was purely contemplative.) The second way invokes our own truth property; his beliefs have that property even though he is not acting on them and would not do so.

62. It will be helpful to have a more detailed account of acting upon a belief. Person S acts upon the belief that *p* if and only if

(1) S believes that *p*.
(2) There is a result *R* such that (a) S wants or desires that *R*, and (b) S believes that: if *p* then (if S does *A*, *R* results).

And

(3) S does *A* because of (1)–(2).

(There are many refinements one might add to this schema, for instance concerning what S believes are the consequences of his actions if not-*p* holds, e.g., S believes that if not-*p*, then there is an alternative action *B* whose results will be better (more preferred) than the results of *A* would be in that situation. However, such refinements are not needed for our purposes here.)

Now to explain the success of action upon *p*, add:

(4) *p*.

(5) If *p* then (if S does *A*, *R* results).

It follows that

(6) If S does *A*, *R* results (from [4] and [5]).

And therefore that

(7) *R* results (from [3] and [6]).

Success in achieving the goal of the action is *assured* when the belief in (1) is true and also when the belief in (2b) is true. And when one is acting upon the belief that *p*, success in achieving the goal is statistically more likely (though not assured) when *p* is true.

To see this, consider the case of success in goal achievement when the belief *p* that is acted upon is *false*, so that what holds is:

(4′) Not-*p*.

If the goal is achieved in this case, then this achievement will depend upon

(5′) If not-*p* then (if S does *A*, *R* results)

and so on up until

(7) *R* results (but this time from [4′], [5′], and [3]).

(Or *R* might result from some other route based upon some narrower *q* rather than simply upon not-*p*.)

Why then is success in goal achievement more likely in acting upon a true belief than upon a false one? Because the conditional probability of (5) given (1)–(4) is greater than the conditional probability of (5′) given (1)–(3) and (4′). More frequently, a true belief dovetails with your means-end belief so as to achieve the goals of the action (i.e., the means-end belief holds true) than does a false belief dovetail with an unbelieved means-end fact that holds.

63. One subset *S* of (successful) beliefs has as its truth property the property *P* (e.g., correspondence with the facts). (*S* might be a majority of these successful beliefs, but it could even be a minority.) The explanation of success with the geocentric theory *G* is this: there is some other statement *G'* such that *G'* has property *P* *and* the consequences of *G* are approximately equal to the consequences of *G'* in a restricted domain with regard to successful navigation. When all this is true of *G* (i.e., that there is a *G'* such that . . .), let us say that *G* has the property *Q*. However, I do not say that the truth property is *Q* or that it is (*P* or *Q*). Rather, the truth property is *P*, and the success of *G* is explained in terms of *P*, namely, by the partial matching of the consequences of *G* to the consequences of *G'*, which *does* have the property *P*. Even when *S* is a minority of the successful beliefs, this may be the neatest (simplest, most powerful and unifying, etc.) overall explanation of successful action.

Does *Q* also fail to satisfy the Tarski condition (where *S* is a term referring to the sentence substituted for "p") that *S* is true if and only if *p* (or its appropriate weakening within the theory that truth is rooted in space and time), and so fail to be a truth property?

64. Or instead, we might base our notion of truth only upon those statements whose truth is independent of belief, where the probability of success in action depends only upon the action in the world as it is, and not upon the action's actually being prompted by that belief.

65. Plato, *Phaedrus* 265E.

66. I mean described by positive applications of some terms. Negative applications of terms *T* would be even more widespread, as in "The world contains no *T*'s."

67. This point holds even if there are no intrinsic natures out there, and no uniquely compelled linguistic descriptions.

68. Bruno Latour has emphasized that one cannot explain why scientists accept a statement by saying that it is true. (See Bruno Latour and Steven Woolgar, *Laboratory Life: The Social Construction of Scientific Facts* [1979; reprint, Princeton: Princeton University Press, 1986]. See also Bruno Latour, *Science in Action* [Cambridge, Mass.: Harvard University Press, 1987]; Andrew Pickering, *Constructing Quarks* [Chicago: University of Chicago Press, 1984].) But it does seem legitimate to say that a statement or theory is accepted because it is well supported by experiments and theoretical arguments, it has passed difficult observational tests, etc. Do the constructionists have plausible explanations that omit such evidential factors? Such evidential explanations even could satisfy the constructionist's much-discussed principle of symmetry—explain the acceptance of true theories and of false theories by the same factors—in that false theories also might be accepted on the basis of significant supporting evidence. Having weighty evidence in its favor is no guarantee of its truth, and gives it no immunity from being replaced by a theory that is even better supported.

69. One completely accurate positive truth, at any rate. Perhaps even when the inaccurate metaphysical assumptions are deeply rooted, the negation of the application of a metaphysically infected predicate would count as true—unless the operation of negation is metaphysically contaminated as well.

70. See Paul Churchland, *A Neurocomputational Perspective* (Cambridge, Mass.: MIT Press, 1989), chaps. 1, 6; Patricia Churchland, *Neurophilosophy* (Cambridge, Mass.: MIT Press, 1989), pp. 299–313. See also Robert McCauly, ed., *The Churchlands and Their Critics* (Oxford: Blackwell, 1996). Sydney Shoemaker holds that if folk psychology is an innate theory of mind, this might explain the accessibility of psychological states to conscious awareness. As we evolved to have the states, we also evolved to think of them in that folk way (Sydney Shoemaker, *The First Person Perspective and Other Essays* [Cambridge: Cambridge University Press, 1996], p. 129). However, we might have evolved to have an inaccurate but good enough theory, or rather, to be in the neurophysiological state that comes closest to having such a theory, and so we may not actually *have* those kinds of folk-states.

71. See Barbara Herrnstein Smith, *Belief and Resistance* (Cambridge, Mass.: Harvard University Press, 1997), pp. 6, 17. Yet Herrnstein Smith also writes, "This is not

to say that the characterization of some judgment as (relatively) objective is meaningless . . . The perspectives reflected in some judgments are certainly more widely shared, stable and/or recurrent than those reflected in others, some judgments are certainly more responsive than others to a broader range of relevant considerations and/or reflect greater than usual effort to identify and control the operation of irrelevant factors, and people sometimes, perhaps quite often, indicate such matters of degree by praising such judgments as (more) 'objective'" (p. 6).

Does Herrnstein Smith mean by "relevant considerations" and "irrelevant factors" simply what is *thought* to be irrelevant—and what is it that is thought when this is thought? (Thought to be *what?*) If the theorist wishes to say that there are degrees of objectivity, that any degree might be surpassed by a greater degree, and that there is no top and unsurpassable degree (despite what the foundationalist believed), then why go on to call anything short of the unreachable and nonexistent topmost objectivity "relativism"? Couldn't one just as well call anything above the greatest extreme of subjectivism "objective"? Since Herrnstein Smith grants that there are degrees of objectivity (see also her p. 17), we might ask whether it is an objective, nonrelative fact that one belief is more objective than another. If there is agreement about the "more objective than" relation, then it is a more minor matter to decide where along the continuous scale a line is to be drawn between the objective and the nonobjective.

72. Richard Rorty, "Solidarity or Objectivity," in *Objectivity, Relativism and Truth*, vol. 1 of Rorty, *Philosophical Papers* (New York: Cambridge University Press, 1991), pp. 21–34.

73. Robert Nozick, *The Examined Life* (New York: Simon and Schuster, 1989), pp. 249–250.

74. See Quine, "Two Dogmas of Empiricism."

75. Perhaps the relevant kind of explanation is marked in part by the property's satisfying some weakening of the Tarski condition.

76. C. I. Lewis suggested that each relative statement corresponds to an absolute one, viz. the one that makes the relativity explicit. If X's having property *P* is relative to factor *F*, then it is a nonrelative truth that *X has P relative to F.* (See C. I. Lewis, *Mind and the World Order* [New York: Scribner's, 1929], pp. 167–194.) However, Einstein uncovered a nonrelative truth that was not of this sort. Einstein noted that spatial intervals and temporal intervals were relative to the velocity of the inertial observer, but the invariant statement that he discovered was not simply the explicit statement (à la C. I. Lewis) of this relativity. He discovered another interval that was invariant, namely, the square root of [the square of the time separation minus the square of the spatial separation]; the content of Einstein's nonrelative statement does not refer to a relation to an observer.

77. Compare the discussion of whether "exists" is univocal or has different senses when physical objects, mathematical objects, etc. are involved, in Morton White, *Toward Reunion in Philosophy* (Cambridge, Mass.: Harvard University Press, 1956), chap. 4.

78. Solubility is a relational notion, solubility in a particular liquid (e.g., water),

but the property that underlies and explains solubility in water is nonrelational, viz. having a certain chemical structure.

79. Even within the rule of maximizing expected utility, one property of belief might fit maximizing *causally* expected utility while another property might fit maximizing *evidentially* expected utility. For a discussion of these two decision rules and a proposal of a compromise between them, see Nozick, *The Nature of Rationality*, chap. 2.

80. If not, should we say that the truth property for a being, even an irrational one, is what would explain its successful action if it followed one of the rational decision rules? Could a being's truth property *change* so that it was no longer correspondence? What could show us that our truth property is now not correspondence, or now is no longer whatever it once was? Could we change our truth property by changing our decision rules?

81. If the coherence theory of truth specifies truth by coherence with particular (kinds of) statements, and these kinds might vary from group to group, then the coherence theory would leave additional room for relativism about truth. For two groups, the truth property might be coherence, but if the groups held different (kinds of) core beliefs with which other beliefs must cohere, then the specification of this truth property would differ between the two groups. (I am indebted to Talbot Brewer for raising the issue of how the coherence theory is related to relativism.)

82. However, if the constraints of actual *social* environments need to be included to converge to one truth property, if human nature and natural environments are not enough for such convergence, then this seems to leave further room for *social* relativism about truth, in that the truth property can vary across imaginable social environments. Whether that counts as relativism may depend upon the kinds of reasons why the imaginable social environments are restricted to the actual ones, e.g., is it because the powerful people artificially restrict the forms and developments of society in order to serve their own interests or because of the functional necessities of any ongoing society?

The relativist might claim that there is an additional explanatory issue (not just the one concerning success in achieving the goals of action) dividing him from the absolutist about truth. This is the question of what explains why people disagree in their beliefs. The relativist will claim that some disagreements in belief are explained by the relativity of truth. Everyone in his own situation is believing the truth, but these are different truths that hold relative to different factors. The absolutist, on the other hand, will maintain that *all* disagreements in belief are to be accounted for by *other* factors: people differ in their information and evidence because of what they have encountered; they differ in how they process information and reach conclusions because of their history; they encounter different conditions that temporarily or continuously distort or bias the process by which they reach their beliefs; and so forth. The issue of relativism versus absolutism about truth therefore seems to be an empirical one with two explanatory components, one concerning the explanation of success in achieving the goals of action, the other concerning the explanation of differences in belief. Those of us—I am one—who believe that all people have the same truth property also will expect that the differences in belief among people will eventually be explained without the introduction of truths that are relative to social factors. However, since some differences *will* be explained as matters of relative truth—for instance, the differences in length attributions between observers traveling at different inertial velocities with respect to the same object—it remains a possibility that some specific differences in belief will turn on truths that are socially relative. (And so the position that denies that this possibility holds has Popperian empirical content.)

83. It is tempting to add that convergence is the reasonable presumption in the absence of strong evidence to the contrary, but I cannot see why it constitutes a more appropriate presumption, or default position, than linearity. It may simply be the novelty or recent salience of nonlinearity that gives it a lesser presumptive status. What should the presumption be if it turns out that *most* phenomena involve nonlinear relations?

The methodological maxim not to posit a difference without a reason is of no help here. First, there *is* some difference in people's admittedly similar situations; the question is whether such differences constitute a reason to think that their truth properties too are merely similar, that is, only somewhat different too. The second, and structurally more interesting, point is this. The methodological maxim says that difference in a domain D_2 (such as truth properties) should be related to and projected from differences in another domain (such as situations). But is the relation between these two domains a linear one, a nonlinear one, or one of convergence? The maxim itself assumes a linear relation between domains, I think. But if our question is which of these kinds of relation should be presumed to hold, it seems unhelpful to answer this question by begging it.

84. For a discussion that emphasizes the environmental constraints throughout the universe, to which life anywhere would be adapted, see Roger Shepard, "Evolution of a Mesh between Principles of the Mind and Regularities of the World," in *The Latest on the Best*, ed. John Dupré (Cambridge, Mass.: MIT Press, 1987), pp. 51–276.

85. I have said that the nature and situations of actual people are similar enough that the same truth property explains their success in acting upon beliefs. I noted earlier that if people's situations and natures are similar enough, this might show that merely *similar* truth properties explain their success in action. Convergence means that the correct explanation isn't so *sensitive* to the variation in people and their situations, so that one and the same explanatory factor applies in a range of cases. If there were greater sensitive dependence, would the truth property vary slightly from group to group or person to person, or would the truth property be the same, e.g., a particular correspondence relation, but it be the facts that vary slightly? Is there theoretical leeway about where we can place the variation, whether to place it in the truth property or in the facts themselves, and are there methodological maxims that might determine where the variation should be placed?

86. We can graph the range of worlds where we would keep the same truth property, and also the range of beings who differ from us to various extents yet who

share the truth property we have. Worlds can differ along many different dimensions, and the range of beings who differ from us also can vary along many dimensions. Let us simplify, however, and imagine that worlds vary along only one dimension, and that beings capable of belief vary along only one dimension. Place the range of worlds along the x-axis, and the range of beings along the y-axis (with ourselves in our world at the coordinate origin). We then can graph which beings over which worlds share our truth property, and also mark the limit of our truth property, the world such that beyond that world we would have a different truth property, at least for a long stretch. (And we also can mark how much further along those worlds we go with that second truth property before we encounter a third one.)

Our theory need not be so humanocentric. In addition to the many possible beings, and the many possible environments, there are many possible truth properties. Assign different colors to these different properties, with closeness among the colors matching "closeness" among the truth properties. (Do the truth properties indeed shade off into closely related ones, or are there gulfs and discontinuities between the properties?) The colored-in space shows the truth property for each being in each world. What will this space look like, what shapes will the color-islands take, are all the points of any one color connected? Total absolutism holds that all of this multidimensional space has the same color. That is a far-reaching and highly implausible theory. A full theory of truth and its relativity would present this variegated multicolored space and explain its features. Such a theory would be more plausible, more interesting, and more illuminating, than a simple yes-or-no answer to the question of whether or not truth is relative.

Instead of focusing upon all possible combinations of environments and beings, we might wish to focus upon the evolutionarily possible combinations, those that combine beings with environments in which they could have evolved. We also can pursue our more practical parochial concerns with human beings. How widely across worlds and beings does the color-island that we inhabit extend? Do all people now inhabit the same island?

We have treated the value of truth in belief as leading statistically to greater success in the achievement of the goals of action, and we have identified the truth property as that property of beliefs that explains their tendency to underlie successful goal achievement. The property that actually underlies it for us is, let us suppose, correspondence to the facts; but if a different property (satisfying some general condition that makes it a candidate for a truth property) had underlain it, that different property would be the truth property. If a different property does underlie it for other beings, then they do have a different truth property; truth is different for them. To this it might be objected that truth is not whatever *might* underlie beliefs' success in goal achievement but, rather, whatever *does* underlie such success *for us*. In terms of Kripke's notion of a rigid designator, the term "truth" would rigidly designate the property that does underlie our beliefs' success. (Why ours, rather than mine now?) But this is an uninteresting way to close the question of relativism. If ethics appropriately varied for different societies or in different possible worlds, that would seem to establish relativism, even if there was some term ("correct ethics"? "morally right"?) that rigidly designated what the ethics of our society now fixed as right. If the notion of truth is a rigid designator, then *derigidify* it, and then ask whether *that* nonrigid term is relative in that it encompasses different truth properties.

87. To the extent that people do act upon scientific beliefs, this tendency to uniformity in truth property does actually hold, and it also holds subjunctively, in that, across cultures, people would be more successful in their actions if they did base them upon scientific beliefs.

88. By his using the property, I mean only that it is the property of his beliefs that underlies his success in achieving the goals of his actions.

89. See J. L. Austin, *Sense and Sensibilia* (Oxford: Clarendon Press, 1962), pp. 124–131.

90. A focus upon intermediate cognitive mechanisms is the mark of evolutionary psychology in distinction to the sociobiology that it builds upon and modifies. See Leda Cosmides and John Tooby, "From Evolution to Behavior: Evolutionary Psychology as the Missing Link," in Dupré, *The Latest on the Best,* pp. 277–306.

91. Richard Kirkham, *Theories of Truth* (Cambridge, Mass.: MIT Press, 1992).

92. Semantic theories that proceed in terms of truth conditions utilize the notion of truth but do not provide a theory of it.

93. Tarski held that a definition of truth must satisfy two conditions. (See Alfred Tarski, "The Concept of Truth in Formalized Languages," in his *Logic, Semantics, Metamathematics* [Oxford: Oxford University Press, 1956], pp. 152–278; idem, "The Semantic Conception of Truth and the Foundations of Semantics," *Philosophy and Phenomenological Research* 4 [1944]: 341–375.) First, it must not entail contradictions, such as the paradox of the liar. Since natural languages contain the resources to refer to each term and sentence of the language, and to form the semantical predicates "true" and "false," such open languages would allow the formulation of the liar paradox and hence generate contradictions. Tarski's solution was to limit his definitions to artificial languages without such strong resources, and to formulate the definition of truth in a metalanguage that includes resources to speak of the sentences of the (artificial) object-language (but does not contain the resources to speak thus of all of its *own* sentences).

Second, the definition of truth (along with logic) must enable one to *prove* every sentence of the form: *S* is true if and only if *p*, where a declarative sentence is substituted for "*p*," and a name of that declarative sentence (or term referring to that sentence) is substituted for "*S*." A definition meeting these two criteria, consistency and the derivation of all sentences of the above form, will be adequate, Tarski held.

If there were a finite number of sentences $s_1, \ldots, s_n$ in the language L, Tarski would be willing to define (in the metalanguage) truth in L as follows:

Let $x_1, \ldots, x_n$ be expressions in the metalanguage referring to the above sentences of the object language, each x_i referring to s_i. Then x is true if and only if $x = x_1$ and s_1, or $x = x_2$ and s_2, or $\ldots$, or $x = x_n$ and s_n.

Because there are not a finite number of sentences, Tarski must use a recursive procedure, and because not all sentences are built up from other closed sentences, he must utilize open sentences and the notion of satisfaction. So much is familiar to those who have studied Tarski's technical construction of a "truth-definition."

However, notice that Tarski would be content with the above definition if there *were* a finite number of sentences, where the truth part of the definition just repeats the statement *p*. And notice that Tarski's own definition of satisfaction does involve a similar using of a sentence. An entity Fido satisfies "*x* is a dog" if and only if Fido is a dog. But what is it for *that* to hold? What in general must hold, if *p*? Tarski does not tell us. However, a theory of truth, as we shall see, can make good use of Tarski's recursive construction.

94. The metaphysics of the making-true of statements has been extensively discussed in the twentieth century. See Bertrand Russell, "The Philosophy of Logical Atomism" I, II, *The Monist* 28 (1918): 495–527 and 29 (1919): 32–63, 190–222, 345–380, reprinted in R. C. Marsh, ed., *Logic and Knowledge, Essays 1901–1950* (London: Allen and Unwin, 1956); Ludwig Wittgenstein, *Tractatus Logico-Philosophicus* (London: Routledge, 1922); Kit Fine, "First Order Modal Theories—III: Facts," *Synthèse* 53 (1982): 43–122; David Armstrong, *A World of States of Affairs* (Cambridge: Cambridge University Press, 1996); David Lewis, "A World of Truthmakers?" reprinted in his *Papers in Metaphysics and Epistemology* (Cambridge: Cambridge University Press, 1999), essay 13 (and see also essays 1, 3, 4, and 12). These discussions are extremely instructive, but it is not my purpose to resolve these tangled issues here, as the reader will see later.

95. Austin's original paper is J. L. Austin, "Truth," in his *Philosophical Papers* (Oxford: Clarendon Press, 1961), pp. 85–101. Strawson's criticism is made in P. F. Strawson, "Truth," *Proceedings of the Aristotelian Society,* suppl. vol. 24 (1950): 129–156. Austin replies in J. L. Austin, "Unfair to Facts," in his *Philosophical Papers,* pp. 102–122.

I do not think Strawson is correct in this criticism, even apart from the points to be made in the text. The statement that John is exactly six feet tall and the statement that John is exactly seventy-two inches tall state the same fact. The statement that Jim is exactly five feet tall and the statement that Jim is exactly sixty inches tall also state the same fact, different from the first fact. John's height is John's height, Jim's height is Jim's height, and John's and Jim's heights stand in the ratio 6/5, no matter what unit we use in our scale of measurement (provided that the unit remains constant). The same facts can be stated in different ways. If every true statement corresponds to a fact, not every one corresponds to a different fact. The mapping of true statements onto facts is not 1:1.

The Special Theory of Relativity teaches the same lesson. Two reports of the magnitude of a spatial or of a temporal interval may differ, depending upon the state of motion of the inertial observer, yet there will be one invariant fact underlying these two different reports. The two statements of relative truths will state the same nonrelative fact concerning the Einstein-interval, the square root of the [temporal separation squared minus the spatial separation squared].

This does not mean that there are more true statements than facts, for there may be further facts underlying the equivalence of each statement with another. But these further facts underlying a statement's equivalence will not be *stated* by that very statement, and will not be the fact it corresponds to.

96. This does not mean that not-*p* corresponds to, and is made true by, a higher-order fact, viz. the fact that no facts make *p* true. Rather, not-*p* is true when there are no facts that make *p* true. Something even more complicated would need to be said for views that deny the law of excluded middle.

97. See Ernest Nagel, *The Structure of Science* (New York: Harcourt, Brace and World, 1961), chap. 11; Paul Churchland, "Reduction, Qualia, and the Direct Introspection of Brain States, I," *Journal of Philosophy* 82 (January 1985), reprinted in his *A Neurocomputational Perspective* (Cambridge, Mass.: MIT Press, 1989), pp. 47–52; C. A. Hooker, "Towards a General Theory of Reduction" I–III, *Dialogue* 20 (1981): 38–59, 201–236, 496–529. See also Jaegwon Kim, *Mind in a Physical World* (Cambridge, Mass.: MIT Press, 1998), chap. 4.

98. For these analyses of identity through time, and of knowledge, see Robert Nozick, *Philosophical Explanations* (Cambridge, Mass.: The Belknap Press of Harvard University Press, 1981), chaps. 1 and 3.

99. Different notions of supervenience have been distinguished in the literature. A contingent statement S is weakly supervenient in world w_i upon $q_1, \ldots, q_n$ when for every x and y in world w_i, necessarily if x and y agree on $q_1, \ldots, q_n$ then x and y agree on S. A contingent statement S is strongly supervenient upon $q_1, \ldots, q_n$ when for *all* worlds w_i and w_j, and for all x and y, if x and y agree on $q_1, \ldots, q_n$ then x and y agree on S. See Jaegwon Kim, "Supervenience," in *A Companion to the Philosophy of Mind*, ed. Samuel Guttenplan (Oxford: Blackwell, 1994), pp. 575–583; idem, *Supervenience and Mind* (Cambridge: Cambridge University Press, 1993), chaps. 4–9, 10, 14.

100. Must there also be a second fact, that the one fact is supervenient upon the other? Does this mean that there is no reduction in the total number of facts, or would one general second fact (that the facts of one sort are supervenient upon facts of another) do multiple duty and so cut down on the total number?

101. On the question of what exactly Tarski's accomplishment was, see Hartrey Field, "Tarski's Theory of Truth," *Journal of Philosophy* 69 (1972): 347–375; John Etchemendy, "Tarski on Truth and Logical Consequence," *Journal of Symbolic Logic* 53 (1988): 51–79; Richard Heck, "Tarski, Truth, and Semantics," *Philosophical Review* 106 (1997): 533–554.

102. "Grass is green" (in English, as it is used in the actual world) is true in world w if and only if grass is green in world w. "Grass is green" (in English, as it is used in the actual world) is true in the actual world A if and only if grass is green in A. "Grass is green" (in English, as it is used in the actual world) is true *simpliciter* if and only if grass is green. But for this last statement to hold, for its righthand clause to pick out the right condition, the statement, since it does not explicitly refer to the actual world A, must be made *within* that actual world A.

103. Although we do not yet have a complete theory of the makes-true relation, it has been given enough content already to dispel Ian Hacking's claim (and endorsement of the objection) that the "core objection to a correspondence theory is that

there is no way to identify the facts to which a statement corresponds, independently of the statement itself." (See Ian Hacking, "Statistical Language, Statistical Truth, and Statistical Reason," in *The Social Dimensions of Science,* ed. Ernan McMullan [Notre Dame: University of Notre Dame Press, 1992], p. 134.)

There is an argument, which has come to be known as the "slingshot" argument, which holds that, on plausible assumptions, all true statements state (or are made true by) the same one fact. (See Donald Davidson, *Inquiries into Truth and Interpretation* [Oxford: Oxford University Press, 1984], chaps. 2, 3; K. R. Olson, *An Essay on Facts* [Stanford: Center for the Study of Language and Information, 1987], pp. 83–100. Versions of the argument can be found in earlier writings by Frege, Kurt Godel, and Alonzo Church.) All versions of this argument depend upon the assumption that co-referential expressions can be substituted in the statement of a fact without changing the fact that is stated. If two referring expressions r_1 and r_2 refer to the same entity, and statement (S2) can be obtained from statement (S1) by substituting (not necessarily uniformly) r_2 for r_1 in (S1), then (S2) states the same fact that (S1) does. However, consider the statement

(S1) If there is exactly one x such that P_x then [the individual x that is P = the individual x that is P].

Statement (S1) is a logical truth, a necessary truth. Now suppose in addition that (as a contingent matter of fact) the one individual that is P is identical with the one individual that is Q. Since "the one individual that is Q" refers to the same entity as "the one individual that is P," we can substitute the former for one occurrence of the latter in (S1), and thereby get

(S2) If there is exactly one x such that P_x then [the individual x that is P = the individual x that is Q].

According to the assumption of the slingshot argument, it should follow that (S2) states the same fact that (S1) does. However, (S2) is not a logical truth, and it is not a necessary truth. In these respects it differs from (S1), and on no plausible view does a logically true necessary statement state the same fact as a nonlogically true contingent statement. Hence we have a counterexample to the co-referentiality assumption underlying the slingshot argument, and see therefore that this argument to the conclusion that there can be only one fact is *invalid.* The proponent of the slingshot argument might reply that the argument at least shows that facts are not extensional entities—here he extends the notion of extensionality from linguistic contexts to entities—and that the nature of these entities is unclear.

104. A proponent of facts might say it will be necessary to add that *it is a fact* that these components are in that combination.

2. Invariance and Objectivity

1. A person can believe a statement whose content is objective via an objective process. And a person can have a subjective belief about an objective fact. (While traveling, he believes that the hurricane did not pass through his home city on the

previous day, because he very strongly desires that it not have done so.) A person can have an objective belief about a subjective fact (she believes that his motive is concern because he told her so, and he generally is reliable in what he says). And a person can believe a statement whose content is subjective on subjective grounds (his belief that he has certain motivations is shaped by his desire to be someone who does have those motivations; as it happens, he also has the motivations).

The category of subjective facts raises intricate issues that will be taken up later. If we say that the content of a fact is subjective when its content is so determined in its character by intrinsically subjective states such as those pertaining to consciousness, desires, and emotions, then a statement that is explicitly about consciousness ("he is conscious now") would seem then to be subjective. However, on the identity theory of the mind-body relation, wherein being conscious is identical with being in a certain physical state, that statement may be objective in that its content is wholly determined in its character by the features of objects. This overlap between the categories of objective and subjective facts could be avoided if one defined as objective all facts about subjectivity that have such wholly objective determinants. I discuss the nature of subjective facts in this chapter's section on intersubjectivity; the question of whether there are (irreducible) first-person perspectival facts is treated in Chapter 4.

2. There can be multiple access to a fact without the different routes' revealing precisely the same thing. The differently angled pieces of information can, in general, confirm one another, being concordant enough to be about the same fact, yet lead to a mutual modification that brings them into more complete harmony. And under some circumstances, rough information from different routes can lead to a sharper picture than any one route can present. See the discussion of coarse coding in Chapter 4.

3. Although quantum mechanics clouds the question of whether there is an independently existing objective world, it may clarify the question of the nature of objects. It can seem that it is arbitrary that we divide the world up one way rather than another, dividing it into these categories rather than those crosscutting ones, dividing objects as we do rather than holding that there is an object consisting of half of one of our standard objects and one-quarter of another, and not countenancing all sums (according to the calculus of individuals) of any of our objects also to be objects.

Not every "entity," however, constitutes an object that will exhibit certain quantum-mechanical behavior. Suppose that a measurement is made by an apparatus of a particle in a linear superposition. According to the Schrodinger equation, there will be a linear evolution of the ensemble of component systems, particle, and measuring apparatus. The final state, after the interaction with the measuring apparatus, will not be one in which either the particle or the apparatus (or any ensemble of these) is in a specific state. Now the particle and the measuring apparatus are entangled, and their final state is a linear superposition of product vectors. The two together, particle and measuring apparatus, now form a joint entity in that neither subsystem alone now has a particular state, and the state of the whole is not analyzable into the sum of the state of the parts.

Suppose we now consider some arbitrary sum of the measuring apparatus plus some other chosen object, e.g., a table in the corner (before the measurement interaction takes place). Each has its own state, represented by a state vector, and the two together, apparatus and table, are in a composite state represented by a product vector, indicating that the state of the whole is analyzable into the sum of the states of its two distinguishable parts. Now the measuring apparatus interacts with a particle in a linear superposition. As we have seen, the apparatus plus particle will now enter into an entangled state. But what of the apparatus + table plus particle? After the measurement, the table will not be entangled with the particle + apparatus. The state of the table will still be represented by its own distinct and separable vector. The supposed entity apparatus plus table does not behave, in interaction, as a quantum-mechanical object. One portion can get entangled with another entity without the other portion's doing so. The apparatus can get entangled with a particle without the table's doing so. Thus, the apparatus and the table (their sum in the calculus of individuals) do not together constitute an entity.

Quantum-mechanical categories and quantum-mechanical interactions give us the means to delineate objects, to see which boundaries and which combinations are *in nature* and which are artificial conceptual constructions. When nature is to be "cut at its joints," to use the expression frequent in recent philosophical discussions, it is at its quantum-mechanical joints that it must be cut.

4. P. A. M. Dirac, *The Principles of Quantum Mechanics,* 3d ed. (Oxford: Clarendon Press, 1947), preface to the first edition, p. vii.

5. Hermann Minkowski, "Space and Time," reprinted in H. A. Lorentz, A. Einstein, H. Minkowski, and H. Weyl, *The Principle of Relativity* (New York: Dover Publications, 1952), p. 75.

6. All this, apart from the fact that *hotness* may be a psychological notion, and that psychological judgments of "twice as hot" may not mesh smoothly with temperature measurement scales.

7. One can define the objective shape of a two-dimensional object as its spatial structure that is invariant under these transformations: *translations,* which change only its position; *rotations,* which change only its orientation; *dilations, expansions, and contractions,* which change only its size; *reflections,* which change only its handedness; and any combination of the foregoing transformations. And an object's objective three-dimensional shape is its spatial structure, which is invariant under three-dimensional versions of the above transformations. See Stephen Palmer, *Vision Science* (Cambridge, Mass.: MIT Press, 1999), p. 364.

8. See James J. Gibson, *The Senses Considered as Perceptual Systems* (Boston: Houghton Mifflin, 1966), pp. 3, 52–54, 81–84, 156–163, 186–223, 250–265, 284–286. For further work on ecological psychology, following Gibson, see William Warren Jr. and Robert Shaw, *Persistence and Change* (Hillsdale, N.J.: Erlbaum, 1985); and Viki McCabe and Gerald Balzano, *Event Cognition* (Hillsdale, N.J.: Erlbaum, 1986). On the connection between invariancies in the world and our psychology, see Roger Shepard, "Evolution of a Mesh between Principles of the Mind and Regularities of the World," in *The Latest on the Best,* ed. John Dupré (Cambridge, Mass.: MIT Press, 1987), pp. 251–276; also Roger Shepard, "The Perceptual Organization of Colors:

An Adaptation to Regularities of the Terrestrial World?" in *The Adapted Mind,* ed. Jerome Barlow, Leda Cosmides, and John Tooby (New York: Oxford University Press, 1992), pp. 495–532.

For a suggestive survey of invariance in several areas, see Ernst Cassirer's essay of the 1930s, translated as "The Concept of Group and the Theory of Perception," in *Philosophy and Phenomenological Research* 5, no. 1 (1944): 1–35.

9. For discussion of this theory, see David Hubel, *Eye, Brain, and Vision* (New York: W. H. Freeman, 1995), chap. 8; and Semir Zeki, *A Vision of the Brain* (Oxford: Blackwell Scientific, 1993), chaps. 23, 25.

10. Hilary Putnam has argued that the notions of an object, and of the number of objects there are, are relative to a method of description and to a choice of primitive terms. (See Hilary Putnam, "Reflections on Goodman's *Ways of Worldmaking,*" in his *Philosophical Papers,* vol. 3: *Realism and Reason* [Cambridge: Cambridge University Press, 1983], pp. 155–169.) Different partitionings of the world will count different numbers of objects. However, if there are transformations linking these different descriptions, then there also may be invariances under these transformations. For instance, although there is disagreement about how many objects there are in room A and how many in room B, all persons may agree on the ratio of the number of objects in room A to the number in room B. That something varies does not entail that no more complicated relationship is invariant.

11. The true statement "Object O has length L in reference frame R" also is objective, even though the Lorentz transformations do not apply directly to it, for the transformations pair this statement with other true statements asserting other lengths for O in other reference frames. Observers in *any* reference frame can use the transformations to derive, from O's length in their own reference frame, that the length of O is L in reference frame R. (Similarly, they can derive the length of O in any other given reference frame.) Thus, according to the transformations, it is an objective fact that O has L *in reference frame R.*

12. Perhaps also a transformation can be a *subjunctive difference,* such that if the members of the domain *were* different in some way, some properties or relations would still hold true of them, and hence be invariant under that subjunctive difference.

13. See Abram Pais, *Subtle Is the Lord: The Science and the Life of Albert Einstein* (Oxford: Clarendon Press, 1982), chaps. 6–8; Michael Friedman, *Foundations of Space-Time Theories* (Princeton: Princeton University Press, 1983), pp. 149, 155–159, and (on the transition to general relativity), 192–195.

We have held that new admissible transformations can be discovered so that something, previously thought to be objective, is concluded not to be so because it is not invariant under these new transformations. Can the reverse happen? The new theory satisfies transformations $T_2, \ldots, T_n$ but not transformation T_1, which previously was held to be an admissible transformation but no longer is so held. Will a property P_1, previously excluded by T_1 as objective (because it was not invariant under T_1), now come to be thought objective, because it *is* invariant under transformations $T_2, \ldots, T_n$, which (now) are all the admissible transformations? It has been suggested by John Bell that, in order to accommodate the results of the Aspect experiment (confirming Bell's work) and so allow superluminal information transfer, one might drop the requirement of Lorentz invariance. This would give a preferred frame of reference within which something can travel faster than light, the Fitzgerald contractions would be dynamical effects, and "behind the apparent Lorentz invariance of the phenomena, there is a deeper level that is not Lorentz invariant." See the interview with John Bell in P. C. W. Davies and J. R. Brown, *The Ghost in the Atom* (Cambridge: Cambridge University Press, 1986), pp. 48–49. See also J. S. Bell, *Speakable and Unspeakable in Quantum Mechanics* (Cambridge: Cambridge University Press, 1987), pp. 154–155, 179–180, 206–209. For further discussion, see Tim Maudlin, *Quantum Non-Locality and Relativity* (Oxford: Blackwell, 1994), pp. 99–112, 202–204.

14. See Eugene Wigner, *Symmetries and Reflections* (Bloomington: Indiana University Press, 1967), chaps. 1–5; Bas Van Fraassen, *Laws and Symmetry* (New York: Oxford University Press, 1989), chaps. 10, 11; Shlomo Sternberg, *Group Theory and Physics* (Cambridge: Cambridge University Press, 1994). The laws of physics are invariant with respect to displacement in time and space, and also with respect to rotation—physical space is isotropic. The equations of physics are invariant with respect to infinitesimal displacements and rotations in space-time. From this follow the conservation laws for linear momentum and energy, for angular momentum and the motion of the center of mass (Wigner, p. 8). Electromagnetic interaction is gauge invariant; strong interactions are invariant under the SU3 Lie group. The laws of nature of electroweak theory are invariant under specific changes of the fields of electrons and neutrinos, with mixed fields, and corresponding changes in other particles. (See Steven Weinberg, *Dreams of a Final Theory* [New York: Pantheon Books, 1992], chap. 8.) Various "broken symmetries" hold in the area of elementary particles; symmetrical equations yield a symmetrical set of possible solutions (which solutions themselves may be asymmetric), while actuality may show only one asymmetric solution. The Hamiltonian of the theory is invariant under some symmetry, but the symmetry is broken because the vacuum state of the Hamiltonian is not invariant. (See Michio Kaku, *Quantum Field Theory* [New York: Oxford University Press, 1993], pp. 321, 357, 559–565.) An example of a broken symmetry is that relating the weak and electromagnetic forces in the Weinberg-Salam model. So-called Grand Unification theories (GUT), still speculative, use powerful symmetries (such as SU[5]) that give a scenario of breakdown of symmetries to the standard model's $SU(3) \times SU(2) \times SU(1)$. And string theories, even more speculative and untestable by current means, formulate and investigate new symmetry principles, developing a further structure of spontaneous symmetry breaking. Some symmetries such as those of parity and of charge conjugation are violated individually, but quantum field theory is invariant under the combined operation of parity, charge conjugation, and time reversal symmetry (CPT), provided two very general conditions are met. (The two conditions are [1] that the theory must be local, possess a Hermitian Lagrangian, and be invariant under proper Lorentz transformations; and [2] that the theory must be quantized with commutators for integral spin fields and quantized with anticommutators for half-integral spin field. See Kaku, *Quantum Field Theory*, pp. 120–121.)

15. Weinberg, *Dreams of a Final Theory,* pp. 158–159.

16. The historical success of thought experiments such as Galileo's and Einstein's might appear to support the *a priori* character of the admissible transformations. But do thought experiments actually do better than chance in leading to true or subsequently confirmed theories? Hypothetical thought experiments might be devised, after a fact is empirically discovered, to arrive at that fact by "pure thought" guided by symmetry and invariance considerations. Since there are many different dimensions along which a phenomenon can be described, it is not surprising that after a fact has been discovered to hold, we can find *some* description of the situation relative to which symmetric and similar reasoning leads us to this fact. If a different incompatible fact had been discovered to hold, we also could have found some *other* description of the situation relative to which symmetric and similar reasoning would lead us to that second fact rather than to the first one. But don't the thought experiments of Galileo and Einstein, which occurred before the relevant facts were discovered and confirmed, show us that facts can be discovered by pure thought? We hear about and record the successful thought experiments, the ones that did lead to hypotheses that subsequently were confirmed, and we do not, in general, hear of the thought experiments that led to predictions that turned out empirically not to hold. It is unclear whether thought experiments have been more successful than chance would predict.

17. That the set of admissible transformations T forms a group means the following. There is a binary operation $*$ *on* T that maps the Cartesian product $T \times T$ into T; that is, it maps each pair (T_i, T_j) of elements of T to an element T_i*T_j, which is an element of T. This binary operation $*$ is associative:

(1) $(T_i*T_j)*T_k = T_i*(T_j*T_k)$.

Moreover, T has a unit element e. That is,

(2)   There is an element e in T such that, for every T_i in T, $e*T_i = T_i$, and $T_i*e = T_i$.

And every element of T has an inverse, that is,

(3)   For every element T_i of T, there is an element $I(T_i)$ in T such that $T_i*I(T_i) = e$, and $I(T_i)*T_i = e$.

We refer to this group itself as $[T,*]$, the ordered pair of the set T and the binary operation $*$. If, moreover, the group satisfies the commutative law, that is, if

(4)   For every T_i and T_j in T, $T_i*T_j = T_j*T_i$,

then the group is an Abelian group.

It is worth considering what might *explain* why the transformations marking objectivity do (as it turns out) form a group; and what their forming a group tells us about the nature of objective fact.

18. It seems that the requirement that a space-time theory be capable of a covariant formulation does not exert any significant constraint upon it beyond the use of differential geometry. (For a discussion of the empirical content of covariance requirements, see John Norton, "The Physical Content of General Covariance,"

in *Studies in the History of General Relativity,* ed. Jean Eisenstaedt and A. J. Kox [Boston: Birkhauser, 1992], pp. 281–315. See also Friedman, *Foundations of Space-Time Theories,* pp. 46–61.) However, it does not follow that covariance does not help limn objective reality, for, as stated in the text, the properties and magnitudes (such as the tensors) in a covariant formulation can be held to be the objective properties that it speaks of.

The special interest of speaking of covariance with regard to general relativity is not that special relativity cannot be given a covariant formulation—it can—but that general relativity cannot be given a formulation that is Lorentz invariant; it can be given a covariant formulation only. General relativity *requires* a covariant formulation, while other theories that can be given one do not require it.

However, see also Robert Wald, *General Relativity* (Chicago: University of Chicago Press, 1984), pp. 57–59, who formulates the requirement of general covariance to require that the metric of space is the only quantity pertaining to space that can appear in the laws of physics. Apparently nontensorial equations can be made tensorial by explicitly incorporating extra geometrical structure into the equation, but then additional quantities pertaining to space will have been incorporated.

Steven Weinberg writes: "It should be stressed that general covariance by itself is empty of physical content. Any equation can be *made* generally covariant by writing it in any one coordinate system, and then working out what it looks like in other arbitrary coordinate systems . . . The significance of the Principle of General Covariance lies in its statement about the effects of gravitation, that a physical equation by virtue of its general covariance will be true in a gravitational field if it is true in the absence of gravitation"; Weinberg, *Gravitation and Cosmology* (New York: John Wiley, 1972), p. 92.

19. Lorentz invariance does not apply globally within the general theory of relativity because such invariance expresses certain relations between global orthogonal rectilinear coordinate systems, and within the general theory of relativity (and in most non-Euclidean spaces) there do not exist such coordinate systems (because, under General Relativity, mass distorts the flatness of the space). Local Lorentz invariance, however, does apply. (See Maudlin, *Quantum Non-Locality and Relativity,* pp. 228–229.) Maudlin goes on to claim (p. 230) that what is common to the special and the general theories of relativity is the commitment that "the only structure intrinsic to space-time itself is the metrical structure."

20. I thank Ady Stern for the points and questions of this paragraph.

21. John Earman (personal communication) has emphasized to me how the thesis that a fact is objective when it is invariant under all admissible transformations might intertwine with other issues, for instance, whether space and time are substantival or relational. On a substantival (container) view of space-time, that a particle has a particular world line in space-time or that its four-velocity at a certain moment is such-and-such will be an objective fact, yet not one that is invariant under Lorentz transformations (viewed not as a change of coordinates that redescribes the same physical system but as a "boost" of the original system). On a relational view of space-time, the objective facts will be invariant under all transformations, for Lo-

rentz transformations do not reposition world lines of particles but instead generate another description of the same physical situation (provided all relative particular quantities are preserved).

I myself would prefer not to have to decide among these contrasting views of space-time. (On the complexity of these issues, see John Earman, *World Enough and Space-Time* [Cambridge, Mass.: MIT Press, 1989].) The thesis that objective facts are the ones invariant under all admissible transformations might be reformulated so as to leave such issues open, pulling in its horns so as not to gore (or be gored by) these other scientific-metaphysical questions. However, this reformulation fits ill with our desire, expounded in the next section, to fashion not a theory for all possible universes but one encapsulating the essence of objectivity (or scientific laws, or truth, etc.) as it is exhibited in this universe. (And such a retrenchment would forgo the virtue of a theory having Popperian boldness.) So let us forswear any such cautious reformulation.

It could conceivably turn out that our fundamental scientific theories (on their proper interpretation) countenance a framework that is not affected by the dynamical interactions spoken of within the theory but rather is the framework within which dynamical interactions take place (for instance, the metric of special relativity or the absolute time of Newtonian mechanics), and that this framework itself does not exhibit such invariance under transformations. This framework structure would be an absolute object. (The distinction between absolute and dynamical objects was introduced by J. L. Anderson and is discussed and clarified in Friedman, *Foundations of Space-Time Theories*, pp. 56–60.) And in that case, the thesis that the objective facts are those invariant under all admissible transformation, while it held for lower levels, would not be correct or illuminating for the most fundamental level of objective fact. We should not then insist on retaining on all levels the notion of objectivity as invariance under admissible transformations. Since that construal of objectivity was suggested by particular physical theories and then generalized, it also can be overturned by other, compelling physical theories that do not fit this generalization.

22. Music theorists have applied some notions from elementary group theory, but it is unclear what role, if any, the structures they delineate play in our experience of works of music.

23. See Eugene Wigner, "Invariance in Physical Theory," in *Symmetries and Reflections*, pp. 3–4.

24. It is often said that scientific laws support counterfactuals, but one must tread cautiously here in stating the precise content of the supported counterfactual. It is a law that whenever two successive measurements (without any intervening measurement or tampering) are made of an observable of a particle, they yield the same result. At time t_2, a measurement of an observable is made and yields result R. You can infer that if an observation were to be made at a close later time t_3 with no intervening measurement of another observable and no tampering, it would yield the result R. However, you *cannot* infer that if an observation had been made at a time t_1 earlier than t_2, and no measurement of another observable and no tampering occurred

between t_1 and t_2, then the result of the measurement at t_1 would have been R. This last counterfactual is not true. The actual measurement at t_2 collapsed the wave packet, and a later measurement would yield the same result. But an earlier measurement at t_1 might have collapsed the wave packet differently, yielding a different result. For a discussion of this, see Bernard d'Espagnat, *Veiled Reality* (Reading, Mass.: Addison-Wesley, 1994), pp. 136–137.

25. See Robert Stalnaker, "A Theory of Conditionals," in *Studies in Logical Theory*, ed. N. Rescher (Oxford: Blackwell, 1968); David Lewis, *Counterfactuals* (Cambridge, Mass.: Harvard University Press, 1973); and, for the notion of the closest band of possible worlds, Robert Nozick, *Philosophical Explanations* (Cambridge, Mass.: The Belknap Press of Harvard University Press, 1981), pp. 680–681.

26. Here are some examples from mathematics of invariance under transformations. A property of a topological space is a topological (or topologically invariant) property if, whenever it is true for one space X, it also is true for every space homeomorphic to X. (A homeomorphism is a continuous 1:1 map from X onto Y such that the inverse mapping of Y onto X also is continuous.) Topological structures, i.e., properties expressible in terms of set operations and open sets, are exactly those that are preserved under homeomorphisms. Some topological properties hold of all topological spaces, e.g., the cardinality of the point set. Other topological invariants hold only of some spaces (and of those spaces homeomorphic to these), for example, connectedness, local connectedness, compactness, continuity, convergence, closure, having a particular dimensionality. Whether or not a space is metrizable is a topological property of the space, but particular metric properties will depend upon the particular metric chosen and not be invariant under homeomorphisms. The boundedness of a set is not a topological property; it depends upon the particular metric used.

Some properties, such as being a Cauchy sequence, being complete, being uniformly continuous, are preserved under *uniform* homeomorphisms (between metric spaces), i.e., under homeomorphisms wherein the function and its inverse are not only continuous but uniformly continuous. These properties, called "uniform properties," are not topological properties, since they are not invariant under all homeomorphisms, only under uniform ones. H. L. Royden, *Real Analysis*, 3d ed. (New York: Macmillan, 1988), pp. 187–188, places uniform properties between topological and metrical ones.

Algebraic topology investigates more sophisticated topological invariants that distinguish topological spaces, invariants such as Poincaré's fundamental group, homology groups, cohomology groups, and the cohomology ring.

Invariance under transformations plays a major role throughout mathematics, not just in topology. Felix Klein's Erlanger Program investigated, and defined, geometries through their automorphism groups of relation-preserving mappings. (See Felix Klein, "A Comparative Review of Recent Researches in Geometry," *Bulletin of the New York Mathematical Society*, July 1893, pp. 215–249. See also H. Behnke, F. Bachmann, K. Fladt, and H. Kunle, eds., *Fundamentals of Mathematics*, vol. 2: *Geometry* [Cambridge, Mass.: MIT Press, 1974], pp. 460–515; Louis Narens, "Meaningfulness and the Erlanger Program of Felix Klein," *Math. Infl. Sci. hum.* 26, no. 101 [1988]: 61–71.) In topology, a homeomorphism is a bijective correspondence that preserves the topological structure involved. In algebra, an isomorphism between algebraic objects (such as groups or rings) is a bijective correspondence that preserves the algebraic structure involved. (See James Munkres, *Topology* [Hillsdale, N.J.: Prentice-Hall, 1975], p. 105.)

According to Robert Goldblatt (*Topoi: The Categorical Analysis of Logic,* rev. ed. [Amsterdam: North Holland, 1984], p. 42): "Isomorphic groups look exactly the same, *as groups;* homeomorphic topological spaces are indistinguishable by any topological property, and so on. Within any mathematical theory, isomorphic objects are indistinguishable in terms of that theory. The aim of that theory is to identify and study constructions and properties that are 'invariant' under the isomorphisms of the theory . . . Category theory then is the subject that provides an abstract formulation of the idea of mathematical isomorphism and studies notions that are invariant under all forms of isomorphism."

27. We also might consider restricting the ordering criterion of objectiveness so that it speaks not of inclusion relations between sets of any and all transformations but only of inclusion relations between sets of the admissible transformations, as these are fixed by the bootstrapping process described earlier.

An instance of the inclusion relation among sets of transformations is provided by the currently speculative theory of superstrings, which has its own symmetries and corresponding invariances, its gauge groups. Michio Kaku writes, "The symmetries found in particle physics and general relativity therefore emerge as a tiny subset of the symmetries of the superstring"; *Quantum Field Theory,* p. 699. By the partial-ordering criterion, superstrings therefore would count as more objective.

When parity was overthrown, something became less objective according to our ordering criterion, since the symmetry group was lessened.

28. The set-inclusion criterion, as a sufficient condition of greater objectiveness, may require further elaboration or qualification. Under that criterion, a combination of things may be less objective than the parts combined, for the mode of combination may lead the whole to vary under transformations each part separately is invariant under. (I owe this point to Mark Steiner, who also makes the interesting suggestion that the superset criterion perhaps should apply only when some transformations of the superset operate upon a greater dimensionality than do any members of the subset.) How should the objectiveness of a whole be a function of the degree of objectiveness of its parts, and the degree of objectiveness of the mode of their combination? (I am content to let the mathematicians work out the needed technical details in the territory of irreducible representations of groups.) Should the superset criterion be responsive to all transformations or only to the *admissible* ones (and should these be the ones not excluded by the measurement procedure, or the transformations that actually are possible to do, given fixed facts, or the ones that have got into the set of admissible transformations through the bootstrapping process described above)?

29. Perhaps we can correlate each set of transformations with a mapping from

possible worlds to triplets of objectiveness scores along the three usual components. Something's degree of objectiveness then would be the set of *all* its mappings, rather than just its three objectiveness scores in the actual world.

30. We discussed earlier the social relativist position about truth, which holds that the truth property, which explains people's success in achieving their goals when acting upon beliefs, varies from group to group. Suppose that invariance under transformations does indeed explain the intersubjective agreement that exists in a group. Might objectiveness nevertheless be relative in that (because of cultural factors in which groups differ) it is invariance under *different* transformations that explains the intersubjective agreement in different groups? Could different groups have different "objectiveness properties"?

31. Our treatment of subjectiveness has taken it to be objectiveness' polar opposite. Another treatment might independently define it, for instance, as involving (being about? being dependent upon?) psychological feelings and emotions. One then could investigate the contentful question of whether low objectiveness is coextensive with high subjectiveness, and whether high objectiveness is coextensive with low subjectiveness.

32. Ludwig Wittgenstein, *Philosophical Investigations*, sec. 312.

33. See Paul Churchland, *A Neurocomputational Perspective* (Cambridge, Mass.: MIT Press, 1989). Notice that something's being relative to an observer is different from its being subjective. And of course, the fact of something's being relative to an observer may itself be an objective fact that is accessible to different observers.

There also may be a positive point to having some states that are epistemically private, where this privacy makes it impossible for other organisms, in situations of conflict of interest, to predict your behavior that depends upon such states. Hence, there might be selection for such states' not being manifested externally in a way that would make them open to detection by others. (See Chapter 5.)

34. See David Albert, *Quantum Mechanics and Experience* (Cambridge, Mass.: Harvard University Press, 1992), chap. 8. "There are going to [be] combinations of things that any particular observer can (in principle) simultaneously know about the world, and that nobody else can simultaneously know about it; what those things are will depend on the identity of the observer in question, and some of those things will invariably be things that are about that observer herself" (p. 186).

35. Perhaps the process need not even be more effective than not. If no available process is likely to yield true beliefs of a desired degree of specificity, then if I need to have a belief about the matter and if the belief is arrived at by (what is close to) the most effective such process, it might count as rational, even if the desired result is not more likely than not. See Robert Nozick, *The Nature of Rationality* (Princeton: Princeton University Press, 1993), pp. 65–66.

36. Biasing factors may be only a subclass of the factors that lead one away from the truth. Being nearsighted or being prone to fallacies of reasoning may tend to make one's beliefs unreliable, but it is not clear that it makes them nonobjective. Biasing factors sometimes involve a desire for a particular result. Further work needs to be done in demarcating biasing factors, even among those factors that vary

from person to person, and that tend to point away from the truth in a particular direction. Do selection effects which produce evidence that is a biased sample of a total population (because the procedure by which the evidence was gathered is especially prone to, or can only, gather certain kinds of evidence) count as the kind of bias that makes a resultant belief nonobjective?

37. Something can be identified as a biasing factor when it operates within a system that constrains it from leading away from the truth, when the factor is of a sort that in a wide range of situations *tends* to lead one away from the truth, consistently pointing in the same direction. (It need not actually do so, or even tend to do so, in every situation.)

If you ask everyone what the best religion is, everyone will vote for his own, probably the one he was raised in, but if you ask everyone what the second-best religion is, that result may tell us which the best is. The consensus of everyone's second choice, having eliminated the home-religion bias, plausibly will represent an unbiased judgment of merit—or at least a less biased judgment. (To be sure, biased voters who know the nature of the system that has been structured to counteract bias might then falsify their beliefs or preferences and engage in strategic voting in order to maximize the chances that their actual first choice will win.)

38. Israel Scheffler, *In Praise of the Cognitive Emotions* (New York: Routledge, 1991), pp. 3–17. Moreover, emotional responses may have knowledge built into them, knowledge that we do not explicitly possess. Random variation over stable evolutionary time, which exceeds the lifetimes of many individual organisms, can produce emotion-behavior combinations that are advantageous (on average) for reasons that we could not ourselves have learned on the basis of our own evidence and experiences. Emotions (such as disgust at certain smells or being repelled by incest) may propel or exclude behavior with beneficial consequences for organisms that do not know, and could not even understand, the connections or the benefits. (However, since those benefits might not hold under current conditions or might be outweighed, we would want to be careful about acting solely on the basis of emotion.) There can be a cognitive function to things that are psychologically subjective, even if not to their *being* subjective.

39. This expected divergence would be defined as the sum of each extent of divergence from the truth that a biasing factor might produce, weighted by the probability that it would produce exactly that extent of divergence.

40. See Nozick, *The Nature of Rationality,* pp. 107–110; and Chapter 3 of this volume.

41. See Ernest Nagel, *The Structure of Science* (New York: Harcourt, Brace, 1961), pp. 485–502.

42. Andy Clark, *Being There* (Cambridge, Mass.: MIT Press, 1997), p. 132.

43. An organism also might use a feature *F* of an object or situation as a sign of objectiveness without testing further for that, if its ancestors over time evolved in an environment in which that feature *F* was strongly connected to objectiveness. Over evolutionary time, the testing would already have been done, and the present organism is wired to benefit from the existing correlation without needing itself to dis-

cover it. Even then, however, the organism might test for the objectiveness of the presence of the feature *F* before taking action appropriate to the further objective facts that *F* indicates.

44. This gives us an ordering of objectiveness, but the ordering thus attained is only a partial ordering. It does not enable us to compare degrees of objectiveness when neither set of transformations is included in the other. However, we can suppose that further criteria and weightings might extend this partial ordering to a complete one.

45. It would be a mistake to say that science is concerned with the invariant, art with the variant. Darwin's theory of evolution focuses upon the crucial importance of variation—if there is no variation, there is nothing differentially to select—and works of literature often depict deep commonalities of human nature, invariant across cultures and times. Nevertheless, this statistical generalization may hold: the special strength of science is in its delineation of the invariant (Darwin found the invariant structure in the evolutionary process whose material was variation), and the special strength of art is in its depiction of the variant. Works of art do call our attention to both kinds of feature, the invariant and the variant, yet their greatest interest often is in the portrayal of particularities of personality or character or appearance to be found in no other person or place. Over historical time, works of visual art have gone from presenting the generic form of a thing to representing its individual, sometimes quite evanescent, particularity. Some great works of art present both the universal and the particular, in equal measure, and, mysteriously, they present the universal *through* the particular.

46. If each type of truth has its proper role to play, why have philosophers concentrated only upon one combination of dimensional positions, extolling the virtues of absoluteness, objectiveness, and objectivity (and, as we shall see later, of necessity over contingency)? The particular goal philosophers themselves seek and serve is deeper *understanding,* and so philosophers have aimed to uncover structures that best provide that kind of understanding. In presenting the view that different types of truths have their own purposes and virtues, I too have aimed at objectively true statements that are not dependent upon my own particular position or upon currently highly contingent facts, and so have formulated a quite objective theory of subjectivity, a quite nonrelative theory of relativity. That philosophical and scientific statements aim at a high degree of objectiveness and absoluteness does not mean that all other statements should do the same. Other purposes, other types of truth.

At the close of his *Nicomachean Ethics* Aristotle seems to hold that the contemplation of philosophical and scientific truths constitutes the whole of the supremely happy life. Earlier in that work, though, he sees a happy life as a life guided by practical reason to a diversity of valuable ends—intellectual understanding would be only one of these. The pragmatist philosophers, on the other hand, hold that intellectual understanding's whole purpose is to serve the guidance of life, but it is unclear why intellectual understanding cannot itself be one of life's appropriate goals and thus be an end as well as a means.

47. Later literature referred to this as "the received view." When I was a graduate student, this was not the "received view"; it was simply "the truth." In philosophy,

something gets called "the received view" only when it is on the way out, by those attempting to push it out. The view I am describing currently is so far out of favor, it no longer is "received" in polite company.

48. See Karl Popper, *The Logic of Scientific Discovery* (New York: Basic Books, 1959), chap. 10; and idem, *Objective Knowledge* (Oxford: Clarendon Press, 1972), pp. 18–21.

49. See once again Popper, *Logic of Scientific Discovery,* chap. 10.

50. Couldn't we then continue, in conformity with Popper's methodology, to formulate a general statistical hypothesis about the instance falsification of hypotheses, to the effect that the probability of falsification of a hypothesis *H* on the *next* test in an area goes down in proportion to the severity of similar tests in that area that the hypothesis already has passed; and couldn't we then go on to severely test *this* statistical hypothesis (where it is most likely to show its falsity), so that it accrues its own degree of corroboration, with the consequence that the probability would have lessened of falsifying it on the next test in an area where it already has passed tests? Thus the inductivist camel takes up residence in the Popperian tent.

51. Imre Lakatos, "Falsification and the Methodology of Scientific Research Programs," in *Criticism and the Growth of Knowledge,* ed. Imre Lakatos and Alan Musgrave (Cambridge: Cambridge University Press, 1970), pp. 91–196.

52. Here is an example of theory-laden observation, or rather of theory-laden nonobservation, or at least of theory-laden report, that I have uncovered. The well known Muller-Lyer visual illusion involves two equally long straight lines placed parallel to each other, one with arrowheads at each end pointing outward, the second with arrowheads at each end extending beyond the line and pointing inward. Subjects see the second line as longer than the first. My one informal foray into empirical research involved presenting two similar such lines to psychologists, except that one of my lines (the one with arrowheads pointing inward) *was* slightly longer than the other. When asked which line was longer, many psychologists replied that they were of equal length. Their beliefs about what was before them shaped, not their observations—I do not think that they *saw* the two lines as equal—but their reports of their observations.

53. Under this rubric fall Thomas Kuhn (on the usual, though not on his own, interpretation), Paul Feyerabend, Bruno Latour, Andrew Pickering, Barry Barnes, and David Bloor.

54. Under this rubric fall Israel Scheffler, Dudley Shapere, Larry Laudan, W. H. Newton Smith, and perhaps Philip Kitcher.

55. For a discussion of Carl G. Hempel's views of scientific rationality and objectivity as they fall under this rubric, see Robert Nozick, "The Objectivity and the Rationality of Science," in *Science, Explanation, and Rationality,* ed. James Fetzer (Oxford: Oxford University Press, 2000), pp. 292–295.

56. See Patricia Churchland and Terrence Sejnowski, *The Computational Brain* (Cambridge, Mass.: MIT Press, 1992), p. 146.

57. Are some reports of the exhibition of halos by figures of religious attention, who frequently are stared at fixedly, an illustration of the Mach band phenomenon?

58. Kuhn writes, "To see the reason for the importance of these more subjective

and aesthetic considerations, remember what a paradigm debate is about. When a new candidate for paradigm is first proposed, it has seldom solved more than a few of the problems that confront it, and most of those solutions are still far from perfect . . . Ordinarily, it is only much later, after the new paradigm has been developed, accepted, and exploited that apparently decisive arguments—the Foucault pendulum to demonstrate the rotation of the earth or the Fizeau experiment to show that light moves faster in air than in water—are developed. Producing them is part of normal science and their role is not in paradigm debate but in postrevolutionary texts"; Thomas Kuhn, *The Structure of Scientific Revolutions,* 3d ed. (Chicago: University of Chicago Press, 1996), p. 156. But why is it that earlier, without knowing of explicitly decisive grounds for their choice, the scientists move to a new paradigm that later will be supported by decisive arguments? What makes them such good early predictors of what later will decisively be shown to be better than what they replace, if not an awareness of grounds that do indicate this? Kuhn, of course, does not say that these theories *are* later shown to be decisively better than the ones they replace, only that the later arguments and experiments are "apparently decisive," for it would be very awkward for his position if indeed they constituted a decisive showing of superiority. Perhaps Kuhn believes that it is merely because of the numbers of people who work on this new paradigm for many years that the apparently decisive arguments and experiments surface, and that if the same energy had continued to be poured into the old paradigm, it too would have generated apparently decisive arguments in its own favor. This would be a very strong counterfactual claim about the history of science. But without such a strong general claim, Kuhn and his followers have a difficult time in explaining why the paradigm that wins out on contemporaneous, supposedly insufficient grounds (almost?) always later turns out to be decisively better.

59. If the old theory satisfied *D* better than the new theory does, there would be oscillation between the two theories and the two paradigms.

60. The various gimmicky methods for always being able to modify one potential explanation to produce a second might be excluded by contentful conditions, based upon what we previously have learned (or are justified in believing) about the nature of the world, that are imposed upon explanations.

David Albert suggests that underdetermination may be a significant problem in the case of quantum mechanics. There, any solution involving a collapse of the wave packet can in principle be distinguished from any noncollapse solution. But, supposing that some noncollapse solution holds, there then are many theories that disagree about highly nontrivial questions (such as determinism versus indeterminism, whether or not Special Relativity is true, and nonlocality), yet there may be *no* consideration that could decide (to the satisfaction of their proponents) between the several conceptually different yet observationally equivalent noncollapse theories. See Albert, *Quantum Mechanics and Experience,* pp. 176–179.

61. We learn a fact about patients' responses to drugs and henceforth require that medical experimentation be blind; we learn a fact about experimenters' "detection" of results and henceforth require that medical experiments be double-blind.

62. Should philosophical methods also become more specialized to fit what we have learned is the nature of the world? Which ones have done so?

63. Or do we come to detect this of specific methods, not *through* their operation but by noticing that those methods are not working well?

64. Before concluding that this construal gives insufficient weight to the role of *reasons* in scientific practice, see the earlier discussion of externalist views of reasons and of the objectivity of belief, and see also Nozick, *The Nature of Rationality*, chap. 3.

65. I leave aside certain qualifications about tradeoff situations. Some human or methodological factor would not cause science to be nonobjective, even though it leads away from certain kinds of truths, if it is maintained because of its greater effectiveness in arriving at many other kinds of truths.

66. Science will be objective, it might appear, (only) when it follows procedures that make its theories (T) and explanations a function of the world (W), and only of the world, and not of any distorting factors. $T = f(W)$. It will not suffice, however, if its theories are a function of the world by providing the negation of truths about the world. The function f must be an accurate one. For an aspect p of the world, the theory about p, term this $T(p)$, must be an accurate function of p alone, stating the way p is. $T(p) = $ "p." (This notation is, of course, strictly nonsense, since the final p with quotation marks around it refers to the sixteenth letter of the alphabet.) Whenever p is true, the theory says "p." For all p, $T(p)$ if and only if p. So runs the function that the theory must be of the world, it seems, if the theory is to be objective. This we recognize as Tarski's truth condition, one of his two criteria of adequacy for a definition of truth.

To *prove* that science is objective would be to prove the generalization, or to prove each statement of that form. This would be to offer a Tarski truth-definition. Such a proof cannot be given *a priori*; it would have to take place *within* science. However, we already know from a theorem of Tarski that this cannot be done without inconsistency. Within just one system, we cannot prove, for each and every p, that $T(p)$ if and only if p, without giving rise to a version of the liar paradox. So our ability to prove the objectivity of science must fall short, if objectivity is interpreted as above. The rest of this section continues by considering a more attainable notion of objectivity.

3. Necessity and Contingency

1. If truths can be in space and time, then perhaps it needs to be added that a necessary truth not only is true in every possible world, but is true at every place,time in each one. (And also true at all place,times in each one that it is true in all worlds at all their place,times? And . . . ?)

2. How does the necessary/contingent distinction mesh with the two earlier distinctions: between absolute and relative, and between objective and subjective? Of the eight possible combinations of objective/subjective, relative/absolute, and necessary/contingent, five of these present no problems, at least according to standard

views. It is absolute, objective, and necessary that $2 + 2 = 4$. It is absolute, objective, and contingent that the General Theory of Relativity holds. It is contingent, objective, and (according to the Special Theory of Relativity) relative that the length of the space between those two flagpoles is 25 feet. It is contingent, subjective, and relative that chocolate ice cream tastes good. It is contingent, subjective, and absolute that I feel pleasure now.

But is any necessary truth relative? It would appear not, for if a proposition's truth is relative to a factor, that factor may vary or fail to hold in some possible world, in which case the proposition will not be true in that possible world, and so will not be true in all possible worlds. But could there be a statement that does hold true in all possible worlds, as a relative truth in some of these worlds, an absolute one in others? A particular truth can be relative in one possible world, absolute in another, for instance, the statement that a table is five feet long, relative in this world, absolute in some possible Newtonian world. (Or, despite our claim later in this chapter, perhaps water = H_2O is a necessary truth that is relative, relative to the chemical composition in the actual world. Although a truth is not relative merely because it is dependent upon a fact, necessity might be.)

3. Ernest Nagel asks how possible worlds can be independently identified; Quine writes skeptically about the notion of necessity. See Ernest Nagel, "Logic without Ontology," in his *Logic without Metaphysics* (Glencoe, Ill.: Free Press, 1957), essay 4, pp. 60–64; and W. V. Quine, "Necessary Truth," in *The Ways of Paradox* (New York: Random House, 1996), pp. 68–76.

4. Write the necessity operator as N and possibility operator as P. The propositional modal logic system (commonly called T) has, in addition to the usual propositional logic, the axioms

(1)   If Np then p.
(2)   If N (if p then q) then (if Np then Nq).

plus the rule of necessitation:

(3)   If p is a thesis then Np is a thesis.

If we add

(4)   If Np then NNp

we get the system S_4, while if we add

(5)   If Pp then NPp

we get the system S_5. These are the major systems, but there are intermediate and alternative ones. If we add to S_4

If PNp then NPp

we get a system between S_4 and S_5; if we add to S_4

If NPp then PNp

we get a system stronger than S_5 yet independent of S_5 (i.e., not having all of S_5 as theorems yet containing some theorems S_5 does not). We can weaken S_4 by replacing (4) above by weaker forms of it, e.g., if NNp then $NNNp$, or the even weaker: if $NNNp$ then $NNNNp$, etc. There has been no agreement over which system correctly captures the notion of necessity. (See Nathan Salmon, *Reference and Essence* [Princeton: Princeton University Press, 1981], chap. 7 and app. 1; and idem, "The Logic of What Might Have Been," *Philosophical Review* 98 [1989]: 3–34; Graeme Forbes, "Origin and Identity," *Philosophical Studies* 37 [1980]: 353–362; and idem, "Two Solutions to Chisholm's Paradox," *Philosophical Studies* 46 [1984]: 171–187.)

Within quantified modal logic, is the Barcan formula

B: If $(x)NFx$ then $N(x)FX$

valid, and is the converse of this formula valid?

CB: If $N(x)Fx$ then $(x)NFx$.

How shall identity be treated? Will the following formulas be valid?

If (NFa and $a = b$) then NFb.
If $x = y$ then $N(x = y)$.

Once again, disagreement reigns. Different modal systems embody different answers.

Stig Kanger developed a model-theoretic interpretation of modal logic using a notion of relative possibility between possible worlds, and Saul Kripke devised and elaborated semantic methods for distinguishing some of these modal systems and investigating their formal properties. This involves a set of possible worlds, an accessibility relation R between possible worlds, and a valuation that for each sentence and each world assigns a truth value for that sentence in that world. (See Stig Kanger, *Provability and Logic* [Stockholm: Almkvist and Wicksell, 1957]; and Saul Kripke, "Semantical Considerations on Modal Logic," *Acta Philosophica Fennica* 16 [1963]: 83–94.) Depending upon the properties of the accessibility relation R (is it reflexive, symmetrical, transitive?) different modal systems result (as Kanger had shown in some cases). (When the accessibility relation R is transitive then it will hold true that if Np then NNp; when R is reflexive, then it will hold true that if p then Pp; when R is symmetric then it will hold true that if p then NPp; when R is symmetric and transitive then it will hold true that if Pp then NPp.)

Yet the Kanger-Kripke semantics (as Fullesdal terms it) does not settle the questions about which modal systems and formalisms are correct. Is necessity such that if p is necessary then it is necessary that p is necessary; and such that if p is possible then it is necessary that p is possible? Reflections on accessibility do not help, for here finally we encounter a notion about which we have no firm intuitions at all! (Kripke himself denies the claim that the semantic formalism will settle the substantive questions. "The main and the original motivation for the 'possible worlds analysis'—and the way it clarified modal logic—was that it enabled modal logic to be treated by the same set theoretic techniques of model theory that proved so successful when applied to extensional logic. It is also useful in making certain concepts clear"; *Naming and Necessity* [Cambridge, Mass.: Harvard University Press, 1980], p. 19, n. 18.) Moreover, as we shall see, a particular semantic formalism may be elegant and structurally interesting yet still be misleading.

5. If we had a systematic method for examining all possible counterexamples, and for telling when a case *was* a counterexample, and if this method would reach a point in time when all possible counterexamples had been examined and determined to be a counterexample or not, then if the method failed to find a counterexample to a particular statement we could conclude that the statement was necessarily true. Beth's semantic tableaux is a method of proof in quantification theory by systematic search for counterexample. If the search fails, the statement is logically true, and one can construct a proof of it by tracing the route of the failed search for a counterexample. See E. W. Beth, *The Foundations of Mathematics* (Amsterdam: North Holland, 1959), chaps. 8, 11.

6. See the discussion of whether robot cats really are cats, in Hilary Putnam, "It Ain't Necessarily So," reprinted in his *Philosophical Papers,* vol. 1: *Mathematics, Matter and Method* (Cambridge: Cambridge University Press, 1975), pp. 237–239; and Jerrold J. Katz, *Cogitations* (New York: Oxford University Press, 1986), pp. 32–35.

Not all necessities will be known *a priori,* some philosophers have argued, and I shall discuss some such claims later. Note that in the philosophical debate over these claims, once again we find the generation of possible cases, the attempt to produce examples where the statement fails, and the disagreement over whether some cases indeed are possible.

7. It is implausible that a faculty of reasoning and inference that covers all possibilities would have been evolutionarily instilled because it is simpler and sleeker than any faculty that covers only some possibilities.

8. Robert Nozick, *The Nature of Rationality* (Princeton: Princeton University Press, 1993), pp. 107–114. The remainder of this section is taken from that earlier book.

9. W. V. Quine, "Truth by Convention," in *Philosophical Essays for A. N. Whitehead,* ed. O. H. Lee (New York: Longmans, 1936), reprinted in Quine, *The Ways of Paradox,* pp. 77–106.

10. In contrast, Saul Kripke writes, "Of course, some philosophers think that something's having intuitive content is very inconclusive evidence in favor of it. I think it is very heavy evidence in favor of anything, myself. I really don't know, in a way, what more conclusive evidence one can have about anything, ultimately speaking"; *Naming and Necessity,* p. 42.

11. I refer here to what the literature calls *de re* necessities. I first raised these issues in a conversation with Saul Kripke at Rockefeller University in 1988 or 1989.

12. Consider as an analogy, the Jewish and the Christian calendars. If the question is asked, did this event occurring today occur on the same day last year, the answer will vary depending upon the calendar. Christmas comes on the same day each year according to the Christian calendar, namely December 25, but not according to the

Jewish calendar. Rosh Hashanah comes on the same day each year according to the Jewish calendar but not according to the Christian one. Each calendar places a day in a different network, involving different repetitions.

13. This nonmodal criterion of essentiality diverges from the more usual modal criteria, but, on the other hand, it has the virtue of being reasonably clear.

14. It might be said that attributions of necessity are relative to a classificatory scheme, but that the true necessities are specified by the *correct* classificatory scheme. However, since the existence of such necessities is what is in question, the criterion of the correctness of a classificatory scheme cannot be that it gets the necessities right. The remaining criteria of classificatory correctness, however, seem unlikely (even if they do ground just one classificatory scheme) to be able to ground necessities that cut sufficiently deeply to count as metaphysical.

15. We might see Roger Shepard's work as investigating those features that will be common to any ecological niche anywhere in the universe, hence as identifying features of any organism's scheme of classification—any organism that is a product of an evolutionary process. (See Roger Shepard, "Evolution of a Mesh between Principles of the Mind and Regularities of the World," in *The Latest on the Best: Essays on Evolution and Optimality,* ed. John Dupré [Cambridge, Mass.: MIT Press, 1987], pp. 251–276; and idem, "The Perceptual Organization of Colors: An Adaptation to Regularities of the Terrestrial World?" in *The Adapted Mind,* ed. Jerome Bardow, Leda Cosmides, and John Tooby [New York: Oxford University Press, 1992], pp. 495–532.) So Shepard might be taken to deny the existence of such radical cross-classification. However, this is frail comfort for the theorist of necessities about an object. Even if such a radical cross-classification were not possible for organisms produced by the evolutionary process in this universe, it remains a logically possible classification, and that is sufficient to raise our questions.

16. Although we and the Alpha Centaurians classify x with different things, in different equivalence classes, we do agree (or can be brought to agree) what (non-modal) predicates are true of x, what the truths are about it. However, we disagree about what the important and salient truths are (a subset of all the truths about x) that need to be given a unified explanation. We say it is $P_1, \ldots, P_n$; they say it is $Q_1, \ldots, Q_m$. And since the essential properties of x are those in the explanation of the important truths, we will disagree about what the essential properties are. We say E_1; they say A_2.

17. On the other hand, if the identity of objects is a function *not* of essential properties but rather of considerations about the individuation of objects, and if individuation also depends upon needs, purposes, and contexts, then a similar argument about what is based upon what applies to shake the purportedly fundamental status of necessities about an object.

It might be asked how we know that the Alpha Centaurians are engaged in *explaining* the properties that are salient to them. But if our notion of essence also depends upon our notion of explaining (which also depends upon our sortal and identity conditions) then it comes even later in the dependence chain than was indicated above, and so too late to be ontologically fundamental. Moreover, the more the purported necessity resembles "necessary under a concept or under a description," the closer it comes to being a necessity concerning our speech about an object rather than a necessity concerning the object itself. Any relativity that is built into the notion of explanation adds further grist to the mill that yields the relativity of necessity.

For this and for other reasons, we would not want modal properties to figure in an application of Leibniz's law to conclude that objects are distinct.

18. See Kripke, *Naming and Necessity,* pp. 116–144; Hilary Putnam, "The Meaning of Meaning," in his *Philosophical Papers,* vol. 2: *Mind, Language and Reality* (Cambridge: Cambridge University Press, 1975), pp. 215–271; and for Putnam's later thoughts, see his "Possibility and Necessity," in his *Philosophical Papers,* vol. 3: *Realism and Reason* (Cambridge: Cambridge University Press, 1983, especially pp. 63–64, and his "Is Water Necessarily H_2O," reprinted in his *Realism with a Human Face* (Cambridge, Mass.: Harvard University Press, 1990), pp. 54–79.

19. The conclusion of the argument follows from the truth of the premises (1), (2), and (4); (3) follows from (1) and (2); (5) follows from (3) and (4). All that is needed for the cogency of the argument is the *truth* of the premises. As a secondary matter, however, it is interesting to look also at the modal and epistemological statuses of the premises themselves. After the argument concludes, we are to think that (1) is necessary but *a posteriori.* What of premiss (2)? Is it necessary and known *a priori?* Affirmative answers might be held to follow from "water"'s being a natural-kind term and a rigid designator, referring in any possible world to what it refers to in the actual world (if that thing does exist in that possible world). However, much is built into the notion of a natural kind, and it does not seem to hold of anything as a *de re* necessity that it is a natural kind; moreover, that does not seem to be something that is knowable *a priori.* (And is it knowable *a priori* that "water" is a rigid designator; is it necessarily a rigid designator?)

20. Some writers also have denied premiss (2) of the argument. They hold that the term "water" is not a rigid designator, and that (in some other possible world) anything having certain characteristics of water would itself be water. Let us add the proviso that this other world is one in which H_2O does not exist, and is one in which no other substance also has those characteristics of water. We might say that what is water in some other possible world is what is the "best candidate" there for being water. And so perhaps it is not necessary even to require that H_2O not exist in that possible world, for it might exist there yet not be the best candidate for being water there. Some support for this is offered by the following line of thought.

Is it also supposed to follow from water = H_2O that in any possible world in which H_2O exists, it is water? But consider a possible world in which the laws of nature are very different, so that H_2O has *none* of the surface properties of water in that world. It cannot be in the liquid state, it is poisonous to people if ingested, it is black in color, etc.; whereas, in that possible world ZPQ does have most of the properties that water actually has in our actual world: a colorless liquid that puts out fires, etc. Now, in that world, is H_2O water? Is ZPQ water? It seems plausible to say that in another world, water is H_2O *if* H_2O there has most of the (important) properties of water (where this does not simply mean what property of chemical composition it has), whereas otherwise, in that world, water is whatever has most of the important properties water has here, if there is one such substance there, even when H_2O, having very different properties, also exists there.

Hilary Putnam is careful to restrict his thesis that necessarily water is H_2O to physically possible worlds, that is, to worlds where the laws of nature are the same as they actually are here. However, isn't this an *ad hoc* restriction that gives weight to surface qualities of just the sort that other theorists thought were definitional of water?

In *this* universe, the laws might vary from place to place, or one fundamental law might have different manifestations in different places, depending on the mass density of the local stars. So in another place in this universe, H_2O might manifest different surface qualities—there it might be a black poisonous sludge. In that case, is it water there? Or should we interpret Putnam's "physically possible" to mean, not in accordance with the actual laws of our universe, but rather in accordance with the laws as they actually operate locally, right around here? Again, won't the point of this *ad hoc* restriction be just to give water the surface qualities we know it to have?

21. It is not sufficient to express the dependence in terms of subjunctives or counterfactuals. For it might be held that if water weren't H_2O in another possible world, then it wouldn't be (wouldn't have been) H_2O in the actual world. This last subjunctive is akin to subjunctives that backtrack in time. This one backtracks across possible worlds. It must either be excluded or be avoided by a "because." Since there is no causal interaction between the possible worlds, the asymmetry involved in the dependence is established by the actuality of only one of the worlds. See further the next note.

22. Are any truths imported into the actual world from some other possible world? The actual world is the sole exporter of truths. There is an asymmetry between the actual world and every other possible world. The actual world is unique; only it is in a position to export. (We do not accept David Lewis's modal realism, wherein each possible world has the same status.)

23. On the current proposal, *Np* if and only if *p* is nonimportedly true in all (accessible) possible worlds. Accepting the standard equivalence, *Pp* if and only if not-*Nnot-p*, it follows that *Pp* if and only if *p* is true in some (accessible) possible world *or* not-*p*'s truth is imported into some possible world. So, in contrast to the standard view, *Pp* is *not* equivalent to just the *first* disjunct.

24. We might distinguish a property's being part of something's essence from that property's holding necessarily of that thing. (See Kit Fine, "Essence and Modality," *Philosophical Perspectives* 8 [1994]: 1–16.) Earlier we specified an object's essential properties as those that underlie and explain the object's other properties. Kripke and Putnam might be right, then, that it is part of water's essence (on earth) that it is H_2O, even though it is not necessary that water is H_2O.

In the section on cross-classifications, I concluded that we and the Alpha

Centaurians would have different views of a thing's essential properties, and hence disagree about *de re* necessities. Once we distinguish essential from necessary properties, the issue of *de re* necessity is altered, shifting perhaps to whether the object has the property indigenously in all (accessible) possible worlds in which it exists.

25. James Pryor has called my attention to the fact that Gareth Evans proposed a structure wherein he speaks of the deep contingency of something that is superficially necessary. See Gareth Evans, "Reference and Contingency," *Monist* 62 (1979): 161–189, reprinted in his *Collected Papers* (Oxford: Clarendon Press, 1985), pp. 178–213.

26. It might be objected to this view that what is exported from our world to other worlds is not the *truth* of water $= H_2O$, but the content of the proposition that water $= H_2O$. That proposition is fixed in its content and meaning by what holds true in our actual world (and in particular by the chemical composition of water here). But once that proposition is fixed and determinate, *it* holds true in other worlds because of facts about those worlds, and does not (further) depend upon what holds true in this actual world. That particular proposition (that water is H_2O) was raised in the actual world, but once it grows up it travels elsewhere to independently seek its fortune and truth value, without any further support from home.

But what is the content of that statement, fixed here, and is there some way to state this that does not beg the question about the statement's necessity? (Does the semantic content become "H_2O is H_2O," and so become a logical truth rather than a synthetic necessary one?) If our concept of "water" has been shaped to be a rigid designator, what of importance about the nature of anything in the world follows from the particular way we have shaped our concept? On this issue, see Nathan Salmon, *Reference and Essence* (Princeton: Princeton University Press, 1981).

27. For on this philosopher's view, it might be that one cannot specify the structure water actually has without listing its distinct chemical compositions in various or in all other possible worlds. (For every chemical composition, there is a possible world of different laws such that a substance of that composition behaves much as water does in the actual world.) Moreover, we can imagine further that it is true that water has different compositions in different worlds yet it is impossible in this world to discover this, because the different compositions of water in other worlds do not reflect themselves in anything about the behavior of water in this world. These reflections reinforce our conclusion that it is not a necessary truth that water is H_2O.

28. It seems that any arguments for saying that the term "space" designates whatever fills the abstract space role (which different geometries can fill) could be paralleled equally by arguments that the term "water" designates whatever fills the water role.

29. Since writing this, I have discovered that a similar point is made about the gravitational constant in Michael Levin, "Rigid Designators: Two Applications," *Philosophy of Science* 54 (1987): 283–294.

30. Some philosophers may accept the conclusion of this purported *reductio*, but this raises the question of whether, in their view, there is *anything* which is such that it could be true yet could not be necessary. Once an example of such a thing is pro-

duced, we can see whether a similar and equally persuasive argument can be produced for *its* necessity, thereby demonstrating to them the ultimate unpersuasiveness of that *form* of argument.

31. Writers in philosophy of law and political philosophy have distinguished between the concept of, e.g., justice and the conception of it, which is a more particular way of spelling out something falling under the concept.

32. The existence of two distinct admissible conceptions of being the same thing is an additional claim that does not follow automatically from the distinction between concept and conception.

33. See Kurt Godel, "A Remark about the Relationship between Relativity Theory and Idealistic Philosophy," in *Albert Einstein: Philosopher-Scientist,* ed. P. A. Schilpp (New York: Tudor, 1949), pp. 555–563; John Earman, *Bangs, Crunches, Whimpers, and Shrieks: Singularities and Acausalities in Relativistic Spacetimes* (New York: Oxford University Press, 1995).

34. Whatever is metaphysically impossible is physically impossible, but not vice versa. Similarly, whatever is logically impossible is metaphysically impossible, but not vice versa.

35. What about moral necessities? Judith Jarvis Thomson claims that moral truths are necessarily true, true in all possible worlds (*The Realm of Rights* [Cambridge, Mass.: Harvard University Press, 1990], pp. 15–21). She offers this as an example of a necessary moral truth: torturing infants to death just for fun is morally impermissible. However, it is not clear that there is *no* possible world in which torturing infants for fun is morally permissible. Consider the world where unfortunately adults are blocked from any source of pleasure other than that they find in torturing infants. The infants later forget the torture and are not permanently harmed. Each adult in the society has been tortured as an infant, and each one thinks it is better to allow this torture, giving the adults some modicum of pleasure in their lives, even though this endorses the fact that they themselves were tortured as infants. (In that world, only those adults who have themselves been tortured are allowed to torture infants. The guardians of infants, who have their best interests at heart, might consent to their being tortured as infants in order to acquire for them the right to do such torturing later.) It seems plausible that one could elaborate this—admittedly extremely gruesome—story so that in *that* possible world, torturing infants for fun would be morally permissible. But torturing them *to death*? The process of torture might hold some small risk of death—the guardians consent to this risk—and when it eventuates, the infant permissibly has been tortured (as it unfortunately turned out) to death, for fun.

Fundamental facts in our world make it wrong ever to torture infants: we do have other sources of pleasure, etc. But these fundamental facts do not hold in all possible worlds, and so neither does our reaction or the moral principle that is based upon these facts. In any case, the collection of such necessities forms a scattered group, not a systematic theory.

36. See Saul Kripke, *Naming and Necessity,* Harvard University Press, Cambridge, 1980, pp. 97–105, 107–110.

37. Standardly, it is held to lack denotation in a possible world in which *a* does not exist. If it might denote something else there, then two rigid designators R_1 and R_2 that denote the same entity *a* in the actual world might denote two different entities in some other possible world in which *a* does not exist. It therefore would not be a necessary truth (one that holds in every possible world) that $R_1 = R_2$.

38. Suppose that R_1 and R_2 are rigid designators denoting *a* in the actual world *A*. Suppose also that R_1 denotes *b* in world W_2. Thus, we have the identity holding that: *a* in *A* = *b* in W_2. Suppose also that R_2 denotes *c* in W_2. Thus, we have the identity holding that: *a* in *A* = *c* in W_2. Does it follow necessarily that *b* in W_2 = *c* in W_2? If not, if identity across possible worlds need not be transitive, then even identity statements with rigid designators that are true in the actual world do not hold as necessary truths. (And if they are necessary, will such identity statements be more than linguistically informative?)

We should distinguish the question of whether identity is transitive across possible worlds from the question of whether it must be. If it is, but need not be, then on some accounts identity statements will be necessary but it will not be necessary that they are necessary. Perhaps the mark of a deep ontological truth is that it is necessary all the way down the line.

For discussion from another angle of the purported necessity of some identity statements, see Robert Nozick, *Philosophical Explanations* (Cambridge, Mass.: The Belknap Press of Harvard University Press, 1981), n. 9, pp. 656–659.

39. I leave aside trivial metastatements about the structure of possibilities, e.g., "There is a possible world."

40. At best, there may be a very large but incompletable disjunction of the possibilities that hold. Even with the logical truths such as "*p* or not-*p*," "not both (*p* and not-*p*)," we might hold that these do not hold in all possibilities, and that we can extend the range where they hold—though still not to *all* possibilities—by adding further disjunctions, so as to get, e.g., "*p* or not-*p* or not-(*p* or not-*p*)," "[not both (*p* and not-*p*)] or [*p* and not-*p*]." (See also the doctrine in Buddhist philosophy of four-cornered negation.)

41. See Arthur Pap, *Semantics and Necessary Truth* (New Haven: Yale University Press, 1958), pp. 237–249; Hilary Putnam, "Reds, Greens and Logical Analysis," *Philosophical Review,* April 1956; Pap, "Once More: Colors and the Synthetic A Priori," *Philosophical Review,* January 1957; and Putnam, "Reds and Greens Again: a Reply to Arthur Pap," *Philosophical Review,* January 1957.

42. Brent Berlin and Paul Kay, *Basic Color Terms: Their Universality and Evolution* (Berkeley: University of California Press, 1969).

43. Another example of the complexity of the relation between the phenomenology and the physics of color is the phenomenon of metamerism, wherein different complex physical light stimuli (and surface reflectances) are phenomenally indistinguishable under certain illumination conditions.

44. On color as surface spectral reflectance, see D. R. Hilbert, *Color and Color Perception* (Stanford: Stanford University Center for the Study of Language and Information, 1984). The amount of a waveband of light, the intensity of light of that

waveband, that reaches the eye from the surface of an object depends upon the amount of that waveband that is reflected from that surface. The amount that is reflected from the surface depends upon two things: the amount that reaches that surface, and the percentage of the amount reaching the surface that the surface reflects. The amount reaching the surface depends upon the illumination that the object is under. However, the percentage of the amount of a waveband reaching a surface which that surface reflects is a *constant* feature of that surface. That amount, the percentage of light of a waveband reflected from the surface, is known as the *reflectance* of that surface for that waveband. A surface can have different reflectances for different wavelengths, e.g., a high percentage reflected for long wavelengths and a low percentage for middle and short wavelengths. However, the reflectance for any given wavelength is a constant physical property of the surface. For critical reflections on the identification of color with surface spectral reflectance, see Evan Thompson, *Colour Vision* (New York: Routledge, 1995), pp. 115–133, 178–205.

45. It is possible to construe some features of color as objective, other features as subjective or as relative. (See C. L. Hardin, *Color for Philosophers* [Indianapolis: Hackett, 1988].) One could hold that colors *are* surface reflectances (or a wavelength phenomenon defined still more broadly), yet these are perceived in a certain way, as a result of the structure of human receptors and the structure of the cells (e.g., double opponent) and the details of the wiring that shapes the later processing of information. These human biological structures give rise to certain features (such as bands, color opposition, the nonexistence of reddish green and of bluish yellow) that are not objective features of the external objects. These features hold only relative to our perceptual apparatus (or to similar ones). However, this does not mean that these color-experiential features are not structurally isomorphic to *neurological* features and reducible to them. Still, the subjective psychological features due to our neural processing also can be *relative features of the external objects,* features these external objects have relative to our neural apparatus. Thus we can hold that an object's color *is* its surface spectral reflectance (or some broader wavelength notion), and its color has certain features only in relation to, only relative to, our neural apparatus, and other features relative to different organisms' neural apparatuses.

46. The retina of the human eye contains three types of sensory cone cells, each containing a different pigment. These three pigments differ in their ability to absorb different wavelengths of light. Each one absorbs some wavelengths better than other wavelengths, and, although their receptive ranges largely overlap, the three pigments differ in which wavelengths they absorb best. It is not one precise wavelength that a pigment absorbs but a range of wavelengths. Over this range, a pigment absorbs some wavelengths better than others. The three pigments differ not only in which wavelengths they absorb best, but also in the range of wavelengths that they absorb.

In the early 1950s Stephen Kuffler discovered that some cells (in the retina and the lateral geniculate nucleus) have a center-surround receptive field organized like a doughnut. An on-center cell is excited when light shines on a circular area in the center, and it is inhibited when light shines in the surrounding band. An off-center cell is excited when light shines on the surrounding band, and inhibited when light shines in the center circle. Such cells compare the amount of light hitting a spot on the retina with the average amount of light in the immediate surround.

Let us consider how cone cells can feed into center-surround cells, a topic studied by David Hubel, Torsten Wiesel, and Margaret Livingstone. The Red and Green cones pair in their feeding into concentric single-opponent cells (in the retina or lateral geniculate nucleus), which may be of the on-center or the off-center kind. One feeds into the center, the other into the surround, and their actions are opponent, one exciting when the other inhibits. Feeding into concentric broadband cells, both types of cells can act in either the center or the antagonistic surround. Less common are the coextensive single-opponent cells, which have an undifferentiated receptive field (with no center-surround doughnutlike structure) where the Blue cones are antagonized by the Green and Red cones acting together. In the visual cortex there are concentric double-opponent cells, which receive inputs from single-opponent cells. These cells have an antagonistic center-surround receptive field, with each type of cone operating in all parts of the receptive field, to different effects. A Red cone may excite in the center and inhibit in the surround, while Green cones have the opposite action. Such a cell would respond best to a red spot centered against a green background. Other double-opponent cells, depending upon how the cones feed into them, respond best to a green spot in a red background, still others to a blue spot in a yellow background, or to a yellow spot in a blue background. The information in this and the following two notes comes from David Hubel, *Eye, Brain, and Vision* (New York: Scientific American Library, 1995).

47. Thus, this cellular mechanism realizes Ewald Hering's earlier hypothesis of opponent processes in the eye and brain. However, the fit is less than perfect between the psychological phenomenon of the perceptual coding into opponent hues and the spectral responses of the neurons; perhaps a more perfect fit will be found in the neural organization further in the central visual pathways.

48. A change in the wavelength will change the center and the surround of a receptive field in a similar fashion, and hence not alter the fact of a contrast to which such a cell responds. These explanations of color constancy and of opponent colors continue to apply even if, as now is thought, the nature of the surround overlaps the center, and so is filled rather than being doughnut shaped. And the retinex theory of Edwin Land, which is based upon comparisons between a region and its surround for each of the cone wavebands, can also be adapted to color-opponent mechanisms and double-opponent cells.

49. Still, it might be said that there is a necessity in the fact that a point of a surface cannot simultaneously reflect different percentages of incident energy of the same given wavelength. But this necessity, if it exists, will not be any peculiar color necessity but perhaps a mathematical or logical necessity.

50. Or rather, what is left may be only a relative necessity: *if* these *contingent* facts hold then it must be that those other facts also hold, and that certain further things cannot hold.

51. See Jerry Fodor, *The Language of Thought* (New York: Crowell, 1975), pp. 27–53; Z. W. Pylyshyn, *Computation and Cognition* (Cambridge, Mass.: MIT Press,

1984), pp. 95–106, 130–145; Paul Smolensky, "Computational Models of Mind," in *A Companion to the Philosophy of Mind,* ed. Samuel Guttenplan (Oxford: Blackwell, 1994), pp. 176–185; Stephen Kosslyn and Oliver Koenig, *Wet Mind* (New York: Free Press, 1992), pp. 128–166; Stephen Kosslyn, *Image and Mind* (Cambridge, Mass.: Harvard University Press, 1980), pp. 29–91, 139–173; idem, *Image and Brain* (Cambridge, Mass.: MIT Press, 1994), pp. 1–52, 335–377; Andy Clark, *Being There* (Cambridge, Mass.: MIT Press, 1997).

52. In the case of computers, we grossly distinguish particular software from functional architecture from hardware. Undoubtedly there will be other relevant distinctions, and new ones special to particular modes of representation.

53. W. V. Quine's well-taken objections, in his 1935 essay "Truth by Convention" (reprinted in *The Ways of Paradox,* pp. 77–106), to explaining all necessary truths as due to convention do not apply to explaining necessities, perhaps even all necessities, as due to convention. The question is which property one is explaining, truth or necessity. Truths are needed in the explanation via convention (to mark what follows from the conventions), so not all truths of this sort can be explained by such explanations. But necessities are not needed in the explanation, for it need not be held that what follows by the conventions, what holds true when the conventions do, follows necessarily. So it is left open that all necessities could be so explained.

54. For an exposition see Stan Wagon, *The Banach-Tarski Paradox* (Cambridge: Cambridge University Press, 1985).

55. See Eugene Wigner, "The Unreasonable Effectiveness of Mathematics in the Natural Sciences," in his *Symmetries and Reflections* (Bloomington: Indiana University Press, 1967), pp. 222–237; Andrew Gleason, "How Does One Get So Much Information from So Few Assumptions?" in *Science, Computers and the Information Onslaught,* ed. Donald Kerr (New York: Academic Press, 1984), pp. 83–89.

56. If an explanation of the truth of mathematics was powerful enough to establish, along the way, its necessity as well, then there would be no need for an additional explanation of (apparent) necessity. Still, some weakening of this powerful explanation might accomplish the first task yet not the second, and this weaker explanation, combined with an additional explanation of apparent necessity, might be superior to the ontologically or metaphysically stronger (but more dubious) explanation.

57. It is instructive to consider, in the most general terms, the model of something's being projected within projective geometry or, more generally, by language or another method of representation. If we suppose that this is what is happening with the logical and mathematical necessities also, we then might follow the hypotheticodeductive method and try to explain what could give rise to the particular mathematical and logical truths we find compelling. Suppose our world W to be a *projected* entity, having features N that appear to hold necessarily of it. What is the reality R and what is the process or method of projection P such that this method, applied to that reality, yields a world with features N? Our task is to hypothesize a process P and a reality R such that $P(R) = N$. Finding such a P and R would explain necessity.

Or would it? Is the operation of the process P applied to the reality R something that *must* give rise to N, so that we can prove the result that $P(R) = N$ as a mathematical theorem? But then there will be a necessity that is unaccounted for, namely the necessity of this theorem. So, instead, it will be a contingent truth that $P(R) = N$. That process of projection applied to that reality just does happen to give rise to N. Are there then any limits or constraints upon our hypothesizing? If P does not have to look like anything that would give rise to N when applied to R, won't any arbitrary P and R fit the bill? For instance, R is a twenty-seven-dimensional sphere of protons and P is process of its being sat upon by a twenty-eight-dimensional walrus. Why does that produce our world with its apparently necessary logical and mathematical features N? It is a contingent truth that it just does. Theorizing is empty and indistinguishable from fairy tales in the absence of any constraints.

It could be, however, that some of the very regularities N that appear necessary in this world, call this subset N', hold of the reality R and of the process P, although they hold of R and P contingently, not necessarily. When P acts on R, this gives rise, in accordance with (contingent) general truths N', to a world W that must have features N. These apparent necessities N turn out to be merely relative necessities, things that will hold if R, which happens to exist, is acted upon by P, which happens to operate, in accordance with N', which happens to hold. Some contingent features of P and R, namely N', would project themselves down as (among the) necessary features of our world W.

Let us say in this case that our world *reflects* the reality R, in that some of what our world shows as necessary does hold (though contingently) of the reality R. Other things that our world shows as necessary might not hold of R at all.

If we hold or suppose that our world is a reflective world, this does impose some constraints upon the explanation of necessities here, namely, the hypothesized process P and reality R must be such as to yield $P(R) = N$ as a mathematical or logical result or theorem. This will not mean, however, that any necessity is left unexplained. All that is supposed is that $P(R) = N$ is projected here as a necessary truth, not that it starts out there as one.

It is an interesting question to ask what contingent truths, holding of a process and a reality, would be projected as necessary truths here. In the case of propositional logic, we might turn to metatruths such as that there are just two truth values, true and false, and that every statement has exactly one of these truth values; every statement is either true or false, and no statement is both true and false. These help to yield the law of excluded middle (p or not-p) and the principle of noncontradiction [not(p and not-p)]. It is not that these *justify* the first-level logical truths—that would appear to be circular. But if the metatruths contingently hold, then the first-level truths will hold necessarily—as relative necessities.

The project of explaining necessities as reflective truths is an interesting one. However, there is no guarantee that even if necessities are projected truths, they are projected as reflections of some truths that hold of the reality and the process of projection. And then we are back to the case of no constraints, of *any* P's and R's possibly giving rise to N.

Necessity does not inhere *qua necessity* in the reality (things in themselves). It may or may not be that (some of) the necessities here do in fact hold of the reality. We seem to have taken a long way around to the structure of Kant's explanation of necessity, though without limiting the projective process to activities of our synthesizing and judging faculties.

But how can generalizing our earlier explanations have led us to face only these two unsatisfactory theoretical alternatives, either real necessities or an unknowable thing in itself, when our earlier explanations did not seem to involve either unpalatable option? Our generalization took too literally the analogy to projective geometry as it imagined a reality and a method of projection both of which were independent of the world as we know it. This indeed might be appropriate if we were developing a theory of our world as a projected entity, with no constraints on either the underlying reality or the method of projection. Then the Kantian inaccessibility of the underlying reality would indeed be a consequence.

However, a particular hypothesis about the method of projection, for instance, that it is associated with language or methods of representation, will go along with particular theories about how that projection operates and what it imprints. With that method of projection fixed, we can ask what world (containing no necessities) would yield, when projected, the world as we know it with the necessities it appears to have. The answer will no doubt be underdetermined, but the usual desiderata in selecting among theories will guide our choice here as well. And perhaps our initial question should have been this somewhat different one. Given a fixed method of projection, what world is most like the one we know (but containing no necessities) that would yield the world we know with its apparent necessities? Here, without being threatened by the specter of the Kantian thing-in-itself, we have returned to the interesting and substantive project of investigating how necessities might be impressed upon our representation or linguistic depiction of a wholly contingent world by features we have independent reason to think internal to our methods of representation or linguistic depiction.

58. See James Bogen and James Woodward, "Saving the Phenomena," *Philosophical Review* 97 (1988): 303–352.

59. Silvano Arieti, *Interpretation of Schizophrenia*, 2d ed. (New York: Basic Books, 1974). Quine attributes the Levy-Bruhl hypothesis of "prelogical peoples" to bad translation; see W. V. Quine, *Word and Object* (Cambridge, Mass.: MIT Press, 1960), pp. 58–59.

60. For a survey of alternative logics to cope with vagueness, see Timothy Williamson, *Vagueness* (London: Routledge, 1994). On paraconsistent logics, see Graham Priest, *In Contradiction* (Dordrecht: Nijhoff, 1987).

61. The filtering account does not even have the consequence that there are no necessary truths. Someone still could maintain that some of the statements whose apparent necessity is accounted for, nevertheless, really are necessary, or at least might be so. (This would be akin to a Kantian's holding that some statements about appearances really do or might apply to things in themselves.) But his reasons for saying this presumably would involve something other than the apparent necessity of these statements.

62. See W. B. Starbuck, "Level of Aspiration," *Psychological Review* 70 (1963): 51–

60; and idem, "Level of Aspiration Theory and Economic Behavior," *Behavioral Sciences* 8 (1963): 128–136.

63. There is an odd curiosity about the definition of the notion of an ordered pair within set theory. An ordered pair has been defined in different ways. In the standard definition proposed by Kuratowski, the ordered pair $<x,y>$ is defined as $\{(x),(x,y)\}$. This definition has the property of unique decomposition, which standardly is the sole criterion of adequacy for a definition of the ordered pair. Such a definition uniquely encodes both what x and y are and what order they are in. If $<x,y> = <u,v>$, then $x = u$ and $y = v$.

The Kuratowski definition defines the ordered pair $<x,y>$, in that order. But the very same Kuratowski definition could have equally well been used to define the ordered pair $<y,x>$, in *that* order! Unique decomposition would continue to hold if we used the Kuratowski definition to define the opposite ordering of the very same members. (Could it be that all the while, theorists who thought they were speaking of x and y in that order were really speaking of y and x in *that* order?) Is there a criterion in addition to uniquely decomposable that a definition of ordered pair must satisfy?

A tripartite classification seems appropriate. A *simple pair* is any set consisting of two (distinct) members, and the Kuratowski definition does define something that is different from this (that is, the Kuratowski ordered pair of x and y does not have x and y as its two members). The Kuratowski definition gives us a pair with one member structurally distinguished from another. Call this a *distinguished pair.* Finally, there is an *ordered pair,* which is a distinguished pair with a determinate order in which one of the distinguished elements comes first. We do not yet have an adequate definition of an ordered pair. I acknowledge that since a distinguished pair seems adequate for mathematical purposes, there is the question of what additional thing, if any, the ordered pair might be needed to do.

64. Must an arithmetic even assume that the successor operation marks off the same *distance* between numbers every time that it is applied, that for *every x,* $S(x) - x = S[S(x)] - S(x)$?

65. An example of a proposition that is true of every possible world but one, call that particular one world W_{-165}, is that the world is not identical with W_{-165}.

Timothy Williamson (personal communication) proposes a distinction between our topic here, how contingent it is *that p,* and how contingent it is *whether p,* where it is maximally contingent whether p when the probability of p is $\frac{1}{2}$.

66. If there is a nondenumerable infinity of possible worlds represented by points in a plane, then if a statement holds in all the worlds represented by points in a straight line, and not in the other points in the plane, although the number of worlds in which it holds equals the number in which it does not—in both cases this is the same nondenumerable infinity—it does not seem correct to say that the statement's degree of contingency is equal to $\frac{1}{2}$. Also, if there is a denumerable infinity of possible worlds, and a statement holds in a finite number of these, then taking the ratio of numbers would give the statement a degree of contingency of 1, the maximum amount, no matter how great the (finite) number of worlds in which it holds,

thus yielding the result that a statement that holds only in one world is no more contingent than a statement that holds in 62 billion worlds. It would be nice to avoid this latter result, but none of the proposals I discuss below does so.

67. Given a noncountable number of possible worlds, there will be difficult issues about measures, depending upon the structure of the space of all possible worlds.

68. Rudolf Carnap, *The Logical Foundations of Probability* (Chicago: University of Chicago Press, 1950), pp. 308–309.

69. David Lewis, *Counterfactuals* (Oxford: Blackwell, 1973). Lewis speaks of distances between possible worlds, but we might start earlier and impose some conditions on the *topology* of the space of possible worlds. Beneath the metric conditions will be topological conditions analogous to those defining Hausdorff spaces, regular spaces, normal spaces, etc., i.e., with open sets around possible worlds, neighborhoods, etc. We then can investigate which ones are metrizable and hence can be related to a Lewis distance metric. And we then can investigate the topological analog of Lewis's subjunctives, that is, the corresponding statement that is true in virtue of the topological structure that could give rise to different metrics. Those truths would be invariant across metrics and would depend only upon the topology. Hence they would be less interest-relative than the metricized subjunctives.

70. If such theorists are correct, that makes the current situation *evidence* or a reason to believe that the earlier universe was indeed in such a state. It must earlier have been in a state that would lead to us, since we are here. However, strong anthropic theorists seem also to want to use these considerations to *explain* why the earlier state held. Here it is more difficult to follow their line of reasoning. The explanation of why my great-grandparents married each other (and had sexual relations) is not that I was born in 1938.

Anthropic theorists concentrate on showing that small changes in any one variable would lead to a universe inhospitable to galaxy formation and hence to life. (Their theories never get so far as to discuss conditions differentially relevant to conscious life.) One also would like to know the effects of *large* changes in the value of some variable, and of simultaneous large changes in the values of several variables, in order to assess the degree of particularity of the conditions conducive to life.

71. Stephen Jay Gould, *Wonderful Life: The Burgess Shale and the Nature of History* (New York: W. W. Norton, 1989).

72. Since we are concerned with how contingent a fact S is that holds *here*, we wish to consider possible worlds centered upon the actual one. However, now the target is not just S-worlds but worlds (centered upon the actual world) in which something *similar enough to S* holds true. Call these T-worlds. Initial conditions C actually did lead (in deterministic fashion) to the outcome S holding in the actual world. How varied might the initial conditions have been and yet led to S or to T?

Form a sphere of radius r centered on the actual world. The degree of r-contingency of T is the ratio R, within this sphere, of the measure of the non-T worlds to the measure of all the worlds. What is the appropriate radius r in this case? Large enough to reach worlds in which the initial conditions C do not hold—until then the ratio R will be zero—and large enough also to encompass a belt of non-C worlds, many of which also yield T. So the ratio R will stay low throughout that radius r. Given a chosen cutoff for ratio R, find how large r can be and still maintain that low a ratio R (and beyond which it cannot, at least for a long stretch, so maintain R). The greater radius r (for a given chosen cutoff ratio R), the *less* contingent S (or T). The greater the radius r is (or the further it goes past the C-world), the less does S depend upon the particular initial conditions C. S, or something like it, is not just locally true.

73. See Ernest R. May and Philip D. Zelikow, eds., *The Kennedy Tapes: Inside the White House during the Cuban Missile Crisis* (Cambridge, Mass.: The Belknap Press of Harvard University Press, 1997). Some of the literature on nuclear warfare of some years ago denied this latter claim about extinction. See Herman Kahn, *On Thermonuclear War* (Princeton: Princeton University Press, 1960).

74. The literature critical of Hume's account of a scientific law points out that it is not sufficient that there be a constant conjunction that holds across all of space and time. It might be that never within this universe does there naturally occur a sphere of pure gold with a radius of twenty-five miles, and never does one get artificially constructed. Yet no law stands in the way of doing this, no forces of repulsion prevent this, and no chain reaction would occur to destroy such a sphere. It just happens that no civilization decides to construct it. So it is true (throughout space and time) that for all things and all places, these are not part of a golden sphere with a radius of twenty-five miles. Still, this does not constitute a law of nature. (So runs the objection to Hume.) Nevertheless, the nonexistence of such a sphere may not be highly contingent. It would be very effortful to construct one, drawing upon much physical energy. The closest possible world in which one exists is not very close. Or does this depend upon how distant is the possible world in which the universe contains a dictator with the absolute powers of a Roman emperor able to command the satisfaction of each of his whims, and upon how unlikely it is that such an emperor would command the construction of such a sphere?

75. We might, however, want not only to look at the closest non-S world to today's actual world, but also to take account of other close worlds, perhaps considering all the non-S worlds in a certain r-band of today's actual world. Here we would want to consider the sparseness of such non-S worlds in that band (the sparser they are, the less contingent S is), as well as their degree of closeness. The degree of r-contingency of S in today's actual world might then be the ratio of the average closeness of the non-S worlds in the r-band around the actual world, weighted by a measure of the number of such worlds there, to the average closeness of the S worlds in that r-band, weighted by a measure of the number of such worlds there.

Degree of contingency of S (in today's actual world) $=$
Measure (non-S) $\times$ Average Closeness (non-S) $/$
Measure (S) $\times$ Average Closeness (S).

If having only S-worlds in the denominator rather than *all* worlds creates a problem, the formula can be modified. In this formula, I have suppressed above the needed reference to the *r*-band, which should be explicitly included for completeness. More generally, we can define *S*'s degree of *r*-contingency not only in today's actual world but in any world *W* at a time:

Degree of *r*-contingency of *S* (in world *W* at time *t*) =
Measure in *r*-band around *W* at *t* of (non-*S*) × Average Closeness in *r*-band around *W* at *t* of (non-*S*) /
Measure in *r*-band around *W* at *t* of (*S*) × Average Closeness in *r*-band around *W* at *t* of (*S*).

Finally, we would have to explicitly include reference to *T* which is similar to *S*, in accordance with our earlier considerations.

76. Also, because we have taken the ratio over the weighting of *S* worlds rather than over all possible worlds, it would differ from a probability, but this difference is trivial. Since we have not argued that the ratio taken over the weighted average distance of the *S*-worlds must be the best way to proceed, the denominator could equally well be: Measure in *r*-band around *W* at *t* of (*S*) × Average Closeness in *r*-band around *W* at *t* of (*S*) + Measure in *r*-band around *W* at *t* of (non-*S*) × Average Closeness in *r*-band around *W* at *t* of (non-*S*).

77. See Robert Conquest, *The Great Terror: A Reassessment* (New York: Oxford University Press, 1990).

78. See Dmitri Volkogonov, *Lenin: Life and Legacy* (London: HarperCollins, 1994); Richard Pipes, ed., *The Unknown Lenin* (New Haven: Yale University Press, 1996).

79. See Martin Malia, *The Soviet Tragedy* (New York: Free Press, 1994), chap. 7.

80. See Leonard Schapiro, *The Origin of the Communist Autocracy* (Cambridge, Mass.: Harvard University Press, 1955); Robert V. Daniels, *The Conscience of the Revolution* (Cambridge, Mass.: Harvard University Press, 1960). For an opposing view about the possibilities for dissent in the 1920s, see Stephen Cohen, *Bukharin and the Bolshevik Revolution* (New York: Alfred A. Knopf, 1974).

81. See Richard Pipes, *The Russian Revolution* (New York: Alfred A. Knopf, 1990); Robert V. Daniels, *Red October* (Boston: Beacon Press, 1984).

82. How shall we assess the degree of contingency of a random event, one whose occurrence is irreducibly probabilistic? In the possible-worlds framework, there will be worlds *very* close to the actual one where that event does not occur, but there also will be other close worlds where it does. In this framework, the measures discussed above will serve. Alternatively, we might want to treat an irreducibly random event as having a probability in the actual world, and in some other nearby worlds as well. A formula that assessed the degree of contingency of the event would have to incorporate explicitly these probabilities, perhaps with each probability (between zero and one) weighting the world in the ultimate measure.

83. However, Darwin's explanation of life, which replaced the explanation in terms of God's design, made life and its details *more* contingent than people had previously thought.

84. Richard Miller holds that citing the cause of event *Z*, which is *Y*, is too shallow to explain *Z* when: there is another event *X* such that if *Y* hadn't occurred, then *X*

would have brought about Z in some other way; or when there is an X such that X caused Z by causing Y, and X is close to Z and so is not a remote cause, and Y causes Z only when X holds. (See Richard Miller, *Fact and Method* [Princeton: Princeton University Press, 1987], pp. 98–105.) Miller's account fits our notion that explanation reveals something's maximum degree of noncontingency. We might want to distinguish two questions: why did Z occur? and to what extent did Z *have to* occur, and why did Z have to occur (to that extent)?

85. See Michael Friedman, "Explanation and Scientific Understanding," *Journal of Philosophy* 71 (1974): 5–19; Philip Kitcher, "Explanatory Unification and the Causal Structure of the World," in *Scientific Explanation*, ed. Philip Kitcher and Wesley Salmon (Minneapolis: University of Minnesota, 1989), pp. 410–505.

86. There may be more to the matter (and here I shift the philosophical focus and tone). Perhaps contingency itself is felt as distasteful, not because of any lack of understanding but because of the *insecurity* it brings in its wake. This goes deeper than any satisfaction philosophers may have had with the way things were, accompanied by an unwillingness to see things changed or to contemplate their having always been different. Lucretius wondered why people are especially concerned about death, worrying more about the fact that there is a time after which they will cease to exist than about the fact that there was a time before which they existed. We can add that each of our existences is highly contingent. I suppose that a belief in souls that are bidirectionally eternal and necessarily existing might help. And the same comforting properties might be found in an extrapersonal surrogate with which one can identify or at least feel closely linked. God, for instance. Or, in the case of many philosophers, timeless noncontingent truths.

In an evolutionary context, of course, there would be no selection for the survival of bodily death, for this would not lead to greater reproductive success. Survival would have to be an accidental side effect of what *was* selected for—and this is a highly *unlikely* accident. For consider the (currently) science-fiction scenario of transferring a person's psychology (personality, etc.) to another entity, for instance, to a cloud or a computer. Think how complicated this would be, how easily things could go wrong. It is overwhelmingly unlikely that something this complex could happen as an accidental side effect of some other process. So if we suppose that all our qualities are a result of the evolutionary process (either directly selected for or a side effect of what was selected for), then almost certainly no human being has yet survived bodily death. This does not mean that it is impossible for this to happen in the future, as a result of complicated intentional activity aimed at bringing this about.

Philosophers have aimed at a different kind of survival: to think thoughts about enduring things, thoughts that will endure about topics that will continue to be worth thinking about, thoughts that will be very long-lived, even if not infinitely enduring. Socrates, Plato, Aristotle, as well as others later in the tradition, left such enduringly valuable effects. (This kind of transcendence of the limits of an individual life was achieved also by other titans of the mind and spirit, by Homer, Aeschylus, Sophocles, Thucydides, Michelangelo, Shakespeare, Newton, Darwin, and Einstein.) That is the kind of immortality that we know is possible, and that is worth having. Recall the Herblock editorial cartoon upon the death of Albert Einstein, which shows from a distance the planet Earth, with a stick into it supporting a sign that says "Albert Einstein lived here."

The task of identifying these great accomplishments of consciousness, intelligence, sensitivity, openness, and boldness, and the task of delineating, analyzing, assessing, evaluating, and appreciating them, are among the things a university is for; it is the central thing a liberal-arts education is to accomplish. Deepening our insights into these accomplishments of the past, which also include piercing affirmations of contingency and finitude, is endlessly worth doing, as is attempting to add to them. It is necessary to say and affirm this because, sadly, I write at a time of widespread neglect and even denigration of such accomplishments.

87. See Lewis, *Counterfactuals,* pp. 84–91; idem, *On the Plurality of Worlds* (Oxford: Blackwell, 1986), chaps. 1, 2.

88. Even if this is granted, it alone does not solve the problem, for on certain views, I also exist in other possible worlds, including all those corresponding to alternative ways this world could have been while still containing me. (Some views deny this, holding that in these other possible worlds it is not I but only a counterpart of myself that exists.)

89. See Robert Nozick, "Fiction," *Ploughshares* 6, no. 3 (Fall 1980): 74–77, reprinted in idem, *Socratic Puzzles* (Cambridge, Mass.: Harvard University Press, 1997), pp. 313–316.

90. In *Philosophical Explanations,* I discussed the question "Why is there something rather than nothing?" There I considered the hypothesis that all self-subsuming possibilities are realized that satisfy further (symmetry and invariance) conditions, where this principle itself satisfies those conditions and is self-subsuming. Thereby I hoped that the "brute fact" quality of the most fundamental explanatory principle could be eliminated or at least reduced. I considered, as an example of this, the situation of all possibilities' being realized, and I also said that one need not countenance all possible worlds (or even more than one) as actual if it turned out that those specific conditions were satisfied by only one possible world. The view presented there sketched a structure but did not specify the further conditions. See Nozick, *Philosophical Explanations,* pp. 115–137.

91. See Derek Parfit, "Why Is There a Universe?" I, II, *London Review of Books,* January 15 and February 5, 1998.

92. Should we think of Feynman's method as saying (a) that only one possibility is actual, and which one this is gets determined by the average of all the nonactual possibilities; or does it tell us (b) that what is real is the superposition of all the possible paths, with the one being observed that is their average; or is it (c) that each of the possible paths actually is followed, with the result being determined by constructive and destructive interference?

93. See Nelson Goodman, *Fact, Fiction and Forecast* (Cambridge, Mass.: Harvard University Press, 1954); and Douglas Stalker, ed., *Grue!: The New Riddle of Induction* (Chicago: Open Court, 1994).

94. I draw heavily in my discussion upon the marvelously lucid and fascinating exposition of the current state of string theory (and of M-theory, which treats not just of one-dimensional strings but of multidimensional [mem]branes), in Brian Greene, *The Elegant Universe* (New York: W. W. Norton, 1999).

95. Supersymmetry, whereby charge transforms as a spinor, relates the masses and couplings of fermions and bosons. Eleven dimensions "is the maximum in which supersymmetry can exist [with only one time dimension], since the spinor representations are too large for" dimensions equal to or greater than 12. See Joseph Polchinski, *String Theory,* vol. 2 (Cambridge: Cambridge University Press, 1998), p. 453.

96. The next (but not the last) strikingly *special* order of infinity comes infinitely far up the line of step-by-step ascending infinities, as their limit. I suppose that one might also consider a space of that number of dimensions, if only to see the results of bringing *serious* set theory into physics.

97. See Greene, *The Elegant Universe,* pp. 376–380.

98. Indeed, from this second premiss of nonarbitrariness, it might be possible to derive the first. If we treat the state of nothing existing as equivalent to a zero-dimensional universe—I suppose we then must treat a point of zero dimensions all alone as equivalent to nothing—and if zero is one arbitrary finite number among others, no less arbitrary than 4 or 769, so that it would be arbitrary if a zero-dimensional universe existed, then perhaps we can deduce from the second premiss that there does not exist a state of a zero-dimensional universe, that is, there is not simply a state of nothingness. And so it would be unnecessary to postulate separately that a universe exists.

99. See Alan Guth, *The Inflationary Universe* (Reading, Mass.: Addison-Wesley, 1997); A. D. Linde, *Particle Physics and Inflationary Cosmology* (New York: Harwood, 1990); also idem, "The Self-Reproducing Inflationary Universe," *Scientific American,* May 1994, pp. 32–39.

100. Smolin first published his idea in "Did the Universe Evolve?" *Classical and Quantum Gravity* 9 (1992): 173–191. I take my description from his book *The Life of the Cosmos* (London: Weidenfeld and Nicolson, 1997), pp. 90–106.

101. Martin Rees writes, "Two issues need clearer formulation. First, does the selection process favour universes that generate blackholes at the *maximum rate* (and maximum efficiency), or is the *total number produced by a universe over its lifetime* more relevant? The latter criterion would depend, more than anything else, on how big and long-lived a universe was. The second point concerns the anthropic constraint. Suppose it turned out that black holes were most readily produced in a universe where complex life could never evolve. For instance, stars might more readily form black holes if there were no nuclear energy sources, and no stable elements other than hydrogen. But there would then be no chemistry, and perhaps no complexity. Should that be so, one might reject Smolin's ideas entirely"; Martin Rees, *Before the Beginning: Our Universe and Others* (London: Simon and Schuster, 1997), p. 269, n. 2. Rees continues, "However one could then test a modified prediction: that our universe produces more black holes than any other *in which conditions are*

equally propitious for complex evolution." It is unclear why one would make this further prediction, though, for what would direct the process toward maximum production of conditions propitious to complex evolution?

102. See Gilbert Harman, *Thought* (Princeton: Princeton University Press, 1973), pp. 135–140; Peter Railton, "A Deductive-Nomological Model of Probabilistic Explanation," *Philosophy of Science* 45 (1978): 206–226.

103. Among the issues cosmology investigates is how homogeneity is maintained across a universe. What would occur if such homogeneity were not maintained? Eventually, when these parts do get to interact, might there be clashes sufficiently great to produce an instability that would destroy the existing universe? A certain evenness in the universe then might be necessary for its stability. And that evenness, that homogeneity, might be maintained by nonlocal superluminal influences. If the world were wholly local, divergences among different localities would (we are supposing) arise that eventually would interact, clash, and mutually destruct. Nonlocality thus might enable the universe to maintain a compatible homogeneity across the board, and hence to remain continuingly stable. (This nonlocality would not be due to separated particles that had a common source in each of their past light cones, and so it would be a new phenomenon. What in particular are the nonlocal phenomena that would maintain large-scale but scattered homogeneity of the universe, a homogeneity the cosmologists otherwise have trouble accounting for? Which types of superluminal influences might play a role in the far-flung coordination that is conducive to a universe's long-term survival?) These considerations might point out a desirable effect of the quantum-mechanical character of the universe, but they do not yet explain why this characteristic exists. The position adumbrated here need not run afoul of various no-signaling theorems. The coordination among far-flung places need not be a causal one or subject to signaling. It just has to establish an order that does not allow far-flung pieces to be in sufficient disharmony that when they do eventually come together, via processes that propagate no faster than the speed of light, the clash produces sufficient instability to destroy the system.

104. Is there anything in the cosmological theories that corresponds to competition among the progeny universes, and might quantum mechanics enter there as well? Or is it simply that the quantum-mechanical universes tend to generate more and to last longer, without having any tendency to eliminate each other?

105. See my discussion of the notion of biological function in *The Nature of Rationality,* pp. 117–119.

106. You might expect, however, that we would live in the very longest-lived world, not simply in an average one, even when the process of averaging gives great weight to long-livedness. But it is not most likely that we live in the most stable world rather than in the average world (as specified by the expected value of all the worlds, weighted by stability).

However, there is another issue about combining the evolutionary cosmology that explains the existence of quantum mechanics with an extrapolation of the Feynman path-integral approach. The evolutionary cosmology requires the actual existence of each of the different universes it considers. Whereas the generalization of the path-integral approach countenances only one actuality, which is the average of all the possibilities. (Would it be of any help to see those possibilities as components of some large superposition?) How might the tension between these two approaches be resolved?

107. It would be instructive someday to trace a path from these rudimentary beginnings to the more developed but still most primitive state $[B_0, S_0, T_0]$ of brane theory that we imagined previously. Or starting with this primitive state, could evolutionary cosmology provide an engine to propel it to later brane states?

4. The Realm of Consciousness

1. With virtual-reality devices and their foreseeable future development, actual reality seems to have caught up with my thought experiment in *Anarchy, State, and Utopia* twenty-five years ago of the experience machine (Robert Nozick, *Anarchy, State, and Utopia* [New York: Basic Books, 1974], pp. 42–45). In view of the widespread expectations that such very sophisticated information technology will enhance our knowledge, it is worth noting that it may turn out to *diminish* the amount that we know.

Descartes asked how we could know we are not dreaming or being systematically deceived by an evil demon. His not very satisfactory answer took a long route through attempting to prove the existence of a good God who would not allow us to be constantly deceived. A more up-to-date version of the skeptical question is to ask how we can know we are not (and have not always been) on an experience machine or a virtual-reality machine. It seems we cannot know this on the basis of the experiences we have had, for the machine could produce these very experiences. And if we do not know that we are not in the experience machine, if we do not know that the reality we encounter is not merely virtual, then how can I know that I am actually writing this now, and how can you know that you are actually reading this book right now?

How can we know we are not (and have not always been) on an experience or a virtual-reality machine? In *Philosophical Explanations* (Cambridge, Mass.: The Belknap Press of Harvard University Press, 1981), I held that knowledge that p involves *tracking* the truth that p, so that (among other things) if the proposition p weren't true, you wouldn't believe it. A surprising consequence is this: you don't now know that you are not in a suitably designed experience or virtual-reality machine that is giving you your current experience; however, you *do* know you are reading this page right now. You are tracking this last fact: if it weren't true, you wouldn't believe it. Your tracking this fact depends upon what actually would or might be happening if you weren't reading this page right now.

However, the existence and widespread use in the future of virtual-reality machines changes the situation so that you no longer will be *tracking* such particular truths. No longer will it hold that if you weren't reading this page, you wouldn't believe you were. For you still might believe it, if an experience or virtual-reality machine gave you the reading experience; and that is the kind of thing that well could be happening then. Just as you cannot trust your senses at a convention of magicians, so you cannot trust your beliefs in a world of virtual-reality machines. Therefore, with the widespread existence of virtual-reality machines, the amount of what we *know* will be drastically curtailed. Our true beliefs may expand, but our *tracking of truths*, and hence our knowledge, will greatly contract! The existence and widespread use of these machines will undercut everyone's tracking, including that of people who do not use such machines. The experience machine's mere existence in the society raises the real possibility that, unbeknownst to people, they have been placed on this machine, and that alone is sufficient to interfere with their actual tracking. (For no longer will it hold that if the proposition weren't true they wouldn't believe it; they still might if it were instilled or simulated by an experience or virtual-reality machine.) Thereby, the amount of things people *know* will diminish.

2. Yet, if other ways of doing that thing could easily have arisen in the evolutionary process, we might search for some additional thing that consciousness (somewhat more specially) does, as its function.

3. There has been much recent controversy over the extent to which the evolutionary process is an optimizing process. Not everything has been directly selected for, so the question may be over what percentage of our (interesting) traits and characteristics has a specific (selected-for) function, as opposed to being a side effect of the concatenation of other factors that themselves were directly selected for. Or the question may be over the extent to which those traits and organs that do have a function that was directly selected for, carry out that function in an optimal fashion. (See John Dupre, ed., *The Latest on the Best: Essays on Evolution and Optimality* [Cambridge, Mass.: MIT Press, 1987].) If, as appears evident, evolution is a process of maximizing subject to certain constraints, then it is unclear what the last issue comes to. Sometimes organs and structures will be jerry-built out of what happened to be genetically available for shaping, and these materials will constitute constraints on how well the resulting organ will carry out its function. Nevertheless, it seems a useful research strategy to presume that evolution is an optimizing process, and that organs are maximally performing their functions. When some organ or trait apparently is performing suboptimally, given the known constraining factors and the presumed functions or purposes, that fact should prompt a search for further relevant factors. There may be further constraining factors to add to those previously known, so that relative to these (new) total constraints the performance is now seen to be optimal. And there may be further functions to discover, so that this organ is optimally serving that (new) mix of functions. Or we may discover both further constraints and further functions, so that the organ is performing that new mix of functions optimally given that new combination of constraints. To be sure, one then wants to check these new hypotheses, deriving further testable consequences from them so that they are not simply *ad hoc*. The assumption of optimality, however, drives one toward discovering these further constraints and functions, and it seems likely to be (to use the terminology of Imre Lakatos) a progressive research program.

4. That does not *prove* this to be the function, but its being something that consciousness *does* is a necessary condition for its being consciousness' function.

5. Illusions are useful clues to how a system works; an adequate explanation of the system explains not only its veridical functioning and representations but also its illusions. When a certain perceptual illusion consistently occurs and it can be explained at a neuronal level, in terms of wiring diagrams of certain types of cells, this is an impressive achievement, showing that a certain kind of *experience* is given rise to, not by external phenomena but by the wiring and firing of cells.

6. See Rudiger von der Heydt, "Form Analysis in Visual Cortex," in *The Cognitive Neurosciences,* ed. Michael Gazzaniga (Cambridge, Mass.: MIT Press, 1995), chap. 23, for a discussion of the Kanizsa triangle and illusory contours; Daniel Schacter, *Memory Distortion* (Cambridge, Mass.: Harvard University Press, 1996); Stephen Kosslyn, *Image and Mind* (Cambridge, Mass.: Harvard University Press, 1980); idem, *Image and Brain* (Cambridge, Mass.: MIT Press, 1994).

7. To say that this third notion, being aware of something, is the basic notion is to say that the other notions can be *defined* in terms of it. In an ontological ordering, however, the capacity (for awareness) is more basic than the power (of awareness), which is more basic than the occurrent state (of awareness).

8. See Richard Dawkins, *The Blind Watchmaker* (New York: W. W. Norton, 1986), pp. 71–82.

9. On flow, see Mihaly Csikscentmihalyi, *Beyond Boredom and Anxiety* (San Francisco: Jossey-Bass, 1975); idem, *Flow* (New York: Harper & Row, 1990).

10. We sometimes distinguish mental items themselves (for instance, wishes or desires) as conscious or unconscious. It has been suggested that, rather than seeing this as a distinction in kinds of desires, the conscious kind and the unconscious kind, we should see it instead as a difference in whether or not we are aware *of* that mental item (whose kind does not vary with our awareness of it). (Fred Dretske, *Naturalizing the Mind* [Cambridge, Mass.: MIT Press, 1995], chap. 4, argues for this latter alternative.) That mental item *M* itself may be an awareness of something *S*, a mental registering of *S*. Yet there may be no awareness of *M* itself, no awareness of that registering in turn. In the case of perceptions, we might distinguish two senses of "conscious." In one sense, a perception is conscious when we are consciously aware (through the perception) of the *object* perceived. In another sense, a perception is conscious when we are aware *of the perception,* just as with the mental items beliefs and desires, what makes them conscious is being aware *of* them.

11. See Leo Weisskrantz, *Blindsight* (Oxford: Oxford University Press, 1986). Blindsight patients, in this way, can detect simple patterns, and also the presence and the direction of motion, and the localization of light. "Some subjects claim to be guessing on the basis of no subjective sense whatsoever . . . In other studies, patients report some 'feeling' that guides their responses, but the feeling is not described as specifically visual in nature. For example, patients will state that they felt the onset of a stimulus or felt it to be in a certain location. Shape discriminations between circles and crosses are made on the basis of 'jagged' versus 'smooth' feelings, which are nevertheless not subjectively visual"; Martha Farah, "Visual Percep-

tion and Visual Awareness after Brain Damage," reprinted in *The Nature of Consciousness,* ed. Ned Block, Owen Flanagan, and Guven Guzeldere (Cambridge, Mass.: MIT Press, 1997), p. 208.

12. The psychologist George Sperling reported the following experiment in 1960. Sperling showed psychological subjects a 3-by-3-inch grid of letters for a fraction of a second. The subjects claimed that they could see all the letters but could recall only three or four of them. After the exposure, Sperling asked them to report any randomly cued letter, and the people could accurately report any arbitrary letter, which suggests that they had fleeting access to all of them. (See Bernard Baars, *A Cognitive Theory of Consciousness* [Cambridge: Cambridge University Press, 1988], pp. 15–16, for this description of Sperling's experiment.) We might say that Sperling's procedure seems to uncover a case of registering, and (since the subjects claimed that they could see all the letters) of registering that it registered, but of its not having registered exactly what had registered. The subjects were consciously aware that they had seen everything but were not consciously aware of everything that they had seen. (The universal quantifier does not stand outside their outermost awareness. They are aware that for all x that has registered, they have seen x; but it is not the case that for all x, for each x, that has registered, they are aware that they have seen x.)

13. To be sure, upon some occasions a greater awareness of how one is moving might make one self-conscious and so might interfere with the smooth performance of the action.

14. Did consciousness first evolve for choice, with the function of aiding it, or did it evolve for another reason, but then choice was able to use the machinery of consciousness, which was lying around available to it?

15. It simplifies the wiring to have sensory receptors close to the cells that process their effects, and hence (since their effects give further information when analyzed together) close to each other. Brains are spatial concentrations of the neurons, and heads are the places where the chief sensory organs and the brain are located close together, thereby cutting down on signal transmission time and on reaction time.

16. For an illuminating, more detailed analysis of whether one fixed mode of behavior or instead behavior that contingently varies with the state of nature is optimal, an analysis that takes account of imperfections in the sensory detection mechanism and of the variations in fitness attendant upon different behaviors in different states of nature, see Eliot Sober, "The Adaptive Advantage of Learning versus *a priori* Prejudice," in his *From a Biological Point of View* (Cambridge: Cambridge University Press, 1994), pp. 50–70; and also Peter Godfrey-Smith, *Complexity and the Function of Mind in Nature* (Cambridge: Cambridge University Press, 1996), chaps. 7–8.

17. None of the required specificity will have been selected for—the particular situation has not occurred frequently enough for that—or any that was selected for may have succumbed to a more flexible and more fit procedure.

18. See Kosslyn, *Image and Mind* and *Image and Brain,* chaps. 3 and 10, also pp. 99–101.

19. "Consciousness may be associated only with the higher-quality end of the con-

tinuum of degrees of representation"; Farah, "Visual Perception and Visual Awareness," p. 205.

20. When operant behavior, behavior that is modifiable by its consequences, is rewarded only in the presence of a stimulus, the organism eventually will emit this behavior at a higher rate or magnitude when this stimulus is present than when it is absent. This stimulus then sets the stage for the operant response, and is termed a discriminative stimulus. B. F. Skinner calls this a three-termed contingency because of the three factors involved in this behavioral situation: the rewarding stimulus, the operant behavior that it rewards, and the discriminative stimulus that signals the occurrence of the reward for the behavior.

21. Bernard Baars writes, "Unconscious processors are excellent tools for dealing with whatever is known. Conscious capacity is called upon to deal with any degree of novelty"; and "We expect consciousness to be involved in learning of novel events, or novel connections between known events"; *A Cognitive Theory of Consciousness*, pp. 77, 214. Baars presents an inconclusive discussion on whether consciousness is a necessary condition for learning, and writes, "Even if conscious experience were not a necessary condition but only a helpful adjunct to the learning process . . ." (p. 217).

22. If this hypothesis is correct, then even the conditioning of a rat to press a bar involves its conscious awareness, for positively reinforcing bar pressing will increase the frequency of this activity only if the rat is consciously aware that there is a bar present (or is consciously aware of its bar-pressing muscular motions and spatial orientation toward the bar).

Eric Kandel has performed experiments on *Aplysia* showing habituation, sensitization, and classical conditioning of the gill-withdrawal reflex. (See Eric Kandel, James Schwartz, and Thomas Jessell, *Principles of Neural Science*, 3d ed. [New York: Elsevier, 1991], pp. 1010–18.) But will operant conditioning to a (new) discriminative stimulus appear that low on the evolutionary scale?

Another consequence of our hypothesis is a prediction of the existence of automated behavior, that is, some behavior for whose performance conscious awareness is required at first, but whose later performance can occur in the absence of conscious awareness.

23. It is thus that I would interpret the results in R. Kentridge, C. Heywood, and L. Weiskrantz, "Attention without Awareness in Blindsight," *Proceedings of the Royal Society, London B*, 1999, pp. 1805–11. (I am grateful to Ned Block for this reference.)

24. For this last conjecture, I am indebted to Martin Seligman (personal conversation). On biological preparedness and classical conditioning, see Martin Seligman and Joanne Hager, *Biological Boundaries of Learning* (New York: Appleton-Century-Crofts, 1972).

25. There are various sharpenings of this hypothesis that are possible, corresponding to aspects of stimulus control by a discriminative stimulus. Will conditioning to emit behavior be possible on a (familiar) discriminative stimulus that is new to that behavior (marking a new link between that behavior and reinforcement) but not on an absolutely new discriminative stimulus not heretofore encountered by the organ-

ism? Will the relational position of the stimulus (as opposed to its absolute position) show a greater diminution in control in the case of an impaired striate cortex? Will the differences in function with an impaired striate cortex be greatest with successive discriminations rather than with simultaneous ones? Will the shape of the generalization gradients along one dimension be different if the striate cortex is impaired? Will transfers of learning be interfered with when the relevant dimension is changed (extradimensional shift) so that, when the striate cortex is impaired, it will be more difficult for more-abstract properties to serve as the discriminative stimulus?

For surveys of aspects of stimulus control and discriminative stimuli, see H. S. Terrace, "Stimulus Control," in *Operant Behavior,* ed. Werner Honig (New York: Appleton-Century-Crofts, 1966), pp. 271–344; Mark Rilling, "Stimulus Control and Inhibitory Processes," in *Handbook of Operant Behavior,* ed. Werner Honig and J. E. R. Staddon (Englewood Cliffs, N.J.: Prentice-Hall, 1977), pp. 432–480; N. J. Mackintosh, "Stimulus Control: Attentional Factors," ibid., pp. 481–513; James Mazur, *Learning and Behavior* (Englewood Cliffs, N.J.: Prentice-Hall, 1986), pp. 231–252.

26. Stephen Kosslyn has informed me that there are results showing paired-associate learning during anesthesia, and that Robert Rafal has some results showing that stimuli presented to the blind field in patients with homonymous hemianopia nevertheless can cue detection of a subsequent stimulus in the good field; some similar results with neglect patients show that the time they require to make a decision about a stimulus in the "neglected" field is sensitive to properties of the stimulus, even though the patients are unaware of having seen it.

27. G. E. Hinton, J. L. McClelland, and D. E. Rumelhart, "Distributed Representations," in *Parallel Distributed Processing,* ed. David Rumelhart and James McClelland, vol. 1 (Cambridge, Mass.: MIT Press, 1986), especially pp. 91–96.

28. In William Bechtel and George Graham, eds., *A Companion to Cognitive Science* (Oxford: Blackwell, 1998), see Robert Stufflebeam, "Representation and Computation," pp. 636–648, and Dorrit Billman, "Representations," pp. 649–659. For the view that the vehicles of representation can be syntactic items, connectionist distributed patterns of activity, or complex temporally and spatially extended processes and interactions, provided, in each case, that the functional role of these is that of carrying information, see Andy Clark, *Being There* (Cambridge, Mass.: MIT Press, 1997), chap. 8. There is disagreement in the literature about what constitutes a state's carrying information. One might want to investigate the notion of forming a representation of an item *as a T*, where the representational states are, in general, correlated with *T*'s and are the product of selection for being better correlated with *T*'s, and which function as part of a receptor-effector system that produces and mediates adaptive responses to *T*'s. The representation's function is to be a state that is correlated with *T*'s and that plays a role in producing adaptive responses to *T*'s. Consider the situation of auditory masking, in which a person pays attention to the ambiguous sentence (such as "He went to the bank") that constitutes input into one ear, and reports not hearing what is fed into the other ear, yet when what is fed into

the second ear can disambiguate the sentence in the first (e.g., "water," "money"), this affects his interpretation of what he has heard. The sound that is fed into the ear he is inattentive to is represented below the level of conscious awareness *as* having a particular semantic content. The stranger in town who, in the joke, asks someone what subway stop to get off at, and is told, "Get off one stop before I do," when he reaches that stop, does have a representation of it, but he does not represent it *as* the station one station before the one his informant will disembark at.

29. For those who cannot bear suspense, the condition is this, where common registration is like common knowledge, except with registration in place of knowledge: The representation *R* is commonly registered (in the relevant parts of the brain) as part of a system of such common registration.

30. Let us pause to consider why a subset must be marked for further intensive processing. We do not have sufficient processing power to intensively analyze and process each possibly relevant bit of current and remembered information. If our processing capacity was greater or if our information was less, it might then be possible to process every bit intensively. (Even in that case, though, such extensive processing would require more extensive caloric support, and hence would be inefficient as compared to a more selective processing system.) It is the *ratio* of available information to processing power that necessitates the selective processing of information.

Bernard Baars holds that the limitations of conscious processing capacity in a brain of huge unconscious processing capacity presents a puzzle requiring explanation. Such an explanation is provided, Baars claims, by his global-workspace theory of consciousness. Unconscious processors (and coalitions of them) compete for access to the general facility that broadcasts information to all unconscious processors throughout the system. To be thus generally broadcast is what constitutes something as conscious information. The explanation of the limited capacity of conscious processors then runs as follows. (See Baars, *A Cognitive Theory of Consciousness*, pp. 91–92. The descriptions that follow are paraphrases or quotations from Baars. The parenthesized comments are mine.) Conscious contents must be internally consistent because a broadcast message requires the cooperation of many specialized processors, and if it ran into powerful competition from other unconscious processors, it could not maintain its access to or current control over the broadcasting facility. (We ask: why could not consciousness be inconsistent, broadcasting in parallel?) Because conscious processes must be consistent, Baars writes, they must be serial, for different messages that cannot be unified into a single message can be shown only one after the other. Unconscious processors can operate in parallel, but conscious ones must be serial. (We notice that Baars derives seriality from consistency, whereas his first explanation of consistency *presupposes* seriality, in that the consistency requirement upon global broadcasts would not apply if such broadcasts could be done in parallel.) Conscious processes have limited capacity because they must be internally consistent. An internally consistent message "must exclude irrelevant or contradictory messages that may come up at the same time. Such messages are likely to exist somewhere in some of the distributed processors, and are therefore a part of the system. But they cannot gain access to the blackboard, unless they can drive off the current message, or unless it leaves the blackboard of its own accord." (Again, this presupposes that consciousness is serial rather than parallel; if it could be parallel, none of this would follow. So there remains a puzzle as to why consciousness cannot be parallel, and consequently of much vaster capacity.)

Leaving Baars aside, it might help if we thought of consciousness as *one* processor, rather than as an analog to *all* the unconscious processors together. Still, the question would remain of why more power has not been devoted to consciousness. But do we know how much power and capacity is so devoted? (How would we measure this? By the number of neurons involved? the energetic requirements?) What we know is a limitation of *tasks* at one time, but this holds for each unconscious processor also. The question, then, is why there are not many conscious processors, acting simultaneously in parallel. What would make them all conscious (if no one is watching them all); would it be a *split* consciousness, comparable to split-brain experiences? The alternative of many parallel conscious processors is not completely clear, and so neither is the explanatory question of why consciousness is serial rather than multiply parallel. (Are parallel conscious processors what the "many minds" interpretation of quantum mechanics requires? See David Albert, *Quantum Mechanics and Experience* [Cambridge, Mass.: Harvard University Press, 1992], pp. 130–133, 186–189.)

31. I owe this suggestion to Edward Furshpan (personal conversation).

32. Consider the difference between programming a task in machine language and programming that task in a higher-order programming language. The higher-order language "chunks" groups of machine-language instructions constituting frequently repeated (and semantically interpretable) operations, so that they can be used and built upon as a unit. This chunking makes it feasible to keep track of particular groups of instructions, to combine them into larger units, and to form new operations.

33. See Gilbert Harman, *Change in View* (Cambridge, Mass.: MIT Press, 1986), for a discussion of the unmanageability of such systems.

34. Choice by human beings can involve further processes. Information can be weighed, assessed, and compared to other information. It can be given a weight in decision that depends upon its relation to other factors, and it can enter as reasons or evidence in the weighting of still further factors. Some of this might occur below the level of conscious awareness (through the information's feeding into a mechanical operation of rules of assessment, weighting, and choice), yet it seems that the guidance could occur more subtly and with greater sensitivity if it were conscious.

We have considered the function for the individual of being consciously aware of various internal and external facts. (We shall turn later to the question of the role and function of conscious *experience*.) Does consciousness also have a *social function*? What you are consciously aware of, another can more easily learn, either because you are able intentionally to communicate this, or because your externally observable behavior exhibits better what you are consciously aware of than does what merely registers upon you. When information is transmitted, the benefits of joint action on the basis of shared information become possible, and there are individual benefits each receives from the information transmitted by the other conscious members of the group. You cannot say (or so easily show) what you aren't consciously aware of. Conscious awareness facilitates the transmission of information, and there would be selection among coevolving organisms for the capacity to transmit registered information, and for the capacity to receive such transmission. Merely possessing automatic rules that utilize whatever information unconsciously registers upon you, and being conspecific with organisms exactly like that entails a diminution in each organism's information that is relevant to choice. We would predict, then, that conscious awareness (in a greater degree) would attend and develop in tandem with the capacity to communicate.

Receiving communicated information brings benefits to an individual, without comparable costs. Communicating information also brings benefits when further information is immediately returned. There would be no individual selective advantage for a mutation that could receive but not communicate *any* information; such a mutation would not spread in the gene pool. However, a selective mutation that masked some things the organism was consciously aware of, e.g., an intent to deceive others, might be selected for, as would the ability to detect such masking, in an escalating "arms race." There is a need, therefore, for a game-theoretical analysis of the evolutionary contours of communicated information.

When conscious awareness is attended by or takes the form of phenomenology, that is, of conscious *experience,* this may heighten the transmission of information. This social aspect of conscious awareness and phenomenology might play a role in its being selected for.

Once an ability to communicate beliefs or sensed events exists, others can use the communicated information to check their own beliefs, partially bringing their estimates of the facts into accord with yours (as in Bayesian procedures that produce convergence in belief). Others are as likely to be as correct in their belief as you are, and the probability of your being correct increases as your belief is brought closer to the mean in the group. (So a tendency to conformity in belief, as exhibited in the Solomon Asch experiments, might be of benefit.)

35. The body's homeostatic mechanisms also will have multiple checks of things, such as bodily temperature, that do not rise into consciousness. However, these multiple checks do not get merged or synthesized into a unified representation. They do not pass into the equivalent of *one* three-dimensional image.

36. P. Cavanagh, "Multiple Analyses of Orientation in the Visual System," reprinted in *Frontiers in Cognitive Neuroscience,* ed. Stephen Kosslyn and Richard Andersen (Cambridge, Mass.: MIT Press, 1992), pp. 52–61.

37. See David Hubel, *Eye, Brain, and Vision* (New York: W. H. Freeman, 1995), pp. 206–207; and see also the computational model in Patricia Churchland and Terrence Sejnowski, *The Computational Brain* (Cambridge, Mass.: MIT Press, 1992), pp. 188–221.

38. Andrew Parker et al., "Multiple Cues for Three-dimensional Shape," in Gazzaniga, *The Cognitive Neurosciences,* p. 355.

39. Many interactions between cues can be described by simple linear pooling, but there are exceptions; ibid., p. 362.

40. See Barry Stein et al., "Neural Mechanisms Mediating Attention and Orientation to Multisensory Cues," in Gazzaniga, *The Cognitive Neurosciences*, p. 687. See also Barry Stein and Alex Meredith, *The Merging of the Senses* (Cambridge, Mass.: MIT Press, 1993).

41. On the notion of biological function, see Robert Nozick, *The Nature of Rationality* (Princeton: Princeton University Press, 1993), pp. 117–119. The view in the text would fit in with Stephen Kosslyn's hypothesis that consciousness is a parity check, a sign that neural activity in diverse locations is mutually consistent. See Stephen Kosslyn and Oliver Koenig, *Wet Mind* (New York: Free Press, 1992), pp. 431–437.

42. Some writers have held that consciousness is divided when the corpus callosum is severed, and that this shows there always are two consciousnesses residing in human beings, the two consciousnesses usually being in close communication. We might hold instead that when the hemispheres communicate through the corpus callosum, there is so widespread a synthesis and mutual coordination of representations as to constitute one unified consciousness. When the cut is made, consciousness is *then* divided, for the synthesis no longer takes place to the same degree, but this does not show that consciousness always was divided before the cut, although this division was unnoticed then. To say that *P*'s being absent when *X* is decomposed means that *P* never was there, even when *X* was composed, is to commit the fallacy of decomposition.

Notice that Thomas Nagel's very interesting early article on cerebral commissurotomy insists, when asking how many consciousnesses reside in each hemisphere, that the answer be given as a whole number (Thomas Nagel, "Brain Bisection and the Unity of Consciousness," *Synthèse* 22 [1971]). It also is worth considering fractional answers, for instance, that both before and after bisection there is half in each hemisphere. One even should consider fractional answers that may vary depending upon the actual connections occurring between the hemispheres, for instance, that there is half a consciousness in each hemisphere before bisection, and a whole consciousness in each hemisphere afterward; or, more interestingly, that there is no determinate fraction in either hemisphere before bisection because there is insufficient separation and independence of function then, and there is less than one consciousness in each hemisphere afterward, because of truncated functioning. See also Donald MacKay, "Divided Brains—Divided Minds?" in *Mindwaves*, ed. Colin Blakemore and Susan Greenfield (Oxford: Oxford University Press, 1987), pp. 5–16.

43. We might give this claim a verificationist cast by saying that although some synthesis has taken place, further routes (that should detect the same objective fact, if indeed it exists) fail to reach this fact.

44. Enrico Fermi is said to have remarked of a physicist's talk, "That's not even wrong." One might say of something that it isn't even subjective, i.e., that it is not objective enough to be synthesized and hence to rise to subjective consciousness.

45. Rudiger von der Heydt reports that no one cue guarantees success in detecting the boundaries or occluded contours of objects; what is needed is the convergence of several different cues at once; "Form Analysis in Visual Cortex," p. 375.

46. For a discussion of when an action will be based upon an objective representation of the fact, see the passage from Andy Clark quoted in Chapter 2.

47. However, Semir Zeki makes these separate analyses less surprising. "In order to be able to extract the invariant features of stimuli and thus categorize objects according to these invariant properties, the brain has evolved the not unreasonable strategy of using different compartments (cortical areas) to identify different invariant attributes of our environment, for example, touch and sound, quite simply because the cortical machinery required to extract the invariant features varies according to the property"; *A Vision of the Brain* (Oxford: Blackwell Scientific, 1993), p. 242.

48. A mapping is transitively topographic over all its stages when, for any three stages and any three neurons at each of those stages, X, Y, and Z at the first stage, X', Y' and Z' at an intermediate stage, and X", Y", and Z" at a later stage, if X projects to X', which projects to X", Y projects to Y', which projects to Y", and Z projects to Z', which projects to Z", then if Y is between X and Z, Y" will be between X" and Z".

49. However, Bernard Baars (*A Cognitive Theory of Consciousness*, p. 361) suggests that all consciousness (including of beliefs, intentions, etc.) involves qualia but that we are unaware of this because the qualia are very fleeting and hard to retrieve. That seems a stretch.

50. See the essays by Bizzi, Andersen, Ghez, Sparks, McNaughton, Jordan, and Graziano in Gazzaniga, *The Cognitive Neuroscience*, chaps. 31, 33, 35, 36, 37, 38, and 67.

51. For a start, see the psychological literature on multidimensional scaling, e.g., Roger Shepard, A. Kimball Romney, and Sara Beth Nerlove, *Multidimensional Scaling* (New York: Seminar Press, 1992).

52. On the binding problem and issues of cortical integration, see Zeki, *A Vision of the Brain*, chaps. 29–32; Francis Crick, *The Astonishing Hypothesis* (New York: Scribner, 1994), pp. 203–214; Antonio Damasio, *Descartes' Error* (New York: Putnam, 1994), pp. 94–96; Antonio Damasio and Hanna Damasio, "Brain and Language," *Scientific American*, September 1992, p. 91; Eric Kandel and Thomas Jessell, "Touch," in Kandel, Schwartz, and Jessell, *Principles of Neural Science*, pp. 380–381; Wolf Singer, "Time as Coding Space in Neocortical Processing," in Gazzaniga, *The Cognitive Neurosciences*, chap. 6.

53. After writing this material, I came across Charles Gallistel, *The Organization of Learning* (Cambridge, Mass.: MIT Press, 1990), who cites earlier work by Anne Treisman, and writes (p. 525) that "the time and space coordinates . . . are what enable search processes to move from record to record, assembling a coherent, unified representation of the experience, the kind required for intelligent behavior."

54. There is another suggestion about binding in the current literature, namely that it occurs through temporal coordination, by a correlated firing of neurons. Neurons associated with aspects of one object will fire at the same moment; neu-

rons associated with two distinct objects will fire at two different moments. Crick and Koch suggested that such correlated firing at 40 Hertz, that is, firing every 25 milliseconds, might be the neural correlate of visual awareness. (See Francis Crick and C. Koch, "Towards a Neurobiological Theory of Consciousness," *Seminars in the Neurosciences* 2 [1990], 263–275.) Two different objects that are sensed simultaneously therefore will not, under this hypothesis, register exactly simultaneously further up the line. Suppose object A has properties P_1, P_2, and P_3, and object B has properties Q_1, Q_2, and Q_3. Simultaneous firing binds P_1 with P_2 rather than with Q_2 because the neurons registering P_1 and P_2 fire simultaneously, and at different instants from the neurons registering Q_1 (which also are firing at 40 Hertz). Earlier I spoke of the presumptive principle that two things cannot be in the same place at the same time. This could be combined with the correlated-firing hypothesis to suggest that binding occurs through spatial coordination in different topographic maps, coordinated *temporally* by correlated firings.

55. Once we have a correct theory of binding (not necessarily the one proposed here), we can ask what features of objects as represented or experienced might be side effects of this form of binding. Do external objects actually have these features, or is it an artifact that is imposed by our form of sensory processing? Might some apparently necessary features of objects (e.g., that they are spatio-temporal) be artifactual? Or is it that the binding process makes use of structures that actually are universally present? See also the section "Necessity and Contingency" in Chapter 3.

56. This is meant to be a specification of when there is one particular sort of "conscious awareness," experiential felt phenomenological quality, and it presupposes the more general account of conscious awareness in general, for instance, the one that we complete in the next section.

57. To "register" is to leave a mark, and this notion does not here build in the notion of consciousness. (Cf. the blindsight phenomenon.) Must it not only register there but also have further decisional effects, e.g., be responded to, acted upon, or at least affect behavioral dispositions? It seems plausible to think that degrees of consciousness will correspond, in part, to differences in the amount of data synthesized, the number of different stages of synthesis and of separate branches leading into it, the number and nature of the topographic maps, the degree of binding, and the highest place in the decision apparatus that the representation eventually reaches. The function of conscious awareness, and of felt phenomenology in particular, is to register objective facts in a way in which they may contingently be acted upon. Shall we say that conscious awareness turns a fact that registers into information that can be used?

58. Farah, "Visual Perception and Visual Awareness," especially pp. 203–206.

59. See the Model I presented by Baars in *A Cognitive Theory of Consciousness*.

60. So far as I know, the first statement that game theory needed this infinite layering of knowledge appeared in my doctoral dissertation, *The Normative Theory of Individual Choice* (Princeton University, 1963), published by Garland Publishing (New York, 1990), pp. 273–274. There I wrote:

P1 and P2 are in a finite two-person zero-sum game-theoretic situation vis-à-vis each other iff

(1)(a) P1 knows he has available to him actions $A_1, \ldots, A_n$ (n is greater than or equal to 2)
  (b) P2 knows he has available to him actions $B_1, \ldots, B_m$ (m is greater than or equal to 2)
  (c) neither P1 nor P2 believes that any other actions are available to him.
(2) Denoting the outcome of P1's doing A_i and P2's doing B_j by "$O_{i,j}$" both P1 and P2 know what $O_{1,1}, \ldots, O_{n,m}$ are.
(3) Both P1 and P2 satisfy the von Neumann–Morgenstern postulates (or similar postulates) over the set of outcomes of these actions and probability mixtures of their outcomes.
(4) P1 prefers x to y iff P2 prefers y to x where x and y are outcomes or probability mixtures of outcomes.
  From this and (3) it follows that P1 is indifferent between x and y iff P2 is indifferent between x and y. Furthermore it is possible to define utility functions u_1 (which is P1's) and u_2 (which is P2's) such that for all x, $u_1(x) = -u_2(x)$.
(5) It is not the case that $u_1(O_{i,j}) = u_1(O_{k,l})$ for all i,j,k,l.
(6) It is not the case that both P1 and P2 have actions available to them which dominate all others.
(7)(a) P1 knows (1)–(6)
  (b) P2 knows (1)–(6).
(8)(a) P1 knows (7)(b)
  (b) P2 knows (7)(a).
(9)(a) P1 knows (8)(b)
  (b) P2 knows (8)(a).
  ⋮
(n)(a) P1 knows (n)−(1)(b)
  (b) P2 knows (n)−(1)(a).
  ⋮

When I wrote that game theory presumed this notion of knowledge of knowledge of . . . , etc., going up an infinite number of levels (as represented by the final three dots), I thought of this as a mere finicky detail and did not realize the deep interest of the point. I hope to partially remedy that omission here.

In my dissertation, I specified the notion of common knowledge (without using a special term for it) by an infinite conjunction of knowings about knowings. David Lewis named and specified the notion of common knowledge and, more importantly, put it to fruitful use in his book *Convention* (Cambridge, Mass.: Harvard University Press, 1969). Instead of using an infinite conjunction, he used a self-referential definition (involving what now would be called a fixed point) where S: everyone knows that p and everyone knows that S.

61. A book-length and extremely illuminating, though technical, discussion of the notion of common knowledge and its implications is contained in Ronald Fagin, Joseph Y. Halpern, Yoram Moses, and Moshe Y. Vardi, *Reasoning about Knowledge* (Cambridge, Mass.: MIT Press, 1995).

62. Notice that the account offered earlier might be correct, even if this particular way of filling in the further important condition is not.

63. See Fagin et al., *Reasoning about Knowledge,* pp. 3–7, 24–30.

64. See ibid., pp. 176–183.

65. See Rumelhart and McClelland, *Parallel Distributed Processing,* vol. 1, chaps. 1–3.

66. The broadcasting throughout the system that Bernard Baars describes would continue to face this problem, though.

67. Robert Aumann, "Agreeing to Disagree," *Annals of Statistics* 4 (1976): 1236–39. See also Fagin et al., *Reasoning about Knowledge,* pp. 184–190.

68. See the discussion of "simultaneous Byzantine agreement" in Fagin et al., *Reasoning about Knowledge,* pp. 190–197.

69. When a low E string on an open guitar is plucked, the fundamental E frequency and all its overtones (integer multiples of the fundamental) are excited. Neighboring strings that are tuned to the fundamental or an overtone will then vibrate "sympathetically" because of the coupling through the air.

If a beam of sound containing many frequencies is sent past a tuning fork tuned to a particular number of cycles per second, then the sound of that particular frequency, being in resonance with the fork, will cause the prongs to vibrate as its energy is absorbed.

Another example of interactive vibrations—resonance—would involve two oscillatory systems that are weakly coupled, such as the Earth's atmosphere and the moon.

Physics, of course, it full of examples of, and analyses of, oscillators (harmonic, forced) and of resonance phenomena, down to the atomic and particle level.

70. For surveys of this literature, see Wolfe Singer, "Visual Feature Integration and the Temporal Correlation Hypothesis," *Annual Review of Neuroscience* 18 (1995): 555–586; idem, "Neural Synchronization: A Solution to the Binding Problem?" in *The Mind-Brain Continuum,* ed. Rodolfo Llinas and Patricia Churchland (Cambridge, Mass.: MIT Press, 1996), pp. 101–130; and C. von der Malsburg, "The Binding Problem of Neural Networks," ibid., pp. 131–146.

Singer and others have written: "The system of tangential intracortical connections, or the reciprocal projections from other cortical areas may provide the anatomical substrate for the synchronization of oscillatory responses between remote columns"; C. M. Gray, P. Konig, A. K. Engel, and W. Singer, "Oscillatory Responses in Cat Visual Cortex Exhibit Inter-Columnar Synchronization Which Reflects Global Stimulus Properties," *Nature* 338 (1989): 334–337, reprinted in Kosslyn and Andersen, *Frontiers in Cognitive Science,* pp. 49–51.

71. See Gerald Edelman, *Neural Darwinism* (New York: Basic Books, 1987).

72. "CNS neurons have been shown to generate both action potentials and subthreshold oscillations that cyclically modulate their synaptic responsiveness. Such membrane properties are present in a large variety of interconnected neurons of the thalamus and cerebral cortex, thus promoting network resonance and the emergence of attractor states . . . The neuronal oscillation in specific thalamic nuclei establish cortical resonance through direct activation of pyramidal cells"; Rodolfo

Llinas and D. Pare, "The Brain as a Closed System Modulated by the Senses," in Llinas and Churchland, *The Mind-Brain Continuum,* pp. 9, 12.

73. To be sure, one question is left open by our current view, namely, why the brain does its common registering *that way,* for instance, at 40 megahertz rather than at, say, 80 MHz, or by one particular oscillatory coupling and resonant state rather than another. That is a question for (evolutionary) neuroscientists.

74. Alexander Borbely and Giulio Tononi, "The Quest for the Essence of Sleep," *Daedalus* 127, no. 2 (Spring 1998): 176.

75. Notice that John Searle's and Ned Block's various examples—the Chinese Room, etc.—lack the feature of common registration. See Ned Block, "Troubles with Functionalism," reprinted in *Readings in Philosophy of Psychology,* ed. Ned Block, vol. 1, (Cambridge, Mass.: Harvard University Press, 1980), especially pp. 275–280; John Searle, "Minds, Brains, and Programs," *Behavioral and Brain Sciences* 3 (1980): 417–424; idem, *Minds, Brains, and Science* (Cambridge, Mass.: Harvard University Press, 1984).

76. For a discussion of what can be achieved by various approximations of common knowledge, see Fagin et al., pp. 411–422.

Might consciousness be especially needed for *unreliable* processes, in order to check that they are proceeding correctly? Highly reliable processes can be routinized and handled automatically, or at any rate without conscious checking.

77. A person can be consciously aware of some things although some portion of the brain is missing or contains lesions. The broadcasting and the common registration need not be universal if its scope is sufficiently wide.

78. In Chapter 1, we saw that a particular truth is timeless (and spaceless) only when it registers everywhere and everywhen. All truth is timeless (and spaceless) only when each and every truth *commonly* registers everywhere and everywhen. (If some truth *p* hadn't commonly registered, then there would be some place-time where some particular truth about *p*'s iterated level of registration had not itself registered.) Would this constitute the universe as conscious; is all truth timeless (and spaceless) only in a fully conscious universe? Is this a consequence that proponents of the timelessness of all truth can swallow?

79. See Paul Churchland, *The Engine of Reason, the Seat of the Soul* (Cambridge, Mass.: MIT Press, 1995), chap. 2, for a discussion of vector coding.

80. If, however, there was a name for each sensory receptor and for each level of activation—fourteen names in all—one could arrive at compositional names of their 10,000 possible combinations. Still, seeing and keeping track of the relationships of their referents, or the precise place of one in relation to some others, would continue to constitute an extremely formidable task, in the absence of discernable phenomenological "feels."

81. If underdetermination of theory leads to phenomenology as a specification of an interpretation of the data, one would not expect this to arise at the level of reflex behavior, for no representation of the data, beyond the impinging of the data itself, is necessary to elicit the reflex. So at what behavioral level is a representation of the data first needed (is it Pavlovian conditioning; operant conditioning?) so that phenomenology arises only then?

82. I ignore the complications introduced by Roger Shepard's ascending sequence of sounds. For very detailed investigation, see Carol Krumhansl, *Cognitive Foundations of Musical Pitch* (New York: Oxford University Press, 1990).

83. Other things, not just experiences, can match the stimuli in structure. Among mathematical objects (numbers, vectors, etc.), we can find many structures isomorphic to features of the stimuli. For instance, numbers refer to the amplitude of the incoming waves; the greater the amplitude, the higher the number. The transitivity of the "higher than" relation among the numbers matches the transitivity of the "greater than" relation among the amplitudes.

84. Here is an anecdote of my earliest teaching years, which occurred either in my year as a twenty-four-year-old, not-yet-endoctored instructor, or my year as a twenty-six-year-old assistant professor at Princeton University. I had given a seminar on Nelson Goodman's *The Structure of Appearance* (Cambridge, Mass.: Harvard University Press, 1951) to two third-year undergraduates in philosophy (John Earman, who became a distinguished philosopher of science; and Martin Seligman, who became a distinguished psychologist). When Nelson Goodman came to Princeton to give a talk on the material soon to be published as *Languages of Art,* since I had just given a seminar on this earlier book of his I was asked to introduce him on the occasion of his talk. Goodman had sent written questions ahead for us to think about, and one of these was "Can two paintings be visually indistinguishable yet differ in aesthetic value?" Having learned from *The Structure of Appearance* of the intricacies of the (nontransitive) matching relation, in my introduction of Goodman I predicted that he would make the following argument. Painting A can be visually indistinguishable from painting B, which can be visually indistinguishable from painting C, which . . . can be visually indistinguishable from painting Z, yet A can visually be clearly distinguishable from Z and can differ from it in aesthetic value. *If* being visually indistinguishable was sufficient for having exactly the same aesthetic value, then A would have to have exactly the same aesthetic value as B, B as C, . . . , and Y as Z. Since "having exactly the same aesthetic value" is a transitive relation, A would have to have exactly the same aesthetic value as Z. Since A does not have exactly the same aesthetic value as Z, it follows that two paintings' being visually indistinguishable is *not* sufficient for their having the same aesthetic value, and moreover, that at least once along the line, there were two adjacent visually indistinguishable paintings of different aesthetic value. (This was an argument I would not have thought of had I not read Goodman's *The Structure of Appearance.*) Well, although Goodman *did* say that two paintings could be visually indistinguishable yet differ in aesthetic value (because you cannot be sure now that you will never learn to see a difference between two paintings merely by looking, and because knowing of some difference, such as the artist who painted one of the paintings, might lead you to train yourself to distinguish between them, and hence to scrutinize the two paintings in different ways now), he did *not* offer *this* (Goodmanian) argument for that conclusion in his lecture or later in chapter 3 of his published *Languages of Art* (Indianapolis: Bobbs-Merrill, 1968). A mystery! Once or twice since then I asked Goodman about this, but I did not understand his answer.

85. A very strong stimulus can activate several different kinds of sensory recep-

tors. See John Martin, "Coding and Processing of Sensory Information," in Kandel, Schwartz, and Jesell, *Principles of Neural Science*, chap. 23.

86. Lloyd D. Partridge and Donald L. Partridge, *The Nervous System* (Cambridge, Mass.: MIT Press, 1991), p. 6.

87. See Martin, "Coding and Processing of Sensory Information," p. 337.

88. Compare the situation in which a store sells different items and receives money for each item in a common currency. Each kind of item, bread, candy, ice-cream, pizza, is translated into one common currency. To keep track of what is sold, the owner could put the money into separate drawers or compartments of the cash register, the placement depending upon what kind of item it was earned from, that is, exchanged for.

The nervous system, too, keeps the information separate for a while. The different receptors are sensitive to different kinds of energy (this is called receptor specificity), and the impulses they generate are transmitted along distinct channels. This is termed the "labeled line code." (There also is another, less frequent method that uses different patterns of firing for different modalities.) One also could imagine that the signals from different receptors differ, each carrying a mark indicating the type of receptors they originate in.

89. Telephones *do* work like that. "A telephone mouthpiece first transduces sound waves into movement of a diaphragm and then further transduces this movement into a changing voltage. These voltage changes later result in magnetic field changes in an earpiece, movements of another diaphragm, and finally new sound waves; Partridge and Partridge, *The Nervous System*, p. 7.

90. Mriganka Sur has rewired the brain of the infant ferret so that the visual receptors in its retina project to its auditory thalmus, and visual inputs activate the auditory thalamus and cortex. Cells in the primary auditory cortex come to have visual receptive fields similar to those in the primary visual cortex, and a map of visual space is recorded in the auditory cortex. (See A. Angelucci, F. Bricolo, K. S. Crame, and M. Sur, "Experimentally Induced Retinal Projects to the Ferret Auditory Thalmus," *Journal of Neuroscience* 17 [1997]: 2020–55.) Furthermore, just as the primary visual cortex contains groups of cells that share a preferred stimulus orientation, and are organized into an orderly orientation map, the ferrets' visually responsive neurons in the "rewired" auditory cortex also are organized into (somewhat less orderly) orientation modules (J. Sharma, A. Angelucci, and M. Sur, "Induction of Visual Orientation Modules in Auditory Cortex," *Nature* 404 [2000]: 841–847). And the ferrets seem to respond to visual stimuli to these "rewired" neurons as though they perceive them to be visual rather than auditory (L. von Melchner, S. Pallas, and M. Sur, "Visual Behavior Mediated by Retinal Projections Directed to the Auditory Pathway," *Nature* 404 [2000]: 871–876). What might be done to give the ferret auditory experiences of the visual world?

91. "Yet, it does seem that we would know more if the *particularity* of our experience matched the world. We would know that the world is like *that*." Exactly like that? "Like that in a certain respect, exactly like that in that respect." What is the respect; is it color, for instance, and what do we know about it? "Well, perhaps I don't

know that the world is exactly that color, but I do know that my experience presents exactly that color." What color? "*That* one" (inner ostension), "the one I now am experiencing." But do you know what that precise experiential color is? After all, colors (along with other experiential qualities) are subject to nontransitivities. Color X is indistinguishable from color Y just by looking at the two of them when they are placed side by side, and Y is indistinguishable from Z, but X is not indistinguishable from Z. So we can infer that X and Y do actually differ. (One of them, after all, is distinguishable from Z while the other is not.) But do we know what the difference is between them as experienced qualia?

92. See Frank Jackson, "What Mary Didn't Know," *Journal of Philosophy* 83 (1986): 291–295.

93. Some psychologists seem to want to equate phenomenology with conscious awareness. So having a thought, on this account, would have a phenomenology. However, it does not have sensations, a feel, mental images—recall the controversies about imageless thought—emotions, etc. We therefore can make a distinction between conscious states that have these (sensations, emotions etc.), and conscious states that do not. What if someone reports (as a psychologist has said to me) that thinking feels a certain way? That person is paying attention to thinking that *p*, and so is aware of thinking that *p*. Thinking that *p* may have no phenomenology, while a state of paying attention to thinking that *p* may itself have a phenomenology. Here, the object of attention is not the content of *p* (which it is when one is thinking that *p*) but rather the state of thinking that *p*, and (for that person) this attending to thinking that *p* may have its own phenomenological feel.

94. What it is like to be in a certain brain state is to consciously believe that 2 + 2 = 4. If this itself does not have any phenomenology, that does not require divorcing the connection (made by Thomas Nagel) in current philosophical usage between "what it is like to be" and a phenomenology. For the brain state, on this account, *does* have a phenomenology, namely consciously thinking that 2 + 2 = 4. On the mind-body identity theory, consciously thinking that 2 + 2 = 4 will be identical with that brain state, whose phenomenology it is. Is this is an advantage or a difficulty?

95. See Paul Churchland, "Conceptual Similarity across Sensory and Neural Diversity," *Journal of Philosophy*, January 1998, pp. 5–32.

96. How might *unconscious* thoughts be integrated within this framework?

97. See W. V. Quine, *Word and Object* (Cambridge, Mass.: MIT Press, 1960).

98. If the parallel is to be carried through, then we should be able to apply Quine's description of his linguistic structure (assuming it is apt) also to the case of sensory phenomenology. There is, Quine says, "no fact of the matter" about which thing a person means; the two apparently different meanings are but two ways of describing the same objective facts (behavioral dispositions to respond to stimuli, etc.). Can we say similarly that there is no fact of the matter about which phenomenology a person has, provided that these are structurally and behaviorally the same? It *seems*, however, that a person could notice that a change in his phenomenology had occurred, that the spectrum had been reversed; red now looks green to him, etc. Simi-

larly, could a person notice that he now speaks, and thinks, of temporal stages of objects rather than of continuing objects *simpliciter,* even though he continues to use the same old words?

99. I take this phrase from the wonderful first sentence of Einstein's first paper on Special Relativity. "It is known that Maxwell's electrodynamics—as usually understood at the present time—when applied to moving bodies, leads to asymmetries which do not appear to be inherent in the phenomena"; Albert Einsein, "On the Electrodynamics of Moving Bodies," reprinted in A. Einstein, H. A. Lorentz, H. Minkowski, and H. Weyl, *The Principle of Relativity* (New York: Dover, n.d.), p. 37.

100. Is memory also a constraint on the classifications we use, because we will classify things in ways that we can remember and call up easily?

101. See Elizabeth Loftus, *Eyewitness Testimony* (Cambridge, Mass.: Harvard University Press, 1979).

102. Gilbert Harman has argued that experiences give us awareness of the entities and states they represent, but that we never are aware of the qualities of our experiences themselves. (See Gilbert Harman, "The Intrinsic Quality of Experience," reprinted in his *Reasoning, Meaning and Mind* [Oxford: Oxford University Press, 1999], pp. 244–261.) We do not need to follow Harman in saying that experiences are wholly representational. It is enough for our purposes here to say that we do pay close attention to the particular qualities of an object as they are represented in an experience.

103. One feature of pain is to prompt immediate action. Pain cannot be ignored; people who do not feel pain injure themselves while asleep and not moving. Phenomenology, or some aspects of it, is like vivid advertising; it grabs your attention. Economists have pointed out that advertising does not have merely an informational function, and we do not want it to. We need our attention to be caught by some information. Our purposes would not be well served if we had always to wade through masses of material no more interestingly presented than the New York City telephone directory. See Israel Kirzner, *Competition and Entrepreneurship* (Chicago: University of Chicago Press, 1973).

104. See Donald Campbell, "'Downward Causation' in Hierarchically Organized Biological Systems," in *Studies in the Philosophy of Biology,* ed. F. J. Ayala and T. Dobshzansky (London: Macmillan, 1974), pp. 179–186; and Nozick, *Philosophical Explanations,* pp. 335–341.

105. There are arguments finding their inspiration in the Skolem-Lowenheim theorem to the effect that we cannot refer to *anything* (and not just to experiences) more specifically than what is fixed by its structural features and interconnections. These arguments are technically imposing, but more than technical arguments are needed to show that there is no mode of fixing reference other than the statable ones subject to the theorem. In particular, it needs showing that pointing to an aspect, perhaps an inner pointing in the case of experience, cannot further fix what one is referring to. Here, of course, we encounter the arguments of Wittgenstein against the possibility of such private ostensions ("private languages"). Which aspect is being pointed to, how can it be specified whether it is narrow or wide, particular or a

disjunction, etc.? We might begin with the suggestion that it is "the most specific and determinate nonstructural aspect of my current experience that I now am aware of" (and, perhaps, am consciously aware of being aware of).

106. See Ernest Nagel, *The Structure of Science* (New York: Harcourt, Brace and World, 1961), chap. 11; Paul Churchland, "Reduction, Qualia, and the Direct Introspection of Brain States," I, *Journal of Philosophy* 82 (January 1985), reprinted in his *A Neurocomputational Perspective* (Cambridge, Mass.: MIT Press, 1989), pp. 47–52; C. A. Hooker, "Towards a General Theory of Reduction" I–III, *Dialogue* 20 (1981): 38–59, 201–236, 496–529. See also Jaegwon Kim, *Mind in a Physical World* (Cambridge, Mass.: MIT Press, 1998), chap. 4.

107. Let *b* be any instance of B. When *b* has a feature *F*, then there is a feature *G*, and some instance *a* of A, such that *a* has feature *G*, and there is a type-type correlation of a different sort one level up between *F* and *G*. It is not, according to this further correlation, that anything will have *F* if and only if *it* has *G*. The relation is somewhat more distant. Consider anything *x* that has the first-level property A and also has its correlated first-level property B. Whenever *x* has a second-level feature *F* of A (that is, whenever *x* has a property that itself has feature *F*), it also will have the second-level feature *G* (that is, *x* will have a property that itself has feature *G*). There is a type-type correlation between these second-level features, in that whatever entity, two levels down, has one of these second-level features also will have the other.

108. See Max Black, "The Identity of Indiscernibles," *Mind* 61 (1952): 153–164; and Peter Simons, "Identity of Indiscernibles," in *Routledge Encyclopedia of Philosophy*, ed. Edward Craig, vol. 4 (London: Routledge, 1998), pp. 678–681. The criterion also should not be applied to certain mathematical cases in which extended parallelisms can be constructed at will.

109. Perhaps the denier of identity between mind and body would propose, as the property (of a mental property) that is not paralleled by a physical property, the following: "is a property known noninferentially to be realized." (I thank Bernard Williams for suggesting that this example be discussed.) You know noninferentially that the property of your having a thought is realized, but you do not know noninferentially that some physical property (which purports to reduce your having a thought) is realized. But since terms such as "know" create opaque contexts in which the substitutivity of identity fails, such "properties" cannot be used to demonstrate failures of identity at a lower level.

110. Consider something that is a candidate for having what John Searle has termed a "subjective ontology." (See John Searle, *The Rediscovery of the Mind* [Cambridge, Mass.: MIT Press, 1992], pp. 89–93, 106–112.) It is difficult to be sure what is meant here: something that stands in a certain perspectival or otherwise unique relation to a person or to his psychological state, viz. its seeming that way is sufficient for it, as a matter of subjective ontology, to be that way; or something that the foregoing necessarily holds of; or something that exists only inside the first-person perspective. These specifications are quite murky. An analogy would help.

The indexical first-person pronoun, "I," when uttered or thought, seems to refer to someone from the inside, in a way that is not captured by any accurate third-person description of the person. However, we can see this use of "I" as a certain kind of rigid description from the inside, where this means a term that rigidly refers to the actual producer of that (token) utterance of "I" in virtue of a property bestowed upon the producer by that very act of producing that token. (For more details, see Nozick, *Philosophical Explanations*, pp. 71–78.) This sentence's last part ("in virtue of as property bestowed . . . ") is meant to capture the quality of reference being "from the inside." However, note that nothing here has a distinct ontological status or is irreducibly subjective, at any rate not in a way that cannot be completely understood in objective terms. Is this case of how the term "I" refers merely an analogy, or does it capture the (relevant part of the) subjective aspect? And when it is said that something feels like a subjective slant, is this an intrinsic trait, or is this something we have learned after infancy, by discovering which things other people do (and which they do not) agree with us about, or have access to whenever we do? The quality of "existing within a subjective ontology"—the language gets awkward here (being ontologically subjective? being subjectively ontological?)—might itself be specified in fully objective and unmysterious terms, and, in any case, it might be correlated with some physical aspects of neuronal states and firings, which the identity theorist claims *is* having a subjective ontological status.

111. Donald Davidson argues that there are no type-type psychological-physical identities, because the psychological realm is holistic, since it is guided by charity in rational interpretation. (Does Davidson's position leave beliefs as *real,* since there is so much room for fiddling in their attribution? See Davidson, "Mental Events" and "The Material Mind," both in his *Actions and Events* [Oxford: Oxford University Press, 1980].) However, according to the Duhem-Quine view, the physical also is holistic. Presumably the physical will not jibe with the psychological, because psychological holism is beholden to different criteria, rational-normative ones. But do we know that there is no overall holism of the psychological *and* physical together that does bring them to jibe?

The non–identity theorist may think he has an *a priori* argument against identity: the mental has a property that the physical *could not* have. However, if this is a nonmodal property, why cannot it be paralleled by a physical property (and paralleled all the way up the line)? And if a modal property, it would have to be *de re* if it is even to be a candidate for a successful argument. (An argument for nonidentity based upon *de re* modality is presented by Saul Kripke, *Naming and Necessity* [Cambridge, Mass.: Harvard University Press, 1980], pp. 144–155.) Skeptical reflections on *de re* necessities were presented in Chapter 3.

112. Note that if there were not a parallelism of properties all the way up the line, then Leibniz's law would force the non-identity down to the very first level of properties. Hence it would find non-identity at the lower level of objects.

It might be objected that if some mental event *m* is identical with a physical event *p*, then it will have all the properties of that physical event. (Identity goes in both directions.) But *p* will have physical properties $P_1, \ldots, P_n$ that are unrelated to its being a mental event, e.g., causing the deflection of a compass needle two feet from the person's head. Does the mental event have these properties? We do not need to find a mental property M_i of m that is correlated with each of these physical properties P_i. For the mental event m itself will have each of these physical properties P_i. Not all properties of mental events are mental properties. Someone might attempt to *define* a mental event as something that (necessarily?) has only mental properties, but then it might turn out that there are no mental events (if what we previously classified as mental events are identical with physical ones) or that mental events are relegated to being abstract entities rather than concrete events. Granting these points, there still is the question of what criterion demarcates a *psychological* property.

113. Hilary Putnam, *Philosophical Papers,* vol. 2: *Mind, Language and Reality* (Cambridge: Cambridge University Press, 1975), chaps. 14, 20–21.

114. What, then, is the property that the mental state has that the physical state lacks? The mental state M can be multiply realized in different physical states, whereas patently no one physical state can be. So the mental state M cannot be identical with one physical state P. Consider the possible physical realizations $P_1, P_2, \ldots ,$ P_n of this mental state M. What property does M have that the disjunction of these physical states, P_1 or P_2 or . . . or P_n, does not have? M can take the form of P_3, can be realized as that, but so can the disjunction.

Is it that M can be *realized* as a physical state, but no disjunction of physical states can be realized as one? (Is this a linguistic point about the word "realization"?) However, if M is identical with this disjunction, and if the disjunction cannot be realized, then neither can M.

Is it illegitimate to consider a disjunction of physical states and treat it as a kind? However, if the states are isomorphic or nearly isomorphic, or if their structures stand in various family resemblances, then won't the disjunction be as much of a kind as our ordinary concepts? And doesn't the plausibility of the functionalist point about multiple realization depend upon imagining (almost) the very same structure realized in different physical material? Is it plausible to identify something as, e.g., pain, even when it plays a similar role in causal nexuses, if it does not have anything like the structure of what realizes pain in the human case?

In *Philosophical Explanations,* I suggested that functionalism be modified as follows: "Putnam is correct in saying that the particular material basis is not important, that beings made of different stuff could be in the same mental states as we. However, it does not follow that nothing about the material basis is essential, provided only that the functional interconnections hold . . . In addition to Putnam's macrorequirement of functional isomorphism, two microconditions must be satisfied: first, that the corresponding states under the functional isomorphism are themselves isomorphic in internal structure; and second—what gives the first content—that these corresponding states perform their role in the functional macro-isomorphism in a way that is dependent upon their (isomorphic) internal structures. The structure that the states isomorphically share is what explains each carrying out its macro-role in the functional isomorphism. Martians can be made of sterner stuff, but if they are to have the same mental states we do, their physical states have not only to perform the same external functional role but also to be (internally) configured in the same way as ours" (p. 339).

So doesn't the functionalist also need to speak of the structure of the underlying states, and to find some similarity of structure there? To be sure, the structure must be hooked up to other structures to realize the functional interconnections. Even when hooked up, these interconnections may not always be realized, e.g., people's feeling no pain from a wound in the heat of battle, and people's feeling pain in phantom limbs. If these facts are added to the list of interconnections that define pain, then if the Alpha-Centaurians are discovered to have something otherwise like pain, with a similar underlying structure, but no phenomenon of sensations in phantom limbs or lack of sensations when ignoring wounds in battle, must the functionalist hold that therefore these beings cannot ever have what is pain?

115. See Jaegwon Kim, *Supervenience and Mind* (Cambridge: Cambridge University Press, 1993), chap. 16; and idem, *Mind in a Physical World*, pp. 106–112.

116. In *The Examined Life* (New York: Simon and Schuster, 1989), p. 103, I wrote: "By a pleasure or pleasurable feeling I mean a feeling that is desired (partly) because of its own felt qualities." Complications should be added to the functional characterization in the text above in order to take account of the structural considerations discussed in note 112 above.

117. Even if all mental happenings were physical, not all physical happenings would be mental, and so there would be a need to demarcate which physical ones are mental, and to explain why the mental line occurs at precisely that place within the physical realm.

If the identity theory does get established, then it possibly might lead us to conclude that thinking that $2 + 2 = 4$ does have a phenomenology, after all, if thinking this arithmetical truth is identical with a brain event that turned out to be a member of a (narrow natural) class of brain events that do have a phenomenology. Hence, there would be "something it is like" to believe that $2 + 2 = 4$.

118. The source of such claims is found in Kripke, *Naming and Necessity*. For doubts about the claim, see the sections "On the Supposed Necessity of Water's Being H_2O" and "The Withering of Metaphysical Necessity" in Chapter 3 above, and also Nozick, *Philosophical Explanations*, pp. 656–659. Kripke himself denies the identity of the experience of pain with the physical.

119. But the fact that these are the particular causal consequences of the physical states (which give rise to those particular conscious awarenesses) is not derivable from the more general causal laws that apply to all physical states, including those that are not connected to states of conscious awareness by giving rise to them or being identical with them. Or so we shall suppose soon when we suppose that the physical world is causally closed but not causally unified. Everthing physical that has sufficient causes at all has sufficient physical causes. Yet which physical behaviors are caused by conscious awarenesses (which, by hypothesis, are given rise to or are identical with physical events) depends upon causal laws that are *special* to those kinds

of physical events, namely the kinds that give rise to or are identical with conscious awarenesses.

120. We shall maintain that the causal consequences of the conscious states can depend upon their being states of conscious awareness, because if they were not, then the general laws applying to everything else would apply to them as well, with the result that they would have different causal consequences from the ones they do have.

121. See Joseph Levine, "Materialism and Qualia: The Explanatory Gap," *Pacific Philosophical Quarterly* 64 (1983): 354–361; and idem, "On Leaving Out What It's Like," in Block, Flanagan, and Guzeldere, *The Nature of Consciousness*, pp. 543–555. For a criticism, see Robert Van Gulick, "Understanding the Phenomenal Mind," I, ibid., pp. 559–566.

122. David Chalmers holds that the mental is not identical with the physical but is supervenient upon it, and he also proposes some *irreducible* laws or relations between the mental and the physical. (See David Chalmers, *The Conscious Mind* [New York: Oxford University Press, 1996].) All the laws and relations Chalmers proposes, however, would hold if the *identity* theory were true, and hence would be unsurprising to the identity theorist, and would be welcomed by as showing the truth of necessary conditions for the identity view. Chalmers' proposal does not, and does not try to, isolate the special character of *non*identity.

Nonidentity would stand on firmer ground if it could be distinguished from identity not merely by an additional clause denying identity, but in some systematic structural way. That would open the possibility of confirming or gathering evidence for the hypothesis of nonidentity while still maintaining supervenience.

Here is one speculative possibility. Let P_1 and P_2 be two types of physical events, and M_1 and M_2 be two types of mental events. If M_1 were identical with P_1, we might suppose that the relevant function connecting M_1 to P_1 was a *recursive* one. It would be somewhat surprising if that function were only recursively enumerable, but still that would not be strictly incompatible with identity, if the criterion of identity is interchangeability *salva veritate*. Suppose, however, that M_1 is a recursively enumerable function of P_1, M_2 is a recursively enumerable function of P_2, that there is a *recursive* causal law connecting P_1 and P_2 (P_2 being a recursive function of P_1). The relation between M_1 and M_2, however, is only recursively enumerable, nothing stronger. In this case, M_1 and P_1 are not interchangeably *salva veritate* in the context "P_2 is a recursive function of," nor are P_2 and M_2 interchangeably *salva veritate* in the context "is a recursive function of P_1." This might be one structural way in which supervenient *non*identity might reveal itself.

123. Here and in the next few pages, I draw upon and expand some aspects of my discussion in *Philosophical Explanations*, pp. 333–338.

124. See the discussion of ideas stemming from C. D. Broad's views on emergence in the various essays in Ansgar Beckermann, Hans Flohr, and Jaegwon Kim, eds., *Emergence or Reduction* (New York: de Gruyter, 1992).

125. For an illuminating discussion of problems concerning the causal efficacy of

mental states and the causal closure of the physical realm when it is held that mental states are *not* identical with physical ones, see Kim, *Mind in a Physical World*.

126. See John von Neumann, *Mathematical Foundations of Quantum Mechanics* (Princeton: Princeton University Press, 1955), chaps. 5, 6.

127. In 1961 Eugene Wigner claimed that the decisive collapse occurs only when the measuring device is a conscious observer. See his "Remarks on the Mind-Body Question," reprinted in *Quantum Theory and Measurement*, ed. John Wheeler and Wojciech Zurek (Princeton: Princeton University Press, 1983), pp. 168–181.

128. We are not supposing that the universes somehow interact; that might call for the notion of a universe's inclusive fitness.

129. Sexually reproducing organisms will have no tendency to such unification, because of (whatever are) the relevant benefits of genetic recombination. But this is not the whole story about such unification within cosmological processes, since asexually reproducing organisms on Earth also show no such tendency toward informational unification of their genome.

130. Here I invoke the current notion and understanding of a "representation" within cognitive psychology. When these are improved, the improvements can be inserted into the present theory, improving it in turn.

131. That claim *is* made by Tyler Burge, "Two Kinds of Consciousness," in Block, Flanagan, and Guzeldere, *The Nature of Consciousness*, pp. 427–433.

5. The Genealogy of Ethics

1. It would not be a promising strategy to try to lift ethics by its own bootstraps, by claiming that objectivity in ethics is good because it is an ethical obligation to be objective.

Might one argue that if there *were* ethical truths then they would be discovered or established through this particular "objective" process (modeled on objectivity elsewhere), while if there were no ethical truths, this process would yield only disagreement? So when the process actually yields stable agreement, won't this be evidence that there are ethical truths or, at least, correct answers (in contrast to incorrect ones) to ethical questions? But why use this particular process rather than another one that also yields equally stable but very different results? Do we already know enough about correct ethical answers to know that this process suits their nature and is a suitable process for detecting these answers? Is there then a partial but determinate notion of correct ethical answer, specified independently of this process, that this process then must match? (And what grounds that independent determinate notion?) Is the best explanation of why the process yields universal agreement that there exist objective ethical truths or correct ethical answers? Perhaps the process itself is so strong that it produces agreement all by itself, or in conjunction with our common human nature. Moreover, why should we pick this particular process, and why term the results of this particular process correct, when other processes also would produce different agreements?

2. In that case, the intuitions would fit the earlier social situations of people in

hunter-gatherer societies, that is, the social conditions in which the evolutionary se-lection that shaped our current intuitions took place. (Would justifying norms by such intuitions make them relative to the conditions of hunter-gatherer societies?) How much weight should be placed upon such intuitions? Since they were instilled as surrogates for inclusive fitness, being correlated with it, why not now go directly to calculations of inclusive fitness itself? Or why not, instead, calculate what intu-itions would be installed by an evolutionary process that operated over a long pe-riod in which current social conditions held sway, and then justify our moral beliefs by their confluence with *those* (hypothetical) intuitions, ones better suited to our current situation than the intuitions we have inherited? Or why stay with intuitions instilled by evolution rather than ones instilled by cultural processes, or by some other process we currently find attractive? (But what is the basis of our finding it at-tractive?)

3. Thomas Scanlon seems to make justification central to his view of ethics in *What We Owe to Each Other* (Cambridge, Mass.: The Belknap Press of Harvard Uni-versity Press, 1998). To the extent that notions of justification, or of objectivity, or of moral truth depend upon the notion of support by good (or by the best) moral rea-sons, the status of these will need to be explained. Some might hold that instances of good moral reasons are identified *a priori,* and hence are explanatorily basic and in no need of explanation. In Chapter 3 we saw that the *a priori* nature and apparent self-evidence of the reason relation might be explained as something that was evolutionarily selected for because it matches a type of factual connection between *truths.* If, however, there are no independent ethical truths, this type of account of the *a priori* character of reasons cannot be offered for the moral realm. Where, then, did this supposed *a priori* faculty of identifying good moral reasons come from, and why? How seriously should we take the claim of its presence?

4. I mean to include societies where ethics no longer exists, if it existed there very recently, but where intervening social upheaval, trauma, or catastrophe has caused it to disappear.

5. Why think that there is just *one* function that accounts for the presence of eth-ics? (As we shall see later, once ethics exists it may come to be extended to other functions.) Could not there be four functions that ethics performs, and it exists in every society because either it performs all four functions in each society and it ex-ists in a society when, and only when, it performs all four functions, or although it performs only one function in each society, performing any one of the four is suf-ficient to explain its presence? However, parsimony suggests that we at least begin with the more economical hypothesis of exactly one function.

6. Our discussion here begins high up on the evolutionary ladder. One could be-gin with the (partial) cooperation of genes on a chromosome, with how one ligand affects another's binding to a protein, with an anaerobic procaryote absorbing an aerobic caryote, with the formation of multicellular organisms, etc.

7. I have taken this listing from Lee Alan Dugatkin, *Cooperation among Animals: An Evolutionary Perspective* (Oxford: Oxford University Press, 1997). For a discus-sion of evolutionary shaping for cooperative behavior among animals primates, see

Dorothy Cheney and R. M. Seyfarth, *How Monkeys See the World* (Chicago: University of Chicago Press, 1990), chaps. 2, 3.

8. A gene increases in frequency when the benefit associated with a trait the gene codes for, divided by the cost due to manifesting the trait, is greater than 1 over (Wright's) coefficient of relatedness (written as "r"). See W. D. Hamilton, "The Genetical Evolution of Social Behavior, I, II," *Journal of Theoretical Biology* 7 (1964): 1–52.

9. See Robert Trivers, "The Evolution of Reciprocal Altruism," *Quarterly Review of Biology* 46 (1971): 35–57 and *Social Evolution* (Menlo Park: Benjamin/Cummins, 1985), pp. 361–394.

10. See Elliot Sober and David Sloan Wilson, *Unto Others* (Cambridge, Mass.: Harvard University Press, 1998), pp. 17–54. Group selection models were sharpened to meet the earlier withering critique of George C. Williams in his *Adaptation and Natural Selection* (Princeton: Princeton University Press, 1966).

11. The Hamilton formula operates as effectively when the term r that it contains represents the probability of their sharing the gene.

12. See Steven A. Frank, *Foundations of Social Evolution* (Princeton: Princeton University Press, 1998), chap. 6.

13. See Bernard Williams, "Formal Structures and Social Reality," in his *Making Sense of Humanity* (Cambridge: Cambridge University Press, 1995), especially pp. 115–116.

14. See Daniel B. Klein, ed., *Reputation: Studies in the Voluntary Elicitation of Good Conduct* (Ann Arbor: University of Michigan Press, 1997).

15. For more details on the nature of function, see Robert Nozick, *The Nature of Rationality* (Princeton: Princeton University Press, 1993), pp. 117–119.

Derek Parfit (in personal conversation) asks the pertinent question of what difference is made by something's being the function of ethics. Many things have bad functions (war, slavery, etc.). And even when the function is a good one, as evaluated by the standards instilled to go with cooperation, is normative force added by saying that this good effect of ethical principles (namely, enhancing mutual coordination) also is the *function* of ethics? We shall see.

16. Yet things that serve such coordination may come to be classed as ethical. Consider the psychological disposition of being trustworthy. This may begin as a means to enlarging the extent of cooperative behavior, and later come to be viewed as an ethical character trait.

17. Compare the discussion in John F. Scott, *Internalization of Norms: A Sociological Theory of Moral Commitment* (Englewood Cliffs, N.J.: Prentice-Hall, 1971), chap. 2. Scott goes on to make the more controversial claim that not only are norms learned via reinforcement, they are maintained by reinforcement; without any reinforcement, he says, extinction may be slow but will eventually occur. Without endorsing this claim, it would be useful to develop a notion of the *degree of internalization* of a norm, specifying this in terms of what kind of reinforcement is needed to maintain the internalization of the norm. Complete internalization would re-

quire no further reinforcement for the norm's maintenance, once it has been learned and internalized.

18. Someone may well feel guilt upon violating a moral norm or principle, yet also discover that nevertheless, the heavens do not fall; life otherwise goes on as normal. The second violation will involve less guilt, a third still less, if any at all. I conjecture that people who rehearse violating moral norms in imagination will feel some guilt beforehand when they first do this, yet such a psychological response will have been damped down considerably by the time they actually perform the action. (Are sociopaths people who have done a large amount of such imaginative rehearsal?) Therefore, there might be an argument for very severe penalties for first-time perpetrators of certain kinds of cruel actions (for instance, later violence is often foreshadowed by the torturing of animals) in order to prevent such easy adaptation to the performance of monstrous acts.

19. There also is the theoretical but risky possibility that victims might bargain with highwaymen over their reputation. "Leave me some portion of the money I am carrying or I will tell others that after I acceded, you tried to kill me anyway, thereby making it less likely that you will encounter compliant, that is, cooperative victims in the future."

20. See John Rawls, *A Theory of Justice* (Cambridge, Mass.: Harvard University Press, 1971), p. 4. Rawls proceeds as though it is the total social product that then is open to considerations of justice, rather than the benefits available over and above what individuals or subgroups would gain for themselves in a noncooperative situation. See my discussion in *Anarchy, State, and Utopia* (New York: Basic Books, 1974), pp. 184–185.

21. I say "two-person situations" because the operation of competitive markets might lead to Pareto-optimal situations without the explicit invocation of distributive norms, in accordance with the first theorem of welfare economics.

22. Theories that emphasize the role of mutual benefit in explaining the existence of norms have been presented by Douglas North, *Institutions, Institutional Change and Economic Performance* (Cambridge: Cambridge University Press, 1990); and Andrew Schotter, *The Economic Theory of Social Institutions* (Cambridge: Cambridge University Press, 1981). A theory that emphasizes the struggle over distributive shares in explaining the existence of norms has been presented by Jack Knight, *Institutions and Social Conflict* (Cambridge: Cambridge University Press, 1992).

23. Notice that these explanations presuppose a preexisting asymmetry in position that, while it might itself be brought about through the operation of other norms, traces back to an original asymmetry that will have a non-norm basis, perhaps even a random one.

24. For one philosopher's discussion of the weight of different causes, see Ernest Nagel, *The Structure of Science* (New York: Harcourt, Brace and World, 1961), pp. 582–588. Social scientists might look to the analysis of variance or to path analysis.

25. Very different modes of cooperation might serve to avoid *n*-person prisoners'-dilemma situations, e.g., should the dam to protect the island be built by labor lev-

ies, progressive taxation (at what rate?), proportional taxation, or a flat tax? Therefore, the fact that everyone might prefer some system or other to get the dam built (in preference to the alternative of being flooded) does not guarantee that any particular system will be unanimously agreed to or explain why a certain particular one was instituted.

26. Invisible-hand explanations are discussed in Nozick, *Anarchy, State, and Utopia,* pp. 18–22; and idem, "Invisible Hand Explanations," *American Economic Review* 84 (May 1994): 314–318, reprinted in *Socratic Puzzles* (Cambridge, Mass.: Harvard University Press, 1997), pp. 191–197. A fascinating and promising presentation of computer modeling of how social patterns arise from individual actions is Joshua Epstein and Robert Axtell, *Growing Artificial Societies* (Washington, D.C.: Brookings Institution Press, 1996). The recent literature about the growth and function of institutions and norms is very rich. See, in addition to writings cited in note 22, Ronald Coase, *The Firm, the Market, and the Law* (Chicago: University of Chicago Press, 1988), pp. 5–16, 33–47, 95–156; Mancur Olson, *The Logic of Collective Action* (Cambridge, Mass.: Harvard University Press, 1965), chaps. 1–2; Oliver Williamson, *The Economic Institutions of Capitalism* (New York: Free Press, 1985), pp. 15–42; Paul Milgrom and John Roberts, *Economics, Organization, and Management* (Englewood Cliffs, N.J.: Prentice-Hall, 1992), pp. 19–35, 259–269; Itai Sened, *The Political Institution of Private Property* (Cambridge: Cambridge University Press, 1997), pp. 54–62; Gary Becker, "Norms and the Formation of Preferences," in his *Accounting for Tastes* (Cambridge, Mass.: Harvard University Press, 1996), pp. 225–230; H. L. A. Hart, *The Concept of Law* (Oxford: Clarendon Press, 1961), pp. 189–195; James Coleman, *Foundations of Social Theory* (Cambridge, Mass.: Harvard University Press, 1990), pp. 241–299, 785–828; William Ian Miller, *Bloodtaking and Peacemaking: Feud, Law, and Society in Saga Iceland* (Chicago: University of Chicago Press, 1990), pp. 77–109.

27. See F. A. Hayek, *Individualism and Economic Order* (London: Routledge and Kegan Paul, 1949), chap. 2, "Economics and Knowledge," and chap. 4, "The Uses of Knowledge."

28. See Douglas North, *Structure and Change in Economic History* (New York: W. W. Norton, 1981); Douglas North and Robert Thomas, *The Rise of the Western World* (Cambridge: Cambridge University Press, 1973); and Douglas North, *Institutions, Institutional Change and Economic Performance* (Cambridge: Cambridge University Press, 1990).

29. See Ludwig von Mises, *Human Action* 3d rev. ed. (New Haven: Yale University Press, 1949), chap. 26; and F. A. Hayek, *Individualism and Economic Order* (London: Routledge and Kegan Paul, 1949), chaps. 7–9.

Once upon a recent time, economists in the Marxist tradition proposed state ownership, or at any rate, some decidedly nonmarket process as the best way to organize social coordination, and as the best and most effective route to the evident good of modernization and economic development. Socialism and communism now are universally seen not only as ineffective means to modernization and development but as thwarting it. There is great cognitive dissonance in the following triad of beliefs: communism is good, capitalism is bad, modernization is good. What is to be done? Will the Marxist theorists now embrace capitalism? The story of one prominent *Marxisant* professor of economics at Harvard University is instructive. In the Harvard University *Catalog of Courses of Instruction* for 1996–97, p. 735, we find him offering a course titled "Development and Modernization: A Critical Perspective," with a course description that begins as follows: "What are the assumptions about human beings and our relationships with one another that underlie the conviction that development and modernization constitute progress, and that the developed West shows the way the rest of the world should/must go?" So now, at least, it is acknowledged that the conviction that communism is good and capitalism bad can be maintained (only) if one also holds that development and modernization are bad. I await the next step, the "discovery" that increases in longevity and physical health do not constitute progress.

30. Gilbert Harman, "Moral Relativism," in Gilbert Harman and Judith Jarvis Thomson, *Moral Relativism and Moral Objectivity* (Oxford: Blackwell, 1995), p. 9. The specification of the relevant group need not be quite that trivial; for instance, each such norm will mandate that a person not behave in certain ways to some group that he or she *belongs to.*

31. See Richard Posner, *The Economics of Justice* (Cambridge, Mass.: Harvard University Press, 1981), chap. 3.

32. Herve Moulin, *Axioms of Cooperative Decision Making* (Cambridge: Cambridge University Press, 1988), p. 3.

33. See George Homans, *Social Behavior*, rev. ed. (New York: Harcourt Brace Jovanovich, 1974), chap. 11. Homans emphasizes that even people who accept this principle may well disagree over what constitutes an investment and a contribution.

34. On anonymity, the Pigou-Dalton principle, issue monotonicity, population monotonicity, separability, the core property, the Shapley value, and independence of irrelevant alternatives, see Moulin, *Axioms of Cooperative Decision Making.* On envy-freeness, proportionality, and equitability in divisions, see Steven Brams and Alan Taylor, *Fair Division* (Cambridge: Cambridge University Press, 1996). On the Nash solution to the two-person bargaining game, see R. D. Luce and Howard Raiffa, *Games and Decisions* (New York: John Wiley, 1957), pp. 124–134. On the relative concession solution, see David Gauthier, *Morals by Agreement* (Oxford: Oxford University Press, 1986), chap. 5. Unlike Gauthier's, the account of ethics in this book does not take cooperation to mutual advantage to be the whole of ethics, but includes other layers of ethics as well; it offers a genealogical rather than a justificatory account; and it does not propose one particular rule of dividing benefits either as normatively or as descriptively correct.

35. Kenneth Arrow, *Social Choice and Individual Values* (New York: John Wiley, 1951).

36. Or, somewhat more strongly, to control for complications about partial orderings: and for each of these values the first does at least as well as the second.

37. See my discussion of voluntary cooperation in *Anarchy, State, and Utopia,* pp. 262–265. Those who prefer to substitute a narrower conception will need to for-

mulate one that does not make *every* action nonvoluntary *and* does not (in order to avoid this conceptually dire consequence) draw very significant lines in very arbitrary places.

38. The literature on the core contains the following relevant results. A necessary condition for the core's being nonempty is that the situation be superadditive, in that the sum of the payoffs to the cooperative scheme involving all *n* persons be at least as great as the sum of the payoffs to the subsets in any partitioning (exclusive and exhaustive dividing) of the *n* persons. To arrive at a sufficient condition for the core's being nonempty, we have to add that the payoff to the cooperative scheme involving everyone is at least as great as the weighted payoff to all subsets of the persons, where every subset is weighted between zero and 1 so as to sum the weights of all the persons in the subset, where the total of weights assigned to a person (in each of the subsets he is in, in each of the partitionings) sums to 1. On these necessary and sufficient conditions, see Moulin, *Axioms of Cooperative Decision Making*, pp. 95–96. See also Roger Myerson, *Game Theory* (Cambridge, Mass.: Harvard University Press, 1991), chap. 9. However, although the core may be empty for all *n* persons, it cannot be empty also for all subsets of the *n* persons.

39. What counts as an interaction in the application of these principles? If G2 is merely refraining from invading and enslaving G1, must G1 find a mode of relationship with G2 that benefits G2 as much as G2's aggressive activity would? Doing so might be desirable in that it makes cooperative relations more secure and durable. However, G2's invading and enslaving G1 itself would violate the principles proposed, so they do not have to be rewarded or compensated for refraining from such violations.

40. See also the use of the game-theoretical notion of the core in Nozick, *Anarchy, State, and Utopia*, pp. 299–301.

As a normative matter, we might say that in a game with an empty core, it is no special objection against any particular distribution *D* that some subgroup of its people would do better on its own, or in coalition with others excluded from the benefits of *D*, because (by hypothesis) this holds true of *every* distribution. The question is whether the subgroup that would do better on its own actually would constitute a coalition that was stable.

In many situations, it is important to note, the core is *not* empty. There are potential distributions that are not blocked by any coalition, and unrestricted voluntary coordination and cooperation will tend to settle upon one or another such distribution. The formal study of market models illustrates this point: *any* Walrasian equilibrium is in the core, and (as the number of participants goes to infinity) *only* Walrasian equilibria are in the core. (See Andreu Mas-Colell, Michael Whinston, and Jerry Green, *Microeconomic Theory* [New York: Oxford University Press, 1995], pp. 652–661.) It is enough for our purposes here if the core is not empty for almost all societal situations of concern. (Moreover, we have been concentrating especially upon the question of expansions of the existing domain of social cooperation to include wider groups, and our principles have mandated this when all the parties involved will benefit. The issue of the shrinkage of cooperation when a subgroup wishes to secede or diminish its own external cooperative ties is another, more complex matter.)

41. In *The Right and the Good* (Oxford: Clarendon Press, 1930), Ross lists these *prima facie* duties: of gratitude, of justice, of beneficience, of self-improvement, of nonmaleficence, and the duty to keep promises. See also his *Foundations of Ethics* (Oxford: Oxford University Press, 1939).

42. That is, the kinds of behavior that contravene the principles concerning the core. A fuller statement would have also to take account of the legitimacy of (detrimentally) punishing people for their own previous violations of these principles.

43. The extent to which moral progress with regard to the abolition of slavery, women's rights, the civil rights movement, and gay rights has been propelled by the perception of mutual benefit (at least on the part of a power subgroup), as compared to the extent to which it is propelled by higher layers of ethics (which is discussed in a later section), is a question for empirical historical investigation.

I too want to say, from the perspective of the Enlightenment norms and values of universal human dignity and rights that I accept, that certain extensions should have taken place earlier, even when it did not benefit the extending group. In particular, they should have not interacted detrimentally with others in ways that violated the core principles, even when such abstention was not of benefit to themselves. Yet I realize that it is natural for me to accept these norms as applying universally, along with norms of extending the domain of cooperation, because of the past growth of possibilities for cooperation to substantial mutual benefit, possibilities that have turned out to be so extensive that we assume that *some* way can always be found for large groups to interact nonaggressively to their mutual benefit, and also because of the modes of reasoning and evaluation that such possibilities made salient and encouraged the extension of.

44. On the Shapley index of power in a legislature, the power of a legislator in a weighted voting situation will not be proportional to the number of votes he or she casts. However, under some circumstances, if legislators are allowed to cast a number of votes that are not proportional to the number they have received, this will result in their having power proportional to the number of votes they have received. (See Robert Nozick, "Weighted Voting and One-Man One-Vote," reprinted in his *Socratic Puzzles*, pp. 265–270.) An electorate would have to be mathematically quite sophisticated, and also be adherents of one particular power measure, for this additional institutional complication to be viewed as politically legitimate.

45. For a more precise description, see Nozick, *The Nature of Rationality*, pp. 114–119.

46. We sometimes can choose to use capacities for purposes other than their (biological) function, as when people engage in sexual activities for pleasurable rather than reproductive purposes. If we can accept sexual pleasure as an end in itself, apart from the function of our sexual organs, cannot we accept adhering to ethics as an end in itself, apart from the function of ethics? However, since ethics is in part constraining—that is the context in which the question of why be moral arises—we would need some reason to pursue it apart from its function. If a predisposition to

some mode of arduous behavior had been evolutionarily instilled in Pleistocene times because it kept people's teeth free of decay, then in these days of fluoridated water when such behavior no longer is necessary to carry out its initial function, we would find it strange and irrational if someone now claimed that such behavior was an end in itself, and so did not seek to damp down or avoid altogether its arduous demands. This is not to say that ethics is *not* an end in itself, or that there are not beneficial consequences of holding it to be so; but, given its demands, surely something needs to be said to rationally justify its having this status.

47. We might recall that Adam Smith, writing before the development of evolutionary theory, spoke of "a certain propensity in human nature . . . the propensity to truck, barter, and change one thing for another. Whether this propensity be one of those original principles in human nature of which no further account can be given; or whether, as seems more probable, it be the necessary consequences of the faculties of reason and speech, it belongs not to our present subject to inquire"; Adam Smith, *An Inquiry into the Nature and Causes of the Wealth of Nations,* chap. 2.

48. See Noam Chomsky, *The Logical Structure of Linguistic Theory* (New York: Plenum Press, 1975) and *Syntactic Structures* (The Hague: Mouton, 1957); Erving Goffman, *Behavior in Public Places* (New York: Free Press, 1963).

49. I thank John Tooby for this point.

50. Perhaps not through the whole population, though. Although most of us may have been evolutionarily shaped to live in a normative realm, it is possible that there was frequency-dependent selection for some smaller percentage of people to pursue some other interactive strategy. An explanation of sociopathy in these terms is presented in Linda Mealey, "The Sociobiology of Sociopathy," *Behavioral and Brain Sciences* 18 (1995): 523–599. Must the internalization of norms always be enforced by internally generated psychological penalties (such as the unpleasant emotions of shame, guilt, remorse) for their violation? Mealey cites data that one type of sociopath is deficient in (the capacity for) these emotions.

51. See Amotz Zahavi, *The Handicap Principle* (New York: Oxford University Press, 1997); Helena Cronin, *The Ant and the Peacock* (New York: Cambridge University Press, 1991).

52. See Robert Frank, *Passions within Reason: The Strategic Role of the Emotions* (New York: W. W. Norton, 1988).

53. Writing in the Kantian ethical tradition, Christine Korsgaard (*The Sources of Normativity* [Cambridge: Cambridge University Press, 1996]) attempts to tie normatively binding obligations to the notion of a person's "identity." However, it is difficult to see why anything normatively binding arises from this unless the identity is one that one ought to have. Yet the basis of *that* "ought" cannot also be grounded in that very same identity. And even if some practical identity or other were needed at each time—a dubious claim—it needn't be *that* particular one, and it needn't be the very same (arbitrary?) one over time. So at any given time a person can consider whether to alter or drastically change fundamental aspects of that "practical identity" (and so to think of herself and her projects quite differently), and in that deliberation, the existing identity no longer is normatively binding. We also might won-

der, if the root basis of Kantian ethics turns on our interest in preserving our own identities, whether (on that conception) Kantian ethics is not at heart an egoistic view, and therefore poorly placed to criticize as egoistic the ethics of coordination to mutual benefit.

54. On issues concerning fundamental explanation, see Norwood Russell Hanson, *Patterns of Discovery* (New York: Cambridge University Press, 1958), pp. 119–120, 212; Nozick, *Anarchy, State, and Utopia*, pp. 6–7; idem, *Philosophical Explanations* (Cambridge, Mass.: The Belknap Press of Harvard University Press, 1981), pp. 632–634.

55. See Harry Frankfurt, *The Importance of What We Care About* (Cambridge: Cambridge University Press, 1988), essays 3, 5.

56. This grouping function also is performed by *principles,* and in *The Nature of Rationality,* chap. 1, I discussed how principles function as devices to enable people to resist the operation of particular current desires and temptations.

57. See Nozick, *Philosophical Explanations,* p. 297.

58. See R. M. Hare, *The Language of Morals* (Oxford: Oxford University Press, 1952); idem, *Freedom and Reason* (Oxford: Oxford University Press, 1963).

59. See Robert Nozick, *The Examined Life* (New York: Simon and Schuster, 1989), pp. 212–215.

60. See P. F. Strawson, "Social Morality and Individual Ideal," reprinted in his *Freedom and Resentment* (London: Methuen, 1974), pp. 26–44.

61. Amartya Sen has argued that there cannot be any conflict between equality and liberty because everyone is an egalitarian in some conceptual space or other. (See his *Inequality Reexamined* [Oxford: Clarendon Press, 1992], chap. 1.) However, if this is so, one need not assume that everyone is an egalitarian in the space that he or she takes to be most important. A religious person may say that salvation is the most important matter, yet accept a theology that countenances God's unequal and arbitrary distribution of this. Similarly, someone may be an egalitarian in the space of political rights without holding that these are the most important things. Is there a *presumption,* though, that one will be an egalitarian about what one holds to be the most important thing, so that it requires explaining when one is not?

62. Would it be permissible, though, to require that higher layers be used to break ties at lower levels, for instance, in choosing between two institutional forms that equally well serve the purpose of coordination of activities to mutual benefit, to choose the one that is most responsive to the value of the participant individuals, the one that best enhances their self-respect, etc.?

63. Group selectionist arguments have been advanced to explain the existence of modes of behavior that do not serve the behaving individual's inclusive fitness. Under certain circumstances, societies containing such individuals would do better than societies that do not, and so be selected for. (See Sober and Wilson, *Unto Others,* pp. 17–54.) Genetic variety in a society that enables it to adapt to new conditions also might be group-selected for. That there is some disagreement within a society about ethical matters might also be predicted on group-selectionist grounds. Such differences might especially suit people for different tasks in a society's divi-

sion of labor, or for coping with new kinds of emergencies, and so a society encompassing such variety might do better than societies that do not. Some people who put forth a minority ethical position that disagrees with the vehement social consensus might take comfort from the thought that they exist for a good social reason.

64. A pointed discussion of this gap in Plato's argument is David Sachs, "A Fallacy in Plato's *Republic*," *Philosophical Review* 72 (1963): 141–158, reprinted in Gregory Vlastos, ed., *Plato, II* (Garden City, N.Y.: Doubleday, 1971), pp. 35–51.

65. For a more extensive presentation of the theoretical alternative advanced in this paragraph in the context of a general theory of value see my *Philosophical Explanations*, pp. 403–411 passim.

66. And we might wonder whether the possibilities of coordination to mutual benefit aren't the explanation of (animal and human) *society*, the explanation of *association* rather than the special explanation of ethics. Perhaps there cannot be association or society without some regularities governing association and behavior. Do these regularities themselves depend upon possibilities of coordination to mutual benefit? If so, the question becomes: what produces norms, rules, principles, goals, sanctions, etc., above and beyond the regularities necessary for association and society?

67. Ethical truth would be a very thin notion if it were derived merely from the condition that it is true that *p* if and only if *p*. It is true that murder is wrong if and only if murder is wrong. But what is it for the ethical statement that murder is wrong, or for any other ethical statement, to hold?

If the truth property is coherence, that might seem to leave more room for the admission of ethical truths, but if something other than coherence—correspondence again?—is to ground some of the statements with which all others are to cohere, ethical statements still might encounter difficulties cohering with *those*. If the notion and standards of coherence themselves are ethically neutral—no ethical values are built into them—then in what way do moral statements cohere better with the nonevaluative facts than immoral statements do?

68. Not all facts are objective, we held earlier. Yet the truths that *some* objective processes will be effective at arriving at will be objective facts, that is, true statements that exhibit a high degree of invariance under admissible transformations. Objectivity in the process of arriving at beliefs can yield true beliefs showing objectiveness, that is, invariance.

69. Factors other than personal ties also might impair objectivity, e.g., ideological bias.

70. See Roderick Firth, "Ethical Absolutism and the Ideal Observer," *Philosophy and Phenomenological Research* 12 (1952): 317–345.

71. For when there are n persons in the society, the chooser has a $1/n$ chance of being each person, and so he evaluates a social state in which each person i receives a utility u_i by its expected utility, which is the sum of $1/n \times u_i$, for each i. He prefers one social state to another when it has a higher expected utility. We can multiply the two expected-utility sums by n without changing their order, and this gives the result that the person will prefer that social state with the higher sum of utilities. See

John Harsanyi, "Cardinal Utility in Welfare Economics and in the Theory of Risk-Taking," *Journal of Political Economy* 61 (1953): 434–435, reprinted in his *Essays in Ethics, Social Behavior, and Scientific Explanation* (Dordrecht: Reidl, 1976), pp. 3–5.

72. The structural difference between Rawls and Harsanyi is that Rawls assumes that the person is completely ignorant of which person he is, and so is deciding under "uncertainty," while Harsanyi holds that the person knows he has an equal chance of being each of the people, and so is deciding under "risk." Rawls argues that for this choice under uncertainty about such a fundamental matter, the maximin principle is appropriate—choose that action (corresponding to an organization of society) whose worst outcome is better than the worst outcome of any other action (organization of society)—and so Rawls is led to his "Difference Principle," maximizing the position of the least well-off group in society. See John Rawls, *A Theory of Justice* (Cambridge, Mass: Harvard University Press, 1971), pp. 150–175.

73. An objective process of forming beliefs is one that is effective in arriving at truths, and the objectivity characteristics are the ones such a process exhibits. Our present discussion of ethics, however, starts with a list of objectivity characteristics from the ethical literature that mostly are taken over from the factual arena. These characteristics are not derived from noticing what characteristics are had by a process that is effective in arriving at ethical truths, for we do not have, as yet, a firm notion of ethical *truths*. Rather, our intellectual strategy is the following. Starting with the imported list of objectivity characteristics, to parallel *thoroughly* the structure of the factual realm, and thereupon (tentatively) to conclude that it *is* ethical truths (or sufficiently parallel things) that are uncovered, and so the process with that imported list of objectivity characteristics is indeed an objective process (for arriving at ethical truths or at something sufficiently parallel).

74. Henry Sidgwick, *The Methods of Ethics*, 7th ed. (London: Macmillan, 1907), p. 209.

75. See Amartya Sen, "Information and Invariance in Normative Choice," in *Social Choice and Public Decision Making*, ed. Walter Heller, Ross Starr, and David Starrett (Cambridge: Cambridge University Press, 1986), pp. 29–55, who connects invariance with constraints on what information may be used in social choice: if two objects are taken to be similar in terms of relevant information (the irrelevant information is information that may not be used) then they must be treated in the same way in the exercise of choice or judgment.

76. R. M. Hare faces difficulties in this being a sufficient condition for an acceptable principle because of "fanatics," who are willing to have monstrous things done to themselves if they turn out to occupy the reversed role.

77. We have considered various types of objective process (including distancing features) and invariance properties to show how these categories of things can enter into ethics. Not all the particular ones we mentioned are necessary for widespread coordination to mutual benefit. For instance, the distancing procedures of Harsanyi and of Rawls would involve an extension of ethics beyond this particular function. Each different complete ethical theory would have to specify its own objective process and invariance properties.

78. Coping with additional complications in a fuller discussion no doubt would increase the unloveliness of the theory. Not all principles that thoughtful people adhere to are invariant or maximally invariant. A person legitimately may (within limits) favor the interests of his own children, weighting them more than the interests of strangers or randomly selected human beings. Yet this does show some degree of invariance: I do not think that everyone should favor the interests of *my* children. Each person may give greater weight to the interests of his or her own children. Some have tried to derive this from a more general principle of utilitarianism, which is wholly symmetrical, but this seems not to capture why we hold that it is legitimate to favor the interests of our own children. (Another route might speak of how deeply rooted such feelings are, and hence of the very strong *prima facie* case for allowing them.) Even greater symmetry would require each person to give absolutely equal weight to the interests of all, whether one's own children or strangers, and most of us do not think that morality demands this.

79. Factual beliefs themselves do not each state a separate fact to which they correspond, as we saw in Chapter 1.

80. That is, does the parallelism we have discussed give us "ethical truth," or rather does it give us ethical *X*, where *X*/ethics = truth/factual discourse? Since ethics and factual discourse have different functions, if the things having analogous places in fulfilling these (different) functions turn out not to be exactly the *same*, have we found ethical truth, or something else that is analogous to it? Have we reached America, rather than the India that we set out for? At what level of abstraction is truth to be characterized?

It may be asked why people need to act upon ethical beliefs at all. Why cannot they just act only upon the factual belief that *X* is a means to coordination to mutual benefit (or to whatever other function they attribute to ethics)? However, sometimes *X* will be "adopting and internalizing a particular norm *N*," and a person cannot merely act on the factual belief that doing this will serve coordination to mutual benefit; what he must do is actually adopt and internalize the norm *N*, if coordination to mutual benefit *is* to be served. (Otherwise, *X* will not have been necessary as a means.) The belief the person needs to act upon is: Everyone, or at least I, ought to conform to norm *N*.

81. See Shelley Taylor, *Positive Illusions* (New York: Basic Books, 1989).

82. See Korsgaard, *The Sources of Normativity,* chap. 1; and note 53 above.

83. See Judy Dunn and Robert Plomin, *Separate Lives* (New York: Basic Books, 1990); for an attempt to take account of differences in birth order, see Frank Sulloway, *Born to Rebel* (New York: Pantheon Books, 1996).

84. See Richard Nisbett and Lee Ross, *The Person and the Situation* (Philadelphia: Temple University Press, 1991).

85. Recall that in zero-sum two-person games, which are situations of absolute conflict of interest, a randomized strategy can raise one's security level, and one cannot do better than follow some randomized strategy. And every zero-sum two-person game has an equilibrium point when randomized strategies are permitted.

86. See Thomas Schelling, "The Rationality of Irrationality," in his *The Strategy of Conflict* (Cambridge, Mass.: Harvard University Press, 1960).

87. Other writers, in a related context, have explained the capacity for self-deception, and hence the existence of unconscious motives, as an aid to effectively deceiving others. See Robert Trivers, *Social Evolution* (Menlo Park: Benjamin/Cummings, 1985).

88. On evolutionarily stable strategies, see John Maynard Smith, *Evolution and the Theory of Games* (Cambridge: Cambridge University Press, 1982).

89. See Edna Ullman-Margalit, *The Emergence of Norms* (Oxford: Oxford University Press, 1997).

90. See Dorothy Cheney and Robert Seyfarth, *How Monkeys See the World* (Chicago: University of Chicago Press, 1992), pp. 240–246.

91. Alternatively, it might be that conscious self-awareness is a side effect of having a large and complex brain that developed for other reasons, perhaps for self-guidance and self-regulation in nonsocial circumstances, or perhaps (in an evolutionary arms race) to guide one's own behavior in situations of conflict with others.

92. See Nozick, *Anarchy, State, and Utopia,* pp. 42–45, and *The Examined Life,* pp. 104–108.

93. (I owe this coin example to a student at New York University.) But are there limits to the dissociation possible between (onetime) function and value? Could we come to think that heinous instruments made to torture slaves were aesthetically valuable, and hence valuable in general?

94. The person who wishes to eat his cake without first having it, needs to demonstrate, though, of the functional object that he claims is valuable, that no value does reside in its function, and that it does possess a value distinct from its function.

Index

Absolutism, strong and weak, 309n11
Actuality: and effects, 32; and truth defini-
tion, 72–73, 155–156; ineluctable mo-
dality of the actual?, 156; Lewis's theory,
156; nonsymmetrical theory, 157; expla-
nation of, 157–161; sufficient explana-
tory property, 157–161, 163
Aeschylus, 360n86
Aesthetic value and indistinguishability,
379n84
African Americans, 262
Aharonov, Yakir, 310n28
Albert, David, 305n13, 312n37, 336n34,
340n60, 371n30
Analyticity, apparent, 135–136, 145
Andersen, Richard A., 377n70
Anderson, J. L., 333n21
Angelucci, A., 380n90
Anthropic Principle, 150, 357n70
Arbitrariness, 157–164
Argument, fishy, 130, 164, 362n38
Arieti, Silvano, 355n59
Aristotle, 27–28, 33, 34, 41, 303n1, 314n50,
338n46, 360n86
Armstrong, David, 324n94
Arrow, Kenneth, 258, 393n35
Art, 338n45
Asch, Solomon, 372n34
Attention, 181
Aumann, Robert, 201, 377n67
Austin, J. L., 70, 323n89, 324n95
Awareness, conscious, 171; fitting behavior
to circumstances, 174–176, 180–183,
193; function of, 174–176, 183, 186, 202;
gradations of, 174–176, 183; registering,
175–176; registering of registering, 175,

180, 184–187; and truth, 180; and new
discriminative stimulus, 182–184; existence of, 187; rising to, 189–190, 193;
theories of, 196; underlain by common
registering, 197–198, 202–205. *See also*
Common registering; Consciousness;
Phenomenology
Axtell, Robert, 392n26

Baars, Bernard, 196, 197, 205, 367n12,
368n21, 370n30, 374n49, 375n59
Baldwin effect, 123–124
Balzano, Gerald, 328n8
Banach-Tarski theorem, 141
Barnes, Barry, 339n53
Becker, Gary, 392n26
Behavior, 176–179; fitting to circumstances, 174–176, 180–183, 193; mecha-
nisms for regulating, 274–275; comp-
lexly caused, 294–297; unpredictability
of, 294–298; guided by norms, 298–300
Beliefs: truth property, 44–48, 66–67; act-
ing upon, 45–47, 49–51, 59–60, 66–67,
180, 187, 192, 293–294, 315n56, 316n62;
effectiveness property, 286; function of,
286, 293–294
Bell, John S., 8, 305n14, 330n13
Berlin, Brent, 350n42
Beth, E. W., 344n5
Biasing factors, 94–99, 117, 336nn35,36,
337n37; not intrinsic, 94–95; constraining, 95. *See also* Objective beliefs
Billman, Dorrit, 369n28
Binocular vision, 191
Black, Max, 383n108
Black holes, 36, 165–166

403

Blake, William, 305n11
Blindsight, 173, 175–176, 181–185
Block, Ned, 378n75, 387n121, 388n131
Bloor, David, 339n53
Bogen, James, 355n58
Bohm, David, 8, 9, 305n12
Bohr, Niels, 37
Bolshevik terror, 152
Borbely, Alexander, 378n74
Boslough, Joshua, 312n35
Brain bisection, 373n42
Braithwaite, R. B., 85
Brams, Steven, 393n34
Brewer, Talbot, 320n81
Bricolo, F., 380n90
Bridgeman, P. W., 10
Broad, C. D., 387n124
Brown, Harvey, 313n42
Brown, J. R., 330n13
Buddhist enlightenment, 53
Burge, Tyler, 388n131
Burgess, John, 310n23

Calabi, E., 161
Calabi-Yau spaces, 161–162
Calendars, Jewish and Christian, 344n12
Campbell, Donald, 229, 382n104
Cantor, Georg, 163
Carnap, Rudolf, 148, 306n4, 357n68
Cartesian argument, 156–157
Cassirer, Ernst, 329n8
Category theory, 146
Causal closure, 230
Cavanagh, P., 372n36
Chalmers, David, 387n122
Change, 303–304n1
Chaos, 61, 149–150, 153
Cheney, Dorothy, 390n7, 401n90
Chiao, Raymond, 31
Choices, 177–179; and objective facts, 192
Chomsky, Noam, 396n48
Church, Alonzo, 326n103
Churchland, Patricia, 7, 52, 318n70,
    339n56, 372n37, 378n72

Churchland, Paul, 7, 52, 219, 318n70,
    325n97, 336n33, 378n79, 381n95,
    383n106
Clark, Andy, 99–100, 337n41, 353n51,
    369n28, 374n46
Coase, Ronald, 392n26
Cohen, Paul, 147
Cohen, Stephen, 359n80
Coleman, James, 392n26
Color and color vision, 118, 136–138, 185,
    211–212, 350nn42–44, 351nn45,46,
    352nn47,48
Color incompatibility, 134, 136–138
Common knowledge, 43–44, 197–205; dif-
    ference it makes, 198–202; and ethics,
    298; game-theory infinite layering,
    375n60
Common registering, 43–44, 197–205; un-
    derlies conscious awareness, 197–198;
    and unity of self, 201; physical realiza-
    tion, 202–205; approximations, 204–
    205; and multiple realizability, 224;
    specialness of?, 231
Computer, conscious, 205, 234–235
Conditioning, Pavlovian and operant, 177,
    179, 183–184
Conquest, Robert, 359n77
Consciousness, 10, 171–235; function of,
    171–176, 179–180, 186–190, 201–202,
    229–230; subjective, 171; blindsight,
    173, 175–176, 181–185; fitting behavior
    to circumstances, 174–176, 180–183,
    193; and sensory experience, 174; grada-
    tions of, 175–176, 183; context of, 176–
    180; zoom-lens theory, 180–182; atten-
    tion, 181–182; existence of, 187; and
    self-consciousness, 187, 298–300; and
    objective facts, 190–193; synthesizing
    data, 190–197; unity of conscious sub-
    ject, 201–205; global property of brain,
    202–203; sleep, 203–204; computer, 205,
    234–235; neurological correlate of, 225;
    nomologically special, 230–232; sum-
    mary about, 234–235; roles of, 235;

brain bisection and fractional, 373n42; Chinese room example, 378n35

Contamination Premiss, 95–96

Contingency, degrees of, 148–155; defined, 148–152; of major features of evolution, 149–150; temporal nature of, 149–154; unpreserved under necessary conditionhood, 150–151; and Bolshevik terror, 152; and explanation, 153–154

Contingent truth, 63; water is H_2O, 128–132; and geometry, 130–131; and unification of forces, 161

Contradiction, 2, 26–27, 162, 303n1, 304nn2–4

Cooperation: animal, 240–241; ethical norms, 243–253; evolutionary selection for, 246; division of benefits, 250–252; Pareto-optimality, 251, 257–259, 261–262; evaluation of systems of, 253–259; fair division, 257–258; core principle of ethics, 259–267; extending, 260–267, 395n43; between different groups, 261–263; integrated society, 262; voluntary, 263; descriptive theory, 263; to mutual benefit, 269–270; and predictability, 296–298

Coordination: to mutual benefit, 240–245, 248–249, 264; by ethical norms, 243–253; nonethical coordination, 243–244; security level, 244–245; institutions of, 253–254; behavioral unpredictability, 296–298

Copenhagen interpretation: of quantum mechanics, 37; of determinacy, 38; of truth, 38, 43

Core principle of ethics, 259–267; and function of ethics, 259–260; and ethics of respect, 281–282

Cosmides, Leda, 323n90

Cosmology, 10, 85. *See also* Evolutionary cosmology

Covariance, 83, 86, 331n18

Crame, K. S., 380n90

Crick, Francis, 374n52, 375n54

Cronin, Helena, 396n51

Csikscentmihalyi, Mihaly, 366n9

Cuban missile crisis, 150

Cushing, James, 305n12

Damasio, Antonio, 374n52

Damasio, Hannah, 374n52

Daniels, Robert V., 359nn80,81

Darwin, Charles, 338n45, 359n83, 360n86

Davidson, Donald, 326n103, 384n111

Davies, P. C. W., 330n13

Dawkins, Richard, 175, 366n8

Dead, white, heterosexual males, 75, 98–99

Death, survival after, 171, 360n86

Degrees: 63–64, 101–102; of truth, 47–48; of relativeness, 63–64, 101–102; of objectiveness, 87–90, 99–100; of objectivity, 96–97, 100–101; of contingency, 148–155; of awareness, 175–176; of registering, 205; of supervenience, 226–227; of strong and weak, 309n11. *See also* Ethical relativism

Delayed-choice experiment, 30, 36–38

Dense information, 205–207, 212–214

Descartes, René, 1, 125

Desires, 274–275

Determinateness, 29–30, 33–34, 37–44; not verificationist, 32–33, 40

Determinism, 8–9, 33

Dewey, John, 97

Dimensions of space-time, 161–163

Dirac, P. A. M., 76, 328n4

Discriminative stimulus, 182–184

Dogmatism, 91, 318n68

Downward causation, 229–230

Dretske, Fred, 366n10

Dugatkin, Lee Alan, 389n7

Duhem, Pierre, 9, 104

Dummett, Michael, 311n31

Dunn, Judy, 400n83

Dupré, John, 323n90

Earman, John, 332n21, 349n33, 379n84

Edelman, Gerald, 202, 377n71

Edgeworth box, 263–264

Eells, Ellery, 306n4

Egoism, ethical, 264, 268, 272, 293–294; and self-consciousness, 298–300; tensions in, 299–300

Einstein, Albert, 10, 76, 78, 319n76, 328n5, 331n16, 361n86, 382n99

Emotions, 337n38

Empirical questions, 28, 33, 39, 43, 63

Engel, A. K., 377n70

Epstein, Joshua, 392n26

Erased measurement, 31–32, 35, 37

Espagnat, Bernard d', 310n26, 334n24

Essential properties, 126

Etchemendy, John, 325n101

Ethical relativism, 254–256, 292; invariants?, 255–256; laditudinism, 255; criticism of societies, 267

Ethics, 10, 236–301; ethical facts?, 236, 292; intuitions, 237; justification in, 237–238, 291; reflective equilibrium, 237, 291; norms, 238, 247; anthropological definition, 238–239, 247–248; function of, 238–240, 247, 250–252, 259–260, 266–267, 268, 279–280, 292, 298–300; ubiquity of, 238–240; as end in itself, 239–240, 395n46, 396n53; Kantian, 239, 269, 273–274, 396n53; reductionism, 239–240; coordination to mutual benefit, 240–245, 279–280, 291; coordination by ethical norms, 243–253; progress in, 246, 264–265, 291; internalization, 247–250, 270–271, 390n17; definition of an ethics, 247–248; division of benefits, 250–252; evaluation of norms, 253–259; normative force, 253, 267–274, 283, 298–300, 396n53; invariance and, 254–256; relativism about, 254–256; core principle of, 259–267, 281; value dominance, 259; ethical egoism, 264, 268, 272, 293–294; nonapplicable?, 267; quandaries in ethical theory, 268–269, 293–294; utilitarianism, 268, 288–289, 300; normativity module, 269–272; internal attitude, 270–271; *ought* from *is,*

271–272; and handicap principle?, 273; moral emotions, 273–274; evaluative capacities, 274–278; explanations of, 274; generality, 275–276; higher levels, 278–284; value, 280, 299–300; of caring, 280; of Light, 280; of respect, 280; of responsiveness, 280; enforcing, 281–282; disagreement in, 282–283; value sanction, 283; Principle of Proportional Ranking, 283; unethical person, 283; parallels to factual arena, 285–288, 290; difference principle, 289; veil of ignorance, 289; crucial test of?, 293–294; and common knowledge, 298; and conscious self-awareness, 298–300; necessary truths?, 349n35; violating norms, 391n18; identity and, 396n53; and equality, 397n61. *See also* Cooperation; Coordination; Egoism, ethical; Ethical relativism; Ethics, higher levels of; Evaluative capacities; Normative force; Normativity module

Ethics, higher levels of, 278–284; new functions, 279–280; ethics of caring, 280; ethics of Light, 280; ethics of respect, 280–282; ethics of responsiveness, 280; value, 280

Ethics, objectivity in: and ethical truth, 236–237, 284–294; objectiveness property, 286–287; objectivity, 288–289; specifications of nonbias, 288–289; objectiveness, 289–290; symmetries and invariances, 289–290; ethically admissible transformations, 290

Ethics, truth in, 236–237, 284–294; effectiveness property, 286, 292–294; truthlike, 292–293; acting upon, 293–294

Ethnic conflict, 262–263, 265–266

Euclidean geometry, 7, 8–9, 52, 122, 124, 130

Evaluative capacities, 274–278; desires, 274; goodness, 274–275; controlling actions, 275–276; generality, 275–276; open-ended, 278–281

Evans, Gareth, 348n25

Evolution, 7; shaped sensory detection of invariances, 78, 107–108, 122–125, 142–143, 149, 150, 227–228, 337nn38,43, 360n86; builds theories into observations, 107–108; and useful picture of world, 108, 123–124; did not instill faculty of reason for necessity, 122; and supposed *a priori* knowledge, 122–126; contingency of major evolutionary results?, 149–150; of eye, 175; and behavioral capacities and choices, 177–179; choice point, 177; and detection of objective facts, 192; of cooperative behavior, 240–243; inclusive fitness, 241–243; kin selection, 241–243; reciprocal altruism, 241–242; Hamilton's Rule, 242–243; selection and ethics, 268; of normativity module, 269–272; handicap principle, 273; and behavioral unpredictability, 294–298; arms race, 295–296; optimizing process?, 365n3. *See also* Function; Selection, natural

Evolutionary cosmology, 164–168, 232–233; yields objective worlds, 167–168; and emergent laws, 232–233; and quantum mechanics, 363n103

Evolutionary psychology, 6–7, 323n90

Experience machine, 171, 299–300, 364n1

Explanation, 111–112, 114; and degrees of contingency, 153–154; sufficient explanatory property, 157–161, 163

Eyewitness unreliability, 216

Facts, 22, 25–26, 28, 33–35, 38, 49, 70–72, 73–74, 324n95, 325n103. *See also* Objective facts; Objectiveness

Fagin, Ronald, 376n61, 377nn63,67,68

Farah, Martha, 196, 366n11, 368n19, 375n58

Fermi, Enrico, 373n44

Feyerabend, Paul, 339n53

Feynman, Richard, 159, 167, 361n92

Fiction, 157

Field, Hartrey, 325n101

Filter, 143–146

Fine, Kit, 324n94, 347n24

Firth, Roderick, 288, 398n70

Flanagan, Owen, 387n121, 388n131

Fleming, Gordon, 311n34

Fodor, Jerry, 307n7, 352n51

Folk epistemology, 52

Folk psychology, 7

Food, 222–224

Forbes, Graeme, 343n4

Frank, Robert, 396n52

Frank, Steven A., 390n12

Frankfurt, Harry, 397n55

Frege, Gottlieb, 20, 314n50, 326n103

Freud, Sigmund, 11, 25

Friedman, Michael, 329n13, 332n18, 333n21, 360n85

Friedman, Milton, 23

Function, 172–173; of mode of representation, 142–143; of quantum mechanics, 166–167; of conscious awareness, 174–176, 183, 186, 201, 202–203, 229–230; of neuronal machinery, 178; of phenomenology, 205–218; of ethics, 238–240, 247, 250–252, 259–260, 266–267, 268, 279–280, 292, 298–300; of beliefs, 286, 293–294; of unpredictable behavior, 294–298; and value, 299–300, 390n15. *See also* Evolution; Selection, natural

Furshpan, Edward, 371n31

Future contingencies, 27–28, 33

Galilei, Galileo, 331n16

Gallistel, Charles, 374n53

Game theory, 197, 250, 260–262, 298; core, 260–261; and infinite layering, 375n60

Gauthier, David, 258, 393n34

Gazzaniga, Michael S., 373n40, 374nn50,52

Gibson, James J., 78, 90, 328n8

Gleason, Andrew, 353n55

Godel, Kurt, 133, 162, 304n6, 326n103, 349n33

Godel's Theorem, 162, 232, 304n6

Godfrey-Smith, Peter, 367n16

Goffman, Erving, 396n48

Goldblatt, Robert, 335n26
Goodman, Nelson, 160, 361n93, 379n84
Gould, Stephen Jay, 150, 357n71
Gray, C. M., 377n70
Green, Jerry, 394n40
Greene, Brian, 164, 362nn94,97
Guth, Alan, 362n99
Guzeldere, Guven, 387n121, 388n131

Hacking, Ian, 325n103
Hager, Joanne, 368n24
Halpern, Joseph Y., 376n61
Hamilton, W. D., 241, 390n8
Hanson, Norwood Russell, 397n54
Hardin, C. L., 351n45
Hare, R. M., 289–290, 397n58, 399n76
Harman, Gilbert, 255–256, 363n102,
    371n33, 382n102, 393n30
Harsanyi, John, 288–289, 399nn71,72,77
Hart, H. L. A., 270, 392n26
Hawking, Stephen, 312n35
Hayek, Frederick A., 23, 392n27, 392n29
Heck, Richard, 325n101
Hempel, Carl G., 85, 103, 111, 306n4,
    339n55
Henle, James, 305n14
Hering, Ewald, 352n47
Hesperus and Phosphorus, 134–135
Heydt, Rudiger von der, 366n6, 374n45
Heywood, C., 368n23
Highwayman, 248–249
Hilbert, D. R., 350n44
Hinton, G. E., 369n27
Homans, George, 258, 393n33
Homer, 360n86
Hooker, C. A., 219, 325n97, 383n106
Horgan, John, 310n27
Horwich, Paul, 314n52, 315n56
Hubel, David, 329n9, 352n46, 372n37
Hume, David, 271, 358n74

Identity theory (mind-body), 217–218;
    epistemic criterion of identity, 219, 222;
    objections to, 219–221, 222; scientific re-
    duction, 219, 223; and multiple realiza-

tions, 222–224; partially true?, 225–226;
    and evolutionary selection of neurologi-
    cal states, 227–228; explanatory gap?,
    228; non-identity theory, 228–229,
    387n122; and function of consciousness,
    229–230; and nonreduction, 229–233;
    and quantum mechanics, 231
Immigrants, 262
Imry, Yoseph, 310n28
Indeterminacy of translation, 213–214
Infinity, 162–163
Information: dense, 205–207, 212; digital,
    205, 213; propositional, linguistic, 205–
    206, 212–214; storing only needed, 216
Information-bearing state, 187, 234,
    369n28
Intersubjectivity, 76, 90–93; dogmatism,
    91; priority, 91
Intrinsic value, 97
Intuitions, 7, 125, 162
Invariance, 76–91; evolution and, 78, 80–
    81; outside physical theory, 78, 84–85,
    90; and physical theory, 81–83;
    covariance, 83, 86, 331n18; explains
    three strands, 85, 88–90; and scientific
    laws, 85–87; ontological priority, 91; and
    objective belief, 96; less than maximum,
    99–100; and necessary truth, 120; and
    heritability of physical laws, 168; under
    transformations, 334n26; and topology
    on possible worlds, 357n69. *See also* Eth-
    ics, objectivity in; Symmetry; Variance

Jackson, Frank, 211, 381n92
James, William, 25, 45
Jessell, Thomas, 368n22, 374n52, 380n85
Jury system, 94–95

Kahn, Herman, 358n73
Kaku, Michio, 330n14, 335n27
Kandel, Eric, 368n22, 374n52, 380n85
Kanger, Stig, 343n4
Kant, Immanuel, 7, 10, 269, 289, 305n10
Kaplan, David, 308n9
Katz, Jerrold, 344n6

Kay, Paul, 350n42
Kentridge, R., 368n23
Kierkegaard, Søren, 239
Kim, Jaegwon, 223, 226, 325nn97,99, 383n106, 386n115
Kirkham, Richard, 323n91
Kirzner, Israel, 382n103
Kitcher, Philip, 339n54, 360n85
Klein, Felix, 78, 334n26
Kleinberg, Eugene, 305n14
Knight, Jack, 391n22
Knowledge, 78, 364n42; by body, 187
Koch, C., 375n54
Kochen, Simon, 35, 311n33
Koening, Oliver, 353n51, 373n41
Konig, P., 377n70
Korsgaard, Christine, 396n53, 400n82
Kosslyn, Stephen, 181, 353n51, 366n6, 367n18, 369n26, 373n41, 377n70
Kripke, Saul, 128, 129, 131, 132, 343n4, 344n10, 346n18, 347n24, 349n36, 384n111, 386n118
Kripke-Putnam argument, 128–132
Krumhansl, Carol, 379n82
Kuffler, Stephen, 351n46
Kuhn, Thomas, 23, 104, 110, 339nn53,58
Kuratowski, Kazimierz, 356n63

Lakatos, Imre, 6, 304n8, 339n51, 365n3
Land, Edwin, 78, 352n48
Latour, Bruno, 318n68, 339n53
Laudon, Larry, 339n54
Legislative voting system, 265–266
Leibniz, Gottfried, 9, 121, 129
Lenin, Vladimir, 152
Le Poidevin, Robin, 310n22
Lepore, Ernest, 307n7
Levin, Michael, 348n29
Levine, Joseph, 387n121
Levy, Marion J., 309n12
Levy-Bruhl, Lucien, 355n59
Lewis, C. I., 65, 319n76
Lewis, David, 149, 156, 159, 324n94, 334n25, 347n22, 357n69, 361n87, 376n60

Liberal arts education, 360n86
Livingstone, Margaret, 352n46
Llinas, Rodolfo, 377n72
Locke, John, 10, 210
Loftus, Elizabeth, 382n101
Logic, 37, 60; modal, 120, 342n4; self-evidence and, 124–125; logical truth, 125; as filter, 143–146; and objective facts, 143–146; and meaning of "not," 145. *See also* Contradiction; Necessity, logical
Lorentz, H. A., 328n5, 382n99
Luce, R. D., 393n34
Lucretius, 360n86

Mach bands, 108
MacKay, Donald, 373n42
Mackintosh, N. J., 369n25
Malament, David, 313n47
Malia, Martin, 359n79
Malsburg, C. von der, 377n70
Market, 253–254
Martin, John, 380n85, 380n87
Marxist economic development, 392n29
Mas-Colell, Andreu, 394n40
Maudlin, Tim, 311n34, 313nn42,45, 330n13, 332n19
Mazur, James, 369n25
McCabe, Viki, 328n8
McClelland, J. L., 369n27, 377n65
Mealey, Linda, 396n50
Melchner, L. von, 380n90
Memory, 216
Meredith, Alex, 373n40
Michelangelo, 360n86
Milgrom, Paul, 392n26
Mill, John Stuart, 55
Miller, Richard, 359n84
Miller, William Ian, 392n26
Mind-body relations, 218–235; identity theory, 217–229; empirical question, 218, 224, 229; multiple relations?, 218, 224–225, 229; functionalism, 222–224, 385n114; multiple realizations, 222–224; supervenience, 226–227; non-identity theory, 397n22

Minkowski, Hermann, 77, 328n5, 382n99
Mises, Ludwig von, 392n29
Modal logic, 120, 342n4
Moses, Yoram, 376n61
Motherhood, 135–136
Moulin, Herve, 393nn32,34, 394n38
Muller-Lyer illusion, 339n52
Munkres, James, 335n26
Myerson, Roger, 394n38

Nagel, Ernest, 85, 97–98, 103, 219, 325n97, 337n41, 342n3, 383n106, 391n24
Nagel, Thomas, 2, 304n5, 373n42, 381n94
Narens, Louis, 334n26
Necessary truth, 83–84, 120–148; explanation of, 119, 136–148, 353n53; and invariance, 120; as true in all possible worlds, 120, 128; epistemology of, 121–125; intuition and, 125; cross-classifications, 126–128; water and H$_2$0, 128–132; criterion of, 129, 347n23; not simply truth in all possible worlds, 129, 347n23; and color incompatibility, 134, 136–138; and language, 139; in ethics?, 349n35. *See also* Necessity; Necessity, logical; Necessity, mathematical; Necessity, metaphysical; Possible worlds
Necessity: unclarity in notion, 120; ontological, 121; relative to classification, 126–128; identity and, 131–132, 134–135; and truths of origin, 131–132; explaining away, 136–148; mother of, 136; invariant under reduction, 138; and veridicality, 140–141; looser notion, 154. *See also* Necessary truth
Necessity, logical, 141–146, 167–168
Necessity, mathematical, 141–143, 146–148, 167–168; and epistemic possibilities, 141–142
Necessity, metaphysical, 120–121, 128–136; physics undercuts, 133–134; and identity statements, 134–136
Nerlove, Sara Beth, 374n51
Neurath, Otto, 2

Neuroscience, 172–174; sensory transduction, 173; back-projection and crosstalk, 178, 195, 202; function of neuronal machinery, 178; parallel distributed processing system, 184, 196, 200–202, 212; coarse coding, 185–186; synthesizing and filtering data, 190–197; cerebral hemispheres, 191; binding problem, 193–196; topographic maps, 193–196, 212
Newton, Sir Isaac, 9, 360n86
Newton Smith, W. H., 339n54
Nietzsche, Friedrich, 252
Nisbett, Richard, 400n84
Noether, Amalie Emmy, 81
Nomologically special, 230–233
Non-identity theory, 228–229, 387n122
Nonlocality, 40, 363n103
Normative force, 253, 267–274; bindingness, 272–274; explanations of, 273–274; value sanction, 283; and self-consciousness, 298–300; and identity, 396n53
Normativity module: evolution and, 269–272; benefits, 271; open-ended, 278–281
Norms: adaptable, 243, 276; ethical, 243–253; internalization, 247–250, 390n17; and highwayman, 248–249; normative force, 253, 267–274, 283, 298–300, 3996n53; evaluation of, 253–259; shared, 255–256; of cooperation, 257–265; and Edgeworth box, 263–264; normativity module, 269–272, 278–281; increase predictability, 298; and self-consciousness, 298–300; violating, 391n18
North, Douglas, 391n22, 392n28
Norton, John, 331n18
Nozick, Robert, 379n84; *Anarchy, State, and Utopia,* 364n1, 391n20, 392n26, 393n37, 394n40, 397n54, 401n92; "Experience, Theory, and Language," 307n7; "Fiction," 361n89; "Invisible Hand Explanations," 392n26; *The Nature of Rationality,* 44–45, 122–123, 315n55, 320n79, 336n35, 337n40, 341n64, 344n8,

363n105, 373n41, 390n15, 395n45, 397n56; *The Normative Theory of Individual Choice*, 375n60; "The Objectivity and the Rationality of Science," 339n55; *Philosophical Explanations*, 78, 187, 304n9, 325n98, 334n25, 350n38, 361n90, 382n104, 384n110, 385n114, 386n118, 387n123, 397nn54,57, 398n65; *Socratic Puzzles*, 361n89; "Weighted Voting and One-Man One-Vote," 395n44
Number theory, 147, 162

Objective beliefs, 94–99, 287; connection with rationality, 94; process forming, 94, 96–97; degrees of, 96–97, 100–101; and invariance, 96. *See also* Biasing factors; Ethics, objectivity in
Objective facts, 75–93, 287; three strands, 75–76, 85, 88–90, 90–93; multiple accessibility, 75–76, 90–93, 190–193, 327n2; intersubjective agreement, 76, 90–93, 336n30; independence, 76; invariance, 76–91; and admissible transformations, 79–83; at a level, 83; ordering of, 87–90, 93, 335n28; logic as filter for, 143–146; consciousness fits behavior to, 193. *See also* Invariance; Objectiveness; Transformations
Objectiveness, 10; maximum, 81, 89; metrical properties, 87–88; topological properties, 87–88; ordering of, 87–90; surface, 88–90; underlying, 88–90; levels of, 89–90; objectiveness property, 91, 286–287; interspecies, 93; less than maximum, 99–100; objective world and evolutionary cosmology, 167–168; subjective consciousness as test of, 191–192. *See also* Objective facts
Objective world, 167–168
Objectivity, 94–99, 287, 318–319n71; of science, 45–96, 102–119, 341n66; degrees of, 96–97; of social science, 97–98; intrinsic value of?, 97; desirability of?, 98–99, 102

Objectivity of science, 95–96, 102–119, 341n66
Objects, 327–328n3, 329n10
Observation, 106–108
Olson, K. R., 326n103
Olson, Mancur, 392n26
Omnes, Roland, 10, 305n15
Ontological argument, 130, 362n98; secular surrogate, 164
Ontological question, 155–156
Ontology, 76–77, 78; subjective, 383n110
Ordered pair, 356n63

Pain, 224
Pais, Abram, 329n13
Pallas, S., 380n90
Palmer, Stephen, 328n7
Pap, Arthur, 350n41
Parallel distributed processing system, 184, 196, 200–202, 212–214
Pare, D., 378n72
Pareto-optimality, 251, 257–259, 261–262
Parfit, Derek, 157, 158, 160, 314n53, 361n91, 390n15
Parker, Andrew, 372n38
Partridge, Donald L., 380n86,88
Partridge, Lloyd D., 380n86,88
Peacocke, Christopher, 307n7
Peano arithmetic, 147
Peirce, Charles Sanders, 1, 52, 117, 167
Phenomenology: felt quality, 174, 207, 211–212; and topographic maps, 194, 212; existence of, 196; function of, 205–218, 229–230; represents dense information, 205–207, 212; particularity of, 207–213; structure of, 207–208; tastes, 207; and underdetermination of theory, 207; functionless aspects, 208–211; nontransitivity of matching, 208, 379n84; specificity, 208; valence, 208, 217; and sensory transduction, 209–211; dimensionality of, 211–212; reversed spectrum, 211, 214; linguistic thoughts lack, 212–213; of neural networks, 212–

Phenomenology *(continued)*
213; attention to, 215–217; determined
by function only up to isomorphism,
218; and mind-body problem, 221; and
neurological states, 225; explanatory
gap?, 228

Philosophy: fixed points, 1–3, 52, 300–301;
methods, 1–11, 121–122, 304n9, 321n63,
341n62; wonder of, 1, 301; reason, 2–3,
122; forays, 3–6; opening possibilities, 3,
8–9, 16–17, 27–28, 34, 133–136; proof,
3–4; plausibility, 4–5; metaphysics, 5,
128–136; and belief, 6; concepts, 6–10,
48–49; progress in, 6; conceptual revisions, 9–10; categories, 7, 9; intuitions
in, 7, 125, 161–162; and science, 10–11;
understanding, 10; absolutist, 24; arbitrary terms, 48–49; postmodernism, 52–
55; global arguments, 53–55; breadth of
characterization, 70, 82, 84, 87; depth of
characterization, 70, 83–84, 87; analyses
in, 71–72; two types of account, 83–87;
ranking kinds of truth, 101–102,
338n46; counterexamples in, 121–125;
fishy arguments, 130; and contingency,
155, 360n86; explanations, 304n7. *See
also* Degrees

Philosophy of science, 80–83; circularity,
50; theory-laden data, 62, 104, 105, 107–
109, 114; three-way project, 82–83, 111;
standard model, 102–103; complications, 103; incoherence in Popper's theory, 103; defensive reaction, 105–106;
paradigms, 105, 109–111, 114–115,
339n58; path-dependence, 105, 109–
110; radical reaction, 105; functional
view, 106–119; data interpretation, 108–
109; replication, 108–109; methods of
science, 115–116, 118–119; "received
view," 338n47. *See also* Physical laws;
Quantum mechanics; Science; Special
Theory of Relativity

Physical laws, 40–41, 85–87, 153–154, 165–
168, 358n74; as universe's heritable

structure, 168, 232–233; restricted, 229–
233; emergent, 229–233

Pickering, Andrew, 318n68, 339n53

Pipes, Richard, 359n81

Planck, Max, 109

Plato, 6, 283, 318n65, 360n86

Plomin, Robert, 400n83

Poincaré, Henri, 8

Polchinski, Joseph, 362n95

Popper, Karl, 102–104, 229, 339nn48,49,50

Popperian content, 16, 284

Popper's theory, incoherence in, 103

Posner, Richard, 393n31

Possibilities, 121–122, 133–135; global, 158

Possible worlds, 86–87, 120, 128–132; exportable truth, 129; indigenous truth,
129; and degrees of contingency, 148–
155; metric on, 149; and actual world,
155–161; and average world, 159; and
degrees of supervenience, 226–227; topology on, 357n69

Postmodernism, 54–55

Power subgroup, 263

Predictions, 182–184, 203

Priest, Graham, 355n60

Prima facie duties, 264

Principle of Proportional Ranking, 282–
283

Prior, Arthur, 310n21

Prisoners' dilemma, 391n25

Privileged access, 90–93

Probability, 17–18

Projection, 353n57

Pryor, James, 348n25

Psychology, 294–298; folk, 7

Putnam, Hilary, 128, 304nn2,3, 329n10,
344n6, 346n18, 347nn20,24, 350n41,
385nn113,114

Putnam-Kripke argument, 128–132

Pylyshyn, Z. W., 352n51

Qualia, 174, 207–209; dimensionality of,
211–212; selection related to, 215, 218.
See also Phenomenology

Quantum mechanics: quantum field theory, 5, 330n14; renormalization, 5; Bohm's formulation, 8–9; interpreting, 10, 32, 35, 37; and truth in space and time, 26–44; and determinacy, 29–33; and tense logic, 29–30, 32, 33–34, 36; delayed-choice, 30, 34, 36, 37–38; measurement, 30–32, 35, 37, 230–231; two-slit experiment, 30, 31; erased measurement, 31, 32, 36, 37–38; merging streams, 31; Schrodinger's equation, 31, 35, 230–232; wave-packet collapse, 31, 32, 35–36, 230–231, 305n14; and verificationism, 32–33, 40; stochastic character, 33–34; relative facts?, 34–35; Einstein-Podolsky-Rosen criterion, 37; nonlocality, 40; determination and truth, 41–43; makes truth relative to time, 43; and objective-subjective distinction, 93; many worlds interpretation, 130; Feynman's path integration, 159, 167; why is world quantum mechanical?, 166–167; von Neumann's interpretation, 230–231; and mind-body identity theory, 231; and nature of objects, 327n3

Quine, W. V., 2, 27, 52, 54, 125, 214, 307n7, 310n20, 314n50, 319n74, 342n3, 344n9, 353n53, 355n59, 381n97

Rafal, Robert, 369n26
Raiffa, Howard, 393n34
Railton, Peter, 363n102
Ramsey, Frank, 314nn50,52
Rawls, John, 250, 289, 391n20, 399nn72,77
Reality principle, 25
Reason, 2–3, 111
Reasons, 97, 123–125; moral reasons, 389n3
Reduction, 71, 219; limited, 223; nonreduction, 229–233
Rees, Martin, 362n101
Reflex, simple, 178, 183
Registering, 175–176, 181; registering of registering, 125, 180, 184–187; of internal state, 178; and simple reflex, 183; common, 197–205; depth of, 205; scope of, 205

Reichenbach, Hans, 103
Relativism: about truth, 15–26, 42–43, 44, 46, 55–64, 64–67, 160–161, 322n86; undercuts itself?, 15–17, 42–43, 64–67; is egalitarian, 17–18; relative (property), 17–18, 65–66; and semantics, 19–20, 307n9; proponents of, 21–26; about facts, 34–36; different forms of, 61–62

Religion: vs. secularism, 54–55; anthropological definition, 239; best, 336n37; halos in, 339n57

Representation, 138–141, 162, 180, 186–187; and evolution, 142–143; analog, 193–194; spatial, 194; of dense information, 205–207, 212; linguistic, propositional, 205–206, 212–215; of normative rule, 270–271

Reversed spectrum, 211, 214
Rigid designator, 128–132, 134–135, 346n20, 350nn37,38
Rilling, Mark, 369n25
Ring of Gyges, 283
Rivers, Robert, 401n87
Roberts, John, 392n26
Robinson, Abraham, 9, 305n14
Romney, A. Kimball, 374n51
Rorty, Richard, 52–53, 319n72
Ross, Lee, 400n84
Ross, W. D., 264, 395n41
Royden, H. L., 334n26
Rumelhart, D. E., 369n27, 377n65
Russell, Bertrand, 71, 78, 324n94

Sachs, David, 398n64
Salmon, Nathan, 343n4, 348n26
Scanlon, Thomas, 389n3
Schacter, Daniel, 366n6
Schapiro, Leonard, 359n80
Scheffler, Israel, 95, 337n38, 339n54
Schelling, Thomas, 283, 401n86
Schizophrenia, 143–144

Schotter, Andrew, 391n22

Schwartz, James, 368n22, 380n85

Science: unifies humanity, 63; objectivity of, 95–96, 97–99, 102–119, 341n66; value free?, 95–96; evidence in, 98, 318n68; nonalgorithmic, 98, 104, 110; rationality of, 106–107, 116; intersubjective confirmation, 108–109; theory acceptance in, 109–110, 318n68, 339n58; methods of, 115–116; progress in, 116; veridicality, 116, 118–119, 140–141; explanation in, 153–154. *See also* Philosophy of science; Physical laws; Theory

Scott, John F., 390n17

Scully, Martin, 31

Searle, John, 378n75, 383n110

Security level, 244–245

Sejnowski, Terrence, 339n56, 372n37

Selection, natural, 172, 177; selection for factual relations coming to seem self-evidently valid, 97; of methods of representation, 142–143; of eye, 175; for isomorphisms of experience, 208; of neurological states giving rise to conscious awareness, 227–228; for cooperation, 246; for unpredictable behavior, 294–298; for self-consciousness, 299; over evolutionary time, 337nn8,43; no selection for survival of bodily death, 360n86; group selection, 397–398n63. *See also* Evolution; Function

Self, unity of, 201, 205, 373n42

Self-consciousness, 187, 298–300

Self-evidence, 124–125

Seligman, Martin, 368n24, 379n84

Semantics, 307n9

Sen, Amartya, 397n61, 399n75

Sened, Itai, 392n26

Sensory organs, 175, 178–179

SEP, 157–161, 163; least restrictive description, 158–159

Set theory, 146–147, 362n96

Seyfarth, Robert M., 390n7, 401n90

Shakespeare, William, 360n86

Shapere, Dudley, 339n54

Sharma, J., 380n90

Shaw, Robert, 328n8

Shepard, Roger, 321n84, 328n8, 345n15, 374n51, 379n82

Shoemaker, Sydney, 310n22, 318n70

Sidgwick, Henry, 289, 399n74

Silk purse, 185

Simons, Peter, 383n108

Simplicity, 8–9, 132

Singer, Wolf, 374n52, 377n70

Skinner, B. F., 368n20

Sklar, Lawrence, 311n33

Skolemite argument, 382n105

Slingshot argument, 325n103

Smith, Adam, 288, 396n47

Smith, Barbara Herrnstein, 52, 318n71

Smith, John Maynard, 401n88

Smolensky, Paul, 353n51

Smolin, Lee, 165, 166, 167, 362n100

Sober, Elliott, 367n16, 390n10, 397n63

Social choice theory, 257–259, 289; value dominance, 259

Social construction, 22, 25–26

Socialism, 254

Socrates, 283, 360n86

Solipsism, 190

Sophocles, 360n86

Space-time: ontological entity, 76–77, 332n21; contingency of geometry, 130–131; number of dimensions, 161–163; origin of, 164

Special Theory of Relativity, 18, 39–41, 76–77, 79–80, 111

Sperling, George, 367n12

Spontaneous symmetry breaking, 150–151

Stalin, Joseph, 152

Stalnaker, Robert, 308n9, 334n25

Starbuck, W. B., 355n62

Stein, Barry, 373n40

Steiner, Mark, 335n28

Stern, Ady, 310n28, 332n20

Sternberg, Shlomo, 330n14

Strawson, P. F., 49, 70, 324n95, 397n60

String theory, 5, 161–164

Stufflebeam, Robert, 369n28
Subjective beliefs, 94–99
Subjective consciousness as test of objectiveness, 191–192
Subjective ontology, 383n110
Subjective truths, 75, 91–93, 99–102, 326n1
Subjunctives, 86–87, 333n24
Subvenience, absolute, 72, 156
Sulloway, Frank, 400n83
Supervenience, 72, 325n99; degrees of, 226–227
Sur, Mriganka, 380n90
Survival after death, 171, 360n86
Symmetry, 81–83, 159; broken, 86–87. *See also* Invariance

Tarski, Alfred, 71, 72–73, 155, 314n50, 323n93, 341n66
Taylor, Alan, 393n34
Taylor, Shelley, 400n81
Tense logic, 29, 36–37
Terrace, H. S., 369n25
Theory: fundamental, 82–83; least arbitrary, 159; ultimate, 161–168; unification, 161, 233
Thomas, Robert, 392n28
Thompson, Evan, 351n44
Thomson, Judith Jarvis, 349n35, 393n30
Thorne, Kip S., 311n35
Thought experiments, 331n16
Thucydides, 360n86
Tononi, Giulio, 378n74
Tooby, John, 323n90, 396n49
Topographic maps, 193–196; and phenomenology, 196, 202, 212
Transformations, 76–93; Lorentz, 76–77, 86; temperature, 77; admissible, 79–83, 99–100, 331n17; types of, 79; and conservation, 81; superset criterion, 87–90, 335n28; weighting of, 87–90; form group, 331n17
Transformations, admissible, 79–83; not *a priori*, 79; stepwise process, 79–80
Treisman, Anne, 374n53

Trivers, Robert, 242, 390n9
Truth, 10, 15–74, 305–326; absolutism about, 15–16, 21–22, 24, 60–64, 65–66; and relativism, 15–26, 42–43; social relativism of?, 19, 20–21, 46, 55–64, 322n86; in space and time, 26–44; timelessness of?, 26–44; correspondence theory of, 28, 34, 44, 45, 57, 66–67, 67–74, 284–285; and determinateness, 29–30, 33–34, 37–44; is tentative, 38; spacelessness of?, 39–44; Platonism about, 43–44; strongly spatiotemporal, 43; weakly spatiotemporal, 43; acting upon, 45–47, 49–51, 59–60, 66–67, 180, 187, 192, 293–294, 315n56, 316n62; degrees of, 47–48; and language, 48–49, 51; folk notion?, 52; and decision rule, 59–60; Tarski condition, 65; connection to representation, 67; general characterization, 68–70; makes-true relation, 70–74; Tarski on, 72–73, 323n93; dimensions of, 99–102. *See also* Actuality; Facts; Necessary truth; Relativism; Truth, dimensions of; Truth property
Truth, dimensions of, 99–102; degree of relativeness, 63–64, 101; degree of objectiveness, 99–100; degree of objectivity, 100–101
Truth, theory of, 67–74; conditions of adequacy, 41–42, 46; presenting truth property, 45; possibility of?, 48–55; undesirable?, 52–53; definition of, 67–70, 72–73, 155–156; coherence theory, 68–69; actuality, 72–73; deflationist and redundancy theories, 314n52, 315n56
Truth property, 44–48, 66–67; differences in, 55–64, 284–285, 321nn83,85, 321n86; and decision rule, 59–60; and awareness, 180
Truth value, 19–20, 307n9
Two-slit experiment, 30

Ullman-Margalit, Edna, 401n89
Underdetermination, 105, 111–114; and phenomenology, 207

Understanding, 338n46
Unity of self, 201, 205, 373n42
Universes, 164–168, 232–233

Value dominance, 259
Value-free science, 95–96
Van Fraassen, Bas, 330n14
Van Gulick, Robert, 387n121
Vardi, Moshe Y., 376n61
Variance, 77–78, 102
Verificationism, 32–33, 40
Virtual reality, 364n1
Visual image, 181
Volkogonov, Dmitri, 359n78
von Neumann, John, 35, 230, 388n126
Voting system, 265–266

Wagon, Stan, 353n54
Wald, Robert, 332n18
Warren, William, Jr., 328n8
Water and H_2O, 128–131
Wave-packet collapse, 31–32, 35, 37
Weierstrass, Karl, 5, 9
Weinberg, Steven, 81–82, 330n14, 331n15, 332n18

Weiskrantz, Lawrence, 366n11, 368n23
Weyl, H., 328n5, 382n99
Wheeler, John A., 30, 34, 37, 133, 164–165, 310n25
Whinston, Michael, 394n40
White, Morton, 319n77
Wiesel, Torsten, 352n46
Wigner, Eugene, 82, 85, 111, 330n14, 333n23, 353n55, 388n127
Williams, Bernard, 383n109, 390n13
Williams, George C., 390n10
Williamson, Oliver, 392n26
Williamson, Timothy, 355n60, 356n65
Wilson, David Sloan, 390n10, 397n63
Winner take proportional all, 265–266
Wittgenstein, Ludwig, 92, 138, 324n94, 336n32, 382n105
Woodward, James, 355n58
Woolgar, Steven, 318n68

Yau, S.-T., 161

Zahavi, Amotz, 396n51
Zeki, Semir, 329n9, 374nn47,52
Zero, 162